LETTERS FROM **VIVEKANANDA**

Discovery Publisher

2019, Discovery Publisher

All rights reserved. No part of this book may be reproduced in any form or by any electronic or mechanical means including information storage and retrieval systems, without permission in writing from the publisher.

DISCOVERY PUBLISHER

616 Corporate Way, Suite 2-4933
Valley Cottage, New York, 10989
www.discoverypublisher.com
books@discoverypublisher.com
facebook.com/DiscoveryPublisher
twitter.com/DiscoveryPB

New York • Tokyo • Paris • Hong Kong

Table of Contents

1888 — 2

India — 4

1888.1 — Sir — 4
1888.2 — Sir — 4
1888.3 — Sir — 5
1888.4 — Sir — 6

1889 — 8

1889.1 — Sir — 10
1889.2 — M__ — 10
1889.3 — Sir — 11
1889.4 — Sir — 11
1889.5 — Sir — 12
1889.6 — Sir — 12
1889.7 — Sir — 14
1889.8 — Sir — 15
1889.9 — Sir — 18
1889.10 — Sir — 18
1889.11 — Sir — 19
1889.12 — Shri Balaram Bose — 19
1889.13 — Sir — 20
1889.14 — Sir — 21
1889.15 — Shri Balaram Bose — 22
1889.16 — Sir — 22

1890 — 24

1890.1 — Fakir — 26
1890.2 — Sir — 26
1890.3 — Sir — 27
1890.4 — Shri Balaram Bose — 28
1890.5 — Sir — 29
1890.6 — Sir — 29
1890.7 — Sir — 30
1890.8 — Sir — 31
1890.9 — Sir — 32
1890.10 — Sir — 32
1890.11 — Sir — 33
1890.12 — Shri Balaram Bose — 33
1890.13 — Gupta — 34
1890.14 — Sir — 35
1890.15 — Akhandananda — 35
1890.16 — Sir — 38
1890.17 — Sir — 39
1890.18 — Sir — 39
1890.19 — Sir — 41
1890.20 — Balaram Babu — 42
1890.21 — Shri Balaram Bose — 42
1890.22 — Atul Babu — 43
1890.23 — Akhandananda — 43
1890.24 — Akhandananda — 44
1890.25 — Sir — 45
1890.26 — Kali — 46
1890.27 — Sir — 46
1890.28 — Sir — 47
1890.29 — Tulsiram — 47
1890.30 — Sir — 48
1890.31 — Sir — 50
1890.32 — Sharat — 50
1890.33 — Sharat — 52

1891 — 54

1891.1 — Govinda Sahay — 56
1891.2 — Govinda Sahay — 56
1891.3 — Govinda Sahay — 56

1892 — 58

1892.1 — Diwanji Saheb — 60
1892.2 — Diwanji Saheb — 60
1892.3 — Diwanji Saheb — 61
1892.4 — Panditji Maharaj — 62
1892.5 — Diwanji Saheb — 63

1893   66

1893.1 — Alasinga   68
1893.2 — Doctor   68
1893.3 — Diwanji Saheb   69
1893.4 — Diwanji Saheb   70
1893.5 — Mother   71
1893.6 — Diwanji Saheb   71

Japan   73

1893.7 — Alasinga   73

U.S.A   77

1893.8 — Alasinga   77
1893.9 — Adhyapakji   82
1893.10 — Adhyapakji   82
1893.11 — Adhyapakji   85
1893.12 — Mrs. Tannatt Woods   87
1893.13 — Adhyapakji   88
1893.14 — Alasinga   88
1893.15 — Mrs. Woods   92
1893.16 — Mother   92
1893.17 — Mother   93
1893.18 — Haripada   93
1893.19 — Haripada   95

1894   98

1894.1 — Swami Ramakrishnanda   100
1894.2 — Miss Bell   103
1894.3 — Friends   103
1894.4 — Diwanji Saheb   105
1894.5 — Mother   107
1894.6 — Mother   108
1894.7 — Mother   109
1894.8 — Mother   109
1894.9 — Sisters   110
1894.10 — Babies   111
1894.11 — Mother   112
1894.12 — Sister   113
1894.13 — Sister Mary   113
1894.14 — Shashi   114
1894.15 — Mother   118
1894.16 — Brother   118
1894.17 — Sister   119
1894.18 — Mother   120
1894.19 — Alasinga   121
1894.20 — Mother   122
1894.21 — Professor   124
1894.22 — Sister   124
1894.23 — Akhandananda   125
1894.24 — Sister   126
1894.25 — Adhyapakji   127
1894.26 — Mother   127
1894.27 — Mother   128
1894.28 — Mother   128
1894.29 — Mother   129
1894.30 — Sharat   130
1894.31 — Adhyapakji   130
1894.32 — Alasinga   131
1894.33 — Adhyapakji   133
1894.34 — Mother   134
1894.35 — Adhyapakji   134
1894.36 — Diwanji Saheb   135
1894.37 — Sir   138
1894.38 — Sisters   138
1894.39 — Alasinga   139
1894.40 — Dear __   141
1894.41 — Mother   143
1894.42 — Mother   144
1894.43 — Alasinga   145
1894.44 — Sisters   146
1894.45 — Mother   147
1894.46 — Mother   148
1894.47 — Babies   149
1894.48 — Sisters   150
1894.49 — Mother   152
1894.50 — Dear and Beloved   153
1894.51 — Mother   157
1894.52 — Mother   157
1894.53 — Sisters   158
1894.54 — Sister   159
1894.55 — Mother   160
1894.56 — Mother   161
1894.57 — Mother   163
1894.58 — Sister   165

1894.59—Alasinga	165	1894.103—Mother	208
1894.60—Mother	167	1894.104—Blessed and Beloved	209
1894.61—Mother	168	1894.105—Mrs. Bull	209
1894.62—Mr. Bhattacharya	168	1894.106—Sister	210
1894.63—Mother	173	1894.107—Dharmapala	210
1894.64—Mother	173	1894.108—Alasinga	211
1894.65—Leon	174	1894.109—Maharaja of Khetri	213
1894.66—Sister	175	1894.110—Brothers	214
1894.67—Mother Sara	176	1894.111—Govinda Sahay	217
1894.68—Mother	176	1894.112—Govinda Sahay	217
1894.69—Alasinga	177	1894.113—Brother Shivananda	218
1894.70—Kidi	178	1894.114—Brahmananda	220
1894.71—Mother	178		
1894.72—Brother disciples	179	***1895***	***222***
1894.73—Mrs. Bull	184		
1894.74—Sister	184	1895.1—Mrs. Bull	224
1894.75—Alasinga	185	1895.2—G. G.	224
1894.76—Mother	185	1895.3—Alasinga	226
1894.77—Alasinga	186	1895.4—Miss Thursby	227
1894.78—Diwanji Saheb	187	1895.5—Sarada	228
1894.79—Diwanji Saheb	187	1895.6—Mrs. Ole Bull	229
1894.80—Mother	188	1895.7—Shashi	230
1894.81—Mother	188	1895.8—Sister	236
1894.82—Mrs. Bull	189	1895.9—Adhyapakji	238
1894.83—Swami Ramakrisnana	190	1895.10—Sanyal	239
1894.84—Vehemia	190	1895.11—Alasinga	239
1894.85—Sister	191	1895.12—Mrs. Bull	240
1894.86—Miss Thursby	191	1895.13—Mother	241
1894.87—Blessed and Beloved	192	1895.14—Sister	242
1894.88—Mother	193	1895.15—Alasinga	242
1894.89—Mrs. Bull	194	1895.16—Mother	243
1894.90—Mother	194	1895.17—Mother	243
1894.91—Sister	194	1895.18—Mrs. Bull	244
1894.92—Mother	195	1895.19—Sister	245
1894.93—Diwanji Saheb	196	1895.20—Alasinga	246
1894.94—Mother	198	1895.21—Friend	246
1894.95—Alasinga	198	1895.22—Friend	247
1894.96—Kidi	200	1895.23—Friend	248
1894.97—Dear and Beloved	200	1895.24—Brother	249
1894.98—Kali	201	1895.25—Mrs. Bull	249
1894.99—Diwanji	204	1895.26—Mother	250
1894.100—Mother	206	1895.27—Mother	251
1894.101—Sister	207	1895.26—Brother	251
1894.102—Sister	207	1895.29—Mother	252

1895.30 — S__	252	1895.74 — Rakhal	284
1895.31 — Friend	253	1895.75 — Friend	285
1895.32 — Friend	254	1895.76 — Brother Disciples	285
1895.33 — Babies	254	1895.77 — Mrs. Bull	287
1895.34 — Alasinga	255		
1895.35 — Mrs. Bull	257	## France	288
1895.36 — Alasinga	258		
1895.37 — Mother	258	1895.78 — Friend	288
1895.38 — Alasinga	259	1895.79 — Rakhal	288
1895.39 — Mother	259	1895.80 — Friend	292
1895.40 — Sir	260	1895.81 — Alasinga	292
1895.41 — Mrs. Bull	260		
1895.42 — Dear __	261	## England	294
1895.43 — Mother	261		
1895.44 — Mrs. Bull	261	1895.82 — Akhandananda	294
1895.45 — Sister	262	1895.83 — Mrs. Bull	295
1895.46 — Friend	262	1895.84 — Mrs. Bull	295
1895.47 — Sister	263	1895.85 — Joe Joe	296
1895.48 — Kidi	264	1895.86 — Dear __	296
1895.49 — Sister	265	1895.87 — Rakhal	297
1895.50 — Sister	265	1895.88 — Mrs. Bull	298
1895.51 — Joe	267	1895.89 — Joe Joe	299
1895.52 — Mrs. Bull	268	1895.90 — Kali	299
1895.53 — Doctor	268	1895.91 — Mother	301
1895.54 — Shashi	269	1895.92 — Rakhal	302
1895.55 — Alasinga	270	1895.93 — Shashi	303
1895.56 — Mother	271	1895.94 — Rakhal	304
1895.57 — Mother	272	1895.95 — Joe Joe	306
1895.58 — Friend	273	1895.96 — Isabelle McKindley	306
1895.59 — Alberta	274	1895.97 — Alasinga	307
1895.60 — Maharaja of Khetri	274	1895.98 — Joe Joe	308
1895.61 — Mother	275	1895.99 — Friend	308
1895.62 — Mrs. William Sturges	276	1895.100 — Friend	309
1895.63 — Mother	276	1895.101 — Friend	310
1895.64 — Mother	277	1895.102 — Akhandananda	310
1895.65 — Friend	278	1895.103 — Alasinga	311
1895.66 — Mother	278	1895.104 — Mrs. Bull	312
1895.67 — Mrs. G. W. Hale	279		
1895.68 — Friend	279	## U.S.A	313
1895.69 — Friend	280		
1895.70 — Christina	282	1895.105 — Blessed and Beloved	313
1895.71 — Mother	283	1895.106 — Mrs. Alberta	313
1895.72 — Sister Christine	283	1895.107 — Sturdy	314
1895.73 — Alasinga	284	1895.108 — Mrs. Bull	316

1895.109 — Christina	316	1896.24 — Alasinga	350
1895.110 — Friend	317	1896.25 — Christina	351
1895.111 — Joe Joe	317	1896.26 — Mrs. Bull	351
1895.112 — Christina	318	1896.27 — Mrs. Bull	352
1895.113 — Mrs. Bull	319	1896.28 — Sarada	352
1895.114 — Christina	319	1896.29 — Dr. Nanjunda Rao	353
1895.115 — Your Highness	319	1896.30 — Sisters	354
1895.116 — Sir	320		
1895.117 — Blessed and Beloved	320	## England	355
1895.118 — Alasinga	321		
1895.119 — Sharat	322	1896.31 — Sisters	355
1895.120 — Christina	323	1896.32 — Christina	355
1895.121 — Mrs. Ole Bull	324	1896.33 — Dear	356
1895.122 — Sister	324	1896.34 — Sturdy	360
1895.123 — Friend	325	1896.35 — Shashi	360
1895.124 — Rakhal	325	1896.36 — Mrs. Bull	361
1895.125 — Alasinga	326	1896.37 — Adhyapakji	362
		1896.38 — Sister	362
## 1896	330	1896.39 — Mary	363
		1896.40 — Mrs. Bull	364
1896.1 — Mrs. Bull	332	1896.41 — Mrs. Bull	364
1896.2 — Mrs. Funkey	332	1896.42 — Miss Noble	365
1896.3 — Sister	332	1896.43 — Shashi	366
1896.4 — Mrs. Bull	334	1896.44 — Shashi	366
1896.5 — Blessed and Beloved	334	1896.45 — Friend and Brother	367
1896.6 — Alasinga	335	1896.46 — Frankincense	367
1896.7 — Christina	336	1896.47 — Sir	369
1896.8 — Sarada	337	1896.48 — Mrs. Bull	369
1896.9 — Yogen	338	1896.49 — Mother	370
1896.10 — Mrs. Bull	338	1896.50 — Babies	370
1896.11 — Blessed and Beloved	339	1896.51 — Mrs. Bull	371
1896.12 — Mrs. Bull	340	1896.52 — Sir	371
1896.13 — Sister	341	1896.53 — Dr. Nanjunda Rao	372
1896.14 — Blessed and Beloved	342	1896.54 — Mrs. Bull	372
1896.15 — Alasinga	344		
1896.16 — Miss Thursby	345	## Switzerland	374
1896.16 — Friend	345		
1896.17 — Sarada	346	1896.55 — Blessed and Beloved	374
1896.18 — Blessed and Beloved	347	1896.56 — Mrs. Bull	374
1896.19 — Sister	348	1896.57 — Sahji	374
1896.20 — Christina	348	1896.58 — Blessed and Beloved	375
1896.21 — Mrs. Funkey	349	1896.59 — Blessed and Beloved	376
1896.22 — Alasinga	349	1896.60 — Dear __	376
1896.23 — Alasinga	350	1896.61 — Alasinga	377

1896.62 — Goodwin	378
1896.63 — Blessesd and Beloved	380
1896.64 — Alasinga	381
1896.65 — Blessed and Beloved	382
1896.66 — Shashi	382
1896.67 — Mrs. Bull	384
1896.68 — Blessed and Beloved	385
1896.69 — Nanjunda Rao	386

Germany 387

1896.70 — Friend	387

England 388

1896.71 — Sister	388
1896.72 — Sister	389
1896.73 — Alasinga	391
1896.74 — Alasinga	392
1896.75 — Alasinga	394
1896.76 — Indian Mirror	394
1896.77 — Christina	395
1896.78 — Joe Joe	396
1896.79 — Miss S. E. Waldo	397
1896.80 — Mrs. Bull	398
1896.81 — Noble	399
1896.82 — Mary	399
1896.83 — Alasinga	402
1896.84 — Mrs. Bull	402
1896.85 — Alasinga	403
1896.86 — Lalaji	404
1896.87 — Dear __	404
1896.88 — Sisters	405
1896.89 — Joe	406
1896.90 — Alberta	406
1896.91 — Miss Noble	407
1896.92 — Mrs. Bull	407
1896.93 — FRANKINCENSE	408
1896.94 — Madam	408

Italy 409

1896.95 — Alberta	409
1896.96 — Rakhal	409

1896.97 — Sir	410

1897 *412*

India 414

1897.1 — Mary	414
1897.2 — Christina	415
1897.3 — Madras Comittee	415
1897.4 — Mary	416
1897.5 — Rakhal	416
1897.6 — Gentlemen	417
1897.7 — Mrs. Bull	417
1897.8 — Christina	418
1897.9 — Sharat Chandra Chakravarti	419
1897.10 — Mrs. Bull	420
1897.11 — Ram Ram	420
1897.12 — Miss Noble	421
1897.13 — Honoured Madam	421
1897.14 — Lalajee	423
1897.15 — Shashi	423
1897.16 — Mary	424
1897.17 — Mrs. Bull	426
1897.18 — Miss Noble	427
1897.19 — Rakhal	428
1897.20 — Sudhir	430
1897.21 — Doctor Shashi	430
1897.22 — Sir	431
1897.23 — Badri Sah	433
1897.24 — Mr.__	433
1897.25 — Shuddhananda	434
1897.26 — Marie	435
1897.27 — Miss Noble	437
1897.28 — Rakhal	437
1897.29 — Akhandananda	438
1897.30 — Rakhal	439
1897.31 — Miss Noble	439
1897.32 — Mother	440
1897.33 — Mrs. Bull	441
1897.34 — Friend	441
1897.35 — Sarat Chandra	441
1897.36 — Miss Noble	443
1897.37 — Shivananda	443
1897.38 — Sister	445

1897.39—Joe Joe	447	**1898**		**486**
1897.40—Rakhal	448			
1897.41—Shuddhananda	450	1898.1—Sister Christine	488
1897.42—Rakhal	451	1898.2—Miss Noble	488
1897.43—Miss Noble	453	1898.3—Rajaji	488
1897.44—Akhandananda	454	1898.4—Shashi	489
1897.45—Marie	454	1898.5—Mary	491
1897.46—Mother	456	1898.6—Christina	492
1897.47—Shashi	457	1898.7—Margaret	493
1897.48—Miss Noble	458	1898.8—Shashi	493
1897.49—Akhandananda	459	1898.9—Dhira Mata	494
1897.50—Joe	460	1898.10—Jagmohan	495
1897.51—Shashi	460	1898.11—Joe Joe	495
1897.52—Mrs. Bull	461	1898.12—Miss MacLeod	496
1897.53—Mother	462	1898.13—Sir	496
1897.54—Rakhal	463	1898.14—Rakhal	497
1897.55—Rakhal	463	1898.15—Joe Joe	497
1897.56—Shuddhananda	465	1898.16—Margot	498
1897.57—Haripada	466	1898.17—Rakhal	498
1897.58—Miss MacLeod	466	1898.18—J. J. Goodwin's Mother	500
1897.59—Rakhal	466	1898.19—Your Highness	500
1897.60—Shashi	468	1898.20—Friend	501
1897.61—Rakhal	469	1898.21—Sturdy	501
1897.62—Margo	469	1898.22—Miss Macleod, Mrs. Bull	502
1897.63—Sarada	470	1898.23—Rakhal	502
1897.64—Akhandananda	471	1898.24—Your Highness	503
1897.65—Rakhal	472	1898.25—Rakhal	504
1897.66—Jagmohanlal	472	1898.26—Your Highness	505
1897.67—Rakhal	473	1898.27—Margot	505
1897.68—Rakhal	475	1898.28—Mary	506
1897.69—M__	476	1898.29—Haripada	507
1897.70—Miss Noble	476	1898.30—Your Highness	508
1897.71—Rakhal	477	1898.31—Haripada	508
1897.72—Mother	477	1898.32—Christina	509
1897.73—Rakhal	478	1898.33—Your Highness	509
1897.74—Mother	479	1898.34—Your Highness	510
1897.75—Baburam	479	1898.35—Joe	510
1897.76—M. __	480	1898.36—Your Highness	511
1897.77—Rakhal	480	1898.37—Your Highness	512
1897.78—Rakhal	481	1898.38—Dear __	513
1897.79—Rakhal	482	1898.39—Dhira Mata	513
1897.80—Christina	482		
1897.81—Shivananda	483		

1899 — 516

1899.1 — Mother	518	
1899.2 — Margot	520	
1899.3 — Nivedita	520	
1899.4 — Christina	521	
1899.5 — Joe	521	
1899.6 — Raja	522	
1899.7 — S__	522	
1899.8 — Margot	523	
1899.9 — Margot	523	
1899.10 — Sir	524	
1899.11 — Mary	524	
1899.12 — Dear __	525	
1899.13 — Madam	526	
1899.14 — Christina	527	
1899.15 — Friend	527	
1899.16 — Miss Macleod	528	

England — 529

1899.17 — Christina	529
1899.18 — Sturdy	529
1899.19 — Christina	530
1899.20 — Sister Christine	531
1899.21 — Joe	531
1899.22 — Mother	532
1899.23 — Rakhal	533
1899.24 — Marie	534

U.S.A — 536

1899.25 — Isabel	536
1899.26 — Mrs. Bull	536
1899.27 — Mother	536
1899.28 — Sturdy	537
1899.29 — Christina	538
1899.30 — Mary	538
1899.31 — Mary	540
1899.32 — Mother Church	540
1899.33 — Mother	541
1899.34 — Christina	542
1899.35 — Christina	542
1899.36 — Optimist	543
1899.37 — Margot	544
1899.38 — Christina	545
1899.39 — Christina	545
1899.40 — Mrs. Bull	546
1899.41 — Christina	546
1899.42 — Margot	547
1899.43 — Sturdy	547
1899.44 — Sturdy	550
1899.45 — Mrs. Bull	551
1899.46 — Rakhal	551
1899.47 — Mary	552
1899.48 — Christina	552
1899.49 — Brahmananda	553
1899.50 — Mrs. Leggett	553
1899.51 — Dhira Mata	554
1899.52 — Mother	554
1899.53 — Mother	555
1899.54 — Margot	555
1899.55 — Mother	556
1899.56 — Margot	556
1899.57 — Christina	557
1899.58 — Mrs. Bull	558
1899.59 — Brahmananda	559
1899.60 — Dhira Mata	559
1899.61 — Margot	560
1899.62 — Christina	561
1899.63 — Dhira Mata	562
1899.64 — Mary	563

1900 — 566

1900.1 — Dhira Mata	568
1900.2 — Margot	569
1900.3 — Margo	569
1900.4 — Dhira Mata	570
1900.5 — Nivedita	570
1900.6 — Mary	572
1900.7 — Akhandananda	572
1900.8 — Joe	575
1900.9 — Mary	576
1900.10 — Dhira Mata	576
1900.11 — Nivedita	577
1900.12 — Dhira Mata	577
1900.13 — Joe	579

1900.14—Christina	580
1900.15—Rakhal	580
1900.16—Mary	581
1900.17—Dhira Mata	582
1900.18—Mother	582
1900.19—Mother	583
1900.20—Mary	584
1900.21—Nivedita	584
1900.22—Margot	585
1900.23—Mary	586
1900.24—Haribhai	587
1900.25—Joe	587
1900.26—Haribhai	588
1900.27—Joe	589
1900.28—Dhira Mata	590
1900.29—Margot	591
1900.30—American Friend	592
1900.31—Mother	592
1900.32—Dhira Mata	593
1900.33—Sister Christine	594
1900.34—Joe	594
1900.35—American Friend	595
1900.36—Mr. Leggett	596
1900.37—Joe	596
1900.38—Joe	598
1900.39—Mary	599
1900.40—Mary	600
1900.41—Aunt Roxy	600
1900.42—Nivedita	600
1900.43—Margot	601
1900.44—Margot	602
1900.45—Mother	602
1900.46—Christina	603
1900.47—Abhedananda	603
1900.48—Nivedita	604
1900.49—Christina	604
1900.50—Christina	605
1900.51—Christina	606
1900.52—Mary	606
1900.53—Nivedita	608
1900.54—Mary	608
1900.55—Christina	609
1900.56—Mrs. Hansbrough	610
1900.57—Nivedita	610
1900.58—Sister Christine	611
1900.59—Mrs. Hansbrough	611
1900.60—Sister	611
1900.61—Turiyananda	612
1900.62—Joe	612
1900.63—Joe	613
1900.64—Abhedananda	613
1900.65—Turiyananda	614
1900.66—Dear __	614

France 616

1900.67—Christina	616
1900.68—Mrs. Leggett	616
1900.69—Hari	617
1900.70—Christine	617
1900.71—John Fox	618
1900.72—Nivedita	618
1900.73—Christine	619
1900.74—Nivedita	619
1900.75—Nivedita	620
1900.76—Brother Hari	621
1900.77—Hari	621
1900.78—Mother	623
1900.79—Alberta	624
1900.80—Christina	625
1900.81—Turiyananda	625
1900.82—Alberta	626
1900.83—Mademoiselle	627
1900.84—Sister Christine	627
1900.85—Mother	629

India 630

1900.86—Alberta	630
1900.87—Margo	630
1900.88—Christina	630
1900.89—Sister Christine	631
1900.90—Joe	631
1900.91—Joe	632
1900.92—Mother	632
1900.93—Nivedita	633
1900.94—Joe	633
1900.95—Shashi	634

1900.96 — Your Highness	635

1901   *638*

1901.1 — Mother	640
1901.2 — Sturdy	641
1901.3 — Mother	642
1901.4 — Shashi	642
1901.5 — Mother	643
1901.6 — Joe	643
1901.7 — Joe	644
1901.8 — Mother	644
1901.9 — Mother	645
1901.10 — Sir	646
1901.11 — Margot	646
1901.12 — Christine	647
1901.13 — Introduction	648
1901.14 — Christine	648
1901.15 — Mother	649
1901.16 — Swarup	649
1901.17 — Mary	650
1901.18 — Shashi	651
1901.19 — Mrs. Hansbrough	651
1901.20 — Joe	652
1901.21 — Friend	653
1901.22 — Joe	654
1901.23 — Joe	654
1901.24 — Christina	655
1901.25 — Mary	655
1901.26 — Christine	656
1901.27 — Christine	657
1901.28 — Christine	658
1901.29 — Mary	658
1901.30 — Blessed and Beloved	659
1901.31 — Christine	660
1901.32 — Nivedita	662
1901.33 — Blessed and Beloved	662
1901.34 — Christine	663
1901.35 — Christina	664
1901.36 — Christina	664
1901.37 — Joe	665
1901.38 — Margo	666
1901.39 — Christina	667
1901.40 — Christine	668
1901.41 — Christine	669
1901.42 — Christine	669
1901.43 — Christine	671
1901.44 — Sister Christine	672

1902   *674*

1902.1 — Swarup	676
1902.2 — Mrs. Ole Bull	677
1902.3 — Sister Nivedita	678
1902.4 — Rakhal	678
1902.5 — Rakhal	679
1902.6 — Rakhal	680
1902.7 — Brahmananda	680
1902.8 — Joe	681
1902.9 — Joe	681
1902.10 — Dhira Mata	682
1902.11 — Christine	682
1902.12 — Christine	683
1902.13 — Christine	684
1902.14 — Christine	685

Name Index   *688*

Index of Proper Names   690

1888

Note: Before leaving for the U.S.A. Swamiji used to change his name very often. In earlier years, he signed as Narendra or Naren; then for some time as Vividishananda or Sachchidananda. But for the convenience of the readers, these volumes use the more familiar name of Vivekananda.

India

1888.1 — SIR[1]

Vrindaban,
12th Aug., 1888.

DEAR SIR,

Leaving Ayodhya I have reached the holy Vrindaban, and am putting up at Kâlâ Bâbu's Kunja. In the town the mind feels contracted. Places like Râdhâ-kunda, I have heard, are delightful; but they are at some distance from the town. I have a mind to proceed very shortly to Hardwar. In case you have any acquaintance there, you would be doing me a great favour if you would kindly write him an introduction for me. What about your visiting this place? Please reply early and oblige.

Yours etc.,
Vivekananda.

1888.2 — SIR[2]

Vrindaban,
20th Aug., 1888.

DEAR SIR,

An aged brother-disciple of mine who has just come back to Vrindaban after visiting Kedarnath and Badrinath met Gangadhar. Twice did Gangadhar ascend up to Tibet and Bhutan. He is in great happiness and felt overwhelmed and wept at the meeting. He spent the winter at Kankhal. The Karoâ (waterpot) you gave him, he still keeps with him. He is coming back and is expected at Vrindaban this very month. So in the hope of meeting him, I postpone my going to Hardwar for some days. Please convey my deepest respects to the Brahmin devotee of Shiva who is with you and accept the same yourself.

Yours etc.,
Vivekananda.

---

1. These letters are translated from Bengali letters written to Pramadadas Mitra of Varanasi, an orthodox Hindu, for whose profound erudition and piety Swamiji had the highest regard. These letters are most interesting being written (except the last) at a time when, after his Master's passing away, Swamiji was leading a wandering monk's life. In the early days he used to sign his name as Narendranath, though his now famous name, Vivekananda, is printed in all these pages for easy comprehension

2. See Note above.

1888.3 — SIR[1]

Salutation to Bhagavan Ramakrishna!

The Baranagore Math,
19th Nov., 1888.

RESPECTED SIR,

I have received the two books sent by you and am filled with joy to read your wonderfully affectionate letter which betokens your broad, generous heart. No doubt, it is due to good merit of my previous births that you show, sir, so much kindness to a mendicant like me who lives on begging. By sending your gift of the "Vedanta", you have laid under lifelong obligation not only myself but the whole group of Shri Ramakrishna's Sannyasins. They all bow down to you in respect. It is not for my own sake alone that I asked of you the copy of Pânini's grammar; a good deal of study, in fact, is given to Sanskrit scriptures in this Math. The Vedas may well be said to have fallen quite out of vogue in Bengal. Many here in this Math are conversant with Sanskrit, and they have a mind to master the Samhitâ portions of the Vedas. They are of opinion that what has to be done must be done to a finish. So, believing that a full measure of proficiency in the Vedic language is impossible without first mastering Panini's grammar, which is the best available for the purpose, a copy of the latter was felt to be a necessity. The grammatical work Mugdhabodha, which we studied in our boyhood, is superior in many respects to Laghukaumudi. You are yourself, however, a deeply learned man and, therefore, the best judge we can have in this matter. So if you consider the Ashtâdhyâyi (Panini's) to be the most suitable in our case, you will lay us under a debt of lifelong gratitude by sending the same (provided you feel it convenient and feel so inclined). This Math is not wanting in men of perseverance, talent, and penetrative intellect. I may hope that by the grace of our Master, they will acquire in a short time Panini's system and then succeed in restoring the Vedas to Bengal. I beg to send you two photographs of my revered Master and two parts of some of his teachings as given in his homely style compiled, and published by a certain gentleman — hoping you will give us the pleasure of your acceptance. My health is now much improved, and I expect the blessings of meeting you within two or three months…

Yours etc.,
Vivekananda.

---

1. See Note page 4.

1888.4 — SIR[2]

Baghbazar, Calcutta,
28th November, 1888.

DEAR SIR, (Shri Pramadadas Mitra)

I have received the book of Pânini which you so kindly sent me. Please accept my gratitude for the same.

I had an attack of fever again—hence I could not reply to you immediately. Please excuse. I am ailing much. I am praying to the Divine Mother to keep you happy physically and mentally.

Your servant,
Vivekananda.

---

2 See Note page 4.

1889

1889.1 — SIR[1]

Victory to God!

Baranagore,
4th Feb., 1889.

DEAR SIR,

For some reason I had been feeling today agitated and cramped in my mind, when your letter of invitation to the heavenly city of Varanasi reached me. I accept it as the call of Vishveshvara. (The Lord of the Universe, or Shiva, as installed in the leading temple of Varanasi or Kashi.) I am going now on a pilgrimage to the place of my Master's nativity, and after a sojourn of a few days there, I shall present myself to you. He must be made of stone whose mind does not melt at the sigh of Kashi and its Lord! I feel now much improved in health. My regards to Jnanananda. I am coming as soon as I can. It all depends ultimately on Vishveshvara's will... More when we meet.

Yours etc.,
Vivekananda.

1889.2 — M__

Auntpur,
7th February, 1889.

DEAR M__,

Thanks a hundred thousand times, Master! You have hit Ramakrishna in the right point.

Few, alas, few understand him!

Yours etc.,
Vivekananda.

PS — My heart leaps with joy, and it is a wonder that I do not go mad when I find anybody thoroughly launched into the midst of the doctrine which is to shower peace on earth hereafter.

---

1. See Note 1, p. 4.

1889.3 — SIR

Baranagore,
22nd February, 1889.

DEAR SIR, (Shri Pramadadas Mitra)

I had intended to go to Varanasi, and I planned to reach there after visiting the birthplace of my Master. But unluckily on the way to that village I had an attack of high fever followed by vomiting and purging as in cholera. There was again fever after three or four days—and as the body is now so weak that I can barely walk even two steps, I have been compelled now to give up my previous intention. I do not know what is God's will, but my body is quite unfit for treading on this path. Anyway, the body is not everything. Recovering my health after a few days here, I entertain the hope of visiting you there. The will of Vishweshwara, the Lord of the universe, will prevail—whatever that may be. You also kindly bless me. My respects to you and brother Jnanananda.

Your servant,
Vivekananda.

1889.4 — SIR

Baghbazar, Calcutta,
21st March, 1889.

RESPECTED SIR, (Shri Pramadadas Mitra)

It is several days since I received your last letter. Please excuse the delay in replying, which was due to some special reasons. I am very ill at present; there is fever now and then, but there is no disorder in the spleen or other organs. I am under homeopathic treatment. Now I have had to give up completely the intention of going to Varanasi. Whatever God dispenses will happen later on, according to the state of the body. If you meet brother Jnanananda, please tell him not to be held up there in expectation of my coming. My going there is very uncertain. My regards to you and Jnanananda.

Yours sincerely,
Vivekananda.

1889.5 — SIR[1]

Shri Durgâ be my Refuge!

Baranagore,
26th June, 1889.

DEAR SIR,

For sundry reasons I have been unable to write to you for long, for which please excuse me. I have now obtained news of Gangadhar. He met one of my brother disciples, and both are now staying in the Uttarakhanda (the sacred Himalayas). Four of us from here are in the Himalayas now, and with Gangadhar they are five. One brother-disciple named Shivananda came across Gangadhar at Srinagara on the way to holy Kedarnath, and Gangadhar has sent two letters here. During his first year in the Himalayas, he could not secure permission to enter Tibet, but he got it the next year. The Lamas love him much, and he had picked up the Tibetan language. He says the Lamas form ninety per cent of the population, but they mostly practice Tântrika forms of worship. The country is intensely cold — eatables there are scarcely any — only dried meat; and Gangadhar had to travel and live on that food. My health is passable, but the state of mind is terrible!

Yours etc.,
Vivekananda.

1889.6 — SIR[2]

Victory to God!

Baghbazar, Calcutta,
4th July, 1889.

DEAR SIR,

It pleased me highly to know all the news in your letter yesterday. You have asked me to request Gangadhar to write to you, but I see no chance thereof, for though they are sending us letters, they do not stop anywhere for more than two or three days and therefore do not receive any of ours.

Some relative of my former life[3] has purchased a bungalow at Simultala (near Baidyanath). The place being credited with a healthy climate, I stayed there for some time. But the summer heat growing excessive, I had an attack of acute diarrhoea, and I have just fled away from the place.

Words fail to describe how strong is the desire in my mind to go to Varanasi and have my soul blessed by meeting you and sojourning with you in good converse, but everything rests on His will! I wonder what linking of heart existed between us,

1. See Note 1, p. 4.
2. See Note 1, p. 4.
3. The life he has renounced.

sir, from some previous incarnation that, receiving as I do the love and affection of not a few men of wealth and position in this city of Calcutta, I am apt to feel so much bored by their society, while only through one day's interview my heart felt charmed enough to accept you as a near relative and friend in spiritual life! One reason is that you are a favoured servant of God. Another perhaps is:

तच्चेतसा स्मरति नूनमबोधपूर्वं भावस्थिराणि जननान्तरसौहृदानि ।[1]

I am indebted to you for the advice which comes from you as the outcome of your experience and spiritual practice. It is very true, and I have also found it so very often, that one has to suffer at times for holding in one's brain novel views of all sorts.

But with me it is a different malady this time. I have not lost faith in a benign Providence — nor am I going ever to lose it — my faith in the scriptures is unshaken. But by the will of God, the last six or seven years of my life have been full of constant struggles with hindrances and obstacles of all sorts. I have been vouchsafed the ideal Shâstra; I have seen the ideal man; and yet fail myself to get on with anything to the end — this is my profound misery.

And particularly, I see no chance of success while remaining near Calcutta. In Calcutta live my mother and two brothers. I am the eldest; the second is preparing for the First Arts Examination, and the third is young.

They were quite well off before, but since my father's death, it is going very hard with them — they even have to go fasting at times! To crown all, some relatives, taking advantage of their helplessness, drove them away from the ancestral residence. Though a part of it is recovered through suing at the High Court, destitution is now upon them — a matter of course in litigation.

Living near Calcutta I have to witness their adversity, and the quality of Rajas prevailing, my egotism sometimes develops into the form of a desire that rises to plunge me into action; in such moments, a fierce fighting ensues in my mind, and so I wrote that the state of my mind was terrible. Now their lawsuit has come to an end. So bless me that after a stay here in Calcutta for a few days more to settle matters, I may bid adieu to this place for ever.

आपूर्यमाणमचलप्रतिष्ठं समुद्रमापः प्रविशन्ति यद्वत् ।
तद्वत्कामा यं प्रविशन्ति सर्वे स शान्तिमाप्नोति न कामकामी ॥[2]

Bless me that my heart may wax strong with supreme strength Divine, and that all forms of Mâyâ may drop off from me for aye: "We have taken up the Cross, Thou hast laid it upon us and grant us strength that we bear it unto death. Amen!" — Imitation of Christ.

I am now staying in Calcutta. My address is: c/o Balaram Babu, 57 Ramkanta Bose's Street, Baghbazar, Calcutta.

1. Kalidasa's **Shakuntalam**, Act V: "It must be the memories, unwittingly recalled, of affinities firmly established in previous incarnations through depths of heart."

2. The Gitâ, II.70: "Not he that lusteth after objects of desire but he alone obtaineth peace in whom desires lose themselves like river-water flowing into the ocean but leaving it unaffected and unmodified in spite of constant accession."

1889.7 — SIR[3]

All Glory to God!

Baranagore, Calcutta,
7th Aug., 1889.

DEAR SIR,

It is more than a week since I received your letter, but having had another attack of fever, I could not send a reply all this time, for which please excuse me. For an interval of a month and a half I kept well, but I have suffered again for the last ten days; now I am doing well.

I have certain questions to put, and you, sir, have a wide knowledge of Sanskrit; so please favour me with answers to the following:

1. Does any narrative occur about Satyakâma, son of Jabâlâ, and about Jânashruti, anywhere else in the Vedas excepting the Upanishads[4]?

2. In most cases where Shankaracharya quotes Smriti in his commentary on the Vedânta-Sutras, he cites the authority of the Mahâbhârata. But seeing that we find clear proofs about caste being based on qualification both in the Bhishmaparva of the Mahabharata and in the stories there of the Ajagara and of Umâ and Maheshvara, has he made any mention in his writings of this fact?

3. The doctrine of caste in the *Purusha-Sukta* of the Vedas does not make it hereditary — so what are those instances in the Vedas where caste has been made a matter of hereditary transmission?

4. The Achârya could not adduce any proof from the Vedas to the effect that the Shudra should not study the Vedas. He only quotes "यज्ञेऽनवकॢप्तः"[5] (Tai. Samhita, VII. i. 1. 6) to maintain that when he is not entitled to perform Yajnas, he has neither any right to study the Upanishads and the like. But the same Acharya contends with reference to "अथातो ब्रह्मजिज्ञासा"[6], (*Vedânta-Sutras*, I. i. 1) that the word अथ (Ath) here does not mean "subsequent to the study of the Vedas", because it is contrary to proof that the study of the Upanishad is not permissible without the previous study of the Vedic Mantras and *Brâhmanas* and because there is no intrinsic sequence between the Vedic Karma-kânda and Vedic Janâna-kânda. It is evident, therefore, that one may attain to the knowledge of Brahman without having studied the ceremonial parts of the Vedas. So if there is no sequence between the sacrificial practices and Jnana, why does the Acharya contradict his own statement when it is a case of the Shudras, by inserting the clause "by force of the same

---

3. See Note 1, p. 4.

4. Shankarâchârya in his commentary on the *Vedanta-Sutras*, I. iii. 34-37, interprets the aphorisms to prove that Upanishadic wisdom was imparted to Janashruti and Satyakama, only because they were not Shudras, as borne out by actual texts. But as these texts are doubtful even after Shankaracharya's explanation, Swamiji wants to be referred to other similar Vedic texts.

5. "The Shudra is not conceived of as a performer of Yajna or Vedic sacrifices."

6. "Now then commences hence the inquiry about Brahman."

logic"? Why should the Shudra not study the Upanishad?

I am mailing you, sir, a book named *Imitation of Christ* written by a Christian Sannyasin. It is a wonderful book. One is astonished to find that such renunciation, Vairâgya, and Dâsya-Bhakti have existed even among the Christians. Probably you may have read this book before; if not, it will give me the greatest pleasure if you will kindly read it.

Yours etc.,
Vivekananda.

1889.8 — SIR[1]

Baranagore,
17th Aug., 1889.

DEAR SIR,

You have expressed embarrassment in your last favour for being addressed reverentially. But the blame attaches not to me but to your own excellent qualities. I wrote in one letter before that from the way I feel attracted by your lofty virtues, it seems we had some affinity from previous births. I make no distinction as to householder or Sannyasin in this, that for all time my head shall bend low in reverence wherever I see greatness, broadness of heart, and holiness — Shântih! Shântih! Shântih! My prayer is that among the many people embracing Sannyâsa nowadays, greedy of honour, posing renunciation for the sake of a living, and fallen off from the ideal on both sides, may one in a lakh at least become high-souled like you! To you my Brahmin fellow-disciples who have heard of your noble virtues tender their best prostrations.

About one amongst my several questions to which you sent your replies, my wrong idea is corrected. For this I shall remain indebted to you for ever. Another of these questions was: Whether Acharya Shankara gives any conclusion regarding caste based on Gunas as mentioned in Puranâs like the Mahabharata. If he does, where is it to be found? I have no doubt that according to the ancient view in this country, caste was hereditary, and it cannot also be doubted that sometimes the Shudras used to be oppressed more than the helots among the Spartans and the negroes among the Americans! As for myself, I have no partiality for any party in this caste question, because I know it is a social law and is based on diversity of Guna and Karma. It also means grave harm if one bent on going beyond Guna and Karma cherishes in mind any caste distinctions. In these matters, I have got some settled ideas through the grace of my Guru but, if I come to know of your views, I may just confirm some points or rectify others in them. One doesn't have honey dripping unless one pokes at the hive — so I shall put you some more questions; and looking upon me as ignorant and as a boy, please give proper replies without taking any offence.

1. See Note 1, p. 4.

1. Is the Mukti, which the Vedanta-Sutras speaks of, one and the same with the Nirvana of the Avadhuta-Gitâ and other texts?

2. What is really meant by Nirvana if, according to the aphorism, "Without the function of creating etc."[2] (ibid., IV. iv. 7), none can attain to the fullest Godhead?

3. Chaitanya-deva is said to have told Sârvabhauma at Puri, "I understand the Sutras (aphorisms) of Vyasa, they are dualistic; but the commentator makes them, monistic, which I don't understand." Is this true? Tradition says, Chaitanya-deva had a dispute with Prakashananda Sarasvati on the point, and Chaitanya-deva won. One commentary by Chaitanya-deva was rumoured to have been existing in Prakashananda's Math.

4. In the Tantra, Acharya Shankara has been called a crypto-Buddhist; views expressed in Prajnâparamitâ, the Buddhist Mâhâyana book, perfectly tally with the Vedantic views propounded by the Acharya. The author of Panchadashi also says, "What we call Brahman is the same truth as the Shunya of the Buddhist." What does all this mean?

5. Why has no foundation for the authority of the Vedas been adduced in the Vedanta-Satras? First, it has been said that the Vedas are the authority for the existence of God, and then it has been argued that the authority for the Vedas is the text: "It is the breath of God." Now, is this statement not vitiated by what in Western logic is called an argument in a circle?

6. The Vedanta requires of us faith, for conclusiveness cannot be reached by mere argumentation. Then why, has the slightest flaw, detected in the position of the schools of Sânkhya and Nyâya, been overwhelmed with a fusillade of dialectics? In whom, moreover, are we to put our faith? Everybody seems to be mad over establishing his own view; if, according to Vyasa, even the great Muni Kapila, "the greatest among perfected souls",[3] is himself deeply involved in error, then who would say that Vyasa may not be so involved in a greater measure? Did Kapila fail to understand the Vedas?

7. According to the Nyaya, "Shabda or Veda (the criterion of truth), is the word of those who have realised the highest"; so the Rishis as such are omniscient. Then how are they proved, according to the Surya-siddhânta, to be ignorant of such simple astronomical truths? How can we accept their intelligence as the refuge to ferry

---

2. जगद्व्यापारवर्जं परकरगादसंनहितित्वाच्च— "Having regard to the context which ascribes the threefold function relating to the universe only to God, and because the fact of their conscious mental distinction comes between that function and their liberated state, we have to conclude that the state of final liberation or Mukti in the case of men is devoid of the capacity to create, preserve, and dissolve the universe." So if this capacity is reserved only for God, what is meant, Swamiji asks, by saying that in Nirvana the human merges completely into the Divine? We must remember that many of the questions here reflect the intellectual stages through which Swamiji was reaching out in those days towards that plenitude of Vedantic wisdom which was his in future years. We also find a glimpse of those processes through which his intellect was growing towards a fuller understanding of our ancient scriptures and customs.

3. Kapila is so spoken of in Shvetâshvatara Upanishad, V.2 In his commentary of **Vedanta-Sutras**, II. i. 1, Shankara doubts the identity of the Vedic Kapila with the Sankhyan Kapila.

us across the ocean of transmigratory existence, seeing that they speak of the earth as triangular, of the serpent Vâsuki as the support of the earth and so on?

8. If in His acts of creation God is dependent on good and evil Karmas, then what does it avail us to worship Him? There is a fine song of Nareshchandra, where occurs the following: "If what lies in one's destiny is to happen anyhow, O Mother, then what good all this invoking by the holy name of Durgâ?"

9. True, it is improper to hold many texts on the same subject to be contradicted by one or two. But why then are the long-continued customs of Madhuparka[1] and the like repealed by one or two such texts as, "The horse sacrifice, the cow sacrifice, Sannyasa, meat-offerings in Shrâddha", etc.? If the Vedas are eternal, then what are the meaning and justification of such specifications as "this rule of Dharma is for the age of Dvâpara," "this for the age of Kali", and so forth?

10. The same God who gives out the Vedas becomes Buddha again to annul them; which of these dispensations is to be obeyed? Which of these remains authoritative, the earlier or the later one?

11. The Tantra says, in the Kali-Yuga the Veda-Mantras are futile. So which behest of God, the Shiva, is to be followed?

12. Vyasa makes out in the Vedanta-Sutras that it is wrong to worship the tetrad of divine manifestation, Vâsudeva, Sankarshana, etc., and again that very Vyasa expatiates on the great merits of that worship in the Bhâgavata! Is this Vyasa a madman?

I have many doubts besides these, and, hoping to have them dispelled from my mind through your kindness, I shall lay them before you in future. Such questions cannot be all set forth except in a personal interview; neither can as much satisfaction be obtained as one expects to. So I have a mind to lay before you all these facts when presenting myself to you, which I expect will be very soon, by the grace of the Guru.

I have heard it said that without inner progress in the practice of religion, no true conclusion can be reached concerning these matters, simply by means of reasoning; but satisfaction, at least to some extent, seems to be necessary at the outset.

Yours etc.,
Vivekananda.

---

1. Madhuparka was a Vedic ceremony, usually in honour of guest, in which a respectful offering was to be made consisting, among other dainties, of beef. The text which Swamiji partially quotes forbids such food. The full text means that in the Kali-Yuga the following five customs are to be forsaken: The horse sacrifice, cow-killing ceremonies, meat-offerings in Shraddha, Sannyasa, and maintaining the line of progeny through the husband's younger brother in case of failure through the husband.

1889.9 — SIR[2]

Baghbazar, Calcutta,
2nd Sept., 1889.

DEAR SIR,

Some days ago I received your two kind letters. I am very much pleased to find in you a wonderful harmony of Jnana and Bhakti. Your advice to me to give up arguing and disputing is very true indeed, and that is really the goal of life for the individual — "Sundered are the knots of the heart, torn off are all his doubts, and the seeds of his Karma wear off, when the sight of the Transcendent One is gained." (Mundakonapanishad, II. ii. 8.) But then, as my Master used to say, when a pitcher is being filled (by immersion), it gurgles, but when full, it is noiseless; know my condition to be the same. Within two or three weeks perhaps, I shall be able to meet you — may God fulfil that wish!

Yours etc.,
Vivekananda.

1889.10 — SIR[3]

Baghbazar,
3rd Dec., 1889.

DEAR SIR,

I have not heard from you for a long time, I hope you are doing well in body and mind. Two of my brother disciples are shortly leaving for Varanasi. One is Rakhal by name, the other is Subodh. The first-named was beloved of my Master and used to stay much with him. Please recommend them to some Satra (house of alms.) during their stay in the city, if you find it convenient. You will hear from them all my news.

With my best regards and greetings.

Yours etc.,
Vivekananda.

PS — Gangadhar is now proceeding to Kailas. The Tibetans wanted to slash him up on the way, taking him to be a spy of the foreigners. Eventually some Lamas kindly set him free. We obtain this news from a Tibet-going trader. Gangadhar's blood won't cool down before seeing Lhasa. The gain is that his physical endurance has grown immensely — one night he passed uncovered on a bed of snow, and that without much hardship.

---

2. See Note 1, p. 4.
3. See Note 1, p. 4.

1889.11 — SIR[1]

Baranagore, Calcutta,
13th Dec., 1889.

DEAR SIR,

I have all particulars from your letter; and from Rakhal's which followed, I came to know of your meeting. I have received the pamphlet written by you. A kind of scientific Advaitism has been spreading in Europe ever since the theory of the conservation of energy was discovered, but all that is Parinâmavâda, evolution by real modification. It is good you have shown the difference between this and Shankara's Vivartavâda (progressive manifestation by unreal superimposition). I can't appreciate your citing Spencer's parody on the German transcendentalists; he himself is fed much on their doles. It is doubtful whether your opponent Gough understands his Hegel sufficiently. Anyway, your rejoinder is very pointed and thrashing.

Yours etc.,
Vivekananda.

1889.12 — SHRI BALARAM BOSE[2]

Glory to Ramakrishna!

Baidyanath,
25th December, 1889.

DEAR SIR, (Shri Balaram Bose)

I have been staying for the last few days at Baidyanath in Purna Babu's Lodge. It is not so cold, and my health too is indifferent. I am suffering from indigestion, probably due to excess of iron in the water. I have found nothing agreeable here — neither the place, nor the season, nor the company. I leave for Varanasi tomorrow. Achyutananda stopped at Govinda Chaudhury's place at Deoghar, and the latter, as soon as he got news of us, earnestly insisted on our becoming his guests. Finally, he met us once again and prevailed on us to accede to his request. The man is a great worker, but has a number of women with him — old women most of them, of the ordinary Vaishnava type... His clerks too revere us much; some of them are very much ill-disposed towards him, and they spoke of his misdeeds. Incidentally, I raised the topic of __. You have many wrong ideas or doubts about her; hence I write all this after particular investigation. Even the aged clerks of this establishment highly respect and revere her. She came to stop with __ while she was a mere child, and ever lived as his wife... Everyone admits in one voice that her character is spotless. She was all along a perfectly chaste woman and never behaved with __ in any relation but that of wife to husband, and she was absolutely

---

1. See Note 1, p. 4.
2. Translated from Bengali.

faithful. She came at too early an age to have incurred any moral taint. After she had separated from __, she wrote to him to say that she had never treated him as anything but her husband, but that it was impossible for her to live with a man with a loose character. His old office-bearers too believe him to be satanic in character; but they consider __ a Devi (angel), and remark that it was following her departure that __ lost all sense of shame.

My object in writing all this is that formerly I was not a believer in the tale of the lady's early life. The idea that there might be such purity in the midst of a relation which society does not recognise, I used to consider as romance. But after thorough investigation I have come to know that it is all right. She is very pure, pure from her infancy — I have not the least doubt about it. For entertaining those doubts, you and I and everyone are guilty to her; I make repeated salutations to her, and ask her pardon for my guilt. She is not a liar.

I take this opportunity to record that such courage is impossible in a lying and unchaste woman. I have also been told that she had a lifelong ardent faith in religion also.

Well, your disease is not yet improving! I don't think this is a place for patients unless one is ready to spend a good deal of money. Please think out some judicious course. Here every article will have to be procured from elsewhere.

Yours affectionately,
Vivekananda.

1889.13 — SIR[3]

Baidyanath,
26th Dec., 1889.

DEAR SIR,

After a long attempt, I think, I am now in a position to present myself before you. In a day or two I take myself to your feet at holy Kashi.

I have been putting up here for some days with a gentleman of Calcutta, but my mind is much longing for Varanasi. My idea is to remain there for some time, and to watch how Vishvanâtha and Annapurnâ[4] deal it out to my lot. And my resolve is something like "either to lay down my life or realise my ideal"[5] — so help me the Lord of Kashi.

Yours etc.,
Vivekananda.

---

3. See Note 1, p. 4.
4. Shiva and His Divine Spouse as installed in Varanasi.
5. "शरीरं वा पातयामि मन्त्रं वा साधयामि।"

1889.14 — SIR[1]

Allahabad,
30th Dec., 1889.

DEAR SIR,

I wrote in a letter to you that I was to go to Varanasi in a day or two, but who can nullify the decree of Providence? News reached me that a brother-disciple, Yogen by name, had been attacked with smallpox after arriving here from a pilgrimage to Chitrakuta, Omkarnath, etc., and so I came to this place to nurse him. He has now completely recovered. Some Bengali gentlemen here are of a greatly pious and loving disposition. They are very lovingly taking care of me, and their importunate desire is that I should stay here during the month of Mâgha (Jan.-Feb.) keeping the Kalpa vow[2]. But my mind is very keenly harping on the name of Varanasi and is quite agog to see you. Yes, I am going to try my best to slip away and avoid their importunities in a day or two and betake myself to the holy realm of the Lord of Varanasi. If one of my monastic brother-disciples, Achyutananda Sarasvati by name, calls on you to enquire of me, please tell him I am soon coming to Varanasi. He is indeed a very good man and learned. I was obliged to leave him behind at Bankipore. Are Rakhal and Subodh still there in Varanasi? Please inquire and inform me whether the Kumbha fair this year is going to be held at Hardwar or not.

Many a man of wisdom, of piety, many a Sâdhu (holy man) and Pundit have I met in so many places, and I have been very much favoured by them, but "भिन्नरुचिर्हि लोकाः — Men are of varying tastes" — Raghuvamsham. I know not what sort of soul-affinity there is between us, for nowhere else does it seem so pleasing and agreeable as with you. Let me see how the Lord of Kashi disposes.

Yours etc.,
Vivekananda.

My address is:
C/o Govinda Chandra Basu, Chauk, Allahabad.

---

1. See Note 1, p. 4.
2. Special ablutions and worship regularly performed in that holy confluence — a very solemn and sacred practice.

1889.15 — SHRI BALARAM BOSE[3]

Glory to Ramakrishna!

Allahabad,
30th December, 1889.

DEAR SIR, (Shri Balaram Bose)

Gupta left a slip when coming and the next day a letter from Yogananda gave me all the news and I immediately started for Allahabad which I reached the day after, to find that Yogananda had completely recovered. He had chicken-pox (with one or two smallpox rashes also). The doctor is a noble soul, and they have got a brotherhood, who are all great pious men and highly devoted to the service of Sâdhus. They are particularly anxious that I pass the month of Mâgh here, but I am leaving for Varanasi... How are you? I pray to God for the welfare of yourself and your family. Please convey my compliments to Tulasiram, Chuni Babu, and the rest.

Yours affectionately,
Vivekananda.

1889.16 — SIR[4]

Simla (Calcutta),
14th July, 1889.

RESPECTED SIR, (Shri Pramadadas Mitra)

I was very glad to get your letter. In such circumstances many give the advice to incline towards the worldly life. But you are truthful and have an adamantine heart. I have been highly comforted by your encouraging and cheering words. My difficulties here have almost come to a close—only I have engaged the services of a broker for the sale of a piece of land, and I hope the sale will be over soon. In that case, I shall be free from all worry and shall at once go straight off to you to Varanasi.

Your servant,
Vivekananda.

---

3 Translated from Bengali.
4 Translated from Bengali.

1890

1890.1 — FAKIR[1]

Allahabad,
5th January, 1890.

MY DEAR FAKIR[2],

...A word for you. Remember always, I may not see you again. Be moral. Be brave. Be a heart-whole man. Strictly moral, brave unto desperation. Don't bother your head with religious theories. Cowards only sin, brave men never, no, not even in mind. Try to love anybody and everybody. Be a man and try to make those immediately under your care, namely Ram, Krishnamayi, and Indu, brave, moral, and sympathising. No religion for you, my children, but morality and bravery. No cowardice, no sin, no crime, no weakness — the rest will come of itself... And don't take Ram with you ever or ever allow him to visit a theatre or any enervating entertainment whatever.

Yours affectionately,
Vivekananda.

MY DEAR RAM, KRISHNAMAYI, AND INDU,

Bear in mind, my children, that only cowards and those who are weak commit sin and tell lies. The brave are always moral. Try to be moral, try to be brave, try to be sympathising.

Yours,
Vivekananda.

1890.2 — SIR

Salutation to Shri Ramakrishna!

Allahabad,
5th January, 1890.

MY DEAR SIR, (Sj. Balaram Bose)

I am very sorry to hear of your illness from your kind note. The gist of the letter I wrote to you about your change to Baidyanath was that it would be impossible for a man of weak and extremely delicate physique like you to live in that place unless you spent a good deal of money. If change be really advisable for you, and if you have deferred it so long simply to select a cheaper place and that sort of thing, it is certainly a matter of regret... Baidyanath is excellent so far as the air is concerned, but the water is not good, it upsets the stomach. I used to suffer from acidity every day. I have already written you a letter; have you got it, or finding it a bearing letter,

---

1 Translated from Bengali.
2. Shri Yajneshwar Bhattacharya.

have you left it to its fate? In my opinion, if you have to go away for a change, the sooner the better. But, pardon me, you have a tendency to expect that everything should fit in exactly with your requirements, but unfortunately, such a state of things is very rare in this world. "आत्मानं सततं रक्षेत्—One must save oneself under any circumstances." "Lord have mercy", is all right, but He helps him who helps himself. If you simply try to save your purse, will the Lord arrange the change for you by drawing on His ancestral capital? If you think you have so much reliance on the Lord, don't call in the doctor, please... If that does not suit you, you should go to Varanasi. I would have already left this place, but the local gentlemen would not give me leave to depart!... But let me repeat once more, if change is actually decided upon, please do not hesitate out of miserliness. That would be suicide. And not even God can save a suicide. Please convey my compliments to Tulasi Babu and the rest.

With best regards,

Yours etc.,
Vivekananda.

1890.3 — SIR[1]

C/O Babu Satish Chandra Mukherji, Gorabazar, Ghazipur,
21st Jan., 1890.

DEAR SIR,

I reached Ghazipur three days ago. Here I am putting up in the house of Babu Satish Chandra Mukherji, a friend of my early age. The place is very pleasant. Close by flows the Ganga, but bathing there is troublesome, for there is no regular path, and it is hard work wading through sands. Babu Ishan Chandra Mukherji, my friend's father, that noble-hearted man of whom I spoke to you, is here. Today he is leaving for Varanasi whence he will proceed to Calcutta. I again had a great mind to go over to Kashi, but the object of my coming here, namely, an interview with the Bâbâji (Pavhâri Bâbâ, the great saint.), has not yet been realised, and. hence the delay of a few days becomes necessary. Everything here appears good. The people are all gentlemen, but very much Westernised; and it is a pity I am so thoroughly against every affectation of the Western idea. Only my friend very little affects such ideals. What a frippery civilisation is it indeed that the foreigners have brought over here! What a materialistic illusion have they created! May Vishvanâtha save these weak-hearted! After seeing Babaji, I shall send you a detailed account.

Yours etc.,
Vivekananda.

PS—Alas for the irony of our fate, that in this land of Bhagavân Shuka's birth, renunciation is looked down upon as madness and sin!

1. See Note 1, p. 4.

1890.4 — SHRI BALARAM BOSE[2]

Ghazipur,
30th January, 1890.

REVERED SIR, (Shri Balaram Bose)

I am now stopping with Satish Babu at Ghazipur. Of the few places I have recently visited, this is the healthiest. The water of Baidyanath is very bad — it leads to indigestion. Allahabad is very congested. The few days I passed at Varanasi, I suffered from fever day and night — the place is so malarious! Ghazipur has a very salubrious climate — specially the quarter I am living in. I have visited Pavhari Baba's house — there are high walls all round, and it is fashioned like an English bungalow. There is a garden inside and big rooms and chimneys, etc. He allows nobody to enter. If he is so inclined, he comes up to the door and speaks from inside — that is all. One day I went and waited and waited in the cold and had to return. I shall go to Varanasi on Sunday next. If the meeting with the Babaji takes place in the meantime, all right, otherwise I bid him good-bye. About Pramada Babu's place I shall write definitely from Varanasi. If Kali Bhattacharya is determined to come, let him do so after I leave for Varanasi on Sunday, but he should rather not. After a few days' stay at Varanasi, I shall start for Hrishikesh. Pramada Babu may accompany me. Please accept all of you my cordial greetings — and blessing to Fakir, Ram, Krishnamayi, etc.

Yours affectionately,
Vivekananda.

PS — In my opinion, it will do you much good if you come and stay for some time at Ghazipur. Here Satish will be able to secure a bungalow for you, and there is a gentleman, Gagan Chandra Ray by name, who is the head of the Opium Office and is exceedingly courteous, philanthropic, and social — they will arrange for everything. The house-rent is fifteen to twenty rupees; rice is dear, and milk sells at sixteen to twenty seers a rupee; all other things are very cheap. Besides, under the care of these gentlemen, there is no chance of any difficulty. But it is slightly expensive — it will cost over forty to fifty rupees. Varanasi is horribly malarious. I have never lived in Pramada Babu's garden. He likes to have me always in his company. The garden is indeed very beautiful, richly laid out, spacious, and open. This time when I go, I shall live there and report to you.

---

2 Translated from Bengali.

1890.5 — SIR[1]

Ghazipur,
31st Jan., 1890.

DEAR SIR,

It is so very difficult to meet the Babaji. He does not step out of his home; and, when willing to speak at all, he just comes near the door to speak from inside. I have come away with having just a view of his garden-house with chimneys tapering above and encircled by high walls — no means of admittance within! People say there are cave-like rooms within where he dwells; and he only knows what he does there, for nobody has had a peep. I had to come away one day sorely used up with waiting and waiting, but shall take my chance again. On Sunday, I leave for holy Varanasi — only the Babus here won't let me off; otherwise all my fancy to see the Babaji has flattened down. I am prepared to be off today, but anyhow, I am leaving on Sunday. What of your plan of going to Hrishikesh?

Yours etc.,
Vivekananda.

PS — The redeeming feature is that the place seems healthy.

1890.6 — SIR[2]

Ghazipur,
4th Feb., 1890.

DEAR SIR,

Received your kind note, and through supreme good fortune, I have obtained an interview with Babaji. A great sage indeed! — It is all very wonderful, and in this atheistic age, a towering representation of marvellous power born of Bhakti and Yoga! I have sought refuge in his grace; and he has given me hope — a thing very few may be fortunate enough to obtain. It is Babaji's wish that I stay on for some days here, and he would do me some good. So following this saint's bidding I shall remain here for some time. No doubt, this will give you also much pleasure. I don't mention them in a letter, but the facts are very strange indeed — to be disclosed when we meet. Unless one is face to face with the life of such men, faith in the scriptures does not grow in all its real integrity.

Yours etc.,
Vivekananda.

---

1. See Note 1, p. 4.
2. See Note 1, p. 4.

1890.7 — SIR[3]

To Balaram Bose:

Glory to Ramakrishna!

Ghazipur,
February 6, 1890.

RESPECTED SIR,

I have talked with Pavhari Baba. He is a wonderful saint — the embodiment of humility, devotion, and Yoga. Although he is an orthodox Vaishnava, he is not prejudiced against others of different beliefs. He has tremendous love for Mahâprabhu Chaitanya, and he [Pavhari Baba] speaks of Shri Ramakrishna as "an incarnation of God". He loves me very much, and I am going to stay here for some days at his request.

Pavhari Baba can live in Samâdhi for from two to six months at a stretch. He can read Bengali and has kept a photograph of Shri Ramakrishna in his room. I have not yet seen him face to face, since he speaks from behind a door, but I have never heard such a sweet voice. I have many things to say about him but not just at present.

Please try to get a copy of Chaitanya-Bhâgavata for him and send it immediately to the following address: Gagan Chandra Roy, Opium Department, Ghazipur. Please don't forget.

Pavhari Baba is an ideal Vaishnava and a great scholar; but he is reluctant to reveal his learning. His elder brother acts as his attendant, but even he is not allowed to enter his room.

Please send him a copy of Chaitanya-Mangala also, if it is still in print. And remember that if Pavhari Baba accepts your presents, that will be your great fortune. Ordinarily, he does not accept anything from anybody. Nobody knows what he eats or even what he does.

Please don't let it be known that I am here and don't send news of anyone to me. I am busy with an important work.

Your servant,
Vivekananda.

---

[3] Translated from Bengali.

1890.8 — SIR[1]

Ghazipur,
7th Feb., 1890.

DEAR SIR,

I feel very happy to hear from you just now. Apparently in his features, the Babaji is a Vaishnava the embodiment, so to speak, of Yoga, Bhakti, and humility. His dwelling has walls on all sides with a few doors in them. Inside these walls, there is one long underground burrow wherein he lays himself up in Samâdhi. He talks to others only when he comes out of the hole. Nobody knows what he eats, and so they call him Pavhâri (One living on air.) Bâbâ. Once he did not come out of the hole for five years, and people thought he had given up the body. But now again he is out. But this time he does not show himself to people and talks from behind the door. Such sweetness in speech I have never come across! He does not give a direct reply to questions but says, "What does this servant know?" But then fire comes out as the talking goes on. On my pressing him very much he said, "Favour me highly by staying here some days." But he never speaks in this way; so from this I understood he meant to reassure me and whenever I am importunate, he asks me to stay on. So I wait in hope. He is a learned man no doubt but nothing in the line betrays itself. He performs scriptural ceremonials, for from the full-moon day to the last day of the month, sacrificial oblations go on. So it is sure, he is not retiring into the hole during this period. How can I ask his permission, (Evidently for a proposed visit to the saint by the correspondent, Pramadadas Mitra of Varanasi.). for he never gives a direct reply; he goes on multiplying such expressions as "this servant", "my fortune", and so on. If you yourself have a mind, then come sharp on receipt of this note. Or after his passing away, the keenest regret will be left in your mind. In two days you may return after an interview—I mean a talk with him ab intra. My friend Satish Babu will receive you most warmly. So, do come up directly you receive this; I shall meanwhile let Babaji know of you.

Yours etc.,
Vivekananda.

PS—Even though one can't have his company, no trouble taken for the sake of such a great soul can ever go unrewarded.

---

1. See Note 1, p. 4.

1890.9 — SIR[2]

To Balaram Bose:

Glory to Ramakrishna!

Ghazipur,
February 11, 1890.

RESPECTED SIR,

I have received your book. In Hrishikesh, Kali [Swami Abhedananda] has had a relapse and is again suffering from what seems to be malaria. Once it comes, the fever does not easily leave those who have never had it before. I too suffered the same way when I first had the attack of fever. Kali has never had the fever before. I have not received any letter from Hrishikesh. Where is … ?

I am suffering terribly from a backache which began in Allahabad. I had recovered from it some time back, but it has recurred. So I will have to stay here awhile longer because of my back and also because Babaji [Pavhari Baba] has requested it.

What you have written about uncooked bread is true. But a monk dies that way, not like the breaking of a cup and saucer. This time I am not going to be overcome by weakness in any way. And if I die, that will be good for me. It is better to depart from this world very soon.

Your servant,
Vivekananda.

1890.10 — SIR[3]

Ghazipur,
13th Feb., 1890.

DEAR SIR,

I am in anxiety to hear of your illness. I am also having some sort of a pain in the loins which, being aggravated of late, gives much trouble. For two days I could not go out to meet Babaji, and so a man came from him to inquire about me. For this reason, I go today. I shall convey your countless compliments. "Fire comes out" that is, a wonderful devotion to Guru and resignation are revealed; and such amazing endurance and humility I have never seen. Whatever good things I may come by, sure, you have your share in them.

Yours etc.,
Vivekananda.

---

2 Translated from Bengali.
3. See Note 1, p. 4.

1890.11 — SIR[1]

Ghazipur,
14th Feb., 1890.

DEAR SIR,

In my note of yesterday I perhaps forgot to ask you to return brother Sharat's letter. Please send it. I have heard from brother Gangadhar. He is now in Rambag Samadhi, Srinagar, Kashmir. I am greatly suffering from lumbago.

Yours etc.,
Vivekananda.

PS — Rakhal and Subodh have come to Vrindaban after visiting Omkar, Girnar, Abu, Bombay, and Dwarka.

1890.12 — SHRI BALARAM BOSE[2]

Salutation to Bhagavan Ramakrishna!

C/O Satish Mukherji,
Gorabazar, Ghazipur.
14th February, 1890.

REVERED SIR, (Shri Balaram Bose)

I am in receipt of your letter of contrition. I am not leaving this place soon — it is impossible to avoid the Babaji's request. You have expressed remorse at not having reaped any appreciable results by serving the Sadhus. It is true, and yet not true; it is true if you look towards ideal bliss; but if you look behind to the place from which you started, you will find that before you were an animal, now you are a man, and will be a god or God Himself in future. Moreover, that sort of regret and dissatisfaction is very good; it is the prelude to improvement. Without this none can rise. He who puts on a turban and immediately sees the Lord, progresses thus far and no farther. You are blessed indeed to have that constant dissatisfaction preying upon your mind — rest assured that there is no danger for you... You are a keenly intelligent man, and know full well that patience is the best means of success. In this respect I have no doubt that we light-headed boys have much to learn from you... You are a considerate man, and I need not add anything. Man has two ears but one mouth. You specially are given to plain-speaking and are chary of making large promises — things that sometimes make me cross with you, but upon reflection I find that it is you who have acted with discretion. "Slow but sure." "What is lost in power is gained in speed." However, in this world everything depends upon one's words. To get an insight behind the words (specially, with your economical

---

1. See Note 1, p. 4.
2 Translated from Bengali.

spirit masking all) is not given to all, and one must associate long with a man to be able to understand him... Religion is not in sects, nor in making a fuss—why do you forget these teachings of our revered Master? Please help as far as it lies in you, but to judge what came of it, whether it was turned to good or evil account, is perhaps beyond our jurisdiction... Considering the great shock which Girish Babu has received, it will give him immense peace to serve Mother at this moment. He is a very keen-witted person. And our beloved Master had perfect confidence in you, used to dine nowhere else except at your place, and, I have heard, Mother too has the fullest confidence in you. In view of these, you will please bear and forbear all shortcomings of us fickle boys, treating them as if they were done by your own boy. This is all I have got to say. Please let me know by return of post when the Anniversary is to take place. A pain in the loins is giving me much trouble. In a few days the place will look exceedingly beautiful, with miles and miles of rose-banks all in flower. Satish says he will then send some fresh roses and cuttings for the Festival... May the Lord ordain that your son becomes a man, and never a coward!

Yours affectionately,
Vivekananda.

PS—If Mother has come, please convey to her my countless salutations, and ask her to bless me that I may have unflinching perseverance. Or, if that be impossible in this body, may it fall off soon!

1890.13 — GUPTA[3]

Ghazipur,
14th Feb., 1890.

MY DEAR GUPTA, (Swami Sadananda)

I hope you are doing well. Do your own spiritual exercises, and knowing yourself to be the humblest servant of all, serve them. Those with whom you are staying are such that even I am not worthy to call myself their humblest servant and take the dust of their feet. Knowing this, serve them and have devotion for them. Don't be angry even if they abuse or even hurt you grievously. Never mix with women. Try to be hardy little by little, and gradually accustom yourself to maintaining the body out of the proceeds of begging. Whoever takes the name of Ramakrishna, know him to be your Guru. Everyone can play the role of a master, but it is very difficult to be a servant. Specially you should follow Shashi. Know it for certain that without steady devotion for the Guru and unflinching patience and perseverance, nothing is to be achieved. You must have strict morality. Deviate an inch from this, and you are gone forever.

Yours affectionately,
Vivekananda.

---

3 Translated from Bengali.

1890.14 — SIR[1]

Victory to the Lord!

Ghazipur,
19th Feb., 1890.

DEAR SIR,

I wrote a letter to brother Gangadhar asking him to stop his wandering and settle down somewhere and to send me an account of the various Sadhus he had come across in Tibet and their ways and customs. I enclose the reply that came from him. Brother Kali is having repeated attacks of fever at Hrishikesh. I have sent him a wire from this place. So if from the reply I find I am wanted by him, I shall be obliged to start direct for Hrishikesh from this place, otherwise I am coming to you in a day or two. Well, you may smile, sir, to see me weaving all this web of Mâyâ—and that is no doubt the fact. But then there is the chain of iron, and there is the chain of gold. Much good comes of the latter; and it drops off by itself when all the good is reaped. The sons of my Master are indeed the great objects of my service, and here alone I feel I have some duty left for me. Perhaps I shall send brother Kali down to Allahabad or somewhere else, as convenient. At your feet are laid a hundred and one faults of mine—"I am as thy son, so guide me who have taken refuge in thee." (An adaptation from the Gitâ, II. 7.)

Yours etc.,
Vivekananda.

1890.15 — AKHANDANANDA

Salutation to Bhagavan Ramakrishna!

Ghazipur,
February, 1890.

BELOVED AKHANDANANDA,

Very glad to receive your letter. What you have written about Tibet is very promising, and I shall try to go there once. In Sanskrit Tibet is called the Uttarakuru-varsha, and is not a land of Mlechchhas. Being the highest tableland in the world, it is extremely cold, but by degrees one may become accustomed to it. About the manners and customs of the Tibetans you have written nothing. If they are so hospitable, why did they not allow you to go on? Please write everything in detail, in a long letter. I am sorry to learn that you will not be able to come, for I had a great longing to see you. It seems that I love you more than all others. However, I shall try to get rid of this Maya too.

The Tântrika rites among the Tibetans that you have spoken of arose in India

---

1. See Note 1, p. 4.

itself, during the decline of Buddhism. It is my belief that the Tantras, in vogue amongst us, were the creation of the Buddhists themselves. Those Tantrika rites are even more dreadful than our doctrine of Vâmâchâra; for in them adultery got a free rein, and it was only when the Buddhists became demoralised through immorality that they were driven away by Kumârila Bhatta. As some Sannyasins speak of Shankara, or the Bâuls of Shri Chaitanya, that he was in secret an epicure, a drunkard, and one addicted to all sorts of abominable practices—so the modern Tantrika Buddhists speak of the Lord Buddha as a dire Vamâchâri and give an obscene interpretation to the many beautiful precepts of the *Prajnâpâramitâ*, such as the *Tattvagâthâ* and the like. The result of all this has been that the Buddhists are divided into two sects nowadays; the Burmese and the Sinhalese have generally set the Tantras at naught, have likewise banished the Hindu gods and goddesses, and at the same time have thrown overboard the Amitâbha Buddha held in regard among the Northern School of Buddhists. The long and the short of it is that the Amitabha Buddha and the other gods whom the Northern School worship are not mentioned in books like the *Prajnaparamita*, but a lot of gods and goddesses are recommended for worship. And the Southern people have wilfully transgressed the Shâstras and eschewed the gods and goddesses. The phase of Buddhism which declares "Everything for others", and which you find spread throughout Tibet, has greatly struck modern Europe. Concerning that phase, however, I have a good deal to say—which it is impossible to do in this letter. What Buddha did was to break wide open the gates of that very religion which was confined in the Upanishads to a particular caste. What special greatness does his theory of Nirvana confer on him? His greatness lies in his unrivalled sympathy. The high orders of Samadhi etc., that lend gravity to his religion are, almost all there in the Vedas; what are absent there are his intellect and heart, which have never since been paralleled throughout the history of the world.

The Vedic doctrine of Karma is the same as in Judaism and all other religions, that is to say, the purification of the mind through sacrifices and such other external means—and Buddha was the first man who stood against it. But the inner essence of the ideas remained as of old—look at that doctrine of mental exercises which he preached, and that mandate of his to believe in the Suttas instead of the Vedas. Caste also remained as of old (caste was not wholly obsolete at the time of Buddha), but it was now determined by personal qualifications; and those that were not believers in his religion were declared as heretics, all in the old style. "Heretic" was a very ancient word with the Buddhists, but then they never had recourse to the sword (good souls!) and had great toleration. Argument blew up the Vedas. But what is the proof of your religion? Well, put faith in it!—the same procedure as in all religions. It was however an imperative necessity of the times; and that was the reason of his having incarnated himself. His doctrine is like that of Kapila. But that of Shankara, how far more grand and rational! Buddha and Kapila are always saying the world is full of grief and nothing but that—flee from it—ay, for your life, do! Is happiness altogether absent here? It is a statement of the nature of what the Brahmos say—the world is full of happiness! There is grief, forsooth, but what can be done? Perchance some will suggest that grief itself will appear as happiness when you become used to it by constant suffering. Shankara does not take this line of argument. He says: This world *is* and is *not*—*manifold* yet one; *I shall unravel its mystery—I shall know whether grief be there, or anything else*; I do not flee from it as from a bugbear. I will know all about it as to the infinite pain that attends its search, well, I am embracing it in its fullest measure. Am I a beast that you frighten me with happiness and misery, decay and death, which are but the outcome of the senses? I will know about it—will give up my life for it. There is nothing to know about in this world—therefore, if there be anything beyond this relative existence—what the Lord Buddha has designated as *Prajnâpâra*—the transcendental—if such there be, I want that alone. Whether happiness attends it or grief, I do not care. What a lofty idea! How grand! The religion of Buddha has reared itself on the Upanishads, and upon that also the philosophy of Shankara. Only, Shankara had not the slightest bit of Buddha's wonderful heart, dry intellect merely! For fear of the Tantras, for fear of the mob, in his attempt to cure a boil, he amputated the very arm itself[1]! One has to write a big volume if one has to write about them at all—but I have neither the learning nor the leisure for it.

The Lord Buddha is my Ishta—my God. He preached no theory about Godhead—he was himself God, I fully believe it. But no one has the power to put a limit to God's infinite glory. No, not even God Himself has the power to make Himself limited. The translation of the *Gandâra-Sutta* that you have made from the *Suttanipâta*, is excellent. In that book there is another *Sutta*—the *Dhaniya-Sutta*—which has got a similar idea. There are many passages in the Dhammapada too, with similar ideas. But that is at the last stage when one has got perfectly satisfied with knowledge and realisation, is the same under all circumstances and has gained mastery over his senses—"ज्ञानविज्ञानतृप्तात्मा कूटस्थो विजितेन्द्रियः" (Gita, VI. 8.). He who has not the least regard for his body as something to be taken care of—it is he who may roam about at pleasure like the mad elephant caring for naught. Whereas a puny creature like myself should practice devotion, sitting at one spot, till he attains realization; and then only should he behave like that; but it is a far-off question—very far indeed.

चिन्ताशून्यमदैन्यभैक्ष्यमशनं पानं सरिद्वारिपि
स्वातन्त्र्येण निरंकुशा स्थितिरभीर्निद्रा श्मशाने वने।
वस्त्रं क्षालनशोषणादिरहितं दिग्वास्तु शय्या मही
संचारो निगमान्तवीथिषु वदां क्रीडा परे ब्रह्मणि॥
विमानमालम्ब्य शरीरमेतद्
भुनक्त्यशेषान्विषयानुपस्थितान् ।

---

1. In his anxiety to defend the purity of the Vedic religion against the excesses of Tantrikism, which as capturing the rank and file of his countrymen, Shankara neglected the problem of the latter, stigmatised as Shudras by the Vedicists. This is perhaps the meaning of Swamiji. It seems he could never forgive Shankara for applying in his commentary on the Brahma-Sutras the old logic of forbidding Vedic rituals to the Shudras to the more modern question of their right to higher modes of worship (Upâsanâ) and knowledge (Jnâna) of the Jnâna-kânda.

परेच्छया बालवदात्मवेत्ता
योऽव्यक्तलिङ्गोऽननुपक्तबाह्यः ॥
दिगम्बरो वापि च साम्बरो वा
त्वगम्बरो वापि चिदिम्बरस्थः।
उन्मत्तवद्वापि च बालवद्वा
पिशाचवद्वापि चरत्यवन्याम्॥

(*Vivekachudmani*, 538-40)

—To a knower of Brahman food comes of itself, without effort—he drinks wherever he gets it. He roams at pleasure everywhere—he is fearless, sleeps sometimes in the forest, sometimes in a crematorium and, treads the Path which the Vedas have taken but whose end they have not seen. His body is like the sky; and he is guided, like a child, by others' wishes; he is sometimes naked, sometimes in gorgeous clothes, and at times has only Jnana as his clothing; he behaves sometimes like a child, sometimes like a madman, and at other times again like a ghoul, indifferent to cleanliness.

I pray to the holy feet of our Guru that you may have that state, and you may wander like the rhinoceros.

Yours etc.,
Vivekananda.

1890.16 — SIR[2]

Victory to the Lord!

Ghazipur,
25th Feb., 1890.

DEAR SIR,

The lumbago is giving a good deal of trouble, or else I would have already sought to come to you. The mind does not find rest here any longer. It is three days since I came away from Babaji's place, but he inquires of me kindly almost every day. As soon as the lumbago is a little better, I bid good-bye to Babaji. Countless greetings to you.

Yours etc.,
Vivekananda.

---

2 Translated from Bengali.

1890.17 — SIR[1]

To Balaram Bose:
Salutation to Bhagavan Shri Ramakrishna!

Ghazipur,
February, 1890.

RESPECTED SIR,

I have received an anonymous letter which I have been unable to trace back to the gigantic soul who wrote it. Indeed, one should pay homage to such a man. He who considers a great soul like Pavhari Baba to be no more than water in a hoof print, he who has nothing to learn in this world and who feels it a disgrace to be taught by any other man—truly, such a new incarnation must be visited. I hope that if the government should discover the identity of this person, he will be handled with special care and be placed in the Alipore garden [zoo]. If you happen to know this man, please ask him to bless me, so that even a dog or a jackal may be my Guru—not to speak of a great soul like Pavhari Baba.

I have many things to learn. My master used to say: "As long as I live, so long do I learn". Also please tell this fellow that unfortunately I do not have the time to "cross the seven seas and thirteen rivers" or to go to Sri Lanka in order to sleep after having put oil in the nostrils.

Your servant,
Vivekananda.

PS—Please have the rose-water brought from Ishan Babu's [Ishan Chandra Mukherjee's] residence if there is delay [in their sending it to the Baranagore Math]. The roses are still not in bloom. The rose-water has just been sent to the residence of Ishan Babu.

1890.18 — SIR[2]

Victory to the Lord!

Ghazipur,
3rd March, 1890.

DEAR SIR,

Your kind letter comes to hand just now. You know not, sir, I am a very soft-natured man in spite of the stern Vedantic views I hold. And this proves to be my undoing. At the slightest touch I give myself away; for howsoever I may try to think only of my own good, I slip off in spite of myself to think of other peoples' interests. This time it was with a very stern resolve that I set out to pursue my own good, but I had to run off at the news of the illness of a brother at Allahabad! And now

1 Translated from Bengali.
2 Translated from Bengali.

comes this news from Hrishikesh, and my mind has run off with me there. I have wired to Sharat, hut no reply yet — a nice place indeed to delay even telegrams so much! The lumbago obstinately refuses to leave me, and the pain is very great. For the last few days I haven't been able to go to see Pavhariji, but out of his kindness he sends every day for my report. But now I see the whole matter is inverted in its bearings! While I myself have come, a beggar, at his door, he turns round and wants to learn of me! This saint perhaps is not yet perfected — too much of rites, vows, observances, and too much of self-concealment. The ocean in its fullness cannot be contained within its shores, I am sure. So it is not good, I have decided not to disturb this Sâdhu (holy man) for nothing, and very soon I shall ask leave of him to go. No help, you see; Providence has dealt me my death to make me so tender! Babaji does not let me off, and Gagan Babu (whom probably you know — an upright, pious, and kindhearted man) does not let me off. If the wire in reply requires my leaving this place, I go; if not, I am coming to you at Varanasi in a few days. I am not going to let you off — I must take you to Hrishikesh — no excuse or objections will do. What are you saying about difficulties there of keeping clean? Lack of water in the hills or lack of room!! Tirthas (places of pilgrimage) and Sannyasins of the Kali-Yuga — you know what they are. Spend money and the owners of temples will fling away the installed god to make room for you; so no anxiety about a resting-place! No trouble to face there, I say; the summer heat has set in there now, I believe, though not that degree of it as you find at Varanasi — so much the better. Always the nights are quite cool there, from which good sleep is almost a certainty.

Why do you get frightened so much? I stand guarantee that you shall return home safe and that you shall have no trouble anywhere. It is my experience that in this British realm no fakir or householder gets into any trouble.

Is it a mere idle fancy of mine that between us there some connection from previous birth? Just see how one letter from you sweeps away all my resolution and, I bend my steps towards Varanasi leaving all matters behind!...

I have written again to brother Gangadhar and have asked him this time to return to the Math. If he comes, he will meet you. How is the climate at Varanasi now? By my stay here I have been cured of all other symptoms of malaria, only the pain in the loins makes me frantic; day and night it is aching and chafes me very much. I know not how I shall climb up the hills. I find wonderful endurance in Babaji, and that's why I am begging something of him; but no inkling of the mood to give, only receiving and receiving! So I also fly off.

Yours etc.,
Vivekananda.

PS — To no big person am I going any longer — "Remain, O mind, within yourself, go not to anybody else's door; whatever you seek, you shall obtain sitting at your ease, only seek for it in the privacy of your heart. There is the supreme Treasure, the philosophers' stone and He can give whatever you ask for; for countless gems, O mind, lie strewn about the portals of His abode. He is the wishing-stone that confers boons at the mere thought." Thus says the poet Kamalâkânta.

So now the great conclusion is that Ramakrishna has no peer; nowhere else in this world exists that unprecedented perfection, that wonderful kindness for all that does not stop to justify itself, that intense sympathy for man in bondage. Either he must be the Avatâra as he himself used to say, or else the ever-perfected divine man whom the Vedanta speaks of as the free one who assumes a body for the good of humanity. This is my conviction sure and certain; and the worship of such a divine man has been referred to by Patanjali in the aphorism: "Or the goal may be attained by meditating on a saint." (Patanjali's aphorism has "Ishvara" in place of "saint". Nârada has an aphorism which runs thus: Bhakti (Supreme Love) is attainable chiefly through the grace of a saint, or by a bit of Divine Grace.)

Never during his life did he refuse a single prayer of mine; millions of offences has he forgiven me; such great love even my parents never had for me. There is no poetry, no exaggeration in all this. It is the bare truth and every disciple of his knows it. In times of great danger, great temptation, I wept in extreme agony with the prayer, "O God, do save me," but no response came from anybody; but this wonderful saint, or Avatara, or anything else he may be, came to know of all my affliction through his powers of insight into human hearts and lifted it off — in spite of my desire to the contrary — after getting me brought to his presence. If the soul be deathless, and so, if he still lives, I pray to trim again and again: "O Bhagavan Ramakrishna, thou infinite ocean of mercy and my only refuge, do graciously fulfil the desires of my esteemed friend, who is every inch a great man." May he impart to you all good, he whom alone I have found in this world to be like an ocean of unconditioned mercy! Shântih, Shântih, Shântih.

Please send a prompt reply.

Yours etc.,
Vivekananda.

1890.19 — SIR[1]

Victory to God!

Ghazipur,
8th March, 1890.

DEAR SIR,

Your note duly reached met and so I too shall be off to Prayag. Please write to inform where you mean to put up while there.

PS — In case Abhedananda reaches your place in a day or two, I shall be much obliged if you will start him on his way to Calcutta.

Yours etc.,
Vivekananda.

---

1 Translated from Bengali.

1890.20 — BALARAM BABU[2]

To Balaram Bose:

Ghazipur,
March 12, 1890.

BALARAM BABU,

As soon as you get the railway receipt, please send someone to the railway warehouse at Fairlie Place (Calcutta) to pick up the roses and send them on to Shashi. See that there is no delay in bringing or sending them.

Baburam is going to Allahabad soon. I am going elsewhere.

Vivekananda.

PS — Know it for certain that everything will be spoiled if delayed.

1890.21 — SHRI BALARAM BOSE[3]

Glory to Ramakrishna!

Ghazipur,
15th March, 1890.

REVERED SIR, (Shri Balaram Bose)

Received your kind note yesterday. I am very sorry to learn that Suresh Babu's illness is extremely serious. What is destined will surely happen. It is a matter of great regret that you too have fallen ill. So long as egoism lasts, any shortcoming in adopting remedial measures is to be considered as idleness — it is a fault and a guilt. For one who has not that egoistic idea, the best course is to forbear. The dwelling-place of the Jivâtman, this body, is a veritable means of work, and he who converts this into an infernal den is guilty, and he who neglects it is also to blame. Please act according to circumstances as they present themselves, without the least hesitation.

— "The highest duty consists in doing the little that lies in one's power, seeking neither death nor life, and biding one's time like a servant ready to do any behest."

There is a dreadful outbreak of influenza at Varanasi and Pramada Babu has gone to Allahabad. Baburam has suddenly come here. He has got fever; he was wrong to start under such circumstances… I am leaving this place tomorrow… My countless salutations to Mother. You all bless me that I may have sameness of vision, that after avoiding the bondages which one is heir to by one's very birth, I may not again get stuck in self-imposed bondages. If there be any Doer of good and if He have the power and the opportunity, may He vouchsafe the highest blessings unto you all — this is my constant prayer.

Yours affectionately,
Vivekananda.

---

2 Translated from Bengali.

3 Translated from Bengali.

1890.22 — ATUL BABU[1]

Ghazipur,
15th March, 1890.

DEAR ATUL BABU, (Atul Chandra Ghosh)

I am extremely sorry to hear that you are passing through mental afflictions. Please do only what is agreeable to you.

— "While there is birth there is death, and again entering the mother's womb. This is the manifest evil of transmigration. How, O man, dost thou want satisfaction in such a world!"

Yours affectionately,
Vivekananda.

PS — I am leaving this place tomorrow. Let me see which way destiny leads!

1890.23 — AKHANDANANDA[2]

Salutation to Bhagavan Ramakrishna!

Ghazipur,
March, 1890.

BELOVED AKHANDANANDA,

Very glad to receive your letter yesterday. I am at present staying with the wonderful Yogi and devotee of this place, called Pavhariji. He never comes out of his room and holds conversations with people from behind the door. Inside the room there is a pit in which he lives. It is rumoured that he remains in a state of Samadhi for months together. His fortitude is most wonderful. Our Bengal is the land of Bhakti and of Jnana, where Yoga is scarcely so much as talked of even. What little there is, is but the queer breathing exercises of the Hatha-Yoga — which is nothing but a kind of gymnastics. Therefore I am staying with this wonderful Raja-Yogi — and he has given me some hopes, too. There is a beautiful bungalow in a small garden belonging to a gentleman here; I mean to stay there. The garden is quite close to Babaji's cottage. A brother of the Babaji stays there to look after the comforts of the Sadhus, and I shall have my Bhikshâ at his place. Hence, with a view to seeing to the end of this fun, I give up for the present my plan of going to the hills. For the last two months I have had an attack of lumbago in the waist, which also makes it impossible to climb the hills now. Therefore let me wait and see what Babaji will give me.

My motto is to learn whatever good things I may come across anywhere. This leads many friends to think that it will take away from my devotion to the Guru.

1 Translated from Bengali.
2 Translated from Bengali.

These ideas I count as those of lunatics and bigots. For all Gurus are one and are fragments and radiations of God, the Universal Guru.

If you come to Ghazipur, you have but to inquire at Satish Babu's or Gagan Babu's at Gorabazar, and you know my whereabouts. Or, Pavhari Baba is so well-known a person here that everyone will inform you about his Ashrama at the very mention of his name, and you have only to go there and inquire about the Paramahamsa, and they will tell you of me. Near Moghul Sarai there is a station named Dildarnagar, where you have to change to a short branch railway and get down at Tarighat, opposite Ghazipur; then you have to cross the Ganga to reach Ghazipur.

For the present, I stay at Ghazipur for some days, and wait and see what the Babaji does. If you come, we shall stay together at the said bungalow for some time, and then start for the hills, or for any other place we may decide upon. Don't, please, write to anyone at Baranagore that I am staying at Ghazipur.

With blessings and best wishes,

Ever yours,
Vivekananda.

1890.24 — AKHANDANANDA[3]

Salutation to Bhagavan Ramakrishna!

Ghazipur,
March, 1890.

BELOVED AKHANDANANDA,

Received another letter of yours just now, and with great difficulty deciphered the scribblings. I have written everything in detail in my last letter. You start immediately on receipt of this. I know the route to Tibet via Nepal that you have spoken of. As they don't allow anyone to enter Tibet easily, so they don't allow anybody to go anywhere in Nepal, except Katmandu, its capital, and one or two places of pilgrimage. But a friend of mine is now a tutor to His Highness the Maharaja of Nepal, and a teacher in his school, from whom I have it that when the Nepal government send their subsidy to China, they send it via Lhasa. A Sadhu contrived in that way to go to Lhasa, China, Manchuria, and even to the holy seat of Târâ Devi in north China. We, too, can visit with dignity and respect Tibet, Lhasa, China, and all, if that friend of mine tries to arrange it. You therefore start immediately for Ghazipur. After a few days' stay here with the Babaji, I shall correspond with my friend, and, everything arranged, I shall certainly go to Tibet via Nepal.

You have to get down at Dildarnagar to come to Ghazipur. It is three or four stations from Moghul Sarai I would have sent you the passage if I could have collected it here; so you get it together and come. Gagan Babu with whom I am putting up, is an exceedingly courteous, noble, and generous-minded man. No sooner did he

3 Translated from Bengali.

come to know of Kali's illness than he sent him the passage at Hrishikesh; he has besides spent much on my account. Under the circumstances it would be violating a Sannyasin's duty to tax him for the passage to Kashmir, and I desist from it. You collect the fare and start as soon as you receive this letter. Let the craze for visiting Amarnath be put back for the present.

Yours affectionately,
Vivekananda.

1890.25 — SIR[1]

Ghazipur,
31st March, 1890.

DEAR SIR,

I haven't been here for the last few days and am again going away today. I have asked brother Gangadhar to come here; and if he comes, we go over to you together. For some special reasons, I shall continue to stay in secret in a village some distance from this place, and there's no facility for writing any letter from that place, owing to which I could not reply to your letter so long. Brother Gangadhar is very likely to come, otherwise the reply to my note would have reached me. Brother Abhedananda is putting up with Doctor Priya at Varanasi. Another brother of mine had been with me, but has left for Abhedananda's place. The news of his arrival has not yet been received, and, his health being bad, I am rather anxious for his sake. I have behaved very cruelly towards him — that is, I have harassed him much to make him leave my company. There's no help, you see; I am so very weak-hearted, so much overmastered by the distractions of love! Bless me that I may harden. What shall I say to you about the condition of my mind! Oh, it is as if the hell-fire is burning there day and night! Nothing, nothing could I do yet! And this life seems muddled away in vain; I feel quite helpless as to what to do! The Babaji throws out honeyed words and keeps me from leaving. Ah, what shall I say? I am committing hundreds of offenses against you — please excuse them as so many misdoings of a man driven mad with mental agonies. Abhedananda is suffering from dysentery. I shall be very much obliged if you will kindly inquire about his condition and send him down to our Math in case he wants to go there with our brother who has come from here. My Gurubhais must be thinking me very cruel and selfish. Oh, what can I do? Who will see deep down into my mind? Who will know how much I am suffering day and night? Bless me that I may have the most unflinching patience and perseverance.

PS — Abhedananda is staying in Doctor Priya's house at Sonarpura. My lumbago is as before.

Yours etc.,
Vivekananda.

---

1 Translated from Bengali.

1890.26 — KALI[2]

Ghazipur,
2nd April, 1890.

MY DEAR KALI, (Abhedananda)

Glad to receive your letter as well as Pramada Babu's and Baburam's (Premananda's). I am doing pretty well here. You have expressed a desire to see me. I too have a similar longing, and it is this that makes me afraid of going. Moreover, the Babaji forbids me to do so. I shall try to go on a few days' leave from him. But there is this fear that by so doing I shall be drawn up to the hills by the attraction I have for Hrishikesh, and it will be very difficult to shake it off, specially for one weak-minded, you see, like myself. The attack of lumbago, too, will not leave me on any account — a botheration! But then I am getting used to it. Please convey my countless salutations to Pramada Babu; his is a friendship which greatly benefits both my mind and body. And I am particularly indebted to him. Things will turn up some way, anyhow.

With best wishes,

Yours affectionately,
Vivekananda.

1890.27 — SIR[3]

Ghazipur,
2nd April, 1890.

DEAR SIR,

Where shall I get that renunciation you speak of in your advice to me? It is for the sake of that very thing that I am out a tramp through the earth. If ever I get this true renunciation, I shall let you know; and if you get anything of the kind, please remember me as a partner thereof.

Yours,
Vivekananda.

---

2 Translated from Bengali.
3 Translated from Bengali.

1890.28 — SIR[1]

Victory to Ramakrishna!

Baranagore,
10th May, 1890.

DEAR SIR,

I could not write to you because of various distractions and a relapse of fever. Glad to learn from Abhedananda's letter that you are doing well. Gangadhar (Akhandananda) has probably arrived at Varanasi by this time. King Death happens here to be casting into his jaws these days many of our friends and own people, hence I am very much taken up. Perhaps no letter for me has arrived there from Nepal. I know not how and when Vishvanâtha (the Lord of Kashi) would choose to vouchsafe some rest to me. Directly the hot weather relaxes a little, I am off from this place, but I am still at a loss where to go. Do please pray for me to Vishvanatha that He may grant me strength. You are a devotee, and I beseech you with the Lord's words coming to my mind, "Those who are the devoted ones to My devotees, are indeed considered the best of My devotees."

Yours etc.,
Vivekananda.

1890.29 — TULSIRAM

To Tulsiram Ghosh:

Ghazipur,
10 May, 1890.

DEAR TULSIRAM,

A basket of roses will be sent to you in a few days at Chitpur. Do you please send them up immediately to Shashi [Swami Ramakrishnananda, at the Baranagore Math]. They would not be sent to the care of Balaram Basu, for there would be such nice delays and that would be death to the flowers. I think if sent to Chitpur, to your depot, it would reach you there at the very place; if not, write sharp. Baburam [Swami Premananda] is here, going up in a day or two to Allahabad. I too am going off from this place very soon. I go perhaps to Bareilly and up. What is Balaram Babu [Balaram Bose] doing?

My Pranâms etc. to you all.

Yours affectionately,
Vivekananda.

---

1 Translated from Bengali.

1890.30 — SIR[2]

57, Ramakanta Bose's Street,
Baghbazar, Calcutta,
26th May, 1890.

DEAR SIR,

I write this to you while caught in a vortex of many untoward circumstances and great agitation of mind; with a prayer to Vishvanatha, please think of the propriety and possibility, or otherwise, of all that I set forth below and then oblige me greatly by a reply.

1. I already told you at the outset that I am Ramakrishna's slave, having laid my body at his feet "with Til and Tulasi leaves", I cannot disregard his behest. If it is in failure that that great sage laid down his life after having attained to superhuman heights of Jnana, Bhakti, Love, and powers, and after having practiced for forty years stern renunciation, non-attachment, holiness, and great austerities, then where is there anything for us to count on? So I am obliged to trust his words as the words of one identified with truth.

2. Now his behest to me was that I should devote myself to the service of the order of all-renouncing devotees founded by him, and in this I have to persevere, come what may, being ready to take heaven, hell, salvation, or anything that may happen to me.

3. His command was that his all-renouncing devotees should group themselves together, and I am entrusted with seeing to this. Of course, it matters not if any one of us goes out on visits to this place or that, but these shall be but visits, while his own opinion was that absolute homeless wandering suited him alone who was perfected to the highest point. Before that state, it is proper to settle somewhere to dive down into practice. When all the ideas of body and the like are dissolved of themselves, a person may then pursue whatever state comes to him. Otherwise, it is baneful for a practicing aspirant to be always wandering.

4. So in pursuance cf this his commandment, his group of Sannyasins are now assembled in a dilapidated house at Baranagore, and two of his lay disciples, Babu Suresh Chandra Mitra and Babu Balaram Bose, so long provided for their food and house-rent.

5. For various reasons, the body of Bhagavan Ramakrishna had to be consigned to fire. There is no doubt that this act was very blamable. The remains of his ashes are now preserved, and if they be now properly enshrined somewhere on the banks of the Ganga, I presume we shall be able in some measure to expiate the sin lying on our head. These sacred remains, his seat, and his picture are every day worshipped in our Math in proper form; and it is known to you that a brother-disciple of mine, of Brahmin parentage, is occupied day and night with the task. The expenses of the worship used also to be borne by the two great souls mentioned above.

2 Translated from Bengali.

6. What greater regret can there be than this that no memorial could yet be raised in this land of Bengal in the very neighbourhood of the place where he lived his life of Sâdhanâ — he by whose birth the race of Bengalees has been sanctified, the land of Bengal has become hallowed, he who came on earth to save the Indians from the spell of the worldly glamour of Western culture and who therefore chose most of his all-renouncing disciples from university men?

7. The two gentlemen mentioned above had a strong desire to have some land purchased on the banks of the Ganga and see the sacred remains enshrined on it, with the disciples living there together; and Suresh Babu had offered a sum of Rs. 1,000 for the purpose, promising to give more, but for some inscrutable purpose of God he left this world yesternight! And the news of Balaram Babu's death is already known to you.

8. Now there is no knowing as to where his disciples will stand with his sacred remains and his seat (and you know well, people here in Bengal are profuse in their professions, but do not stir out an inch in practice). The disciples are Sannyasins and are ready forthwith to depart anywhere their way may lie. But I, their servant, am in an agony of sufferings, and my heart is breaking to think that a small piece of land could not be had in which to install the remains of Bhagavan Ramakrishna.

9. It is impossible with a sum of Rs. 1,000 to secure land and raise a temple near Calcutta. Some such land would at least cost about five to seven thousands.

10. You remain now the only friend and patron of Shri Ramakrishna's disciples. In the NorthWestern Province great indeed is your fame, your position, and your circle of acquaintance. I request you to consider, if you feel like it, the propriety of your getting the affair through by raising subscriptions from well-to-do pious men known to you in your province. If you deem it proper to have some shelter erected on the bangs of the Ganga in Bengal for Bhagavan Ramakrishna's sacred remains and for his disciples, I shall with your leave report myself to you, and I have not the slightest qualm to beg from door to door for this noble cause, for the sake of my Lord and his children. Please give this proposal your best thoughts with prayers to Vishvanatha. To my mind, if all these sincere, educated, youthful Sannyasins of good birth fail to dive up to the ideals of Shri Ramakrishna owing to want of an abode and help, then alas for our country!

11. If you ask, "You are a Sannyasin, so why do you trouble over these desires?" — I would then reply, I am Ramakrishna s servant, and I am willing even to steal and rob, if by doing so I can perpetuate his name in the land of his birth and Sâdhanâ (spiritual struggle) and help even a little his disciples to practice his great ideals. I know you to be my closest in kinship, and I lay my mind bare to you. I returned to Calcutta for this reason. I had told you this before I left, and now I leave it to you to do what you think best.

12. If you argue that it is better to have the plan carried out in some place like Kashi, my point is, as I have told you, it would be the greatest pity if the memorial shrine could not be raised in the land of his birth and Sadhana! The condition of

Bengal is pitiable. The people here cannot even dream what renunciation truly means—luxury and sensuality have been so much eating into the vitals of the race! May God send renunciation and unworldliness into this land! They have here nothing to speak of, while the people of the North-Western Province, specially the rich there as I believe, have great zeal in noble causes like this. Please send me such reply as you think best. Gangadhar has not yet arrived today, and may do so tomorrow. I am so eager to see him again.

Please write to the address given above.

Yours etc.,
Vivekananda.

1890.31 — SIR[1]

Baghbazar, Calcutta,
4th June, 1890.

RESPECTED SIR, (Shri Pramadadas Mitra)

I got your letter. There is no doubt that your advice is very wise. It is quite true that the Lord's Will will prevail. We also are spreading out here and there in small groups of two or three. I also got two letters from brother Gangadhar. He is at present in the house of Gagan Babu suffering from an attack of influenza. Gagan Babu is taking special care of him. He will come here as soon as he recovers. Our respectful salutations to you.

Your servant,
Vivekananda.

PS—Abhedananda and others are all doing well.

1890.32 — SHARAT

Baghbazar, Calcutta,
July 6, 1890.

DEAR SHARAT (SARADANANDA) and KRIPANANDA,

Your letters have duly reached us. They say Almora is healthiest at this time of the year, yet you are taken ill! I hope it is nothing malarious...

I find Gangadhar the same pliant child with his turbulence moderated by his wanderings, and with a greater love for us and for our Lord. He is bold, brave, sincere, and steadfast. The only thing needed is a guiding mind to whom he would instinctively submit with reverence, and a fine man would be the result.

I had no wish to leave Ghazipur this time, and certainly not to come to Calcutta, but Kali's illness made me go to Varanasi, and Balaram's sudden death brought

[1] Translated from Bengali.

me to Calcutta. So Suresh Babu and Balaram Babu are both gone! G. C. Ghosh is supporting the Math...I intend shortly, as soon as I can get my fare, to go up to Almora and thence to some place in Gharwal on the Ganga where I can settle down for a long meditation. Gangadhar is accompanying me. Indeed it was with this desire and intention that I brought him down from Kashmir.

I don't think you ought to be in any hurry about coming down to Calcutta. You have done with roving; that's good, but you have not yet attempted the one thing you should do, that is, be resolved to sit down and meditate. I don't think Jnana is a thing like rousing a maiden suddenly from sleep by saying, "Get up, dear girl, your marriage ceremony is waiting for you!" as we say. I am strongly of opinion that very few persons in any Yuga (age) attain Jnana, and therefore we should go on striving and striving even unto death. That's my old-fashioned way, you know. About the humbug of modern Sannyasins' Jnana I know too well. Peace be unto you and strength! Daksha, who is staying at Vrindaban with Rakhal (Brahmananda), has learnt to make gold and has become a pucca Jnani, so writes Rakhal. God bless him, and you may say, amen!

I am in fine health now, and the good I gained by my stay in Ghazipur will last, I am sure, for some time. I am longing for a flight to the Himalayas. This time I shall not go to Pavhari Baba or any other saint—they divert one from his highest purpose. Straight up!

How do you find the climate at Almora? Neither S—nor you need come down. What is the use of so many living together in one place and doing no good to one's soul? Don't be fools always wandering from place to place; that's all very good, but be heroes.

निर्मानमोहा जितसङ्गदोषा
अध्यात्मनित्या विनिवृत्तकामाः ।
द्वन्द्वैर्विमुक्ताः सुखदुःखसंज्ञै-
र्गच्छन्त्यमूढाः पदमव्ययं तत् ॥

—"Free from pride and delusion, with the evil of attachment conquered, ever dwelling in the Self, with desires completely receded, liberated from the pairs of opposites known as pleasure and pain, the undeluded reach that Goal Eternal" (Gita, XV. 5).

Who advises you to jump into fire? If you don't find the Himalayas a place for Sadhana, go somewhere else then. So many gushing inquiries simply betray a weak mind. Arise, ye mighty one, and be strong! Work on and on, struggle on and on! Nothing more to write.

Yours affectionately,
Vivekananda.

1890.33 — SHARAT

To Swami Saradananda:

Salutation to Bhagavan Ramakrishna!

Calcutta, 32 Ashadha,
July 15, 1890.

MY DEAR SHARAT,

I am sorry to learn that [Vaikunthanath] Sanyal's habits are as yet not Pucca [firm]; and what about Brahmacharya? I don't understand you. If so, the best thing for you both is to come down and live here. The widow of Mohindra Mukherjee is trying head and heart to erect a Math for you, and Surendranath Mitra has left another thousand so that you are very likely soon to get a beautiful place on the river. As for all the hardships up there, I reserve my own opinions.

It was not at all my intention to come down, only the death of Balaram Bose had made me have a peep here and go back. If the mountains be so bad, there is more than enough place for me; only I leave Bengal. If one does not suit, another will. So that is my determination. Everyone here will be so glad at your return here, and from your letter I see it would be downright injurious to you if you didn't come down. So come down at your earliest opportunity. I will leave this place before this letter reaches you; only I won't go to Almora. I have my own plans for the future and they shall be a secret.

As for Sanyal, I do not see how I can benefit him. Of course, you are at liberty to hold your own opinion about the Sanga [holy company] here. That I can find places Sudrishya [having scenic beauty] and Subhiksha [where alms are available] is enough. Sanga is not much, or, I think, not at all necessary for me.

Yours, etc.,
Vivekananda.

1891

1891.1 — GOVINDA SAHAY

Ajmer,
14th April, 1891.

DEAR GOVINDA SAHAY,

…Try to be pure and unselfish — that is the whole of religion…

Yours with love,
Vivekananda.

1891.2 — GOVINDA SAHAY

Mount Abu,
30th April, 1891.

DEAR GOVINDA SAHAY,

Have you done the Upanayana of that Brahmin boy? Are you studying Sanskrit? How far have you advanced? I think you must have finished the first part…Are you diligent in your Shiva Pujâ? If not, try to be so. "Seek ye first the kingdom of God and all good things will be added unto you." Follow God and you shall have whatever you desire…To the two Commander Sahebs my best regards; they being men of high position were very kind to a poor fakir like me. My children, the secret of religion lies not in theories but in practice. To be good and to do good — that is the whole of religion. "Not he that crieth 'Lord', 'Lord', but he that doeth the will of the Father". You are a nice band of young men, you Alwaris, and I hope in no distant future many of you will be ornaments of the society and blessings to the country you are born in.

Yours with blessings,
Vivekananda.

PS — Don't be ruffled if now and then you get a brush from the world; it will be over in no time, and everything will be all right.

1891.3 — GOVINDA SAHAY

Mount Abu,
1891.

DEAR GOVINDA SAHAY,

You must go on with your Japa whatever direction the mind takes. Tell Harbux that he is to begin with the Prânâyâma in the following way.

Try hard with your Sanskrit studies.

Yours with love,
Vivekananda.

1892

1892.1 — DIWANJI SAHEB

Baroda,
26th April, 1892.

DEAR DIWANJI SAHEB, (Shri Haridas Viharidas Desai)

Very happy to receive your kind letter even here. I had not the least difficulty in reaching your house from the station of Nadiad. And your brothers, they are what they should be, your brothers. May the Lord shower his choicest blessings on your family. I have never found such a glorious one in all my travels. Your friend Mr. Manibhai has provided every comfort for me; but, as to his company, I have only seen him twice; once for a minute, the other for ten minutes at the most when he talked about the system of education here. Of course, I have seen the Library and the pictures of Ravi Varma, and that is about all worth seeing here. So I am going off this evening to Bombay. My thanks to the Diwanji here (or to you) for his kind behaviour. More from Bombay.

Yours in affection,
Vivekananda.

PS — At Nadiad I met Mr. Manilal Nabhubhai. He is a very learned and pious gentleman, and I enjoyed his company much.

1892.2 — DIWANJI SAHEB

Ellapa Balaram's House,
C/O. Thakore of Limdi,
Neutral Line, Poona,
15th June, 1892.

DEAR DIWANJI SAHEB, (Shri Haridas Viharidas Desai)

It is a long time since I heard from you. I hope I have not offended you anyway. I came down with the Thakore Saheb of Mahabaleshwar, and I am living here with him. I would remain here a week or more and then proceed to Rameshwaram via Hyderabad.

Perhaps by this time every hitch has been removed from your way in Junagad; at least I hope so. I am very anxious to learn about your health, especially that sprain, you know.

I saw your friend the Surti tutor to the Prince of Bhavnagar. He is a perfect gentleman. It was quite a privilege to make his acquaintance; he is so good and noble-natured a man.

My sincerest greetings to your noble-minded brothers and to our friends there. Kindly send to Mr. Nabhubhai my earnest good wishes in your letter home. I hope you would gratify me by a speedy reply.

With my sincerest respects and gratitude and prayers for you and yours, I remain,

Yours faithfully,
Vivekananda.

1892.3 — DIWANJI SAHEB

Bombay,
22nd August, 1892.

DEAR DIWANJI SAHEB, (Shri Haridas Viharidas Desai)

I am very much gratified on receiving your letter, especially as that is the proof that you have the same kindness towards me.

About the kindness and gentlemanliness of your friend Mr. Bederkar of Indore and of the Dakshinis in general, the less said the better; but of course there are Dakshinis and Dakshinis, and I would only quote to you what Shankar Pandurang wrote me at Mahabaleshwar on my informing him that I had found shelter with the Limdi Thakore:

"I am so glad to learn that you have found Limdi Thakore there, else you would have been in serious troubles, our Maratha people not being so kind as the Gujaratis." So kind? heaven and hell!

I am very glad that your joint has now been nearly perfectly cured. Kindly tell your noble brother to excuse my promise-breaking as I have got here some Sanskrit books and help, too, to read, which I do not hope to get elsewhere, and am anxious to finish them. Yesterday I saw your friend Mr. Manahsukharam who has lodged a Sannyâsin friend with him. He is very kind to me and so is his son.

After remaining here for 15 to 20 days I would proceed toward Rameshwaram, and on my return would surely come to you.

The world really is enriched by men, high-souled, noble-minded, and kind, like you; the rest are "only as axes which cut at the tree of youth of their mothers', as the Sanskrit poet puts it.

It is impossible that I should ever forget your fatherly kindness and care of me, and what else can a poor fakir like me do in return to a mighty minister but pray that the Giver of all gifts may give you all that is desirable on earth and in the end — which may He postpone to a day long, long ahead — may take you in His shelter of bliss and happiness and purity infinite.

Yours,
Vivekananda.

PS — One thing that I am very sorry to notice in these parts is the thorough want of Sanskrit and other learning. The people of this part of the country have for their religion a certain bundle of local superstitions about eating, drinking, and bathing, and that is about the whole of their religion.

Poor fellows! Whatever the rascally and wily priests teach them — all sorts of mummery and tomfoolery as the very gist of the Vedas and Hinduism (mind you, neither these rascals of priests nor their forefathers have so much as seen a volume of the Vedas for the last 400 generations) — they follow and degrade themselves. Lord help them from the Râkshasas in the shape of the Brahmins of the Kaliyuga.

I have sent a Bengali boy to you. Hope he would be treated kindly.

1892.4 — PANDITJI MAHARAJ

Bombay,
20th September, 1892.

DEAR PANDITJI MAHÂRÂJ[1],

Your letter has reached me duly. I do not know why I should be undeservingly praised. "None is good, save One, that is, God", as the Lord Jesus bath said. The rest are only tools in His hands. "Gloria in Excelsis", "Glory unto God in the highest", and unto men that deserve, but not to such an undeserving one like me. Here "the servant is not worthy of the hire"; and a Fakir, especially, has no right to any praise whatsoever, for would you praise your servant for simply doing his duty?

... My unbounded gratitude to Pandit Sundarlalji, and to my Professor[2] for this kind remembrance of me.

Now I would tell you something else. The Hindu mind was ever deductive and never synthetic or inductive. In all our philosophies, we always find hair-splitting arguments, taking for granted some general proposition, but the proposition itself may be as childish as possible. Nobody ever asked or searched the truth of these general propositions. Therefore independent thought we have almost none to speak of, and hence the dearth of those sciences which are the results of observation and generalization. And why was it thus? — From two causes: The tremendous heat of the climate forcing us to love rest and contemplation better than activity, and the Brâhmins as priests never undertaking journeys or voyages to distant lands. There were voyagers and people who travelled far; but they were almost always traders, i.e. people from whom priestcraft and their own sole love for gain had taken away all capacity for intellectual development. So their observations, instead of adding to the store of human knowledge, rather degenerated it; for their observations were bad and their accounts exaggerated and tortured into fantastical shapes, until they passed all recognition.

So you see, we must travel, we must go to foreign parts. We must see how the engine of society works in other countries, and keep free and open communication with what is going on in the minds of other nations, if we really want to be a nation

---

1. Pandit Shankarlal of Khetri.
2. With whom he read the Mahâ-Bhâshya on Pânini.

again. And over and above all, we must cease to tyrannise. To what a ludicrous state are we brought! If a Bhângi comes to anybody as a Bhangi, he would be shunned as the plague; but no sooner does he get a cupful of water poured upon his head with some mutterings of prayers by a Pâdri, and get a coat on his back, no matter how threadbare, and come into the room of the most orthodox Hindu—I don't see the man who then dare refuse him a chair and a hearty shake of the hands! Irony can go no further. And come and see what they, the Pâdris, are doing here in the Dakshin (south). They are converting the lower classes by lakhs; and in Travancore, the most priestridden country in India—where every bit of land is owned by the Brahmins... nearly one-fourth has become Christian! And I cannot blame them; what part have they in David and what in Jesse? When, when, O Lords shall man be brother to man?

Yours,
Vivekananda.

1892.5 — DIWANJI SAHEB

Bombay,
1892

DEAR DIWANJI SAHEB, (Shri Haridas Viharidas Desai)

The bearer of this letter, Babu Akshaya Kumar Ghose, is a particular friend of mine. He comes of a respectable family of Calcutta. I found him at Khandwa where I made his acquaintance, although I knew his family long before in Calcutta.

He is a very honest and intelligent boy and is an undergraduate of the Calcutta University. You know how hard the struggle is in Bengal nowadays, and the poor boy has been out in search of some job. Knowing your native kindness of heart, I think I am not disturbing you by asking and entreating you to do something for this young man. I need not write more. You will find him an honest and hard-working lad. If a single act of kindness done to a fellow creature renders his whole life happy, I need not remind you that this boy is a Pâtra (a person quite deserving of help), noble and kind as you are.

I hope you are not disturbed and troubled by this request of mine. This is the first and the last of its kind and made only under very peculiar circumstances. Hoping and relying on your kind nature, I remain,

Yours faithfully,
Vivekananda.

1893

1893.1 — ALASINGA

To Shri Alasinga Perumal:

C/O Babu Madhusudan Chattopadhyaya Superintending Engineer
Khartabad, Hyderabad,
11th February, 1893.

DEAR ALASINGA,

Your friend, the young graduate, came to receive me at the station, so also a Bengali gentleman. At present I am living with the Bengali gentleman; tomorrow I go to live with your young friend for a few days, and then I see the different sights here, and in a few days you may expect me at Madras. For I am very sorry to tell you that I cannot go back at present to Rajputana. It is so very dreadfully hot here already. I do not know how hot it would be at Rajputana, and I cannot bear heat at all. So the next thing, I would do, would be to go back to Bangalore and then to Ootacamund to pass the summer there. My brain boils in heat.

So all my plans have been dashed to the ground. That is why I wanted to hurry off from Madras early. In that case I would have months left in my hands to seek out for somebody amongst our northern princes to send me over to America. But alas, it is now too late. First, I cannot wander about in this heat — I would die. Secondly, my fast friends in Rajputana would keep me bound down to their sides if they get hold of me and would not let me go over to Europe. So my plan was to get hold of some new person without my friends' knowledge. But this delay at Madras has dashed all my hopes to the ground, and with a deep sigh I give it up, and the Lord's will be done! However, you may be almost sure that I shall see you in a few days for a day or two in Madras and then go to Bangalore and thence to Ootacamund to see "if" the M — Maharaja sends me up. "If" — because you see I cannot be sure of any promise of a Dakshini (southern) Raja. They are not Rajputs. A Rajput would rather die than break his promise. However, man learns as he lives, and experience is the greatest teacher in the world.

"Thy will be done on earth as it is in heaven, for Thine is the glory and the kingdom for ever and ever." My compliments to you all.

Yours affectionately,
Vivekananda.

1893.2 — DOCTOR

Khetri,
27th April, 1893.

DEAR DOCTOR, (Dr. Nanjunda Rao, M.D.)

Your letter has just reached me. I am very much gratified by your love for my unworthy self. So, so sorry to learn that poor Bâlâji has lost his son. "The Lord gave and the Lord bath taken away; blessed be the name of the Lord." We only know that nothing is lost or can be lost. For us is only submission, calm and perfect. The soldier has no right to complain, nay murmur, if the general orders him into the cannon's mouth. May He comfort Balaji in his grief, and may it draw him closer and closer to the breast of the All-merciful Mother!

As to my taking ship from Madras, I do not think it feasible, as I have already made arrangements from Bombay. Tell Bhattacharya that the Raja (The Maharaja of Khetri, Rajputana.) or my Gurubhâis would be the last men to put any obstacles in my way. As for the Rajaji, his love for me is simply without limit.

May the Giver of all good bless you all here and hereafter, will be the constant prayer of

Vivekananda.

1893.3 — DIWANJI SAHEB

To Shri Haridas Viharidas Desai:

Khetri,
28th April, 1893.

DEAR DIWANJI SAHEB,

On my way here, I wanted to go to your place at Nadiad and redeem my pledge, but certain circumstances prevented me, and the greatest of them was that you were not there; and to play Hamlet leaving Hamlet's part out is a ridiculous affair; and as I know for certain that you are to return in a few days to Nadiad, and as I am shortly going back to Bombay, say in 20 days, I thought it better to postpone my visit for that time.

Here the Khetri Rajaji was very, very anxious to see me and had sent his Private Secretary to Madras; and so I was bound to leave for Khetri. But the heat is quite intolerable, and so I am flying off very soon.

By and by, I have made the acquaintances of nearly all the Dakshini Rajas and have seen most queer sights in many places of which I would tell you in extenso when we meet next. I know your love for me and am sure that you would excuse my not going down to your place. However, I am coming to you in a few days.

One thing more. Have you got lion's cubs now in Junagad? Can you lend me one for my Raja? He can give you some Rajputana animals in exchange, if you like.

I saw Ratilalbhai in the train. He is the same nice and kind gentleman; and what more shall I wish for you, my dear Diwanji Saheb, but that the Lord would be your all in all in your well-merited, well-applauded and universally respected latter end of a life which was ever holy, good, and devoted to the service of so many of the sons and daughters of the great Father of Mercies. Amen!

Yours affectionately,
Vivekananda.

1893.4 — DIWANJI SAHEB

To Shri Haridas Viharidas Desai:

Bombay,
22nd May, 1893.

DEAR DIWANJI SAHEB,

Reached Bombay a few days ago and would start off in a few days. Your friend, the Banya gentleman to whom you wrote for the house accommodation, writes to say that his house is already full of guests and some of them are ill and that he is very sorry he cannot accommodate me. After all we have got a nice, airy place.

... The Private Secretary of H. H. of Khetri and I are now residing together. I cannot express my gratitude to him for his love and kindness to me. He is what they call a Tazimi Sardar in Rajputana, i.e. one of those whom the Rajas receive by rising from their seats. Still he is so simple, and sometimes his service for me makes me almost ashamed.

... Often and often, we see that the very best of men even are troubled and visited with tribulations in this world; it may be inexplicable; but it is also the experience of my life that the heart and core of everything here is good, that whatever may be the surface waves, deep down and underlying everything, there is an infinite basis of goodness and love; and so long as we do not reach that basis, we are troubled; but having once reached that zone of calmness, let winds howl and tempests rage. The house which is built on a rock of ages cannot shake. I thoroughly believe that a good, unselfish and holy man like you, whose whole life has been devoted to doing good to others, has already reached this basis of firmness which the Lord Himself has styled as "rest upon Brahman" in the Gita.

May the blows you have received draw you closer to that Being who is the only one to be loved here and hereafter, so that you may realise Him in everything past, present, and future, and find everything present or lost in Him and Him alone. Amen!

Yours affectionately,
Vivekananda.

1893.5 — MOTHER

Bombay,
24th May, 1893.

DEAR MOTHER, (Shrimati Indumati Mitra)

Very glad to receive your letter and that of dear Haripada. Please do not be sorry that I could not write to you very often. I am always praying to the Lord for your welfare. I cannot go to Belgaum now as arrangements are all ready for my starting for America on the 31st next. The Lord willing, I shall see you on returning from my travels in America and Europe. Always resign yourselves to the Lord Shri Krishna. Always remember that we are but puppets in the Lord's hands. Remain pure always. Please be careful not to become impure even in thought, as also in speech and action; always try to do good to others as far as in you lies. And remember that the paramount duty of a woman is to serve her husband by thought, word, and deed. Please read the Gita every day to the best of your opportunity. Why have you signed yourself as … Dâsi (maidservant)? The Vaishya and the Shudra should sign as Dâsa and Dâsi, but the Brahmin and Kshatriya should write Deva and Devi (goddess). Moreover, these distinctions of caste and the like have been the invention of our modern sapient Brahmins. Who is a servant, and to whom? Everyone is a servant of the Lord Hari. Hence a woman should use her patronymic, that is, the surname of her husband. This is the ancient Vedic custom, as for example, such and such Mitra, or the like. It is needless to write much, dear mother; always know that I am constantly praying for your well-being. From America I shall now and then write you letters with descriptions of the wonderful things there. I am now at Bombay, and shall stay here up to the 31st. The private Secretary to the Maharaja of Khetri has come here to see me off.

With blessings,

Yours sincerely,
Vivekananda.

1893.6 — DIWANJI SAHEB

To Shri Haridas Viharidas Desai:

Khetri
May, 1893.

DEAR DIWANJI SAHEB,

Surely my letter had not reached you before you wrote to me. The perusal of your letter gave me both pleasure and pain simultaneously: pleasure, to see that I have the good fortune to be loved by a man of your heart, power, and position; and pain, to see that my motive has been misinterpreted throughout. Believe me, that I love you and respect you like a father and that my gratitude towards you and your family is surely unbounded. The fact is this. You may remember that I had from before a desire to go to Chicago. When at Madras, the people there, of their own accord, in conjunction with H.H. of Mysore and Ramnad made every arrangement to send me up. And you may also remember that between H.H. of Khetri and myself there are the closest ties of love. Well, I, as a matter of course, wrote to him that I was going to America. Now the Raja of Khetri thought in his love that I was bound to see him once before I departed, especially as the Lord has given him an heir to the throne and great rejoicings were going on here; and to make sure of my coming he sent his Private Secretary all the way to Madras to fetch me, and of course I was bound to come. In the meanwhile I telegraphed to your brother at Nadiad to know whether you were there, and, unfortunately, the answer I could not get; therefore, the Secretary who, poor fellow, had suffered terribly for his master in going to and from Madras and with his eye wholly on the fact that his master would be unhappy if we could not reach Khetri within the Jalsa (festival), bought tickets at once for Jaipur. On our way we met Mr. Ratilal who informed me that my wire was received and duly answered and that Mr. Viharidas was expecting me. Now it is for you to judge, whose duty it has been so long to deal even justice. What would or could I do in this connection? If I would have got down, I could not have reached in time for the Khetri rejoicings; on the other hand, my motives might be misinterpreted. But I know you and your brother's love for me, and I knew also that I would have to go back to Bombay in a few days on my way to Chicago. I thought that the best solution was to postpone my visit till my return. As for my feeling affronted at not being attended by your brothers, it is a new discovery of yours which I never even dreamt of; or, God knows, perhaps, you have become a thought-reader. Jokes apart, my dear Diwanji Saheb, I am the same frolicsome, mischievous but, I assure you, innocent boy you found me at Junagad, and my love for your noble self is the same or increased a hundredfold, because I have had a mental comparison between yourself and the Diwans of nearly all the states in Dakshin, and the Lord be my witness how my tongue was fluent in your praise (although I know that my powers are quite inadequate to estimate your noble qualities) in every Southern court. If this be not a sufficient explanation, I implore you to pardon me as a father pardons a son, and let me not be haunted with the impression that I was ever ungrateful to one who was so good to me.

Yours,
Vivekananda.

PS — I depend on you to remove any misconception in the mind of your brother about my not getting down and that, even had I been the very devil, I could not forget their kindness and good offices for me.

As to the other two Swamis, they were my Gurubhais, who went to you last at Junagad; of them one is our leader. I met them after three years, and we came together as far as Abu and then I left them. If you wish, I can take them back to Nadiad on my way to Bombay. May the Lord shower His blessings on you and yours.

Japan

1893.7 — ALASINGA

Oriental Hotel, Yokohama.
10th July, 1893.

Dear Alasinga, Balaji, G. G., Banking Corporation, and All My Madras Friends,

Excuse my not keeping you constantly informed of my movements. One is so busy every day, and especially myself who am quite new to the life of possessing things and taking care of them. That consumes so much of my energy. It is really an awful botheration.

From Bombay we reached Colombo. Our steamer remained in port for nearly the whole day, and we took the opportunity of getting off to have a look at the town. We drove through the streets, and the only thing I remember was a temple in which was a very gigantic Murti (image) of the Lord Buddha in a reclining posture, entering Nirvâna...

The next station was Penang, which is only a strip of land along the sea in the body of the Malaya Peninsula. The Malayas are all Mohammedans and in old days were noted pirates and quite a dread to merchantmen. But now the leviathan guns of modern turreted battleships have forced the Malayas to look about for more peaceful pursuits. On our way from Penang to Singapore, we had glimpses of Sumatra with its high mountains, and the Captain pointed out to me several places as the favourite haunts of pirates in days gone by. Singapore is the capital of the Straits Settlements. It has a fine botanical garden with the most splendid collection of palms. The beautiful fan-like palm, called the traveller's palm, grows here in abundance, and the bread-fruit tree everywhere. The celebrated mangosteen is as plentiful here as mangoes in Madras, but mango is nonpareil. The people here are not half so dark as the people of Madras, although so near the line. Singapore possesses a fine museum too.

Hong Kong next. You feel that you have reached China, the Chinese element predominates so much. All labour, all trade seems to be in their hands. And Hong Kong is real China. As soon as the steamer casts anchor, you are besieged with hundreds of Chinese boats to carry you to the land. These boats with two helms are rather peculiar. The boatman lives in the boat with his family. Almost always, the wife is at the helms, managing one with her hands and the other with one of her feet. And in ninety per cent of cases, you find a baby tied to her back, with the hands and feet of the little Chin left free. It is a quaint sight to see the little John

Chinaman dangling very quietly from his mother's back, whilst she is now setting with might and main, now pushing heavy loads, or jumping with wonderful agility from boat to boat. And there is such a rush of boats and steamlaunches coming in and going out. Baby John is every moment put into the risk of having his little head pulverised, pigtail and all; but he does not care a fig. This busy life seems to have no charm for him, and he is quite content to learn the anatomy of a bit of rice-cake given to him from time to time by the madly busy mother. The Chinese child is quite a philosopher and calmly goes to work at an age when your Indian boy can hardly crawl on all fours. He has learnt the philosophy of necessity too well. Their extreme poverty is one of the causes why the Chinese and the Indians have remained in a state of mummified civilisation. To an ordinary Hindu or Chinese, everyday necessity is too hideous to allow him to think of anything else.

Hong Kong is a very beautiful town. It is built on the slopes of hills and on the tops too, which are much cooler than the city. There is an almost perpendicular tramway going to the top of the hill, dragged by wire-rope and steam-power.

We remained three days at Hong Kong and went to see Canton, which is eighty miles up a river. The river is broad enough to allow the biggest steamers to pass through. A number of Chinese steamers ply between Hong Kong and Canton. We took passage on one of these in the evening and reached Canton early in the morning. What a scene of bustle and life! What an immense number of boats almost covering the waters! And not only those that are carrying on the trade, but hundreds of others which serve as houses to live in. And quite a lot of them so nice and big! In fact, they are big houses two or three storeys high, with verandahs running round and streets between, and all floating!

We landed on a strip of ground given by the Chinese Government to foreigners to live in. Around us on both sides of the river for miles and miles is the big city — a wilderness of human beings, pushing, struggling, surging, roaring. But with all its population, all its activity, it is the dirtiest town I saw, not in the sense in which a town is called dirty in India, for as to that not a speck of filth is allowed by the Chinese to go waste; but because of the Chinaman, who has, it seems, taken a vow never to bathe! Every house is a shop, people living only on the top floor. The streets are very very narrow, so that you almost touch the shops on both sides as you pass. At every ten paces you find meat-stalls, and there are shops which sell cat's and dog's meat. Of course, only the poorest classes of Chinamen eat dog or cat.

The Chinese ladies can never be seen. They have got as strict a zenana as the Hindus of Northern India; only the women of the labouring classes can be seen. Even amongst these, one sees now and then a woman with feet smaller than those of your youngest child, and of course they cannot be said to walk, but hobble.

I went to see several Chinese temples. The biggest in Canton is dedicated to the memory of the first Buddhistic Emperor and the five hundred first disciples of Buddhism. The central figure is of course Buddha, and next beneath Him is seated the Emperor, and ranging on both sides are the statues of the disciples, all beautifully carved out of wood.

From Canton I returned back to Hong Kong, and from thence to Japan. The first port we touched was Nagasaki. We landed for a few hours and drove through the town. What a contrast! The Japanese are one of the cleanliest peoples on earth. Everything is neat and tidy. Their streets are nearly all broad, straight, and regularly paved. Their little houses are cage-like, and their pine-covered evergreen little hills form the background of almost every town and village. The short-statured, fair-skinned, quaintly-dressed Japs, their movements, attitudes, gestures, everything is picturesque. Japan is the land of the picturesque! Almost every house has a garden at the back, very nicely laid out according to Japanese fashion with small shrubs, grass-plots, small artificial waters, and small stone bridges.

From Nagasaki to Kobe. Here I gave up the steamer and took the land-route to Yokohama, with a view to see the interior of Japan.

I have seen three big cities in the interior — Osaka, a great manufacturing town, Kyoto, the former capital, and Tokyo, the present capital. Tokyo is nearly twice the size of Calcutta with nearly double the population.

No foreigner is allowed to travel in the interior without a passport.

The Japanese seem now to have fully awakened themselves to the necessity of the present times. They have now a thoroughly organised army equipped with guns which one of their own officers has invented and which is said to be second to none. Then, they are continually increasing their navy. I have seen a tunnel nearly a mile long, bored by a Japanese engineer.

The match factories are simply a sight to see, and they are bent upon making everything they want in their own country. There is a Japanese line of steamers plying between China and Japan, which shortly intends running between Bombay and Yokohama.

I saw quite a lot of temples. In every temple there are some Sanskrit Mantras written in Old Bengali characters. Only a few of the priests know Sanskrit. But they are an intelligent sect. The modern rage for progress has penetrated even the priesthood. I cannot write what I have in my mind about the Japs in one short letter. Only I want that numbers of our young men should pay a visit to Japan and China every year. Especially to the Japanese, India is still the dreamland of everything high and good. And you, what are you? ... talking twaddle all your lives, vain talkers, what are you? Come, see these people, and then go and hide your faces in shame. A race of dotards, you lose your caste if you come out! Sitting down these hundreds of years with an ever-increasing load of crystallised superstition on your heads, for hundreds of years spending all your energy upon discussing the touchableness or untouchableness of this food or that, with all humanity crushed out of you by the continuous social tyranny of ages — what are you? And what are you doing now? ... promenading the sea-shores with books in your hands — repeating undigested stray bits of European brainwork, and the whole soul bent upon getting a thirty-rupee clerkship, or at best becoming a lawyer — the height of young India's ambition — and every student with a whole brood of hungry children cackling at his heels and asking for bread! Is there not water enough in the sea to drown you, books, gowns, university diplomas, and all?

Come, be men! Kick out the priests who are always against progress, because they would never mend, their hearts would never become big. They are the offspring of centuries of superstition and tyranny. Root out priest craft first. Come, be men! Come out of your narrow holes and have a look abroad. See how nations are on the march! Do you love man? Do you love your country? Then come, let us struggle for higher and better things; look not back, no, not even if you see the dearest and nearest cry. Look not back, but forward!

India wants the sacrifice of at least a thousand or her young men — men, mind, and not brutes. The English Government has been the instrument, brought over here by the Lord, to break your crystallised civilisation, and Madras supplied the first men who helped in giving the English a footing. How many men, unselfish, thorough-going men, is Madras ready now to supply, to struggle unto life and death to bring about a new state of things sympathy for the poor, and bread to their hungry mouths, enlightenment to the people at large — and struggle unto death to make men of them who have been brought to the level of beasts, by the tyranny of your forefathers?

Yours etc.,
Vivekananda.

PS — Calm and silent and steady work, and no newspaper humbug, no name-making, you must always remember.

U.S.A

1893.8 — ALASINGA

Breezy Meadows, Metcalf, Mass.,
20th August, 1893.

DEAR ALASINGA,

Received your letter yesterday. Perhaps you have by this time got my letter from Japan. From Japan I reached Vancouver. The way was by the Northern Pacific. It was very cold and I suffered much for want of warm clothing. However, I reached Vancouver anyhow, and thence went through Canada to Chicago. I remained about twelve days in Chicago. And almost every day I used to go to the Fair. It is a tremendous affair. One must take at least ten days to go through it. The lady to whom Varada Rao introduced me and her husband belong to the highest Chicago society, and they were so very kind to me. I took my departure from Chicago and came to Boston. Mr. Lâlubhâi was with me up to Boston. He was very kind to me...

The expense I am bound to run into here is awful. You remember, you gave me £170 in notes and £9 in cash. It has come down to £130 in all!! On an average it costs me £1 every day; a cigar costs eight annas of our money. The Americans are so rich that they spend money like water, and by forced legislation keep up the price of everything so high that no other nation on earth can approach it. Every common coolie earns nine or ten rupees a day and spends as much. All those rosy ideas we had before starting have melted, and I have now to fight against impossibilities. A hundred times I had a mind to go out of the country and go back to India. But I am determined, and I have a call from Above; I see no way, but His eyes see. And I must stick to my guns, life or death...

Just now I am living as the guest of an old lady in a village near Boston. I accidentally made her acquaintance in the railway train, and she invited me to come over and live with her. I have an advantage in living with her, in saving for some time my expenditure of £1 per day, and she has the advantage of inviting her friends over here and showing them a curio from India! And all this must be borne. Starvation, cold, hooting in the streets on account of my quaint dress, these are what I have to fight against. But, my dear boy, no great things were ever done without great labour.

... Know, then, that this is the land of Christians, and any other influence than that is almost zero. Nor do I care a bit for the enmity of any — ists in the world. I am here amongst the children of the Son of Mary and the Lord Jesus will help me. They like much the broad views of Hinduism and my love for the Prophet of

Nazareth. I tell them that I preach nothing against the Great One of Galilee. I only ask the Christians to take in the Great Ones of Ind along with the Lord Jesus, and they appreciate it.

Winter is approaching and I shall have to get all sorts of warm clothing, and we require more warm clothing than the natives... Look sharp, my boy, take courage. We are destined by the Lord to do great things in India. Have faith. We will do. We, the poor and the despised, who really feel, and not those...

In Chicago, the other day, a funny thing happened The Raja of Kapurthala was here, and he was being lionised by some portion of Chicago society. I once met the Raja in the Fair grounds, but he was too big to speak with a poor Fakir. There was an eccentric Mahratta Brâhmin selling nail-made pictures in the Fair, dressed in a dhoti. This fellow told the reporters all sorts of things against the Raja—, that he was a man of low caste, that those Rajas were nothing but slaves, and that they generally led immoral lives, etc., etc. And these truthful (?) editors, for which America is famous, wanted to give to the boy's stories some weight; and so the next day they wrote huge columns in their papers about the description of a man of wisdom from India, meaning me — extolling me to the skies, and putting all sorts of words in my mouth, which I never even dreamt of, and ascribing to me all those remarks made by the Mahratta Brahmin about the Raja of Kapurthala. And it was such a good brushing that Chicago society gave up the Raja in hot haste... These newspaper editors made capital out of me to give my countryman a brushing. That shows, however, that in this country intellect carries more weight than all the pomp of money and title.

Yesterday Mrs. Johnson, the lady superintendent of the women's prison, was here. They don't call it prison but reformatory here. It is the grandest thing I have seen in America. How the inmates are benevolently treated, how they are reformed and sent back as useful members of society; how grand, how beautiful, You must see to believe! And, oh, how my heart ached to think of what we think of the poor, the low, in India. They have no chance, no escape, no way to climb up. The poor, the low, the sinner in India have no friends, no help — they cannot rise, try however they may. They sink lower and lower every day, they feel the blows showered upon them by a cruel society, and they do not know whence the blow comes. They have forgotten that they too are men. And the result is slavery. Thoughtful people within the last few years have seen it, but unfortunately laid it at the door of the Hindu religion, and to them, the only way of bettering is by crushing this grandest religion of the world. Hear me, my friend, I have discovered the secret through the grace of the Lord. Religion is not in fault. On the other hand, your religion teaches you that every being is only your own self multiplied. But it was the want of practical application, the want of sympathy — the want of heart. The Lord once more came to you as Buddha and taught you how to feel, how to sympathise with the poor, the miserable, the sinner, but you heard Him not. Your priests invented the horrible story that the Lord was here for deluding demons with false doctrines! True indeed, but we are the demons, not those that believed. And just as the Jews denied the Lord Jesus and are since that day wandering over the world as homeless beggars, tyrannised over by everybody, so you are bond-slaves to any nation that thinks it worth while to rule over you. Ah, tyrants! you do not know that the obverse is tyranny, and the reverse slavery. The slave and the tyrant are synonymous.

Balaji and G. G. may remember one evening at Pondicherry—we were discussing the matter of sea-voyage with a Pandit, and I shall always remember his brutal gestures and his Kadâpi Na (never)! They do not know that India is a very small part of the world, and the whole world looks down with contempt upon the three hundred millions of earthworms crawling upon the fair soil of India and trying to oppress each other. This state of things must be removed, not by destroying religion but by following the great teachings of the Hindu faith, and joining with it the wonderful sympathy of that logical development of Hinduism—Buddhism.

A hundred thousand men and women, fired with the zeal of holiness, fortified with eternal faith in the Lord, and nerved to lion's courage by their sympathy for the poor and the fallen and the downtrodden, will go over the length and breadth of the land, preaching the gospel of salvation, the gospel of help, the gospel of social raising-up—the gospel of equality.

No religion on earth preaches the dignity of humanity in such a lofty strain as Hinduism, and no religion on earth treads upon the necks of the poor and the low in such a fashion as Hinduism. The Lord has shown me that religion is not in fault, but it is the Pharisees and Sadducees in Hinduism, hypocrites, who invent all sorts of engines of tyranny in the shape of doctrines of Pâramârthika and Vyâvahârika.

Despair not; remember the Lord says in the Gita, "To work you have the right, but not to the result." Gird up your loins, my boy. I am called by the Lord for this. I have been dragged through a whole life full of crosses and tortures, I have seen the nearest and dearest die, almost of starvation; I have been ridiculed, distrusted, and have suffered for my sympathy for the very men who scoff and scorn. Well, my boy, this is the school of misery, which is also the school for great souls and prophets for the cultivation of sympathy, of patience, and, above all, of an indomitable iron will which quakes not even if the universe be pulverised at our feet. I pity them. It is not their fault. They are children, yea, veritable children, though they be great and high in society. Their eyes see nothing beyond their little horizon of a few yards—the routine-work, eating, drinking, earning, and begetting, following each other in mathematical precision. They know nothing beyond—happy little souls! Their sleep is never disturbed, their nice little brown studies of lives never rudely shocked by the wail of woe, of misery, of degradation, and poverty, that has filled the Indian atmosphere—the result of centuries of oppression. They little dream of the ages of tyranny, mental, moral, and physical, that has reduced the image of God to a mere beast of burden; the emblem of the Divine Mother, to a slave to bear children; and life itself, a curse. But there are others who see, feel, and shed tears of blood in their hearts, who think that there is a remedy for it, and who are ready to apply this remedy at any cost, even to the giving up of life. And "of such is the kingdom of Heaven". Is it not then natural, my friends, that they have no time to look down from their heights to the vagariese of these contemptible little insects, ready every moment to spit their little venoms?

Trust not to the so-called rich, they are more dead than alive. The hope lies in you—in the meek, the lowly, but the faithful. Have faith in the Lord; no policy, it is nothing. Feel for the miserable and look up for help—it shall come. I have travelled twelve years with this load in my heart and this idea in my head. I have gone from door to door of the so-called rich and great. With a bleeding heart I have crossed half the world to this strange land, seeking for help. The Lord is great. I know He will help me. I may perish of cold or hunger in this land, but I bequeath to you, young men, this sympathy, this struggle for the poor, the ignorant, the oppressed. Go now this minute to the temple of Pârthasârathi[1], and before Him who was friend to the poor and lowly cowherds of Gokula, who never shrank to embrace the Pariah Guhaka, who accepted the invitation of a prostitute in preference to that of the nobles and saved her in His incarnation as Buddha—yea, down on your faces before Him, and make a great sacrifice, the sacrifice of a whole life for them, for whom He comes from time to time, whom He loves above all, the poor, the lowly, the oppressed. Vow, then, to devote your whole lives to the cause of the redemption of these three hundred millions, going down and down every day.

It is not the work of a day, and the path is full of the most deadly thorns. But Parthasarathi is ready to be our Sârathi—we know that. And in His name and with eternal faith in Him, set fire to the mountain of misery that has been heaped upon India for ages—and it shall be burned down. Come then, look it in the face, brethren, it is a grand task, and we are so low. But we are the sons of Light and children of God. Glory unto the Lord, we will succeed. Hundreds will fall in the struggle, hundreds will be ready to take it up. I may die here unsuccessful, another will take up the task. You know the disease, you know the remedy, only have faith. Do not look up to the so-called rich and great; do not care for the heartless intellectual writers, and their cold-blooded newspaper articles. Faith, sympathy—fiery faith and fiery sympathy! Life is nothing, death is nothing, hunger nothing, cold nothing. Glory unto the Lord—march on, the Lord is our General. Do not look back to see who falls—forward—onward! Thus and thus we shall go on, brethren. One falls, and another takes up the work.

From this village I am going to Boston tomorrow. I am going to speak at a big Ladies' Club here, which is helping Ramâbâi. I must first go and buy some clothing in Boston. If I am to live longer here, my quaint dress will not do. People gather by hundreds in the streets to see me. So what I want is to dress myself in a long black coat, and keep a red robe and turban to wear when I lecture. This is what the ladies advise me to do, and they are the rulers here, and I must have their sympathy. Before you get this letter my money would come down to somewhat about £70 of £60. So try your best to send some money. It is necessary to remain here for some time to have any influence here. I could not see the phonograph for Mr. Bhattacharya as I got his letter here. If I go to Chicago again, I will look for them.

---

1. Shri Krishna as Sârathi, charioteer, of Pârtha or Arjuna.

I do not know whether I shall go back to Chicago or not. My friends there write me to represent India. And the gentleman, to whom Varada Rao introduced me, is one of the directors of the Fair; but then I refused as I would have to spend all any little stock of money in remaining more than a month in Chicago.

In America, there are no classes in the railway except in Canada. So I have to travel first-class, as that is the only class; but I do not venture in the Pullmans. They are very comfortable — you sleep, eat, drink, even bathe in them, just as if you were in a hotel — but they are too expensive.

It is very hard work getting into society and making yourself heard. Now nobody is in the towns, they are all away in summer places. They will all come back in winter. Therefore I must wait. After such a struggle, I am not going to give up easily. Only try your best to help me as much as you can; and even if you cannot, I must try to the end. And even if I die of cold or disease or hunger here, you take up the task. Holiness sincerity, and faith. I have left instructions with Cooks to forward any letter or money to me wherever I am. Rome was not built in a day. If you can keep me here for six months at least, I hope everything will come right. In the meantime I am trying my best to find any plank I can float upon. And if I find out any means to support myself, I shall wire to you immediately.

First I will try in America; and if I fail, try in England; if I fail, go back to India and wait for further commands from High. Ramdas's father has gone to England. He is in a hurry to gone home. He is a very good man at heart, only the Baniya roughness on the surface. It would take more than twenty days for the letter to reach. Even now it is so cold in New England that every day we have fires night and morning. Canada is still colder. I never saw snow on such low hills as there.

Gradually I can make my way; but that means a longer residence in this horribly expensive country. Just now the raising of the Rupee in India has created a panic in this country, and lots of mills have been stopped. So I cannot hope for anything just now, but I must wait.

Just now I have been to the tailor and ordered some winter clothings, and that would cost at least Rs. 300 and up. And still it would not be good clothes, only decent. Ladies here are very particular about a man's dress, and they are the power in this country. They... never fail the missionaries. They are helping our Ramabai every year. If you fail in keeping me here, send some money to get me out of the country. In the meantime if anything turns out in my favour, I will write or wire. A word costs Rs. 4 in cable!!

Yours,
Vivekananda.

1893.9 — ADHYAPAKJI

Salem (U.S.A.),
30th Aug., 1893.

DEAR ADHYAPAKJI (Honourable Professor), (Prof. John Henry Wright)

I am going off from here today. I hope you have received some reply from Chicago. I have received an invitation with full directions from Mr. Sanborn. So I am going to Saratoga on Monday. My respects to your wife. And my love to Austin and all the children. You are a real Mahâtmâ (a great soul) and Mrs. Wright is nonpareil.

Yours affectionately,
Vivekananda.

1893.10 — ADHYAPAKJI

Salem,
Saturday, 4th Sept., 1893.

DEAR ADHYAPAKJI, (Prof. John Henry Wright)

I hasten to tender my heartfelt gratitude to you for your letters of introduction. I have received a letter from Mr. Theles of Chicago giving me the names of some of the delegates and other things about the Congress.

Your professor of Sanskrit in his note to Miss Sanborn mistakes me for Purushottama Joshi and states that there is a Sanskrit library in Boston the like of which can scarcely be met with in India. I would be so happy to see it.

Mr. Sanborn has written to me to come over to Saratoga on Monday and I am going accordingly. I would stop then at a boarding house called Sanatorium. If any news come from Chicago in the meanwhile I hope you will kindly send it over to the Sanatorium, Saratoga.

You and your noble wife and sweet children have made an impression in my brain which is simply indelible, and I thought myself so much nearer to heaven when living with you. May He, the giver of all gifts, shower on your head His choicest blessings.

Here are a few lines written as an attempt at poetry. Hoping your love will pardon this infliction.

Ever your friend,
Vivekananda.

O'er hill and dale and mountain range,
In temple, church, and mosque,
In Vedas, Bible, Al Koran
I had searched for Thee in vain.
Like a child in the wildest forest lost
I have cried and cried alone,
"Where art Thou gone, my God, my love?"
The echo answered, "gone."

And days and nights and years then passed—
A fire was in the brain;
I knew not when day changed in night,
The heart seemed rent in twain.
I laid me down on Gangâ's shore,
Exposed to sun and rain;
With burning tears I laid the dust
And wailed with waters' roar.

I called on all the holy names
Of every clime and creed,
"Show me the way, in mercy, ye
Great ones who have reached the goal".

Years then passed in bitter cry,
Each moment seemed an age,
Till one day midst my cries and groans
Some one seemed calling me.

A gentle soft and soothing voice
That said "my son", "my son",
That seemed to thrill in unison
With all the chords of my soul.

I stood on my feet and tried to find
The place the voice came from;
I searched and searched and turned to see
Round me, before, behind.
Again, again it seemed to speak—
The voice divine to me.
In rapture all my soul was hushed,

Entranced, enthralled in bliss.
A flash illumined all my soul;
The heart of my heart opened wide.
O joy, O bliss, what do I find!
My love, my love, you are here,

And you are here, my love, my all!
And I was searching thee!
From all eternity you were there

Enthroned in majesty!
From that day forth, where'er I roam,
I feel Him standing by
O'er hill and dale, high mount and vale,

Far far away and high.
The moon's soft light, the stars so bright,
The glorious orb of day,
He shines in them; His beauty — might —
Reflected lights are they.
The majestic morn, the melting eve,
The boundless billowy sea,
In nature's beauty, songs of birds,

I see through them — it is He.
When dire calamity seizes me,
The heart seems weak and faint,
All nature seems to crush me down,

With laws that never bend.
Meseems I hear Thee whispering sweet
My love, "I am near", "I am near".
My heart gets strong. With Thee, my love,
A thousand deaths no fear.
Thou speakest in the mother's lay
That shuts the baby's eye;
When innocent children laugh and play

I see Thee standing by.
When holy friendship shakes the hand,
He stands between them too;

He pours the nectar in mother's kiss

And the baby's sweet "mama".

Thou wert my God with prophets old;

All creeds do come from Thee;

The Vedas, Bible, and Koran bold

Sing Thee in harmony.

"Thou art", "Thou art" the Soul of souls

In the rushing stream of life.

"Om tat Sat om." (Tat Sat means that only real existence. [*Swamiji's note*].) Thou art my God.

My love, I am thine, I am thine.

1893.11 — ADHYAPAKJI

Chicago,
2nd October, 1893.

DEAR ADHYAPAKJI, (Prof. John Henry Wright)

I do not know what you are thinking of my long silence. In the first place I dropped in on the Congress in the eleventh hour, and quite unprepared; and that kept me very very busy for some time. Secondly, I was speaking almost every day in the Congress and had no time to write; and last and greatest of all — my kind friend, I owe so much to you that it would have been an insult to your ahetuka (unselfish) friendship to have written you business-like letters in a hurry. The Congress is now over.

Dear brother, I was so so afraid to stand before that great assembly of fine speakers and thinkers from all over the world and speak; but the Lord gave me strength, and I almost every day heroically (?) faced the platform and the audience. If I have done well, He gave me the strength for it; if I have miserably failed — I knew that beforehand — for I am hopelessly ignorant.

Your friend Prof. Bradley was very kind to me and he always cheered me on. And oh! everybody is so kind here to me who am nothing — that it is beyond my power of expression. Glory unto Him in the highest in whose sight the poor ignorant monk from India is the same as the learned divines of this mighty land. And how the Lord is helping me every day of my life, brother — I sometimes wish for a life of [a] million million ages to serve Him through the work, dressed in rags and fed by charity.

Oh, how I wished that you were here to see some of our sweet ones from India — the tender-hearted Buddhist Dharmapala, the orator Mazoomdar — and realise that in that far-off and poor India there are hearts that beat in sympathy to yours, born and brought up in this mighty and great country.

My eternal respects to your holy wife; and to your sweet children my eternal love and blessings.

Col. Higginson, a very broad man, told me that your daughter had written to his daughter about me; and he was very sympathetic to me. I am going to Evanston tomorrow and hope to see Prof. Bradley there.

May He make us all more and more pure and holy so that we may live a perfect spiritual life even before throwing off this earthly body.

Vivekananda.

[The letter continues on a separate sheet of paper:]

I am now going to be reconciled to my life here. All my life I have been taking every circumstance as coming from Him and calmly adapting myself to it. At first in America I was almost out of my water. I was afraid I would have to give up the accustomed way of being guided by the Lord and cater for myself — and what a horrid piece of mischief and ingratitude was that. I now clearly see that He who was guiding me on the snow tops of the Himalayas and the burning plains of India is here to help me and guide me. Glory unto Him in the highest. So I have calmly fallen into my old ways. Somebody or other gives me a shelter and food, somebody or other comes to ask me to speak about Him, and I know He sends them and mine is to obey. And then He is supplying my necessities, and His will be done!

"He who rests [in] Me and gives up all other self-assertion and struggles I carry to him whatever he needs" (Gitâ).

So it is in Asia. So in Europe. So in America. So in the deserts of India. So in the rush of business in America. For is He not here also? And if He does not, I only would take for granted that He wants that I should lay aside this three minutes' body of clay — and hope to lay it down gladly.

We may or may not meet, brother. He knows. You are great, learned, and holy. I dare not preach to you or your wife; but to your children I quote these passages from the Vedas —

"The four Vedas, sciences, languages, philosophy, and all other learnings are only ornamental. The real learning, the true knowledge is that which enables us to reach Him who is unchangeable in His love."

"How real, how tangible, how visible is He through whom the skin touches, the eyes see, and the world gets its reality!"

"Hearing Him nothing remains to be heard,
Seeing Him nothing remains to be seen,
Attaining Him nothing remains to be attained."

"He is the eye of our eyes, the ear of our ears, the Soul of our souls."

He is nearer to you, my dears, than even your father and mother. You are innocent and pure as flowers. Remain so, and He will reveal Himself unto you. Dear

Austin, when you are playing, there is another playmate playing with you who loves you more than anybody else; and Oh, He is so full of fun. He is always playing—sometimes with great big balls which we call the sun and earth, sometimes with little children like you and laughing and playing with you. How funny it would be to see Him and play with Him! My dear, think of it.

Dear Adhyapakji, I am moving about just now. Only when I come to Chicago, I always go to see Mr. and Mrs. Lyons, one of the noblest couples I have seen here. If you would be kind enough to write to me, kindly address it to the care of Mr. John B. Lyon, 262 Michigan Ave., Chicago.

"He who gets hold of the One in this world of many—the one constant existence in a world of flitting shadows—the one life in a world of death—he alone crosses this sea of misery and struggle. None else, none else" (Vedas).

"He who is the Brahman of the Vedântins, Ishvara of the Naiyâyikas, Purusha of the Sânkhyas, cause of the Mimâmsakas, law of the Buddhists, absolute zero of the Atheists, and love infinite unto those that love, may [He] take us all under His merciful protection": Udayanâchârya—a great philosopher of the Nyâya or Dualistic school. And this is the Benediction pronounced at the very beginning of his wonderful book Kusumânjali (A handful of flowers), in which he attempts to establish the existence of a personal creator and moral ruler of infinite love independently of revelation.

Your ever grateful friend,
Vivekananda.

1893.12—MRS. TANNATT WOODS

Chicago,
10th October, 1893.

DEAR MRS. TANNATT WOODS,

I received your letter yesterday. Just now I am lecturing about Chicago—and am doing as I think very well; it is ranging from 30 to 80 dollars a lecture, and just now I have been so well advertised in Chicago gratis by the Parliament of Religions that it is not advisable to give up this field now. To which I am sure you will agree. However I may come soon to Boston, but when I cannot say. Yesterday I returned from Streator where I got 87 dollars for a lecture. I have engagements every day this week. And hope more will come by the end of the week. My love to Mr. Woods and compliments to all our friends.

Yours truly,
Vivekananda.

1893.13 — ADHYAPAKJI

C/O J. Lyon,
262 Michigan Avenue, Chicago,
26th October, 1893.

DEAR ADHYAPAKJI, (Prof. John Henry Wright)

You would be glad to know that I am doing well here and that almost everybody has been very kind to me, except of course the very orthodox. Many of the men brought together here from far-off lands have got projects and ideas and missions to carry out, and America is the only place where there is a chance of success for everything. But I thought better and have given up speaking about my project entirely — because I am sure now — the heathen draws more than his project. So I want to go to work earnestly for my own project only keeping the project in the background and working like any other lecturer.

He who has brought me hither and has not left me yet will not leave me ever I am here. You will be glad to know that I am doing well and expect to do very well in the way of getting money. Of course I am too green in the business but would soon learn my trade. I am very popular in Chicago. So I want to stay here a little more and get money.

Tomorrow I am going to lecture on Buddhism at the ladies' fortnightly club — which is the most influential in this city. How to thank you my kind friend or Him who brought you to me; for now I think the success of my project probable, and it is you who have made it so.

May blessings and happiness attend every step of your progress in this world.

My love and blessings to your children.

Yours affectionately ever,
Vivekananda.

1893.14 — ALASINGA

Chicago,
2nd November, 1893.

DEAR ALASINGA,

I am so sorry that a moment's weakness on my part should cause you so much trouble; I was out of pocket at that time. Since then the Lord sent me friends. At a village near Boston I made the acquaintance of Dr. Wright, Professor of Greek in the Harvard University. He sympathised with me very much and urged upon me the necessity of going to the Parliament of Religions, which he thought would give me an introduction to the nation. As I was not acquainted with anybody, the Professor undertook to arrange everything for me, and eventually I came back to

Chicago. Here I, together with the oriental and occidental delegates to the Parliament of Religions, were all lodged in the house of a gentleman.

On the morning of the opening of the Parliament, we all assembled in a building called the Art Palace, where one huge and other smaller temporary halls were erected for the sittings of the Parliament. Men from all nations were there. From India were Mazoomdar of the Brâhmo Samâj, and Nagarkar of Bombay, Mr. Gandhi representing the Jains, and Mr. Chakravarti representing Theosophy with Mrs. Annie Besant. Of these, Mazoomdar and I were, of course, old friends, and Chakravarti knew me by name. There was a grand procession, and we were all marshalled on to the platform. Imagine a hall below and a huge gallery above, packed with six or seven thousand men and women representing the best culture of the country, and on the platform learned men of all the nations of the earth. And I, who never spoke in public in my life, to address this august assemblage!! It was opened in great form with music and ceremony and speeches; then the delegates were introduced one by one, and they stepped up and spoke. Of course my heart was fluttering, and my tongue nearly dried up; I was so nervous and could not venture to speak in the morning. Mazoomdar made a nice speech, Chakravarti a nicer one, and they were much applauded. They were all prepared and came with ready-made speeches. I was a fool and had none, but bowed down to Devi Sarasvati and stepped up, and Dr. Barrows introduced me. I made a short speech. I addressed the assembly as "Sisters and Brothers of America", a deafening applause of two minutes followed, and then I proceeded; and when it was finished, I sat down, almost exhausted with emotion. The next day all the papers announced that my speech was the hit of the day, and I became known to the whole of America. Truly has it been said by the great commentator Shridhara—"मूकं करोति वाचालं—Who maketh the dumb a fluent speaker."

His name be praised! From that day I became a celebrity, and the day I read my paper on Hinduism, the hall was packed as it had never been before. I quote to you from one of the papers: "Ladies, ladies, ladies packing every place—filling every corner, they patiently waited and waited while the papers that separated them from Vivekananda were read", etc. You would be astonished if I sent over to you the newspaper cuttings, but you already know that I am a hater of celebrity. Suffice it to say, that whenever I went on the platform, a deafening applause would be raised for me. Nearly all the papers paid high tributes to me, and even the most bigoted had to admit that "This man with his handsome face and magnetic presence and wonderful oratory is the most prominent figure in the Parliament", etc., etc. Sufficient for you to know that never before did an Oriental make such an impression on American society.

And how to speak of their kindness? I have no more wants now, I am well off, and all the money that I require to visit Europe I shall get from here... A boy called Narasimhâchârya has cropped up in our midst. He has been loafing about the city for the last three years. Loafing or no loafing, I like him; but please write to me all about him if you know anything. He knows you. He came in the year of the Paris

Exhibition to Europe...

I am now out of want. Many of the handsomest houses in this city are open to me. All the time I am living as a guest of somebody or other. There is a curiosity in this nation, such as you meet with nowhere else. They want to know everything, and their women — they are the most advanced in the world. The average American woman is far more cultivated than the average American man. The men slave all their life for money, and the women snatch every opportunity to improve themselves. And they are a very kind-hearted, frank people. Everybody who has a fad to preach comes here, and I am sorry to say that most of these are not sound. The Americans have their faults too, and what nation has not? But this is my summing up: Asia laid the germs of civilization, Europe developed man, and America is developing the woman and the masses. It is the paradise of the woman and the labourer. Now contrast the American masses and women with ours, and you get the idea at once. The Americans are fast becoming liberal. Judge them not by the specimens of hard-shelled Christians (it is their own phrase) that you see in India. There are those here too, but their number is decreasing rapidly, and this great nation is progressing fast towards that spirituality which is the standard boast of the Hindu.

The Hindu must not give up his religion, but must keep religion within its proper limits end give freedom to society to grow. All the reformers in India made the serious mistake of holding religion accountable for all the horrors of priestcraft and degeneration and went forth with to pull down the indestructible structure, and what was the result? Failure! Beginning from Buddha down to Ram Mohan Roy, everyone made the mistake of holding caste to be a religious institution and tried to pull down religion and caste all together, and failed. But in spite of all the ravings of the priests, caste is simply a crystallised social institution, which after doing its service is now filling the atmosphere of India with its stench, and it can only be removed by giving back to the people their lost social individuality. Every man born here knows that he is a man. Every man born in India knows that he is a slave of society. Now, freedom is the only condition of growth; take that off, the result is degeneration. With the introduction of modern competition, see how caste is disappearing fast! No religion is now necessary to kill it. The Brâhmana shopkeeper, shoemaker, and wine-distiller are common in Northern India. And why? Because of competition. No man is prohibited from doing anything he pleases for his livelihood under the present Government, and the result is neck and neck competition, and thus thousands are seeking and finding the highest level they were born for, instead of vegetating at the bottom.

I must remain in this country at least through the winter, and then go to Europe. The Lord will provide everything for me. You need not disturb yourself about it. I cannot express my gratitude for your love.

Day by day I am feeling that the Lord is with me, and I am trying to follow His direction. His will be done... We will do great things for the world, and that for the sake of doing good and not for name and fame.

"Ours not to reason why, ours but to do and die." Be of good cheer and believe that we are selected by the Lord to do great things, and we will do them. Hold yourself in readiness, i.e. be pure and holy, and love for love's sake. Love the poor, the miserable, the downtrodden, and the Lord will bless you.

See the Raja of Ramnad and others from time to time and urge them to sympathise with the masses of India. Tell them how they are standing on the neck of the poor, and that they are not fit to be called men if they do not try to raise them up. Be fearless, the Lord is with you, and He will yet raise the starving and ignorant millions of India. A railway porter here is better educated than many of your young men and most of your princes. Every American woman has far better education than can be conceived of by the majority of Hindu women. Why cannot we have the same education? We must.

Think not that you are poor; money is not power, but goodness, holiness. Come and see how it is so all over the world.

Yours with blessings,
Vivekananda.

PS — By the bye, your uncle's paper was the most curious phenomenon I ever saw. It was like a tradesman's catalogue, and it was not thought fit to be read in the Parliament. So Narasimhacharya read a few extracts from it in a side hall, and nobody understood a word of it. Do not tell him of it. It is a great art to press the largest amount of thought into the smallest number of words. Even Manilal Dvivedi's paper had to be cut very short. More than a thousand papers were read, and there was no time to give to such wild perorations. I had a good long time given to me over the ordinary half hour, ... because the most popular speakers were always put down last, to hold the audience. And Lord bless them, what sympathy they have, and what patience! They would sit from ten o'clock in the morning to ten o'clock at night — only a recess of half an hour for a meal, and paper after paper read, most of them very trivial, but they would wait and wait to hear their favourites.

Dharmapâla of Ceylon was one of the favourites But unfortunately he was not a good speaker. He had only quotations from Max Müller and Rhys Davids to give them. He is a very sweet man, and we became very intimate during the Parliament.

A Christian lady from Poona, Miss Sorabji, and the Jain representative, Mr. Gandhi, are going to remain longer in the country end make lecture tours. I hope they will succeed. Lecturing is a very profitable occupation in this country and sometimes pays well.

Mr. Ingersoll gets five to six hundred dollars a lecture. He is the most celebrated lecturer in this country. Do not publish this letter. After reading, send it to the Maharaja (of Khetri). I have sent him my photograph in America.

1893.15 — MRS. WOODS

541 Dearborn Avenue, Chicago,
19th November, 1893.

DEAR MRS. WOODS,

Excuse my delay in answering your letter. I do not know when I will be able to see you again. I am starting tomorrow for Madison and Minneapolis.

The English gentleman you speak of is Dr. Momerie of London. He is a well-known worker amongst the poor of London and is a very sweet man. You perhaps do not know that the English church was the only religious denomination in the world who did not send to us a representative, and Dr. Momerie came to the Parliament in spite of the Archbishop of Canterbury's denouncing of the Parliament of Religions.

My love for you, my kind friend, and your noble son is all the same whether I write pretty often or not.

Can you express my books and the cover-all to the care of Mr. Hale? I am in need of them. The express will be paid here.

The blessings of the Lord on you and yours.

Ever your friend,
Vivekananda.

PS — If you have the occasion to write to Miss Sanborn and others of our friends in the east, kindly give them my deepest respects.

1893.16 — MOTHER

To Mrs. G. W. Hale:

Minneapolis,
21 November, 1893.

DEAR MOTHER,

I reached Madison safely, went to a hotel, and sent a message to Mr. Updike. He came to see me. He is a Congregational and so, of course, was not very friendly at first; but in the course of an hour or so became very kind to me, and took me over the whole place and the University. I had a fine audience and $100. Immediately after the lecture I took the night train to Minneapolis.

I tried to get the clergymen's ticket, but they could not give me any, not being the headquarters. The thing to be done is to get a permit from every head office of every line in Chicago. Perhaps it is possible for Mr. Hale to get the permits for me. If it is so, I hope he will take the trouble to send them over to me to Minneapolis if they can reach me by the 25th, or to Des Moines if by the 29th. Else I would do it the next time in Chicago. I have taken the money in a draft on the bank, which cost me 40¢.

May you be blessed for ever, my kind friend; you and your whole family have made such a heavenly impression on me as I would carry all my life.

Yours sincerely,
Vivekananda.

1893.17 — MOTHER

To Mrs. G. W. Hale:

Minneapolis,
24 November, 1893.

DEAR MOTHER,

I am still in Minneapolis. I am to lecture this afternoon, and the day after tomorrow go to Des Moines.

The day I came here they had their first snow, and it snowed all through the day and night, and I had great use for the arctics. (A waterproof overshoe.) I went to see the frozen Minnehaha Falls. They are very beautiful. The temperature today is 21° below zero, but I had been out sleighing and enjoyed it immensely. I am not the least afraid of losing the tips of my ears or nose.

The snow scenery here has pleased me more than any other sight in this country.

I saw people skating on a frozen lake yesterday.

I am doing well. Hoping this will find you all the same, I remain yours obediently,

Vivekananda

1893.18 — HARIPADA[1]

C/O George W. Hale Esq.,
541 Dearborn Avenue, Chicago,
28th December, 1893.

DEAR HARIPADA[2],

It is very strange that news of my Chicago lectures has appeared in the Indian papers; for whatever I do, I try my best to avoid publicity. Many things strike me here. It may be fairly said that there is no poverty in this country. I have never seen women elsewhere as cultured and educated as they are here. Well-educated men

1 Translated from Bengali.
2. Haripada Mitra.

there are in our country, but you will scarcely find anywhere women like those here. It is indeed true, that "the Goddess Herself lives in the houses of virtuous men as Lakshmi". I have seen thousands of women here whose hearts are as pure and stainless as snow. Oh, how free they are! It is they who control social and civic duties Schools and colleges are full of women, and in our country women cannot be safely allowed to walk in the streets! Their kindness to me is immeasurable. Since I came here, I have been welcomed by them to their houses. They are providing me with food, arranging for my lectures, taking me to market, and doing everything for my comfort and convenience. I shall never be able to repay in the least the deep debt of gratitude I owe to them.

Do you know who is the real "Shakti-worshipper"? It is he who knows that God is the omnipresent force in the universe and sees in women the manifestation of that Force. Many men here look upon their women in this light. Manu, again, has said that gods bless those families where women are happy and well treated. Here men treat their women as well as can be desired, and hence they are so prosperous, so learned, so free, and so energetic. But why is it that we are slavish, miserable, and dead? The answer is obvious.

And how pure and chaste are they here! Few women are married before twenty or twenty-five, and they are as free as the birds in the air. They go to market, school, and college, earn money, and do all kinds of work. Those who are well-to-do devote themselves to doing good to the poor. And what are we doing? We are very regular in marrying our girls at eleven years of age lest they should become corrupt and immoral. What does our Manu enjoin? "Daughters should be supported and educated with as much care and attention as the sons." As sons should be married after observing Brahmacharya up to the thirtieth year, so daughters also must observe Brahmacharya and be educated by their parents. But what are we actually doing? Can you better the condition of your women? Then there will be hope for your well-being. Otherwise you will remain as backward as you are now.

If anybody is born of a low caste in our country, he is gone for ever, there is no hope for him. Why? What a tyranny it is! There are possibilities, opportunities, and hope for every individual in this country. Today he is poor, tomorrow he may become rich and learned and respected. Here everyone is anxious to help the poor. In India there is a howling cry that we are very poor, but how many charitable associations are there for the well-being of the poor? How many people really weep for the sorrows and sufferings of the millions of poor in India? Are we men? What are we doing for their livelihood, for their improvement? We do not touch them, we avoid their company! Are we men? Those thousands of Brâhmanas—what are they doing for the low, downtrodden masses of India? "Don't touch", "Don't touch", is the only phrase that plays upon their lips! How mean and degraded has our eternal religion become at their hands! Wherein does our religion lie now? In "Don't-touchism" alone, and nowhere else!

I came to this country not to satisfy my curiosity, nor for name or fame, but to see if I could find any means for the support of the poor in India. If God helps me, you will know gradually what those means are.

As regards spirituality, the Americans are far inferior to us, but their society is far superior to ours. We will teach them our spirituality and assimilate what is best in their society.

With love and best wishes,

Yours,
Vivekananda.

1893.19 — HARIPADA[1]

To Shri Haripada Mitra:

Margaon,
1893.

DEAR HARIPADA,

I just now received a letter from you. I reached here safe. I went to visit Panjim and a few other villages and temples near by. I returned just today. I have not given up the intention of visiting Gokarna, Mahabaleshwar, and other places. I start for Dharwar by the morning train tomorrow. I have taken the walking-stick with me. Doctor Yagdekar's friend was very hospitable to me. Please give my compliments to Mr. Bhate and all others there. May the Lord shower His blessings on you and your wife. The town of Panjim is very neat and clean. Most of the Christians here are literate. The Hindus are mostly uneducated.

Yours affectionately,
Sachchidananda.

(Swamiji used to call himself such in those days.)

---

[1] Translated from Bengali.

1894

1894.1 — SWAMI RAMAKRISHNANDA[1]

C/O George W. Hale, Esq.,
541 Dearborn Avenue, Chicago,
(Beginning of?) 1894.

MY DEAR __, (Swami Ramakrishnananda)

Very glad to receive your letter. I am very sorry to hear of Mazoomdar's doings. One always behaves thus in trying to push oneself before all others. I am not much to blame. M — came here ten years ago, and got much reputation and honour; now I am in flying colours. Such is the will of the Guru, what shall I do? It is childishness on M — 's part to be annoyed at this. Never mind, उपेक्षितव्यं तद्वचनं भवत्सट्टशानां महात्मनाम्। अपि कीटदंशनभीरुका वयं रामकृष्ण तनयास्तद्दृहृदयरुधिरपोषिताः। "अलोकसामान्यमचिन्त्यहेतुकं हनिदन्ती मन्दाश्चरितं महात्मनाम्" — Great men like you should pay no heed to what he says. Shall we, children of Shri Ramakrishna, nourished with his heart's blood, be afraid of worm-bites? "The wicked criticise the conduct of the magnanimous, which is extraordinary and whose motives are difficult to fathom" (Kalidasa's Kumârasambhavam.) — remember all this and forgive this fool. It is the will of the Lord that people of this land have their power of introspection roused, and does it lie in anybody to check His progress? I want no name — I want to be a voice without a form. I do not require anybody to defend me —

— who am I to check or to help the course of His march? And who are others also? Still, my heartfelt gratitude to them.

— "Established in which state a man is not moved even by great misfortune" (Gita) — that state he has not reached; think of this and look upon him with pity. Through the Lord's will, the desire for name and fame has not yet crept into my heart, and I dare say never will. I am an instrument, and He is the operator. Through this instrument He is rousing the religious instinct in thousands of hearts in this far-off country. Thousands of men and women here love and revere me..." the lame cross mountains." I am amazed at His grace. Whichever town I visit, it is in an uproar. They have named me "the cyclonic Hindu". Remember, it is His will — I am a voice without a form.

The Lord knows whether I shall go to England or any other blessed place. He will arrange everything. Here a cigar costs one rupee. Once you get into a cab, you have to pay three rupees, a coat costs a hundred rupees; the hotel charge is nine rupees a day. The Lord provides everything... The Lord be praised, I know nothing. "—Truth alone triumphs, not falsehood. Through Truth alone lies the path of Devayâna." You must be fearless. It is the coward who fears and defends himself. Let no one amongst us come forward to defend me. I get all news of Madras and Rajputana from time to time... There are eyes that can see at a distance of fourteen thousand miles. It is quite true. Keep quiet now, everything will see the light in time, as far as He wills it. Not one word of His proves untrue. My brother, do men

---

1 Translated from Bengali.

grieve over the fight of cats and dogs? So the jealousy, envy, and elbowing of common men should make no impression on your mind. For the last six months I have been saying, the curtain is going up, the sun is rising. Yes, the curtain is lifting by degrees, slow but sure; you will come to know it in time. He knows. One cannot speak out one's mind. These are things not for writing... Never let go your hold of the rudder, grasp it firm. We are steering all right, no mistaking that, but landing on the other shore is only a question of time. That's all. Can a leader be made my brother? A leader is born. Do you understand? And it is a very difficult task to take on the role of a leader.—One must be accommodate a thousand minds. There must not be a shade of jealousy or selfishness, then you are a leader. First, by birth, and secondly, unselfish—that's a leader. Everything is going all right, everything will come round. He casts the net all right, and winds it up likewise best instrument. Love conquers in the long run. It won't do to become impatient—wait, wait—patience is bound to give success...

I tell you brother, let everything go on as it is, only take care that no form becomes necessary—unity in variety—see that universality be not hampered in the least. Everything must be sacrificed, if necessary, for that one sentiment, universality. Whether I live or die, whether I go back to India or not, remember this specially, that universality—perfect acceptance, not tolerance only—we preach and perform. Take care how you trample on the least rights of others. Many a huge ship has foundered in that whirlpool. Remember, perfect devotion minus its bigotry—this is what we have got to show. Through His grace everything will go all right... Everybody wants to be a leader, but it is the failure to grasp that he is born, that causes all this mischief...

Our matrons are all hale and hearty, I hope? Where is Gour-Mâ? We want a thousand such Mothers with that noble stirring spirit... We want all. It is not at all necessary that all should have the same faith in our Lord as we have, but we want to unite all the powers of goodness against all the powers of evil... A besetting sin with Sannyasins is the taking pride in their monastic order. That may have its utility during the first stages, but when they are full-grown, they need it no more. One must make no distinction between householders and Sannyasins—then only one is a true Sannyasin...

A movement which half a dozen penniless boys set on foot and which now bids fair to progress in such an accelerated motion—is it a humbug or the Lord's will? If it is, then let all give up party-spirit and jealousy, and unite in action. A universal religion cannot be set up through party faction...

If all understand one day for one minute that one cannot become great by the mere wish, that he only rises whom He raises, and he falls whom He brings down then all trouble is at an end. But there is that egotism—hollow in itself, and without the power to move a finger: how ludicrous of it to say, "I won't let anyone rise!" That jealousy, that absence of conjoint action is the very nature of enslaved nations. But we must try to shake it off. The terrible jealousy is characteristic of us... You will be convinced of this if you visit some other countries. Our fellows in this respect are the enfranchised negroes of this country—if but one amongst them rises to greatness, all the others would at once set themselves against him and try to level him down by making a common cause with the whites...

At any cost, any price, any sacrifice, we must never allow that to creep in among ourselves. Whether we be ten or two, do not care, but those few must be perfect characters... "It is not good to ask of one's father if the Lord keeps His promise (to look after His devotees)." And the Lord will do so, get your minds easy on that score... We must spread his name in Rajputana, Punjab, U.P., Madras, and such other provinces—yes, in Raiputana, where still there are people who can say, "Such has ever been the custom with Raghu's line that they keep their word even at the cost of life."

A bird, in the course of its flight, reaches a spot whence it looks on the ground below with supreme calmness, Have you reached that spot? He who has not reached there has no right to teach others. Relax your limbs and float with the current, and you are sure to reach your destination.

Cold is making itself scarce by degrees, and I have been almost through the winter. Here in winter the whole body becomes charged with electricity. In shaking hands one feels a shock, accompanied by a sound. You can light the gas with your finger. And about the cold I have written to you already. I am coursing through the length and breadth of the country, but Chicago is my "Math" (monastery), where I always return after my wanderings. I am now making for the east. He knows where the bark will reach the shore...

Has Dashu the same sort of love for you. Does he see you frequently? How is Bhavanath, and what is he doing. Do you visit him, and look upon him with an eye of regard? Yes, brother, the distinction between Sannyasin and layman is a fiction, etc.—"He makes the dumb fluent," etc. My friend it is difficult to judge what is in a particular individual. Shri Ramakrishna has spoken highly of him; and he deserves our respect. Fie upon you if you have no faith even after so much experience. Does he love you? Please convey to him my hearty love and esteem. My love to Kalikrishna Babu, he is a very noble soul. How is Ramlal (Nephew of Shri Ramakrishna.)? He has got a little faith and devotion? My love and greetings to him. Sanyal is moving all right with the mill, I suppose? Ask him to have patience, and the mill will go on all right.

My heart's love to all.

Ever yours in love,
Vivekananda.

1894.2 — MISS BELL

To Miss Isabelle McKindley:

528, 5th Ave., New York,
24th Jan., 1895.

DEAR MISS BELL,

I hope you are well...

My last lecture was not very much appreciated by the men but awfully so by vemen. You know this Brooklyn is the centre of anti-women's rights movements; and when I told them that women deserve and are fit for everything, they did not like it of course. Never mind, the women were in ecstasies.

I have got again a little cold. I am going to the Guernseys. I have got a room downtown also where I will go several hours to hold my classes etc. Mother Church must be all right by this time, and you are all enjoying this nice weather. Give Mrs. Adams mountain high love and regard from me when you see her next.

Send my letters as usual to the Guernseys.

With love for all,

Ever your affectionate brother,
Vivekananda.

1894.3 — FRIENDS

C/O George W. Hale Esq.,
541 Dearborn Avenue, Chicago,
24th January, 1894.

DEAR FRIENDS[1],

Your letters have reached me. I am surprised that so much about me has reached you. The criticism you mention of the Interior is not to be taken as the attitude of the American people. That paper is almost unknown here, and belongs to what they call a "blue-nose Presbyterian paper", very bigoted. Still all the "blue-noses" are not ungentlemanly. The American people, and many of the clergy, are very hospitable to me. That paper wanted a little notoriety by attacking a man who was being lionised by society. That trick is well known here, and they do not think anything of it. Of course, our Indian missionaries may try to make capital out of it. If they do, tell them, "Mark, Jew, a judgment has come upon you!" Their old building is tottering to its foundation and must come down in spite of their hysterical shrieks. I pity them — if their means of living fine lives in India is cut down by the influx of oriental religions here. But not one of their leading clergy is ever against me. Well, when I am in the pond, I must bathe thoroughly.

1. His disciples in Madras.

I send you a newspaper cutting of the short sketch of our religion which I read before them. Most of my speeches are extempore. I hope to put them in book form before I leave the country. I do not require any help from India, I have plenty here. Employ the money you have in printing and publishing this short speech; and translating it into the vernaculars, throw it broadcast; that will keep us before the national mind. In the meantime do not forget our plan of a central college, and the starting from it to all directions in India. Work hard…

About the women of America, I cannot express my gratitude for their kindness. Lord bless them. In this country, women are the life of every movement, and represent all the culture of the nation, for men are too busy to educate themselves.

I have received Kidi's letters. With the question whether caste shall go or come I have nothing to do. My idea is to bring to the door of the meanest, the poorest, the noble ideas that the human race has developed both in and out of India, and let them think for themselves. Whether there should be caste or not, whether women should be perfectly free or not, does not concern me. "Liberty of thought and action is the only condition of life, of growth and well-being." Where it does not exist, the man, the race, the nation must go down.

Caste or no caste, creed or no creed, any man, or class, or caste, or nation, or institution which bars the power of free thought and action of an individual — even so long as that power does not injure others — is devilish and must go down.

My whole ambition in life is to set in motion a machinery which will bring noble ideas to the door of everybody, and then let men and women settle their own fate. Let them know what our forefathers as well as other nations have thought on the most momentous questions of life. Let them see specially what others are doing now, and then decide. We are to put the chemicals together, the crystallization will be done by nature according to her laws. Work hard, be steady, and have faith in the Lord. Set to work, I am coming sooner or later. Keep the motto before you — "Elevation of the masses without injuring their religion".

Remember that the nation lives in the cottage. But, alas! nobody ever did anything for them. Our modern reformers are very busy about widow remarriage. Of course, I am a sympathiser in every reform, but the fate of a nation does not depend upon the number of husbands their widows get, but upon the condition of the masses. Can you raise them? Can you give them back their lost individuality without making them lose their innate spiritual nature? Can you become an occidental of occidentals in your spirit of equality, freedom, work, and energy, and at the same time a Hindu to the very backbone in religious culture and instincts? This is to be done and we will do it. You are all born to do it. Have faith in yourselves, great convictions are the mothers of great deeds. Onward for ever! Sympathy for the poor, the downtrodden, even unto death — this is our motto. Onward, brave lads!

Yours affectionately,
Vivekananda.

PS—Do not publish this letter; but there is no harm in preaching the idea of elevating the masses by means of a central college, and bringing education as well as religion to the door of the poor by means of missionaries trained in this college. Try to interest everybody.

I send you a few newspaper cuttings—only from the very best and highest. The one by Dr. Thomas is very valuable as written by one of the, if not the leading clergymen of America. The Interior with all its fanaticism and thirst for notoriety was bound to say that I was the public favourite. I cut a few lines from that magazine also.

1894.4 — DIWANJI SAHEB

To Shri Haridas Viharidas Desai:

Chicago,
29th January, 1894.

DEAR DIWANJI SAHEB,

Your last letter reached me a few days ago. You had been to see my poor mother and brothers. I am glad you did. But you have touched the only soft place in my heart. You ought to know, Diwanji, that I am no hard-hearted brute. If there is any being I love in the whole world, it is my mother. Yet I believed and still believe that without my giving up the world, the great mission which Ramakrishna Paramahamsa, my great Master came to preach would not see the light, and where would those young men be who have stood as bulwarks against the surging waves of materialism and luxury of the day? These have done a great amount of good to India, especially to Bengal, and this is only the beginning. With the Lord's help they will do things for which the whole world will bless them for ages. So on the one hand, my vision of the future of Indian religion and that of the whole world, my love for the millions of beings sinking down and down for ages with nobody to help them, nay, nobody with even a thought for them; on the other hand, making those who are nearest and dearest to me miserable; I choose the former. "Lord will do the rest." He is with me, I am sure of that if of anything. So long as I am sincere, nothing can resist me, because He will be my help. Many and many in India could not understand me; and how could they, poor men? Their thoughts never strayed beyond the everyday routine business of eating and drinking. I know only a few noble souls like yourself appreciate me. Lord bless your noble self. But appreciation or no appreciation, I am born to organise these young men; nay, hundreds more in every city are ready to join me; and I want to send them rolling like irresistible waves over India, bringing comfort, morality, religion, education to the doors of the meanest and the most downtrodden. And this I will do or die.

Our people have no idea, no appreciation. On the other hand, that horrible jealousy and suspicious nature which is the natural outcome of a thousand years of slavery make them stand as enemies to every new idea. Still the Lord is great.

About the Ârati as well as other things you speak of, it is the form in every one of the monasteries in all parts of India, and the worshipping of Guru is the first duty inculcated in the Vedas. It has its bad and good sides. But you must remember we are a unique company, nobody amongst us has a right to force his faith upon the others. Many of us do not believe in any form of idolatry; but they have no right to object when others do it, because that would break the first principle of our religion. Again, God can only be known in and through man. Vibrations of light are everywhere, even in the darkest corners; but it is only in the lamp that it becomes visible to man. Similarly God, though everywhere, we can only conceive Him as a big man. All ideas of God such as merciful preserver, helper, protector — all these are human ideas, anthropomorphic; and again these must cling to a man, call him a Guru or a Prophet or an Incarnation. Man cannot go beyond his nature, no more than you can jump out of your body. What harm is there in some people worshipping their Guru when that Guru was a hundred times more holy than even your historical prophets all taken together? If there is no harm in worshipping Christ, Krishna, or Buddha, why should there be any in worshipping this man who never did or thought anything unholy, whose intellect only through intuition stands head and shoulders above all the other prophets, because they were all one-sided? It was he that brought first to the world this idea of truth, not in but of every religion, which is gaining ground all over the world, and that without the help of science or philosophy or any other acquirement.

But even this is not compulsory, none of the brethren has told you that all must worship his Guru. No, no, no. But again none of us has a right to object when another worships. Why? Because that would overthrow this most unique society the world has ever seen, ten men of ten different notions and ideas living in perfect harmony. Wait, Diwanji, the Lord is great and merciful, you will see more.

We do not only tolerate but accept every religion, and with the Lord's help I am trying to preach it to the whole world.

Three things are necessary to make every man great, every nation great:

1. Conviction of the powers of goodness.
2. Absence of jealousy and suspicion.
3. Helping all who are trying to be and do good.

Why should the Hindu nation with all its wonderful intelligence and other things have gone to pieces? I would answer you, jealousy. Never were there people more wretchedly jealous of one another, more envious of one another's fame and name than this wretched Hindu race. And if you ever come out in the West, the absence of this is the first feeling which you will see in the Western nations.

Three men cannot act in concert together in India for five minutes. Each one struggles for power, and in the long run the whole organisation comes to grief. Lord! Lord! When will we learn not to be jealous! In such a nation, and especially in Bengal, to create a band of men who are tied and bound together with a most undying love in spite of difference — is it not wonderful? This band will increase.

This idea of wonderful liberality joined with eternal energy and progress must spread over India. It must electrify the whole nation and must enter the very pores of society in spite of the horrible ignorance, spite, caste-feeling, old boobyism, and jealousy which are the heritage of this nation of slaves.

You are one of the few noble natures who stand as rocks out of water in this sea of universal stagnation. Lord bless you for ever and ever!

Yours ever faithfully,
Vivekananda.

1894.5 — MOTHER

To Mrs. G. W. Hale:

Detroit,
14 February, 1894.

DEAR MOTHER,

Arrived safely night before last at 1 o'clock a.m. The train was seven hours late, being blocked by snowdrifts on the way. However, I enjoyed the novelty of the sight: several men cutting and clearing the snow and two engines tugging and pulling was a new sight to me.

Here I met Mr. Bagley, the youngest [Paul F. Bagley], waiting for me at the station; and, it being very late in the night, Mrs. Bagley had retired, but the daughters sat up for me.

They are very rich, kind and hospitable. Mrs. Bagley is especially interested in India. The daughters are very good, educated and good-looking. The eldest gave me a luncheon at a club where I met some of the finest ladies and gentlemen of the city. Last evening there was a reception given here in the house. Today I am going to speak for the first time. Mrs. Bagley is a very nice and kind lady. I hope the lectures will please her. With my love and regards for you all, I remain,

Yours sincerely,
Vivekananda.

PS — I have received a letter from Slayton in reply to that in which I wrote to him that I cannot stay. He gives me hope. What is your advice? I enclose the letter [from Narasimhacharya] in another envelope.

1894.6 — MOTHER

To Mrs. G. W. Hale:

Detroit,
20 February, 1894.

DEAR MOTHER,

My lectures here are over. I have made some very good friends here, amongst them Mr. Palmer, President of the late World's Fair. I am thoroughly disgusted with this Slayton business and am trying hard to break loose. I have lost at least $5,000 by joining this man. Hope you are all well. Mrs. Bagley and her daughters are very kind to me. I hope to do some private lecturing here and then go to Ada and then back to Chicago. It is snowing here this morning. They are very nice people here, and the different clubs took a good deal of interest in me.

It is rather wearisome, these constant receptions and dinners; and their horrible dinners — a hundred dinners concentrated into one — and when in a man's club, why, smoking on between the courses and then beginning afresh. I thought the Chinese alone make a dinner run through half a day with intervals of smoking!!

However, they are very gentlemanly men and, strange to say, an Episcopal clergyman and a Jewish rabbi take great interest in me and eulogize me. Now the man who got up the lectures here got at least a thousand dollars. So in every place. And this is Slayton's duty to do for me. Instead, he, the liar, had told me often that he has agents everywhere and would advertise and do all that for me. And this is what he is doing. His will be done. I am going home. Seeing the liking the American people have for me, I could have, by this time, got a pretty large sum. But Jimmy Mills and Slayton were sent by the Lord to stand in the way. His ways are inscrutable.

However, this is a secret. President Palmer has gone to Chicago to try to get me loose from this liar of a Slayton. Pray that he may succeed. Several judges here have seen my contract, and they say it is a shameful fraud and can be broken any moment; but I am a monk — no self-defence. Therefore, I had better throw up the whole thing and go to India.

My love to Harriets, Mary, Isabelle, Mother Temple, Mr. Matthews, Father Pope and you all.

Yours obediently,
Vivekananda.

1894.7 — MOTHER

To Mrs. G. W. Hale:

Detroit,
February 22, 1894.

DEAR MOTHER,

I have got the $200 for the engagements, $175 and $117 by private lectures and $100 as a present from a lady.

This sum will be sent to you tomorrow in cheques by Mrs. Bagley. Today, the banks being closed, we could not do it.

I am going tomorrow to lecture at Ada, Ohio. I do not know whether I will go to Chicago from Ada or not. However, kindly let not Slayton know anything about the rest of the money, as I am going to separate myself from him.

Yours obediently,
Vivekananda.

1894.8 — MOTHER

To Mrs. G. W. Hale:

Detroit,
10 March, 1894.

DEAR MOTHER,

Reached Detroit safely yesterday evening. The two younger daughters were waiting for me with a carriage. So everything was all right. I hope the lecture will be a success, as one of the girls said the tickets are selling like hot cakes. Here I found a letter from Mr. Palmer awaiting me with a request that I should come over to his house and be his guest.

Could not go last night. He will come in the course of the day to take me over. As I am going over to Mr. Palmer's, I have not opened the awfully-packed bag. The very idea of repacking seems to me to be hopeless. So I could not shave this morning. However, I hope to shave during the course of the day. I am thinking of going over to Boston and New York just now, as the Michigan cities I can come and take over in summer; but the fashionables of New York and Boston will fly off. Lord will show the way.

Mrs. Bagley and all the family are heartily glad at my return and people are again coming in to see me.

The photographer here has sent me some of the pictures he made. They are positively villainous — Mrs. Bagley does not like them at all. The real fact is that between the two photos my face has become so fat and heavy — what can the poor photographers do?

Kindly send over four copies of photographs. Not yet made any arrangement with Holden. (A lecture agent at Detroit.) Everything promises to be very nice. "Ssenator Ppalmer" is a very nice gentleman and very kind to me. He has got a French chef—Lord bless his stomach! I am trying to starve and the whole world is against me!! He used to give the best dinners in all Washington! Hopeless! I am resigned!

I will write more from Mr. Palmer's house.

If the Himalayas become the inkpot, the ocean ink, if the heavenly eternal Devadaroo becomes the pen, and if the sky itself becomes paper, still I would not be able to write a drop of the debt of gratitude I owe to you and yours. Kindly convey my love to the four full notes and the four half notes of the Hale gamut.

May the blessings of the Lord be upon you and yours ever and ever.

Ever yours in grateful affection,
Vivekananda.

1894.9 — SISTERS

To the Hale Sisters:

Detroit,
12th March, 1894.

DEAR SISTERS,

I am now living with Mr. Palmer. He is a very nice gentleman. He gave a dinner the night before last to a group of his old friends, each more than 60 years of age, which he calls his "old boys' club". I spoke at an opera house for two hours and a half. People were very much pleased. I am going to Boston and New York. I will get here sufficient to cover my expenses there. I have forgotten the addresses of both Flagg and Prof. Wright. I am not going to lecture in Michigan, Mr. Holden tried to persuade me this morning to lecture in Michigan but I am quite bent upon seeing a little of Boston and New York. To tell you the truth, the more I am getting popularity and facility in speaking, the more I am getting fed up. My last address was the best I ever delivered. Mr. Palmer was in ecstasies and the audience remained almost spellbound, so much so that it was after the lecture that I found I had spoken so long. A speaker always feels the uneasiness or inattention of the audience. Lord save me from such nonsense, I am fed up. I would take rest in Boston or New York if the Lord permits. My love to you all. May you ever be happy!

Your affectionate brother,
Vivekananda.

1894.10 — BABIES

To the Hale Sisters:

Detroit,
15th March, 1894.

DEAR BABIES,

I am pulling on well with old Palmer. He is a very jolly, good old man. I got only 127 dollars by my last lecture. I am going to speak again in Detroit on Monday. Your mother asked me to write to a lady in Lynn. I have never seen her. Is it etiquette to write without any introduction? Please post me a little letter about this lady. Where is Lynn? The funniest thing said about me here was in one of the papers which said, "The cyclonic Hindu has come and is a guest with Mr. Palmer. Mr. Palmer has become a Hindu and is going to India; only he insists that two reforms should be carried out: firstly that the Car of Jagannath should be drawn by Percherons raised in Mr. Palmer's Loghouse Farm, and secondly that the Jersey cow be admitted into the pantheon of Hindu sacred cows." Mr. Palmer is passionately fond of both Percheron horse and Jersey cow and has a great stock of both in his Loghouse Farm.

The first lecture was not properly managed, the cost of the hall being 150 dollars. I have given up Holden. Here is another fellow cropped up; let me see if he does better. Mr. Palmer makes me laugh the whole day. Tomorrow there is going to be another dinner party. So far all is well; but I do not know — I have become very sad in my heart since I am here — do not know why.

I am wearied of lecturing and all that nonsense. This mixing with hundreds of varieties of the human animal has disturbed me. I will tell you what is to my taste; I cannot write, and I cannot speak, but I can think deeply, and when I am heated, can speak fire. It should be, however, to a select, a very select — few. Let them, if they will, carry and scatter my ideas broadcast — not I. This is only a just division of labour. The same man never succeeded both in thinking and in scattering his thoughts. A man should be free to think, especially spiritual thoughts.

Just because this assertion of independence, this proving that man is not a machine, is the essence of all religious thought, it is impossible to think it in the routine mechanical way. It is this tendency to bring everything down to the level of a machine that has given the West its wonderful prosperity. And it is this which has driven away all religion from its doors. Even the little that is left, the West has reduced to a systematic drill.

I am really not "cyclonic" at all. Far from it. What I want is not here, nor can I longer bear this "cyclonic" atmosphere. This is the way to perfection, to strive to be perfect, and to strive to make perfect a few men and women. My idea of doing good is this: to evolve out a few giants, and not to strew pearls before swine, and so lose time, health, and energy.

Just now I got a letter from Flagg. He cannot help me in lecturing. He says, "First go to Boston." Well, I do not care for lecturing any more. It is too disgusting, this attempt to bring me to suit anybody's or any audience's fads. However, I shall come back to Chicago for a day or two at least before I go out of this country. Lord bless you all.

Ever gratefully your brother,
Vivekananda.

1894.11 — MOTHER

To Mrs. G. W. Hale:

Detroit,
16 March, 1894.

DEAR MOTHER,

Since my last, there has been nothing of interest here. Except that Mr. Palmer is a very hearty, jolly, good old man and very rich. He has been uniformly kind to me. Tomorrow I go back to Mrs. Bagley's because I am afraid she is rather uneasy at my long stay here. I am shrewd enough to know that in every country in general, and America in particular, "she" is the real operator at the nose string.

I am going to lecture here on Monday and in two places near the town on Tuesday and Wednesday. I do not remember the lady you refer me to, and she is in Lynn; what is Lynn, where on the globe its position is — I do not know. I want to go to Boston. What good would it do me by stopping at Lynn? Kindly give me a more particular idea. Nor could I read the name of the lady at whose house you say I met the lady. However, I am in no way very anxious. I am taking life very easy in my natural way. I have no particular wish to go anywhere, Boston or no Boston. I am just in a nice come-what-may mood. Something should turn up, bad or good. I have enough now to pay my passage back and a little sight-seeing to boot. As to my plans of work, I am fully convinced that at the rate it is progressing I will have to come back four or five times to put it in any shape.

As to informing others and doing good that way, I have failed to persuade myself that I have really anything to convey to the world. So I am very happy just now and quite at my ease. With almost nobody in this vast house and a cigar between my lips, I am dreaming just now and philosophising upon that work fever which was upon me. It is all nonsense. I am nothing, the world is nothing, the Lord alone is the only worker. We are simply tools in His hands etc., etc., etc. Have you got the Alaska information? If so, kindly send it to me c/o Mrs. Bagley.

Are you coming to the East this summer? With eternal gratitude and love,

Yours son,
Vivekananda.

1894.12 — SISTER

Detroit,
17th March, 1894.

DEAR SISTER, (Miss Harriet McKindley of Chicago)

Got your package yesterday. Sorry that you send those stockings — I could have got some myself here. Glad that it shows your love. After all, the satchel has become more than a thoroughly stuffed sausage. I do not know how to carry it along.

I have returned today to Mrs. Bagley's as she was sorry that I would remain so long with Mr. Palmer. Of course in Palmer's house there was real "good time". He is a real jovial heartwhole fellow, and likes "good time" a little too much and his "hot Scotch". But he is right along innocent and childlike in his simplicity.

He was very sorry that I came away, but I could not help. Here is a beautiful young girl. I saw her twice, I do not remember her name. So brainy, so beautiful, so spiritual, so unworldly! Lord bless her! She came this morning with Mrs. M'cDuvel and talked so beautifully and deep and spiritually — that I was quite astounded. She knows everything about the Yogis and is herself much advanced in practice!!

"Thy ways are beyond searching out." Lord bless her — so innocent, holy, and pure! This is the grandest recompense in my terribly toilsome, miserable life — the finding of holy happy faces like you from time to time. The great Buddhist prayer is, "I bow down to all holy men on earth". I feel the real meaning of this prayer whenever I see a face upon which the finger of the Lord has written in unmistakable letters "mine". May you all be happy, blessed, good and pure as you are for ever and ever. May your feet never touch the mud and dirt of this terrible world. May you live and pass away like flowers as you are born — is the constant prayer of your brother.

1894.13 — SISTER MARY

To Miss Mary Hale:

Detroit,
18th March, 1894.

DEAR SISTER MARY,

My heartfelt thanks for your kindly sending me the letter from Calcutta. It was from my brethren at Calcutta, and it is written on the occasion of a private invitation to celebrate the birthday of my Master about whom you have heard so much from me — so I send it over to you. The letter says that Mazoomdar has gone back to Calcutta and is preaching that Vivekananda is committing every sin under the sun in America... This is your America's wonderful spiritual man! It is not their fault; until one is really spiritual, that is, until one has got a real insight into the nature of one's own soul and has got a glimpse of the world of the soul, one cannot distinguish chaff from seed, tall talk from depth, and so on. I am sorry for poor Mazoomdar that he should stoop so low! Lord bless the old boy!

The address inside the letter is in English and is my old, old name as written by a companion of my childhood who has also taken orders. It is a very poetic name. That written in the letter is an abbreviation, the full name being Narendra meaning the "Chief of men" ("nara" means "man", and "indra" stands for "ruler", "chief") — very ludicrous, isn't it? But such are the names in our country; we cannot help, but I am glad I have given that up.

I am all right. Hoping it is same with you.

I remain your brother,
Vivekananda.

1894.14 — SHASHI[1]

Salutation to Bhagavan Ramakrishna!

C/O George W. Hale, Esq.,
541 Dearborn Avenue, Chicago,
19th March, 1894.

MY DEAR SHASHI, (Ramakrishnananda)

I have not written to you since coming to this country. But Haridas Bhai's[2] letter gives me all the news. It is excellent that G. C. Ghosh[3] and all of you have treated him with due consideration.

I have no wants in this country, but mendicancy has no vogue here, and I have to labour, that is, lecture in places. It is as cold here as it is hot. The summer is not a bit less hot than in Calcutta. And how to describe the cold in winter! The whole country is covered with snow, three or four feet deep, nay, six or seven feet at places! In the southern parts there is no snow. Snow, however, is a thing of little consideration here. For it snows when the mercury stands at 32° F. In Calcutta it scarcely comes down to 60,° and it rarely approaches zero in England. But here, your mercury sinks to minus 4° or 5°. In Canada, in the north, mercury becomes condensed, when they have to use the alcohol thermometer. When it is too cold, that is, when the mercury stands even below 20°F, it does not snow. I used to think that it must be an exceedingly cold day on which the snow falls. But it is not so, it snows on comparatively warm days. Extreme cold produces a sort of intoxication. No carriages would run; only the sledge, which is without wheels, slides on the

---

1 Translated from Bengali.

2. Ex-Dewan of Junagarh. Shortly before Swamiji left India for America, he became intimately acquainted with this gentleman, and was introduced by him to many Indian princes.

3. Girish Chandra Ghosh, the great actor-dramatist of Bengal, and a staunch devotee of Shri Ramakrishna.

ground! Everything is frozen stiff—even an elephant can walk on rivers and canals and lakes. The massive falls of Niagara, of such tremendous velocity, are frozen to marble!! But I am doing nicely. I was a little afraid at first, but necessity makes me travel by rail to the borders of Canada one day, and the next day finds me lecturing in south U.S.A.! The carriages are kept quite warm, like your own room, by means of steam pipes, and all around are masses of snow, spotlessly white. Oh, the beauty of it!

I was mortally afraid that my nose and ears would fall off, but to this day they are all right. I have to go out, however, dressed in a heap of warm clothing surmounted by a fur-coat, with boots encased in a woollen jacket, and so on. No sooner do you breathe out than the breath freezes among the beard and moustache! Notwithstanding all this, the fun of it is that they won't drink water indoors without putting a lump of ice into it. This is because it is warm indoors. Every room and the staircase are kept warm by steam pipes. They are first and foremost in art and appliances, foremost in enjoyment and luxury, foremost in making money, and foremost in spending it. The daily wages of a coolie are six rupees, as also are those of a servant; you cannot hire a cab for less than three rupees, nor get a cigar for less than four annas. A decent pair of shoes costs twenty-four rupees, and a suit, five hundred rupees. As they earn, so they spend. A lecture fetches from two hundred up to three thousand rupees. I have got up to five hundred[1]. Of course now I am in the very heyday of fortune. They like me, and thousands of people come to hear me speak.

As it pleased the Lord, I met here Mr. Mazoomdar. He was very cordial at first, but when the whole Chicago population began to flock to me in overwhelming numbers, then grew the canker in his mind!... The priests tried their utmost to snub me. But the Guru (Teacher) is with me, what could anybody do? And the whole American nation loves and respects me, pays my expenses, and reveres me as a Guru... It was not in the power of your priests to do anything against me. Moreover, they are a nation of scholars. Here it would no longer do to say, "We marry our widows", "We do not worship idols", and things of that sort. What they want is philosophy, learning; and empty talk will no more do.

Dharmapala is a fine boy. He has not much of learning but is very gentle. He had a good deal of popularity in this country.

Brother, I have been brought to my senses... ये नधिनन्ति निरिर्थकं परहितं ते के न जानीमहे—We do not know what sort of people they are who for nothing hinder the welfare of others" (Bhartrihari). Brother, we can get rid of everything, but not of that cursed jealousy... That is a national sin with us, speaking ill of others, and burning at heart at the greatness of others. Mine alone is the greatness, none else should rise to it!!

Nowhere in the world are women like those of this country. How pure, inde-

---

1. For some time after the Chicago addresses, Swamiji lectured on behalf of a lecture bureau. He soon gave it up as curtailing his independence, and devoted most of the money thus earned to various charitable works in the U.S.A. and India.

pendent, self-relying, and kindhearted! It is the women who are the life and soul of this country. All learning and culture are centred in them. The saying, "या श्रीः स्वयं सुकृतिनां भवनेषु—Who is the Goddess of Fortune Herself in the families of the meritorious" (Chandi)—holds good in this country, while that other, "अलक्ष्मीः पापात्मनां—The Goddess of ill luck in the homes of the sinful" (ibid.)—applies to ours. Just think on this. Great God! I am struck dumb with wonderment at seeing the women of America. "त्वं श्रीस्त्वमीश्वरी त्वं ह्रीः etc.—Thou art the Goddess of Fortune, Thou art the supreme Goddess, Thou art Modesty" (ibid.)," "या देवी सर्वभूतेषु शक्तिरूपेण संस्थिता—The Goddess who resides in all beings as Power" (ibid.)—all this holds good here. There are thousands of women here whose minds are as pure and white as the snow of this country. And look at our girls, becoming mothers below their teens!! Good Lord! I now see it all. Brother, "यत्र नार्यस्तु पूज्यन्ते रमन्ते तत्र देवताः—The gods are pleased where the women are held in esteem"—says the old Manu. We are horrible sinners, and our degradation is due to our calling women "despicable worms", "gateways to hell", and so forth. Goodness gracious! There is all the difference between heaven and hell!! "याथातथ्यतोऽर्थान् व्यदधात्—He adjudges gifts according to the merits of the case" (Isha, 8). Is the Lord to be hoodwinked by idle talk? The Lord has said, "त्वं स्त्री त्वं पुमानसि त्वं कुमार उत वा कुमारी—Thou art the woman, Thou art the man, Thou art the boy and the girl as well." (Shvetâshvatara Upa.) And we on our part are crying, "दूरमपसर रे चण्डाल—Be off, thou outcast!" "केनेषा निर्मिता नारी मोहिनी etc.—Who has made the bewitching woman?" My brother, what experiences I have had in the South, of the upper classes torturing the lower! What Bacchanalian orgies within the temples! Is it a religion that fails to remove the misery of the poor and turn men into gods! Do you think our religion is worth the name? Ours is only Don't touchism, only "Touch me not", "Touch me not." Good heavens! A country, the big leaders of which have for the last two thousand years been only discussing whether to take food with the right hand or the left, whether to take water from the right-hand side or from the left, ... if such a country does not go to ruin, what other will? "कालः सुप्तेषु जागर्ति कालो हि दुरतिक्रमः—Time keeps wide awake when all else sleeps. Time is invincible indeed!" He knows it; who is there to throw dust in His eyes, my friend?

A country where millions of people live on flowers of the Mohuâ plant, and a million or two of Sadhus and a hundred million or so of Brahmins suck the blood out of these poor people, without even the least effort for their amelioration—is that a country or hell? Is that a religion, or the devil's dance? My brother, here is one thing for you to understand fully—I have travelled all over India, and seen this country too—can there be an effect without cause? Can there be punishment without sin?

सर्वशास्त्रपुराणेषु व्यासस्य वचनं ध्रुवम् ।
परोपकारः पुण्याय पापाय परपीडनम् ॥

—"Amidst all the scriptures and Purânas, know this statement of Vyâsa to be true, that doing good to others conduces to merit, and doing harm to them leads to sin."

Isn't it true?

My brother, in view of all this, specially of the poverty and ignorance, I had no sleep. At Cape Comorin sitting in Mother Kumari's temple, sitting on the last bit of Indian rock—I hit upon a plan: We are so many Sannyasins wandering about, and teaching the people metaphysics—it is all madness. Did not our Gurudeva use to say, "An empty stomach is no good for religion"? That those poor people are leading the life of brutes is simply due to ignorance. We have for all ages been sucking their blood and trampling them underfoot.

... Suppose some disinterested Sannyasins, bent on doing good to others, go from village to village, disseminating education and seeking in various ways to better the condition of all down to the Chandâla, through oral teaching, and by means of maps, cameras, globes, and such other accessories—can't that bring forth good in time? All these plans I cannot write out in this short letter. The long and the short of it is—if the mountain does not come to Mohammed, Mohammed must go to the mountain. The poor are too poor to come to schools and Pâthashâlâs, and they will gain nothing by reading poetry and all that sort of thing. We, as a nation, have lost our individuality, and that is the cause of all mischief in India. We have to give back to the nation its lost individuality and raise the masses. The Hindu, the Mohammedan, the Christian, all have trampled them underfoot. Again the force to raise them must come from inside, that is, from the orthodox Hindus. In every country the evils exist not with, but against, religion. Religion therefore is not to blame, but men.

To effect this, the first thing we need is men, and the next is funds. Through the grace of our Guru I was sure to get from ten to fifteen men in every town. I next travelled in search of funds, but do you think the people of India were going to spend money!... Selfishness personified—are they to spend anything? Therefore I have come to America, to earn money myself, and then return to my country and devote the rest of my days to the realisation of this one aim of my life.

As our country is poor in social virtues, so this country is lacking in spirituality. I give them spirituality, and they give me money. I do not know how long I shall take to realise my end... These people are not hypocrites, and jealousy is altogether absent in them. I depend on no one in Hindusthan. I shall try to earn the wherewithal myself to the best of my might and carry out my plans, or die in the attempt. "सन्नमित्ते वरं त्यागो विनाशे नियते सति—When death is certain, it is best to sacrifice oneself for a good cause."

You may perhaps think what Utopian nonsense all this is! You little know what is in me. If any of you help me in my plans, all right, or Gurudeva will show me the way out... We cannot give up jealousy and rally together. That is our national sin!! It is not to be met with in this country, and this is what has made them so great.

Nowhere in the world have I come across such "frogs-in-the-well" as we are. Let anything new come from some foreign country, and America will be the first to accept it. But we?—oh, there are none like us in the world, we men of Aryan blood!!

Where that heredity really expresses itself, I do not see... Yet they are descendants of the Aryans?

Ever yours,
Vivekananda.

1894.15 — MOTHER

To Mrs. G. W. Hale:

Detroit,
Tuesday, 27 March, 1894.

DEAR MOTHER,

Herewith I send two cheques of $114 and $75 to be put in the banks for me. I have endorsed them to your care.

I am going to Boston in a day or two. I have got $57 with me. They will go a long way. Something will turn up, as it always does. I do not know where I go from Boston. I have written to Mrs. [Francis W.] Breed but as yet heard nothing from her. His will be done. Not I but Thou — that is always the motto of my life.

With my eternal gratitude, love, and admiration for Mother Church and all the dignitaries,

I remain your son,
Vivekananda.

1894.16 — BROTHER

Detroit,
29th March, 1894.

DEAR BROTHER,

Your letter just reached me here. I am in a hurry, so excuse a few points which I would take the liberty of correcting you in.

In the first place, I have not one word to say against any religion or founder of religion in the world — whatever you may think of our religion. All religions are sacred to me. Secondly, it is a misstatement that I said that missionaries do not learn our vernaculars. I still stick to my statement that few, if any, of them pay any attention to Sanskrit; nor is it true that I said anything against any religious body — except that I do insist on my statement that India can never be converted to Christianity, and further I deny that the conditions of the lower classes are made any better by Christianity, and add that the majority of southern Indian Christians are not only Catholics, but what they call themselves, caste Christians, that is, they stick close to their castes, and I am thoroughly persuaded that if the Hindu society gives up its exclusive policy, ninety per cent of them would rush back to Hinduism with all its defects.

Lastly, I thank you from the bottom of my heart for calling me your fellow-countryman. This is the first time any European foreigner, born in India though he be, has dared to call a detested native by that name — missionary or no missionary. Would you dare call me the same in India? Ask your missionaries, born in India, to do the same — and those not born, to treat them as fellow human beings. As to the rest, you yourself would call me a fool if I admit that my religion or society submits to be judged by strolling globe-trotters or story-writers' narratives.

My brother — excuse me — what do you know of my society or religion, though born in India? It is absolutely impossible — the society is so closed; and over and above, everyone judges from his preconceived standard of race and religion, does he not? Lord bless you for calling me a fellow-countryman. There may still come a brotherly love and fellowship between the East and West.

Yours fraternally,
Vivekananda.

1894.17 — SISTER

To Miss Mary Hale:

Detroit,
30th March, 1894.

DEAR SISTER,

Your and Mother Church's letters came together just now, acknowledging the receipt of the money. I am very glad to receive the Khetri letter, which I send back for your perusal. You would find from it that he wants some newspaper clippings. I do not think I have any except the Detroit one, which I will send to him. If you can get hold of some others, kindly send some over to him if it be possible and convenient. You know his address — H. H. the Maharajah of Khetri, Rajputana, India. Of course, this letter is for the perusal of the holy family alone. Mrs. Breed wrote to me a stiff burning letter first, and then today I got a telegram from her inviting me to be her guest for a week. Before this I got a letter from Mrs. Smith of New York writing on her behalf and another lady Miss Helen Gould and another Dr.___ to come over to New York. As the Lynn Club wants me on the 17th of next month, I am going to New York first and come in time for their meeting at Lynn.

Next summer, if I do not go away, which Mrs. Bagley insists I should not, I may go to Annisquam where Mrs. Bagley has engaged a nice house. Mrs. Bagley is a very spiritual lady, and Mr. Palmer a spirituous gentleman but very good. What shall I write more? I am all right in nice health of body and mind. May you all be blessed, ever blessed, my dear, dear sisters. By the by, Mrs. Sherman has presented me with a lot of things amongst which is a nail set and letter holder and a little satchel etc., etc. Although I objected, especially to the nail set, as very dudish with mother-of-pearl handles, she insisted and I had to take them, although I do not know what to do with that brushing instrument. Lord bless them all. She gave me one advice — never to wear this Afrikee dress in society. Now I am a society man! Lord! What comes next? Long life brings queer experiences! My inexpressible love for you all, my holy family.

Your brother,
Vivekananda.

1894.18 — MOTHER

To Mrs. G. W. Hale:

C/O Dr. Guernsey,
528 Fifth Avenue, New York,
2 April, 1894.

DEAR MOTHER,

I am in New York. The gentleman [Dr. Guernsey] whose guest I am is a very nice and learned and well-to-do man. He had an only son whom he lost last July. Has only a daughter now. The old couple have received a great shock, but they are pure and God-loving people and bear it manfully. The lady of the house is very, very kind and good. They are trying to help me as much as they can and they will do a good deal, I have no doubt.

Awaiting further developments. This Thursday [April 5] they will invite a number of the brainy people of the Union League Club and other places of which the Doctor is a member, and see what comes out of it. Parlour lectures are a great feature in this city, and more can be made by each such lecture than even platform talks in other cities.

It is a very clean city. None of that black smoke tarring everyone in five minutes; and the street in which the Doctor lives is a nice, quiet one.

Hope the sisters are doing well and enjoying their music, both in the opera and the parlour. I am sure I would have appreciated the music at the opera about which Miss Mary wrote to me. I am sure the opera musicians do not show the interior anatomy of their throats and lungs.

Kindly give brother Sam my deep love. I am sure he is bewaring of the vidders. Some of the Baby Bagleys are going to Chicago. They will go to see you, and I am sure you would like them very much.

Nothing more to write. With all respect, love and obedience,

Your son,
Vivekananda.

PS—I have not to ask now for addresses. Mrs. Sherman (Mrs. Bagley's married daughter.) has given me a little book with A., B., C., etc., marks and has written under them all the addresses I need; and I hope to write all the future addresses in the same manner. What an example of self-help I am!!

1894.19 — ALASINGA

New York,
9th April, 1894.

DEAR ALASINGA,

I got your last letter a few days ago. You see I am so very busy here, and have to write so many letters every day, that you cannot expect frequent communications from me. But I try my best to keep you in touch with whatever is going on here. I will write to Chicago for one of the books on the Parliament of Religions to be sent over to you. But by this time you have got two of my short speeches.

Secretary Saheb writes me that I must come back to India, because that is my field. No doubt of that. But my brother, we are to light a torch which will shed a lustre over all India. So let us not be in a hurry; everything will come by the grace of the Lord. I have lectured in many of the big towns of America, and have got enough to pay my passage back after paying the awful expenses here. I have made a good many friends here, some of them very influential. Of course, the orthodox clergymen are against me; and seeing that it is not easy to grapple with me, they try to hinder, abuse, and vilify me in every way; and Mazoomdar has come to their help. He must have gone mad with jealousy. He has told them that I was a big fraud, and a rogue! And again in Calcutta he is telling them that I am leading a most sinful life in America, specially unchaste! Lord bless him! My brother, no good thing can be done without obstruction. It is only those who persevere to the end that succeed...I believe that the Satya Yuga (Golden Age) will come when there will be one caste, one Veda, and peace and harmony. This idea of Satya Yuga is what would revivify India. Believe it. One thing is to be done if you can do it. Can you convene a big meeting in Madras, getting Ramnad or any such big fellow as the President, and pass a resolution of your entire satisfaction at my representation of Hinduism here, and send it to the Chicago Herald, Inter-Ocean, and the New York Sun, and the Commercial Advertiser of Detroit (Michigan). Chicago is in Illinois. New York Sun requires no particulars. Detroit is in the State of Michigan. Send copies to Dr. Barrows, Chairman of the Parliament of Religions, Chicago. I have forgotten his number, but the street is Indiana Avenue. One copy to Mrs. J. J. Bagley of Detroit, Washington Ave.

Try to make this meeting as big as possible. Get hold of all the big bugs who must join it for their religion and country. Try to get a letter from the Mysore Maharaja and the Dewan approving the meeting and its purpose—so of Khetri—in fact, as big and noisy a crowd as you can.

The resolution would be of such a nature that the Hindu community of Madras, who sent me over, expressing its entire satisfaction in my work here etc.

Now try if it is possible. This is not much work. Get also letters of sympathy from all parts you can and print them and send copies to the American papers — as quickly as you can. That will go a long way, my brethren. The B — S — fellows here are trying to talk all sorts of nonsense. We must stop their mouths as fast as we can.

Up boys, and put yourselves to the task! If you can do that, I am sure we will be able to do much in future. Old Hinduism for ever! Down with all liars and rogues! Up, up, my boys, we are sure to win!

As to publishing my letters, such parts as ought to be published may be published for our friends till I come. When once we begin to work, we shall have a tremendous "boom", but I do not want to talk without working. I do not know, but G. C. Ghosh and Mr. Mitra of Calcutta can get up all the sympathisers of my late Gurudeva to do the same in Calcutta. If they can, so much the better. Ask them, if they can, to pass the same resolutions in Calcutta. There are thousands in Calcutta who sympathise with our movement. However I have more faith in you than in them.

Nothing more to write. Convey my greetings to all our friends — for whom I am always praying.

Yours with blessings,
Vivekananda.

1894.20 — MOTHER

To Mrs. G. W. Hale:

[C/O Dr. Egbert Guernsey,
528 Fifth Avenue], New York,
10 April, 1894.

DEAR MOTHER,

I just now received your letter. I have the greatest regard for the Salvationists; in fact, they and the Oxford Mission gentlemen are the only Christian missionaries for whom I have any regard at all. They live with the people, as the people, and for the people of India. Lord bless them. But I would be very, very sorry of any trick being played by them. I never have heard of any Lord in India, much less in Ceylon. (Now Sri Lanka.) The people of Ceylon and northern India differ more than Americans and Hindus. Nor is there any connection between the Buddhist priest and the Hindu. Our dress, manners, religion, food, language differ entirely from southern India, much less to speak of Ceylon. You know already that I could not speak a word of Narasimha's language!! Although that was only Madras. Well, you have Hindu princesses; why not a Lord, which is not a higher title.

There was a certain Mrs. Smith in Chicago. I met her at Mrs. Stockham's. She has introduced me to the Guernseys. Dr. Guernsey is one of the chief physicians of this city and is a very good old gentleman. They are very fond of me and are very nice people. Next Friday I am going to Boston. I have not been lecturing in New York at all. I will come back and do some lecturing here.

For the last few days I was the guest of Miss Helen Gould — daughter of the rich Gould — at her palatial country residence, an hour's ride from the city. She has one of the most beautiful and large green-houses in the world, full of all sorts of curious plants and flowers. They are Presbyterians, and she is a very religious lady. I had a very nice time there.

I met my friend Mr. Flagg (William Joseph Flagg.) several times. He is flying merrily. There is another Mrs. Smith here who is very rich and pious. She has invited me to dine today.

As for lecturing, I have given up raising money. I cannot degenerate myself any more. When a certain purpose was in view, I could work; with that gone I cannot earn for myself. I have sufficient for going back. I have not tried to earn a penny here, and have refused some presents which friends here wanted to make to me. Especially Flagg — I have refused his money. I had in Detroit tried to refund the money back to the donors, and told them that, there being almost no chance of my succeeding in my enterprise, I had no right to keep their money; but they refused and told me to throw that into the waters if I liked. But I cannot take any more conscientiously. I am very well off, Mother. Everywhere the Lord sends me kind persons and homes; so there is no use of my going into beastly worldliness at all.

The New York people, though not so intellectual as the Bostonians, are, I think, more sincere. The Bostonians know well how to take advantage of everybody. And I am afraid even water cannot slip through their closed fingers!!! Lord bless them!!! I have promised to go and I must go; but, Lord, make me live with the sincere, ignorant and the poor, and not cross the shadow of the hypocrites and tall talkers who, as my Master used to say, are like vultures who soar high and high in their talks, but the heart is really on a piece of carrion on the ground.

I would be the guest of Mrs. Breed for a few days and, after seeing a little of Boston, I would come back to New York.

Hope the sisters are all right and enjoying their concerts immensely. There is not much of music in this city. That is a blessing (?) Went to see Barnum's circus the other day. It is no doubt a grand thing. I have not been as yet downtown. This street is very nice and quiet.

I heard a beautiful piece of music the other day at Barnum's — they call it a Spanish Serenada. Whatever it be, I liked it so much. Unfortunately, Miss Guernsey is not given to much thumping, although she has a good assortment of all the noisy stuffs in the world — and so she could not play it, which I regret ever so much.

Yours obediently,
Vivekananda.

PS — Most probably I will go to Annisquam as Mrs. Bagley's guest. She has got a nice house there this summer. Before that, I will go back to Chicago once more if I can.

1894.21 — PROFESSOR

New York,
25th April, 1894.

DEAR PROFESSOR, (Prof. John Henry Wright)

I am very very grateful for your invitation. And will come on May 7th. As for the bed — my friend, your love and noble heart can convert the stone into down.

I am sorry I am not going to the authors' breakfast at Salem.

I am coming home by May 7th.

Yours truly,
Vivekananda.

1894.22 — SISTER

New York,
26th April, 1894.

DEAR SISTER, (Miss Isabelle McKindley)

Your letter reached me yesterday. You were perfectly right — I enjoyed the fun of the lunatic Interior, (Chicago Interior, a Presbyterian newspaper which opposed Swamiji. — Ed.) but the mail you sent yesterday from India was really, as Mother Church says in her letter, a good news after a long interval. There is a beautiful letter from Dewanji. The old man — Lord bless him — offers as usual to help me. Then there was a little pamphlet published in Calcutta about me — revealing that once at least in my life the prophet has been honoured in his own country. There are extracts from American and Indian papers and magazines about me. The extracts printed from Calcutta papers were especially gratifying, although the strain is so fulsome that I refuse to send the pamphlet over to you. They call me illustrious, wonderful, and all sorts of nonsense, but they forward me the gratitude of the whole nation. Now I do not care what they even of my own people say about me — except for one thing. I have an old mother. She has suffered much all her life and in the midst of all she could bear to give me up for the service of God and man; but to have given up the most beloved of her children — her hope — to live a beastly immoral life in a far distant country, as Mazoomdar was telling in Calcutta, would have simply killed her. But the Lord is great, none can injure His children.

The cat is out of the bag — without my seeking at all. And who do you think is the editor of one of our leading papers which praise me so much and thank God that I came to America to represent Hinduism? Mazoomdar's cousin!! — Poor Mazoomdar — he has injured his cause by telling lies through jealousy. Lord knows I never attempted any defence.

I read the article of Mr. Gandhi in the Forum before this.

If you have got the Review of Reviews of last month — read to mother the testimony about the Hindus in connection with the opium question in India by one of the highest officials of the English in India. He compares the English with the Hindus and lauds the Hindu to the skies. Sir Lepel Griffin was one of the bitterest enemies of our race. What made this change of front?

I had a very good time in Boston at Mrs. Breed's — and saw Prof. Wright. I am going to Boston again. The tailor is making my new gown. I am going to speak at Cambridge University [Harvard] and would be the guest of Prof. Wright there. They write grand welcomes to me in the Boston papers.

I am tired of all this nonsense. Towards the latter part of May I will come back to Chicago, and after a few day's stay would come back to the East again.

I spoke last night at the Waldorf hotel. Mrs. Smith sold tickets at $2 each. I had a full hall which by the way was a small one. I have not seen anything of the money yet. Hope to see in the course of the day.

I made a hundred dollars at Lynn which I do not send because I have to make my new gown and other nonsense.

Do not expect to make any money at Boston. Still I must touch the brain of America and stir it up if I can.

Your loving brother,
Vivekananda.

1894.23 — AKHANDANANDA[1]

Salutation to Bhagavan Ramakrishna!

(March or April?) 1894.

MY DEAR AKHANDANANDA,

I am very glad to receive your letter. It is a great pleasure to me to learn that you have regained your health to a great extent by your stay at Khetri.

Brother Tarak (Shivananda) has done a good deal of work in Madras. Very agreeable news indeed! I heard much praise of him from the people of Madras...

Try to develop spirituality and philanthropy amongst the Thakurs in the different places of Rajputana. We must work, and this cannot be done by merely sitting idle. Make a trip now and then to Malsisar, Alsisar, and all the other "sars" that are there. And carefully learn Sanskrit and English. Gunanidhi is in the Punjab, I presume. Convey my special love to him and bring him to Khetri. Learn Sanskrit

1 Translated from Bengali.

with his help, and teach him English. Let me have his address by all means…

Go from door to door amongst the poor and lower classes of the town of Khetri and teach them religion. Also, let them have oral lessons on geography and such other subjects. No good will come of sitting idle and having princely dishes, and saying "Ramakrishna, O Lord!" — unless you can do some good to the poor. Go to other villages from time to time, and teach the people the arts of life as well as religion. Work, worship, and Jnana (knowledge) — first work, and your mind will be purified; otherwise everything will be fruitless like pouring oblations on a pile of ashes instead of in the sacred fire. When Gunanidhi comes, move from door to door of the poor and the destitute in every village of Rajputana. If people object to the kind of food you take, give it up immediately. It is preferable to live on grass for the sake of doing good to others. The Geruâ robe is not for enjoyment. It is the banner of heroic work. You must give your body, mind, and speech to "the welfare of the world". You have read — "मातृदेवो भव, पितृदेवो भव — Look upon your mother as God, look upon your father as God" — but I say "दरिद्रदेवो भव, मूर्खदेवो भव — The poor, the illiterate, the ignorant, the afflicted — let these be your God." Know that service to these alone is the highest religion.

Ever yours, with blessings,
Vivekananda.

1894.24 — SISTER

New York,
2nd [actually 1st] May, 1894.

DEAR SISTER, (Miss Isabelle McKindley)

I am afraid I cannot send you the pamphlet just now. But I got a little bit of a newspaper cutting from India yesterday which I send you up. After you have read it kindly send it over to Mrs. Bagley. The editor of this paper is a relative of Mr. Mazoomdar. I am now sorry for poor Mazoomdar!! (The last two sentences were written crosswise on the left margin.)

I could not find the exact orange colour of my coat here, so I have been obliged to satisfy myself with the next best — a cardinal red with more of yellow.

The coat will be ready in a few days.

Got about $70 the other day by lecturing at Waldorf. And hope to get some more by tomorrow's lecture.

From 7th to 19th there are engagements in Boston, but they pay very little.

Yesterday I bought a pipe for $13 — meerschaum do not tell it to father Pope. The coat will cost $30. I am all right getting food… and money enough. Hope very soon to put something in the bank after the coming lecture.

…in the evening I am going to speak in a vegetarian dinner! Well, I am a vegetarian…, because I prefer it when I can get it. I have another invitation to lunch with

Lyman Abbott day after tomorrow. After all, I am having very nice time and hope to have very nice time in Boston — only that nasty nasty lecturing — disgusting. However as soon as 19th is over — one leap from Boston ... to Chicago ... and then I will have a long long breath and rest, rest for two three weeks. I will simply sit down and talk — talk and smoke.

By the by, your New York people are very good — only more money than brains.

I am going to speak to the students of the Harvard University. Three lectures at Boston, three at Harvard — all arranged by Mrs. Breed. They are arranging something here too, so that I will, on my way to Chicago, come to New York once more — give them a few hard raps and pocket the boodle and fly to Chicago.

If you want anything from New York or Boston which cannot be had at Chicago — write sharp. I have plenty of dollars now. I will send you over anything you want in a minute. Don't think it would be indelicate anyway — no humbug about me. If I am a brother so I am. I hate only one thing in the world — hypocrisy.

Your affectionate brother,
Vivekananda.

1894.25 — ADHYAPAKJI

New York,
4th May, 1894.

DEAR ADHYAPAKJI, (Prof. John Henry Wright)

I have received your kind note just now. And it is unnecessary for me to say that I will be very happy to do as you say.

I have also received Col. Higginson's letter. I will reply to him.

I will be in Boston on Sunday [May 6]. On Monday I lecture at the Women's Club of Mrs. Howe.

Yours ever truly,
Vivekananda.

1894.26 — MOTHER

To Mrs. G. W. Hale:

C/O Miss Florence Guernsey,
528 Fifth Avenue,
New York,
4 May, 1894.

DEAR MOTHER,

Herewith I send over $125 in a cheque upon the 5th Avenue Bank to be deposited at your leisure.

I am going to Boston on Sunday, day after tomorrow, and write to you from Boston. With my love to all the family.

I remain yours truly,
Vivekananda.

1894.27 — MOTHER

To Mrs. John J. Bagley:

Hotel Bellevue, European Plan,
Boston,
May 8, 1894.

DEAR MOTHER,

I have arrived in Boston again. Last afternoon [I] spoke at Mrs. Julia Ward Howe's club — of course for nothing, but it gives me a prestige. I saw there Mrs. [Ednah Dean] Cheney. Would you not write a letter to her for me? Although I told her I had a card from you, I think a letter is better.

Yours truly,
Vivekananda.

1894.28 — MOTHER

To Mrs. G. W. Hale:

Hotel Bellevue, European Plan,
Beacon Street, Boston,
11 May, 1894.

DEAR MOTHER,

I have been since the 7th, lecturing here every afternoon or evening. At Mrs. Fairchild's I met the niece of Mrs. Howe. She was here today to invite me to dinner with her today. I have not seen Mr. Volkinen as yet. Of course, the pay for lecture is here the poorest, and everybody has an axe to grind. I got a long letter full of the prattles of the babies. Your city, i.e. New York, pays far better than Boston, so I am trying to go back there. But here one can get work almost every day.

I think I want some rest. I feel as if I am very much tired, and these constant journeyings to and fro have shaken my nerves a little, but hope to recoup soon. Last few days I have been suffering from cold and slight fever and lecturing for all that; hope to get rid of it in a day or two.

I have got a very nice gown at $30. The colour is not exactly that of the old one, but cardinal, with more of yellow — could not get the exact old colour even in New York.

I have not much to write, for it is the repetition of the old story: talking, talking, talking. I long to fly to Chicago and shut up my mouth and give a long rest to mouth and lungs and mind. If I am not called for in New York, I am coming soon to Chicago.

Yours obediently,
Vivekananda.

1894.29 — MOTHER

To Mrs. G. W. Hale:

Hotel Bellevue European Plan,
Beacon Street, Boston,
14 May, 1894.

DEAR MOTHER,

Your letter was so, so pleasing instead of being long; I enjoyed every bit of it.

I have received a letter from Mrs. Potter Palmer (Social queen of Chicago who made Swami Vivekananda's acquaintance at the Parliament of Religions, in which she had been active. Vide Complete Works, VI.) asking me to write to some of my countrywomen about their society etc. I will see her personally when I come to Chicago; in the meanwhile I will write her all I know. Perhaps you have received $125 sent over from New York. Tomorrow I will send another $100 from here. The Bostonians want to grind their own axes!!

Oh, they are so, so dry—even girls talk dry metaphysics. Here is like our Benares where all is dry, dry metaphysics!! Nobody here understands "my Beloved". Religion to these people is reason, and horribly stony at that. I do not care for anybody who cannot love my "Beloved". Do not tell it to Miss Howe—she may be offended.

The pamphlet I did not send over because I do not like the quotations from the Indian newspapers—especially, they give a haul over coal to somebody. Our people so much dislike the Brâhmo Samâj that they only want an opportunity to show it to them. I dislike it. Any amount of enmity to certain persons cannot efface the good works of a life. And then they were only children in Religion. They never were much of religious men—i.e. they only wanted to talk and reason, and did not struggle to see the Beloved; and until one does that I do not say that he has any religion. He may have books, forms, doctrines, words, reasons, etc., etc., but not religion; for that begins when the soul feels the necessity, the want, the yearning after the "Beloved", and never before. And therefore our society has no right to expect from them anything more than from an ordinary "house-holder".

I hope to come to Chicago before the end of this month. Oh, I am so tired.

Yours affectionately,
Vivekananda.

1894.30 — SHARAT

U. S. A.,
20th May, 1894.

MY DEAR SHARAT, (Saradananda)

I am in receipt of your letter and am glad to learn that Shashi (Ramakrishnananda) is all right. Now I tell you a curious fact. Whenever anyone of you is sick, let him himself or anyone of you visualise him in your mind, and mentally say and strongly imagine that he is all right. That will cure him quickly. You can do it even without his knowledge, and even with thousands of miles between you. Remember it and do not be ill any more. You have received the money by this time. If you all like, you can give to Gopal Rs. 300 from the amount I sent for the Math. I have no more to send now. I have to look after Madras now.

I cannot understand why Sanyal is so miserable on account of his daughters' marriage. After all, he is going to drag his daughters through the dirty Samsâra (world) which he himself wants to escape! I can have but one opinion of that — condemnation! I hate the very name of marriage, in regard to a boy or a girl. Do you mean to say that I have to help in putting someone into bondage, you fool! If my brother Mohin marries, I will throw him off. I am very decided about that…

Yours in love,
Vivekananda.

1894.31 — ADHYAPAKJI

541 Dearborn Ave., Chicago,
24th May, 1894.

DEAR ADHYAPAKJI, (Prof. John Henry Wright)

Herewith I forward to you a letter from one of our ruling princes of Rajputana, His Highness the Maharaja of Khetri, and another from the opium commissioner, late minister of Junagad, one of the largest states in India, and a man who is called the Gladstone of India. These I hope would convince you of my being no fraud.

One thing I forgot to tell you. I never identified myself anyway with Mr. Mazoomdar's party chief. (Evidently, Keshab Chandra Sen.) If he says so, he does not speak the truth.

I hope, after your perusal, you will kindly send the letters over to me, except the pamphlet which I do not care for.

I am bound, my dear friend, to give you every satisfaction of my being a genuine Sannyasin, but to you alone. I do not care what the rabbles say or think about me.

"Some would call you a saint, some a chandala; some a lunatic, others a demon. Go on then straight to thy work without heeding either" — thus saith one of our great Sannyasins, an old emperor of India, King Bhartrihari, who joined the order in old times.

May the Lord bless you for ever and ever. My love to all your children and my respects to your noble wife.

I remain ever your friend,
Vivekananda.

PS—I had connection with Pundit Shiva Nath Shastri's party—but only on points of social reform. Mazoomdar and Chandra Sen—I always considered as not sincere, and I have no reason to change my opinion even now. Of course in religious matters even with my friend Punditji I differed much, the chief being, I thinking Sannyasa or (giving up the world) the highest ideal, and he, a sin. So the Brahmo Samajists consider becoming a monk a sin!!

The Brahmo Samaj, like Christian Science in your country, spread in Calcutta for a certain time and then died out. I am not sorry, neither glad that it died. It has done its work—viz social reform. Its religion was not worth a cent, and so it must die out. If Mazoomdar thinks I was one of the causes of its death, he errs. I am even now a great sympathiser of its reforms; but the "booby" religion could not hold its own against the old "Vedanta". What shall I do? Is that my fault? Mazoomdar has become childish in his old age and takes to tactics not a whit better than some of your Christian missionaries. Lord bless him and show him better ways.

When are you going to Annisquam? My love to Austin and Bime. My respects to your wife; and for you my love and gratitude is too deep for expression.

1894.32 — ALASINGA

Chicago,
28th May, 1894.

DEAR ALASINGA,

I could not reply to your note earlier, because I was whirling to and fro from New York to Boston, and also I awaited Narasimha's letter. I do not know when I am going back to India. It is better to leave everything in the hands of Him who is at my back directing me. Try to work without me, as if I never existed. Do not wait for anybody or anything. Do whatever you can. Build your hope on none. Before writing about myself, I will tell you about Narasimha. He has proved a complete failure... However he wrote to me for help in the last stage, and I will try to help him as much as is in my power. Meanwhile you tell his people to send money as soon as they can for him to go over... He is in distress. Of course I will see that he does not starve.

I have done a good deal of lecturing here... The expenses here are terrible; money has to fly, although I have been almost always taken care of everywhere by the nicest and the highest families.

I do not know whether I shall go away this summer or not. Most probably not. In the meantime try to organise and push on our plans. Believe you can do everything. Know that the Lord is with us, and so, onward, brave souls!

I have had enough appreciation in my own country. Appreciation or no appreciation, sleep not, slacken not. You must remember that not a bit even of our plans has been as yet carried out.

Act on the educated young men, bring them together, and organise them. Great things can be done by great sacrifices only. No selfishness, no name, no fame, yours or mine, nor my Master's even! Work, work the idea, the plan, my boys, my brave, noble, good souls — to the wheel, to the wheel put your shoulders! Stop not to look back for name, or fame, or any such nonsense. Throw self overboard and work. Remember, "The grass when made into a rope by being joined together can even chain a mad elephant." The Lord's blessings on you all! His power be in you all — as I believe it is already. "Wake up, stop not until the goal is reached", say the Vedas. Up, up, the long night is passing, the day is approaching, the wave has risen, nothing will be able to resist its tidal fury. The spirit, my boys, the spirit; the love, my children, the love; the faith, the belief; and fear not! The greatest sin is fear.

My blessings on all. Tell all the noble souls in Madras who have helped our cause that I send them my eternal love and gratitude, but I beg of them not to slacken. Throw the idea broadcast. Do not be proud; do not insist upon anything dogmatic; do not go against anything — ours is to put chemicals together, the Lord knows how and when the crystal will form. Above all, be not inflated with my success or yours. Great works are to be done; what is this small success in comparison with what is to come? Believe, believe, the decree has gone forth, the fiat of the Lord has gone forth — India must rise, the masses and the poor are to be made happy. Rejoice that you are the chosen instruments in His hands. The flood of spirituality has risen. I see it is rolling over the land resistless, boundless, all-absorbing. Every man to the fore, every good will be added to its forces, every hand will smooth its way, and glory be unto the Lord!...

I do not require any help. Try to get up a fund, buy some magic-lanterns, maps, globes, etc., and some chemicals. Get every evening a crowd of the poor and low, even the Pariahs, and lecture to them about religion first, and then teach them through the magic-lantern and other things, astronomy, geography, etc., in the dialect of the people. Train up a band of fiery young men. Put your fire in them and gradually increase the organization, letting it widen and widen its circle. Do the best you can, do not wait to cross the river when the water has all run down. Printing magazines, papers, etc., are good, no doubt, but actual work, my boys even if infinitesimal, is better than eternal scribbling and talking. Call a meeting at Bhattacharya's. Get a little money and buy those things I have just now stated, hire a hut, and go to work. Magazines are secondary, but this is primary. You must have a hold on the masses. Do not be afraid of a small beginning, great things come afterwards. Be courageous. Do not try to lead your brethren, but serve them. The brutal mania for leading has sunk many a great ship in the waters of life. Take care especially of that, i.e. be unselfish even unto death, and work. I could not write all I was going to say, but the Lord will give you all understanding, my brave boys. At it, my boys! Glory unto the Lord!...

Yours affectionately,
Vivekananda.

1894.33 — ADHYAPAKJI

17 Beacon Street, Boston,
May, 1894.

DEAR ADHYAPAKJI, (Prof. John Henry Wright)

By this time you have got the pamphlet and the letters. If you like, I would send you over from Chicago some letters from Indian Princes and ministers — one of these ministers was one of the Commissioners of the late opium commission that sat under Royal Commission in India. If you like, I will have them write to you to convince you of my not being a cheat. But, my brother, our ideal of life is to hide, to suppress, and to deny.

We are to give up and not to take. Had I not the "Fad" in my head, I would never have come over here. And it was with a hope that it would help my cause that I joined the Parliament of Religions — having always refused it when our people wanted to send me for it. I came over telling them — "that I may or may not join that assembly — and you may send me over if you like". They sent me over leaving me quite free.

You did the rest.

I am morally bound to afford you every satisfaction, my kind friend; but for the rest of the world I do not care what they say — the Sannyasin must not have self-defence. So I beg of you not to publish or show anybody anything in that pamphlet or the letters. I do not care for the attempts of the old missionary; but the fever of jealousy which attacked Mazoomdar gave me a terrible shock, and I pray that he would know better — for he is a great and good man who has tried all his life to do good. But this proves one of my Master's sayings, "Living in a room covered with black soot — however careful you may be — some spots must stick to your clothes." So, however one may try to be good and holy, so long he is in the world, some part of his nature must gravitate downwards.

The way to God is the opposite to that of the world. And to few, very few, are given to have God and mammon at the same time.

I was never a missionary, nor ever would be one — my place is in the Himalayas. I have satisfied myself so far that I can with a full conscience say, "My God, I saw terrible misery amongst my brethren; I searched and discovered the way out of it, tried my best to apply the remedy, but failed. So Thy will be done."

May his blessings be on you and yours for ever and ever.

Yours affectionately,
Vivekananda.

I go to Chicago tomorrow or day after.

1894.34 — MOTHER

To Mrs. G. W. Hale:

541 Dearborn Avenue, Chicago,
9 June, 1894.

DEAR MOTHER,

We are all doing very well here. Last night the sisters (The daughters of Mrs. Hale: Mary and Harriet.) invited me and Mrs. Norton and Miss Howe and Mr. Frank Howe. We had a grand dinner and softshell crab and many other things, and a very nice time. Miss Howe left this morning.

The sisters and Mother Temple (Mrs. James Matthews, Mr. Hale's sister.>) are taking very good care of me. Just now I am going to see my "oh-my-dear" Gandhi. Narasimha was here yesterday; he wanted to go to Cincinnati where he says he has more chances of success than anywhere else in the world. I gave him the passage, and so I hope I have got the white elephant out of my hands for the time being. How is Father Pope doing now? Hope he has been much benefited by the mudfish business.

I had a very beautiful letter from Miss Guernsey of New York, giving you her regards. I am going downtown to buy a new pair of shoes as well as to get some money, my purse having been made empty by Narasimha.

Nothing more to write. Yes, we went to see the "Charley's Aunt". I nearly killed myself with laughing. Father Pope will enjoy it extremely. I had never seen anything so funny.

Yours affectionately,
Vivekananda.

1894.35 — ADHYAPAKJI

541 Dearborn Avenue,
18th June, 1894.

DEAR ADHYAPAKJI, (Prof. John Henry Wright)

Excuse my delay in sending the other letters; I could not find them earlier. I am going to New York in a week.

I do not know whether I will come to Annisquam or not. The letters need not be sent over to me until I write you again. Mrs. Bagley seems to be unsettled by that article in the Boston paper against me. She sent me over a copy from Detroit and has ceased correspondence with me. Lord bless her. She has been very kind to me.

Stout hearts like yours are not common, my brother. This is a queer place — this world of ours. On the whole I am very very thankful to the Lord for the amount of kindness I have received at the hands of the people of this country — I, a complete stranger here without even "credentials". Everything works for the best.

Yours ever in gratitude,
Vivekananda.

PS — The East India stamps are for your children if they like.

1894.36 — DIWANJI SAHEB

To Shri Haridas Viharidas Desai:

Chicago,
20th June, 1894.

DEAR DIWANJI SAHEB,

Your very kind note came today. I am so sorry that I could have caused pain to such a noble heart as yours with my rash and strong words. I bow down to your mild corrections. "Thy son am I, teach me thus bowing" — Gita. But you well know, Diwanji Saheb, it was my love that prompted me to say so. The backbiters, I must tell you, have not indirectly benefited me; on the other hand, they have injured me immensely in view of the fact that our Hindu people did not move a finger to tell the Americans that I represented them. Had our people sent some words thanking the American people for their kindness to me and stating that I was representing them!... have been telling the American people that I have donned the Sannyasin's garb only in America and that I was a cheat, bare and simple. So far as reception goes, it has no effect on the American nation; but so far as helping me with funds goes, it has a terrible effect in making them take off their helping hands from me. And it is one year since I have been here, and not one man of note from India has thought it fit to make the Americans know that I am no cheat. There again the missionaries are always seeking for something against me, and they are busy picking up anything said against me by the Christian papers of India and publishing it here. Now you must know that the people here know very little of the distinction in India between the Christian and the Hindu.

Primarily my coming has been to raise funds for an enterprise of my own. Let me tell it all to you again.

The whole difference between the West and the East is in this: They are nations, we are not, i.e., civilisation, education here is general, it penetrates into the masses. The higher classes in India and America are the same, but the distance is infinite between the lower classes of the two countries. Why was it so easy for the English to conquer India? It was because they are a nation, we are not. When one of our great men dies, we must sit for centuries to have another; they can produce them as fast as they die. When our Diwanji Saheb will pass away (which the Lord may delay long for the good of my country), the nation will see the difficulty at once of filling his place, which is seen even now in the fact that they cannot dispense with your services. It is the dearth of great ones. Why so? Because they have such a bigger field of recruiting their great ones, we have so small. A nation of 300 millions has the smallest field of recruiting its great ones compared with nations of thirty, forty, or sixty millions, because the number of educated men and women in those nations is so great. Now do not mistake me, my kind friend, this is the great defect in our nation and must be removed.

Educate and raise the masses, and thus alone a nation is possible. Our reformers do not see where the wound is, they want to save the nation by marrying the widows; do you think that a nation is saved by the number of husbands its widows get? Nor is our religion to blame, for an idol more or less makes no difference. The whole defect is here: The real nation who live in cottage have forgotten their manhood, their individuality. Trodden under the foot of the Hindu, Mussulman, or Christian, they have come to think that they are born to be trodden under the foot of everybody who has money enough in his pocket. They are to be given back their lost individuality. They are to be educated. Whether idols will remain or not, whether widows will have husbands enough or not, whether caste is good or bad, I do not bother myself with such questions. Everyone must work out his own salvation. Our duty is to put the chemicals together, the crystallisation will come through God's laws. Let us put ideas into their heads, and they will do the rest. Now this means educating the masses. Here are these difficulties. A pauper government cannot, will not, do anything; so no help from that quarter.

Even supposing we are in a position to open schools in each village free, still the poor boys would rather go to the plough to earn their living than come to your school. Neither have we the money, nor can we make them come to education. The problem seems hopeless. I have found a way out. It is this. If the mountain does not come to Mohammed, Mohammed must go to the mountain. If the poor cannot come to education, education must reach them at the plough, in the factory, everywhere. How? You have seen my brethren. Now I can get hundreds of such, all over India, unselfish, good, and educated. Let these men go from village to village bringing not only religion to the door of everyone but also education. So I have a nucleus of organising the widows also as instructors to our women.

Now suppose the villagers after their day's work have come to their village and sitting under a tree or somewhere are smoking and talking the time away. Suppose two of these educated Sannyasins get hold of them there and with a camera throw astronomical or other pictures, scenes from different nations, histories, etc. Thus with globes, maps, etc.—and all this orally—how much can be done that way, Diwanji? It is not that the eye is the only door of knowledge, the ear can do all the same. So they would have ideas and morality, and hope for better. Here our work ends. Let them do the rest. What would make the Sannyasins do this sacrifice, undertake such a task? — religious enthusiasm. Every new religious wave requires a new centre. The old religion can only be revivified by a new centre. Hang your dogmas or doctrines, they never pay. It is a character, a life, a centre, a God-man that must lead the way, that must be the centre round which all other elements will gather themselves and then fall like a tidal wave upon the society, carrying all before it, washing away all impurities. Again, a piece of wood can only easily be cut along the grain. So the old Hinduism can only be reformed through Hinduism, and not through the new-fangled reform movements. At the same time the reformers must be able to unite in themselves the culture of both the East and the West. Now do you not think that you have already seen the nucleus of such a great movement, that you have heard the low rumblings of the coming tidal wave? That centre, that God-man to lead was born in India. He was the great Ramakrishna Paramahamsa, and round him this band is slowly gathering. They will do the work. Now, Diwanji Maharaj, this requires an organisation, money — a little at least to set the wheel in motion. Who would have given us money in India? — So, Diwanji Maharaj, I crossed over to America. You may remember I begged all the money from the poor, and the offers of the rich I would not accept because they could not understand my ideas. Now lecturing for a year in this country, I could not succeed at all (of course, I have no wants for myself) in my plan for raising some funds for setting up my work. First, this year is a very bad year in America; thousands of their poor are without work. Secondly, the missionaries and the Brahmo Samajists try to thwart all my views. Thirdly, a year has rolled by, and our countrymen could not even do so much for me as to say to the American people that I was a real Sannyasin and no cheat, and that I represented the Hindu religion. Even this much, the expenditure of a few words, they could not do! Bravo, my countrymen! I love them, Diwanji Saheb. Human help I spurn with my foot. He who has been with me through hills and dales, through deserts or forests, will be with me, I hope; if not, some heroic soul would arise some time or other in India, far abler than myself, and carry it out. So I have told you all about it. Diwanji, excuse my long letter, my noble friend, one of the few who really feel for me, have real kindness for me. You are at liberty, my friend, to think that I am a dreamer, a visionary; but believe at least that I am sincere to the backbone, and my greatest fault is that I love my country only too, too well. May you and yours be blessed ever and ever, my noble, noble friend. May the shadow of the Almighty ever rest on all those you love. I offer my eternal gratitude to you. My debt to you is immense, not only because you are my friend, but also because you have all your life served the Lord and your motherland so well.

Ever yours in gratitude,
Vivekananda.

1894.37 — SIR

Chicago,
23rd June, 1894.

DEAR SIR, (Rao Bahadur Narasimhachariar)

Your kindness to me makes me venture to take a little advantage of it. Mrs. Potter Palmer is the chief lady of the United States. She was the lady president of the World's Fair. She is much interested in raising the women of the world and is at the head of a big organisation for women. She is a particular friend of Lady Dufferin and has been entertained by the Royalties of Europe on account of her wealth and position. She has been very kind to me in this country. Now she is going to make a tour in China, Japan, Siam, and India. Of course she will be entertained by the Governors and other high people in India. But she is particularly anxious to see our society apart from English official aid. I have on many occasions told her about your noble efforts in raising the Indian women, of your wonderful College in Mysore. I think it is our duty to show a little hospitality to such personages from America in return for their kindness to our countrymen who came here. I hope she will find a warm reception at your hands and be helped to see a little of our women as they are. And I assure you she is no missionary, nor Christian even as to that. She wants to work apart from all religions to ameliorate the conditions of women all over the world. This would also be helping me a great deal in this country. May the Lord bless you!

Yours for ever and ever, affectionately,
Vivekananda.

1894.38 — SISTERS

C/O George W. Hale, Esq.,
541 Dearborn Avenue, Chicago,
26th June, 1894.

DEAR SISTERS, (Misses Mary and H. Hale)

The great Hindi poet, Tulasidâsa, in his benediction to his translation of the Râmâyana, says, "I bow down to both the wicked and holy; but alas! for me, they are both equally torturers — the wicked begin to torture me as soon as they come in contact with me — the good, alas! take my life away when they leave me." I say amen to this. To me, for whom the only pleasure and love left in the world is to love the holy ones of God, it is a mortal torture to separate myself from them.

But these things must come. Thou Music of my Beloved's flute, lead on, I am following. It is impossible to express my pain, my anguish at being separated from you, noble and sweet and generous and holy ones. Oh! how I wish I had succeeded in becoming a Stoic! Hope you are enjoying the beautiful village scenery. "Where the world is awake, there the man of self-control is sleeping. Where the world sleeps, there he is waking." May even the dust of the world never touch you, for, after all the poets may say, it is only a piece of carrion covered over with garlands. Touch it not—if you can. Come up, young ones of the bird of Paradise, before your feet touch the cesspool of corruption, this world, and fly upwards.

"O those that are awake do not go to sleep again."

"Let the world love its many, we have but one Beloved—the Lord. We care not what they say; we are only afraid when they want to paint our Beloved and give Him all sorts of monstrous qualities. Let them do whatever they please—for us He is only the beloved—my love, my love, my love, and nothing more."

"Who cares to know how much power, how much quality He has—even that of doing good! We will say once for all: We love not for the long purse, we never sell our love, we want not, we give."

"You, philosopher, come to tell us of His essences His powers, His attributes—fool! We are here dying for a kiss of His lips."

"Take your nonsense back to your own home and send me a kiss of my Love—can you?"

"Fool! whom art thou bending thy tottering knees before, in awe and fear? I took my necklace and put it round His neck; and, tying a string to it as a collar, I am dragging Him along with me, for fear He may fly away even for a moment that necklace was the collar of love; that string the ecstasy of love. Fool! you know not the secret—the Infinite One comes within my fist under the bondage of love." "Knowest thou not that the Lord of the Universe is the bond slave of love?" "Knowest thou not that the Mover of the Universe used to dance to the music of the ringing bracelets of the shepherdesses of Vrindaban?"

Excuse my mad scribbling, excuse my foolery in trying to express the inexpressible. It is to be felt only.

Ever with blessings,

Your brother,
Vivekananda.

1894.39 — ALASINGA

541 Dearborn Avenue,
Chicago, 1894.

DEAR ALASINGA,

Your letter just to hand... I was mistaken in asking you to publish the scraps I sent you. It was one of my awful mistakes. It shows a moment's weakness. Money can be raised in this country by lecturing for two or three years. But I have tried a little, and although there is much public appreciation of my work, it is thoroughly uncongenial and demoralising to me...

I have read what you say about the Indian papers and their criticisms, which are natural. Jealousy is the central vice of every enslaved race. And it is jealousy and want of combination which cause and perpetuate slavery. You cannot feel the truth of this remark until you come out of India. The secret of Westerners' success is this power of combination, the basis of which is mutual trust and appreciation. The weaker and more cowardly a nation is, so much the more is this sin visible... But, my son, you ought not to expect anything from a slavish race. The case is almost desperate no doubt, but let me put the case before you all. Can you put life into this dead mass—dead to almost all moral aspiration, dead to all future possibilities—and always ready to spring upon those that would try to do good to them? Can you take the position of a physician who tries to pour medicine down the throat of a kicking and refractory child?... An American or a European always supports his countrymen in a foreign country... Let me remind you again, "Thou hast the right to work but not to the fruits thereof." Stand firm like a rock. Truth always triumphs. Let the children of Shri Ramakrishna be true to themselves and everything will be all right. We may not live to see the outcome, but as sure as we live, it will come sooner or later. What India wants is a new electric fire to stir up a fresh vigour in the national veins. This was ever, and always will be, slow work. Be content to work, and, above all, be true to yourself. Be pure, staunch, and sincere to the very backbone, and everything will be all right. If you have marked anything in the disciples of Shri Ramakrishna, it is this—they are sincere to the backbone. My task will be done, and I shall be quite content to die, if I can bring up and launch one hundred such men over India. He, the Lord, knows best. Let ignorant men talk nonsense. We neither seek aid nor avoid it—we are the servants of the Most High. The petty attempts of small men should be beneath our notice. Onward! Upon ages of struggle a character is built. Be not discouraged. One word of truth can never be lost; for ages it may be hidden under rubbish, but it will show itself sooner or later. Truth is indestructible, virtue is indestructible, purity is indestructible. Give me a genuine man; I do not want masses of converts. My son, hold fast! Do not care for anybody to help you. Is not the Lord infinitely greater than all human help? Be holy—trust in the Lord, depend on Him always, and you are on the right track; nothing can prevail against you...

Let us pray, "Lead, Kindly Light"—a beam will come through the dark, and a hand will be stretched forth to lead us. I always pray for you: you must pray for me. Let each one of us pray day and night for the downtrodden millions in India who are held fast by poverty, priestcraft, and tyranny—pray day and night for them. I care more to preach religion to them than to the high and the rich. I am no metaphysician, no philosopher, nay, no saint. But I am poor, I love the poor. I see what they call the poor of this country, and how many there are who feel for them! What an immense difference in India! Who feels there for the two hundred millions of men and women sunken for ever in poverty and ignorance? Where is the way out? Who feels for them? They cannot find light or education. Who will bring the light to them—who will travel from door to door bringing education to them? Let these people be your God—think of them, work for them, pray for them incessantly—the Lord will show you the way. Him I call a Mahâtman (great soul) whose heart bleeds for the poor, otherwise he is a Durâtman (wicked soul). Let us unite our wills in continued prayer for their good. We may die unknown, unpitied, unbewailed, without accomplishing anything—but not one thought will be lost. It will take effect, sooner or later. My heart is too full to express my feeling; you know it, you can imagine it. So long as the millions live in hunger and ignorance, I hold every man a traitor who, having been educated at their expense, pays not the least heed to them! I call those men who strut about in their finery, having got all their money by grinding the poor, wretches, so long as they do not do anything for those two hundred millions who are now no better than hungry savages! We are poor, my brothers, we are nobodies, but such have been always the instruments of the Most High. The Lord bless you all.

With all love,
Vivekananda.

1894.40 — DEAR __

To a Madras disciple:

541 Dearborn Ave., Chicago,
28 June, 1894.

DEAR __,

The other day I received a letter from G. G., Mysore. G. G. unfortunately thinks that I am all-knowing, else he would have written his Canarese address on the top of the letter more legibly. Then again it is a great mistake to address me letters to any other place but Chicago. It was my mistake of course at first, because I ought to have thought of the fine Buddhi (intellect) of our friends who are throwing letters at me anywhere they find an address at the top. But tell our Madras Brihaspatis (i.e. wise fellows) that they already knew full well that before their letters reach, I may be 1000 miles away from that particular place, for I am continuously travelling. In Chicago there is a friend whose house is my headquarters.

Now as to my prospects here—it is well-nigh zero. Why, because although I had the best purpose, it has been made null and void by these causes. All that I get about India is from Madras letters. Your letters say again and again how I am being praised in India. But that is between you and me, for I never saw a single Indian paper writing about me, except the three square inches sent to me by Alasinga. On the other hand, everything that is said by Christians in India is sedulously gathered by the missionaries and regularly published, and they go from door to door to make my friends give me up. They have succeeded only too well, for there is not one word for me from India. Indian Hindu papers may laud me to the skies, but not a word of that ever came to America, so that many people in this country think me a fraud. In the face of the missionaries and with the jealousy of the Hindus here to back them, I have not a word to say.

I now think it was foolish of me to go to the Parliament on the strength of the urging of the Madras boys. They are boys after all. Of course, I am eternally obliged to them, but they are after all enthusiastic young men without any executive abilities. I came here without credentials. How else to show that I am not a fraud in the face of the missionaries and the Brahmo Samaj? Now I thought nothing so easy as to spend a few words; I thought nothing would be so easy as to hold a meeting of some respectable persons in Madras and Calcutta and pass a resolution thanking me and the American people for being kind to me and sending it over officially, i.e. through the Secretary of the function, to America, for instance, sending one to Dr. Barrows and asking him to publish it in the papers and so on, to different papers of Boston, New York, and Chicago. Now after all, I found that it is too terrible a task for India to undertake. There has not been one voice for me in one year and every one against me, for whatever you may say of me in your homes, who knows anything of it here? More than two months ago I wrote to Alasinga about this. He did not even answer my letter. I am afraid his heart has grown lukewarm. So you must first think of that and then show this letter to the Madras people. On the other hand, my brethren foolishly talk nonsense about Keshab Sen; and the Madrasis, telling the Theosophists anything I write about them, are creating only enemies... Oh! If only I had one man of some true abilities and brains to back me in India! But His will be done. I stand a fraud in this country. It was my foolishness to go to the Parliament without any credentials, hoping that there would be many for me. I have got to work it out slowly.

On the whole, the Americans are a million times nobler than the Hindus, and I can work more good here than in the country of the ingrate and the heartless. After all, I must work my Karma out. So far as pecuniary circumstances go I am all right and will be all right. The number of Theosophists in all America is only 625 by the last census. Mixing up with them will smash me in a minute rather than help me in any way. What nonsense does Alasinga mean by my going to London to see Mr. Old etc. Fool! the boys there don't know what they are talking. And this pack of Madras babies cannot even keep a counsel in their blessed noodles! Talk nonsense all day, and when it comes to the least business, they are nowhere! Boobies, who cannot get up a few meetings of 50 men each and send up a few empty words only to help me, talk big about influencing the world. I have written to you about the phonograph. Now there is here an electric fan costing $20 and working beautifully. The battery works 100 hours and then can be replenished at any electric plant. Good-bye, I have had enough of the Hindus. Now His will be done, I obey and bow down to my Karma. However, do not think me ungrateful... The Madras people have done for me more than I deserved and more than was in their power. It was my foolishness — the forgetting for a moment that we Hindus have not yet become human beings and giving up for a moment my self-reliance and relying upon the Hindus — that I came to grief. Every moment I expected something from India. No, it never came. Last two months especially I was in torture at every moment. No, not even a newspaper from India! My friends waited — waited month after month; nothing came, not a voice. Many consequently grew cold and at last gave me up. But it is the punishment for relying upon man and upon brutes, for our countrymen are not men as yet. They are ready to be praised, but when their turn comes even to say a word, they are nowhere.

My thanks eternal to the Madras young men. May the Lord bless them for ever. America is the best field in the world to carry on my idea; so I do not think of leaving America soon. And why? Here I have food and drink and clothes, and everybody so kind, and all this for a few good words! Why should I give up such a noble nation to go to the land of brutes and ingrates and the brainless boobies held in eternal thraldom of superstitious, merciless, pitiless wretches? So good-bye again. You may show this letter to the people with discretion, even Alasinga upon whom I built so much. By the by, will you kindly send up a few copies of the sketch of Ramakrishna Paramahamsa's life written by Mazumdar to Chicago? They have lots in Calcutta. Don't forget the address 541 Dearborn Avenue (not Street), Chicago, or c/o Thomas Cook, Chicago. Any other address would cause much delay and confusion, as I am continually travelling, and Chicago is my headquarters, although even this much did not come to the brains of our Madras friends. Kindly give G. G., Alasinga, Secretary, and all others my eternal blessings. I am always praying for their welfare, and I am not in the least displeased with them, but I am not pleased with myself. I committed a terrible error — of calculating upon others' help — once in my life — and I have paid for it. It was my fault and not theirs. Lord bless all the Madras people. They are at least far superior to the Bengalis, who are simply fools and have no souls, no stamina at all. Good-bye, good-bye. I have launched my boat in the waves, come what may. Regarding my brutal criticisms, I have really no right to make them. You have done for me infinitely more than I deserve. I must bear my own Karma, and that without a murmur. Lord bless you all.

Yours truly,
Vivekananda.

PS — I am afraid Alasinga's college has closed, but I have no intimation of it, and he never gave me his home address. Kidi has dropped out, I am afraid.

1894.41 — MOTHER

To Mrs. G. W. Hale:

New York,
28 June, 1894.

DEAR MOTHER,

Arrived safely two hours ago. Landsberg was waiting at the station. Came to Dr.

Guernsey's house. Nobody was there except a servant. I took a bath and strolled with Landsberg to some restaurant where I had a good meal. Then, I have just now returned to Landsberg's rooms in the Theosophical Society and am writing you this letter.

I haven't been to see my other friends yet. After a good and long rest through the night I hope to see most of them tomorrow. My Love to you all. By the by, somebody stepped on my umbrella on board the train and broke its nose off.

Your affectionate son,
Vivekananda.

PS — I have not settled myself. So as to direct letters to me, they can be directed c/o Leon Landsberg, 144 Madison Ave., New York.

1894.42 — MOTHER

To Mrs. G. W. Hale:

C/O Leon Landsberg,
144 Madison Avenue, New York,
1 July, 1894.

DEAR MOTHER,

Hope you are settled down in peace by this time. The babies are doing well in Mudville (Kenosha, Wisconsin) — in their nunnery, I am sure. It is very hot here, but now and then a breeze comes up which cools it down. I am now with Miss [Mary A.] Phillips. Will move off from here on Tuesday to another place.

Here I find a quotation from a speech by Sir Monier Williams, professor of Sanskrit in the Oxford University. It is very strange as coming from one who every day expects to see the whole of India converted to Christianity. "And yet it is a remarkable characteristic of Hinduism that it neither requires nor attempts to make converts. Nor is it at present by any means decreasing in numbers, nor is it being driven out of the field by two such proselytizing religions as Mahomedanism [sic] and Christianity. On the contrary, it is at present rapidly increasing. And far more remarkable than this is that, it is all-receptive, all-embracing and all-comprehensive. It claims to be the one religion of humanity, of human nature, of the entire world. It cares not to oppose the progress of Christianity nor of any other religion. For it has no difficulty in including all other religions within its all-embracing arms and ever-widening fold. And in real fact Hinduism has something to offer which is suited to all minds. Its very strength lies in its infinite adaptability to the infinite diversity of human characters and human tendencies. It has its highly spiritual and abstract side suited to the philosophical higher classes. Its practical and concrete side suited to the man of affairs and the man of the world. Its aesthetic and ceremonial side suited to the man of poetic feeling and imagination. Its quiescent and contemplative side suited to the man of peace and lover of seclusion.

"Indeed, the Hindus were Spinozists 2,000 years before the birth of Spinoza, Darwinians centuries before the birth of Darwin, and evolutionists centuries before the doctrine of evolution had been accepted by the Huxleys of our time, and before any word like evolution existed in any language of the world."

This, as coming from one of the staunchest defenders of Christianity, is wonderful indeed. But he seems to have got the idea quite correct.

Now I am going to send up the orange coat today; as for the books that came to me from Philadelphia, I do not think they are worthy of being sent at all. I do not know what I am going to do next. Patiently wait and resign myself unto His guidance—that is my motto. My love to you all.

Your affectionate son,
Vivekananda.

1894.43—ALASINGA

U. S. A.,
11th July, 1894.

DEAR ALASINGA,

You must never write to me anywhere else but 541 Dearborn Ave., Chicago. Your last letter has travelled the whole country to come to me, and this was only because I am so well known. Some of the resolutions are to be sent to Dr. Barrows with a letter thanking him for his kindness to me and asking him to publish the letter in some American newspapers—as that would be the best refutation of the false charges of the missionaries that I do not represent anybody. Learn business, my boy. We will do great things yet! Last year I only sowed the seeds; this year I mean to reap. In the meanwhile, keep up as much enthusiasm as possible in India. Let Kidi go his own way. He will come out all right in time. I have taken his responsibility. He has a perfect right to his own opinion. Make him write for the paper; that will keep him in good temper! My blessings on him.

Start the journal and I will send you articles from time to time. You must send a paper and a letter to Professor J. H. Wright of Harvard University, Boston, thanking him as having been the first man who stood as my friend and asking him to publish it in the papers, thus giving the lie to the missionaries.

In the Detroit lecture I got $900, i.e. Rs. 2,700. In other lectures, I earned in one, $2,500, i.e. Rs. 7,500 in one hour, but got only 200 dollars! I was cheated by a roguish Lecture Bureau. I have given them up. I spent a good deal here; only about $3,000 remains.

I shall have to print much matter next year. I am going regularly to work... The sheer power of the will will do everything... You must organise a society which should regularly meet, and write to me about it as often as you can. In fact, get up as much enthusiasm as you can. Only, beware of falsehood. Go to work, my boys, the fire will come to you! The faculty of organisation is entirely absent in our nature, but this has to be infused. The great secret is — absence of jealousy. Be always ready to concede to the opinions of your brethren, and try always to conciliate. That is the whole secret. Fight on bravely! Life is short! Give it up to a great cause. Why do you not write anything about Narasimha? He is almost starving. I gave him something. Then he went over to somewhere, I do not know where, and does not write. Akshaya is a good boy. I like him very much. No use quarrelling with the Theosophists. Do not go and tell them all I write to you... Theosophists are our pioneers, do you know? Now Judge is a Hindu and Col. a Buddhist, and Judge is the ablest man here. Now tell the Hindu Theosophists to support Judge. Even if you can write Judge a letter, thanking him as a co-religionist and for his labours in presenting Hinduism before Americans; that will do his heart much good. We must not join any sect, but we must sympathise and work with each... Work, work — conquer all by your love!...

Try to expand. Remember the only sign of life is motion and growth. You must send the passed resolution to Dr. J. H. Barrows..., Dr. Paul Carus..., Senator Palmer..., Mrs. J. J. Bagley..., it must come officially... I write this because I do not think you know the ways of foreign nations... Keep on steadily. So far we have done wonderful things. Onward, brave souls, we will gain! Organise and found societies and go to work, that is the only way.

At this time of the year there is not much lecturing to be done here; so I will devote myself to my pen and write. I shall be hard at work all the time, and then, when the cold weather comes and people return to their homes, I shall begin lecturing again and at the same time organise societies.

My love and blessings to you all. I never forget anybody, though I do not write often. Then again, I am now, continuously travelling, and letters have to be redirected from one place to another.

Work hard. Be holy and pure and the fire will come.

Yours affectionately,
Vivekananda.

1894.44 — SISTERS

To the Hale Sisters (about the Calcutta meeting of 5th Sept., 1894):

New York
9th July (Sept.?), 1894.

O MY SISTERS,

Glory unto Jagadambâ (Mother of the Universe)! I have gained beyond expectations. The prophet has been honoured and with a vengeance. I am weeping like a child at His mercy — He never leaves His servant, sisters. The letter I send you will explain all, and the printed things are coming to the American people. The names there are the very flower of our country. The President was the chief nobleman of Calcutta, and the other man Mahesh Chandra Nyâyaratna is the principal of the Sanskrit College and the chief Brahmin in all India and recognised by the Government as such. The letter will tell you all. O sisters! What a rogue am I that in the face of such mercies sometimes the faith totters — seeing every moment that I am in His hands. Still the mind sometimes gets despondent. Sister, there is a God — a Father — a Mother who never leaves His Children, never, never, never. Put uncanny theories aside and becoming children take refuge in Him. I cannot write more — I am weeping like a woman.

Blessed, blessed art Thou, Lord God of my soul!

Yours affectionately,
Vivekananda.

1894.45 — MOTHER

To Mrs. G. W. Hale:

C/O Dr. E. Guernsey, Cedar Lawn,
Fishkill On The Hudson,
19 July, 1894.

DEAR MOTHER,

Your kind note reached me here yesterday evening. I am so glad to hear the babies are enjoying. I got the Interior and am very glad to see my friend Mazoomdar's (Pratap Chandra Mazumdar.) book spoken of so highly. Mazoomdar is a great and a good man and has done much for his fellow beings.

It is a lovely summer place, this Cedar Lawn of the Guernseys. Miss Guernsey has gone on a visit to Swampscott. I had also an invitation there, but I thought [it] better to stay here in the calm and silent place full of trees and with the beautiful Hudson flowing by and mountain in the background.

I am very thankful for Miss Howe's suggestion, and I am also thinking of it. Most probably I will go to England very soon. But between you and me, I am a sort of mystic and cannot move without orders, and that has not come yet. Mr. [Charles M.] Higgins, a rich young lawyer and inventor of Brooklyn, is arranging some lectures for me. I have not settled whether I will stop for them or not.

My eternal thanks to you for your kindness. My whole life cannot repay my debt to you. (Original letter: your debt.) You may see from the letter from Madras that there is not a word about Narasimha. What can I do more? I did not get the cheque cashed yet, for there was no necessity. Miss Phillips was very kind to me. She is an old lady, about 50 or more. You need not feel any worry about my being taken care of. The Lord always takes care of His servants; and so long as I am really His servant and not the world's, I am very confident of getting everything that would be good for me. The Guernseys love me very much, and there are many families in New York and Brooklyn who would take the best care of me.

I had a beautiful letter from Mr. Snell, saying that a sudden change for the better has taken place in his fortunes and offering me thrice the money I lent him as a contribution to my work. And he also has beautiful letters from Dharmapala and others from India. But, of course, I politely refused his repayment.

So far so good. I have seen Mr. [Walter Hines] Page, the editor of the Forum here. He was so sorry not to get the article on missionaries. But I have promised to write on other interesting subjects. Hope I will have patience to do so.

I had a letter yesterday from Miss Harriet, (Mrs. Hale's daughter.) from which I learn that they are enjoying Kenosha (A port in southwest Wisconsin, on Lake Michigan.) very much. Lord bless you and yours, Mother Church, for ever and ever. I cannot even express my gratitude to you.

As for me, you need not be troubled in the least. My whole life is that of a vagabond — homeless, roving tramp; any fare, good or bad, in any country, is good enough for me.

Yours ever in love and obedience,
Swami Vivekananda.

1894.46 — MOTHER

To Mrs. G. W. Hale:

Swampscott, Massachusetts,
23 July, 1894.

DEAR MOTHER,

I think I have all your questions answered and you are in good humour again.

I am enjoying this place very much; going to Greenacre today or tomorrow and on our way back I intend to go to Annisquam, to Mrs. Bagley's — I have written to her. Mrs. Breed (Mrs. Francis W. Breed of Lynn, Massachusetts.) says, "You are very sensitive".

Now, I fortunately did not cash your check in New York. I wanted to cash it here, when lo! you have not signed your name to it. The Hindu is a dreamer no doubt, but when the Christian dreams he dreams with a vengeance.

Do not be distressed. Somebody gave me plenty of money to move about. I would be taken care of right along. I send herewith the cheque back to you. I had a very beautiful letter from Miss Mary. My love to them.

What is Father Pope doing? Is it very hot in Chicago? I do not care for the heat of this country. It is nothing compared to our India heat. I am doing splendidly. The other day I had the summer cholera; and cramp, etc. came to pay their calls to me. We had several hours nice talk and groans and then they departed.

I am on the whole doing very well. Has the meerschaum pipe reached Chicago? I had nice yachting, nice sea bathing, and am enjoying myself like a duck. Miss Guernsey went home just now. I do not know what more to write.

Lord bless you all.

Affectionately,
Vivekananda.

1894.47 — BABIES

To the Hale Sisters:

Swampscott,
26th July, 1894.

DEAR BABIES,

Now don't let my letters stray beyond the circle, please. I had a beautiful letter from sister Mary. See how I am getting the dash, sister Jeany teaches me all that. She can jump and run and play and swear like a devil and talk slang at the rate of 500 a minute; only she does not much care for religion, only a little. She is gone today home, and I am going to Greenacre. I had been to see Mrs. Breed. Mrs. Stone was there, with whom is residing Mrs. Pullman and all the golden bugs, my old friends hereabouts. They are kind as usual. On my way back from Greenacre I am going to Annisquam to see Mrs. Bagley for a few days.

Darn it, forget everything. I had duckings in the sea like a fish. I am enjoying every bit of it. What nonsense was the song Harriet taught me "dans la plaine" the deuce take it. I told it to a French scholar and he laughed and laughed till the fellow was well-nigh burst at my wonderful translation. That is the way you would have taught me French! You are a pack of fools and heathens, I tell you. Now are you gasping for breath like a huge fish stranded? I am glad that you are sizzling. Oh! how nice and cool it is here, and it is increased a hundred-fold when I think about the gasping, sizzling, boiling, frying four old maids, and how cool and nice I am here. Whooooooo!

Miss Phillips has a beautiful place somewhere in N.Y. State — mountain, lake, river, forest altogether — what more? I am going to make a Himalayas there and start a monastery as sure as I am living — I am not going to leave this country without throwing one more apple of discord into this already roaring, fighting, kicking, mad whirlpool of American religion. Well, dear old maids, you sometimes have a glimpse of the lake and on every hot noon, think of going down to the bottom of the lake, down, down, down, until it is cool and nice, and then to lie down on the bottom, with that coolness above and around, and lie there still, silent, and just doze — not sleep, but dreamy dozing half unconscious sort of bliss — very much like that which opium brings; that is delicious; and drinking lots of iced water. Lord bless my soul — I had such cramps several times as would have killed an elephant. So I hope to keep myself away from the cold water.

May you be all happy, dear fin de siècle young ladies, is the constant prayer of.

Vivekananda.

1894.48 — SISTERS

Greenacre Inn, Elliot, Maine,
31st July, 1894.

DEAR SISTERS,

I have not written you long, and I have not much to write. This is a big inn and farm-house where the Christian Scientists are holding a session. Last spring in New York I was invited by the lady projector of the meeting to come here, and after all I am here. It is a beautiful and cool place, no doubt, and many of my old friends of Chicago are here. Mrs. Mills, Miss Stockham, and several other ladies and gentlemen live in tents which they have pitched on the open ground by the river. They have a lively time and sometimes all of them wear what you call your scientific dress the whole day. They have lectures almost every day. One Mr. Colville from Boston is here; he speaks every day, it is said, under spirit control. The Editor (?) of the Universal Truth has settled herself down here. She is conducting religious services and holding classes to heal all manner of diseases, and very soon I expect them to be giving eyes to the blind, and the like! After all, it is a queer gathering. They do not care much about social laws and are quite free and happy. Mrs. Mills is quite brilliant, and so are many other ladies... Another lady from Detroit — very cultured and with beautiful black eyes and long hair is going to take me to an island fifteen miles out at sea. I hope we shall have a nice time... I may go over to Annisquam from here, I suppose. This is a beautiful and nice place and the bathing is splendid. Cora Stockham has made a bathing dress for me, and I am having as good a time in the water as a duck this is delicious even for the denizens of mud Ville. I do not find anything more to write. Only I am so busy that I cannot find time enough to write to Mother Church separately. My love and respects to Miss Howe.

There is here Mr. Wood of Boston who is one of the great lights of your sect. But he objects to belong to the sect of Mrs. Whirlpool. So he calls himself a mental healer of metaphysico-chemico-physico-religiosio what not! Yesterday there was a tremendous cyclone which gave a good "treatment" to the tents. The big tent under which they had the lectures had developed so much spirituality, under the "treatment", that it entirely disappeared from mortal gaze, and about two hundred chairs were dancing about the grounds under spiritual ecstasy! Mrs. Figs of Mills company gives a class every morning; and Mrs. Mills is jumping all about the place; they are all in high spirits. I am especially glad for Cora, for they have suffered a good deal last winter and a little hilarity would do her good. You will be astounded with the liberty they enjoy in the camps, but they are very good and pure people there—a little erratic and that is all. I shall be here till Saturday next…

…The other night the camp people went to sleep beneath a pine tree under which I sit every morning a la Hindu and talk to them. Of course I went with them, and we had a nice night under the stars, sleeping on the lap of mother earth, and I enjoyed every bit of it. I cannot describe to you that night's glories—after a year of brutal life that I have led, to sleep on the ground, to meditate under the tree in the forest! The inn people are more or less well-to-do, and the camp people are healthy, young, sincere, and holy men and women. I teach them Shivo'ham, Shivo'ham, and they all repeat it, innocent and pure as they are and brave beyond all bounds. And so I am happy and glorified. Thank God for making me poor, thank God for making these children in the tents poor. The Dudes and Dudines are in the Hotel, but iron-bound nerves and souls of triple steel and spirits of fire are in the camp. If you had seen them yesterday, when the rain was falling in torrents and the cyclone was overturning everything, hanging by their tent strings to keep them from being blown down, and standing on the majesty of their souls—these brave ones—it would have done your hearts good. I will go a hundred miles to see the like of them. Lord bless them! I hope you are enjoying your nice village life. Never be anxious for a moment. I will be taken care of, and if not, I will know my time has come and shall pass out.

"Sweet One! Many people offer to You many things, I am poor—but I have the body, mind, and soul. I give them over to You. Deign to accept, Lord of the Universe, and refuse them not."—So have I given over my life and soul once for all. One thing—they are a dry sort of people here—and as to that very few in the whole world are there that are not. They do not understand "Mâdhava", the Sweet One. They are either intellectual or go after faith cure, table turning, witchcraft, etc., etc. Nowhere have I heard so much about "love, life, and liberty" as in this country, but nowhere is it less understood. Here God is either a terror or a healing power, vibration, and so forth. Lord bless their souls! And these parrots talk day and night of love and love and love!

Now, good dreams, good thoughts for you. You are good and noble. Instead of materialising the spirit, that is, dragging the spiritual to the material plane as these folks do, convert the matter into spirit, catch a glimpse at least, every day, of that world of infinite beauty and peace and purity—the spiritual, and try to live in it day and night. Seek not, touch not with your toes even, anything that is uncanny. Let your souls ascend day and night like an "unbroken string" unto the feet of the Beloved whose throne is in your own hearts and let the rest take care of themselves, that is the body and everything else. Life is evanescent, a fleeting dream; youth and beauty fade. Say day and night, "Thou art my father, my mother, my husband, my love, my lord, my God—I want nothing but Thee, nothing but Thee, nothing but Thee. Thou in me, I in Thee, I am Thee. Thou art me." Wealth goes, beauty vanishes, life flies, powers fly—but the Lord abideth for ever, love abideth for ever. If here is glory in keeping the machine in good trim, it is more glorious to withhold the soul from suffering with the body—that is the only demonstration of your being "not matter", by letting the matter alone.

Stick to God! Who cares what comes to the body or to anything else! Through the terrors of evil, say — my God, my love! Through the pangs of death, say — my God, my love! Through all the evils under the sun, say — my God, my love! Thou art here, I see Thee. Thou art with me, I feel Thee. I am Thine, take me. I am not of the world's but Thine, leave not then me. Do not go for glass beads leaving the mine of diamonds! This life is a great chance. What, seekest thou the pleasures of the world? — He is the fountain of all bliss. Seek for the highest, aim at that highest, and you shall reach the highest.

Yours with all blessings,
Vivekananda.

1894.49 — MOTHER

To Mrs. George W. Hale:

C/O Dr. E. Guernsey,
Fishkill Landing, N.Y.,
July, 1894.

DEAR MOTHER,

I came yesterday to this place, and shall remain here a few days. I received in New York a letter from you but did not receive any Interior, for which I am glad, because I am not perfect yet, and knowing the "unselfish love" the Presbyterian priests, especially the Interior has for "me", I want to keep aloof from rousing bad feelings towards these "sweet Christian gentlemen" in my heart.

Our religion teaches that anger is a great sin, even if it is "righteous". Each must follow his own religion. I could not for my soul distinguish ever the distinction between "religious anger" and "commonplace anger", "religious killing" and "commonplace killing", "religious slandering and irreligious", and so forth. Nor may that "fine" ethical distinction ever enter into the ethics of our nation! Jesting apart, Mother Church, I do not care the least for the gambols these men play, seeing as I do through and through the insincerity, the hypocrisy, and love of self and name that is the only motive power in these men.

As to the photographs, the first time the Babies got a few copies, and the second time you brought a few copies; you know they are to give 50 copies in all. Sister Isabelle knows better than I.

With my sincerest love and respects for you and Father Pope.

I remain,

Yours,
Vivekananda.

PS — How are you enjoying the heat? I am bearing the heat very well here. I had an invitation to Swampscott on the sea from a very rich lady whose acquaintance I made last winter in New York, but I declined with thanks. I am very careful not to take the hospitality of anybody here, especially the rich. I had a few other invitations from some very rich people here. I refused; I have by this time seen the whole business through. Lord bless you and yours, Mother Church, for your sincerity. Oh! it is so rare in this world.

1894.50 — DEAR AND BELOVED[1]

Salutation to Bhagavan Ramakrishna!

(Summer?) 1894.

DEAR AND BELOVED, (The brother-disciples at Alambazar monastery)

Your letter gives me all the news over there. I am grieved to hear of the bereavement Balaram Babu's wife has sustained. Such is the Lord's will. This is a place for action, not enjoyment, and everyone will go home when his task is done — some earlier, and some later, that is all. Fakir has gone — well, such is the will of the Lord!

It is a welcome news that Shri Ramakrishna's festival has come off with great éclat; the more his name is spread, the better it is. But there is one thing to know: Great sages come with special messages for the world, and not for name; but their followers throw their teachings overboard and fight over their names — this is verily the history of the world. I do not take into any consideration whether people accept his name or not, but I am ready to lay down my life to help his teachings, his life, and his message spread all over the world. What I am most afraid of is the worship-room. It is not bad in itself, but there is a tendency in some to make this all in all and set up that old-fashioned nonsense over again — this is what makes me nervous. I know why they busy themselves with those old, effete ceremonials. Their spirit craves for work, but having no outlet they waste their energy in ringing bells and all that.

I am giving you a new idea. If you can work it out, then I shall know you are men and will be of service... Make an organised plan. A few cameras, some maps, globes, and some chemicals, etc., are needed. The next thing you want is a big hut. Then you must get together a number of poor, indigent folk. Having done all this, show them pictures to teach them astronomy, geography, etc., and preach Shri Ramakrishna to them. Try to have their eyes opened as to what has taken place or is taking place in different countries, what this world is like and, so forth. You have got lots of poor and ignorant folk there. Go to their cottages, from door to door, in the evening, at noon, any time and open their eyes. Books etc., won't do — give them oral teaching. Then slowly extend your centres. Can you do all this? Or only bell-ringing?

I have heard everything about Brother Tarak from Madras. They are highly

---

1 Translated from Bengali.

pleased with him. Dear Brother Tarak, if you go to Madras and live there for some time, a lot of work will be done. But before you go, start this work there first. Can't the lady devotees convert some widows; into disciples? And can't you put a bit of learning into their heads? And can't you then send them out to preach Sari Ramakrishna from door to door, and impart education along with it?...

Come! Apply yourselves heart and soul to it. The day of gossip and ceremonials is gone, my boy, you must work now. Now, let me see how far a Bengali's religion will go. Niranjan writes that Latu (Adbhutananda) wants some warm clothing. The people here import winter clothing from Europe and India. You will get a woollen wrap in Calcutta at one-fourth of the price at which I might buy it here... I don't know when I shall go to Europe, everything is uncertain with me — I am getting on somehow in this country, that is all.

This is a very funny country. It is now summer; this morning it was as hot as April in Bengal, but now it is as cold as February at Allahabad! So much fluctuation within four hours! The hotels of this country beggar description. For instance there is a hotel in New York where a room can be hired for up to Rs. 5,000 a day, excluding boarding charges. Not even in Europe is there a country like this in point of luxury. It is indeed the richest country in the world, where money is drained off like water. I seldom live in hotels, but am mostly the guest of big people here. To them I am a widely known man. The whole country knows me now; so wherever I go they receive me with open arms into their homes. Mr. Hale's home is my centre in Chicago. I call his wife mother, and his daughters call me brother. I scarcely find a family so highly pure and kind. Or why should God shower His blessings on them in such abundance, my brother? Oh, how wonderfully kind they are! If they chance to learn that a poor man is in a strait at such and such a place, there they will go ladies and gentlemen, to give him food and clothing and find him some job! And what do we do!

In summer they leave their homes to go to foreign lands, or to the seaside. I, too, shall go somewhere, but have not yet fixed a place. In other points, they are just as you see Englishmen. They have got books and things of that sort, but very dear. You can have five times those things In Calcutta for the same price. In other words, these people will not let foreign goods be imported into the country. They set a heavy tax on them, and as a result, the market goes up enormously. Besides, they are not much in the way of manufacturing clothing etc. They construct tools and machinery, and grow wheat, rice, cotton, etc., which are fairly cheap.

By the bye, nowadays we have plenty of Hilsâ fish here. Eat your fill, but everything digests. There are many kinds of fruits; plantain, lemon, guava, apple, almond, raisin, and grape are in abundance; besides many other fruits come from California. There are plenty of pineapples but there are no mangoes or lichis, or things of that sort.

There is a kind of spinach, which, when cooked, tastes just like our Noté of Bengal, and another class, which they call asparagus, tastes exactly like the tender Dengo herb, but you can't have our Charchari made of it here. There is no Kalâi or any other pulse; they do not even know of them. There is rice, and bread, and numerous varieties of fish and meat, of all descriptions. Their menu is like that of the French. There is your milk, rarely curd, but plenty of whey. Cream is an article of everyday use. In tea and coffee and everything there is that cream — not the hardened crust of boiled milk, mind you — and there is your butter, too, and ice-water — no matter whether it is summer or winter, day or night, whether you have got a bad cold or fever — you have ice-water in abundance. These are scientific people and laugh when they are told that ice-water aggravates cold. The more you take, the better. And there is plenty of ice-cream, of all sorts of shapes. I have seen the Niagara Falls seven or eight times, the Lord be praised! Very grand no doubt, but not quite as you have heard them spoken of. One day, in winter, we had the aurora borealis.

…Only childish prattle! I have not much time to listen to that sort of thing in this life; it will be time enough to see if I can do that in the next. Yogen has completely rallied by this time, I hope? The vagabond spirit of Sarada (Trigunâtita) is not yet at an end, I see. What is wanted is a power of organisation — do you understand me? Have any of you got that much brain in your head? If you do, let your mind work. Brother Tarak, Sharat, and Hari will be able to do it. — has got very little originality, but is a very good workman and persevering — which is an essential necessity, and Shashi (Ramakrishnananda) is executive to a degree…We want some disciples — fiery young men — do you see? — intelligent and brave, who dare to go to the jaws of Death, and are ready to swim the ocean across. Do you follow me? We want hundreds like that, both men and women. Try your utmost for that end alone. Make converts right and left, and put them into our purity-drilling machine.

…What made you communicate to the Indian Mirror that Paramahamsa Deva used to call Narendra such and such, and all sorts of nonsense? — As if he had nothing else to do but that! Only thought-reading and nonsensical mystery-mongering!…It is excellent that Sanyal is visiting you often. Do you write letters to Gupta? Convey to him my love, and take kind care of him. Everything will come right by degrees. I don't find much time to write heaps of letters. As for lectures and so forth, I don't prepare them beforehand. Only one I wrote out, which you have printed. The rest I deliver off-hand, whatever comes to my lips — Gurudeva backs me up. I have nothing to do with pen and paper. Once at Detroit I held forth for three hours at a stretch. Sometimes I myself wonder at my own achievement — to think that there was such stuff in this pate! They ask me here to write a book. Well, I think I must do something that way, this time. But that's the botheration; who will take the trouble of putting things in black and white and all that!…We must electrify society, electrify the world. Idle gossip and barren ceremonials won't do. Ceremonials are meant for householders, your work is the distribution and propagation of thought-currents. If you can do that, then it is all right…

Let character be formed and then I shall be in your midst. Do you see? We want two thousand Sannyasins, nay ten, or even twenty thousand — men and women, both. What are our matrons doing? We want converts at any risk. Go and tell them, and try yourselves, heart and soul. Not householder disciples, mind you, we want Sannyasins. Let each one of you have a hundred heads tonsured — young educated men, not fools. Then you are heroes. We must make a sensation. Give up your passive attitude, gird your loins and stand up. Let me see you make some electric circuits between Calcutta and Madras. Start centres at places, go on always making converts. Convert everyone into the monastic order whoever seeks for it, irrespective of sex, and then I shall be in your midst. A huge spiritual tidal wave is coming — he who is low shall become noble, and he who is ignorant shall become the teacher of great scholars — through HIS grace. "— Arise! Awake! and stop not till the goal is reached." Life is ever expanding, contraction is death. The self-seeking man who is looking after his personal comforts and leading a lazy life — there is no room for him even in hell. He alone is a child of Shri Ramakrishna who is moved to pity for all creatures and exerts himself for them even at the risk of incurring personal damnation, — others are vulgar people. Whoever, at this great spiritual juncture, will stand up with a courageous heart and go on spreading from door to door, from village to village, his message, is alone my brother, and a son of his. This is the test, he who is Ramakrishna's child does not seek his personal good. "the point of death." Those that care for their personal comforts and seek a lazy life, who are ready to sacrifice all before their personal whims, are none of us; let them pack off, while yet there is time. Propagate his character, his teaching, his religion. This is the only spiritual practice, the only worship, this verily is the means, and this the goal. Arise! Arise! A tidal wave is coming! Onward! Men and women, down to the Chandâla (Pariah) — all are pure in his eyes. Onward! Onward! There is no time to care for name, or fame, or Mukti, or Bhakti! We shall look to these some other time. Now in this life let us infinitely spread his lofty character, his sublime life, his infinite soul. This is the only work — there is nothing else to do. Wherever his name will reach, the veriest worm will attain divinity, nay, is actually attaining it; you have got eyes, and don't you see it? Is it a child's play? Is it silly prattle? Is it foolery?" back. I cannot write any more. — Onward! I only tell you this, that whoever reads this letter will imbibe my spirit! Have faith! Onward! Great Lord!... I feel as if somebody is moving my hand to write in this way. Onward! Great Lord! Everyone will be swept away! Take care, he is coming! Whoever will be ready to serve him — no, not him but his children — the poor and the downtrodden, the sinful and the afflicted, down to the very worm — who will be ready to serve these, in them he will manifest himself. Through their tongue the Goddess of Learning Herself will speak, and the Divine Mother — the Embodiment of all Power — will enthrone Herself in their hearts. Those that are atheists, unbelievers, worthless, and foppish, why do they call themselves as belonging to his fold...

Yours affectionately,
Vivekananda.

PS — ... The term organisation means division of labour. Each does his own part, and all the parts taken together express an ideal of harmony...

1894.51 — MOTHER

To Mrs. G. W. Hale:

Greenacre Inn, Eliot, Maine,
5 August, 1894.

DEAR MOTHER,

I have received your letter and am very much ashamed at my bad memory. I unfortunately forgot all about the cheque. Perhaps you have come to know by this time of my being in Greenacre. I had a very nice time here and am enjoying it immensely. In the fall I am going to lecture in Brooklyn, New York. Yesterday I got news that they have completed all the advertising there. I have an invitation today from a friend in New York to go with him to some mountains north of this state of Maine. I do not know whether I will go or not. I am doing pretty well. Between lecturing, teaching, picnicking and other excitements the time is flying rapidly. I hope you are doing very well and that Father Pope is in good trim. It is a very beautiful spot — this Greenacre — and [I] have very nice company from Boston: Dr. Everett Hale, you know, of Boston, and Mrs. Ole Bull, of Cambridge. I do not know whether I will accept the invitation of my friend of New York or not.

So far only this is sure, that I will go to lecture in New York this coming fall. And Boston, of course, is a good field. The people here are mostly from Boston and they all like me very much. Are you having a good time, and Father Pope? Has your house-painting been finished? The Babies, I am sure, are enjoying their Mudville.

I am in no difficulty for money. I have plenty to eat and drink.

With my best love and gratitude to you and Father Pope and the Babies.

Yours affectionately,
Vivekananda.

Excuse this hasty scrawl. The pen is very bad.

The Harrison people sent me two "nasty standing" photos — that is all I have out of them, when they ought to give me 40 minus the 10 or 15 I have got already!!!

1894.52 — MOTHER

To Mrs. G. W. Hale:

Greenacre Inn, Eliot, Maine,
8 August, 1894.

DEAR MOTHER,

I have received the letter you sent over to me coming from India.

I am going to leave this place on Monday next for Plymouth [Massachusetts], where the Free Religious Association is holding its session. They will defray my expenses, of course.

I am all right, enjoying nice health, and the people here are very kind and nice to me. Up to date I had no occasion to cash any cheque as everything is going on smoothly. I have not heard anything from the Babies. Hope they are doing well. You also had nothing to write; however, I feel that you are doing well.

I would have gone over to another place, but Mr. Higginson's invitation ought to be attended to. And Plymouth is the place where the fathers of your country first landed. I want, therefore, to see it.

I am all right. It is useless reiterating my love and gratitude to you and yours — you know it all. May the Lord shower His choicest blessings on you and yours.

This meeting is composed of the best professors of your country and other people, so I must attend it; and then they would pay me. I have not yet determined all my plans, only I am going to lecture in New York this coming fall; every arrangement is complete for that. They have printed advertisements at their own expense for that and made everything ready.

Give my best love to the Babies, to Father Pope, and believe me ever in gratitude and love,

Your Son,
Vivekananda.

PS — I am very much obliged to the sisters for asking me to tell them if I want anything. I have no want anyway — I have everything I require and more to spare.

"He never gives up His servants."

My thanks and gratitude eternal to the sisters for their kindness in asking about my wants.

1894.53 — SISTERS

To the Hale Sisters:

Greenacre,
11th August, 1894.

DEAR SISTERS,

I have been all this time in Greenacre. I enjoyed this place very much. They have been all very kind to me. One Chicago lady, Mrs. Pratt of Kenilworth, wanted to give me $500; she became so much interested in me; but I refused. She has made me promise that I would send word to her whenever I need money, which I hope the Lord will never put me in. His help alone is sufficient for me. I have not heard anything from you nor from Mother. Neither have I any news from India as to the arrival of the phonograph.

If there was anything in my letter to you which was offensive, I hope you all know that I meant everything in love. It is useless to express my gratitude to you for your kindness. Lord bless you and shower His choicest blessings on you and those you love. To your family I am ever, ever beholden. You know it. You feel it. I cannot express it. On Sunday I am going to lecture at Plymouth at the "Sympathy of Religions" meetings of Col. Higginson. Herewith I send a photograph Cora Stockham took of the group under the tree. It is only a proof and will fade away under exposure, but I cannot get anything better at present. Kindly tender my heartfelt love and gratitude to Miss Howe. She has been so, so kind to me. I do not need anything at present. I shall be very glad to let you know if I need anything. I think I am going to Fishkill from Plymouth, where I will be only a couple of days. I will write you again from Fishkill. Hope you are all happy, or rather I know you are. Pure and good souls can never be unhappy. I shall have a very nice time the few weeks I am here. I will be in New York next fall. New York is a grand and good place. The New York people have a tenacity of purpose unknown in any other city. I had a letter from Mrs. Potter Palmer asking me to see her in August. She is a very gracious and kind lady, etc. I have not much to say. There is my friend Dr. Janes of New York, President of the Ethical Culture Society, who has begun his lectures. I must go to hear him. He and I agree so much. May you be always happy!

Ever your well-wishing brother,
Vivekananda.

1894.54 — SISTER

Annisquam,
20th August, 1894.

DEAR SISTER[1],

Your very kind letter duly reached me at Annisquam. I am with the Bagleys once more. They are kind as usual. Professor Wright was not here. But he came day before yesterday and we have very nice time together. Mr. Bradley of Evanston, whom you have met at Evanston, was here. His sister-in-law had me sit for a picture several days and had painted me. I had some very fine boating and one evening overturned the boat and had a good drenching—clothes and all.

I had very very nice time at Greenacre. They were all so earnest and kind people. Fanny Hartley and Mrs. Mills have by this time gone back home I suppose.

From here I think I will go back to New York. Or I may go to Boston to Mrs. Ole Bull. Perhaps you have heard of Mr. Ole Bull, the great violinist of this country. She is his widow. She is a very spiritual lady. She lives in Cambridge and has a fine big parlour made of woodwork brought all the way from India. She wants me to come over to her any time and use her parlour to lecture. Boston of course is the great field for everything, but the Boston people as quickly take hold of anything

---

1. Isabelle McKindley.

as give it up; while the New Yorkers are slow, but when they get hold of anything they do it with a mortal grip.

I have kept pretty good health all the time and hope to do in the future. I had no occasion yet to draw on my reserve, yet I am rolling on pretty fair. And I have given up all money-making schemes and will be quite satisfied with a bite and a shed and work on.

I believe you are enjoying your summer retreat. Kindly convey my best regards and love to Miss Howe and Mr. Frank Howe.

Perhaps I did not tell you in my last how I slept and lived and preached under the trees and for a few days at least found myself once more in the atmosphere of heaven.

Most probably I will make New York my centre for the next winter; and as soon as I fix on that, I will write to you. I am not yet settled in my ideas of remaining in this country any more. I cannot settle anything of that sort. I must bide my time. May the Lord bless you all for ever and ever is the constant prayer of your ever affectionate brother,

Vivekananda.

1894.55 — MOTHER

To Mrs. G. W. Hale:

C/O Mrs. J. J. Bagley, Annisquam,
20 August, 1894.

DEAR MOTHER,

Your letters just now reached me. I had some beautiful letters from India. The letter from Ajit Singh (The Raja of Khetri, a very devoted disciple of the Swami.) shows that the phonograph has not reached yet, and it was dated 8th June. So I do not think it is time yet to get an answer. I am not astonished at my friends' asking Cook & Sons to hunt for me; I have not written for a long time.

I have a letter from Madras which says they will soon send money to Narasimha (Narasimhacharya. Vide the letter dated February 14, 1894.) — in fact, as soon as they get a reply to their letter written to Narasimha. So kindly let Narasimha know it. The photographs have not reached me — except two of Fishkill when I was there last. Landsberg (Leon Landsberg. Vide the letter dated June 28, 1894.) has kindly sent over the letters. From here I will probably go over to Fishkill. The meerschaum was not sent over by me direct, but I left it to the Guernseys. And they are a lazy family in that respect.

I have beautiful letters from the sisters.

By the by, your missionaries try to make me a malcontent before the English government in India, and the Lieutenant Governor of Bengal in a recent speech hinted that the recent revival of Hinduism was against the government. Lord bless the missionary. Everything is fair in love and (religion?).

The word Shri means "of good fortune", "blessed", etc. Paramahamsa is a title for a Sannyâsi who has reached the goal, i.e. realized God. Neither am I blessed nor have I reached the goal; but they are courteous, that is all. I will soon write to my brothers in India. I am so lazy, and I cannot send over the newspaper nonsense day after day.

I want a little quiet, but it is not the will of the Lord, it seems. At Greenacre I had to talk on an average 7 to 8 hours a day — that was rest, if it ever was. But it was of the Lord, and that brings vigour along with it.

I have not much to write, and I do not remember anything of what I said or did all these places over. So I hope to be excused.

I will be here a few days more at least, and therefore I think it would be better to send over my mail here.

I have now almost become dizzy through the perusal of a heavy and big mail, so excuse my hasty scrawl.

Ever affectionately yours,
Swami Vivekananda.

1894.56 — MOTHER

To Mrs. G. W. Hale:

Annisquam,
23 August, 1894.

DEAR MOTHER,

The photographs reached safely yesterday. I cannot tell exactly whether Harrison ought to give me more or not. They had sent only two to me at Fishkill — not the pose I ordered, though.

Narasimha has perhaps got his passage by this time. He will get it soon, whether his family gives him the money or not. I have written to my friends in Madras to look to it, and they write me they will.

I would be very glad if he becomes a Christian or Mohammedan or any religion that suits him; but I am afraid for some time to come none will suit our friend. Only if he becomes a Christian he will have a chance to marry again, even in India — the Christians there permitting it. I am so sorry to learn that it is the "bondage of heathen India" that, after all, was the cause of all this mischief. We learn as we live. So we were all this time ignorantly and blindly blaming our much suffering, persecuted, saintly friend Narasimha, while all the fault was really owing to the "bondage of heathen India"!!!!

But to give the devil his due, this heathen India has been supplying him with money to go on a spree again and again. And this time too "heathen India" will [take] or already has taken our "enlightened" and persecuted friend from out of his present scrape, and not "Christian America"!! Mrs. Smith's plan is not bad after all — to turn Narasimha into a missionary of Christ. But unfortunately for the world, many and many a time the flag of Christ has been entrusted to such hands. But I would beg to add that he will then be only a missionary of Smithian American Christianity, not Christ's. Arrant humbug! That thing to preach Lord Jesus!!! Is He in want of men to uphold His banner? Pooh! the very idea is revolting. Do good to India indeed! Thank your charity and call back your dog — as the tramp said. Keep such good workers for America. The Hindus will have a quarantine against all such [outcasting] to protect their society. I heartily advise Narasimha to become a Christian — I beg your pardon, a convert to Americanism — because I am sure such a jewel is unsaleable in poor India. He is welcome to anything that will fetch a price. I know the gentleman whom you name perfectly well, and you may give him any information about me you like. I do not care for sending scraps and getting a boom for me. And these friends from India bother me enough for newspaper nonsense. They are very devoted, faithful and holy friends. I have not much of these scraps now. After a long search I found a bit in a Boston Transcript. I send it over to you. This public life is such a botheration. I am nearly daft.

Where to fly? In India I have become horribly public — crowds will follow me and take my life out. I got an Indian letter from Landsberg. Every ounce of fame can only be bought at the cost of a pound of peace and holiness. I never thought of that before. I have become entirely disgusted with this blazoning. I am disgusted with myself. Lord will show me the way to peace and purity. Why, Mother, I confess to you: no man can live in an atmosphere of public life, even in religion, without the devil of competition now and then thrusting his head into the serenity of his heart. Those who are trained to preach a doctrine never feel it, for they never knew religion. But those that are after God, and not after the world, feel at once that every bit of name and fame is at the cost of their purity. It is so much gone from that ideal of perfect unselfishness, perfect disregard of gain or name or fame. Lord help me. Pray for me, Mother. I am very much disgusted with myself. Oh, why the world be so that one cannot do anything without putting himself to the front; why cannot one act hidden and unseen and unnoticed? The world has not gone one step beyond idolatry yet. They cannot act from ideas, they cannot be led by ideas. But they want the person, the man. And any man that wants to do something must pay the penalty — no hope. This nonsense of the world. Shiva, Shiva, Shiva.

By the by, I have got such a beautiful edition of Thomas à Kempis. How I love that old monk. He caught a wonderful glimpse of the "behind the veil" — few ever got such. My, that is religion. No humbug of the world. No shilly-shallying, tall talk, conjecture — I presume, I believe, I think. How I would like to go out of this piece of painted humbug they call the beautiful world with Thomas à Kempis — beyond, beyond, which can only be felt, never expressed.

That is religion. Mother, there is God. There all the saints, prophets and incarnations meet. Beyond the Babel of Bibles and Vedas, creeds and crafts, dupes and doctrines—where is all light, all love, where the miasma of this earth can never reach. Ah! who will take me thither? Do you sympathize with me, Mother? My soul is groaning now under the hundred sorts of bondage I am placing on it. Whose India? Who cares? Everything is His. What are we? Is He dead? Is He sleeping? He, without whose command a leaf does not fall, a heart does not beat, who is nearer to me than my own self. It is bosh and nonsense—to do good or do bad or do fuzz. We do nothing. We are not. The world is not. He is, He is. Only He is. None else is. He is.

Om, the one without a second. He in me, I in Him. I am like a bit of glass in an ocean of light. I am not, I am not. He is, He is, He is.

Om, the one without a second.

Yours ever affectionately,
Vivekananda.

1894.57—MOTHER

To Mrs. G. W. Hale:

Annisquam,
[Postmarked: August 28, 1894]

DEAR MOTHER,

I have been for three days at Magnolia. Magnolia is one of the most fashionable and beautiful seaside resorts of this part. I think the scenery is better than that of Annisquam. The rocks there are very beautiful, and the forests run down to the very edge of the water. There is a very beautiful pine forest. A lady of Chicago and her daughter, Mrs. Smith and Mrs. Sawyer, were the friends that invited me up there. They had also arranged a lecture for me, out of which I got $43. I met a good many Boston people—Mrs. Smith Junior, who said she knows Harriet, and Mrs. Smith the elder, [who] knows you well.

In Boston the other day I met a Unitarian clergyman who said he lives next to you in Chicago. I have unfortunately forgotten his name. Mrs. Smith is a very nice lady and treated me with all courtesy. Mrs. Bagley is kind as ever, and I will have to remain here a few days more, I am afraid. Prof. Wright and I are having a good time. Prof. Bradley of Evanston has gone home. If you ever meet him at Evanston, give him my best love and regards. He is really a spiritual man.

I do not find anything more to write.

Some unknown friend has sent me from New York a fountain pen. So I am writing with it to test it. It is working very smoothly and nicely as you can judge from the writing. Perhaps Narasimha's difficulties have been settled by this time, and "heathen India" has helped him out yet, I hope.

What is Father Pope doing? What the Babies are doing and where are they? What news of our Sam? Hope he is prospering. Kindly give him my best love. Where is Mother Temple now?

Well, after all, I could fill up two pages. Yes, there was a Miss Barn (?) who said she met me at your house. She is a young lady of Chicago.

Magnolia is a good bathing place and I had two baths in the sea. A large concourse of men and women go to bathe there every day — the most part men. And strange, women do not give up their coat of mail even while bathing. That is how these mailclad she-warriors of America have got the superiority over men.

Our Sanskrit poets lavish all the power of expression they have upon the soft body of women — the Sanskrit word for women is "Komala", the soft body; but the mailclad ones of this country are "armadillas", I think. You cannot imagine how ludicrous it appears to a foreigner who never saw it before. Shiva, Shiva.

Now Narasimha's Mrs. Smith does not torture you anymore with letters, I hope. Did I tell you I met your friend Mrs. H. O. Quarry at Swampscott? — she can swamp a house for all that, not to speak of a cott — and that I met there the woman that pulls by the nose Mr. Pullman? And I also heard there the best American singer, (Miss Emma Thursby.) they said — she sang beautifully; she sang "Bye Baby Bye". I am having a very, very good time all the time, Lord be praised.

I have written to India not to bother me with constant letters. Why, when I am travelling in India nobody writes to me. Why should they spend all their superfluous energy in scrawling letters to me in America? My whole life is to be that of a wanderer — here or there or anywhere. I am in no hurry. I had a foolish plan in my head unworthy of a Sannyasin. I have given it up now and mean to take life easy. No indecent hurry. Don't you see, Mother Church? You must always remember, Mother Church, that I cannot settle down even at the North Pole, that wander about I must — that is my vow, my religion. So India or North Pole or South Pole — don't care where. Last two years I have been travelling among races whose language even I cannot speak. "I have neither father nor mother nor brothers nor sisters nor friends nor foes, nor home nor country — a traveller in the way of eternity, asking no other help, seeking no other help but God."

Yours ever affectionately,
Vivekananda.

1894.58 — SISTER

To Miss Mary Hale:

C/O. Mrs. Bagley, Annisquam,
31st August, 1894.

DEAR SISTER,

The letter from the Madras people was published in yesterday's Boston Transcript. I hope to send you a copy. You may have seen it in some Chicago paper. I am sure there is some mail for me at Cook & Sons — I shall be here till Tuesday next at least, on which day I am going to lecture here in Annisquam.

Kindly inquire at Cook's for my mail and send it over at Annisquam.

I had no news of you for some time. I sent two pictures to Mother Church yesterday and hope you will like them. I am very anxious about the Indian mail. With love for all,

I am your ever affectionate brother,
Vivekananda.

PS — As I do not know where you are I could not send something else which I have to send over to you.

1894.59 — ALASINGA

U. S. A.,
31st August, 1894.

DEAR ALASINGA,

I just now saw an editorial on me about the circular from Madras in the Boston Transcript. Nothing has reached me yet. They will reach me soon if you have sent them already. So far you have done wonderfully, my boy. Do not mind what I write in some moments of nervousness. One gets nervous sometimes alone in a country 15,000 miles from home, having to fight every inch of ground with orthodox inimical Christians. You must take those into consideration, my brave boy, and work right along.

Perhaps you have heard from Bhattacharya that I received a beautiful letter from G. G. His address was scrawled in such a fashion as to become perfectly illegible to me. So I could not reply to him direct. But I have done all that he desired. I have sent over my photograph and written to the Raja of Mysore. Now I have sent a phonograph to Khetri Raja...

Now send always Indian newspapers about me to me over here. I want to read them in the papers themselves — do you know? Now lastly, you must write to me all about Mr. Charu Chandra who has been so kind to me. Give him my heartfelt thanks; but (between you and me) I unfortunately do not remember him. Would you give me particulars?

The Theosophists here now like me, but they are 650 in all!! There are the Christian Scientists. All of them like me. They are about a million. I work with both, but join none, and will with the Lord's grace would them both after the true fashion; for they are after all mumbling half realised truth. Narasimha, perhaps, by the time this reaches you, will get the money etc.

I have received a letter from Cat, but it requires a book to answer all his queries. So I send him my blessings through you and ask you to remind him that we agree to differ — and see the harmony of contrary points. So it does not matter what he believes in; he must act. Give my love to Balaji, G. G., Kidi, Doctor, and to all our friends and all the great and patriotic souls, who were brave and noble enough to sink their differences for their country's cause.

With a magazine or journal or organ — you become the Secretary thereof. You calculate the cost of starting the magazine and the work, how much the least is necessary to start it, and then write to me giving name and address of the Society, and I will send you money myself, and not only that, I will get others in America to subscribe annually to it liberally. So ask them of Calcutta to do the same. Give me Dharmapala's address. He is a great and good man. He will work wonderfully with us. Now organise a little society. You will have to take charge of the whole movement, not as a leader, but as a servant. Do you know, the least show of leading destroys everything by rousing jealousy?

Accede to everything. Only try to retain all of my friends together. Do you see? And work slowly up. Let G. G. and others, who have no immediate necessity for earning something, do as they are doing, i.e. casting the idea broadcast. G. G. is doing well at Mysore. That is the way. Mysore will be in time a great stronghold.

I am now going to write my mems in a book and next winter will go about this country organising societies here. This is a great field of work, and everything done here prepares England. So far you have done very well indeed, my brave boy — all strength shall be given to you.

I have now Rs. 9,000 with me, part of which I will send over to you for the organisation; and I will get many people to send money to you in Madras yearly, half-yearly, or monthly. You now start a Society and a journal and the necessary apparatus. This must be a secret amongst only a few — but at the same time try to collect funds from Mysore and elsewhere to build a temple in Madras which should have a library and some rooms for the office and the preachers who should be Sannyásins, and for Vairâgis (men of renunciation) who may chance to come. Thus we shall progress inch by inch. This is a great field for my work, and everything done here prepares the way for my coming work in England...

You know the greatest difficulty with me is to keep or even to touch money. It is disgusting and debasing. So you must organise a Society to take charge of the practical and pecuniary part of it. I have friends here who take care of all my monetary concerns. Do you see? It will be a wonderful relief to me to get rid of horrid money affairs. So the sooner you organise yourselves and you be ready as secretary and treasurer to enter into direct communication with my friends and sympathisers here, the better for you and me. Do that quickly, and write to me. Give the society a non-sectarian name... Do you write to my brethren at the Math to organise in a similar fashion... Great things are in store for you Alasinga. Or if you think proper, you get some of the big folks to be named as office-bearers of the Society, while you work in the real sense. Their name will be a great thing. If your duties are too severe and do not let you have any time, let G. G. do the business part, and by and by I hope to make you independent of your college work so that you may, without starving yourself and family, devote your whole soul to the work. So work, my boys, work! The rough part of the work has been smoothened and rounded; now it will roll on better and better every year. And if you can simply keep it going well until I come to India, the work will progress by leaps and bounds. Rejoice that you have done so much. When you feel gloomy, think what has been done within the last year. How, rising from nothing, we have the eyes of the world fixed upon us now. Not only India, but the world outside, is expecting great things of us. Missionaries or M — or foolish officials — none will be able to resist truth and love and sincerity. Are you sincere? unselfish even unto death? and loving? Then fear not, not even death. Onward, my lads! The whole world requires Light. It is expectant! India alone has that Light, not in magic, mummery, and charlatanism, but in the teaching of the glories of the spirit of real religion — of the highest spiritual truth. That is why the Lord has preserved the race through all its vicissitudes unto the present day. Now the time has come. Have faith that you are all, my brave lads, born to do great things! Let not the barks of puppies frighten you — no, not even the thunderbolts of heaven — but stand up and work!

Ever yours affectionately,
Vivekananda.

1894.60 — MOTHER

To Mrs. G. W. Hale:

[Gloucester, Massachusetts]
4 September, 1894.

DEAR MOTHER,

The bundle was the report of the meeting. Hope you will succeed in publishing some in the Chicago papers.

Here is a letter from Dewanji to you which will explain his sending a pamphlet to Mr. Hale The rugs are coming. When they come, take them in, even paying the duty if any. I will pay it to you afterwards. I have plenty of money, more than $150 in pocket. Will get more tonight. Here are some newspaper clippings, and an Indian Mirror I will send later on. Some have been sent to Mr. Barrows; don't hope he will give them publicity. Now for your Mrs. Bartlett.

I am in haste. [Will] write more with the clippings. Write to me always, kind Mother—I become very anxious when I do not hear from you. Write, whether I reply sharp or not.

Yours ever affectionately,
Vivekananda.

1894.61—MOTHER

To Mrs. G. W. Hale:

Annisquam,
5 September, 1894.

DEAR MOTHER,

The news of the arrival of the phonograph from Khetri has not come yet. But I am not anxious, because I just now got another letter from India wherein there is no mention of the photographs I sent, showing that parcels reach later than letters.

Herewith I send you an autograph letter of H.H. the Maharaja of Mysore, the chief Hindu king in India. You may see on the map [that] his territory occupies a very large portion of southern India.

I am very glad that he is slowly being gained over to my side. If he wills, he can set all my plans to work in five days. He has an income of $150 million dollars; think of that.

May Jagadamba [the Mother of the Universe] turn his mind towards the good work. He says he quite appreciates my good words—they were about my plans for educating the poor. Hope he will soon show it in material shape.

My love to all. Why the babies do not prattle?

Your son,
Vivekananda.

1894.62—MR. BHATTACHARYA[1]

U.S.A.
5th September, 1894.

DEAR MR. BHATTACHARYA, (Mr. Manmatha Nath Bhattacharya)

I was much pleased to read your affectionate letter. I shall make inquiries about the weaving machine as soon as I can, and let you know. Now I am resting at Annisquam, a village on the seacoast; soon I shall go to the city and attend to the matter of the machine. These seaside places are filled with people during the sum-

1 Translated from Bengali.

mer; some come to bathe in the sea, some to take rest, and some to catch husbands.

There is a strong sense of decorum in this country.

You have to keep yourself always covered from neck to foot in the presence of women. You cannot so much as mention the normal functions of the body: nobody knows when anyone goes to the toilet—one has to live so circumspectly. In this country, you can blow your nose a thousand times into your handkerchief—there is no harm in that; but it is highly uncivilised to belch. Women sometimes are not embarrassed to expose their bodies above the waist—you must have seen the kind of low-cut gown they wear—but they say that to go bare-foot is as bad as being naked. Just as we always dwell on the soul, so they take care of the body, and there is no end to the cleaning and embellishing of it. One who fails to do this has no place in society.

Our method of cooking with cow-dung fuel and eating on the floor they consider eating like pigs: they say that the Hindus have no sense of disgust and that, like pigs, they eat cow-dung. The word "cow-dung" is taboo in English. On the other hand, numbers of people will drink water with the same glass without thinking of washing it, and they rarely observe the rule that things must be washed before cooking. But should the clothes of the cook be a little soiled, they will throw her out. The table-ware is all spick and span. They are the richest people on earth; their enjoyments and luxuries beggar description.

In Rajputana they imitate the Mohammedans in their mode of dining, which is, on the whole, good. They sit on a low seat and place their plate of rice on a low table. This is much better than spreading a banana leaf on the earthen floor plastered with cow-dung and filth. And how disastrous if the leaf gets torn! The Hindus did not know much about clothes or food. Moreover, whatever Hindu civilisation there was existed in the Punjab and the north-west provinces...

Our women lose caste if they put on shoes, but the Rajput women lose their caste if they don't put on shoes! Says Manu: "One shall always wear shoes". There is no denying that people should have a decent enough standard of living. I say they should be neat and clean even though not luxurious... I say, why do we have to be Englishmen? It is enough for the present if we imitate our brothers of the western provinces. If group after group of Indians travel all over the world and back for some years, the face of India will be changed within twenty years by that alone; nothing else need be done. But how will anything happen if the people of one village do not visit the next? However, everything will take place by and by. By and by, the stubborn Bengali boys will awaken the country. But Manmatha Babu, you will have to stop this shameful business of marrying off nine-year-old girls. That is the root of all sins. It is a very great sin, my boy. Consider further what a terrible thing it was that when the government wanted to pass a law stopping early marriage, our worthless people raised a tremendous howl! If we don't stop it ourselves, the government will naturally intervene, and that is just what it wants to do. All the world cries fie upon us. You remain shut up in your homes, but the people outside spit upon you. How far can I quarrel with them? What a horror—even a father and mother allow their ten-year-old daughter to be given in marriage to a full-grown fat husband! O Lord, is there any punishment unless there has been a sin? It is all the fruit of Karma. If ours were not a terribly sinful nation, then why should it have been booted and beaten for seven hundred years?

Now, just as in our country the parents suffer a lot to have their daughter married, here in the same way the girls suffer—the parents only a little—it is the job of the girls to capture husbands. I am now closely associated with them in all their affairs; I am, as it were, a woman amongst women. Therefore, I have seen, and am seeing, all their play. To give dinners, to dance, to go to musical parties, go to the watering places—all that is all right. But all the while the young women are scheming within themselves how to capture husbands. They hang round the boys. The boys, on the other hand, are so cautious that, though they mingle with the girls and flirt with them all the time, when it is time to surrender they run away. The boys place the girls above themselves; they show them respect and slave for them; but the moment the girls stretch their hands to catch them, they run away beyond their reach. After many efforts of this kind, a girl succeeds in capturing a boy. If the girl has money, then many a boy dances attendance upon her, but the poor have great difficulty. If a poor girl is exceedingly beautiful, she can marry quickly; otherwise, she has to wait all her life. Just as in our country, so here, one marriage in a thousand takes place through love and courtship; the rest are based on money. After that, quarrel, and then, 'Get out!'—divorce. We do not have this; the only way out is to hang oneself. It is the same in all countries. Only, here the girls take matters into their own hands; and in our country, we get the help of the parents to give their married life a decent appearance. The result is the same in either case.

Nowadays, however, American girls don't want to marry. During the Civil War a large number of men were killed and women began to do all kinds of work. Since then, they have not wanted to give up the rights they have acquired. They earn their own living, and therefore they say, "There is no use in marrying. If we truly fall in love, then we shall marry; otherwise, we shall earn and meet our own expenses". Even if the father is a millionaire, the son has to earn enough before he marries. One may not marry depending on an allowance from the father. The girls also want the same thing now. When a son marries he becomes like a stranger to his own family, but when a girl marries she brings her husband, as it were, into her parents' home. Men will visit their wives' parents ten times, but rarely go to their own parents. Yet they are very much afraid of having their mothers-in-law on their neck.

In this country, there are rivers of wealth and waves of beauty, and an abundance of knowledge everywhere. The country is very healthy; they know how to enjoy this earth... When princes of Europe become poor they come to marry here. The average American doesn't like this; but some rich, beautiful women fall for the titles. Yet it is very difficult for American women to live in Europe. The husbands of this country are slaves of their wives; but the European wives are slaves to their husbands—this the American women don't like. In everything, the men here have to say, 'Yes dear'; otherwise the wives lose face before people.

The women in America are very sentimental and have a mania for romance. I am, however, a strange sort of animal who hasn't any romantic feeling, and therefore they could not sustain any such feeling toward me and they show me great respect. I make all of them call me "father" or "brother". I don't allow them to come near me with any other feeling, and gradually they have all been straightened out...

The ministers in this country...are eager to throw sinners into hell. A few of them are very good, however...I have a great reputation among the women in this country. I have not as yet seen a single unchaste girl among the unmarried. It is either a widow or a married woman who turn unchaste. The unmarried girls are exceedingly good, because their future is bright...

Those emaciated Western women, looking like old dried-up fruit, whom you see in India, are English, and the English are an ugly race amongst the Europeans. In America, the best blood strains of Europe have been blended, and therefore, the American women are very beautiful. And how they take care of their beauty! Can a woman retain her beauty if she gives birth to children...every hour from her tenth year on? Damn nonsense! What a terrible sin! Even the most beautiful woman of our country will look like a black owl here. Yet it must be admitted that the women of the Punjab have very well-drawn features. Many of the American women are very well educated and put many a learned professor to shame; nor do they care for anyone's opinion. And as regards their virtues: what kindness, what noble thought and action! Just think, if a man of this country were to visit India, nobody would even touch him; yet here I am allowed to do as I please in the houses of the best families — like their own son! I am like a child; their women shop for me, run errands for me. For example: I have just written to a girl for information about the machine, which she will gather carefully and send to me. Again, a phonograph was sent to the Maharaj of Khetri: the girls managed the whole affair very well. Lord! Lord! It is the difference between heaven and hell! "They are the goddess Lakshmi in beauty and the goddess Saraswati in talents and accomplishments." This cannot be achieved through the study of books. I say, can you send out some men and women to see the world? Only then will the country wake up — not through the reading of books. The men here are very clever in earning wealth. Where others do not see even dust, there they see gold. Whoever will leave India and visit another country will earn great merit.

Keeping aloof from the community of nations is the only cause for the downfall of India. Since the English came, they have been forcing you back into communion with other nations, and you are visibly rising again. Everyone that comes out of the country confers a benefit on the whole nation; for it is by doing that alone that your horizon will expand. And as women cannot avail themselves of this advantage, they have made almost no progress in India. There is no station of rest; either you progress upwards or you go back and die out. The only sign of life is going outward and forward and expansion. Contraction is death. Why should you do good to others? Because that is the only condition of life; thereby you expand beyond your little self; you live and grow. All narrowness, all contraction, all selfishness is simply slow suicide, and when a nation commits the fatal mistake of contracting itself and of thus cutting off all expansion and life, it must die. Women similarly must go forward or become idiots and soulless tools in the hands of their tyrannical lords. The children are the result of the combination of the tyrant and the idiot, and they are slaves. And this is the whole history of modern India. Oh, who would break this horrible crystallisation of death? Lord help us! (This paragraph was written in English.)

Gradually all this will come about: "One should cross a road slowly and cautiously; one should patch a quilt carefully and cautiously; so should one be slow and cautious in crossing a mountain".

The papers have arrived duly and in good shape; there has not been any difficulty about that. The enemy has been silenced. Consider this: They have allowed me, an unknown young man, to live among their grown-up young daughters, and when my own countryman, Mazoomdar, says I am a rogue, they don't pay any attention! How noble they are, and how kind! I shall not be able to repay this debt even in a hundred lives, I am like a foster son to the American women; they are really my mother. If they don't flourish in every way, who would?

A while back several hundred intellectual men and women were gathered in a place called Greenacre, and I was there for nearly two months. Every day I would sit in our Hindu fashion under a tree, and my followers and disciples would sit on the grass all around me. Every morning I would instruct them, and how earnest they were!

The whole country now knows me. The ministers are very angry; but, naturally, not all of them. There are many followers of mine amongst the learned ministers of this country. The ignorant and the stubborn amongst them don't understand anything but only make trouble, and thereby they only hurt themselves. But abusing me, Mazoomdar has lost three-fourths of what little popularity he had in this country. I have been adopted by them. When anyone abuses me he is condemned everywhere by the women.

I cannot say when I shall return to India, possibly next winter. There I shall have to wander, and here also I do the same.

There is nothing more to add. Please don't make this letter public. You understand, I have to be careful about every word I say — I am now a public man. Everybody is watching, particularly the clergy.

Yours faithfully,
Vivekananda.

1894.63 — MOTHER

To Mrs. G. W. Hale:

Hotel Bellevue, European Plan,
Beacon Street, Boston,
12 September, 1894.

DEAR MOTHER,

I hope you will immediately send me over the little scrap from the Indian Mirror about my Detroit lectures which I sent you.

Yours,
Vivekananda.

1894.64 — MOTHER

To Mrs. G. W. Hale:

Hotel Bellevue, Beacon Street, Boston,
13 September, 1894.

DEAR MOTHER,

Your very kind note came just now. I was suffering for the last few days from cold and fever. I am all right now. I am glad all the papers reached you safe. The newspaper clippings are with Mrs. Bagley; only a copy has been sent over to you. By the by, Mrs. Bagley becomes jealous if I send away everything to you. That is between you and me. The Indian Mirror is with Prof. Wright, and he will send it over to you. There is yet no news of the phonograph. Wait one week more and then we will enquire. If you see a letter with the Khetri stamp, then surely the news is coming. I do not smoke one third as much as I used to when Father Pope's eternal box was ready and open day and night. Haridasbhai is to be addressed as Shri only. On the envelope, Dewan Bahadoor ought to be written, as that is a title. Perhaps the note from the Maharaja of Mysore has reached you by this time.

I will remain a few days yet in Boston and the vicinity. The bank book is in the bank. We did not take it out, but the cheque book is with me. I am going to write out my thoughts on religion; in that, no missionaries have any place. I am going to lecture in New York in autumn, but I like teaching small circles better, and there will be enough of that in Boston.

The rugs I wanted to be sent from India; and they will come from Punjab, where the best rugs are made.

I had a beautiful letter from Sister Mary. (Mary Hale.)

Narasimha must have got money or passage by this time, and his people have taken care to send him Thomas Cook's passage from place to place. I think he is gone now.

I do not think the Lord will allow his servant to be inflated with vanity at the appreciation of his countrymen. I am glad that they appreciate me — not for my sake, but that I am firmly persuaded that a man is never improved by abuse but by praise, and so with nations. Think how much of abuse has been quite unnecessarily hurled at the head of my devoted, poor country, and for what? They never injured the Christians or their religion or their preachers. They have always been friendly to all. So you see, Mother, every good word a foreign nation says to them has such an amount of power for good in India. The American appreciation of my humble work here has really done a good deal of benefit to them. Send a good word, a good thought — at least to the down-trodden, vilified, poor millions of India instead of abusing them day and night. That is what I beg of every nation. Help them if you can; if you cannot, at least cease from abusing them.

I did not see any impropriety in the bathing places at the seashore, but only vanity in some: in those that went into water with their corsets on, that was all.

I have not got any copy of the Inter-Ocean yet. (A leading Chicago newspaper.)

With my love to Father Pope, babies, and to you, I remain

Your obedient son,
Vivekananda.

1894.65 — LEON

To Mr. Leon Landsberg:

Hotel Bellevue, Boston,
13th September, 1894.

DEAR LEON,

Forgive me, but I have the right, as your Guru, to advise you, and I insist that you buy some clothes for yourself, as the want of them stands in the way of your doing anything in this country. Once you have a start, you may dress in whatever way you like. People do not object.

You need not thank me, for this is only a duty. According to Hindu law, if a Guru dies, his disciple is his heir, and not even his son — supposing him to have had one before becoming a Sannyasin. This is, you see, an actual spiritual relationship, and none of your Yankee "tutor" business!

With all blessings and prayers for your success,

Yours,
Vivekananda.

1894.66 — SISTER

To Miss Mary Hale:

Hotel Bellevue, Beacon St., Boston,
13th September, 1894.

DEAR SISTER,

Your kind note reached me this morning. I have been in this hotel for about a week. I will remain in Boston some time yet. I have plenty of gowns already, in fact, more than I can carry with ease. When I had that drenching in Annisquam, I had on that beautiful black suit you appreciate so much, and I do not think it can be damaged any way; it also has been penetrated with my deep meditations on the Absolute. I am very glad that you enjoyed the summer so well. As for me, I am vagabondising. I was very much amused the other day at reading Abe Hue's description of the vagabond lamas of Tibet — a true picture of our fraternity. He says they are queer people. They come when they will, sit at everybody's table, invitation or no invitation, live where they will, and go where they will. There is not a mountain they have not climbed, not a river they have not crossed, not a nation they do not know, not a language they do not talk. He thinks that God must have put into them a part of that energy which makes the planets go round and round eternally. Today this vagabond lama was seized with a desire of going right along scribbling, and so I walked down and entering a store bought all sorts of writing material and a beautiful portfolio which shuts with a clasp and has even a little wooden inkstand. So far it promises well. Hope it will continue. Last month I had mail enough from India and am greatly delighted with my countrymen at their generous appreciation of my work. Good enough for them. I cannot find anything more to write. Prof. Wright, his wife, and children were as good as ever. Words cannot express my gratitude to them.

Everything so far is not going bad with me except that I had a bad cold. Now I think the fellow is gone. This time I tried Christian Science for insomnia and really found it worked very well. Wishing you all happiness,

I remain, ever your affectionate brother,
Vivekananda.

PS — Kindly tell Mother that I do not want any coat now.

1894.67 — MOTHER SARA[1]

Salutations to Bhagavan Shri Ramakrishna!

Hotel Belle Vue, Beacon Street, Boston,
19th September, '94.

DEAR MOTHER SARA, (Mrs. Ole Bull)

I did not forget you at all. You do not think I will be ever as ungrateful as that! You did not give me your address, still I have been getting news about you from Landsberg through Miss Phillips. Perhaps you have seen the memorial and address sent to me from Madras. I sent some to be sent to you at Landsberg's.

A Hindu son never lends to his mother, but the mother has every right over the son and so the son in the mother. I am very much offended at your offering to repay me the nasty few dollars. I can never repay my debts to you.

I am at present lecturing in several places in Boston. What I want is to get a place where I can sit down and write down my thoughts. I have had enough of speaking; now I want to write. I think I will have to go to New York for it. Mrs. Guernsey was so kind to me, and she is ever willing to help me. I think I will go to her and sit down and write my book.

Yours ever affectionately,
Vivekananda.

PS — Kindly write me whether the Guernseys have returned to town or are still in Fishkill. — V.

1894.68 — MOTHER

To Mrs. G. W. Hale:

Hotel Bellevue, Beacon S,
Treet , Boston,
19 September, 1894.

DEAR MOTHER,

The huge packet received. It was a few pamphlets sent over to me from my monastery in Calcutta. No news at all about the phonograph. I think it is high time we make them inquire into it.

The two volumes of Todd's [Tod's] history of Rajasthan have been presented to me by Mrs. Potter Palmer. I have asked her to send it over to your care. The babies will like reading it very much, and after they finish I will send it over with my Sanskrit books to Calcutta.

I did not ask you to send me the typewritten news clippings at all, but a little slip

---
1 Translated from Bengali.

I sent over some time ago from the Indian Mirror. Perhaps it did not reach you at all. You need not send the typewritten thing at all.

I do not require any clothes here; there are plenty of them. I am taking good care of my cuffs and collars, etc.

I have more clothes than are necessary. Very soon I will have to disburse myself of half of them at least.

I will write to you before I go to India. I am not flying off without giving you due intimation.

Yours,
Vivekananda.

PS — My love to Babies and Father Pope.

1894.69 — ALASINGA

U. S. A,
21st September, 1894.

DEAR ALASINGA,

... I have been continuously travelling from place to place and working incessantly, giving lectures, holding classes, etc.

I have not been able to write yet for my proposed book. Perhaps I may be able to take it in hand later on. I have made some nice friends here amongst the liberal people, and a few amongst the orthodox. I hope to return soon to India — I have had enough of this country and especially as too much work is making me nervous. The giving of too many public lectures and constant hurry have brought on this nervousness. I do not care for this busy, meaningless, money-making life. So you see, I will soon return. Of course, there is a growing section with whom I am very popular, and who will like to have me here all the time. But I think I have had enough of newspaper blazoning and humbugging of a public life. I do not care the least for it ...

There is no hope for money for our project here. It is useless to hope. No large number of men in any country do good out of mere sympathy. The few who really give money in the Christian lands often do so through priestcraft and fear of hell. So it is as in our Bengali proverb, "Kill a cow and make a pair of shoes out of the leather and give them in charity to a Brahmana". So it is here, and so everywhere; and then, the Westerners are miserly in comparison to our race. I sincerely believe that the Asians are the most charitable race in the world, only they are very poor.

I am going to live for a few months in New York. That city is the head, hand, and purse of the country. Of course, Boston is called the Brahmanical city, and here in America there are hundreds of thousands that sympathise with me ... The New York people are very open. I will see what can be done there, as I have some very influential friends. After all, I am getting disgusted with this lecturing business. It will take a long time for the Westerners to understand the higher spirituality, Everything is £. s. d. to them. If a religion brings them money or health or beauty or long life, they will all flock to it, otherwise not...

Give to Balaji, G. G., and all of our friends my best love.

Yours with everlasting love,
Vivekananda.

1894.70 — KIDI

U. S. A.,
21st September, 1894.

DEAR KIDI,

I am very sorry to hear your determination of giving up the world so soon. The fruit falls from the tree when it gets ripe. So wait for the time to come. Do not hurry. Moreover, no one has the right to make others miserable by his foolish acts. Wait, have patience, everything will come right in time.

Yours with blessings,
Vivekananda.

1894.71 — MOTHER

To Mrs. G. W. Hale:

Hotel Bellevue, Beacon Street, Boston,
24 September, 1894.

DEAR MOTHER,

I have not heard from you a long while. I am still in Boston and will be a few days more.

I am afraid the phonograph has not reached India at all, or something is the matter with it. Kindly ask Mr. — to inquire. The receipt is with you on which they will enquire.

Ever affectionately yours,
Vivekananda.

1894.72 — BROTHER DISCIPLES[1]

New York,
25th September, 1894.

MY DEAR __, (Meant for his brother-disciples)

Glad to receive some letters from you. It gives me great pleasure to learn that Shashi and others are making a stir. We must create a stir, nothing short of this will do. You will be throwing the whole world into convulsion. Victory to the Guru! You know, "श्रेयांसि बहुविघ्नानि—Great undertakings are always fraught with many obstacles." It is these obstacles which knock and shape great characters... Is it in the power of missionaries and people of that sort to withstand this shock?... Should a fool succeed where scholars have failed? It is no go, my boy, set your mind at ease about that. In every attempt there will be one set of men who will applaud, and another who will pick holes. Go on doing your own work, what need have you to reply to any party? "सत्यमेत्र जयते नानृतं सत्येन पन्था वितितो देवयानः—Truth alone triumphs, not falsehood. Through Truth lies Devayâna, the path of gods" (Mundaka, III. i. 6). Everything will come about by degrees.

Here in summer they go to the seaside: I also did the same. They have got almost a mania for boating and yachting. The yacht is a kind of light vessel which everyone, young and old, who has the means, possesses. They set sail in them every day to the sea, and return home, to eat and drink and dance—while music continues day and night. Pianos render it a botheration to stay indoors!

I shall now tell you something of the Hales to whose address you direct my letters. He and his wife are an old couple, having two daughters, two nieces, and a son. The son lives abroad where he earns a living. The daughters live at home. In this country, relationship is through the girls. The son marries and no longer belongs to the family, but the daughter's husband pays frequent visits to his father-in-law's house. They say,

"Son is son till he gets a wife;
The daughter is daughter all her life."

All the four are young and not yet married. Marriage is a very troublesome business here. In the first place, one must have a husband after one's heart. Secondly, he must be a moneyed man... They will probably live unmarried; besides, they are now full of renunciation through my contact and are busy with thoughts of Brahman!

The two daughters arc blondes, that is, have golden hair, while the two nieces are brunettes, that is, of dark hair. They know all sorts of occupations. The nieces are not so rich, they conduct a kindergarten school; but the daughters do not earn. Many girls of this country earn their living. Nobody depends upon others. Even millionaires' sons earn their living; but they marry and have separate establishments of their own. The daughters call me brother; and I address their mother as

---

1 Translated from Bengali.

mother. All my things are at their place; and they look after them, wherever I may go. Here the boys go in search of a living while quite young; and the girls are educated in the universities. So you will find that in a meeting there will be ninety-nine per cent of girls. The boys are nowhere in comparison with them.

There are a good many spiritualists in this country. The medium is one who induces the spirit. He goes behind a screen; and out of this come ghosts of all sizes and all colours. I have witnessed some cases; but they seemed to be a hoax. I shall test some more before I come to a final conclusion. Many of the spiritualists respect me.

Next comes Christian Science. They form the most influential party, nowadays, figuring everywhere. They are spreading by leaps and bounds, and causing heartburn to the orthodox. They are Vedantins; I mean, they have picked up a few doctrines of the Advaita and grafted them upon the Bible. And they cure diseases by proclaiming "So'ham So'ham" — "I am He! I am He!" — through strength of mind. They all admire me highly.

Nowadays the orthodox section of this country are crying for help. "Devil worship"[2] is but a thing of the past. They are mortally afraid of me and exclaim, "What a pest? Thousands of men and women follow him! He is going to root out orthodoxy!" Well, the torch has been applied and the conflagration that has set in through the grace of the Guru will not be put out. In course of time the bigots will have their breath knocked out of them…

The Theosophists have not much power. But they, too, are dead set against the orthodox section.

The Christian Science is exactly like our Kartâbhajâ[3] sect: Say, "I have no disease", and you are whole; and say, "I am He" — "So'ham" — and you are quits — be at large. This is a thoroughly materialistic country. The people of this Christian land will recognise religion if only you can cure diseases, work miracles, and open up avenues to money; and they understand little of anything else. But there are honourable exceptions…

People here have found a new type of man in me. Even the orthodox are at their wit's end. And people are now looking up to me with an eye of reverence. Is there a greater strength than that of Brahmacharya — purity, my boy?

I am now busy writing a reply to the Madras Address, which was published in all the newspapers here and created a sensation. If it be cheap, I shall send it in print, but if dear, I shall send a type-written copy. To you also I shall send a copy; have it published in the Indian Mirror. The unmarried girls of this country are very good and have a good deal of self-respect… These (the people) are come of Virochana's[4]

---

2. The Orthodox Christians brand Hindus and people of other religions with this name and look upon them with scorn.

3. An offshoot of degenerate Vaishnavism, calling God "Kartâ" or Master, and noted for efficiency in faith-cure.

4. The King of the Asuras and son of the saintly Prahlâda. He went to Brahma for Self-knowledge, but misunderstanding His teaching turned a materialist. (Chhândogya Upa., VIII).

race. To them ministering to the body is a great thing: they would trim and polish and give their whole attention to that. A thousand instruments for paring nails, ten thousand for hair-cutting, and who can count the varieties of dress and toilet and perfumery?... They are good-natured, kind, and truthful. All is right with them, but that enjoyment is their God. It is a country where money flows like a river, with beauty as its ripple and learning its waves, and which rolls in luxury.

कांक्षन्तः कर्मणां सिद्धिं यजन्त इह देवताः।
क्षिप्रं हि मानुषे लोके सिद्धिर्भवति कर्मजा॥

—"Longing for success in action, in this world, (men) worship the deities. For success is quickly attained through action in this world of Man." (Gita, IV.12)

Here you have a wonderful manifestation of grit and power—what strength, what practicality, and what manhood! Horses huge as elephants are drawing carriages that are as big as houses. You may take this as a specimen of the gigantic proportions in other things also. Here is a manifestation of tremendous energy... They look with veneration upon women, who play a most prominent part in their lives. Here this form of worship has attained its perfection—that is the long and the short of it. But to come to the point. Well, I am almost at my wit's end to see the women of this country! They take me to the shops and everywhere, Is if I were a child. They do all sorts of work—I cannot do even a sixteenth part of what they do. They are like Lakshmi (the Goddess of Fortune) in beauty, and like Sarasvati (the Goddess of Learning) in virtues—they are the Divine Mother incarnate and worshipping them, one verily attains perfection in everything. Great God! Are we to be counted among men? If I can raise a thousand such Madonnas, Incarnations of the Divine Mother, in our country before I die, I shall die in peace. Then only will your countrymen become worthy of their name...

I am really struck with wonder to see the women here. How gracious the Divine Mother is on them! Most wonderful women, these! They are about to corner the men, who have been nearly worsted in the competition. It is all through Thy grace, O Mother!... I shall not rest till I root out this distinction of sex. Is there any sex-distinction in the Atman (Self)? Out with the differentiation between man and woman—all is Atman! Give up the identification with the body, and stand up! Say, "Asti, Asti"—"Everything is!"—cherish positive thoughts. By dwelling too much upon "Nâsti, Nâsti"—"It is not! It is not!" (negativism), the whole country is going to ruin! "So'ham, So'ham, Shivo'ham"—"I am He! I am He! I am Shiva!" What a botheration! In every soul is infinite strength; and should you turn yourselves into cats and dogs by harbouring negative thoughts? Who dares to preach negativism? Whom do you call weak and powerless? "Shivo'ham, Shivo'ham"—"I am Shiva! I am Shiva!" I feel as if a thunderbolt strikes me on the head when I hear people dwell on negative thoughts. That sort of self-depreciating attitude is another name for disease—do you call that humility? It is vanity in disguise! "न लिङ्गम् धर्मकारणं, समता सर्वभूतेषु एतन्मुक्तस्य लक्षणम्—The external badge does not confer spirituality. It is same-sightedness to all beings which is the test of a liberated soul." "अस्ति अस्ति" (It is, It is), "सोऽहं सोऽहं", "चिदानन्दरूपः शिवोऽहं शिवोऽहं"—"I am

He!", "I am Shiva, of the essence of Knowledge and Bliss!" "निर्गच्छति जगज्जालात् पञ्जरादिव केशरी—He frees himself from the meshes of this world as a lion from its cage!" "नायमात्मा बलहीनेन लभ्यः—This Atman is not accessible to the weak"... Hurl yourselves on the world like an avalanche—let the world crack in twain under your weight! Hara! Hara! Mahâdeva! उद्धरेदात्मनात्मानम्—One must save the self by one's own self"—by personal prowess.

... Will such a day come when this life will go for the sake of other's good? The world is not a child's play—and great men are those who build highways for others with their heart's blood. This has been taking place through eternity, that one builds a bridge by laying down his own body and thousands of others cross the river through its help. "एवमस्तु, एवमस्तु, शिवोऽहं शिवोऽहं—Be it so! Be it so! I am Shiva! I am Shiva!"

It is welcome news that Madras is in a stir.

Were you not going to start a paper or something of that sort, what about that? We must mix with all, and alienate none. All the powers of good against all the powers of evil—this is what we want. Do not insist upon everybody's believing in our Guru... You shall have to edit a magazine, half Bengali and half Hindi—and if possible, another in English... It won't do to be roaming aimlessly. Wherever you go, you must start a permanent preaching centre. Then only will people begin to change. I am writing a book. As soon as it is finished, I run for home!... Always remember that Shri Ramakrishna came for the good of the world—not for name or fame. Spread only what he came to teach. Never mind his flame—it will spread of itself. Directly you insist on everybody's accepting your Guru, you will be creating a sect, and everything will fall to the ground—so beware! Have a kind word for all—it spoils work to show temper. Let people say whatever they like, stick to your own convictions, and rest assured, the world will be at your feet. They say, "Have faith in this fellow or that fellow", but I say, "Have faith in yourself first", that's the way. Have faith in yourself—all power is in you—be conscious and bring it out. Say, "I can do everything." "Even the poison of a snake is powerless if you can firmly deny it." Beware! No saying "nay", no negative thoughts! Say, "Yea, Yea," "So'ham, So'ham"—"I am He! I am He!"

किंनाम रोदिषि सखे त्वयि सर्वशक्तिरामन्त्रयस्व भगवन् भगदं स्वरूपम्।
त्रैलोक्यमेतदखिलं तव पादमूले आत्मैव हि प्रभवते न जडः कदाचित्॥

—"What makes you weep, my friend? In you is all power. Summon up your all-powerful nature, O mighty one, and this whole universe will lie at your feet. It is the Self alone that predominates, and not matter."

To work, with undaunted energy! What fear! Who is powerful enough to thwart you!" कूर्मस्तारकचर्वणं त्रिभुवनमुत्पाटयामो बलात् , किं भो न विजानास्यस्मान् रामकृष्णदासा वयम्—We shall crush the stars to atoms, and unhinge the universe. Don't you know who we are? We are the servants of Shri Ramakrishna." Fear?

Whom to fear, forsooth?

कृपीणाः स्म दीनाः सकरुणा जल्पन्ति मूढा जना

नास्तिकियन्त्ववदिन्तु अहह देहात्मवादातुराः।
प्राताः स्म वीरा गतभया अभयं प्रतिष्ठां यदा
अस्तिकियन्त्ववदिन्तु वनिमः रामकृष्णदासा वयम्॥
पीत्वा पीत्वा परममृतं वीतसंसाररागाः
हित्वा हित्वा सकलकलहप्रापणीं स्वार्थसिद्धिम् ।
ध्यात्वा ध्यात्वा गुरुवरपदं सर्वकल्याणरूपम्
नत्वा नत्वा सकलभुवनं पातुमामन्त्रयामः॥
प्राप्तं यद्वै त्वनादिनिधनं वेदोदधिं मथित्वा
दत्तं यस्य प्रकरणे हरिहिरब्रह्मादिदेर्बलम्।
पूर्णं यत्तु प्राणसारैर्भौमनारायणानां
रामकृष्णास्तनुं धत्ते तत्पूर्णपात्रमिदं भोः ॥

—"It is those foolish people who identify themselves with their bodies, that piteously cry, 'We are weak, we are low.' All this is atheism. Now that we have attained the state beyond fear, we shall have no more fear and become heroes. This indeed is theism which we, the servants of Shri Ramakrishna, will choose.

"Giving up the attachment for the world and drinking constantly the supreme nectar of immortality, for ever discarding that self-seeking spirit which is the mother of all dissension, and ever meditating on the blessed feet of our Guru which are the embodiment of all well-being, with repeated salutations we invite the whole world to participate in drinking the nectar.

"That nectar which has been obtained by churning the infinite ocean of the Vedas, into which Brahmâ, Vishnu, Shiva, and the other gods have poured their strength, which is charged with the life-essence of the Avataras—Gods Incarnate on earth—Shri Ramakrishna holds that nectar in his person, in its fullest measure!"

We must work among the English educated young men. "त्यागेनेके अमृतत्वमानशुः—Through renunciation alone some (rare ones) attained immortality." Renunciation!—Renunciation!—you must preach this above everything else. There will be no spiritual strength unless one renounces the world…

Why are Baburam and Yogen suffering so much? It is owing to their negative, their self-abasing spirit. Tell them to brush aside their illness by mental strength, and in an hour it will disappear! I the Atman smitten with disease! Off with it! Tell them to meditate for an hour at a stretch, "I am the Atman, how can I be affected by disease!"—and everything will vanish. Think all of you that you are the infinitely powerful Atman, and see what strength comes out… Self-depreciation! What is it for? I am the child of the Infinite, the all-powerful Divine Mother. What means disease, or fear, or want to me? Stamp out the negative spirit as if it were a pestilence, and it will conduce to your welfare in every way. No negative, all positive, affirmative. I am, God is, everything is in me. I will manifest health, purity, knowledge, whatever I want. Well, these foreign people could grasp my teachings, and you are suffering from illness owing to your negative spirit! Who says you are ill—what is disease to you? Brush it aside! वीर्यमसि वीर्य मयि धेहि, बलमसि बल मयि धेहि, ओजोऽसि ओजो मयि धेहि, सहोऽसि सहो मयि धेहि—Thou art Energy, impart energy unto me. Thou art Strength, impart strength unto me. Thou art Spirituality, impart spirituality unto me. Thou art Fortitude, impart fortitude unto me!" The ceremony of steadying the seat (Âsana-pratishthâ) that you perform every day when you sit down to worship the Lord — "आत्मानमच्छिद्रं भावयेत्—One must think of oneself as strong and invulnerable," and so forth — what does it all mean? Say, "Everything is in me, and I can manifest it at will." Repeat to yourself that such and such are Atman, that they are infinite, and how can they have any disease? Repeat this an hour or so, on a few successive days, and all disease and trouble will vanish into nought.

Yours ever,
Vivekananda.

1894.73 — MRS. BULL

Boston,
26th Sept., 1894.

DEAR MRS. BULL,

I have received both of your kind notes. I will have to go back to Melrose on Saturday and remain there till Monday. On Tuesday I will come over to your place. But I have forgotten the exact location. If you kindly write me that, I cannot express my gratitude for your kindness. For that is exactly what I wanted, a quiet place to write. Of course, much less space will suffice me than what you have kindly proposed to put at my disposal, I can bundle myself up anywhere and feel quite comfortable.

Yours very sincerely,
Vivekananda.

1894.74 — SISTER

Boston,
26th Sept, 1894.

DEAR SISTER[1],

Your letter with the India mail just to hand. A quantity of newspaper clippings were sent over to me from India. I send them back for your perusal and safe keeping.

I am busy writing letters to India last few days. I will remain a few days more in Boston.

With my love and blessings,

Yours ever affly.,
Vivekananda.

---

1. Isabelle Mckindley.

1894.75 — ALASINGA

U. S. A.
27th September, 1894.

DEAR ALASINGA,

... One thing I find in the books of my speeches and sayings published in Calcutta. Some of them are printed in such a way as to savour of political views; whereas I am no politician or political agitator. I care only for the Spirit — when that is right everything will be righted by itself... So you must warn the Calcutta people that no political significance be ever attached falsely to any of my writings or sayings. What nonsense I... I heard that Rev. Kali Charan Banerji in a lecture to Christian missionaries said that I was a political delegate. If it was said publicly, then publicly ask the Babu for me to write to any of the Calcutta papers and prove it, or else take back his foolish assertion. This is their trick! I have said a few harsh words in honest criticism of Christian governments in general, but that does not mean that I care for, or have any connection with politics or that sort of thing. Those who think it very grand to print extracts from those lectures and want to prove that I am a political preacher, to them I say, "Save me from my friends." ...

... Tell my friends that a uniform silence is all my answer to my detractors. If I give them tit for tat, it would bring us down to a level with them. Tell them that truth will take care of itself, and that they are not to fight anybody for me. They have much to learn yet, and they are only children. They are still full of foolish golden dreams — mere boys!

... This nonsense of public life and newspaper blazoning has disgusted me thoroughly. I long to go back to the Himalayan quiet.

Ever yours affectionately,
Vivekananda.

1894.76 — MOTHER

To Mrs. G. W. Hale:

Hotel Bellevue, Beacon Street, Boston,
27 September, 1894.

DEAR MOTHER,

The bundles all came safely. One was newspapers from India. The other was the short sketch of my Master published by Mr. Mazumdar long ago. In the latter bundle there are two sextos or pamphlets. One, my Master's sketch; the other, a short extract to show how what Mr. [Keshab] Chandra Sen and [Pratap Chandra] Mazumdar preached as their "New Dispensation" was stolen from my Master's life. The latter therefore you need not distribute, but I hope you will distribute my

Master's life to many good people.

I beg you to send some to Mrs. Guernsey, Fishkill on the Hudson, N.Y.; Mrs. Arthur Smith and Mrs. [Miss Mary A.] Phillips, 19 West 38th Street, New York (both); to Mrs. Bagley, Annisquam, Mass.; and Prof. J. Wright, Professor of Greek, Harvard, Mass.

The newspapers — you may do whatever you like, and I hope you will send any newspaper scrap you get about me to India.

Yours etc.,
Vivekananda.

1894.77 — ALASINGA

U. S. A.,
29th September, 1894.

DEAR ALASINGA,

You all have done well, my brave unselfish children. I am so proud of you... Hope and do not despair. After such a start, if you despair you are a fool...

Our field is India, and the value of foreign appreciation is in rousing India up. That is all... We must have a strong base from which to spread... Do not for a moment quail. Everything will come all right. It is will that moves the world.

You need not be sorry, my son, on account of the young men becoming Christians. What else can they be under the existing social bandages, especially in Madras? Liberty is the first condition of growth. Your ancestors gave every liberty to the soul, and religion grew. They put the body under every bondage, and society did not grow. The opposite is the case in the West — every liberty to society, none to religion. Now are falling off the shackles from the feet of Eastern society as from those of Western religion.

Each again will have its type; the religious or introspective in India, the scientific or out-seeing in the West. The West wants every bit of spirituality through social improvement. The East wants every bit of social power through spirituality. Thus it was that the modern reformers saw no way to reform but by first crushing out the religion of India. They tried, and they failed. Why? Because few of them ever studied their own religion, and not one ever underwent the training necessary to understand the Mother of all religions. I claim that no destruction of religion is necessary to improve the Hindu society, and that this state of society exists not on account of religion, but because religion has not been applied to society as it should have been. This I am ready to prove from our old books, every word of it. This is what I teach, and this is what we must struggle all our lives to carry out. But it will take time, a long time to study. Have patience and work. उध्दरेदात्मनात्मानम् — Save yourself by yourself.

Yours etc.,
Vivekananda.

PS — The present Hindu society is organised only for spiritual men, and hopelessly crushes out everybody else. Why? Where shall they go who want to enjoy the world a little with its frivolities? Just as our religion takes in all, so should our society. This is to be worked out by first understanding the true principles of our religion and then applying them to society. This is the slow but sure work to be done.

1894.78 — DIWANJI SAHEB

Chicago,
September, 1894.

DEAR DIWANJI SAHEB, (Shri Haridas Viharidas Desai)

Your kind letter reached long ago, but as I had not anything to write I was late in answering.

Your kind note to G. W. Hale has been very gratifying, as I owed them that much. I have been travelling all over this country all this time and seeing everything. I have come to this conclusion that there is only one country in the world which understands religion — it is India; that with all their faults the Hindus are head and shoulders above all other nations in morality and spirituality; and that with proper care and attempt and struggle of all her disinterested sons, by combining some of the active and heroic elements of the West with the calm virtues of the Hindus, there will come a type of men far superior to any that have ever been in this world.

I do not know when I come back; but I have seen enough of this country, I think, and so soon will go over to Europe and then to India.

With my best love, gratitude to you and all your brothers,

I remain, yours faithfully,
Vivekananda.

1894.79 — DIWANJI SAHEB

Chicago(?),
September, 1894(3?),

DEAR DIWANJI SAHEB, (Shri Haridas Viharidas Desai)

Very kind of you to send up a man inquiring about my health and comfort. But that's quite of a piece with your fatherly character. I am all right here. Your kindness has left nothing more to be desired here. I hope soon to see you in a few days. I don't require any conveyance while going down. Descent is very bad, and the ascent is the worst part of the job, that's the same in everything in the world. My heartful gratitude to you.

Yours faithfully,
Vivekananda.

1894.80 — MOTHER

To Mrs. G. W. Hale:

C/O Mrs. Ole Bull,
168 Brattle Street, Cambridge, Mass.
5 October, 1894.

DEAR MOTHER,

I have not heard from you for long. Have you received the huge packages I sent over to you? Have you heard anything about the phonograph from the express office?

I will be with Mrs. Ole Bull a few days, and then I go to New York to Mrs. Guernsey's.

Yours ever affectionately,
Vivekananda.

1894.81 — MOTHER

To Mrs. G. W. Hale:

C/O Mrs. Ole Bull,
Riverview, 168 Brattle Street, Cambridge, Mass.,
[Postmarked: Oct. 10, 1894, 4:30 a.m.]

DEAR MOTHER,

Received two letters from you and a large number from India but none from Khetri.

I am sorry the sisters have got bad colds and more sorry for your getting worried over it. Nothing can make a Christian worry. I hope Narasimha will be a good boy this time forth. Sister Mary is coming to Boston — good. I am going off from here tomorrow to Baltimore. I had enough to pay all my expenses here; and since I am living with Mrs. Bull, there is no expense. She is a rich and highly cultured lady. She has given me $500 for my work or anything I like. As I am not going west very soon, I will have a bank account here in Boston. From Philadelphia I go to Washington, and then I will run between New York and Boston. So I do not think I will be able to see you, except perhaps Sister Mary. I want so very much that Mary will see Mrs. Bull and others of my friends here. I have the fat of the land as usual, and my dinner is cooking very well both here and in India. Do not make it public, Mother — that is between you and me and the babies — and do not worry yourself about anything. All things come to him that waits. I am going to send the greater part of the money I have got to India and then money will come faster. I have always found that the faster I spend, the faster it comes. Nature abhors a vacuum. I am in very good spirits, only you must not stop keeping me informed about yourself, Babies and Father Pope from time to time.

Perhaps you remember the two letters that came from Mysore — I want one of those envelopes with the Mysore King's seal on the outside to be sent to Miss Phillips, 19 West 38th Street, New York.

I cannot go to New York now nor to Chicago, although I had a number of invitations and offers from both the places. I must see now the capital and the other cities. I am in His Hands. If Miss Mary be in Boston, sometime I may hope to see her.

I am glad that Narasimha was never fast — hope he will never be.

From India they always write me to come, come, come. They do not know the secret. I am acting more from here than I will ever do from there.

Kindly send my letters to this address and they will reach me safe wherever I be. This will be one of my homes when I am in Boston.

Lord bless you all, dear Mother.

Yours ever affectionately,
Vivekananda.

1894.82 — MRS. BULL

To Mrs. Ole Bull:

1123 Saint Paul Street, Baltimore,
17 October, 1894.

DEAR MRS. BULL,

I could not find time earlier to write you — I was so incessantly knocking about. We had a nice meeting last Sunday at Baltimore and [are] going to have one more next Sunday. Of course, they do not financially help me a bit; but as I promised to help them and like the idea, I speak for them.

In the letters you sent over from India was an address sent over to me from Calcutta by my fellow citizens for my work here and a number of newspaper cuttings. I will send them on to you later.

Yesterday I went to see Washington and met Mrs. Colville and Miss Young, who were very kind to me.

I am going to speak at Washington again and then will go over to Philadelphia and from there to New York.

Your affectionate Son,
Vivekananda.

1894.83 — SWAMI RAMAKRISNANANDA[1]

Baltimore, U.S.A.,
22nd October, 1894.

DEAR __, (Swami Ramakrishnananda)

Glad to receive your letter and go through the contents. I received today a letter of Akshay Kumar Ghosh from London, which also gives me some information...

Now you have come to know your own powers. Strike the iron while it is hot. Idleness won't do. Throw overboard all idea of jealousy and egotism, once for all. Come on to the practical field with tremendous energy; to work, in the fullness of strength! As to the rest, the Lord will point out the way. The whole world will be deluged by a tidal wave. Work, work, work — let this be your motto. I cannot see anything else. There is no end of work here — I am careering all over the country. Wherever the seed of his power will find its way, there it will fructify — आद्य वा अब्दशतान्ते वा — be it today, or in a hundred years." You must work in sympathy with all, then only it will lead to quick results...

Our object is to do good to the world, and not the trumpeting of our own names. Why doesn't Niranjan (Niranjanananda) learn Pali in Ceylon, and study Buddhist books? I cannot make out what good will come of aimless rambling. Those that have come under his protection, have virtue, wealth, desires, and freedom lying at their feet. मामे: मामे: — Courage! Everything will come about by degrees. From all of you I want this that you must discard for ever self-aggrandisement, faction-mongering, and jealousy. You must be all-forbearing, like Mother Earth. If you can achieve this, the world will be at your feet...

Try to give less of material food in the anniversary celebrations, and give some food for the brain instead...

Yours affectionately,
Vivekananda.

1894.84 — VEHEMIA

Washington,
23rd October, 1894.

DEAR VEHEMIA CHAND LIMBDI,

I am going on very well in this country. By this time I have become one of their own teachers. They all like me and my teachings... I travel all over the country from one place to another, as was my habit in India, preaching and teaching. Thousands and thousands have listened to me and taken my ideas in a very kindly spirit. It is the most expensive country, but the Lord provides for me everywhere I go.

With my love to you and all my friends there (Limbdi, Rajputana).

1 Translated from Bengali.

1894.85 — SISTER

Washington,
C/O Mrs. T. Totten. 1708 W I Street,
26th (?) October, 1894.

DEAR SISTER[1],

Excuse my long silence; but I have been regularly writing to Mother Church. I am sure you are all enjoying this nice cool weather. I am enjoying Baltimore and Washington very much. I will go hence to Philadelphia. I thought Miss Mary was in Philadelphia, and so I wanted her address. But as she is in some other place near Philadelphia, I do not want to give her the trouble to come up to see me, as Mother Church says.

The lady with whom I am staying is Mrs. Totten, a niece of Miss Howe. I will be her guest more than a week yet; so you may write to me to her care.

I intend going over to England this winter somewhere in January or February. A lady from London with whom one of my friends is staying has sent an invitation to me to go over as her guest; and from India they are urging me every day to come back.

How did you like Pitoo in the cartoon? Do not show it to anybody. It is too bad of our people to caricature Pitoo that way.

I long ever so much to hear from you, but take a little more care to make your letter just a bit more distinct. Do not be angry for the suggestion.

Your ever loving brother,
Vivekananda.

1894.86 — MISS THURSBY

To Miss Emma Thursby:

[Washington, D.C.,
26 October, 1894]

DEAR MISS THURSBY,

I received your kind note and the introductory letters. I will make it a point to see the ladies and hope to be benefitted much by it.

I had a beautiful letter from Mr. Flagg. I am soon coming to N.Y. where I hope to see you.

With my deepest love and gratitude,

I remain yours faithfully,
Vivekananda.

---

1. Isabelle Mckindley.

1894.87 — BLESSED AND BELOVED

Washington,
27th October, 1894.

BLESSED AND BELOVED[2],

By this time you must have received my other letters. You must excuse me for certain harshness of tone sometimes, and you know full well how I love you. You have asked me often to send over to you all about my movements in this country and all my lecture reports. I am doing exactly here what I used to do in India. Always depending on the Lord and making no plans ahead... Moreover you must remember that I have to work incessantly in this country, and that I have no time to put together my thoughts in the form of a book, so much so, that this constant rush has worn my nerves, and I am feeling it. I cannot express my obligation to you, G. G., and all my friends in Madras, for the most unselfish and heroic work you did for me. But it was not at all meant to blazon me, but to make you conscious of your own strength. I am not an organiser, my nature tends towards scholarship and meditation. I think I have worked enough, now I want rest and to teach a little to those that have come to me from my Gurudeva (venerable Guru). You have known now what you can do, for it is really you, young men of Madras, that have done all; I am only the figurehead. I am a Tyâgi (detached) monk. I only want one thing. I do not believe in a God or religion which cannot wipe the widow's tears or bring a piece of bread to the orphan's mouth. However sublime be the theories, however well-spun may be the philosophy — I do not call it religion so long as it is confined to books and dogmas. The eye is in the forehead and not in the back. Move onward and carry into practice that which you are very proud to call your religion, and God bless you!

Look not at me, look to yourselves. I am happy to have been the occasion of rousing an enthusiasm. Take advantage of it, float along with it, and everything will come right. Love never fails, my son; today or tomorrow or ages after, truth will conquer. Love shall win the victory. Do you love your fellow men? Where should you go to seek for God — are not all the poor, the miserable, the weak, Gods? Why not worship them first? Why go to dig a well on the shores of the Gangâ? Believe in the omnipotent power of love. Who cares for these tinsel puffs of name? I never keep watch of what the newspapers are saying. Have you love? — You are omnipotent. Are you perfectly unselfish? If so, you are irresistible. It is character that pays everywhere. It is the Lord who protects His children in the depths of the sea. Your country requires heroes; be heroes! God bless you!

Everybody wants me to come over to India. They think we shall be able to do more if I come over. They are mistaken, my friend. The present enthusiasm is only a little patriotism, it means nothing. If it is true and genuine, you will find in a short time hundreds of heroes coming forward and carrying on the work. Therefore know that you have really done all, and go on. Look not for me. Akshoy

2. Alasinga Perumal.

Kumar Ghosh is in London. He sent a beautiful invitation from London to come to Miss Müller's. And I hope I am going in January or February next. Bhattacharya writes me to come over. Here is a grand field. What have I to do with this "ism" or that "ism"? I am the servant of the Lord, and where on earth is there a better field than here for propagating all high ideas? Here, where if one man is against me, a hundred hands are ready to help me; here, where man feels for man, weeps for his fellow-men and women are goddesses! Even idiots may stand up to hear themselves praised, and cowards assume the attitude of the brave when everything is sure to turn out well, but the true hero works in silence. How many Buddhas die before one finds expression! My son, I believe in God, and I believe in man. I believe in helping the miserable. I believe in going even to hell to save others. Talk of the Westerners? They have given me food, shelter, friendship, protection—even the most orthodox Christians! What do our people do when any of their priests go to India? You do not touch them even, they are Mlechchhas! No man, no nation, my son, can hate others and live; India's doom was sealed the very day they invented the word Mlechchha and stopped from communion with others. Take care how you foster that idea. It is good to talk glibly about the Vedanta, but how hard to carry out even its least precepts!

Ever yours with blessings,
Vivekananda.

PS—Take care of these two things—love of power and jealousy. Cultivate always "faith in yourself".

1894.88—MOTHER

To Mrs. G. W. Hale:

[Washington, D.C.,
October 27, 1894]

DEAR MOTHER,

I received your very kind note and all the India letters just now. I will make it a point to see Mrs. Whitland [?]. I have been very kindly treated by Mrs. [Enoch] Totten.

Will you kindly order 100 photographs from Harrison, and send them over to India to Ramdayal Chakravarty, c/o Swami Ramakrishnananda, Varahanagar Math, Alambazar, Calcutta? I will pay for it when I come to Chicago.

I have nothing especial to write—except I had good treatment everywhere. How I long to give up this life of weariness and blazoning day and night.

I will go from here to New York and will come back to see you in Chicago before I start for England.

Yours etc.,
Vivekananda.

1894.89 — MRS. BULL

C/O Mrs. E. Totten,
1708, 1st Street, Washington, D.c.,
27th Oct., 1894.

DEAR MRS. BULL,

Many thanks for your kindness in sending me the introduction to Mr. Frederic Douglas. You need not be sorry on account of the ill-treatment I received at the hands of a low class hotel-keeper at Baltimore. It was the fault of the Vrooman brothers. Why should they take me to a low hotel?

And then the American women, as everywhere, came to my rescue, and I had a very good time.

In Washington I am the guest of Mrs. E. Totten who is an influential lady here and a metaphysician. She is moreover the niece of one of my Chicago friends. So everything is going on all right. I also saw Mrs. Colville and Miss Young here.

With my eternal love and gratitude for you,
I remain,

Yours etc.,
Vivekananda.

1894.90 — MOTHER

To Mrs. George W. Hale:

1125 St. Paul St., Baltimore,
October, 1894.

DEAR MOTHER,

You see where I am now. Did you see a telegram from India in the Chicago Tribune? Did they print the address from Calcutta? From here I go to Washington, thence to Philadelphia and then to New York; send me the address of Miss Mary in Philadelphia so that I may look in on my way to New York. Hope your worry is over.

Yours affectionately,
Vivekananda.

1894.91 — SISTER

To Miss Mary Hale:

C/O Mrs. E. Totten,
1703, 1st Street, Washington,
[November 1(?), 1894]

DEAR SISTER,

I have received two letters which you were very kind to take the trouble to write. I am going to talk here today, tomorrow at Baltimore, then again Monday at Baltimore, and Tuesday at Washington again. So I will be in Philadelphia a few days after that. I shall write to you the day I start from Washington. I shall be in Philadelphia a few days only to see Prof. Wright, and then I go to New York and run for a little while between New York and Boston, and then go to Chicago via Detroit; and then "whist"..., as Senator Palmer says, to England.

The word "Dharma" means religion. I am very sorry they treated Petro very badly in Calcutta. I have been very well treated here and am doing very well. Nothing extraordinary in the meantime except I got vexed at getting loads of newspapers from India; so after sending a cart-load to Mother Church and another to Mrs. Guernsey, I had to write them to stop sending their newspapers. I have had "boom" enough in India. Alasinga writes that every village all over the country now has heard of me. Well, the old peace is gone for ever and no rest anywhere from heretofore. These newspapers of India will be my death, I am sure. They will now talk what I ate on such and such a date and how I sneezed. Lord bless them, it was all my foolery. I really came here to raise a little money secretly and go over but was caught in the trap and now no more of a reserved life.

Wishing you all enjoyments,

I remain, yours affectionately,
Vivekananda.

1894.92 — MOTHER

To Mrs. G. W. Hale:

Baltimore, [Maryland],
3 November, 1894.

DEAR MOTHER,

I do not know what to say about this phonograph business. It takes six months to go to India!! and the company cannot get an inquiry in another six months!!! American express, indeed!! Well — however, they are bound to make good my money. Mother, do not lose the receipt of the express company.

I am going to New York as soon as possible.

Yours affectionately,
Vivekananda.

1894.93 — DIWANJI SAHEB

Chicago,
15th November, 1894(3?).

DEAR DIWANJI SAHEB, (Shri Haridas Viharidas Desai)

I here received your kind note. So very kind of you to remember me even here, I have not seen your Narayan Hemchandra. He is not in America, I believe. I have seen many strange sights and grand things. I am glad that there is a good chance of your coming over to Europe. Avail yourself of it by any means. The fact of our isolation from all the other nations of the world is the cause of our degeneration and its only remedy is getting back into the current of the rest of the world. Motion is the sign of life. America is a grand country. It is a paradise of the poor and women. There is almost no poor in the country, and nowhere else in the world women are so free, so educated, so cultured. They are everything in society.

This is a great lesson. The Sannyasin has not lost a bit of his Sannyasinship, even his mode of living. And in this most hospitable country, every home is open to me. The Lord who guides me in India, would He not guide me here? And He has.

You may not understand why a Sannyasin should be in America, but it was necessary. Because the only claim you have to be recognised by the world is your religion, and good specimens of our religious men are required to be sent abroad to give other nations an idea that India is not dead.

Some representative men must come out of India and go to all the nations of the earth to show at least that you are not savages. You may not feel the necessity of it from your Indian home, but, believe me, much depends upon that for your nation. And a Sannyasin who has no idea of doing good to his fellows is a brute, not a Sannyasin.

I am neither a sightseer nor an idle traveller; but you will see, if you live to see, and bless me all your life.

Mr. Dvivedi's papers were too big for the Parliament, and they had to be cut short.

I spoke at the Parliament of Religions, and with what effect I may quote to you from a few newspapers and magazines ready at hand. I need not be self-conceited, but to you in confidence I am bound to say, because of your love, that no Hindu made such an impression in America, and if my coming has done nothing, it has done this that the Americans have come to know that India even today produces men at whose feet even the most civilised nations may learn lessons of religion and morality. Don't you think that is enough to say for the Hindu nation sending over here their Sannyasin? You would hear the details from Virchand Gandhi.

These I quote from the journals: "But eloquent as were many of the brief speeches, no one expressed as well the spirit of the Parliament (of religions) and its limitations as the Hindu monk. I copy his address in full, but I can only suggest its effect upon the audience; for he is an orator by Divine right, and his strong intelligent face in its picturesque setting of yellow and orange was hardly less interesting than these earnest words and the rich rhythmical utterance he gave them." (Here the speech is quoted in extenso.) New York Critique.

"He has preached in clubs and churches until his faith has become familiar to us... His culture, his eloquence, and his fascinating personality have given us a new idea of Hindu civilisation... His fine, intelligent face and his deep musical voice, prepossessing one at once in his favour... He speaks without notes, presenting his facts and his conclusions with the greatest art and the most convincing sincerity, and rising often to rich inspiring eloquence." (ibid.)

"Vivekananda is undoubtedly the greatest figure in the Parliament of Religions. After hearing him we feel how foolish it is to send missionaries to this learned nation." Herald (the greatest paper here).

I cease from quoting more lest you think me conceited; but this was necessary to you who have become nearly frogs in the well and would not see how the world is going on elsewhere. I do not mean you personally, my noble friend, but our nation in general.

I am the same here as in India, only here in this highly cultural land there is an appreciation, a sympathy which our ignorant fools never dream of. There our people grudge us monks a crumb of bread, here they are ready to pay one thousand rupees a lecture and remain grateful for the instructions for ever.

I am appreciated by these strangers more than I was ever in India. I can, if I will, live here all my life in the greatest luxury; but I am a Sannyasin, and "India, with all thy faults I love thee still". So I am coming back after some months, and go on sowing the seeds of religion and progress from city to city as I was doing so long, although amongst a people who know not what appreciation and gratefulness are.

I am ashamed of my own nation when I compare their beggarly, selfish, unappreciative, ignorant ungratefulness with the help, hospitality, sympathy, and respect which the Americans have shown to me, a representative of a foreign religion. Therefore come out of the country, see others, and compare.

Now after these quotations, do you think it was worth while to send a Sannyasin to America?

Please do not publish it. I hate notoriety in the same manner as I did in India.

I am doing the Lord's work, and wherever He leads I follow. lame cross a mountain, He will help me. I do not care for human help. He is ready to help me in India, in America, on the North Pole, if He thinks fit. If He does not, none else can help me. Glory unto the Lord for ever and ever.

Yours with blessings,
Vivekananda.

1894.94 — MOTHER

To Mrs. G. W. Hale:

New York,
18 November, 1894.

DEAR MOTHER,

I have been very late this time in writing you as Sister Mary has already written to you, no doubt, about me.

The clothes have all reached safe, only I will send over some of the summer and other clothes as it will be impossible to carry the burden all along with me.

The certainty about going to Europe this December has gone; so I am uncertain when I go.

Sister Mary has improved a great deal from what I saw her last. She lives with a number of fox-hunting squires and is quite happy. I hope she will marry one of those fellows with long pockets. I am going again to see her tomorrow at Mrs. Spalding's — I was there last afternoon. I will be in N.Y. this month; then I go to Boston and perhaps will be there all through December. When I was sick in Boston last spring, I went over to Chicago, and not to Detroit as Mrs. Bagley expected. So this time I am going to Detroit first and then to Chicago, if possible. Else I altogether give up the plan of going to the West soon.

There is more chance of working my plans out in the East than in the West, as it now appears.

I have got news of the phonograph — it has reached safe, and the Râjâ wrote to me a very nice letter on that. I have a lot of addresses and other nonsense from India. I have written home to them not to send any more newspapers. My love to the babies at home and I am going to visit the baby abroad.

Mrs. Guernsey has been at death's door. She is now recovering slowly. I have not seen her yet. She is not strong enough to see anybody. Hope she will soon be strong.

My love to Father Pope and everyone.

Your ever affectionate son,
Vivekananda.

1894.95 — ALASINGA

U. S. A.,
30th November, 1894.

DEAR ALASINGA,

I am glad to leant that the phonograph and the letter have reached you safely. You need not send any more newspaper cuttings. I have been deluged with them. Enough of that. Now go to work for the organisation. I have started one already in New York and the Vice-President will soon write to you. Keep correspondence with them. Soon I hope to get up a few in other places. We must organise our forces not to make a sect — not on religious matters, but on the secular business part of it. A stirring propaganda must be launched out. Put your heads together and organise.

What nonsense about the miracle of Ramakrishna!... Miracles I do not know nor understand. Had Ramakrishna nothing to do in the world but turning wine into the Gupta's medicine? Lord save me from such Calcutta people! What materials to work with! If they can write a real life of Shri Ramakrishna with the idea of showing what he came to do and teach, let them do it, otherwise let them not distort his life and sayings. These people want to know God who see in Shri Ramakrishna nothing but jugglery!... Now let Kidi translate his love, his knowledge, his teachings, his eclecticism, etc. This is the theme. The life of Shri Ramakrishna was an extraordinary searchlight under whose illumination one is able to really understand the whole scope of Hindu religion. He was the object-lesson of all the theoretical knowledge given in the Shâstras (scriptures). He showed by his life what the Rishis and Avatâras really wanted to teach. The books were theories, he was the realisation. This man had in fifty-one years lived the five thousand years of national spiritual life and so raised himself to be an object-lesson for future generations. The Vedas can only be explained and the Shastras reconciled by his theory calf Avasthâ or stages — that we must not only tolerate others, but positively embrace them, and that truth is the basis of all religions. Now on these lines a most impressive and beautiful life can be written. Well, everything in good time. Avoid all irregular indecent expressions about sex etc..., because other nations think it the height of indecency to mention such things, and his life in English is going to be read by the whole world. I read a Bengali life sent over. It is full of such words... So take care. Carefully avoid such words and expressions. The Calcutta friends have not a cent worth of ability; but they have their assertions of individuality. They are too high to listen to advice. I do not know what to do with these wonderful gentlemen. I have not got much hope in that quarter. His will be done. I am simply ashamed of the Bengali book. The writer perhaps thought he was a frank recorder of truth and keeping the very language of Paramahamsa. But he does not remember that Ramakrishna would never use that language before ladies. And this man expects his work to be read by men and women alike! Lord, save me from fools! They, again, have their own freaks; they all knew him! Bosh and rot... Beggars taking upon themselves the air of kings! Fools thinking they are all wise! Puny slaves thinking that they are masters! That is their condition. I do not know what to do. Lord save me. I have all hope in Madras. Push on with your work; do not be governed by the Calcutta people. Keep them in good humour in the hope that some one of them may turn good. But push on with your work independently. "Many come to sit at dinner when it is cooked." Take care and work on.

Yours ever with blessings,
Vivekananda.

1894.96 — KIDI

U. S. A.
30th November, 1894.

DEAR KIDI,

... As to the wonderful stories published about Shri Ramakrishna, I advise you to keep clear of them and the fools who write them. They are true, but the fools will make a mess of the whole thing, I am sure. He had a whole world of knowledge to teach, why insist upon unnecessary things as miracles really are! They do not prove anything. Matter does not prove Spirit. What connection is there between the existence of God, Soul, or immortality, and the working of miracles? ... Preach Shri Ramakrishna. Pass the Cup that has satisfied your thirst ... Preach Bhakti. Do not disturb your head with metaphysical nonsense, and do not disturb others by your bigotry ...

Yours ever with blessings,
Vivekananda.

1894.97 — DEAR AND BELOVED

U.S.A.,
30th November, 1894.

DEAR AND BELOVED, (Dr. Nanjunda Rao)

Your beautiful letter just came to hand. I am so glad that you have come to know Shri Ramakrishna. I am very glad at the strength of your Vairâgya. It is the one primary necessity in reaching God. I had always great hopes for Madras, and still I have the firm belief that from Madras will come the spiritual wave that will deluge India. I can only say Godspeed to your good intentions; but here, my son, are the difficulties. In the first place, no man ought to take a hasty step. In the second place, you must have some respect for the feelings of your mother and wife. True, you may say that we, the disciples of Ramakrishna, had not always shown great deference to the opinions of our parents. I know, and know for sure, that great things are done only by great sacrifices. I know for certain that India requires the sacrifice of her highest and best, and I sincerely hope that it will be your good fortune to be one of them.

Throughout the history of the world you find great men make great sacrifices and the mass of mankind enjoy the benefit. If you want to give up everything for your own salvation, it is nothing. Do you want to forgo even your own salvation for the good of the world? You are God, think of that. My advice to you is to live the life of a Brahmacharin, i.e. giving up all sexual enjoyments for a certain time live in the house of your father; this is the "Kutichaka" stage. Try to bring your wife to consent to your great sacrifice for the good of the world. And if you have burning faith and all-conquering love and almighty purity, I do not doubt that you will shortly succeed. Give yourself body and soul to the work of spreading the teachings of Shri Ramakrishna, for work (Karma) is the first stage. Study Sanskrit diligently as well as practice devotion. For you are to be a great teacher of mankind, and my Guru Maharaja used to say, "A penknife is sufficient to commit suicide with, but to kill others one requires guns and swords." And in the fullness of time it will be given unto you when to go forth out of the world and preach His sacred name. Your determination is holy and good. Godspeed to you, but do not take any hasty step. First purify yourself by work and devotion India has suffered long, the Religion Eternal has suffered long. But the Lord is merciful. Once more He has come to help His children, once more the opportunity is given to rise to fallen India. India can only rise by sitting at the feet of Shri Ramakrishna. His life and his teachings are to be spread far and wide, are to be made to penetrate every pore of Hindu society. Who will do it? Who are to take up the flag of Ramakrishna and march for the salvation of the world? Who are to stem the tide of degeneration at the sacrifice of name and fame, wealth and enjoyment—nay of every hope of this or other worlds? A few young men have jumped in the breach, have sacrificed themselves. They are a few; we want a few thousands of such as they, and they will come. I am glad that our Lord has put it in your mind to be one of them Glory unto him on whom falls the Lord's choice. Your determination is good, your hopes are high, your aim is the noblest in the world—to bring millions sunk in darkness to the light of the Lord.

But, my son, here are the drawbacks. Nothing shall be done in haste. Purity, patience, and perseverance are the three essentials to success and, above all, love. All time is yours, there is no indecent haste. Everything will come right if you are pure and sincere. We want hundreds like you bursting upon society and bringing new life and vigour of the Spirit wherever they go. Godspeed to you.

Yours with all blessings,
Vivekananda.

1894.98—KALI[1]

U.S.A.
(November?) 1894.

DEAR KALI, (Abhedananda)

Thanks for all that I come to know from your letter. I had no news of the telegram in question having appeared in the Tribune. It is six months since I left Chicago, and I have not been yet free to return. So I could not keep myself well posted. You have taken great pains indeed! And for this how can I thank you adequately? You have all evinced a wonderful capacity for work. And how can Shri Ramakrishna's words prove false?—You have got wonderful spirit in you. About

---

[1] Translated from Bengali.

Shashi Sanyal, I have already written. Nothing remains undetected, through the grace of Shri Ramakrishna. But let him found a sect or whatever he will, what harm? " — May blessings attend your path!" Secondly, I could not catch the drift of your letter. I shall collect my own funds to build a monastery for ourselves, and if people criticise me for it, I see nothing in this to affect us either way. You have your minds pitched high and steady, it will do you no harm. May you have exceeding love for one another among yourselves, and it would be enough to have an attitude of indifference towards public criticisms. Kalikrishna Babu has deep love for the cause and is a great man. Please convey my special love to him. So long as there is no feeling of disunion amongst you, through the grace of the Lord, I assure you, there is no danger for you, " mountains". " — All noble undertakings are fraught with obstacles". It is quite in the nature of things. Keep up the deepest mental poise. Take not even the slightest notice of what puerile creatures may be saying against you. Indifference, indifference, indifference! I have already written to Shashi (Ramakrishnananda) in detail. Please do not send newspapers and tracts any more. "Take the husking hammer to heaven, and there it will do its husking", as the Bengali saying goes. The same trudging about here as it was in India, only with the carrying of others' loads added! How can I procure customers for people's books in this land? I am only one amongst the many here and nothing more. Whatever the papers and things of that sort in this country write about me, I make an offering of to the Fire-God. You also do the same. That is the proper course.

A bit of public demonstration was necessary for Guru Maharaja's work. It is done, and so far so good. Now you must on no account pay any heed to what the rabble may be prattling about us. Whether I make my pile or do whatever else I am reported to, shall the opinions of the riff-raff stand in the way of His work? My dear brother, you are yet a boy, while I am growing grey. What regard I have for the pronouncements and opinions of such people, you should guess from this. So long as you gird up your loins and rally behind me, there is no fear even if the whole world combine against us. This much I understand that I shall have to take up a very lofty attitude, I should not, I think, write to anyone except to you. By the by, where is Gunanidhi? Try to find him out and bring him to the Math with all kindness. He is a very sincere man and highly learned. You must try your best to secure two plots of land, let people say what they will. Let anyone write anything for or against me in the papers; you shouldn't take the slightest notice. And my dear brother, I beseech you repeatedly not to send me any more newspapers by the basketful. How can you talk of rest now? We shall have rest awhile only when we give up this body. Just do once get up the celebration, brother, in that spirit, so that all the country around may burn with enthusiasm. Bravo! Capital indeed! The whole band of scoffers will be swept away by the tidal wave of love. You are elephants, forsooth, what do you fear from an ant-bite?

The address (The Address presented by the citizens of Calcutta who gathered at a meeting at the Town Hall on September 5, 1894, under the Presidentship of Raja Pyari Mohan Mookherjee.) you sent me reached me long ago and the reply to it has also been despatched to Pyari Babu (18 Nov. 1894).

Bear in mind—the eyes are two in number and so the ears, but the mouth is but one! Indifference, indifference, indifference! "—The doer of good deeds never comes to grief, my dear". Ah! To fear! and whom are we going to fear, brother? Here the missionaries and their ilk have howled themselves into silence—and the whole world will but do likewise.

—Whether people skilled in policy praise or blame, whether the Goddess of Fortune favours or goes her way, whether death befalls today or after hundreds of years—persons of steady mind never swerve from the path of righteousness" (Bhartrihari, Nitishataka)

You need not even mix with the humdrub people, nor beg of them either. The Lord is supplying everything and will do so in future. What fear, my brother? All great undertakings are achieved through mighty obstacles.

—You valiant one, put forth your manly efforts; wretched people under the grip of lust and gold deserve to be looked upon with indifference. Now I have got a firm footing in this country, and therefore need no assistance. But my one prayer to you all is that you should apply to the service of the Lord that active impulse of manliness which your eagerness to help me through brotherly love has brought out in you. Do not open out your mind, unless you feel it will be positively beneficial. Use agreeable and wholesome language towards even the greatest enemy. The desire for fame, for riches, for enjoyment is quite natural to every mortal, dear brother, and if that agrees well with serving both ways (i.e. serving both God and mammon), why, all men would exhibit great zeal! It is only the great saint who can work, making a mountain of an atom of virtue in others and cherishing no desire but that of the good of the world—"Bhartrihari, Nitishataka."

Therefore let dullards whose intellect is steeped in ignorance and who look upon the non-Self as all in all, play out their boyish pranks. They will of themselves leave off the moment they find it too hot. Let them try to spit upon the moon—it will but recoil upon themselves.—Godspeed to them! If they have got anything substantial in them, who can bar their success? But if it be only empty swagger due to jealousy, then all will be in vain. Haramohan has sent rosaries. All right. But you should know that religion of the type that obtains in our country does not go here. You must suit it to the taste of the people. If you ask them to become Hindus, they will all give you a wide berth and hate you, as we do the Christian missionaries. They like some of the ideas of the Hindu scriptures—that is all. Nothing more than that, you should know. The men, most of them, do not trouble about religion and all that. The women are a little interested—that is all, but no large doses of it! A few thousands of people have faith in the Advaita doctrine. But they will give you the go-by if you talk obscure mannerisms about sacred writings, caste, or women. Everything proceeds slowly, by degrees. Patience, purity, perseverance.

Yours etc.,
Vivekananda.

1894.99 — DIWANJI

541 Dearborn Avenue, Chicago,
(November,)? 1894.

DEAR DIWANJI, (Shri Haridas Viharidas Desai)

Your letter pleased me extremely. I, of course, understand the joke, but I am not the baby to be put off with a joke; now take more.

The secret of success of the Westerners is the power of organisation and combination. That is only possible with mutual trust and co-operation and help. Now here is Virchand Gandhi, the Jain, whom you well knew in Bombay. This man never takes anything but pure vegetables even in this terribly cold climate, and tooth and nail tries to defend his countrymen and religion. The people of this country like him very well, but what are they doing who sent him over? They are trying to outcast him. Jealousy is a vice necessarily generated in slaves. Again it is jealousy that holds them down.

Here were...; they were all trying to lecture and get money thereby. They did something, but I succeeded better than they — why, I did not put myself as a bar to their success. It was the will of the Lord. But all these... except... have fabricated and circulated the most horrible lies about me in this country, and behind my back. Americans will never stoop to such meanness.

...If any man tries to move forward here, everybody is ready to help him. In India you may try tomorrow by writing a single line of praise for me in any of our papers (Hindu), and the next day they would be all against me. Why? It is the nature of slaves. They cannot suffer to see any one of their brethren putting his head the least above their rank... Do you mean to compare such stuff with these children of liberty, self-help, and brotherly love? The nearest approach to our people are the freed slaves of the U.S.A., the Negroes. Why, in the South they are about twenty millions and are now free. The whites are a handful, still the whites hold them down all the same. Why, even when they have every right by law, a bloody war between the brothers has been fought to free these slaves? The same defect — jealousy. Not one of these Negroes would bear to see his brother-Negro praised or pushing on. Immediately they would join the whites to crush him down. You can have no idea about it until you come out of India. It is all right for those who have plenty of money and position to let the world roll on such, but I call him a traitor who, having been educated, nursed in luxury by the heart's blood of the downtrodden millions of toiling poor, never even takes a thought for them. Where, in what period of history your rich men, noblemen, your priests and potentates took any thought for the poor — the grinding of whose faces is the very life-blood of their power?

But the Lord is great, the vengeance came sooner or later, and they who sucked the life-blood of the poor, whose very education was at their expense, whose very power was built on their poverty, were in their turn sold as slaves by hundreds and thousands, their wives and daughters dishonoured, their property robbed for the last 1,000 years, and do you think it was for no cause?

Why amongst the poor of India so many are Mohammedans? It is nonsense to say, they were converted by the sword. It was to gain their liberty from the...zemindars and from the...priest, and as a consequence you find in Bengal there are more Mohammedans than Hindus amongst the cultivators, because there were so many zemindars there. Who thinks of raising these sunken downtrodden millions? A few thousand graduates do not make a nation, a few rich men do not make a nation. True, our opportunities are less, but still there is enough to feed and clothe and made 300 millions more comfortable, nay, luxurious. Ninety per cent of our people are without education—who thinks of that?—these Babus, the so-called patriots?

Now, let me tell you—still there is a God, no joke. He is ordering our lives, and although I know a nation of slaves cannot but try to bite at the hand that wants to give them medicine, yet, pray with me, you—one of the few that have real sympathy for everything good, for everything great, one at least whom I know to be a man of true ring, nobility of nature, and a thorough sincerity of head and heart—pray with me:

"Lead, kindly Light,

amid th' encircling gloom."

I do not care what they say. I love my God, my religion, my country, and above all, myself, a poor beggar. I love the poor, the ignorant, the downtrodden, I feel for them—the Lord knows how much. He will show me the way. I do not care a fig for human approbation or criticism. I think of most of them as ignorant, noisy children—they have not penetrated into the inner nature of sympathy, into the spirit which is all love.

I have that insight through the blessing of Ramakrishna. I am trying to work with my little band, all of these poor beggars like me, you have seen them. But the Lord's works have been always done by the lowly, by the poor. You bless me that I may have faith in my Guru, in my God, and in myself.

The only way is love and sympathy. The only worship is love.

May He help you and yours ever and ever!

With prayers and blessings,
Vivekananda.

1894.100 — MOTHER

To Mrs. G. W. Hale:

C/O Mrs. Ole Bull,
168 Brattle Street, Cambridge, Mass.,
6 December, 1894.

DEAR MOTHER,

I have not heard long from you. What is the matter with you? I am here in Cambridge and will be here for three weeks to come and will have to lecture and hold classes. Here is a Chicago lady, Mrs. [Milward] Adams, who lectures on tone building etc.

Today we had a lecture from Lady Henry Somerset on Woman Suffrage. Miss Willard of Chicago was here and Julia Ward Howe.

Col. Higginson, Dr. [J. Estlin] Carpenter of Eng. and many other friends were present. Altogether it was a grand affair. I have received a letter from India informing me that the phonograph was duly received.

I have sent part of my money to India and intend sending nearly the whole of it very soon. Only, I will keep enough for the passage back. Saw Mother Temple several times in New York. She was kind as usual. So was Mrs. Spalding.

Sister Mary wrote me a letter from Brookline [Massachusetts]. I am sure she would have enjoyed Lady Somerset's lecture so much. I wrote her about it, but I have not heard from her yet.

I will go to see her the first day I get some time. I am very busy. Hope the sisters at home are enjoying themselves. I will try to run into Chicago for a few days if I can.

Please write me all about the holy family as soon as you get time.

Mrs. Guernsey was very ill and still so weak that she cannot get out of her room.

Miss Helen Bagley was seized with diphtheria in New York and suffered a good deal. She has recovered, however, and the Bagleys have gone home to Detroit.

With my Love to you all, I remain,

Ever yours affectionately,
Vivekananda.

PS — Kindly send my India mail c/o Mrs. Sara Ole Bull, 168 Brattle Street, Cambridge, Mass.

1894.101 — SISTER

To Miss Mary Hale:

168, Brattle Street, Cambridge,
8th December, 1894.

DEAR SISTER,

I have been here three days. We had a nice lecture from Lady Henry Somerset. I have a class every morning here on Vedanta and other topics. Perhaps you have got the copy of Vedantism by this time which I left with Mother Temple to be sent over. I went to dine with the Spaldings another day. That day they urged me, against my repeated protests, to criticise the Americans. I am afraid they did not relish it. It is of course always impossible to do it. What about Mother Church and the family at Chicago? I had no letters from them a long time. I would have run into town to see you before this, had I time. I am kept pretty busy the whole day. Then there is the fear of not meeting you.

If you have time, you may write, and I shall snatch the first opportunity to see you. My time of course is always in the afternoon, so long I shall be here, that is until the 27th or 28th of this month; I will have to be very busy in the morning till 12 or 1.

With my love to you all,

Ever your affectionate brother,
Vivekananda.

1894.102 — SISTER

To Miss Mary Hale:

Cambridge,
21st December, 1894.

DEAR SISTER,

I had not anything from you since your last. I am going away next Tuesday to New York. You must have received Mrs. Bull's letter in the meanwhile. If you cannot accept it, I shall be very glad to come over any day — I have time now as the lectures are at an end, except Sunday next.

Yours ever affectionately,
Vivekananda.

1894.103 — MOTHER

To Mrs. G. W. Hale:

[Cambridge, Mass.,
21 December, 1894]

DEAR MOTHER,

I am glad that Haridas Viharidas (The Dewan of Junagadh.) has sent the rugs. I am afraid they will take a long time to reach here. The Raja (Maharaja Ajit Singh, the Raja of Khetri.) was very much pleased with the phonograph, as he writes, and has heard my voice several times. Hope he will bring it into life.

I have not seen Sister Mary yet, but hope to see her this week as I am going away to New York next Tuesday. Cannot come by any means to Chicago now, for I expect to go to Washington from New York and hope to be pretty busy in New York.

If I can snatch up a few days between the lecture in Brooklyn on the 30th and the next series in New York, I will fly to Chicago for a few days. If I had time just now, it would have been better for me, for the half—fare ticket will expire after this month.

I have been kept very busy here this month so could not go to Boston even for a day. Now I have time and hope to see Sister Mary.

How are the babies at home? Mrs. M. Adams of Chicago, who lectures on voice building and walking etc., has been lecturing here all this time. She is a very great lady in every respect and so intelligent. She knows all of you and likes the "Hale girls" very much. Sister Isabel[le] knows her especially, I think.

Do not you see, Mother — I am determined to work my project out. I must see the light. India can cheer alone — but no money. In the East and South I am getting slowly friends who will help me in my work, I am sure, as they have done already. They all like me more and more.

I have made friends of Lady Somerset and Miss Willard, you will be glad to know. So you see, Mother, you are the only attraction in Chicago; and so long I am in this country, wherever you live is my home. As soon as I have time I will run in to see you and the sisters. But I have no other hopes in the West; nor will you advise me to destroy the only hope I have of success in these parts of the country by giving it up and going to Chicago to be idle as the day is long.

Mrs. Bull and a few other ladies here who are helping me on are not only sincere and love me but they have the power to do as leaders of society. Would that you had millions.

With my love to you all,

Your ever affectionate Son,
Vivekananda.

1894.104 — BLESSED AND BELOVED

U. S. A.,
26th December, 1894.

BLESSED AND BELOVED[1],

...In reference to me every now and then attacks are made in missionary papers (so I hear), but I never care to see them. If you send any of those made in India, I should throw them into the waste-paper basket. A little agitation was necessary for our work. We have had enough. Pay no more attention to what people say about me, whether good or bad. You go on with your work and remember that "Never one meets with evil who tries to do good" (Gita, VI. 40).

Every day the people here are appreciating me. And between you and me, I am more of an influence here than you dream of. Everything must proceed slowly... I have written to you before, and I write again, that I shall not pay heed to any criticism or praise in the newspapers. They are consigned to the fire. Do you do the same. Pay no attention whatsoever to newspaper nonsense or criticism. Be sincere and do your duty. Everything will come all right Truth must triumph...

Missionary misrepresentations should be beneath sour notice... Perfect silence is the best refutation to them and I wish you to maintain the same... Make Mr. Subrahmanya Iyer the President of your Society. He is one of the sincerest and noblest men I know; and in him intellect and emotion are beautifully blended. Push on in your work, without counting much on me; work on your own account... As for me, I do not know when I shall go back; I am working here and in India as well...

With my love to you all.

Yours ever with blessings,
Vivekananda.

1894.105 — MRS. BULL

Brooklyn,
28th Dec., 1894.

DEAR MRS. BULL,

I arrived safely in New York where Landsberg met me at the depot. I proceeded at once to Brooklyn where I arrived in time.

We had a nice evening. Several gentlemen belonging to the Ethical Culture Society came to see me.

Next Sunday we shall have a lecture. Dr. Janes was as usual very kind and good, and Mr. Higgins is as practical as ever. Here alone in New York I find more men interested in religion than in any other city, and do not know why here the interest is more amongst men than women...

---

1. Alasinga Perumal.

Herewith I send a copy of that pamphlet Mr. Higgins has published about me. Hope to send more in the future.

With my love to Miss Farmer and all the holy family,

I remain yours obediently,
Vivekananda.

1894.106 — SISTER

To Miss Mary Hale:

Cambridge,
December, 1894.

DEAR SISTER,

I received your letter just now. If it is not against the rules of your society, why do you not come to see Mrs. Ole Bull, Miss Farmer, and Mrs. Adams the physical culturist from Chicago?

Any day you will find them there.

Yours ever affectionately,
Vivekananda.

1894.107 — DHARMAPALA

U. S. A.,
1894.

DEAR DHARMAPALA,

I have forgotten your address in Calcutta; so I direct this to the Math. I heard about your speeches in Calcutta and how wonderful was the effect produced by them. A certain retired missionary here wrote me a letter addressing me as brother and then hastily went to publish my short answer and make a show. But you know what people here think of such gentlemen. Moreover, the same missionary went privately to some of my friends to ask them not to befriend me. Of course he met with universal contempt. I am quite astonished at this man's behaviour — a preacher of religion to take to such underhand dealings! Unfortunately too much of that in every country and in every religion. Last winter I travelled a good deal in this country although the weather was very severe. I thought it would be dreadful, but I did not find it so after all. You remember Col. Neggenson, President of the Free Religious Society. He makes very kind inquiries about you. I met Dr. Carpenter of Oxford (England) the other day. He delivered an address on the ethics of Buddhism at Plymouth. It was very sympathetic and scholarly. He made inquiries about you and your paper. Hope, your noble work will succeed. You are a worthy servant of Him who came Bahujana Hitâya Bahujana Sukhâya (for the good of the many, for the happiness of the many).

... The Christianity that is preached in India is quite different from what one sees here; you will be astonished to hear, Dharmapala, that I have friends in this country amongst the clergy of the Episcopal and even Presbyterian churches, who are as broad, as liberal, and as sincere as you are in your own religion. The real spiritual man is broad everywhere. His love forces him to be so. Those to whom religion is a trade are forced to become narrow and mischievous by their introduction into religion of the competitive, fighting, and selfish methods of the world.

Yours ever in brotherly love,
Vivekananda.

1894.108 — ALASINGA

U. S. A.,
1894.

DEAR ALASINGA,

Listen to an old story. A lazy tramp sauntering along the road saw an old man sitting at the door of his house and stopped to inquire of him the whereabouts of a certain place. "How far is such and such a village?" he asked. The old man remained silent. The man repeated his query several times. Still there was no answer. Disgusted at this, the traveller turned to go away. The old man then stood up and said, "The village of — is only a mile from here." "What!" said the tramp, "Why did you not speak when I asked you before?" "Because then", said the old man, "you seemed so halting and careless about proceeding, but now you are starting off in good earnest, and you have a right to an answer."

Will you remember this story, my son? Go to work, the rest will come: "Whosoever not trusting in anything else but Me, rests on Me, I supply him with everything he needs" (Gitâ, IX. 22). This is no dream.

... The work should be in the line of preaching and serving, at the present time. Choose a place of meeting where you can assemble every week holding a service and reading the Upanishads with the commentaries, and so slowly go on learning and working. Every thing will come to you if you put your shoulders to the wheel ...

Now, go to work! G. G.'s nature is of the emotional type, you have a level head; so work together; plunge in; this is only the beginning. Every nation must save itself; we must not depend upon funds from America for the revival of Hinduism, for that is a delusion. To have a centre is a great thing; try to secure such a place in a large town like Madras, end go on radiating a living force in all directions. Begin slowly. Start with a few lay missionaries; gradually others will come who will devote their whole lives to the work. Do not try to be a ruler. He is the best ruler who can serve well. Be true unto death. The work we want — we do not seek wealth, name or fame... Be brave... Endeavour to interest the people of Madras in collecting funds for the purpose, and then make a beginning... Be perfectly unselfish and you will be sure to succeed... Without losing the independence in work, show all regards to your superiors. Work in harmony... My children must be ready to jump into fire, if needed, to accomplish their work. Now work, work, work! We will stop and compare notes later on. Have patience, perseverance, and purity.

I am writing no book on Hinduism just now. I am simply jotting down my thoughts. I do not know if I shall publish them. What is in books? The world is too full of foolish things already. If you could start a magazine on Vedantic lines, it would further our object. Be positive; do not criticise others. Give your message, teach what you have to teach, and there stop. The Lord knows the rest...

Do not send me any more newspapers, as I do not notice the missionary criticisms on myself; and here the public estimation of me is better for that reason.

...If you are really my children, you will fear nothing, stop at nothing. You will be like lions. We must rouse India and the whole world. No cowardice. I will take no nay. Do you understand? Be true unto death!... The secret of this is Guru-Bhakti — faith in the Guru unto death! Have you that? I believe with all my heart that you have, and you know that I have confidence in you — so go to work. You must succeed. My prayers and benedictions follow every step you take. Work in harmony. Be patient with everybody. Every one has my love. I am watching you. Onward! Onward! This is just the beginning. My little work here makes a big echo in India, do you know? So I shall not return there in a hurry. My intention is to do something permanent here, and with that object I am working day by day. I am every day gaining the confidence of the American people... Expand your hearts and hopes, as wide as the world. Study Sanskrit, especially the three Bhâshyas (commentaries) on the Vedanta. Be ready, for I have many plans for the future. Try to be a magnetic speaker. Electrify the people. Everything will come to you if you have faith. So tell Kidi, in fact, tell all my children there. In time they will do great things at which the world will wonder. Take heart and work. Show me something you have done. Show me a temple, a press, a paper, a home for me. Where shall I come to if you cannot make a home for me in Madras? Electrify people. Raise funds and preach. Be true to your mission. Thus far you promise well, so go on and do better and better still.

...Do not fight with people; do not antagonise anyone. Why should we mind if Jack and John become Christians? Let them follow whatever religion suits them. Why should you mix in controversies? Bear with the various opinions of everybody. Patience, purity, and perseverance will prevail.

Yours etc.,
Vivekananda.

1894.109 — MAHARAJA OF KHETRI

From a letter written to H. H. the Maharaja of Khetri.

America,
1894.

... "It is not the building that makes the home, but it is the wife that makes it,"[1] says a Sanskrit poet, and how true it is! The roof that affords you shelter from heat and cold and rain is not to be judged by the pillars that support it — the finest Corinthian columns though they be — but by the real spirit-pillar who is the centre, the real support of the home — the woman. Judged by that standard, the American home will not suffer in comparison with any home in the world.

I have heard many stories about the American home: of liberty running into licence, of unwomanly women smashing under their feet all the peace and happiness of home-life in their mad liberty-dance, and much nonsense of that type. And now after a year's experience of American homes, of American women, how utterly false and erroneous that sort of judgment appears! American women! A hundred lives would not be sufficient to pay my deep debt of gratitude to you! I have not words enough to express my gratitude to you. "The Oriental hyperbole" alone expresses the depth of Oriental gratitude — "If the Indian Ocean were an inkstand, the highest mountain of the Himalaya the pen, the earth the scroll and time itself the writer"[2] still it will not express my gratitude to you!

Last year I came to this country in summer, a wandering preacher of a far distant country, without name, fame, wealth, or learning to recommend me — friendless, helpless, almost in a state of destitution and American women befriended me, gave me shelter and food, took me to their homes and treated me as their own son, their own brother. They stood my friends even when their own priests were trying to persuade them to give up the "dangerous heathen" — even when day after day their best friends had told them not to stand by this "unknown foreigner, may be, of dangerous character". But they are better judges of character and soul — for it is the pure mirror that catches the reflection.

And how many beautiful homes I have seen, how many mothers whose purity of character, whose unselfish love for their children are beyond expression, how many daughters and pure maidens, "pure as the icicle on Diana's temple", and withal with much culture, education, and spirituality in the highest sense! Is America then full of only wingless angels in the shape of women? There is good and bad everywhere, true — but a nation is not to be judged by its weaklings called the wicked, as they are only the weeds which lag behind, but by the good, the noble, and the pure who indicate the national life-current to be flowing clear and vigorous.

Do you judge of an apple tree and the taste of its fruits by the unripe, undeveloped, worm-eaten ones that strew the ground, large even though their number be

---
1. "न गृहं गृहमित्याहुर्गृहिणी गृहमुच्यते ।"
2. Adapted from the *Shiva-Mahimnah-Stotram*.

sometimes? If there is one ripe developed fruit, that one would indicate the powers, the possibility and the purpose of the apple tree and not hundreds that could not grow.

And then the modern American women — I admire their broad and liberal minds. I have seen many liberal and broad-minded men too in this country, some even in the narrowest churches, but here is the difference — there is danger with the men to become broad at the cost of religion, at the cost of spirituality — women broaden out in sympathy to everything that is good everywhere, without closing a bit of their own religion. They intuitively know that it is a question of positivity and not negativity, a question of addition and not subtraction. They are every day becoming aware of the fact that it is the affirmative and positive side of everything that shall be stored up, and that this very act of accumulating the affirmative and positive, and therefore soul-building forces of nature, is what destroys the negative and destructive elements in the world.

What a wonderful achievement was that World's Fair at Chicago! And that wonderful Parliament of Religions where voices from every corner of the earth expressed their religious ideas! I was also allowed to present my own ideas through the kindness of Dr. Barrows and Mr. Bonney. Mr. Bonney is such a wonderful man! Think of that mind that planned and carried out with great success that gigantic undertaking, and he, no clergyman, a lawyer, presiding over the dignitaries of all the churches — the sweet, learned, patient Mr. Bonney with all his soul speaking through his bright eyes...

Yours etc.,
Vivekananda.

1894.110 — BROTHERS[3]

Salutations to Bhagavan Shri Ramakrishna!

1894.

DEAR BROTHERS, (Brother-disciples of Swamiji)

Before this I wrote to you a letter which for want of time was very incomplete. Rakhal (Brahmananda) and Hari (Turiyananda) wrote in a letter from Lucknow that Hindu newspapers were praising me, and that they were very glad that twenty thousand people had partaken of food at Shri Ramakrishna's anniversary. I could do much more work but for the Brahmos and missionaries who have been opposing me unceasingly, and the Hindus of India too did nothing for me. I mean, if the Hindus of Calcutta or Madras had held a meeting and passed a resolution recognising me as their representative, and thanking the American people for receiving me with kindness, things would have progressed appreciably. But it is over a year, and nothing done. Of course I never relied on the Bengalis, but the Madrasis

3 Translated from Bengali.

couldn't do anything either...

There is no hope for our nation. Not one original idea crosses anyone's brains, all fighting over the same old, threadbare rug — that Ramakrishna Paramahamsa was such and such — and cock-and-bull stories — stories having neither head nor tail. My God! Won't you do something to show that you are in any way removed from the common run of men! — Only indulging in madness!...Today you have your bell, tomorrow you add a horn, and follow suit with a chowry the day after; or you introduce a cot today, and tomorrow you have its legs silver-mounted, and people help themselves to a rice-porridge, and you spin out two thousand cock-and-bull stories — in short, nothing but external ceremonials. This is called in English imbecility. Those into whose heads nothing but that sort of silliness enters are called imbecile. Those whose heads have a tendency to be troubled day and night over such questions as whether the bell should ring on the right or on the left, whether the sandal-paste mark should be put on the head or anywhere else, whether the light should be waved twice or four times — simply deserve the name of wretches, and it is owing to that sort of notion that we are the outcasts of Fortune, kicked and spurned at, while the people of the West are masters of the whole world...There is an ocean of difference between idleness and renunciation.

If you want any good to come, just throw your ceremonials overboard and worship the Living God, the Man-God — every being that wears a human form — God in His universal as well as individual aspect. The universal aspect of God means this world, and worshipping it means serving it — this indeed is work, not indulging in ceremonials. Neither is it work to cogitate as to whether the rice-plate should be placed in front of the God for ten minutes or for half an hour — that is called lunacy. Millions of rupees have been spent only that the templedoors at Varanasi or Vrindaban may play at opening and shutting all day long! Now the Lord is having His toilet, now He is taking His meals, now He is busy on something else we know not what...And all this, while the Living God is dying for want of food, for want of education! The banias of Bombay are erecting hospitals for bugs — while they would do nothing for men even if they die! You have not the brain to understand this simple thing — that it is a plague with our country, and lunatic asylums are rife all over...Let some of you spread like fire, and preach this worship of the universal aspect of the Godhead — a thing that was never undertaken before in our country. No quarrelling with people, we must be friends with all...

Spread ideas — go from village to village, from door to door — then only there will be real work. Otherwise, lying complacently on the bed and ringing the bell now and then is a sort of disease, pure and simple...Be independent, learn to form independent judgments. — That such and such a chapter of such and such a Tantra has prescribed a standard length for the handle of a bell, — what matters it to me? Through the Lord's will, out of your lips shall come millions of Vedas and Tantras and Purânas...If now you can show this in practice, if you can make three or four hundred thousand disciples in India within a year, then only I may have some hope...

By the bye, you know the boy who had his head shaven and went with Brother Tarak from Bombay to Rameswaram? He calls himself a disciple of Ramakrishna Paramahamsa! Let Brother Tarak initiate him ... He had never even met Shri Ramakrishna in his life, and yet a disciple! — What impudence! Without an unbroken chain of discipleship — Guruparampara — nothing can be done. Is it a child's play? To have no connection whatsoever and call oneself a disciple! The idiot! If that boy refuses to go on in the right way, turn him out. Nothing, I say, can be done without the chain of discipleship, that is, the power that is transmitted from the Guru to the disciple, and from him to his disciple, and so on. Here he comes and proclaims himself a disciple of Ramakrishna — is it tomfoolery? Jagamohan told me of somebody calling himself a brother-disciple of mine. I have now a suspicion that it is that boy. To pose as a brother-disciple! He feels humiliated to call himself a disciple, I dare say, and would fain turn a Guru straightway! Turn him out if he does not follow the established procedure.

Talking of the restlessness of Tulasi (Nirmalananda) and Subodh (Subodhananda) it all means that they have got no work to do ... Go from village to village, do good to humanity and to the world at large. Go to hell yourself to buy salvation for others. There is no Mukti on earth to call my own. Whenever you think of yourself, you are bound to feel restless. What business have you to do with peace, my boy? You have renounced everything. Come! Now is the turn for you to banish the desire for peace, and that for Mukti too! Don't worry in the least; heaven or hell, or Bhakti or Mukti — don't care for anything, but go, my boy, and spread the name of the Lord from door to door! It is only by doing good to others that one attains to one's own good, and it is by leading others to Bhakti and Mukti that one attains them oneself. Take that up, forget-your own self for it, be mad over the idea. As Shri Ramakrishna used to love you, as I love you, come, love the world like that. Bring all together. Where is Gunanidhi? You must have him with you. My infinite love to him. Where is Gupta (Sadananda)? Let him join if he likes. Call him in my name. Remember these few points:

1. We are Sannyasins, who have given up everything — Bhakti, and Mukti, and enjoyment, and all.

2. To do the highest good to the world, everyone down to the lowest — this is our vow. Welcome Mukti or hell, whichever comes of it.

3. Ramakrishna Paramahamsa came for the good of the world. Call him a man, or God, or an Incarnation, just as you please. Accept him each in your own light.

4. He who will bow before him will be converted into purest gold that very moment. Go with this message from door to door, if you can, my boy, and all your disquietude will be at an end. Never fear — where's the room for fear? — Caring for nothing whatsoever is a part of your life. You have so long spread his name and your character all around, well and good. Now spread them in an organised way. The Lord is with you. Take heart!

Whether I live or die, whether I go back to India or not, you go on spreading love,

love that knows no bounds. Put Gupta too to this task. But remember one needs weapons to overcome others. "सन्नमित्ते वरं त्यागो विनाशे नियते सति—When death is so certain, it is better to die for a good cause."

Yours affly.,
Vivekananda.

PS—Remember my previous letter—we want both men and women. There is no distinction of sex in the soul. It won't do merely to call Shri Ramakrishna an Incarnation, you must manifest power. Where are Gour-Mâ, Yogin-Mâ, and Golap-Mâ? Tell them to spread these ideas. We want thousands of men and thousands of women who will spread like wild fire from the Himalayas to Cape Comorin, from the North Pole to the South Pole—all over the world. It is no use indulging in child's play—neither is there time for it. Let those who have come for child's play be off now, while there is time, or they will surely come to grief. We want an organisation. Off with laziness. Spread! Spread! Run like fire to all places. Do not depend upon me. Whether I live or die, go on spreading, yourselves.

1894.111—GOVINDA SAHAY

C/O G. W. Hale, Esq.,
Chicago, U.S.A.,

DEAR GOVINDA SAHAY,

Do you keep any correspondence with my Gurubhâis of Calcutta? Are you progressing morally, spiritually, and in your worldly affairs?... Perhaps you have heard how for more than a year I have been preaching Hindu religion in America. I am doing very well here. Write to me as soon as you can and as often as you like.

Yours with love,
Vivekananda.

1894.112—GOVINDA SAHAY

U.S.A.,
1894.

DEAR GOVINDA SAHAY,

...Honesty is the best policy, and a virtuous man must gain in the end...You must always bear in mind, my son, that however busy or however distant, or living with men however high in position I may be, I am always praying, blessing, and remembering everyone of my friends, even the humblest.

Yours, with blessings,
Vivekananda.

1894.113 — BROTHER SHIVANANDA[1]

U. S. A.,
1894.

DEAR BROTHER SHIVANANDA,

Your letter just reached me. Perhaps by this time you have received my other letters and learnt that it is not necessary to send anything to America any more. Too much of everything is bad. This newspaper booming has given me popularity no doubt, but its effect is more in India than here. Here, on the other hand, constant booming creates a distaste in the minds of the higher class people; so enough. Now try to organise yourselves in India on the lines of these meetings. You need not send anything more in this country. As to money, I have determined first to build some place for Mother, (Holy Mother, Shri Sarada Devi.) for women require it first ... I can send nearly Rs. 7,000 for a place for Mother. If the place is first secured, then I do not care for anything else. I hope to be able to get Rs. 1,600 a year from this country even when I am gone. That sum I will make over to the support of the Women's place, and then it will grow. I have written to you already to secure a place ...

I would have, before this, returned to India, but India has no money. Thousands honour Ramakrishna Paramahamsa, but nobody will give a cent — that is India ... In the meanwhile live in harmony at any price. The world cares little for principles. They care for persons. They will hear with patience the words of a man they like, however nonsense, and will not listen to anyone they do not like. Think of this and modify your conduct accordingly. Everything will come all right. Be the servant if you will rule. That is the real secret. Your love will tell even if your words be harsh. Instinctively men feel the love clothed in whatever language. (These two paragraphs and the last half of the fourth were written in English.)

My dear brother, that Ramakrishna Paramahamsa was God incarnate, I have not the least doubt; but then you must let people find out for themselves what he used to teach — you cannot thrust these things upon them — this is my only objection.

Let people speak out their own opinions, why should we object? Without studying Ramakrishna Paramahamsa first, one can never understand the real import of the Vedas, the Vedanta, of the Bhâgavata and the other Purânas. His life is a searchlight of infinite power thrown upon the whole mass of Indian religious thought. He was the living commentary to the Vedas and to their aim. He had lived in one life the whole cycle of the national religious existence in India.

Whether Bhagavân Shri Krishna was born at all we are not sure; and Avataras like Buddha and Chaitanya are monotonous; Ramakrishna Paramahamsa is the latest and the most perfect — the concentrated embodiment of knowledge, love, renunciation, catholicity, and the desire to serve mankind. So where is anyone to compare with him? He must have been born in vain who cannot appreciate him! My supreme good fortune is that I am his servant through life after life. A single

1 Translated from Bengali.

word of his is to me far weightier than the Vedas and the Vedanta.—Oh, I am the servant of the servants of his servants. But narrow bigotry militates against his principles, and this makes me cross. Rather let his name be drowned in oblivion, and his teachings bear fruit instead! Why, was he a slave to fame? Certain fishermen and illiterate people called Jesus Christ a God, but the literate people killed him. Buddha was honoured in his lifetime by a number of merchants and cowherds. But Ramakrishna has been worshipped in his lifetime—towards the end of this nineteenth century—by the demons and giants of the university as God incarnate... Only a few things have been jotted down in the books about them (Krishna, Buddha, Christ, etc.). "One must be a wonderful housekeeper with whom we have never yet lived!" so the Bengali proverb goes. But here is a man in whose company we have been day and night and yet consider him to be a far greater personality than any of them. Can you understand this phenomenon?

You have not yet understood the wonderful significance of Mother's life—none of you. But gradually you will know. Without Shakti (Power) there is no regeneration for the world. Why is it that our country is the weakest and the most backward of all countries?—Because Shakti is held in dishonour there. Mother has been born to revive that wonderful Shakti in India; and making her the nucleus, once more will Gârgis and Maitreyis be born into the world. Dear brother, you understand little now, but by degrees you will come to know it all. Hence it is her Math that I want first... Without the grace of Shakti nothing is to be accomplished. What do I find in America and Europe?—the worship of Shakti, the worship of Power. Yet they worship Her ignorantly through sense-gratification. Imagine, then, what a lot of good they will achieve who will worship Her with all purity, in a Sattvika spirit, looking upon Her as their mother! I am coming to understand things clearer every day, my insight is opening out more and more. Hence we must first build a Math for Mother. First Mother and Mother's daughters, then Father and Father's sons—can you understand this?...To me, Mother's grace is a hundred thousand times more valuable than Father's. Mother's grace, Mother's blessings are all paramount to me... Please pardon me. I am a little bigoted there, as regards Mother. If but Mother orders, her demons can work anything. Brother, before proceeding to America I wrote to Mother to bless me. Her blessings came, and at one bound I cleared the ocean. There, you see. In this terrible winter I am lecturing from place to place and fighting against odds, so that funds may be collected for Mother's Math. Baburam's mother must have lost her sense owing to old age and that is why she is about to worship Durga in the earthen image, ignoring the living one. (Viz. Holy Mother Shri Sarada Devi.) Brother, faith is very difficult to achieve. Brother, I shall show how to worship the living Durga and then only shall I be worthy of my name. I shall be relieved when you will have purchased a plot of land and established there the living Durga, the Mother. Till then I am not returning to my native land. As soon as you can do that, I shall have a sigh of relief after sending the money. Do you accomplish this festival of Durga of mine by making all the necessary arrangements. Girish Ghosh is adoring the Mother splendidly; blessed is he, and blessed are his followers. Brother, often enough, when

I am reminded of the Mother, I ejaculate, "What after all is Rama?" Brother, that is where my fanaticism lies, I tell you. Of Ramakrishna, you may aver, my brother, that he was an Incarnation or whatever else you may like but fie on him who has no devotion for the Mother. Niranjan has a militant disposition, but he has great devotion for Mother and all his vagaries I can easily put up with. He is now doing the most marvellous work. I am keeping myself well posted. And you too have done excellently in co-operating with the Madrasis. Dear brother, I expect much from you, you should organise all for conjoint work. As soon as you have secured the land for Mother, I go to India straight. It must be a big plot; let there be a mud-house to begin with, in due course I shall erect a decent building, don't be afraid.

The chief cause of malaria lies in water. Why do you not construct two or three filters? If you first boil the water and then filter it, it will be harmless... Please buy two big Pasteur's bacteria-proof filters. Let the cooking be done in that water and use it for drinking purposes also, and you will never hear of malaria any more... On and on, work, work, work, this is only the beginning.

Yours ever,
Vivekananda.

1894.114 — BRAHMANANDA[1]

1894.

DEAR AND BELOVED, (Swami Brahmananda)

... Well, do you think there is any religion left in India! The paths of knowledge, devotion, and Yoga — all have gone, and now there remains only that of Don't touchism — "Don't touch me! Don't touch me!" The whole world is impure, and I alone am pure. Lucid Brahmajnâna! Bravo! Great God! Nowadays Brahman is neither in the recesses of the heart, nor in the highest heaven, nor in all beings — now He is in the cooking-pot. Formerly the characteristic of a noble-minded man was "— Pleasing the whole universe by one's numerous acts of service" but now it is — I am pure and the whole world is impure — go and get money and set it at my feet... Tell the sapient sage who writes to me to finish my preaching work here and return home, ... that this country is more my home. What is there in Hindusthan? Who appreciates religion? Who appreciates learning?

To return home! Where is the home! I do not care for liberation, or for devotion, I would rather go to a hundred thousand hells, "— this is my religion. I do not want to have any connection with lazy, hard-hearted, cruel and selfish men. He whose good fortune it is, may help in this great cause.

... Please convey to all my love, I want the help of everyone. Neither money pays, nor name, nor fame, nor learning; it is character that can cleave through adamantine walls of difficulties. Bear this in mind...

Yours ever,
Vivekananda.

---

1 Translated from Bengali.

1895

1895.1 — MRS. BULL

541 Dearborn Avenue, Chicago,
3rd January, 1895.

DEAR MRS. BULL,

I lectured at Brooklyn last Sunday, Mrs. Higgins gave a little reception the evening I arrived, and some of the prominent members of the Ethical Society including Dr. Jain [Janes] were there. Some of them thought that such Oriental religious subjects will not interest the Brooklyn public.

But the lecture, through the blessings of the Lord, proved a tremendous success. About 800 of the élite of Brooklyn were present, and the very gentlemen who thought it would not prove a success are trying for organising a series in Brooklyn. The New York course for me is nearly ready, but I do not wish to fix the dates until Miss Thursby comes to New York. As such Miss Phillips who is a friend of Miss Thursby's and who is arranging the New York course for me will act with Miss Thursby in case she wants to get up something in New York.

I owe much to the Hale family and I thought to give them a little surprise by dropping in on New Year's day. I am trying to get a new gown here. The old gown is here, but it is so shrunken by constant washings that it is unfit to wear in public. I am almost confident of finding the exact thing in Chicago.

I hope your father is all right by this time.

With my love to Miss Farmer, Mr. and Mrs. Gibbons and the rest of the holy family, I am ever yours,

Affectionately,
Vivekananda.

PS — I saw Miss Couring at Brooklyn. She was as kind as ever. Give her my love if you write her soon.

1895.2 — G. G.

Chicago,
11th January, 1895.

DEAR G. G, (G. G. NARASIMHACHARIAR)

Your letter just to hand... The Parliament of Religions was organised with the intention of proving the superiority of the Christian religion over other forms of faith, but the philosophic religion of Hinduism was able to maintain its position notwithstanding. Dr. Barrows and the men of that ilk are very orthodox, and I do not look to them for help... The Lord has sent me many friends in this country, and they are always on the increase. The Lord bless those who have tried to injure me... I have been running all the time between Boston and New York, two great centres of this country, of which Boston may be called the brain and New York, the purse. In both, my success is more than ordinary. I am indifferent to the newspaper reports, and you must not expect me to send any of them to you. A little boom was necessary to begin work. We have had more than enough of that.

I have written to Mani Iyer, and I have given you my directions already. Now show me what you can do. No foolish talk now, but actual work; the Hindus must back their talk with real work; if they cannot they do not deserve anything; that is all. America is not going to give you money for your fads. And why should they? As for me, I want to teach the truth; I do not care whether here or elsewhere.

In future do not pay any heed to what people say either for or against you or me. Work on, be lions; and the Lord will bless you. I shall work incessantly until I die, and even after death I shall work for the good of the world. Truth is infinitely more weighty than untruth; so is goodness. If you possess these, they will make their way by sheer gravity.

I have no connection with the Theosophists. And Judge will help me — pooh! ... Thousands of the best men do care for me; you know this, and have faith in the Lord. I am slowly exercising an influence in this land greater than all the newspaper blazoning of me can do. The orthodox feel it, but they cannot help it. It is the force of character, of purity, and of truth — of personality. So long as I have these things, you can feel easy; no one will be able to injure a hair of my head. If they try, they will fail, saith the Lord... Enough of books and theories. It is the life that is the highest and the only way to stir the hearts of people; it carries the personal magnetism... The Lord is giving me a deeper and deeper insight every day. Work, work, work... Truce to foolish talk; talk of the Lord. Life is too short to be spent in talking about frauds and cranks

You must always remember that every nation must save itself; so must every man; do not look to others for help. Through hard work here, I shall be able now and then to send you a little money for your work; but that is all. If you have to look forward to that, better stop work. Know also that this is a grand field for my ideas, and that I do not care whether they are Hindus or Mohammedans or Christians, but those that love the Lord will always command my service.

... I like to work on calmly and silently, and the Lord is always with me. Follow me, if you will, by being intensely sincere, perfectly unselfish, and, above all, by being perfectly pure. My blessings go with you. In this short life there is no time for the exchange of compliments. We can compare notes and compliment each other to our hearts' content after the battle is finished. Now, do not talk; work, work! work! I do not see anything permanent you hare done in India — I do not see any centre you have made — I do not see any temple or hall you have erected — I do not see anybody joining hands with you. There is too much talk, talk, talk! We are great, we are great! Nonsense! We are imbeciles; that is what we are! This hankering after name and fame and all other humbugs — what are they to me? What do I care about them? I should like to see hundreds coming to the Lord! Where are they? I want them, I want to see them. You must seek them out. You only give me name and fame. Have done with name and fame; to work, my brave men, to work! You have not caught my fire yet — you do not understand me! You run in the old ruts of sloth and enjoyments. Down with all sloth, down with all enjoyments here or hereafter. Plunge into the fire and bring the people towards the Lord.

That you may catch my fire, that you may be intensely sincere, that you may die the heroes' death on the field of battle — is the constant prayer of Vivekananda.

PS — Tell Alasinga, Kidi, Dr. Balaji, and all the others not to pin their faith on what Tom, Dick, and Harry say for or against us, but to concentrate all their energy on work.

1895.3 — ALASINGA

U.S.A.,
12th January, 1895.

DEAR ALASINGA,

I am sorry you still continue to send me pamphlets and newspapers, which I have written you several times not to do. I have no time to peruse them and take notice of them. Please send them no more. I do not care a fig for what the missionaries or the Theosophists say about me. Let them do as they please. The very taking notice of them will be to give them importance. Besides, you know, the missionaries only abuse and never argue.

Now know once and for all that I do not care for name or fame, or any humbug of that type. I want to preach my ideas for the good of the world. You have done a great work; but so far as it goes, it has only given me name and fame. My life is more precious than spending it in getting the admiration of the world. I have no time for such foolery. What work have you done in the way of advancing the ideas and organising in India? None, none, none!

An organisation that will teach the Hindus mutual help and appreciation is absolutely necessary. Five thousand people attended that meeting that was held in Calcutta, and hundreds did the same in other places, to express an appreciation of my work here — well and good! But if you asked them each to give an anna, would they do it? The whole national character is one of childish dependence. They are all ready to enjoy food if it is brought to their mouth, and even some want it pushed down... You do not deserve to live if you cannot help yourselves.

I have given up at present my plan for the education of the masses. It will come by degrees. What I now want is a band of fiery missionaries. We must have a College in Madras to teach comparative religions, Sanskrit, the different schools of Vedanta, and some European languages; we must have a press, and papers printed in English and in the Vernaculars. When this is done, then I shall know that you have accomplished something. Let the nation show that they are ready to do. If you cannot do anything of the kind in India, then let me alone. I have a message to give, let me give it to the people who appreciate it and who will work it out. What care I who takes it? "He who doeth the will of my Father," is my own…

My name should not be made prominent; it is my ideas that I want to see realised. The disciples of all the prophets have always inextricably mixed up the ideas of the Master with the person, and at last killed the ideas for the person. The disciples of Shri Ramakrishna must guard against doing the same thing. Work for the idea, not the person. The Lord bless you.

Yours ever with blessings,
Vivekananda.

1895.4 — MISS THURSBY

To Miss Emma Thursby:

Chicago, 541 Dearborn Avenue,
17 January, 1895.

DEAR MISS THURSBY,

I am very sorry to learn about the passing on of Mr. Thorp. Mrs. Bull must have felt it deeply. Still he has passed on after a good and useful life. All is for the best.

I have been lecturing every day to a class in Mrs. Adams's rooms at the Auditorium. Today I also lecture there and in the Evening to a class of Miss Josephine Locke's at the Plaza Hotel.

Have you seen Mrs. Peake in New York? She is lecturing to a class at Mrs. Guernsey's.

Miss Locke is as kind as usual. She is enamoured of Mrs. Peake as are many of Miss Locke's friends, you will be glad to learn.

Mrs. Peake has made a very favourable impression on Chicago. So she does wherever she goes.

Mrs. Adams invited me to an organ concert in the Auditorium. She is so good and kind to me. Lord bless her.

I have not seen Mr. Young, nor, I am afraid, [will] I have time to see [him,] as I start for New York on Friday next.

I will hear him once in New York.

I was so busy here these two weeks.

I have got a new scarlet coat but can get no orange here.

Ever with blessings,

Your brother,
Vivekananda.

1895.5 — SARADA[1]

228 W.39, New York,
17th Jan., 1895.

DEAR SARADA,

Your two letters are to hand, as also the two of Ramdayal Babu. I have got the bill of lading; but it will be long before the goods arrive. Unless one arranges for the prompt despatch of goods they take about six months to come. It is four months since Haramohan wrote that the Rudrâksha beads and Kusha mats had been despatched, but there is no news of their whereabouts yet. The thing is, when the goods reach England, the agent of the company here gives me notice; and about a month later, the goods arrive. I received your bill of lading about three weeks ago, but no sign of the notice! Only the goods sent by Raja of Khetri arrive quickly. Most probably he spends a lot of money for them. However it is a matter of congratulation that goods do arrive without fail in this region of Pâtâla, at the other end of the globe. I shall let you know as soon as the goods come. Now keep quiet for at least three months.

Now is the time for you to apply yourself to start the magazine. Tell Ramdayal Babu that though the gentleman of whom he speaks be a competent person, I am not in a position to have anybody in America at present... What about your article on Tibet? When it is published in the Mirror, send me a copy... Come, here is a task for you, conduct that magazine. Thrust it on people and make them subscribe to it, and don't be afraid. What work do you expect from men of little hearts? — Nothing in the world! You must have an iron will if you would cross the ocean. You must be strong enough to pierce mountains. I am coming next winter. We shall set the world on fire — let those who will, join us and be blessed, and those that won't come, will lag behind for ever and ever; let them do so. You gird up your loins and keep yourself ready... Never mind anything! In your lips and hands the Goddess of Learning will make Her seat; the Lord of infinite power will be seated on your chest; you will do works that will strike the world with wonder. By the bye, can't you shorten your name a bit, my boy? What a long, long name — a single name enough to fill a volume! Well, you hear people say that the Lord's name keeps away death! It is not the simple name Hari, mind you. It is those deep and sonorous names, such as (Destroyer of Agha, Bhaga, and Naraka) (Subduer of the pride of Tripura, demon of the "three cities"), and (Giver of infinite and endless blessings), and so forth — that put to rout King Death and his whole party. Won't it look nice if you simplify yours a little? But it is too late, I am afraid as it has already been abroad. But, believe me, it is a world-entrancing, death-defying name that you have got! (The full name which Swami Trigunatita, to whom this letter was addressed, bore at first was "Swami Trigunatitananda" — hence Swamiji's pleasantry about it.)

Yours affectionately,
Vivekananda.

1 Translated from Bengali.

PS — Throw the whole of Bengal and, for the matter of that, the whole of India into convulsion! Start centres at different places.

The Bhâgavata has reached me — a very nice edition indeed; but people of this country have not the least inclination for studying Sanskrit; hence there is very little hope for its sale. There may be a little in England, for there many are interested in the study of Sanskrit. Give my special thanks to the editor. I hope his noble attempt will meet with complete success. I shall try my best to push his book here. I have sent his prospectus to different places. Tell Ramdayal Babu that a flourishing trade can be set on foot with England and America in Mung Dâl, Arhar Dâl, etc. Dâl soup will have a go if properly introduced. There will be a good demand for these things if they be sent from house to house, in small packets, with directions for cooking on them and a depot started for storing a quantity of them. Similarly Badis (Pellets made of Dal, pounded and beaten.) too will have a good market. We want an enterprising spirit. Nothing is done by leading idle lives. If anyone forms a company and exports Indian goods here and into England, it will be a good trade. But they are a lazy set, enamoured of child marriage and nothing else.

1895.6 — MRS. OLE BULL

Brooklyn,
20th January, 1895.

(Written to Mrs. Ole Bull whom Swamiji called "Dhirâ Mâtâ", the "Steady Mother" on the occasion of the loss of her father.)

... I had a premonition of your father's giving up the old body and it is not my custom to write to anyone when a wave of would-be inharmonious Mâyâ strikes him. But these are the great turning points in life, and I know that you are unmoved. The surface of the sea rises and sinks alternately, but to the observant soul — the child of light — each sinking reveals more and more of the depth and of the beds of pearls and coral at the bottom. Coming and going is all pure delusion. The soul never comes nor goes. Where is the place to which it shall go when all space is in the soul? When shall be the time for entering and departing when all time is *in the soul*?

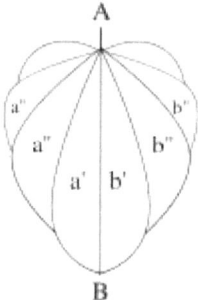

The earth moves, causing the illusion of the movement of the sun; but the sun does not move. So Prakriti, or Maya, or Nature, is moving, changing, unfolding veil after veil, turning over leaf after leaf of this grand book — while the witnessing soul drinks in knowledge, unmoved, unchanged. All souls that ever have been, are, or shall be, are all in the present tense and — to use a material simile — are all standing at one geometrical point. Because the idea of space does occur in the soul, therefore all that were ours, are ours, and will be ours, are always with us, were always with us, and will be always with us. We are in them. They are in us. Take these cells. Though each separate, they are all nevertheless inseparably joined at A B. There they are one. Each is an individual, yet all are one at the axis A B. None can escape from that axis, and however broken or torn the circumference, yet by standing at the axis, we may enter any one of the chambers. This axis is the Lord. There we are one with Him, all in all, and all in God.

The cloud moves across the face of the moon, creating the illusion that the moon is moving. So nature, body, matter moves on, creating the illusion that the soul is moving. Thus we find at last that, that instinct (or inspiration?) which men of every race, whether high or low, have had to feel, viz the presence of the departed about them, is true intellectually also.

Each soul is a star, and all stars are set in that infinite azure, that eternal sky, the Lord. There is the root, the reality, the real individuality of each and all. Religion began with the search after some of these stars that had passed beyond our horizon, and ended in finding them all in God, and ourselves in the same place. The whole secret is, then, that your father has given up the old garment he was wearing and is standing where he was through all eternity. Will he manifest another such garment in this or any other world? I sincerely pray that he may not, until he does so in full consciousness. I pray that none may be dragged anywhither by the unseen power of his own past actions. I pray that all may be free, that is to say, may know that they are free. And if they are to dream again, let us pray that their dreams be all of peace and bliss...

Yours etc.,
Vivekananda.

1895.7 — SHASHI[1]

(Beginning of?) 1895.

Yesterday I received a letter from you in which there was a smattering of news, but nothing in detail. I am much better now. Through the grace of the Lord I am proof against the severe cold for this year. Oh, the terrible cold! But these people keep all down through scientific knowledge. Every house has its cellar underground, in which there is a big boiler whence steam is made to course day and night through every room. This keeps all the rooms warm, but it has one defect, that while it is summer indoors, it is 30 to 40 degrees below zero outside! Most of the rich people

1 Translated from Bengali.

of this country make for Europe during the winter, which is comparatively warm.

Now, let me give you some instructions. This letter is meant for you. Please go through these instructions once a day and act up to them. I have got Sarada's letter—he is doing good work—but now we want organization. To him, Brother Tarak, and others please give my special love and blessings. The reason why I give you these few instructions is that there is an organising power in you—the Lord has made this known to me—but it is not yet fully developed. Through His blessings it will soon be. That you never lose your centre of gravity is an evidence of this, but it must be both intensive and extensive.

1. All the Shâstras hold that the threefold misery that there is in this world is not natural, hence it is removable.

2. In the Buddha Incarnation the Lord says that the root of the Âdhibhautika misery or, misery arising from other terrestrial beings, is the formation of classes (Jâti); in other words, every form of class-distinction, whether based on birth, or acquirements, or wealth is at the bottom of this misery. In the Atman there is no distinction of sex, or Varna or Ashrama, or anything of the kind, and as mud cannot be washed away by mud, it is likewise impossible to bring about oneness by means of separative ideas.

3. In the Krishna Incarnation He says that the root of all sorts of misery is Avidyâ (Nescience) and that selfless work purifies the mind. But "what is no-work" (Gita).

4. Only that kind of work which develops our spirituality is work. Whatever fosters materiality is no-work.

5. Therefore work and no-work must be regulated by a person's aptitude, his country, and his age.

6. Works such as sacrifices were suited to the olden times but are not for the modern times.

7. From the date that the Ramakrishna Incarnation was born, has sprung the Satya-Yuga (Golden Age)...

8. In this Incarnation atheistic ideas...will be destroyed by the sword of Jnana (knowledge), and the whole world will be unified by means of Bhakti (devotion) and Prema (Divine Love). Moreover, in this Incarnation, Rajas, or the desire for name and fame etc., is altogether absent. In other words, blessed is he who acts up to His teachings; whether he accepts Him or not, does not matter.

9. The founders of different sects, in the ancient or modern times, have not been in the wrong. They have done well, but they must do better. Well—better—best.

10. Therefore we must take all up where they are, that is, we must lead them on to higher and higher ideals, without upsetting their own chosen attitude. As to social conditions, those that prevail now are good, but they shall be better—best.

11. There is no chance for the welfare of the world unless the condition of women is improved. It is not possible for a bird to fly on only one wing.

12. Hence, in the Ramakrishna Incarnation the acceptance of a woman as the Guru, hence His practicing in the woman's garb and frame of mind, hence too His

preaching the motherhood of women as representations of the Divine Mother.

13. Hence it is that my first endeavour is to start a Math for women. This Math shall be the origin of Gârgis and Maitreyis, and women of even higher attainments than these...

14. No great work can be achieved by humbug. It is through love, a passion for truth, and tremendous energy, that all undertakings are accomplished.

15. There is no need for quarrel or dispute with anybody. Give your message and leave others to their own thoughts. "—Truth alone triumphs, not falsehood."—Why then fight?

...Combine seriousness with childlike naïveté. Live in harmony with all. Give up all idea of egoism, and entertain no sectarian views. Useless wrangling is a great sin.

...From Sarada's letter I came to know that N—Ghosh has compared me with Jesus Christ, and the like. That kind of thing may pass muster in our country, but if you send such comments here in print, there is a chance of my being insulted! I mean, I do not like to hamper anybody's freedom of thought—am I a missionary? If Kali has not sent those papers to this country, tell him not to do it. Only the Address will do, I do not want the proceedings. Now many respectable ladies and gentlemen of this country hold me in reverence. The missionaries and others of that ilk have tried their utmost to put me down, but finding it useless have now become quiet. Every undertaking must pass through a lot of obstacles. Truth triumphs if only one pursues a peaceful course. I have no need to reply to what a Mr. Hudson has spoken against me. In the first place, it is Unnecessary, and secondly, I shall be bringing myself down to the level of people of Mr. Hudson's type. Are you mad? Shall I fight from here with one Mr. Hudson? Through the Lord's grace, people who are far above Mr. Hudson in rank listen to me with veneration. Please do not send any more papers. Let all that go on in India, it will do no harm. For the Lord's work at one time there was need for that kind of newspaper blazoning. When that is done, there is no more need for it... It is one of the attendant evils of name and fame that you can't have anything private... Before you begin any undertaking, pray to Shri Ramakrishna, and he will show you the right way. We want a big plot of land to begin with, then building and all will come. Slowly our Math is going to raise itself, don't worry abbot it...

Kali and all others have done good work. Give my love and best wishes to all. Work in unison with the people of Madras, and let someone or other amongst you go there at intervals. Give up for ever the desire for name and fame and power. While I am on earth, Shri Ramakrishna is working through me. So long as you believe in this there is no danger of any evil for you.

The Ramakrishna Punthi (Life of Shri Ramakrishna in Bengali verse) that Akshaya has sent is very good, but there is no glorification of the Shakti at the opening which is a great defect. Tell him to remedy it in the second edition. Always bear this in mind that we are now standing before the gaze of the world, and that people are watching every one of our actions and utterances. Remember this and work.

...Be on the look-out for a site for our Math... If it be at some little distance from

Calcutta, no harm. Wherever we shall build our Math, there we shall have a stir made. Very glad to learn about Mahim Chakravarty. The Andes have turned into the holy Gaya, I see! Where is he? Please give him, Sj. Bijoy Goswami, and our other friends my cordial greetings... To beat an opponent one needs a sword and buckler, so carefully learn English and Sanskrit. Kali's English is getting nicer every day, while that of Sarada is deteriorating. Tell Sarada to give up the flowery style. It is extremely difficult to write a flowery style in a foreign tongue. Please convey to him a hundred thousand bravos from me! There's a hero indeed... Well done, all of you! Bravo, lads! The beginning is excellent. Go on in that way. If the adder of jealousy foes not come in, there is no fear!

— Those who serve My devotees are My best devotees." Have all of you a little grave bearing. I am not writing any book on Hinduism at present. But I am jotting down my thoughts. Every religion is an expression, a language to express the same truth, and we must speak to each in his own language. That Sarada has grasped this, is all right. It will be time enough to look to Hinduism later on. Do you think people in this country would be much attracted if I talk of Hinduism? — The very name of narrowness in ideas will scare them away! The real thing is — the Religion taught by Shri Ramakrishna, let the Hindus call it Hinduism — and others call it in their own way. Only you must proceed slowly. "— One must make journeys slowly." Give my blessings to Dinanath, the new recruit. I have very little time to write — always lecture, lecture, lecture. Purity, Patience, Perseverance... You must ask those numerous people who are now paying heed to Shri Ramakrishna's teachings, to help you pecuniarily to a certain extent. How can the Math be maintained unless they help you? You must not be shy of making this plain to all...

There is no gain in hastening my return from this country. In the first place, a little sound made here will resound there a great deal. Then, the people of this country are immensely rich and are bold enough to pay. While the people of our country have neither money nor the least bit of boldness.

You will know everything by degrees. Was Shri Ramakrishna the Saviour of India merely? It is this narrow idea that has brought about India's ruin, and her welfare is an impossibility so long as this is not rooted out. Had I the money I would send each one of you to travel all over the world. No great idea can have a place in the heart unless one steps out of his little corner. It will be verified in time. Every great achievement is done slowly. Such is the Lord's will...

Why didn't any of you write about Daksha and Harish? I shall be glad to know if you watch their whereabouts. That Sanyal is feeling miserable is because his mind is not yet pure like the water of the Ganga. It is not yet selfless, but will be in time. He will have no misery if he can give up the little crookedness and be straightforward. My special loving greetings to Rakhal and Hari. Take great care of them... Never forget that Rakhal was the special object of Shri Ramakrishna's love. Let nothing daunt you. Who on earth has the power to snub us so long as the Lord favours us? Even if you are at your last breath, be not afraid. Work on with the intrepidity of a lion but, at the same time with the tenderness of a flower. Let this year's Shri

Ramakrishna festival be celebrated in great pomp. Let the feeding be quite ordinary — Prasâda being distributed in earthen plates among the devotees standing in rows. There should be readings from Shri Ramakrishna's Life. Place books like the Vedas and the Vedanta together and perform Ârati before them... Avoid issuing invitation cards of the old style.

— With Bhagavan Shri Ramakrishna's blessings and our great esteem we have the pleasure to invite you." Write some such line, and then write that to defray the expenses of Shri Ramakrishna's Birthday Festival and those of the maintenance of the Math, you want his assistance. That if he likes, he may kindly send the money to such and such, at such and such address, and so on. Also add a page in English. The term "Lord Ramakrishna" has no meaning. You must give it up. Write "Bhagavan" in English characters, and add a line or two in English:

THE ANNIVERSARY OF
BHAGAVAN SHRI RAMAKRISHNA

Sir, we have great pleasure in inviting you to join us in celebrating the — th anniversary of Bhagavan Ramakrishna Paramahamsa. For the celebration of this great occasion and for the maintenance of the Alambazar Math funds are absolutely necessary. If you think that the cause is worthy of your sympathy, we shall be very grateful to receive your contribution to the great work.

Yours obediently,
(Name)

If you get more than enough money, spend only a little of it and keep the surplus as a reserve fund to defray your expenses. On the plea of offering the food to the Lord, do not make everybody wait till he is sick, to have a stale and unsavoury dinner. Have two filters made and use that filtered water for both cooking and drinking purposes. Boil the water before filtering. If you do this, you will never more hear of malaria. Keep a strict eye on everybody's health. If you can give up lying on the floor — in other words, if you can get the money to do it, it will be excellent indeed. Dirty clothes are the chief cause of disease... About the food offering, let me tell you that only a little Payasânna (milk-rice with sugar) will do. He used to love that alone. It is true that the worship-room is a help to many, but it is no use indulging in Râjasika and Tâmasika food. Let the ceremonials give place to a certain extent to a little study of the Gita or the Upanishads or other sacred books. What I mean is this — let there be as little materialism as possible, with the maximum of spirituality... Did Shri Ramakrishna come for this or that particular individual, or for the world at large? If the latter, then you must present him in such a light that the whole world may understand him... You must not identify yourselves with any life of his written by anybody nor give your sanction to any. There is no danger so long as such books do not come out associated with our name... "Say yea, yea, to all and stick to your own."

...A thousand thanks to Mahendra Babu for his kindly helping us. He is a very liberal-hearted man... About Sanyal, he will attain the highest good by doing his bit of work attentively, that is, by simply serving Shri Ramakrishna's children... Brother Tarak is doing very good work. Bravo! Well done! That is what we want. Let me see all of you shoot like so many meteors! What is Gangadhar doing? Some Zemindars in Rajputana respect him. Tell him to get some money from them as Bhikshâ; then he is a man...

Just now I read Akshaya's book. Give him a hundred thousand hearty embraces from me. Through his pen Shri Ramakrishna is manifesting himself. Blessed is Akshaya! Let him recite that Punthi before all. He must recite it before all in the Festival. If the work be too large, let him read extracts of it. Well, I do not find a single irrelevant word in it. I cannot tell in words the joy I have experienced by reading his book. Try all of you to give the book an extensive sale. Then ask Akshaya to go from village to village to preach. Well done Akshaya! He is doing his work. Go from village to village and proclaim to all Shri Ramakrishna's teachings, can there be a more blessed lot than this? I tell you, Akshaya's book and Akshaya himself must electrify the masses. Dear, dear, Akshaya, I bless you with all my heart, my dear brother. May the Lord sit in your tongue! Go and spread his teachings from door to door. There is no need whatever of your becoming a Sannyasin... Akshaya is the future apostle for the masses of Bengal. Take great care of Akshaya; his faith and devotion have borne fruit.

Ask Akshaya to write these few points in the third section of his book, "The Propagation of the Faith".

1. Whatever the Vedas, the Vedanta, and all other Incarnations have done in the past, Shri Ramakrishna lived to practice in the course of a single life.

2. One cannot understand the Vedas, the Vedanta, the Incarnations, and so forth, without understanding his life. For he was the explanation.

3. From the very date that he was born, has sprung the Satya-Yuga (Golden Age). Henceforth there is an end to all sorts of distinctions, and everyone down to the Chandâla will be a sharer in the Divine Love. The distinction between man and woman, between the rich and the poor, the literate and illiterate, Brahmins and Chandalas—he lived to root out all. And he was the harbinger of Peace—the separation between Hindus and Mohammedans, between Hindus and Christians, all are now things of the past. That fight about distinctions that there was, belonged to another era. In this Satya-Yuga the tidal wave of Shri Ramakrishna's Love has unified all.

Tell him to expand these ideas and write them in his own style.

Whoever—man or woman—will worship Shri Ramakrishna, be he or she ever so low, will be then and there converted into the very highest. Another thing, the Motherhood of God is prominent in this Incarnation. He used to dress himself as a woman—he was, as it were, our Mother—and we must likewise look upon all women as the reflections of the Mother. In India there are two great evils. Trampling on the women, and grinding the poor through caste restrictions. He was the Saviour of women, Saviour of the masses, Saviour of all, high and low. And let

Akshaya introduce his worship in every home — Brahmin or Chandala, man or woman — everyone has the right to worship him. Whoever will worship him only with devotion shall be blessed for ever.

Tell him to write in this strain. Never mind anything — the Lord will be at his side.

Yours affectionately,
Vivekananda.

PS— ...Ask Sanyal to send me a copy each of the Nârada and Shândilya Sutras, and one of the Yogavâsishtha, that has been translated in Calcutta. I want the English translation of the last, not a Bengali edition...

1895.8 — SISTER

54 W. 33rd Street, N.Y.,
1st February, 1895.

DEAR SISTER[1],

I just received your beautiful note... Well, sometimes it is a good discipline to be forced to work for work's sake, even to the length of not being allowed to enjoy the fruits of one's labour... I am very glad of your criticisms and am not sorry at all. The other day at Miss Thursby's I had an excited argument with a Presbyterian gentleman, who, as usual, got very hot, angry, and abusive. However, I was afterwards severely reprimanded by Mrs. Bull for this, as such things hinder my work. So, it seems, is your opinion.

I am glad you write about it just now, because I have been giving a good deal of thought to it. In the first place, I am not at all sorry for these things — perhaps that may disgust you — it may. I know full well how good it is for one's worldly prospects to be sweet. I do everything to be sweet, but when it comes to a horrible compromise with the truth within, then I stop. I do not believe in humility. I believe in Samadarshitva — same state of mind with regard to all. The duty of the ordinary man is to obey the commands of his "God", society; but the children of light never do so. This is an eternal law. One accommodates himself to surroundings and social opinion and gets all good things from society, the giver of all good to such. The other stands alone and draws society up towards him. The accommodating man finds a path of roses; the non-accommodating, one of thorns. But the worshippers of "Vox populi" go to annihilation in a moment; the children of truth live for ever.

I will compare truth to a corrosive substance of infinite power. It burns its way in wherever it falls — in soft substance at once, hard granite slowly, but it must. What is writ is writ. I am so, so sorry, Sister, that I cannot make myself sweet and accommodating to every black falsehood. But I cannot. I have suffered for it all my life. But I cannot. I have essayed and essayed. But I cannot. At last I have given it

1. Miss Mary Hale.

up. The Lord is great. He will not allow me to become a hypocrite. Now let what is in come out. I have not found a way that will please all, and I cannot but be what I am, true to my own self. "Youth and beauty vanish, life and wealth vanish, name and fame vanish, even the mountains crumble into dust. Friendship and love vanish. Truth alone abides." God of Truth, be Thou alone my guide! I am too old to change now into milk and honey. Allow me to remain as I am. "Without fear—without shopkeeping, caring neither for friend nor foe, do thou hold on to Truth, Sannyâsin, and from this moment give up this world and the next and all that are to come—their enjoyments and their vanities. Truth, be thou alone my guide." I have no desire for wealth or name or fame or enjoyments, Sister—they are dust unto me. I wanted to help my brethren. I have not the tact to earn money, bless the Lord. What reason is there for me to conform to the vagaries of the world around me and not obey the voice of Truth within? The mind is still weak, Sister, it sometimes mechanically clutches at earthly help. But I am not afraid. Fear is the greatest sin my religion teaches.

The last fight with the Presbyterian priest and the long fight afterwards with Mrs. Bull showed me in a clear light what Manu says to the Sannyasin, "Live alone, walk alone." All friendship, all love, is only limitation. There never was a friendship, especially of women, which was not exacting. O great sages! You were right. One cannot serve the God of Truth who leans upon somebody. Be still, my soul! Be alone! and the Lord is with you. Life is nothing! Death is a delusion! All this is not, God alone is! Fear not, my soul! Be alone. Sister, the way is long, the time is short, evening is approaching. I have to go home soon. I have no time to give my manners a finish. I cannot find time to deliver my message. You are good, you are so kind, I will do anything for you; and do not be angry, I see you all are mere children.

Dream no more! Oh, dream no more, my soul! In one word, I have a message to give, I have no time to be sweet to the world, and every attempt at sweetness makes me a hypocrite. I will die a thousand deaths rather than lead a jelly-fish existence and yield to every requirement of this foolish world, no matter whether it be my own country or a foreign country. You are mistaken, utterly mistaken, if you think I have a work, as Mrs. Bull thinks; I have no work under or beyond the sun. I have a message, and I will give it after my own fashion. I will neither Hinduise my message, nor Christianise it, nor make it any "ise" in the world. I will only my-ise it and that is all. Liberty, Mukti, is all my religion, and everything that tries to curb it, I will avoid by fight or flight. Pooh! I try to pacify the priests!! Sister, do not take this amiss. But you are babies and babies must submit to be taught. You have not yet drunk of that fountain which makes "reason unreason, mortal immortal, this world a zero, and of man a God". Come out if you can of this network of foolishness they call this world. Then I will call you indeed brave and free. If you cannot, cheer those that dare dash this false God, society, to the ground and trample on its unmitigated hypocrisy; if you cannot cheer them, pray, be silent, but do not try to drag them down again into the mire with such false nonsense as compromise and becoming nice and sweet.

I hate this world, this dream, this horrible nightmare with its churches and chicaneries, its books and blackguardisms, its fair faces and false hearts, its howling righteousness on the surface and utter hollowness beneath, and, above all, its sanctified shopkeeping. What! measure my soul according to what the bond-slaves of the world say? — Pooh! Sister, you do not know the Sannyasin. "He stands on the heads of the Vedas!" say the Vedas, because he is free from churches and sects and religions and prophets and books and all of that ilk! Missionary or no missionary, let them howl and attack me with all they can, I take them as Bhartrihari says, "Go thou thy ways, Sannyasin! Some will say, 'Who is this mad man?' Others, 'Who is this Chandâla?' Others will know thee to be a sage. Be glad at the prattle of the worldlings." But when they attack, know that, "The elephant passing through the market-place is always beset by curs, but he cares not. He goes straight on his own way. So it is always, when a great soul appears there will be numbers to bark after him."[1]

I am living with Landsberg at 54 W. 33rd Street. He is a brave and noble soul, Lord bless him. Sometimes I go to the Guernseys' to sleep.

Lord bless you all ever and ever — and may He lead you quickly out of this big humbug, the world! May you never be enchanted by this old witch, the world! May Shankara help you! May Umâ open the door of truth for you and take away all your delusions!

Yours with love and blessings,
Vivekananda.

1895.9 — ADHYAPAKJI

To Professor John H. Wright:

54 W. 33 Street, New York,
1 February, 1895.

DEAR ADHYAPAKJI,

You must be immersed in your work now; however, taking advantage of your kindness to me, I want to bother you a little.

What was the original Greek idea of the soul, both philosophical and popular? What books can I consult (Translations, of course) to get it?

So with the Egyptians and Babylonians and Jews?

Will you kindly name me the books? I am sure you are perfectly well and so are Mrs. Wright and the children.

Ever gratefully and fraternally,

Yours,
Vivekananda.

---

1. Tulasidasa.

1895.10 — SANYAL[1]

54 W. 33rd St., New York,
9th February, 1895.

DEAR SANYAL,

... Paramahamsa Deva was my Guru, and whatever I may think of him in point of greatness, why should the world think like me? And if you press the point hard, you will spoil everything. The idea of worshipping the Guru as God is nowhere to be met with outside Bengal, for other people are not yet ready to take up that ideal... Many would fain associate my name with themselves — "I belong to them!" But when it comes to doing something I want, they are nowhere. So selfish is the whole world!

I shall consider myself absolved from a debt of obligation when I succeed in purchasing some land for Mother. I don't care for anything after that.

In this dire winter I have travelled across mountains and over snows at dead of night and collected a little fund; and I shall have peace of mind when a plot is secured for Mother.

Henceforth address my letters as above, which is to be my permanent seat from now. Try to send me an English translation of the Yogavâsishtha Râmâyana... Don't forget those books I asked for before, viz Sanskrit Nârada and Shândilya Sutras.

"Hope is the greatest of miseries, the highest bliss lies in giving up hope."

Yours affectionately,
Vivekananda.

1895.11 — ALASINGA

19 W., 38 St.,
New York, 1895.

DEAR ALASINGA,

... Meddle not with so-called social reform, for there cannot be any reform without spiritual reform first. Who told you that I want social reform? Not I. Preach the Lord — say neither good nor bad about the superstitions and diets. Do not lose heart, do not lose faith in your Guru, do not lose faith in God. So long as you possess these three, nothing can harm you, my child. I am growing stronger every day. Work on, my brave boys.

Ever yours with blessings,
Vivekananda.

---

1 Translated from Bengali.

1895.12 — MRS. BULL

54 W. 33rd St., New York,
14th February, 1895.

DEAR MRS. BULL,

Accept my heartfelt gratitude for your motherly advice. I hope I will be able to carry out them in life.

How can I express my gratitude to you for what you have already done for me and my work, and my eternal gratitude to you for your offering to do something more this year. But I sincerely believe that you ought to turn all your help to Miss Farmer's Greenacre work this year. India can wait as she is waiting centuries and an immediate work at hand should always have the preference.

Again, according to Manu, collecting funds even for a good work is not good for a Sannyasin, and I have begun to feel that the old sages were right. "Hope is the greatest misery, despair is the greatest happiness." It appears like a hallucination. I am getting out of them. I was in these childish ideas of doing this and doing that.

"Give up all desire and be at peace. Have neither friends nor foes, and live alone. Thus shall we travel having neither friends nor foes, neither pleasure nor pain, neither desire nor jealousy, injuring no creatures, being the cause of injury to no creatures—from mountain to mountain, from village to village, preaching the name of the Lord."

"Seek no help from high or low, from above or below. Desire nothing—and look upon this vanishing panorama as a witness and let it pass."

Perhaps these mad desires were necessary to bring me over to this country. And I thank the Lord for the experience.

I am very happy now. Between Mr. Landsberg and me, we cook some rice and lentils or barley and quietly eat it, and write something or read or receive visits from poor people who want to learn something, and thus I feel I am more a Sannyasin now than I ever was in America.

"In wealth is the fear of poverty, in knowledge the fear of ignorance, in beauty the fear of age, in fame the fear of backbiters, in success the fear of jealousy, even in body is the fear of death. Everything in this earth is fraught with fear. He alone is fearless who has given up everything" (Vairâgya-Shatakam, 31).

I went to see Miss Corbin the other day, and Miss Farmer and Miss Thursby were also there. We had a nice half-hour and she wants me to hold some classes in her home from next Sunday.

I am no more seeking for these things. If they come, the Lord be blessed, if not, blessed more be He.

Again accept my eternal gratitude.

Your devoted son,
Vivekananda.

1895.13 — MOTHER

To Mrs. G. W. Hale:

54 W. 33., New York,
18 March, [February?] 1895.

DEAR MOTHER,

I am sure you are all right by this time. The babies write from time to time and so I get your news regularly. Miss Mary is in a lecturing mood now — good for her. Hope she will not let her energies fritter away now — a penny saved is a penny gained. Sister Isabel[le] has sent me the French Books and the Calcutta pamphlets have arrived, but the big Sanskrit books ought to come. I want them badly. Make them payable here, if possible, or I will send you the postage.

I am doing very well. Only some of these big dinners kept me late, and I returned home at 2 o'clock in the morning several days. Tonight I am going to one of these. This will be the last of its kind. So much keeping up the night is not good for me. Every day from 11 to 1 o'clock I have classes in my rooms and I talk [to] them till they [grow] tired. The Brooklyn course ended yesterday. Another lecture I have there next Monday.

Bean soup and rice or barley is now my general diet. I am faring well. Financially I am making the ends meet and nothing more because I do not charge anything for the classes I have in my rooms. And the public lectures have to go through so many hands.

I have a good many lectures planned ahead in New York, which I hope to deliver by and by. Sister Isabel wrote to me a beautiful letter and she does so much for me. My eternal gratitude to her.

Baby has stopped writing; I do not know why.

Kindly tell Baby to send me a little Sanskrit book which came from India. I forgot to bring it over. I want to translate some passages from it.

Mr. [Charles M.] Higgins is full of joy. It was he who planned all this for me, and he is so glad that everything succeeded so well.

Mrs. Guernsey is going to give up this house and going to some other house. Miss [Florence] Guernsey wants to marry but her father and mother do not like it at all. I am very sorry for her, poor "Sister Jenny" — and so many men are after her. Here is a very rich railway gentleman called Mr. [Austin] Corbin; his only daughter, Miss [Anna] Corbin, is very much interested in me. And though she is one of the leaders of the 400, she is very intellectual and spiritual too, in a way. Their house is always chock full of swells and foreign aristocracy. Princes and Barons and whatnot from all over the world. Some of these foreigners are very bright. I am sorry your home-manufactured aristocracy is not very interesting. Behind her parlor she has a long arbour with all sorts of palms and seats and electric light. There I will have a little class next week of a score of long-pockets. The Fun is not bad. "This world is a great humbug after all", Mother. "God alone is real; everything else is a dream only." Mother Temple says she does not like to be bossed by you and that is why she does not come to Chicago. She is very happy nearby. Between swells and Delmonico and Waldorf dinners, my health was going to be injured. So I quickly turned a thorough vegetarian to avoid all invitations. The rich are really the salt of this world — they are neither food nor drink. Goodbye for the present.

Your ever affectionate Son,
Vivekananda.

1895.14 — SISTER

54 West, 33 New York,
25th February, 1895.

DEAR SISTER[1],

I am sorry you had an attack of illness. I will give you an absent treatment though your confession takes half the strength out of my mind.

That you have rolled put of it is all right. All's well that ends well.

The books have arrived in good condition and many thanks for them.

Your ever affectionate bro.,
Vivekananda.

1895.15 — ALASINGA

U. S. A.,
6th March, 1895.

DEAR ALASINGA,

… Do not for a moment think the "Yankees" are practical in religion. In that the Hindu alone is practical, the Yankee in money-making, so that as soon as I depart, the whole thing will disappear. Therefore I want to have a solid ground under my feet before I depart. Every work should be made thorough… You need not insist upon preaching Shri Ramakrishna. Propagate his ideas first, though I know the world always wants the Man first, then the idea… Do not figure out big plans at first, but begin slowly, feel your ground, and proceed up and up.

… Work on, my brave boys. We shall see the light some day.

Harmony and peace! … Let things slowly grow. Rome was not built in a day. The Maharaja of Mysore is dead — one of our greatest hopes. Well! the Lord is great. He will send others to help the cause.

1. Isabelle McKindley. Swamiji took delight in gently teasing the Hale sisters (of whom Isabelle was one) about their study and practice of Christian Science. He wrote this short note from New York, and in this he slyly poked fun at the "'Scientists'" practice of never confessing to sickness.

Send some Kushâsanas (small sitting-mats) if you can.

Yours ever with blessings,
Vivekananda.

1895.16 — MOTHER

To Mrs. G. W. Hale:

54 W. 33rd St., New York,
11 March, 1895.

DEAR MOTHER,

Many thanks for your kind letter. I will be only too glad to have an orange coat, provided it be light as summer is approaching.

I do not remember whether the Cook's letters of credit I have are limited as to their time or not. It is high time we look into them. If they are limited, don't you think it is better to put them in some bank? I have about a thousand dollars in the Boston bank and a few hundred in the New York — they all go to India by this week or next. So it is better that I look into the Cook's letters, and it will be foolish to get into trouble by having them past the date.

There are a few more Sanskrit books which have not been sent — one pretty thick and broad, the other two very thin. Kindly send them as soon as you can.

Mrs. [Milward] Adams, Mrs. [Ole] Bull, and Miss Emma Thursby are gone to Chicago today.

With eternal love to the babies and to you and Father Pope.

I remain ever your affectionate Son,
Vivekananda.

1895.17 — MOTHER

To Mrs. G. W. Hale:

[54 W. 33rd St., New York],
14 March, 1895.

DEAR MOTHER,

The last letter you sent over is a notice from the Chicago post office of a parcel received by them. I think it is some books sent to me from India. The rugs cannot come through the post office (?) I do not know what to do. I send you therefore back this notice, and if they deliver it to you, all right — else I hope you will ask them to send it over to New York and kindly give them my address.

Yours obediently,
Vivekananda.

1895.18 — MRS. BULL

54 W. 33rd St., New York,
21st March, 1895.

DEAR MRS. BULL,

I am astonished to hear the scandals the Ramabai circles are indulging in about me. Don't you see, Mrs. Bull, that however a man may conduct himself, there will always be persons who invent the blackest lies about him? At Chicago I had such things every day against me. And these women are invariably the very Christian of Christians!... I am going to have a series of paid lectures in my rooms (downstairs), which will seat about a hundred persons, and that will cover the expenses. I am in no great hurry about the money to be sent to India. I will wait. Is Miss Farmer with you? Is Mrs. Peake at Chicago? Have you seen Josephine Locke? Miss Hamlin has been very kind to me and does all she can to help me.

My master used to say that these names, as Hindu, Christian, etc., stand as great bars to all brotherly feelings between man and man. We must try to break them down first. They have lost all their good powers and now only stand as baneful influences under whose black magic even the best of us behave like demons. Well, we will have to work hard and must succeed.

That is why I desire so much to have a centre. Organisation has its faults, no doubt, but without that nothing can be done. And here, I am afraid, I will have to differ from you — that no one ever succeeded in keeping society in good humour and at the same time did great works. One must work as the dictate comes from within, and then if it is light and good, society is bound to veer round, perhaps centuries after one is dead and gone. We must plunge heart and soul and body into the work. And until we be ready to sacrifice everything else to one Idea and to one alone, we never, never will see the light.

Those that want to help mankind must take their own pleasure and pain, name and fame, and all sorts of interests, and make a bundle of them and throw them into the sea, and then come to the Lord. This is what all the Masters said and did.

I went to Miss Corbin's last Saturday and told her that I should not be able to come to hold classes any more. Was it ever in the history of the world that any great work was done by the rich? It is the heart and the brain that do it ever and ever and not the purse.

My idea and all my life with it — and to God for help; to none else! This is the only secret of success. I am sure you are one with me here. My love to Mrs. Thursby and Mrs. Adams.

Ever yours in grateful affection,
Vivekananda.

1895.19 — SISTER

54 W., 33 New York,
27th March, 1895.

DEAR SISTER, (Isabelle McKindley)

Your kind note gave me pleasure inexpressible. I was also able to read it through very easily. I have at last hit upon the orange and have got a coat, but could not as yet get any in summer material. If you get any, kindly inform me. I will have it made here in New York. Your wonderful Dearborn Ave misfit tailor is too much even for a monk.

Sister Locke writes me a long letter and perhaps wondering at my delay in reply. She is apt to be carried away by enthusiasm; so I am waiting, and again I do not know what to answer. Kindly tell her from me that it is impossible for me to fix any place just now. Mrs. Peake though noble, grand, and very spiritual, is as much clever in worldly matter as I, yet I am getting cleverer every day. Mrs. Peake has been offered, by some one whom she knows only hazily in Washington, a place for summer.

Who knows that she will not be played upon? This is a wonderful country for cheating, and 99.9 per cent have some motive in the background to take advantage of others. If any one just but closes his eyes for a moment, he is gone!! Sister Josephine is fiery. Mrs. Peake is a simple good woman. I have been so well handled by the people here that I look round me for hours before I take a step. Everything will come to right. Ask Sister Josephine to have a little patience.

You are every day finding kindergarten better than running an old man's home I am sure. You saw Mrs. Bull, and I am sure you were quite surprised to find her so tame and gentle. Do you see Mrs. Adams now and then? Mrs. Bull has been greatly benefited by her lessons. I also took a few, but no use; the ever increasing load in front does not allow me to bend forward as Mrs. Adams wants it. If I try to bend forward in walking, the centre of gravity comes to the surface of the stomach, and so I go cutting front somersaults.

No millionaire coming? Not even a few hundred thousands? Sorry, very sorry!!! I am trying my best; what I can do? My classes are full of women. You of course cannot marry a woman. Well, have patience. I will keep my eyes open and never let go an opportunity. If you do not get one, it would not be owing to any laziness at least on my part.

Life goes on the same old ruts. Sometimes I get disgusted with eternal lecturings and talkings, want to be silent for days and days.

Hoping you the best dreams (for that is the only way to be happy).

I remain ever your loving bro.,
Vivekananda.

1895.20 — ALASINGA

U. S. A.,
4th April, 1895.

DEAR ALASINGA,

Your letter just to hand. You need not be afraid of anybody's attempting to hurt me. So long as the Lord protects me I shall be impregnable. Your ideas of America are very hazy... This is a huge country, the majority do not care much about religion... Christianity holds its ground as a mere patriotism, and nothing more.

... Now my son, do not lose courage... Send me the Vedanta-Sutras and the Bhâshyas (commentaries) of all the sects... I am in His hands. What is the use of going back to India? India cannot further my ideas. This country takes kindly to my ideas. I will go back when I get the Command. In the meanwhile, do you all gently and patiently work. If anybody attacks me, simply ignore his existence... My idea is for you to start a Society where people could be taught the Vedas and the Vedanta, with the commentaries. Work on this line at present... Know that every time you feel weak, you not only hurt yourself but also the Cause. Infinite faith and strength are the only conditions of success.

Be cheerful... Hold on to your own ideal... Above all, never attempt to guide or rule others, or, as the Yankees say, "boss" others. Be the servant of all.

Ever yours with blessings,
Vivekananda.

1895.21 — FRIEND

To Mr. Francis Leggett:

New York,
10th April, 1895.

DEAR FRIEND,

It is impossible to express my gratitude for your kindly inviting me to your country seat [Ridgely]. I am involved in a mistake now and find it impossible for me to come tomorrow. Tomorrow I have a class at Miss Andrews' of 40 W. 9th Street. As I was given to understand by Miss MacLeod that that class could be postponed, I was only too glad at the prospect of joining the company tomorrow. But I find that Miss MacLeod was mistaken and Miss Andrews came to tell me that she could not by any means stop the class tomorrow or even give notice to the members, who are about 50 or 60 in number.

In view of this I sincerely regret my inability and hope that Miss MacLeod and Mrs. Sturges will understand that it is an unavoidable circumstance, and not the will, that stands in the way of my taking advantage of your kind invitation.

I shall only be too glad to come day after tomorrow, or any other day this week, as it suits you.

Ever sincerely yours,
Vivekananda.

1895.22 — FRIEND

To Mr. E. T. Sturdy:

54 W. 33rd Street, New York,
24th April, 1895.

DEAR FRIEND,

I am perfectly aware that although some truth underlies the mass of mystical thought which has burst upon the Western world of late, it is for the most part full of motives, unworthy, or insane. For this reason, I have never had anything to do with these phases of religion, either in India or elsewhere, and mystics as a class are not very favourable to me...

I quite agree with you that only the Advaita philosophy can save mankind, whether in East or West, from "devil worship" and kindred superstitions, giving tone and strength to the very nature of man. India herself requires this, quite as much or even more than the West. Yet it is hard uphill work, for we have first to create a taste, then teach, and lastly proceed to build up the whole fabric.

Perfect sincerity, holiness, gigantic intellect, and an all-conquering will. Let only a handful of men work with these, and the whole world will be revolutionised. I did a good deal of platform work in this country last year, and received plenty of applause, but found that I was only working for myself. It is the patient upbuilding of character, the intense struggle to realise the truth, which alone will tell in the future of humanity. So this year I am hoping to work along this line—training up to practical Advaita realisation a small band of men and women. I do not know how far I shall succeed. The West is the field for work if a man wants to benefit humanity, rather than his own particular sect or country. I agree perfectly as to your idea of a magazine. But I have no business capacity at all to do these things. I can teach and preach, and sometimes write. But I have intense faith in Truth. The Lord will send help and hands to work with me. Only let me be perfectly pure, perfectly sincere, and perfectly unselfish.

"Truth alone triumphs, not untruth; through truth alone stretches the way to the Lord" (Atharva-Veda). He who gives up the little self for the world will find the whole universe his... I am very uncertain about coming to England. I know no one there, and here I am doing some work. The Lord will guide, in His own time.

Yours etc.,
Vivekananda.

1895.23 — FRIEND

To Mr. E. T. Sturdy:

54 W. 33rd Street, New York,
24th April, 1895.

DEAR FRIEND,

I am perfectly aware that although some truth underlies the mass of mystical thought which has burst upon the Western world of late, it is for the most part full of motives, unworthy, or insane. For this reason, I have never had anything to do with these phases of religion, either in India or elsewhere, and mystics as a class are not very favourable to me...

I quite agree with you that only the Advaita philosophy can save mankind, whether in East or West, from "devil worship" and kindred superstitions, giving tone and strength to the very nature of man. India herself requires this, quite as much or even more than the West. Yet it is hard uphill work, for we have first to create a taste, then teach, and lastly proceed to build up the whole fabric.

Perfect sincerity, holiness, gigantic intellect, and an all-conquering will. Let only a handful of men work with these, and the whole world will be revolutionised. I did a good deal of platform work in this country last year, and received plenty of applause, but found that I was only working for myself. It is the patient upbuilding of character, the intense struggle to realise the truth, which alone will tell in the future of humanity. So this year I am hoping to work along this line — training up to practical Advaita realisation a small band of men and women. I do not know how far I shall succeed. The West is the field for work if a man wants to benefit humanity, rather than his own particular sect or country. I agree perfectly as to your idea of a magazine. But I have no business capacity at all to do these things. I can teach and preach, and sometimes write. But I have intense faith in Truth. The Lord will send help and hands to work with me. Only let me be perfectly pure, perfectly sincere, and perfectly unselfish.

"Truth alone triumphs, not untruth; through truth alone stretches the way to the Lord" (Atharva-Veda). He who gives up the little self for the world will find the whole universe his... I am very uncertain about coming to England. I know no one there, and here I am doing some work. The Lord will guide, in His own time.

Yours etc.,
Vivekananda.

1895.24 — BROTHER

54 W. 33 New York,
25th April, 1895.

DEAR BROTHER, (to Dr. I. Janes)

I was away in the Catskill mountains and it was almost impossible to get a letter regularly posted from where I was—so accept my apology for the delay in offering you my most heartfelt thanks for your letter in the "Eagle".

It was so scholarly, truthful and noble and withal so permeated with your natural universal love for the good and true everywhere. It is a great work to bring this world into a spirit of sympathy with each other but it should be done no doubt when such brave souls as you still hold your own. Lord help you ever and ever my brother and may you live long to carry on the mighty work you and your society has undertaken.

With my gratitude and love to you and to the members of the Ethical Society.

I remain Yours ever truly,
Vivekananda.

1895.25 — MRS. BULL

54 W. 33rd St., New York,
25th April, 1895.

DEAR MRS. BULL,

The day before yesterday I received a kind note from Miss Farmer including a cheque for a hundred dollars for the Barbar House lectures. She is coming to New York next Saturday. I will of course tell her to put my name in her circulars; and what is more, I cannot go to Greenacre now; I have arranged to go to the Thousand Islands, wherever that may be. There is a cottage belonging to Miss Dutcher, one of my students, and a few of us will be there in rest and peace and seclusion. I want to manufacture a few "Yogis" out of the materials of the classes, and a busy farm like Greenacre is the last place for that, while the other is quite out of the way, and none of the curiosity-seekers will dare go there.

I am very glad that Miss Hamlin took down the names of the 130 persons who come to the Jnana-Yoga class. There are 50 more who come to the Wednesday Yoga class and about 50 more to the Monday class. Mr. Landsberg had all the names; and they will come anyhow, names or no names... If they do not, others will, and so it will go on—the Lord be praised.

Taking down names and giving notices is a big task, no doubt, and I am very thankful to both of them for doing that for me. But I am thoroughly persuaded that it is laziness on my part, and therefore immoral, to depend on others, and always evil comes out of laziness. So henceforth I will do it all myself…

However, I will be only too glad to take in any one of Miss Hamlin's "right sort of persons", but unfortunately for me, not one such has as yet turned up. It is the duty of the teacher always to turn the "right sort" out of the most "unrighteous sort" of persons. After all, though I am very, very grateful to the young lady, Miss Hamlin, for the great hope and encouragement she gave tine of introducing me to the "right sort of New Yorkers" and for the practical help she has given me, I think I hard better do my little work with my own hands…

I am only glad that you have such a great opinion about Miss Hamlin. I for one am glad to know that you will help her, for she requires it. But, mother, through the mercy of Ramakrishna, my instinct "sizes up" almost infallibly a human face as soon as I see it, and the result is this: you may do anything you please width my affairs, I will not even murmur; — I will be only too glad to take Miss Farmer's advice, in spite of ghosts and spooks. Behind the spooks I see a heart of immense love, only covered with a thin film of laudable ambition — even that is bound to vanish in a few years. Even I will allow Landsberg to "monkey" with my affairs from time to time; but here I put a full stop. Help from any other persons besides these frightens me. That is all I can say. Not only for the help you have given me, but from my instinct (or, as I call it, inspiration of my Master), I regard you as my mother and will always abide by any advice you may have for me — but only personally. When you select a medium, I will beg leave to exercise my choice. That is all.

Herewith I send the English gentleman's letter. I have made a few notes on the margin to explain Hindustani words.

Your obedient son,
Vivekananda.

1895.26 — MOTHER

To Mrs. G. W. Hale:

[New York,
April 25, 1895]

DEAR MOTHER,

I was away a long time in the country. Came back day before yesterday.

I think the summer coat is in Chicago. If so, will you kindly send it over c/o Miss Phillips, 19 W. 38 Str., New York? It is getting hot here every day.

I will remain in New York till the end of May, at least.

Hoping you are all in perfect health. I remain,

Yours truly,
Vivekananda.

1895.27 — MOTHER

To Mrs. G. W. Hale:

54 W. 33., New York,
[April 26, 1895]

DEAR MOTHER,

Perhaps you did not receive my letter asking you to send the Calcutta pamphlets about the Paramahamsa Ramakrishna. Kindly send them to me at 54 W. 33, and also the pamphlets about the Calcutta meeting if you have any. Also the summer coat to the care of Miss Phillips, 19 W. 38.

As I do not see any probability of my going soon to Chicago, I am thinking of drawing all my money from the Chicago bank to New York. Will you kindly ascertain the exact total amount I have in Chicago so that I may draw it out at once and deposit it in some New York bank?

Kindly do these and I will bother you no more. I have written to India long ago about the rugs. I do not know whether Dewanji is alive or dead. I have no information.

I am all right and will be more than a month yet in New York. After that I am going to the Thousand Islands — wherever that place may be — for a little summer quiet and rest. Mrs. Bagley has been down here to see me and attended several of my classes.

The classes are going on with a boom; almost every day I have one, and they are packed full. But no "money" — except they maintain themselves. I charge no fees, except as the members contribute to the rent etc. voluntarily.

It is mostly probable that I will go away this summer.

With my love to all,

Ever gratefully yours,
Vivekananda.

1895.26 — BROTHER

54 W. 33 New York,
25th April, 1895.

DEAR BROTHER, (to Dr. I. Janes)

I was away in the Catskill mountains and it was almost impossible to get a letter regularly posted from where I was — so accept my apology for the delay in offering you my most heartfelt thanks for your letter in the "Eagle".

It was so scholarly, truthful and noble and withal so permeated with your natural universal love for the good and true everywhere. It is a great work to bring this world into a spirit of sympathy with each other but it should be done no doubt when such brave souls as you still hold your own. Lord help you ever and ever my brother and may you live long to carry on the mighty work you and your society has undertaken.

With my gratitude and love to you and to the members of the Ethical Society.

I remain Yours ever truly,
Vivekananda.

1895.29 — MOTHER

To Mrs. G. W. Hale:

54 W. 33 New York,
The 1st of May, 1895.

DEAR MOTHER,

Many, many thanks for sending the coat. Now I am well equipped for summer. I am so sorry the rugs could not come before I leave this country. They will come if Dewanji is alive.

I have been out of town a few days and have now come back all right — healthy as ever.

Lord bless you ever and ever for your untiring kindness to me.

Ever your grateful Son,
Vivekananda.

PS — The History of Rajasthan I present you, and the satchel to the babies.

1895.30 — S__

U. S. A.,
2nd May, 1895.

DEAR S__,

So you have made up your mind to renounce the world. I have sympathy with your desire. There is nothing so high as renunciation of self. But you must not forget that to forgo your own favourite desire for the welfare of those that depend upon you is no small sacrifice. Follow the spotless life and teachings of Shri Ramakrishna and look after the comforts of your family. You do your own duty, and leave the rest to Him.

Love makes no distinction between man and man, between an Aryan and a Mlechchha, between a Brâhmana and a Pariah, nor even between a man and a woman. Love makes the whole universe as one's own home. True progress is slow but sure. Work among those young men who can devote heart and soul to this one duty—the duty of raising the masses of India. Awake them, unite them, and inspire them with this spirit of renunciation; it depends wholly on the young people of India.

Cultivate the virtue of obedience, but you must not sacrifice your own faith. No centralization is possible unless there is obedience to superiors. No great work can be done without this centralization of individual forces. The Calcutta Math is the main centre; the members of all other branches must act in unity and conformity with the rules of that centre.

Give up jealousy and conceit. Learn to work unitedly for others. This is the great need of our country.

Yours with blessings,
Vivekananda.

1895.31—FRIEND

To Mr. E. T. Sturdy:

19 W. 38th St.,
New York

DEAR FRIEND,

I received your last duly, and as I had a previous arrangement to come to Europe by the end of this August, I take your invitation as a Divine Call.

"Truth alone triumphs, not untruth. Through truth alone lies the way to Devayâna (the way to the gods)." Those who think that a little sugar-coating of untruth helps the spread of truth are mistaken and will find in the long run that a single drop of poison poisons the whole mass... The man who is pure, and who dares, does all things. May the Lord ever protect you from illusion and delusion! I am ever ready to work with you, and the Lord will send us friends by the hundred, if only we be our own friends first. "The Atman alone is the friend of the Atman."

Europe has always been the source of social, and Asia of spiritual power; and the whole history of the world is the tale of the varying combinations of those two powers. Slowly a new leaf is being turned in the story of humanity. The signs of this are everywhere. Hundreds of new plans will be created and destroyed. Only the fit will survive. And what but the true and the good is the fit?

Yours etc.,
Vivekananda.

1895.32 — FRIEND

To Mr. Francis H. Leggett:

54 W. 33rd St., New York,
The 4th of May, 1895.

DEAR FRIEND,

Many thanks for your kind present. The cigars are indeed delicious — and a hundred times so, as coming from you.

With everlasting love and regards,

I remain yours truly,
Vivekananda.

1895.33 — BABIES

To the Hale Sisters:

New York,
5th May, 1895.

DEAR BABIES,

What I expected has come. I always thought that although Prof. Max Muller in all his writings on the Hindu religion adds in the last a derogatory remark, he must see the whole truth in the long run. As soon as you can, get a copy of his last book Vedantism; there you will find him swallowing the whole of it — reincarnation and all.

Of course, you will not find it difficult at all to understand, as it is only a part of what I have been telling you all this time.

Many points you will find smack of my paper in Chicago.

I am glad now the old man has seen the truth, because that is the only way to have religion in the face of modern research and science.

Hope you are enjoying Todd's Rajasthan.

With all love, your brother,
Vivekananda.

PS — When is Miss Mary coming to Boston?

1895.34 — ALASINGA

U. S. A.,
6th May, 1895.

DEAR ALASINGA,

This morning I received your last letter and that first volume of the Bhâshya of Râmânujâcharya. A few days ago I received another letter from you. Also I received a letter from Mr. Mani Iyer. I am doing well and going on in the same old rate. You mention about the lectures of Mr. Lund. I do not know who he is or where he is. He may be some one lecturing in Churches; for had he big platforms, we would have heard of him. Maybe, he gets them reported in some newspapers and sends them to India; and the missionaries may be making trade out of it. Well, so far I guess from the tone of your letters. It is no public affair here to call forth any defence from us; for in that case I will have to fight hundreds of them here every day. For India is now in the air, and the orthodox, including Dr. Barrows and all the rest, are struggling hard to put out the fire. In the second place, every one of these orthodox lectures against India must have a good deal of abuse hurled against me. If you hear some of the filthy stories the orthodox men and women invent against me, you will be astonished. Now, do you mean to say that a Sannyâsin should go about defending himself against the brutal and cowardly attacks of these self-seeking men and women? I have some very influential friends here who, now and then, give them their quietus. Again, why should I waste my energies defending Hinduism if the Hindus all go to sleep? What are you three hundred millions of people doing there, especially those that are so proud of their learning etc.? Why do you not take up the fighting and leave me to teach and preach? Here am I struggling day and night in the midst of strangers... What help does India send? Did the world ever see a nation with less patriotism than the Indian? If you could send and maintain for a few years a dozen well-educated strong men to preach in Europe and America, you would do immense service to India, both morally and politically. Every man who morally sympathises with India becomes a political friend. Many of the Western people think of you as a nation of half-naked savages, and therefore only fit to be whipped into civilization. If you three hundred millions become cowed by the missionaries — you cowards — and dare not say a word, what can one man do in a far distant land? Even what I have done, you do not deserve.

Why do you not send your defences to the American magazines? What prevents you? You race of cowards — physical, moral, and spiritual! You animals fit to be treated as you are with two ideas before you — lust and money — you want to prod a Sannyasin to a life of constant fighting, and you are afraid of the "Saheb logs", even missionaries! And you will do great things, pish! Why not some of you write a beautiful defence and send it to the Arena Publishing Company of Boston? The Arena is a magazine which will gladly publish it and perhaps pay you hard money. So far it ends. Think of this when you will be tempted to be a fool. Think that up to date every blackguard of a Hindu that had hitherto come to western lands had too often criticised his own faith and country in order to get praise or money. You know that I did not come to seek name and fame; it was forced upon me. Why shall I go back to India? Who will help me?... You are children, you prattle you do not know what. Where are the men in Madras who will give up the world to preach religion? Worldliness and realization of God cannot go together. I am the one man who dared defend his country, and I have given them such ideas as they never expected from a Hindu. There are many who are against me, but I will never be a coward like you. There are also thousands in the country who are my friends, and hundreds who would follow me unto death; every year they will increase, and if I live and work with them, my ideals of life and religion will be fulfilled. Do you see?

I do not hear much now about the Temple Universal that was to be built in America; yet I have a firm footing in New York, the very centre of American life, and so my work will go on. I am taking several of my disciples to a summer retreat to finish their training in Yoga and Bhakti and Jnâna, and then they will be able to help carry the work on. Now my boys, go to work.

Within a month I shall be in a position to send some money for the paper. Do not go about begging from the Hindu beggars. I will do it all myself with my own brain and strong right hand. I do not want the help of any man here or in India... Do not press too much the Ramakrishna Avatâra.

Now I will tell you my discovery. All of religion is contained in the Vedanta, that is, in the three stages of the Vedanta philosophy, the Dvaita, Vishishtâdvaita and Advaita; one comes after the other. These are the three stages of spiritual growth in man. Each one is necessary. This is the essential of religion: the Vedanta, applied to the various ethnic customs and creeds of India, is Hinduism. The first stage, i.e. Dvaita, applied to the ideas of the ethnic groups of Europe, is Christianity; as applied to the Semitic groups, Mohammedanism. The Advaita, as applied in its Yoga-perception form, is Buddhism etc. Now by religion is meant the Vedanta; the applications must vary according to the different needs, surroundings, and other circumstances of different nations. You will find that although the philosophy is the same, the Shâktas, Shaivas, etc. apply it each to their own special cult and forms. Now, in your journal write article after article on these three systems, showing their harmony as one following after the other, and at the same time keeping off the ceremonial forms altogether. That is, preach the philosophy, the spiritual part, and let people suit it to their own forms. I wish to write a book on this subject, therefore I wanted the three Bhashyas; but only one volume of the Ramanuja (Bhashya) has reached me as yet.

The American Theosophists have seceded from the others, and now they hate India. Poor things! And Sturdy of England who has lately been in India and met my brother Shivananda wrote me a letter wanting to know when I go over to England. I wrote him a nice letter. What about Babu Akshay Kumar Ghosh? I do not hear anything from him more. Give the missionaries and others their dues. Get up some of our very strong men and write a nice, strong, but good-toned article on the present religious revival in India and send it to some American magazine. I am acquainted with only one or two of them. You know I am not much of a writer. I am not in the habit of going from door to door begging. I sit quiet and let things come to me... Now, my children, I could have made a grand success in the way of organising here, if I were a worldly hypocrite. Alas! That is all of religion here; money and name = priest, money and lust = layman. I am to create a new order of humanity here who are sincere believers in God and care nothing for the world. This must be slow, very slow. In the meantime you go on with your work, and I shall steer my boat straight ahead. The journal must not be flippant but steady, calm, and high-toned... Get hold of a band of fine, steady writers... Be perfectly unselfish, be steady and work on. We will do great things; do not fear... One thing more. Be the servant of all, and do not try in the least to govern others. That will excite jealousy and destroy everything... Go on. You have worked wonderfully well. We do not wait for help, we will work it out, my boy, be self-reliant, faithful and patient. Do not antagonise my other friends, live in harmony with all. My eternal love to all.

Ever yours with blessings,
Vivekananda.

PS — Nobody will come to help you if you put yourself forward as a leader... Kill self first if you want to succeed.

1895.35 — MRS. BULL

54 W. 33rd St., New York,
7th May, 1895.

DEAR MRS. BULL,

... I had a newspaper from India with a publication in it of Dr. Barrows' short reply to the thanks sent over from India. Miss Thursby will send it to you. Yesterday I received another letter from India from the President of Madras meeting to thank the Americans and to send me an Address... This gentleman is the chief citizen of Madras and a Judge of the Supreme Court, a very high position in India.

I am going to have two public lectures more in New York in the upper hall of the Mott's Memorial Building. The first one will be on Monday next, on the Science of Religion. The next, on the Rationale of Yoga... Has Miss Hamlin sent you the book on the financial condition of India? I wish your brother will read it and then find out for himself what the English rule in India means.

Ever gratefully your son,
Vivekananda.

1895.36 — ALASINGA

New York,
14th May, 1895.

DEAR ALASINGA,

... Now I have got a hold on New York, and I hope to get a permanent body of workers who will carry on the work when I leave the country. Do you see, my boy, all this newspaper blazoning is nothing? I ought to be able to leave a permanent effect behind me when I go; and with the blessings of the Lord it is going to be very soon... Men are more valuable than all the wealth of the world.

You need not worry about me. The Lord is always protecting me. My coming to this country and all my labours must not be in vain.

The Lord is merciful, and although there are many who try to injure me any way they can, there are many also who will befriend me to the last. Infinite patience, infinite purity, and infinite perseverance are the secret of success in a good cause.

Ever yours with blessings,
Vivekananda.

1895.37 — MOTHER

To Mrs. G. W. Hale:

54 W. 33, New York,
16th May, '95.

DEAR MOTHER,

Your kind note duly reached. The books have arrived safe and more are coming. The Sanskrit books pay no duty, being classics. I expect a big package from Khetri. The big packet was from the Raja of Khetri, sending me an address from a meeting held of Rajput nobility at Mount Abu, for my work in this country.

I do not know whether I will be able to come over to Chicago or not. I am trying to get a free pass; in case I succeed I will come, else not. Financially this winter's work was no success at all — I could barely keep myself up — but spiritually very great. I am going to the Thousand Islands for the summer to visit a friend and some of my pupils will be there.

I have got plenty of books now to read from India, and I will be quite engaged this summer.

The Khetri package will not arrive soon, so kindly make arrangements that it will be received during your absence if you go away. [There] will have to be paid a heavy duty for [it,] I am afraid.

Mrs. [Florence] Adams brought me the love from the [Hale] Sisters on her way to Europe. She started this morning. A large package of books also I expect soon. The original Upanishads — there is no duty on them.

I have had some trouble with my stomach; hope it will be over in a few days.

With love to all,

I am ever your affectionate Son,
Vivekananda.

1895.38 — ALASINGA

C/O MISS PHILIPS,
19 West 38th Street, New York
28th May, 1895.

DEAR ALASINGA,

Herewith I send a hundred dollars or £20-8-7 in English money. Hope this will go just a little in starting your paper. Hoping to do more by and by.

I remain, ever yours, with blessings,
Vivekananda.

PS — Reply immediately to it C/o the above address. New York will be my headquarters henceforth.

I have succeeded in doing something in this country at last.

1895.39 — MOTHER

To Mrs. Ole Bull:

NEW YORK,
The 28th May, '95.

DEAR MOTHER,

Your last kind letter to hand. This week will be the last of my classes. I am going next Tuesday with Mr. Leggett to Maine. He has a fine lake and a forest there. I will be two or three weeks there. Thence I go to the Thousand Islands. Also I have an invitation to speak at a parliament of religions at Toronto, Canada, on July 18th. I will go there from Thousand Islands and return back.

So far everything is going on well with me.

Ever your grateful son,

I am ever your affectionate Son,
Vivekananda.

PS — My regards and love to your daughter and pray for her speedy recovery.

1895.40 — SIR

To Dr. Paul Carus:

19 W. 38th St., New York,
June [May?] 28, '95.
Dr. Paul Carus, La Salle, Ill.

DEAR SIR,

I am just now in receipt of your letter and will be very happy to join the religions Congress at Toronto. Only, as you are well aware of, the financial means of a "Bhikshu" (A Hindu or Buddhist monk.) are very limited. I will be only too glad to do anything in my power to help you and wait further particulars and directions.

Hoping to hear from you soon and thanking you very much for your great sympathy with Buddhistic India.

I remain ever fraternally your,
Vivekananda.

1895.41 — MRS. BULL

54 W. 33rd St., New York,
May, 1895, Thursday.

DEAR MRS. BULL,

The classes are going on; but I am sorry to say, though the attendance is large, it does not even pay enough to cover the rent. I will try this week and then give up.

I am going this summer to the Thousand Islands to Miss Dutcher's, one of my students. The different books on Vedanta are now being sent over to me from India. I expect to write a book in English on the Vedanta Philosophy in its three stages when I am at Thousand Islands, and I may go to Greenacre later on. Miss Farmer wants me to lecture there this summer.

I am rather busy just now in writing a promised article for the Press Association on Immortality.

Yours,
Vivekananda.

1895.42 — DEAR __

54 W. 33 New York,
May, 1895.

DEAR __,

Since writing to you my pupils have come round me with help, and the classes will go on nicely now no doubt.

I was so glad at it because teaching has become a part of my life, as necessary to my life as eating or breathing.

Yours,
Vivekananda.

PS — I saw a lot of things about __ in an English paper, the Borderland. __ is doing good work in India, making the Hindus, very much to appreciate their own religion... I do not find any scholarship in __'s writing, ... nor do I find any spirituality whatever. However Godspeed to anyone who wants to do good to the world.

How easily this world can be duped by humbugs and what a mass of fraud has gathered over the devoted head of poor humanity since the dawn of civilisation.

1895.43 — MOTHER

Mrs. Ole Bull:

4th June '95.

DEAR MOTHER,

Today I leave New York at 5 p.m. by steamer with Mr. Leggett.

The classes were closed on Saturday last [June 1] and so far the work has been very successful, no small part of which is due to you.

Ever praying for you and yours,

I am ever your faithful Son,
Vivekananda.

PS — I will acquaint you with my whereabouts as soon as I know it myself.

1895.44 — MRS. BULL

Percy, New Hampshire,
7th June, 1895.

DEAR MRS. BULL,

I am here at last with Mr. Leggett. This is one of the most beautiful spots I have ever seen. Imagine a lake, surrounded with hills covered with a huge forest, with nobody but ourselves. So lovely, so quiet, so restful! And you may imagine how glad I am to be here after the bustle of cities.

It gives me a new lease of life to be here. I go into the forest alone and read my Gita and am quite happy. I will leave this place in about ten days and go to the Thousand Island Park. I will meditate by the hour there and be all alone to myself. The very idea is ennobling.

Vivekananda.

1895.45 — SISTER

To Miss Mary Hale:

(Written on birch bark)
Percy N. H.,
17 June, 1895.

DEAR SISTER,

Going tomorrow to the Thousand Islands care Miss Dutcher's, Thousand Island Park, N.Y. Where are you now? Where will you all be in summer? I have a chance of going to Europe in August, I will come to see you before I go. So write to me. Also I expect books and letters from India. Kindly send them care Miss Phillips, 19 W. 38th Street, N.Y. This is the bark in which all holy writings are written in India. So I write Sanskrit: May the husband of Uma (Shiva) protect you always.

May you all be blessed ever and ever,
Vivekananda.

1895.46 — FRIEND

C/O Miss Dutcher
Thousand Island Park, N.Y.,
18th June, 1895.

DEAR FRIEND, (Mr. F. Leggett)

A letter reached me from Mrs. Sturges the day before she left, including a cheque for $50. It was impossible to make the acknowledgement reach her the next day; so I take this opportunity to ask you the favour of sending her my thanks and acknowledgement in your next to her.

We are having a nice time here except, as an old Hindu proverb says, that "a pestle must pound even if it goes to heaven". I have to work hard all the same. I am going to Chicago in the beginning of August. When are you starting?

All our friends here send their respects to you. Hoping you all bliss and joy and health, and ever praying for the same.

I remain, yours affectionately,
Vivekananda.

1895.47 — SISTER

To Miss Mary Hale:

54 W. 33rd Street, New York,
22nd June, 1895.

DEAR SISTER,

The letters from India and the parcel of books reached me safe. I am so happy to know of Mr. Sam's arrival. I am sure he is "bewaring of the vidders" nicely. I met a friend of Mr. Sam's one day on the street. He is an Englishman with a name ending in "ni". He was very nice. He said he was living in the same house with Sam somewhere in Ohio.

I am going on pretty nearly in the same old fashion. Talking when I can and silent when forced to be. I do not know whether I will go to Greenacre this summer. I saw Miss Farmer the other day. She was in a hurry to go away, so I had but very little talk with her. She is a noble, noble lady.

How are you going on with your Christian Science lessons? I hope you will go to Greenacre. There you will find quite a number of them and also the Spiritualists, table turnings, palmists, astrologers, etc., etc. You will get all the "cures" and all the "isms" presided over by Miss Farmer.

Landsberg has gone away to live in some other place, so I am left alone. I am living mostly on nuts and fruits and milk, and find it very nice and healthy too. I hope to lose about 30 to 40 lbs. this summer. That will be all right for my size. I am afraid I have forgotten all about Mrs. Adam's lessons in walking. I will have to renew them when she comes again to N.Y. Gandhi has gone to England en route to India from Boston, I suppose.

I would like to know about his "chaperon" Mrs. Howard and her present bereaved state. I am very glad to hear that the rugs did not go down to the bottom of the Atlantic and are at last coming.

This year I could hardly keep my head up, and I did not go about lecturing. The three great commentaries on the Vedanta philosophy belonging to the three great sects of dualists, qualified dualists, and monists are being sent to me from India. Hope they will arrive safe. Then I will have an intellectual feast indeed. I intend to write a book this summer on the Vedanta philosophy. This world will always be a mixture of good and evil, of happiness and misery; this wheel will ever go up and come down; dissolution and resolution is the inevitable law. Blessed are those who struggle to go beyond. Well, I am glad all the babies are doing well but sorry there was no "catch" even this winter, and every winter the chances are dwindling down. Here near my lodgings is the Waldorf-Hotel, the rendezvous of lots of titled but penniless Europeans on show for "Yankee" heiresses to buy. You may have any selection here, the stock is so full and varied. There is the man who talks no English; there are others who lisp a few words which no one can understand; and others are there who talk nice English, but their chance is not so great as that of the dumb ones — the girls do not think them enough foreign who talk plain English fluently.

I read somewhere in a funny book that an American vessel was being foundered in the sea; the men were desperate and as a last solace wanted some religious service being done. There was "Uncle Josh" on board who was an elder in the Presbyterian Church. They all began to entreat, "Do something religious, Uncle Josh! We are all going to die." Uncle Joseph took his hat in his hand and took up a collection on the spot!

That is all of religion he knew. And that is more or less characteristic of the majority of such people. Collections are about all the religion they know or will ever know. Lord bless them. Good-bye for present. I am going to eat something; I feel very hungry.

Yours affectionately,
Vivekananda.

1895.48 — KIDI

19 W 38th St., New York
22nd June, 1895.

DEAR KIDI,

I will write you a whole letter instead of a line. I am glad you are progressing. You are mistaken in thinking that I am not going to return to India; I am coming soon. I am not giving to failures, and here I have planted a seed, and it is going to become a tree, and it must. Only I am afraid it will hurt its growth if I give it up too soon…

Work on, my boy. Rome was not built in a day. I am guided by the Lord, so everything will come all right in the end.

With my love ever and ever to you,

Yours sincerely,
Vivekananda.

1895.49 — SISTER

To Miss Mary Hale:

C/O Miss Dutcher, Thousand Island Park, N.Y.
26th June, 1895.

DEAR SISTER,

Many thanks for the Indian mail. I cannot express in words my gratitude to you. As you have already read in Max Müller's article on Immortality I sent Mother Church, that he thinks that those we love in this life we must have loved in the past, so it seems I must have belonged to the Holy Family in some past life. I am expecting some books from India. I hope they have arrived. If so, will you kindly send them over here? If any postage is due I shall send it as soon as I get intimation. You did not write about the duty on the rugs; there will be another big packet from Khetri containing carpets and shawls and some brocades and other nick-nacks. I have written them to get the duty paid there if it is possible through the American Consul in Bombay. If not I shall have to pay it here. I do not think they will arrive for some months yet. I am anxious about the books. Kindly send them as soon as they arrive.

My love to Mother and Father Pope and all the sisters. I am enjoying this place immensely. Very little eating and good deal of thinking and talking and study. A wonderful calmness is coming over my soul. Every day I feel I have no duty to do; I am always in eternal rest and peace. It is He that works. We are only the instruments. Blessed be His name! The threefold bondage of lust and gold and fame is, as it were, fallen from me for the time being, and once more, even here, I feel what sometimes I felt in India, "From me all difference has fallen, all right or wrong, all delusion and ignorance has vanished, I am walking in the path beyond the qualities." What law I obey, what disobey? From that height the universe looks like a mud-puddle. Hari Om Tat Sat. He exists; nothing else does. I in Thee and Thou in me. Be Thou Lord my eternal refuge! Peace, Peace, Peace! Ever with love and blessings,

Your brother,
Vivekananda.

1895.50 — SISTER

To Miss Mary Hale:

C/O Miss Dutcher, Thousand Island Park, N.Y.
26th June, 1895.

DEAR SISTER,

Many thanks for the Indian mail. It brought a good deal of good news. You are enjoying by this time, I hope, the articles by Prof. Max Müller on the "Immortality of the Soul" which I sent to Mother Church. The old man has taken in Vedanta, bones and all, and has boldly come out. I am so glad to know the arrival of the rugs. Was there any duty to pay? If so I will pay that, I insist on it. There will come another big packet from the Raja of Khetri containing some shawls and brocades and nick-nacks. I want to present them to different friends. But they are not going to arrive before some months, I am sure.

I am asked again and again, as you will find in the letters from India, to go over. They are getting desperate. Now if I go to Europe, I will go as the guest of Mr. Francis Leggett of N.Y. He will travel all over Germany, England, France, and Switzerland for six weeks. From there I shall go to India, or I may return to America. I have a seed planted here and wish it to grow. This winter's work in N.Y. was splendid, and it may die if I suddenly go over to India, so I am not sure about going to India soon.

Nothing noticeable has happened during this visit to the Thousand Islands. The scenery is very beautiful and I have some of my friends here with me to talk about God and soul ad libitum. I am eating fruits and drinking milk and so forth, and studying huge Sanskrit books on Vedanta which they have kindly sent me from India.

If I come to Chicago I cannot come at least within six weeks or more. Baby needn't alter any of her plans for me. I will see you all somehow or other before I go.

You fussed so much over my reply to Madras, but it has produced a tremendous effect there. A late speech by the President of the Madras Christian College, Mr. Miller, embodies a large amount of my ideas and declares that the West is in need of Hindu ideas of God and man and calls upon the young men to go and preach to the West. This has created quite a furore of course amongst the Missions. What you allude to as being published in the Arena I did not see a bit of it. The women did not make any fuss over me at all in New York. Your friend must have drawn on his imagination. They were not of the "bossing" type at all. I hope Father Pope will go to Europe and Mother Church too. Travelling is the best thing in life. I am afraid I shall die if made to stick to one place for a long time. Nothing like a nomadic life!

The more the shades around deepen, the more the ends approach and the more one understands the true meaning of life, that it is a dream; and we begin to understand the failure of everyone to grasp it, for they only attempted to get meaning out of the meaningless. To get reality out of a dream is boyish enthusiasm. "Everything is evanescent, everything is changeful"—knowing this, the sage gives up both pleasure and pain and becomes a witness of this panorama (the universe) without attaching himself to anything.

"They indeed have conquered Heaven even in this life whose mind has become fixed in sameness. God is pure and same to all, therefore they are said to be in God" (Gita, V.19). Desire, ignorance, and inequality—this is the trinity of bondage.

Denial of the will to live, knowledge, and same-sightedness is the trinity of liberation.

Freedom is the goal of the universe.

"Nor love nor hate nor pleasure nor pain nor death nor life nor religion nor irreligion: not this, not this, not this."

Yours ever,
Vivekananda.

1895.51 — JOE

To Miss Josephine MacLeod:

21 W. 34th St., New York,
June, 1895.

DEAR JOE,

Experiences are gathering a bit thick round you. I am sure they will lift many a veil more.

Mr. Leggett told me of your phonograph. I told him to get a few cylinders — I talk in them through somebody's phonograph and send them to Joe — to which he replied that he could buy one, because "I always do what Joe asks me to do." I am glad there is so much of hidden poetry in his nature.

I am going today to live with the Guernseys as the doctor wants to watch me and cure me... Doctor Guernsey, after examining other things, was feeling my pulse, when suddenly Landsberg (whom they had forbidden the house) got in and retreated immediately after seeing me. Dr. Guernsey burst out laughing and declared he would have paid that man for coming just then, for he was then sure of his diagnosis of my case. The pulse before was so regular, but just at the sight of Landsberg it almost stopped from emotion. It is sure only a case of nervousness. He also advises me strongly to go on with Doctor Helmer's treatment. He thinks Helmer will do me a world of good, and that is what I need now. Is not he broad?

I expect to see "the sacred cow" today in town. I will be in New York a few days more. Helmer wants me to take three treatments a week for four weeks, then two a week for four more, and I will be all right. In case I go to Boston, he recommends me to a very good ostad (expert) there whom he would advise on the matter.

I said a few kind words to Landsberg and went upstairs to Mother Guernsey to save poor Landsberg from embarrassment.

Ever yours in the Lord,
Vivekananda.

1895.52 — MRS. BULL

54 W. 33rd St., New York
June, 1895.

DEAR MRS. BULL,

I have just arrived home. The trip did me good, and I enjoyed the country and the hills, and especially Mr. Leggett's country-house in New York State. Poor Landsberg has gone from this house. Neither has he left one his address. May the Lord bless Landsberg wherever he goes! He is one of the few sincere souls I have had the privilege in this life to come across.

All is for good. All conjunctions are for subsequent disjunction. I hope I shall be perfectly able to work alone. The less help from men, the more from the Lord! Just now I received a letter from an Englishman in London who had lived in India in the Himalayas with two of my brethren. He asks me to come to London.

Yours,
Vivekananda.

1895.53 — DOCTOR

To Dr. Paul Carus:

C/O Miss Dutcher, Thousand Island Park, N. Y.,
[June, 1895.]

DEAR DOCTOR,

I am in this place now and had to change some of my plans on account of the Toronto Congress.

I am therefore not quite sure whether I will be able to come to Oak Island Conference. It is very possible, however, that I will be able to do so.

I also hope Mr. [Charles Carroll] Bonney will come. He is a noble, noble soul — one who sincerely wishes the fellowship of all humanity.

Is it not true, Dr., that Mr. Bonney, as I have every reason to think, originated the plan of the parliament of religions?

I will certainly try my best to come.

Thanking you very much for your kindness, I remain

Ever yours in the Lord of Compassion,
Vivekananda.

PS — Will you kindly inform me what lines of thought you want me to take.

1895.54 — SHASHI[1]

1895.

MY DEAR SHASHI,

... I am quite in agreement with what Sarada is doing, but it is not necessary to preach that Ramakrishna Paramahamsa was an Incarnation, and things of that sort. He came to do good to the world; not to trumpet his own name — you must always remember this. Disciples pay their whole attention to the preservation of their master's name and throw overboard his teachings; and sectarianism etc., are the result. Alasinga writes of Charu; but I do not recollect him. Write all about him and convey him my thanks. Write in detail about all; I have no time to spare for idle gossip... Try to give up ceremonials. They are not meant for Sannyasins; and one must work only so long as one does not attain to illumination... I have nothing to do with sectarianism. Or party-forming and playing the frog-in-the-well, whatever else I may do... It is impossible to preach the catholic ideas of Ramakrishna Paramahamsa and form sects at the same time... Only one kind of work I understand, and that is doing good to others; all else is doing evil. I therefore prostrate myself before the Lord Buddha... I am a Vedantist; Sachchidananda — Existence-Knowledge-Bliss Absolute — is my God. I scarcely find any other God than the majestic form of my own Self. By the word "Incarnation" are meant those who have attained that Brahmanhood, in other words, the Jivanmuktas — those who have realised this freedom in this very life. I do not find any speciality in Incarnations: all beings from Brahmâ down to a clump of grass will attain to liberation-in-life in course of time, and our duty lies in helping all to reach that state. This help is called religion; the rest is irreligion. This help is work; the rest is evil-doing — I see nothing else. Other kinds of work, for example, the Vaidika or the Tântrika, may produce results; but resorting to them is simply waste of life, for that purity which is the goal of work is realisable only through doing good to others. Through works such as sacrifices etc., one may get enjoyments, but it is impossible to have the purity of soul... Everything exists already in the Self of all beings. He who asserts he is free, shall be free. He who says he is bound, bound he shall remain. To me, the thought of oneself as low and humble is a sin and ignorance. " — This Atman is not to be attained by one who is weak."

— If you say Brahman is, existence will be the result; if you say Brahman is not, non existent It shall verily become." He who always thinks of himself as weak wild never become strong, but he who knows himself to be a lion,

— rushes out from the world's meshes, as a lion from its cage." Another point, it was no new truth that Ramakrishna Paramahamsa came to preach, though his advent brought the old truths to light. In other words, he was the embodiment of all the past religious thoughts of India. His life alone made me understand what the Shâstras really meant, and the whole plan and scope of the old Shastras.

---

[1] Translated from Bengali.

Missionaries and others could not do much against me in this country. Through the Lord's grace the people here like me greatly and are not to be tricked by the opinions of any particular class. They appreciate my ideas in a manner my own countrymen cannot do, and are not selfish. I mean, when it comes to practical work they will give up jealousy and all those ideas of self-sufficiency. Then all of them agree and act under the direction of a capable man. That is what makes them so great. But then they are a nation of Mammon-worshippers. Money comes before everything. People of our country are very liberal in pecuniary matters, but not so much these people. Every home has a miser. It is almost a religion here. But they fall into the clutches of the priests when they do something bad, and then buy their passage to heaven with money. These things are the same in every country — priestcraft. I can say nothing as to whether I shall go back to India and when. There also I shall have to lead a wandering life as I do here; but here thousands of people listen to and understand my lectures, and these thousands are benefited. But can you say the same thing about India? ... I am perfectly at one with what Sarada is doing. A thousand thanks to him ... In Madras and Bombay I have lots of men who are after my heart. They are learned and understand everything. Moreover they are kind-hearted and can therefore appreciate the philanthropic spirit ... I have printed neither books nor anything of the kind. I simply go on lecturing tours ... When I take a retrospective view of my past life, I feel no remorse. From country to country I have travelled teaching something, however little, to people, and in exchange for that have partaken of their slices of bread. If I had found I had done no work, but simply supported myself by imposing upon people, I would have committed suicide today. Why do those who think themselves unfit to teach their fellow-beings, wear the teacher's garb and earn their bread by cheating them? Is not that a deadly sin? ...

Yours etc.,
Vivekananda.

1895.55 — ALASINGA

U. S. A.,
1st July, 1895.

DEAR ALASINGA,

I received your missionary book and the Ramnad photos. I have written to the Raja as well as the Dewan at Mysore. The missionary pamphlet must have reached here long ago, as the Ramabai circle controversy with Dr. Janes savoured of it, it seems. Now you need not be afraid of anything. There is one misstatement in that pamphlet. I never went to a big hotel in this country, and very few times to any other. At Baltimore, the small hotels, being ignorant, would not take in a black man, thinking him a negro. So my host, Dr. Vrooman, had to take me to a larger one, because they knew the difference between a negro and a foreigner. Let me tell you, Alasinga, that you have to defend yourselves. Why do you behave like babies? If anybody attacks your religion, why cannot, you defend it? As for me, you need not be afraid, I have more friends than enemies here, and in this country one-third are Christians, and only a small number of the educated care about the missionaries. Again, the very fact of the missionaries being against anything makes the educated like it. They are less of a power here now, and are becoming less so every day. If their attacks pain you, why do you behave like a petulant child and refer to me?... Cowardice is no virtue.

Here I have already got a respectable following. Next year I will organise it on a working basis, and then the work will be carried on. And when I am off to India, I have friends who will back me here and help me in India too; so you need not fear. So long as you shriek at the missionary attempts and jump without being able to do anything, I laugh at you; you are little dollies, that is what you are... What can Swami do for old babies!!

I know, my son, I shall have to come and manufacture men out of you. I know that India is only inhabited by women and eunuchs. So do not fret. I will have to get means to work there. I do not put myself in the hands of imbeciles. You need not worry, do what little you can. I have to work alone from top to bottom... "This Âtman (Self) is not to be reached by cowards." You need not be afraid for me. The Lord is with me, you defend yourselves only and show me you can do that; and I will be satisfied. Don't bother me any more with what any one says about me. I am not waiting to hear any fool's judgment of me. You babies, great results are attained only by great patience, great courage, and great attempts... Kidi's mind is taking periodic somersaults, I am afraid...

The brave alone do great things, not the cowards. Know once for all, you faithless ones, that I am in the hands of the Lord. So long as I am pure and His servant, not a hair of my head will be touched... Do something for the nation, then they will help you, then the nation will be with you. Be brave, be brave! Man dies but once. My disciples must not be cowards.

Ever yours with love,
Vivekananda.

1895.56 — MOTHER

To Mrs. G. W. Hale:

C/O Miss Dutcher's, Thousand Island Park, N.Y.,
2nd July, 1895.

DEAR MOTHER,

You did not write to me a single line for a long time. Neither did Sister Mary write about the duty paid on the rugs [from the Dewan of Junagadh]. I am afraid the rugs are small.

Here is another consignment from Raja Ajit Singh [the Maharaja of Khetri] consisting of carpets, shawls, etc., etc., for which the bill of lading you sent me the other day. This consignment has no duty to pay because it was all prepaid in India, and the bill of lading says so expressly. I will send you the bill of lading and the receipt for the duty. Kindly take one more trouble for me and get it out of the express company. And keep it with you till I come. The goods have arrived in New York and I had a notice of that. They are on their way to Chicago.

In two or three days I will send the bill of lading and the receipt for duty paid, to you. I foolishly asked Miss Phillips, as soon as I got the Company's (Original letter: Companies'.) notice, to get them out before I got the bill of lading. Now the bill of lading shows that it is bound for Chicago. So I am bound to give you this trouble. I am so sorry. Again with my usual business instincts — I forgot to note down the name of the express company. So I have written to New York for the letters of the Company. As soon as that comes I will send over to you.

I am going to Europe by the end of August or a little later.

I will come to see you by the end of August.

Lord bless you and yours for ever and ever.

Your ever affectionate Son,
Vivekananda.

1895.57 — MOTHER

To Mrs. G. W. Hale:

Thousand Island Park, N.Y., C/O Miss Dutcher,
July 3, 1895.

DEAR MOTHER,

Herewith I send you the bill of landing and the inventory of the goods sent from India. The duty, as you will find, has been prepaid, so there is no botheration on that score. The goods have reached Hull. They will be here by the middle of this month. And if you see a letter with the Morris American Express Co. name on the envelope, tear it open. You need not forward it to me, for that will be the notice of arrival to Chicago. I am sure Dewanji's carpets were too small, but why do you not write to me about the duty if you had to pay it? I insist upon paying it myself. The Raja's things seem to come very quick. I am so glad too I will have something to present to Mrs. Bagley, Mrs. Bull, etc.

[Enclosed in the above letter was the following note.]

541 DEARBORNAVE.

CHICAGO.

TO THE MORRIS EXPRESS CO. —

DEAR SIR,

Please permit Mrs. G. W. Hale of 541 Dearborn Ave., Chicago, to act for me about the goods sent to me from India and receive the same.

I have the honor to be, sir, your most obedient servant,

Swami Vivekananda.

1895.58 — FRIEND

C/O Miss Dutcher, Thousand Island Park, N. Y.
7th July, 1895.

DEAR FRIEND[1],

I see you are enjoying New York very much, so excuse my breaking into your reverie with a letter.

I had two beautiful letters from Miss MacLeod and Mrs. Sturges. Also they sent over two pretty birch bark books. I have filled them with Sanskrit texts and translations, and they go by today's post.

Mrs. Dora[2] is giving, I hear, some startling performances in the Mahatma line.

Since leaving Percy[3] I have invitations to come over to London from unexpected quarters, and that I look forward to with great expectations.

I do not want to lose this opportunity of working in London. And so your invitation, coupled with the London one, is, I know, a divine call for further work.

I shall be here all this month and only have to go to Chicago for a few days sometime in August.

Don't fret, Father Leggett, this is the best time for expectation — when sure in love.

Lord bless you ever and ever, and may all happiness be yours for ever, as you richly deserve it.

Ever yours in love and affection,
Vivekananda.

---

1. Mr. F. Leggett.

2. Mrs. Dora Rosthlesberger, an occultist who had introduced Miss MacLeod and Mrs. Sturges to Swami Vivekananda.

3. Mr. Leggett's camp in New Hampshire. From here Swami Vivekananda went to Thousand Island Park.

1895.59 — ALBERTA

19 W. 38, New York,
8th July, 1895.

DEAR ALBERTA, (Miss Alberta Sturges)

I am sure you are engrossed in your musical studies now. Hope you have found out all about the scales by this time. I will be so happy to take a lesson on the scales from you next time we meet.

We had such jolly good time up there at Percy with Mr. Leggett — isn't he a saint?

Hollister is also enjoying Germany greatly, I am sure, and I hope none of you have injured your tongues in trying to pronounce German words — especially those beginning with sch, tz, tsz, and other sweet things.

I read your letter to your mother from on board Most possibly I am going over to Europe next September. I have never been to Europe yet. It will not be very much different from the United States after all. And I am already well drilled in the manners and customs of this country.

We had a good deal of rowing at Percy and I learnt a point or two in rowing. Aunt Joe Joe had to pay for her sweetness, for the flies and mosquitoes would not leave her for a moment. They rather gave me a wide berth, I think because they were very orthodox sabbatarian flies and would not touch a heathen. Again, I think, I used to sing a good deal at Percy, and that must have frightened them away. We had such fine birch trees. I got up an idea of making books out of the bark, as was used to be done in ancient times in our country, and wrote Sanskrit verses for your mother and aunt.

I am sure, Alberta, you are going to be a tremendously learned lady very soon.

With love and blessings for both of you,

Ever your affectionate,
Swami Vivekananda.

1895.60 — MAHARAJA OF KHETRI

U. S. A.,
9th July, 1895.

... About my coming to India, the matter stands thus I am, as your Highness[4] well knows, a man of dogged perseverance. I have planted a seed in this country; it is already a plant, and I expect it to be a tree very soon. I have got a few hundred followers. I shall make several Sannyâsins, and then I go to India leaving the work to them. The more the Christian priests oppose me, the more I am determined to

---

4. The Maharaja of Khetri.

leave a permanent mark on their country... I have already some friends in London. I am going there by the end of August... This winter anyway has to be spent partly in London and partly in New York, and then I shall be free to go to India. There will be enough men to carry on the work here after this winter if the Lord is kind. Each work has to pass through these stages — ridicule, opposition, and then acceptance. Each man who thinks ahead of his time is sure to be misunderstood. So opposition and persecution are welcome, only I have to be steady and pure and must have immense faith in God, and all these will vanish...

Vivekananda.

1895.61 — MOTHER

To Mrs. G. W. Hale:

Thousand Island Park, C/O Miss Dutcher, N. Y.,
27th July, '95.

DEAR MOTHER,

I will be ever so much obliged if you kindly look into the "bead" affair. (Rudrâksha beads sent from India. Vide letter dated January 17, 1895 in pay it to you when I come.

I start from here next week. I will be in Detroit a day or two on my way. I will be in by the third or fourth of August.

With Everlasting love, your Son,
Vivekananda.

[Enclosed in the above letter was the following note.]

27th July '95
TO THE STATES EXPRESS COMPANY
FOREIGN DEPARTMENT.

DEAR SIR,

Herewith I authorize Mrs. George W. Hale to take delivery of the "beads" that have been expressed to me from India. Hoping they will be regularly delivered to her, I remain yours obediently,

Swami Vivekananda.

1895.62 — MRS. WILLIAM STURGES

Thousand Island Park,
29th (July?), 1895.

A glorious time to you, dear Mother[1] and I am sure this letter will find you in all health. Many thanks for the $50 you sent; it went a long way.

We have had such a nice time here. Two ladies came up all the way from Detroit to be with us here. They are so pure and good. I am going from the Thousand Island to Detroit and thence to Chicago.

Our class in New York is going on, and they have carried it bravely on, although I was not there.

By the by, the two ladies who have come from Detroit were in the class, and unfortunately were mighty frightened with imps and other persons of that ilk. They have been taught to put a little salt, just a little, in burning alcohol, and if there is a black precipitate, that must be the impurities showing the presence of the imps. However, these two ladies had too much fright from the imps. It is said that these imps are everywhere filling the whole universe. Father Leggett must be awfully downcast at your absence, as I did not hear from him up to date. Well, it is better to let grief have its way. So I do not bother him any more.

Aunt Joe Joe must have had a terrible time at sea. All is well that ends well.

The babies[2] must be enjoying their stay in Germany very much. My shiploads of love to them.

We all here send you love, and I wish you a life that will be like a torch to generations to come.

Your son,
Vivekananda.

1895.63 — MOTHER

C/O Miss Dutcher, Thousand Island Park,
July, 1895.

DEAR MOTHER[3],

I am sure you are in New York by this time, and that it is not very hot there now.

We are having great times here. Marie Louise arrived yesterday. So we are exactly seven now including all that have come yet.

All the sleep of the world has come upon me. I sleep at least two hours during the day and sleep through the whole night as a piece of log. This is a reaction, I

---

1. Mrs. William Sturges.
2. Hollister and Alberta — then at school in Germany.
3. Mrs. Betty Sturges.

think, from the sleeplessness of New York. I am also writing and reading a little, and have a class every morning after breakfast. The meals are being conducted on the strictest vegetarian principles, and I am fasting a good deal.

I am determined that several pounds of my fat shall be off before I leave. This is a Methodist place, and they will have their camp meeting in August. It is a very beautiful spot, but I am afraid it becomes too crowded during the season.

Miss Joe Joe's fly-bite has been cured completely by this time, I am sure Where is... Mother? Kindly give her my best regards when you write her next.

I will always look back upon the delightful time I had at Percy, and always thank Mr. Leggett for that treat I shall be able to go to Europe with him. When you meet him next, kindly give him my eternal love and gratitude The world is always bettered by the love of the likes of him.

Are you with your friend, Mrs. Dora (long German name). She is a noble soul, a genuine Mahâtmâ (great soul). Kindly give her my love and regards.

I am in a sort of sleepy, lazy, happy state now and do not seem to dislike it. Marie Louise brought a little tortoise from New York, her pet. Now, arriving here, the pet found himself surrounded with his natural element. So by dint of persistent tumbling and crawling, he has left the love and fondlings of Marie Louise far, far behind. She was a little sorry at first, but we preached liberty with such a vigour that she had to come round quick

May the Lord bless you and yours for ever and ever is the constant prayer of Vivekananda

PS — Joe Joe did not send the birch bark book. Mrs. Bull was very glad to have the one I had sent her.

I had a large number of very beautiful letters from India Everything is all right there. Send my love to the babies on the other side — the real "innocents abroad".

1895.64 — MOTHER

To Mrs. G. W. Hale:

C/O Miss Dutcher, Thousand Island Park,
30th ~~August,~~ [July,] '95.

DEAR MOTHER,

I was starting for Chicago, Thursday next [August 1], but your letter stopped me. The letter and the package have safely arrived.

Write to me or wire if you want me to come to Chicago. I will then start for Chicago next week, i.e. on Tuesday next [August 6]. I thought Sister Mary was at home. When are the other babies coming? My going to Europe is not yet settled finally. The babies have not written me a line — not one of them.

Oh, Mother, my heart is so, so sad. The letters bring the news of the death of

Dewanji. Haridas Viharidas has left the body. He was as a father to me. Poor man, he was the last 5 years seeking the retirement from business life, and at last he got it but could not enjoy it long. I pray that he may never come back again to this dirty hole they call the Earth. Neither may he be born in heaven or any other horrid place. May he never again wear a body — good or bad, thick or thin. What a humbug and illusion this world is, Mother, what a mockery this life. I pray constantly that all mankind will come to know the reality, i.e. God, and this "Shop" here be closed for ever.

My heart is too full to write more. Write to me or wire if you like.

Your ever obedient Son,
Vivekananda.

PS — We will think of the coming package [from the Maharaja of Khetri] in Chicago. How long will you be in Chicago? If it is only a week or so, I need not come. I will meet you in New York. If more than that, I come to see you.

1895.65 — FRIEND

C/O Miss Dutcher, Thousand Island Park, N. Y.
31st July, 1895.

DEAR FRIEND[1],

I wrote you before this a letter, but as I am afraid it was not posted carefully, I write another.

I shall be in time before the 14th. I shall have to come to New York before the 11th anyway. So there will be time enough to get ready.

I shall go with you to Paris, for my principal object in going with you is to see you married. When you go away for a trip, I go to London. That is all.

It is unnecessary to repeat my everlasting love and blessings for you and yours.

Ever your son,
Vivekananda.

1895.66 — MOTHER

To Mrs. G. W. Hale:

C/O Miss Dutcher, Thousand Island Park, N. Y.,
[July 31, 1895.]

DEAR MOTHER,

I am afraid I can not come to see you and neither will you advise me. I am going with a friend (Mr. Francis Leggett.) to Europe, at his expense. We go first to Paris

1. Francis Leggett.

and from there to London. My friend will go to Italy and I to London. I will, however, come back to New York in September. So I am not going away for good.

I start on the 17th. So you see, it is impossible to come and go that way for 3 or 4 days.

(The goods mentioned in Swami Vivekananda's letter dated July 2, 1895.)

The package from India ought to have reached by this time. If they come, kindly take the delivery and send it back to New York to Miss Mary Phillips, 19 W. 38. If the package does not come to Chicago before you go away, then kindly send the bill of lading etc. to Miss Mary Phillips, 19. W. 38. The babies [the Hale daughters] did not write me a line, nor did they intimate where they are. I absolutely do not know anything about them. As they do not want it, it seems I ought not to disturb them with my letters. But you kindly convey them my love and eternal, undying blessings. So to you, Mother and Father Pope. I will pen a longer epistle in a few days. We will see each other next spring in Chicago, Mother, if we all live.

Ever gratefully your Son,
Vivekananda.

1895.67 — MRS. G. W. HALE

To Mrs. G. W. Hale:

The Western Union Telegraph Company.,
Received At: Plaza Hotel Drug Store,,
North Ave. & Clark Street.,
Thousand Island, N.Y., 2, '95.
[August 2, 1895.]
8 jw ws 11 paid 1.33 p.m.

MRS. G. W. HALE, 541 DEARBORN AVE,

WHY ANY CHARGES DUTY PREPAID (This evidently again refers to the goods sent by the Maharaja of Khetri. Vide the letter addressed to Mrs. G. W. Hale dated July 2, 1895.) YOU HAVE DOCUMENTS WRITE FULL PARTICULARS.

Vivekananda.

1895.68 — FRIEND

To Mr. E. T. Sturdy:

19 WEST 38th ST., NEW YORK,
2nd August, 1895.

DEAR FRIEND,

Your kind note received today. I am going to Paris first with a friend and start for

Europe on the 17th of August. I will however remain in Paris only a week to see my friend married, and then I go over to London.

Your advice about an organisation was very good indeed. And I am trying to act on that line.

I have many strong friends here, but unfortunately they are most of them poor. So the work here must be slow. Moreover it requires a few months more of work in New York to carry it to some visible shape: as such I will have to return to New York early this winter, and in summer I will return to London again. So far as I see now I can stay only a few weeks in London. But if the Lord wills, that small time may prove to be the beginning of great things. From Paris I will inform you by wire when I arrive in England.

Some Theosophists came to my classes in New York, but as soon as human beings perceive the glory of the Vedanta, all abracadabras fall off of themselves. This has been my uniform experience. Whenever mankind attains a higher vision, the lower vision disappears of itself. Multitude counts for nothing. A few heart-whole, sincere, and energetic men can do more in a year than a mob in a century. If there is heat in one body, then those others that come near it must catch it. This is the law. So success is ours, so long as we keep up the heat, the spirit of truth, sincerity, and love. My own life has been a very chequered one, but I have always found the eternal words verified: "Truth alone triumphs, not untruth. Through truth alone lies the way to God."

May the Sat in you be always your infallible guide! May He speedily attain to freedom and help others to attain it!

Ever yours in the Sat,
Vivekananda.

1895.69 — FRIEND

To Mr. E. T. Sturdy:

19, West 38th Street, New York,
9th August, 1895.

DEAR FRIEND,

... It is only just that I should try to give you a little of my views. I fully believe that there are periodic ferments of religion in human society, and that such a period is now sweeping over the educated world. While each ferment, moreover, appears broken into various little bubbles, these are all eventually similar, showing the cause or causes behind them to be the same. That religious ferment which at present is every day gaining a greater hold over thinking men, has this characteristic that all the little thought-whirlpools into which it has broken itself declare one single aim — a vision and a search after the Unity of Being. On planes physical, ethical, and spiritual, an ever-broadening generalisation — leading up to a concept of Unity Eternal—is in the air; and this being so, all the movements of the time may be taken to represent, knowingly or unknowingly, the noblest philosophy of the unity man ever had—the Advaita Vedanta.

Again, it has always been observed that as a result of the struggles of the various fragments of thought in a given epoch, one bubble survives. The rest only arise to melt into it and form a single great wave, which sweeps over society with irresistible force.

In India, America, and England (the countries I happen to know about) hundreds of these are struggling at the present moment. In India, dualistic formulae are already on the wane, the Advaita alone holds the field in force. In America, many movements are struggling for the mastery. All these represent Advaita thought more or less, and that series, which is spreading most rapidly, approaches nearer to it than any of the others. Now if anything was ever clear to me, it is that one of these must survive, swallowing up all the rest, to be the power of the future. Which is it to be?

Referring to history, we see that only that fragment which is fit will survive, and what makes fit to survive but character? Advaita will be the future religion of thinking humanity. No doubt of that. And of all the sects, they alone shall gain the day who are able to show most character in their lives, no matter how far they may be.

Let me tell you a little personal experience. When my Master left the body, we were a dozen penniless and unknown young men. Against us were a hundred powerful organisations, struggling hard to nip us in the bud. But Ramakrishna had given us one great gift, the desire, and the lifelong struggle not to talk alone, but to live the life. And today all India knows and reverences the Master, and the truths he taught are spreading like wild fire. Ten years ago I could not get a hundred persons together to celebrate his birthday anniversary. Last year there were fifty thousand.

Neither numbers nor powers nor wealth nor learning nor eloquence nor anything else will prevail, but purity, living the life, in one word, anubhuti, realisation. Let there be a dozen such lion-souls in each country, lions who have broken their own bonds, who have touched the Infinite, whose whole soul is gone to Brahman, who care neither for wealth nor power nor fame, and these will be enough to shake the world.

Here lies the secret. Says Patanjali, the father of Yoga, "When a man rejects all the superhuman powers, then he attains to the cloud of virtue." He sees God. He becomes God and helps others to become the same. This is all I have to preach. Doctrines have been expounded enough. There are books by the million. Oh, for an ounce of practice!

As to societies and organisations, these will come of themselves. Can there be jealousy where there is nothing to be jealous of? The names of those who will wish to injure us will be legion. But is not that the surest sign of our having the truth? The more I have been opposed, the more my energy has always found expression. I have been driven and worshipped by princes. I have been slandered by priests and laymen alike. But what of it? Bless them all! They are my very Self, and have they not helped me by acting as a spring-board from which my energy could take higher and higher flights?

...I have discovered one great secret—I have nothing to fear from talkers of religion. And the great ones who realise—they become enemies to none! Let talkers talk! They know no better! Let them have their fill of name and fame and money and woman. Hold we on to realisation, to being Brahman, to becoming Brahman. Let us hold on to truth unto death, and from life to life. Let us not pay the least attention to what others say, and if, after a lifetime's effort, one soul, only one, can break the fetters of the world and be free, we have done our work. Hari Om!

...One word more. Doubtless I do love India. But every day my sight grows clearer. What is India, or England, or America to us? We are the servants of that God who by the ignorant is called MAN. He who pours water at the root, does he not water the whole tree?

There is but one basis of well-being, social, political or spiritual—to know that I and my brother are one. This is true for all countries and all people. And Westerners, let me say, will realise it more quickly than Orientals, who have almost exhausted themselves in formulating the idea and producing a few cases of individual realisation.

Let us work without desire for name or fame or rule over others. Let us be free from the triple bonds of lust, greed of gain, and anger. And this truth is with us!

Ever yours in the Lord,
Vivekananda.

1895.70 — CHRISTINA

To Sister Christine:

19 West 38th Street,
9th August '95.

DEAR CHRISTINA,

You must be enjoying the beautiful weather very much. Here, it is extremely hot but it does not worry me much. I had a pleasant journey from Thousand Islands to New York; and though the Engine was derailed, I did not know anything of it, being asleep all the time. Miss Waldo went out of the train at Albany. I did not see her off as I was asleep. I have not heard anything from her yet. Hope to hear soon. Dr. [L. L. Wight] and Miss [Ruth] Ellis must have gone home by this time.

We gave them a telepathic message but Miss Ellis has not got it sure, else she would write.

I am making preparations for my departure.

I came in time for one of the meetings here and had another one last evening—going to have one more this evening and almost every evening till I go over.

What is Mrs. Funkey [Mary Caroline Funke] doing, and Miss [Mary Elizabeth] Dutcher? Do you go to meditate on the mountain as usual? Did you hear from Kripananda?

Write to me as soon as you can — I am so anxious to hear from you.

Ever yours with blessings and love,
Vivekananda.

PS — My love and blessings to Mrs. Funkey and Miss Dutcher.

1895.71 — MOTHER

To Mrs. Ole Bull:

19 West 38th Street, New York,
9th August '95.

DEAR MOTHER,

Your note duly received. I saw also Miss Thursby yesterday. After the hard work at the Thousand Islands, I am taking a few days quiet and preparation for my departure. So I cannot come to Greenacre. I am with Miss Phillips and will be till the 17th, on which day I depart for Europe. I have seen Mr. Leggett. You remember Mrs. Sturges, the widow in black in my classes. She is going to marry Mr. Leggett in Paris. They will be married the 1st week we arrive, and then they go on a tour through Europe, and I, to England. I hope to return in a few weeks — back to New York.

Kindly give to Miss Hamlin [Elizabeth L. Hamlen], to Miss [Sarah] Farmer, Dr. [L. L. Wight] and Miss Howe, and all our friends my greetings, love and good-bye.

Ever sincerely your Son,
Vivekananda.

1895.72 — SISTER CHRISTINE

To Sister Christine:

[The following telegram was sent on Swami Vivekananda's behalf.]

Postal Telegraph-Cable Company,
Received At Main Office, Cor., Griswold,
Lafayette Ave., Detroit, Mich.,
43. NY. FC. W... 10 Paid. 12:45 PM,
New York, N.Y.,
[August 17, 1895.]

MISS CHRISTINA GREENSTIDEL,

418 ALFRED ST., DETROIT, MICH.

SWAMM [SWAMI] LEAVING SENDS YOU AND MRS. FUNKE LOVE AND BLESSING.

Kripananda.

1895.73 — ALASINGA

U. S. A.,
August, 1895.

By the time this reaches you, dear Alasinga, I shall be in Paris... I have done a good deal of work this year and hope to do a good deal more in the next. Don't bother about the missionaries. It is quite natural that they should cry. Who does not when his bread is dwindling away? The missionary funds have got a big gap the last two years, and it is on the increase. However, I wish the missionaries all success. So long as you have love for God and Guru and faith in truth, nothing can hurt you, my son. But the loss of any of these is dangerous. You have remarked well; my ideas are going to work in the West better than in India... I have done more for India than India ever did for me... I believe in truth, the Lord sends me workers by the scores wherever I go — and they are not like the ... disciples either — they are ready to give up their lives for their Guru. Truth is my God, the universe my country I do not believe in duty. Duty is the curse of the Samsâri (householder), not for the Sannyâsin. Duty is humbug. I am free, my bonds are cut; what care I where this body goes or does not go. You have helped me well right along. The Lord will reward you. I sought praise neither from India nor from America, nor do I seek such bubbles. I have a truth to teach, I, the child of God And He that gave me the truth will send me fellow workers from the earth's bravest and best. You Hindus will see in a few years what the Lord does in the West. You are like the Jews of old — dogs in the manger, who neither eat nor allow others to eat. You have no religion your God is the kitchen, your Bible the cooking-pots... You are a few brave lads... Hold on, boys, no cowards among my children... Are great things ever done smoothly? Time, patience, and indomitable will must show. I could have told you many things that would have made your heart leap, but I will not. I want iron wills and hearts that do not know how to quake. Hold on. The Lord bless you.

Ever yours with blessings,
Vivekananda.

1895.74 — RAKHAL[1]

19 West 38th Street, New York,
August, 1895.

BELOVED RAKHAL,

... I am now in New York City. The city is hot in summer, exactly like Calcutta.

1 Translated from Bengali.

You perspire profusely, and there is not a breath of air. I made a tour in the north for a couple of months. Please answer this letter by return of post to England, for which I shall start before this will have reached you.

Yours affectionately,
Vivekananda.

1895.75 — FRIEND

To Mr. Francis Leggett:

[Thousand Island Park, U.S.A.,
August, 1895.]

DEAR FRIEND,

I received your note duly.

Very kind of you and noble to ask me to have my own time to London. Many thanks for that. But I am in no hurry for London and, moreover, I want to see you married in Paris and then I go over to London.

I will be ready, Father Leggett, at hand and in time — never fear.

Yours affectionately ever,
Vivekananda.

1895.76 — BROTHER DISCIPLES[1]

U.S.A.,
(Summer of?) 1895.

MY DEAR __, (Brother-disciples at the Math)

The books that Sanyal sent have arrived. I forgot to mention this. Please inform him about it.

Let me write down something for you all:

1. Know partiality to be the chief cause of all evil. That is to say, if you show towards any one more love than towards somebody else, rest assured, you will be sowing the seeds of future troubles.

2. If anybody comes to you to speak ill of any of his brothers, refuse to listen to him in toto. It is a great sin to listen even. In that lies the germ of future troubles.

3. Moreover, bear with everyone's shortcomings. Forgive offences by the million. And if you love all unselfishly, all will by degrees come to love one another. As soon as they fully understand that the interests of one depend upon those of others, everyone of them will give up jealousy. To do something conjointly is not in our

1 Translated from Bengali.

very national character. Therefore you must try to inaugurate that spirit with the utmost care, and wait patiently. To tell you the truth, I do not find among you any distinction of great or small: everyone has the capacity to manifest, in times of need, the highest energy. I see it. Look for instance how Shashi will remain always constant to his spot; his steadfastness is a great foundation-rock. How successfully Kali and Jogen brought about the Town Hall meeting; it was indeed a momentous task! Niranjan has done much work in Ceylon and elsewhere. How extensively has Sarada travelled and sown seeds of gigantic future works! Whenever I think of the wonderful renunciation of Hari, about his steadiness of intellect and forbearance, I get a new access of strength! In Tulasi, Gupta, Baburam, Sharat, to mention a few, in every one of you there is tremendous energy. If you still entertain any doubt as to Shri Ramakrishna's being a jewel-expert, what then is the difference between you and a madman! Behold, hundreds of men and women of this country are beginning to worship our Lord as the greatest of all Avataras! Steady! Every great work is done slowly...

He is at the helm, what fear! You are all of infinite strength — how long does it take you to keep off petty jealousy or egoistic ideas! The moment such propensity comes, resign yourselves to the Lord! Just make over your body and mind to His work, and all troubles will be at an end for ever.

There will not be room enough, I see, in the house where you are at present living. A commodious building is needed. That is to say, you need not huddle together in one room. If possible, not more than two should live in the same room. There should be a big hall, where the books may be kept.

Every morning there should be a little reading from the scriptures, which Kali and others may superintend by turns. In the evening there should be another class, with a little practice in meditation and Sankirtanas etc. You may divide the work, and set apart one day for Yoga, a day for Bhakti, another for Jnâna, and so forth: It will be excellent if you fix a routine like this, so that outside people also may join in the evening classes. And every Sunday, from ten in the morning up till night, there should be a continuous succession of classes and Sankirtanas etc. That is for the public. If you take the trouble to continue this kind of routine work for some time, it will gradually make itself easy and smooth. There should be no smoking in that hall, for which another place must be set apart. If you can take trouble to bring about this state of things by degrees, I shall think a great advance is made.

What about a certain magazine that Haramohan was trying to publish? If you can manage to start one, it will indeed be nice.

Yours affectionately,
Vivekananda.

1895.77 — MRS. BULL

Thousand Island Park,
August, 1895.

DEAR MRS. BULL,

... Now here is another letter from Mr. Sturdy I send it over to you. See how things are being prepared ahead. Don't you think this coupled with Mr. Leggett's invitation as a divine call? I think so and am following it. I am going by the end of August with Mr. Leggett to Paris, and then I go to London.

What little can be done for my brethren and my work is all the help I want from you now. I have done my duty to my people fairly well. Now for the world that gave me this body — the country that gave me the ideas, the humanity which allows me to be one of them!

The older I grow, the more I see behind the idea of the Hindus that man is the greatest of all beings. So say the Mohammedans too. The angels were asked by Allah to bow down to Adam. Iblis did not, and therefore he became Satan. This earth is higher than all heavens; this is the greatest school in the universe; and the Mars or Jupiter people cannot be higher than we, because they cannot communicate with us. The only so-called higher beings are the departed, and these are nothing but men who have taken another body. This is finer, it is true, but still a man-body, with hands and feet, and so on. And they live on this earth in another Âkâsha, without being absolutely invisible. They also think, and have consciousness, and everything else like us. So they also are men, so are the Devas, the angels. But man alone becomes God; and they all have to become men again in order to become God...

Yours etc.,
Vivekananda.

France

1895.78 — FRIEND

Hotel Continental,
3 Rue Castiglione, Paris,
26th August, 1895.

Aum tat sat

DEAR FRIEND[1],

I arrived here day before yesterday. I came over to this country as the guest of an American friend who is going to be married here next week.

I shall have to stop here with him till that time; and after that I shall be free to come to London. Eagerly anticipating the joy of meeting you, Ever yours in Sat,

Vivekananda.

1895.79 — RAKHAL[2]

Salutation to Bhagavan Ramakrishna!

1895.

DEAR RAKHAL,

I have now got lots of newspapers etc., and you need not send any more. Let the movement now confine itself to India...

It isn't much use getting up a sensation every day. But avail yourselves of this stir that is rife all over the country, and scatter yourselves in all quarters. In other words, try to start branches at different places. Let it not be an empty sound merely. You must join the Madrasis and start associations etc., at different places. What about the magazine which I heard was going to be started? Why are you nervous about conducting it?... Come? Do something heroic! Brother, what if you do not attain Mukti, what if you suffer damnation a few times? Is the saying untrue? —

— There are some saints who full of holiness in thought, word, and bleed, please the whole world by their numerous beneficent acts, and who develop their own hearts by magnifying an atom of virtue in others as if it were as great as a mountain" (Bhartrihari, Nitishataka).

---

1. Mr. E. T. Sturdy.
2 Translated from Bengali.

What if you don't get Mukti? What childish prattle! Lord! They say even the venom of a snake loses its power by firmly denying it. Isn't it true? What queer humility is this to say, "I know nothing!" "I am nothing!" This is pseudo-renunciation and mock modesty, I tell you. Off with such a self-debasing spirit! "If I do not know, who on earth does!" What have you been doing so long if you now plead ignorance? These are the words of an atheist—the humility of a vagabond wretch. We can do everything, and will do everything! He who is fortunate enough will heroically join us, letting the worthless mew like cats from their corner. A saint writes, "Well, you have had enough of blazoning. Now come back home." I would have called him a man if he could build a house and call me. Ten years' experience of such things has made me wiser. I am no more to be duped by words. Let him who has courage in his mind and love in his heart come with me. I want none else. Through Mother's grace, single-handed I am worth a hundred thousand now and will be worth two millions... There is no certainty about my going back to India. I shall have to lead a wandering life there also, as I am doing here. But here one lives in the company of scholars, and there one must live among fools—there is this difference as of the poles. People of this country organise and work, while our undertakings all come to dust clashing against laziness—miscalled "renunciation,"—and jealousy, etc.—writes me big letters now and then, half of which I cannot decipher, which is a blessing to me. For a great part of the news is of the following description—that in such and such a place such and such a man was speaking ill of me, and that he, being unable to bear the same, had a quarrel with him, and so forth. Many thanks for his kind defence of me. But what seriously hinders me from listening to what particular people may be saying about me is—"

An organised society is wanted. Let Shashi look to the household management, Sanyal take charge of money matters and marketing, and Sharat act as secretary, that is, carry on correspondence etc. Make a permanent centre—it is no use making random efforts as you are doing now. Do you see my point? I have quite a heap of newspapers, now I want you to do something. If you can build a Math, I shall say you are heroes; otherwise you are nothing. Consult the Madras people when you work. They have a great capacity for work. Celebrate this year's Shri Ramakrishna festival with such éclat as to make it a record. The less the feeding propaganda is, the better. It is enough if you distribute Prasâda in earthen cups to the devotees standing in rows...

I am going to write a very short sketch of Shri Ramakrishna's life in English, which I shall send you. Have it printed and translated into Bengali and sell it at the festival—people do not read books that are distributed free. Fix some nominal price. Have the festival done with great pomp...

You must have an all-sided intellect to do efficient work. In any towns or villages you may visit, start an association wherever you find a number of people revering Shri Ramakrishna. Have you travelled through so many villages all for nothing? We must slowly absorb the Hari Sabhâs and such other associations. Well, I cannot tell you all—if I could but get another demon like me! The Lord will supply me everything in time... If one has got power, one must manifest it in action... Off with your ideas of Mukti and Bhakti! There is only one way in the world,

— "The good live for others alone", "The wise man should sacrifice himself for others". I can secure my own good only by doing you good. There is no other way, none whatsoever... You are God, I am God, and man is God. It is this God manifested through humanity who is doing everything in this world. Is there a different God sitting high up somewhere? To work, therefore!

Bimala has sent me a book written by Shashi (Sanyal)... From a perusal of that work Bimala has come to know that all the people of this world are impure and that they are by their very nature debarred from having a jot of religion; that only the handful of Brahmins that are in India have the sole right to it, and among these again, Shashi (Sanyal) and Bimala are the sun and moon, so to speak. Bravo! What a powerful religion indeed! In Bengal specially, that sort of religion is very easy to practice. There is no easier way than that. The whole truth about austerities and spiritual exercises is, in a nutshell, that I am pure and all the rest are impure! A beastly, demoniac, hellish religion this! If the American people are unfit for religion, if it is improper to preach religion here, why then ask their help?... What can remedy such a disease? Well, tell Shashi (Sanyal) to go to Malabar. The Raja there has taken his subjects' land and offered it at the feet of Brahmins. There are big monasteries in every village where sumptuous dinners are given, supplemented by presents in cash... There is no harm in touching the non-Brahmin classes when it serves one's purpose; and when you have done with it, you bathe, for the non-Brahmins are as a class unholy and must never be touched on other occasions! Monks and Sannyasins and Brahmins of a certain type have thrown the country into ruin. Intent all the while on theft and wickedness, these pose as preachers of religion! They will take gifts from the people and at the same time cry, "Don't touch me!" And what great things they have been doing! — "If a potato happens to touch a brinjal, how long will the universe last before it is deluged?" "If they do not apply earth a dozen times to clean their hands, will fourteen generations of ancestors go to hell, or twenty-four?" — For intricate problems like these they have been finding out scientific explanations for the last two thousand years — while one fourth of the people are starving. A girl of eight is married to a man of thirty, and the parents are jubilant over it... And if anyone protests against it, the plea is put forward, "Our religion is being overturned." What sort of religion have they who want to see their girls becoming mothers before they attain puberty even and offer scientific explanations for it? Many, again, lay the blame at the door of the Mohammedans. They are to blame, indeed! Just read the Grihya-Sutras through and see what is given as the marriageable age of a girl... There it is expressly stated that a girl must be married before attaining puberty. The entire Grihya-Sutras enjoin this. And in the Vedic Ashvamedha sacrifice worse things would be done... All the Brâhmanas mention them, and all the commentators admit them to be true. How can you deny them?

What I mean by mentioning all this is that there were many good things in the ancient times, but there were bad things too. The good things are to be retained, but the India that is to be, the future India. must be much greater than ancient India. From the day Shri Ramakrishna was born dates the growth of modern India and of the Golden Age. And you are the agents to bring about this Golden Age. To work, with this conviction at heart!

Hence, when you call Shri Ramakrishna an Incarnation and in the same breath plead your ignorance unhesitatingly, I say, "You are false to the backbone!" If Ramakrishna Paramahamsa be true, you also are true. But you must show it... In you all there is tremendous power. The atheist has nothing but rubbish in him. Those who are believers are heroes. They will manifest tremendous power. The world will be swept before them. "Sympathy and help to the poor"; "Man is God, he is Nârâyana"; "In Atman there is no distinction of male or female, of Brahmin or Kshatriya, and the like"; "All is Narayana from the Creator down to a clump of grass." The worm is less manifested, the Creator more manifested. Every action that helps a being manifest its divine nature more and more is good, every action that retards it is evil.

The only way of getting our divine nature manifested is by helping others to do the same.

If there is inequality in nature, still there must be equal chance for all — or if greater for some and for some less — the weaker should be given more chance than the strong.

In other words, a Brahmin is not so much in need of education as a Chandâla. If the son of a Brahmin needs one teacher, that of a Chandala needs ten. For greater help must be given to him whom nature has not endowed with an acute intellect from birth. It is a madman who carries coals to Newcastle. The poor, the downtrodden, the ignorant, let these be your God.

A dreadful slough is in front of you — take care; many fall into it and die. The slough is this, that the present religion of the Hindus is not in the Vedas, nor in the Puranas, nor in Bhakti, nor in Mukti — religion has entered into the cooking-pot. The present religion of the Hindus is neither the path of knowledge nor that of reason — it is "Don't-touchism". "Don't touch me!" "Don't touch me!" — that exhausts its description. See that you do not lose your lives in this dire irreligion of "Don't-touchism". Must the teaching, " — Looking upon all beings as your own self" — be confined to books alone? How will they grant salvation who cannot feed a hungry mouth with a crumb of bread? How will those who become impure at the mere breath of others purify others? Don't-touchism is a form of mental disease. Beware! All expansion is life, all contraction is death. All love is expansions all selfishness is contraction. Love is therefore the only law of life. He who loves lives, he who is selfish is dying. Therefore love for love's sake, because it is the only law of life, just as you breathe to live. This is the secret of selfless love, selfless action and the rest... Try to help Shashi (Sanyal) if you can, in any ways He is a very good and pious man, but of a narrow heart. It does not fall to the lot of all to feel for the misery of others. Good Lord! Of all Incarnations Lord Chaitanya was the greatest, but he was comparatively lacking in knowledge; in the Ramakrishna Incarnation there is knowledge, devotion and love — infinite knowledge, infinite love, infinite work, infinite compassion for all beings. You have not yet been able to understand him. "— Even after hearing about Him, most people do not understand Him." What the whole Hindu race has thought in ages, he lived in one life. His life is the living commentary to the Vedas of all nations. People will come to know him by degrees. My old watchword — struggle, struggle up to light! Onward!

Yours in service,
Vivekananda.

1895.80 — FRIEND

To Mr. E. T. Sturdy:

C/O Miss Macleod,
Hotel Hollande,
Rue de La Paix, Paris,
5th September, 1895.

DEAR AND BLESSED FRIEND,

It is useless to express my gratitude for your kindness; it is too great for expression...

I have a cordial invitation from Miss Müller, and as her place is very near to yours, I think it will be nice to come to her place first for a day or two and then to come over to you.

My body was very ill for a few days, which caused this delay in writing you.

Hoping soon for the privilege of mingling hearts and heads together.

I remain, ever yours in love, and fellowship in the Lord,
Vivekananda.

1895.81 — ALASINGA

Paris,
9th September, 1895.

DEAR ALASINGA,

...I am surprised you take so seriously the missionaries' nonsense... If the people in India want me to keep strictly to my Hindu diet, please tell them to send me a cook and money enough to keep him. This silly bossism without a mite of real help makes me laugh. On the other hand, if the missionaries tell you that I have ever broken the two great vows of the Sannyâsin — chastity and poverty — tell them that they are big liars. Please write to the missionary Hume asking him categorically to write you what misdemeanour he saw in me, or give you the names of his informants, and whether the information was first-hand or not; that will settle the question and expose the whole thing...

As for me, mind you, I stand at nobody's dictation. I know my mission in life, and no chauvinism about me; I belong as much to India as to the world, no humbug about that. I have helped you all I could. You must now help yourselves. What country has any special claim on me? Am I any nation's slave? Don't talk any more silly nonsense, you faithless atheists.

I have worked hard and sent all the money I got to Calcutta and Madras, and then after doing all this, stand their silly dictation! Are you not ashamed? What do I owe to them? Do I care a fig for their praise or fear their blame? I am a singular man, my son, not even you can understand me yet. Do your work; if you cannot, stop; but do not try to "boss" me with your nonsense. I see a greater Power than man, or God, or devil at my back. I require nobody's help. I have been all my life helping others... They cannot raise a few rupees to help the work of the greatest man their country ever produced—Ramakrishna Paramahamsa; and they talk nonsense and want to dictate to the man for whom they did nothing, find who did everything he could for them! Such is the ungrateful world!

Do you mean to say I am born to live and die one of those caste-ridden, superstitious, merciless, hypocritical, atheistic cowards that you find only amongst the educated Hindus? I hate cowardice; I will have nothing to do with cowards or political nonsense. I do not believe in any politics. God and truth are the only politics in the world, everything else is trash.

I am going to London tomorrow...

Yours with blessings,
Vivekananda.

England

1895.82 — AKHANDANANDA[1]

C/O E. T. Sturdy, Esq.,
High View, Caversham,
1895.

BELOVED AKHANDANANDA,

I am glad to go through the contents of your letter. Your idea is grand but our nation is totally lacking in the faculty of organisation. It is this one drawback which produces all sorts of evil. We are altogether averse to making a common cause for anything. The first requisite for organisation is obedience. I do a little bit of work when I feel so disposed, and then let it go to the dogs — this kind of work is of no avail. We must have plodding industry and perseverance. Keep a regular correspondence, I mean, make it a point to write to me every month, or twice a month, what work you are doing and what has been its outcome. We want here (in England) a Sannyasin well-versed in English and Sanskrit. I shall soon go to America again, and he is to work here in my absence. Except Sharat and Shashi — I find no one else for this task. I have sent money to Sharat and written to him to start at once. I have requested Rajaji that his Bombay agent may help Sharat in embarking. I forgot to write — but if you can take the trouble to do it, please send through Sharat a bag of Mung, gram, and Arhar Dâl, also a little of the spice called Methi. Please convey my love to Pundit Narayan Das, Mr. Shankar Lal, Ojhaji, Doctor, and all. Do you think you can get the medicine for Gopi's eyes here? — Everywhere you find patent medicines, which are all humbug. Please give my blessings to him and to the other boys. Yajneshwar has founded a certain society at Meerut and wants to work conjointly with us. By the bye, he has got a certain paper too; send Kali there, and let him start a Meerut centre, if he can and, try to have a paper in Hindi. I shall help a little now and then. I shall send some money when Kali goes to Meerut and reports to me exactly how matters stand. Try to open a centre at Ajmer... Pundit Agnihotri has started some society at Saharanpur. They wrote my a letter. Please keep in correspondence with them. Live on friendly terms with all. Work! Work! Go on opening centres in this way. We have them already in Calcutta and Madras, and it will be excellent if you can start new ones at Meerut and Ajmer. Go on slowly starting centres at different places like that. Here all my letters etc., are to be addressed in care of E. T. Sturdy, Esq., High View, Caversham, Reading, England, and those for America, C/o Miss Phillips, 19 W. 38 Street, New York. By degrees we must spread the world over. The first thing needed is obedience. You

---

1 Translated from Bengali.

must be ready to plunge into fire—then will work be done... Form societies dike that at different villages in Rajputana. There you have a hint.

Yours affectionately,
Vivekananda.

1895.83 — MRS. BULL

C/O E. T. Sturdy, Esq.,
High View, Caversham,
Reading, England,
17th Sept., 1895.

DEAR MRS. BULL,

Mr. Sturdy and I want to get hold of a few of the best, say, strong and intelligent men in England to form a society, and therefore we must proceed slowly. We must take care not to be run over with "fads" from the first. This you will know has been my policy in America too. Mr. Sturdy has been in India living with our Sannyasins in their manner for some time. He is an exceedingly energetic man, educated and well versed in Sanskrit... So far so good... Purity, perseverance, and energy—these three I want, and if I get only half a dozen here, my work will go on. I have a great chance of such a few.

Yours with best wishes,
Vivekananda.

1895.84 — MRS. BULL

Reading, England,
24th Sept., 1895.

DEAR MRS. BULL,

I have not done any visible work as yet except helping Mr. Sturdy in studying Sanskrit... Mr. Sturdy wants me to bring over a monk from India from amongst my brethren to help him when I am away in America. I have written to India for one... So far it is all right. I am waiting for the next wave. "Avoid not and seek not—wait for what the Lord sends", is my motto... I am a slow writer, but the heart is full of gratitude.

Yours with best wishes,
Vivekananda.

1895.85 — JOE JOE

To Miss Josephine MacLeod:

C/O E. T. Sturdy, Esq.,
High View, Caversham,
Reading, England,
September, 1895.

DEAR JOE JOE,

A thousand pardons for not promptly writing to you. I arrived safe in London, found my friend, and am all right in his home. It is beautiful. His wife is surely an angel, and his life is full of India. He has been years there — mixing with the Sannyasins, eating their food, etc., etc.; so you see I am very happy. I found already several retired Generals from India; they were very civil and polite to me. That wonderful knowledge of the Americans that identify every black man with the negro is entirely absent here, and nobody even stares at me in the street.

I am very much more at home here than anywhere out of India. The English people know us, we know them. The standard of education and civilisation is very high here — that makes a great change, so does the education of many generations.

Have the Turtle-doves returned? The Lord bless them and theirs for ever and ever. How are the babies — Alberta and Holister? Give them my oceans of love and know it yourself.

My friend being a Sanskrit scholar, we are busy working on the great commentaries of Shankara etc. Nothing but philosophy and religion here, Joe Joe. I am going to try to get up classes in October in London.

Ever affectionately with love and blessings,
Vivekananda.

1895.86 — DEAR __

Reading, England,
4th Oct., 1895.

DEAR __,

... Purity, patience, and perseverance overcome all obstacles. All great things must of necessity be slow ...

Yours with love,
Vivekananda.

1895.87 — RAKHAL[1]

C/O E. T. Sturdy,
High View, Caversham, Reading
4th October, 1895.

MY DEAR RAKHAL,

You know that I am now in England. I shall stay here for about a month and go back to America. Next summer I shall again come to England. At present there is not much prospect in England, but the Lord is omnipotent. Let us wait and see...

It is impossible for — to come now. The thing is, the money belongs to Mr. Sturdy, and we must have the kind of man he likes. Mr. Sturdy has taken initiation from me, and is a very enterprising and good man.

In the first place we want a man who has a thorough mastery of English and Sanskrit. It is true that will be able to pick up English soon should he come here but I am as yet unable to bring men here to learn. We want them, first, who will be able to teach. In the second place, I trust those that will not desert me in prosperity and adversity alike... The most trustworthy men are needed. Then, after the foundation is laid, let him who will, come and make a noise, there is no fear. — gave no proof of wisdom in being carried away by a hubbub and joining the party of those charlatans. Sir, granted that Ramakrishna Paramahamsa was a sham, granted that it has been a very serious mistake, indeed, to take refuge in him, but what is the way out now? What if one life is spent in vain, but shall a man eat his own words? Can there be such a thing as having a dozen husbands? Any of you may join any party you like, I have no objection, no, not in the least, but travelling this world over I find that save and except his circle alone, everywhere else thought and act are at variance. For those that belong to him, I have the utmost love, the utmost confidence. I have no alternative in the matter. Call me one-sided if you will, but there you have my bona fide avowal. If but a thorn pricks the foot of one who has surrendered himself to Shri Ramakrishna, it makes my bones ache. All others I love; you will find very few men so unsectarian as I am; but you must excuse me, I have that bit of bigotry. If I do not appeal to his name, whose else shall I? It will be time enough to seek for a big Guru in our next birth; but in this, it is that unlearned Brahmin who has bought this body of mine for ever.

I give you a bit of my mind; don't be angry, pray. I am your slave so long as you are his — step a hair's breadth outside that, and you and I are on a par. All the sects and societies that you see, the whole host of them, inside the country or out, he has already swallowed them all, my brother.

"— These have verily been killed by Myself long ago, be only the instrument, O Arjuna." Today or tomorrow they will be merged in your own body. O man of little faith! Through his grace, "— The whole universe becomes a hoof-mark of the cow." Be not traitors, that is a sin past atonement. Name, fame, good deeds,

---

1 Translated from Bengali.

"— Whatever sacrifices you perform, whatever penances you undergo, whatever you eat" — surrender everything to his feet. What on earth do we want? He has given us refuge, what more do we want? Bhakti is verily its own reward — what else is needed? My brother, he who made men of us by feeding and clothing and imparting wisdom and knowledge, who opened the eyes of our self, whom day and night we found the living God — must we be traitors to him!!! And you forget the mercy of such a Lord! The lives of Buddha and Krishna and Jesus are matters of ancient history, and doubts are entertained about their historicity, and you in spite of seeing the greatness of Shri Ramakrishna's life in flesh and blood sometimes lose your head! Fie upon you! I have nothing to say. His likeness is being worshipped in and out of your country, by godless and heartless men, and you are stranded at times on disbelief!! In a breath he will create for himself hundreds of thousands of such as you are. Blessed is your birth, blessed your lineage, and blessed your country that you were allowed to take the dust of his feet. Well I can't help. He is protecting us, forsooth — I see it before my eyes. Insane that you are, is it through my own strength that beauty like that of fairies, and hundreds of thousands of rupees, lose their attraction and appear as nothing to me? Or is it he who is protecting me? He who has no faith in him and no reverence for the Holy Mother will be a downright loser, I tell you plainly.

... Haramohan has written about his troubled circumstances, and says he will be dislodged from his home soon. He has asked for some lectures; but I have none at present, but have still some money left in my purse, which I shall send him. So he need not be afraid. I could send him at once, but I suspect that the money I last sent was miscarried, therefore I postpone sending it. Secondly, I know, besides, of no address to send it to. I see the Madras people have failed to start the paper. Practical wisdom is altogether wanting in the Hindu race, I see. Whenever you promise to do any work, you must do it exactly at the appointed time, or people lose their faith in you. Money matters require a speedy reply ... If Master Mahashaya be willing, tell him to be my Calcutta agent, for I have an implicit faith in him, and he understands a good deal of these things; it is not for a childish and noisy rabble to do it. Tell him to fix upon a centre, an address that will not change every hour, and to which I shall direct all my Calcutta correspondence ... Business is business ...

Yours etc.,
Vivekananda.

1895.88 — MRS. BULL

Reading,
6th Oct., 1895.

DEAR MRS. BULL,

... I am translating a little book on Bhakti with Mr. Sturdy with copious commentaries, which is to be published soon. This month I am to give two lectures in London and one in Maidenhead. This will open up the way to some classes and parlour lectures. We do not wish to make any noise but to go quietly...

Yours with best wishes,
Vivekananda.

1895.89 — JOE JOE

To Miss Josephine MacLeod:

High View, Caversham,
Reading, England,
20th October, 1895.

DEAR JOE JOE,

This note is to welcome the Leggetts to London. This being in a sense my native country, I send you my welcome first, I shall receive your welcome next Tuesday the 22nd at Princes' Hall half past eight p.m.

I am so busy till Tuesday, I am afraid, I shall not be able to run in to see you. I, however, shall come to see you any day after that. Possibly I may come on Tuesday.

With everlasting love and blessings,

Yours,
Vivekananda.

1895.90 — KALI[1]

To Swami Abhedananda:

C/O E. T. Sturdy, Esq.,
High View, Caversham,
Reading, England,
October, 1895.

DEAR KALI,

You may have got my earlier letter. At present send all letters to me at the above address. Mr. Sturdy is known to Târakdâ. He has brought me to his place, and we are both trying to create a stir in England. I shall this year leave again in November for America. So I require a man well-up in Sanskrit and English, particularly the latter language — either Shashi or you or Sâradâ. Now, if you have completely recovered, very well, you come; otherwise send Sharat. The work is to teach the devotees I shall be leaving here, to make them study the Vedanta, to do a little

---

1 Translated from Bengali.

translation work into English, and to deliver occasional lectures. "Work is apt to cloud spiritual vision." X__ is very eager to come, but unless the foundation is strongly laid, there is every likelihood of everything toppling down. I am sending you a cheque along with this letter. Buy clothes and other necessary things — whoever comes. I am sending the cheque in the name of Master Mahashay Mahendra Babu. Gangâdhar's Tibetan choga is in the Math; get the tailor to make a similar choga of gerua colour. See that the collar is a little high, that is, the throat and neck should be covered... Above all, you must have a woolen overcoat, for it is very cold. If you do not put on an overcoat on the ship, you will suffer much... I am sending a second class ticket, as there is not much difference between a first class and a second class berth... If it is decided to send Shashi then inform the purser of the ship beforehand to provide him with vegetarian diet.

Go to Bombay and see Messrs. King, King & Co., Fort, Bombay, and tell them that you are Mr. Sturdy's man. They will then give you a ticket to England. A letter is being sent from here to the Company with instructions. I am writing to the Maharaja of Khetri to instruct his Bombay agent to look after the booking of your passage. If this sum of Rs. 150 is not sufficient for your outfit, get the remainder from Rakhal. I shall send him the amount afterwards. Keep another Rs. 50 for pocket expenses — take it from Rakhal; I shall pay back later. I have not up to now got any acknowledgement of the amount I sent to Chuni Babu. Start as quickly as possible. Inform Mahendra Babu that he is my Calcutta agent. Tell him to send a letter to Mr. Sturdy by next mail informing him that he is ready to look after all business transactions in Calcutta on your behalf. In effect, Mr. Sturdy is my secretary in England, Mahendra Babu in Calcutta, and Alasinga in Madras. Send this information to Madras also. Can any work be done unless all of us gird up our loins? And be up and doing! "Fortune favours the brave and energetic." Don't look back — forward, infinite energy, infinite enthusiasm, infinite daring, and infinite patience — then alone can great deeds be accomplished. We must set the whole world afire.

Now on the day the steamer is due to start, write a letter to Mr. Sturdy informing him by which steamer you are leaving for England. Otherwise there is some likelihood of your having difficulties when you reach London. Take the ship that comes directly to London, for even if it takes a few days longer on the voyage, the fares are less. At the moment our purse is lean. In time we shall send preachers in large numbers to all the quarters of the globe.

Yours affectionately,
Vivekananda.

PS — Write at once to the Maharaja of Khetri, that you are going to Bombay and that you will be glad if his agent attends to the booking of your passage and sees you off the board.

Keep my address with you written in a pocket-book, lest there should be difficulties afterwards.

1895.91 — MOTHER

C/O E. T. Sturdy, Esq.,
High View, Caversham,
Reading, England,
October, 1895.

DEAR MOTHER, (Mrs. F. H. Leggett)

You have not forgotten your son? Where are you now? And Tante and the babies? What about our saintly worshipper at your shrine? Joe Joe is not entering "Nirvana" so soon, but her deep silence almost seems to be a big "Samadhi".

Are you on the move? I am enjoying England very much. I am living with my friend on philosophy, leaving a little margin for eating and smoking. We are getting nothing else but Dualism and Monism and all the rest of them.

Hollister has become very manly, I suppose, in his long trousers; and Alberta is studying German.

The Englishmen here are very friendly. Except a few Anglo-Indians, they do not hate black men at all. Not even do they hoot at me in the streets. Sometimes I wonder whether my face has turned white, but the mirror tells the truth. Yet they are all so friendly here.

Again, the English men and women who love India are more Hindu than the Hindus themselves. I am getting plenty of vegetables cooked, you will be surprised to hear, à la Indienne perfectly. When an Englishman takes up a thing, he goes to its very depths. Yesterday I met a Prof. Fraser, a high official here. He has been half his life in India; and he has lived so much in ancient thought and wisdom that he does not care a fig for anything out of India!! You will be astonished to hear that many of the thoughtful English men and women think that the Hindu caste is the only solution of the social problem. With that idea in their head you may imagine how they hate the socialists and other social democrats!! Again, here the men — and the most highly educated — take the greatest interest in Indian thought, and very few women. The woman's sphere is narrower here than in America. So far everything is going very well with me. I shall let you know any further developments.

With my love to paterfamilias, to the Queen Mother, to Joe Joe (no title), and to the babies,

Ever yours with love and blessings,
Vivekananda.

1895.92 — RAKHAL[1]

C/O E. T. Sturdy, Esq.,
Reading, Caversham, England,
1895.

DEAR RAKHAL,

Glad to receive your letters. There are two defects in the letters which you all write, specially in yours. The first is that very few of the important points I ask are answered. Secondly, there is unusual delay in replying... I have to work day and night, and am always whirling from place to place besides... These are countries where the people are most luxurious, fashionable folk, and nobody would touch a man who has but a speck of dirt on his body... I hoped that somebody would come while I was still here, but as yet nothing has been settled I see... Business is business, that is, you must do everything promptly; delay and shuffling won't do. By the end of next week I shall go to America, so there is no chance of my meeting him who is coming... These are countries of gigantic scholars. Is it a joke to make disciples of such people? You are but children and talk like children. Only this much is needed that there should be someone to teach a little Sanskrit, or translate a bit in my absence, that's all. Why not let Girish Babu visit these lands? It is a good idea. It will cost him but 3000 rupees to visit England and America, and go back. The more people come to these countries, the better. But then it sets my nerves on edge to look at those who don hats and pose as Sahibs!

Black as chimney sweeps, and calling themselves Europeans! Why not wear one's country-dress, as befits gentlemen? — Instead of that, to add to that frightfulness of appearance! Good heavens!... Here, as in our country one has to spend from one's own pocket to give lectures, but one can make good the expenses if one lives long enough and makes a reputation. Another thing, my incessant lecturing tours are making my constitution very nervous, causing insomnia and other troubles. Over and above that, I have to work single-handed. It is no use depending on my countrymen. No one (in Bengal) has hitherto helped me with a penny, nor has a single soul stepped forward to my assistance. Everybody in this world seeks help, and the more you help him, the more he wants. And if you can do no further, he will call you a cheat... I love — and trust him... He will be free from disease through the Lord's grace. I take all his responsibility...

Yours affectionately,
Vivekananda.

---

1 Translated from Bengali.

1895.93 — SHASHI[1]

C/O E. T. Sturdy, Esq.,
Reading, Caversham, England,
1895.

DEAR SHASHI,

...I am in receipt of Rakhal's letter today. I am sorry to hear that — has suffered from gravel. Most probably it was due to indigestion. Gopal's debts have been cleared; now ask him to join the monastic order. The worldly-wise instinct is most difficult to root out...Let him come and work in the Math. One is apt to imbibe a lot of mischievous ideas by concerning oneself too long in worldly affairs. If he refuses to take the monastic vow, please tell him to clear out. I don't want amphibious type of men who will be half monks and half householders...Haramohan has coined a Lord Ramakrishna Paramahamsa, I see. What does he mean? English Lord, or Duke? Tell Rakhal, let people say whatever they will — "Men (who wrongly criticise) are to be treated as worms!" as Shri Ramakrishna used to say. Let there be no disparity between what you profess and what you do, also eschew the very name of Jesuitism. Was I ever an orthodox, Paurânika Hindu, an adherent of social usages? I do not pose as one. You will not have to say things that will be pleasant to any section of people. You must not so much as notice what the Bengalis say for or against us...They could not do a penny-worth of service to him whose birth has sanctified their country where the primary laws of health and sanitation are trampled, and yet they would talk big! What matters is, my brother, what such men have got to say!...It is for you to go on doing your own work. Why look up to men for approbation, look up to God! I hope Sharat will be able to teach them the Gita and the Upanishads and their commentaries somehow, with the help of the dictionary. — Or, is it an empty Vairâgya that you have? The days of such Vairagya are gone! It is not for everyone, my boy, to become Ramakrishna Paramahamsa! I hope Sharat has started by this time. Please send a copy of the Panchadashi, a copy of the Gita (with as many commentaries as possible), a copy each of the Nârada and Shândilya Sutras (published in Varanasi), a translation (good, not worthless) of the Panchadashi — if it is available — and the translation by Kâlivara Vedântavâgisha of Shankara's Commentary. And if there be any translation, Bengali or English (by Shrish Babu of Allahabad), of Pânini's Sutras, or the Kâshikâ-Vritti, or the Phani-Bhâshya, please send a copy of each...Now, just tell your Bengalis to send me a copy of the Vâchaspatya Dictionary, and that will be a good test for those tall-talking people. In England, religious movements make very slow progress. These people here are either bigots or atheists. And the former again have only a bit of formal religion. They say, "Patriotism is our religion." That is all.

Send the books to America, c/o Miss Mary Phillips, 19 West 38th Street, New York, U.S.A. That is my American address. By the end of November I shall go to

---

[1] Translated from Bengali.

America. So send my books etc., there. If Sharat has started immediately on your receipt of my letter, then only I may meet him, otherwise not. Business is business, no child's play. Mr. Sturdy will see to him and accommodate him. This time I have come to England just to probe a little. Next summer I shall try to make some stir. The winter after that, I shall go to India... Correspond regularly with those who are interested in us, so as to keep up their interest. Try to open centres in places all over Bengal... This much for the present. In my next I shall give you more details. Mr. Sturdy is a very nice gentleman, a staunch Vedantist, and understands a smattering of Sanskrit. It is with a good deal of labour that you can do a little bit of work in these countries; a sheer uphill task, with cold and rain into the bargain. Moreover, here you must support yourself and do your labour of love. Englishmen won't spend a penny on lectures or things of that sort. If they do come to listen to you, well, thank your stars — as is the case in our country. Besides, the common people here do not even know of me now. In addition to all this, they will give you a wide berth if you preach God and such things to them. They think this must be another clergyman! Well, you just patiently do one thing — set about collecting everything that books, beginning with the Rig-Veda down to the most insignificant of Puranas and Tantras, have got to say about creation and annihilation of the universe, about race, heaven, and hell, the soul, consciousness, and intellect, etc., the sense-organs, Mukti, transmigration, and suchlike things. No child's play would do, I want real scholarly work. The most important thing is to collect the materials. My love to you all.

Yours affectionately,
Vivekananda.

1895.94 — RAKHAL[2]

1895.

DEAR RAKHAL,

...Your suggestion to me to go back to India is no doubt right, but a seed has been sown in this country, and there is the possibility of its being nipped in the bud if I go away all on a sudden. Hence I have to wait some time. Moreover it will be possible to manage everything nicely from here. Everybody requests me to return to India. It is all right, but don't you see it is not wise to depend upon others. A wise man should stand firm on his own legs and act. Everything will come about slowly. For the present don't forget to be on the look-out for a site. We want a big plot — of about ten to twenty thousand rupees — it must be right on the Ganga. Though my capital is small, I am exceedingly bold. Have an eye on securing the land. At present we shall have to work three centres, one in New York, another in Calcutta and a third in Madras. Then, by degrees, as the Lord will arrange... You

[2] Translated from Bengali.

must keep a strict eye on your health; let everything else be subordinated to that...

Brother Tarak is eager for travel. Well, it is good, but these are very expensive countries; a preacher needs here at least a thousand rupees a month. But Brother Tarak has boldness, and it is God who provides every thing. Quite true, but he must have to improve his English a little. The thing is, one has to snatch one's bread from the jaws of the missionary scholars. That is, one must prevail over these people by dint of learning, or one will be blown off at a puff. They understand neither Sâdhus nor your Sânnyasins, nor the spirit of renunciation. What they do understand is the vastness of learning, the display of eloquence and tremendous activity. Over and above that, the whole country will be searching for flaws, the clergy will day and night try to snub you, through force or guile. You must get rid of these obstructions to preach your doctrines. Through the mercy of the Divine Mother everything is possible. But in my opinion if Brother Tarak goes on starting some societies in the Punjab and Madras, and you become organised, it will be the best thing. It is indeed a great thing to discover a new path, but it is as difficult a task to cleanse that path and make it spacious and nice. If you live for some time in places where I have sown the seeds of our Master's ideals and succeed in developing the seeds into plants, you will be doing much greater work than I did. What will they who cannot manage some ready-made thing do with regard to things that are yet to come? If you cannot add a little salt to a dish almost done, how am I to believe that you will collect all the ingredients? Let Brother Tarak, as an alternative, start a Himalayan Math at Almora and have a library there, so that we may spend some of our spare time in a cool place and practice spiritual exercises. However, I have nothing to say against any particular course which any one may be led to adopt; on the contrary, God-speed — " bit. What's the good of being in a hurry? You shall all travel the whole world. Courage! Brother Tarak has a great capacity for work within him. Hence I expect much of him... You remember, I suppose, how after Shri Ramakrishna's passing away, all forsook us as so many worthless, ragged boys. Only people like Balaram, Suresh, Master, and Chuni Babu were our friends at that hour of need. And we shall never be able to repay our debts to them... Tell Chuni Babu in private that he has nothing to fear, that those who are protected by the Lord must be above fear. I am a puny man, but the glories of the Lord are infinite. — Discard fear. Let not your faith be shaken ... Has danger any power over one whom the Lord has taken into His fold?

Ever yours,
Vivekananda.

1895.95 — JOE JOE

To Miss Josephine MacLeod:

> High View, Caversham,
> Reading, England,
> October, 1895.

DEAR JOE JOE,

I was so glad to hear from you. I was afraid you had forgotten me.

I am going to have a few lectures in and about London. One of them, a public one, will be at Princes' Hall on the 22nd at 8-30.

Come over and try to form a class. I have as yet done almost nothing here. Of course, breaking the ice is slow always. It took me two years in America to work up that little which we had in New York.

With love for all,

> Yours ever,
> Vivekananda.

1895.96 — ISABELLE MCKINDLEY

To Miss Isabelle McKindley:

> 80 Oakley Street,
> Chelsea, S.W., London,
> 24th October, '95.

We meet and part. This is the law and ever ever be. I sadly ask O gentle ones, do you remember me?

I haven't had any news from Chicago, nor did I write as I did not want to bother you — also I did not know where to.

Accompanying is a newspaper notice of a lecture I delivered in London. It is not bad. The London audiences are very learned and critical, and the English nature is far from being effusive. I have some friends here — made some more — so I am going on.

My bed is in the foaming deep

What care I, friend, the dew!

It is a queer life, mine — always travelling, no rest. Rest will be my death — such is the force of habit. Little success here, little there — and a good deal of bumping. Saw Paris a good [deal]. Miss Josephine M'cLeod [MacLeod], a New York friend, showed it all over to me for a month. Even there, the kind American girl! Here in England they know us more. Those that do not like the Hindus, they hate them; those that like, they worship them.

It is slow work here, but sure. Not frothy, not superficial. English women as a rule are not as highly educated as the American women, nor are so beautiful. They are quite submissive wives or hidden-away daughters or church-going mothers—the embodiments of crystallized conventionality. I am going to have some classes at the above address.

Sometimes—and generally when I score a success—I feel a despondence; I feel as if everything is vain—as if this life has no meaning, as if it is a waking dream. Love, friendship, religion, virtue, kindness—everything, a momentary state of mind. I seem to long to go; in spite of myself I say, how far—O how far! Yet the body-and-mind will have to work its Karma out. I hope it will not be bad.

How are you all going on? Where is Mother Church? Is she interviewing the ghosts of the Thotmeses and Rameses in the Pyramids—or calmly going her round of duties at home?

Yet the life seems to grow deep and at the same time lose its hold on itself.

Not disgust, nor joy for life, but a sort of indifference—things will take their course; who can resist—only stand by and look on. Well, I will not talk about myself so much. Egregious egotist! I always was that, you know. How about you all? Great fun this life, isn't it? Don't go to the extremes. A calm, restful, settled married life is good for the majority of mankind. Mr. [Edward T.] Sturdy, the friend with whom I am living now, was in India several times. He mixed with our monks and is very ascetic in his habits, but he is married at last and has settled down. And [he] has got a beautiful little baby. Their life is very nice. The wife, of course, doesn't much care about metaphysics or Sanskrit, but her whole life is in her husband—and husband's soul is in Sanskrit metaphysics! Yet it is a good combination of theory and practice, I think. Write me all about yourselves if you have time and inclination, and give Mother Church my eternal gratitude.

My movements are so, so uncertain. Yet I will be a month more in London.

With never-ending gratitude and love,
Vivekananda.

1895.97 — ALASINGA

London,
24th October, 1895.

DEAR ALASINGA,

…I have already delivered my first address, and you may see how well it has been received by the notice in the Standard. The Standard is one of the most influential conservative papers. I am going to be in London for a month, then I go off to America and shall come back again next summer. So far you see the seed is well sown in England…

Take courage and work on. Patience and steady work—this is the only way. Go on; remember—patience and purity and courage and steady work... So long as you are pure, and true to your principles, you will never fail—Mother will never leave you, and all blessings will be yours.

Yours with love,
Vivekananda.

1895.98 — JOE JOE

To Miss Josephine MacLeod:

80 Oakley Street, Chelsea,
31st October, 1895.

DEAR JOE JOE,

I shall be only too glad to come to lunch on Friday and see Mr. Coit at the Albemarle.

Two American ladies, mother and daughter, living in London came in to the class last night—Mrs. and Miss Netter. They were very sympathetic of course. The class there at Mr. Chamier's is finished. I shall begin at my lodgings from Saturday night next. I expect to have a pretty good-sized room or two for my classes. I have been also invited to Moncure Conways's Ethical Society where I speak on the 10th. I shall have a lecture in the Balboa Society next Tuesday. The Lord will help. I am not sure whether I can go up with you on Saturday. You will have great fun in the country anyway, and Mr. and Mrs. Sturdy are such nice people.

With love and blessings,
Vivekananda.

PS—Kindly order some vegetables for me. I don't care much for rice—bread will do as well. I have become an awful vegetarian now.

1895.99 — FRIEND

80 Oakley St., Chelsea,
31st October, 1895 (5 p.m.).

DEAR FRIEND, (Mr. E. T. Sturdy)

Just now two young gentlemen, Mr. Silverlock and his friend, left. Miss Müller also came this afternoon and left just when these gentlemen came in.

One is an Engineer and the other is in the grain trade. They have read a good deal of modern philosophy and science and have been much struck by the similarity with the latest conclusions of both with the ancient Hindu thought. They are very fine, intelligent, and educated men. One has given up the Church, the other asked me whether he should or not. Now, two things struck me after this interview. First, we must hurry the book through. We will touch a class thereby who are philosophically religious without the least mystery-mongering. Second, both of them want to know the rituals of my creed! This opened my eyes. The world in general must have some form. In fact, in the ordinary sense religion is philosophy concretised through rituals and symbols.

It is absolutely necessary to form some ritual and have a Church. That is to say, we must fix on some ritual as fast as we can. If you can come Saturday morning or sooner, we shall go to the Asiatic Society library or you can procure for me a book which is called Hemâdri Kosha, from which we can get what we want, and kindly bring the Upanishads. We will fix something grand, from birth to death of a man. A mere loose system of philosophy gets no hold on mankind.

If we can get it through, before we have finished the classes, and publish it by publicly holding a service or two under it, it will go on. They want to form a congregation, and they want ritual; that is one of the causes why — will never have a hold on Western people.

The Ethical Society has sent me another letter thanking me for the acceptance of this offer. Also a copy of their forms. They want me to bring with me a book from which to read for ten minutes. Will you bring the Gita (translation) and the Buddhist Jâtaka (translation) with you?

I would not do anything in this matter without seeing you first.

With love and blessings,
Vivekananda.

1895.100 — FRIEND

80 Oakley Street,
Chelsea,
1st November, 1895.

DEAR FRIEND, (Mr. E. T. Sturdy)

The tickets of the Balleren (?) Society are 35 in number.

The subject is "Indian Philosophy and Western Society". Chairman blank.

As you did not ask me to send them over, I do not. I got your letters properly.

Yours in the Sat,
Vivekananda.

1895.101 — FRIEND

2nd November, 1895.

DEAR FRIEND, (Mr. E. T. Sturdy)

I think you are right; we shall work on our own lines and let things grow.

I send you the note of the lecture.

I shall come on Sunday if nothing extraordinary prevents me.

Yours with love,
Vivekananda.

1895.102 — AKHANDANANDA[1]

London,
13th Nov., 1895.

MY DEAR AKHANDANANDA,

I am very glad to receive your letter. It is excellent work that you are doing. R— is very liberal and openhanded, but no advantage should be taken over him for that reason. About the raising of funds by Shrimân—, well, it is a fair enterprise; but my boy, this is a very queer world, where even the World-Gods Brahmâ and Vishnu find it difficult to evade the clutches of lust and gold. Wherever there is any the least concern with money, there is the chance for misunderstanding. Let therefore nobody undertake such work as raising money on behalf of the Math... Whenever you hear of any householder collecting funds in my or our name on the plea of erecting a Math, or some such thing, the first thing you should do is to distrust him, and never set your hand to it. The more so, as householders of poor means take to various tricks to supply their wants. Therefore, if ever a trusty devotee or a householder with a heart, being of affluent circumstances, undertakes such works as the founding of a Math, or if the funds raised be kept in the custody of a trusty householder of wealth—well and good, otherwise never have a hand in it. On the contrary, you must dissuade others from such a thing. You are but a boy and are ignorant of the snare of gold. Opportunities will turn even a staunch moralist into a cheat. This is the way of the world.

It is not at all in our nature to do a work conjointly. It is to this that our miserable condition is due. He who knows how to obey knows how to command. Learn obedience first. Among these Western nations, with such a high spirit of independence, the spirit of obedience is equally strong. We are all of us self-important—which never produces any work. Great enterprise, boundless courage, tremendous energy, and, above all, perfect obedience—these are the only traits that lead to individual and national regeneration. These traits are altogether lacking in us.

1 Translated from Bengali.

Go on with the work as you are doing it, but then you must pay particular attention to study. J—Babu has sent a Hindi magazine, in which Pundit R—of Alwar has published a translation of my Chicago Address. Please convey my special indebtedness and thanks to both.

Let me now address myself to you—take particular care to start a centre in Rajputana. It must be in some central place like Jaipur or Ajmer. Then branches must be established in towns like Alwar and Khetri. You must mix with all, we do not want to quarrel with any. Give my loving embrace to Pundit N—; the man is very energetic, and will be a very practical man in time. Tender my loving regards to Mr. M—and—ji too. A Religious Association or something of the kind has been afoot at Ajmer—what is it? Let me know all about it. M—Babu writes that he and others have written me letters; but I have not received any up till now... About Maths, or centres, or anything of the kind, it is no use starting them in Calcutta; Varanasi is the place for them. I have many plans like that, but all depends on funds. You will know of them by degrees. You might have noticed from the papers that our movement is steadily gaining ground in England. Every enterprise in this country takes some time to have a go. But once John Bull sets his hand to a thing, he will never let it go. The Americans are quick, but they are somewhat like straw on fire, ready to be extinguished. Do not preach to the public that Ramakrishna Paramahamsa was an Incarnation, and things of that sort. I have some followers at—look after them... Infinite power will come unto you—never fear. Be pure, have faith, be obedient.

Teach against the marriage of boys. No scripture ever sanctions it. But for the present say nothing against little girls being married. Directly you stop the marriage of boys, that of girls will stop of itself. Girls surely are not going to marry among themselves! Write to the Secretary, Arya Samaj, Lahore, asking the whereabouts of a Sannyasin named Achyutananda who used to live with them. Make special inquiry of the man... Never fear.

Yours affectionately,
Vivekananda.

1895.103—ALASINGA

London,
18th November, 1895.

DEAR ALASINGA,

... In England my work is really splendid, I am astonished myself at it. The English people do not: talk much in the newspapers, but they work silently. I am sure of more work in England than in America. Bands and bands come, and I have no room for so many; so they squat on the floor, ladies and all. I tell them to imagine that they are under the sky of India, under a spreading banyan, and they like the idea. I shall have to go away next week, and they are so sorry. Some think my work here will be hurt a little if I go away so soon. I do not think so. I do not depend on men or things. The Lord alone I depend upon — and He works through me.

... Please everybody without becoming a hypocrite and without being a coward. Hold on to your own ideas with strength and purity, and whatever obstructions may now be in your way, the world is bound to listen to you in the long run...

I have no time even to die, as the Bengalis say. I work, work, work, and earn my own bread and help my country, and this all alone, and then get only criticism from friends and foes for all that! Well, you are but children, I shall have to bear everything. I have sent for a Sannyâsin from Calcutta and shall leave him to work in London. I want one more for America — I want my own man. Guru-Bhakti is the foundation of all spiritual development.

... I am really tired from incessant work. Any other Hindu would have died if he had to work as hard as I have to... I want to go to India for a long rest...

Ever yours with love and blessings,
Vivekananda.

1895.104 — MRS. BULL

London,
21st Nov., 1895.

DEAR MRS. BULL,

I sail by the Britannic on Wednesday, the 27th. My work so far has been very satisfactory here and I am sure to do splendid work here next summer...

Yours with love,
Vivekananda.

U.S.A

1895.105 — BLESSED AND BELOVED

R.M.S. "BRITANNIC"
End of Nov., 1895.

BLESSED AND BELOVED, (Mr. E. T. Sturdy)

So far the journey has been very beautiful. The purser has been very kind to me and gave me a cabin to myself. The only difficulty is the food—meat, meat, meat. Today they have promised to give me some vegetables.

We are standing at anchor now. The fog is too thick to allow the ship to proceed. So I take this opportunity to write a few letters.

It is a queer fog almost impenetrable though the sun is shining bright and cheerful. Kiss baby for me; and with love and blessings for you and Mrs. Sturdy,

I remain, Yours,
Vivekananda.

PS — Kindly convey my love to Miss Müller. I left the night shirt at Avenue Road. So I shall have to do without any until the trunk is brought out of the hold.

1895.106 — MRS. ALBERTA

R.M.S. "BRITANNIC",
Thursday morning, Dec. 5, 1895.

DEAR ALBERTA,

Received your nice letter last evening. Very kind of you to remember me. I am going soon to see the "Heavenly Pair". Mr. Leggett is a saint as I have told you already, and your mother is a born empress, every inch of her, with a saint's heart inside.

I am so glad you are enjoying the Alps so much They must be wonderful. It is always in such places that the human soul aspires for freedom. Even if the nation is spiritually poor, it aspires for physical freedom. I met a young Swiss in London. He used to come to my classes. I was very successful in London, and though I did not care for the noisy city, I was very much pleased with the people. In your country, Alberta, the Vedantic thought was introduced in the beginning by ignorant "cranks", and one has to work his way through the difficulties created by such introductions. You may have noticed that only a few men or women of the upper classes ever joined my classes in America. Again in America the upper classes being the rich, their whole time is spent in enjoying their wealth and imitating (aping?) the Europeans. On the other hand in England the Vedantic ideas have been introduced by the most learned men in the country, and there are a large number among the upper classes in England who are very thoughtful. So you will be astonished to hear that I found my grounds all prepared, and I am convinced that my work will have more hold on England than America. Add to this the tremendous tenacity of the English character, and judge for yourself. By this you will find that I have changed a good deal of my opinion about England, and I am glad to confess it. I am perfectly sure that we will do still better in Germany. I am coming back to England next summer. In the meanwhile my work is in very able hands. Joe Joe has been the same kind good pure friend to me here as in America, and my debt to your family is simply immense. My love and blessings to Hollister and you. The steamer is standing at anchor on account of fog. The purser has very kindly given me a whole cabin by myself. Every Hindu is a Raja, they think, and are very polite — and the charm will break, of course, when they find that the Raja is penniless!!

Yours with love and blessings,
Vivekananda.

1895.107 — STURDY

To Mr. E. T. Sturdy:

New York,
1895.

The work here is going on splendidly. I have been working incessantly at two classes a day since my arrival. Tomorrow I go out of town with Mr. Leggett for a week's holiday. Did you know Madame Antoinette Sterling, one of your greatest singers? She is very much interested in the work.

I have made over all the secular part of the work to a committee and am free from all that botheration. I have no aptitude for organising. It nearly breaks me to pieces.

... What about the Nârada-Sutra? There will be a good sale of the book here, I am sure. I have now taken up the Yoga-Sutras and take them up one by one and go through all the commentators along with them. These talks are all taken down, and when completed will form the fullest annotated translation of Patanjali in English. Of course it will be rather a big work.

At Trübner's I think there is an edition of Kurma Purâna. The commentator, Vijnâna Bhikshu, is continually quoting from that book. I have never seen the book myself. Will you kindly find time to go and see if in it there are some chapters on

Yoga? If so, will you kindly send me a copy? Also of the Hatha-Yoga-Pradipikâ, Shiva-Samhitâ, and any other book on Yoga? The originals of course. I shall send you the money for them as soon as they arrive. Also a copy of Sânkhya-Kârikâ of Ishwara Krishna by John Davies. Just now your letter reached along with Indian letters. The one man who is ready is ill. The others say that they cannot come over on the spur of the moment. So far it seems unlucky. I am sorry they could not come. What can be done? Things go slow in India!

Ramanuja's theory is that the bound soul or Jiva has its perfections involved, entered, into itself. When this perfection again evolves, it becomes free. The Advaitin declares both these to take place only in show; there was neither involution nor evolution. Both processes were Maya, or apparent only.

In the first place, the soul is not essentially a knowing being. Sachchidânanda is only an approximate definition, and Neti Neti is the essential definition. Schopenhauer caught this idea of willing from the Buddhists. We have it also in Vâsanâ or Trishnâ, Pali tanhâ. We also admit that it is the cause of all manifestation which are, in their turn, its effects. But, being a cause, it must be a combination of the Absolute and Maya. Even knowledge, being a compound, cannot be the Absolute itself, but it is the nearest approach to it, and higher than Vasana, conscious or unconscious. The Absolute first becomes the mixture of knowledge, then, in the second degree, that of will. If it be said that plants have no consciousness, that they are at best only unconscious wills, the answer is that even the unconscious plant-will is a manifestation of the consciousness, not of the plant, but of the cosmos, the Mahat of the Sankhya Philosophy. The Buddhist analysis of everything into will is imperfect, firstly, because will is itself a compound, and secondly, because consciousness or knowledge which is a compound of the first degree, precedes it. Knowledge is action. First action, then reaction. When the mind perceives, then, as the reaction, it wills. The will is in the mind. So it is absurd to say that will is the last analysis. Deussen is playing into the hands of the Darwinists.

But evolution must be brought in accordance with the more exact science of Physics, which can demonstrate that every evolution must be preceded by an involution. This being so, the evolution of the Vasana or will must be preceded by the involution of the Mahat or cosmic consciousness. (See also Vol VIII Sayings and Utterances & Vol V Letter to Mr. Sturdy.) There is no willing without knowing. How can we desire unless we know the object of desire?

The apparent difficulty vanishes as soon as you divide knowledge also into subconscious and conscious. And why not? If will can be so treated, why not its father?

Vivekananda.

1895.108 — MRS. BULL

228 West 39th Street, New York,
8th Dec., 1895.

DEAR MRS. BULL,

Many thanks for your kind note of welcome. I arrived last Friday after ten days of a very tedious voyage. It was awfully rough and for the first time in my life I was very badly seasick...I have left some strong friends in England who will work in my absence expecting my arrival next summer. My plans are not settled yet about the work here. Only I have an idea to run to Detroit and Chicago meanwhile, and then come back to New York. The public lecture plan I intend to give up entirely, as I find the best thing for me to do is to step entirely out of the money question — either in public lectures or private classes. In the long run it does harm and sets a bad example.

In England I worked on this principle and refused even the voluntary collections they made. Mr. Sturdy, being a rich man, bore the major part of the expenses of lecturing in big halls — the rest I bore. It worked well. Again, to use rather a vulgar illustration, even in religion there is no use overstocking the market. The supply must follow the demand, and the demand alone. If people want me, they will get up lectures. I need not bother myself about these things. If you think after consultation with Mrs. Adams and Miss Locke that it would be practicable for me to come to Chicago for a course of lectures, write to me. Of course the money question should be left entirely out.

My idea is for autonomic, independent groups in different places. Let them work on their own account and do the best they can. As for myself, I do not want to entangle myself in any organisation. Hoping you are enjoying good health both physically and mentally,

I am yours, in the Lord,
Vivekananda.

1895.109 — CHRISTINA

To Sister Christine:

228 W. 39th Street, [New York],
8th Dec. '95.

DEAR CHRISTINA,

I am once more on American Soil and have taken lodgings at 228 W. 39, where I begin work from Monday next. Sometime after Christmas I intend to make a tour through Detroit and Chicago.

I do not care for public lecturings at all — and do not think I shall have any more public lectures charging admission. If you will see Mrs. Phelps and others of our friends and arrange some classes (strictly on nonpayment basis), it will facilitate things a good deal.

Write at your earliest opportunity and give Mrs. Phunkey [Funke] and all our friends my deepest love and gratitude.

Yours ever in the Lord,
Vivekananda.

PS — Kripananda is over full of praise of you and Mrs. Funkey [Funke] and sends his loving regards for you.

1895.110 — FRIEND

228 West 39th Street, New York,
8th December, 1895.

DEAR FRIEND, (Mr. E. T. Sturdy)

After ten days of a most tedious and rough voyage I safely arrived in New York. My friends had already engaged some rooms at the above where I am living now and intend to hold classes ere long. In the meanwhile the Theosophists have been alarmed very much and are trying their best to hurt me; but they and their followers are of no consequence whatever.

I went to see Mrs. Leggett and other friends, and they are as kind and enthusiastic as ever.

Did you hear anything from India about the coming Sannyasin?

I will write later fuller particulars of the work here.

Kindly convey my best love to Miss Müller and to Mrs. Sturdy and all the other friends and kiss baby for me.

Yours ever in the Sat,
Vivekananda.

1895.111 — JOE JOE

To Miss Josephine MacLeod:

228 West 39th Street, New York,
8th December, 1895.

DEAR JOE JOE,

After 10 days of the most disastrous voyage I ever had I arrived in New York. I was so so sick for days together.

After the clean and beautiful cities of Europe, New York appears very dirty and miserable. I am going to begin work next Monday. Your bundles have been safely delivered to the heavenly pair, as Alberta calls them. They are as usual very kind. Saw Mrs. and Mr. Salomon and other friends. By chance met Mrs. Peak at Mrs. Guernsey's but yet have no news of Mrs. Rothinburger. Going with the birds of paradise to Ridgely this Christmas. Wish ever so much you were there.

Had you a nice visit with Lady Isabelle? Kindly give my love to all our friends and know oceans yourself.

Excuse this short letter. I shall write bigger ones by the next.

Yours ever in the Lord,
Vivekananda.

1895.112 — CHRISTINA

To Sister Christine:

228 W. 39th Street, [New York,
Dec. 10, 1895.

DEAR CHRISTINA,

Perhaps by this time you have received my first letter. I received yours just now.

I had a splendid success in England and have left a nucleus there to work till my arrival next summer. You will be astonished to learn that some of my strongest friends are big "guns" of the Church of England.

This Christmas I am going away a week, from 24th Decem., to the country with Mr. and Mrs. Leggett — after that I resume my work. In the meanwhile the classes have begun.

I have written to you my intention of taking a quick turn through Detroit and Chicago in the meanwhile and [then] return back.

Give Mrs. Phelps my love and kindly arrange the classes [in Detroit] with her. The best thing is to arrange for a public lecture where I give out my general plan of work. The Unitarian church is available; and if the lecture is free, there will be a big crowd. The collection most possibly will cover the expenses. Then out of this we will get the materials of a big class and then hurry them through, leaving Mrs. Phelps and you and Mrs. Funkey [Funke] to work on with them.

This plan is entirely feasible and if Mrs. Phelps and Mrs. Bagley desire it, they can work it out very quickly.

Ever yours with love and blessings,
Vivekananda.

1895.113 — MRS. BULL

228 W. 39th Street, New York,
10th Dec., 1895.

DEAR MRS. BULL,

I have received the Secretary's letter and will be glad to lecture before the Harvard Philosophical Club as requested. The difficulty in the way is: I have begun to write in earnest, as I want to finish some text-books to form the basis of work when I am gone. I have to hurry through four little books before I go.

This month, notices are out for the four Sunday lectures. The lectures for the first week of February in Brooklyn are being arranged by Dr. Janes and others.

Yours, with best wishes,
Vivekananda.

1895.114 — CHRISTINA

To Sister Christine:

228 W. 39th Street, New York,
12 December, 1895.

DEAR CHRISTINA,

I am going away out of town from the 24th of this month and will come back on the 2nd of January. From the 24th — the 2nd I will not be here. I will settle the dates for Detroit and Chicago after hearing from you and from Chicago.

[Paragraph excised from the original letter.]

My love to Mrs. Phunkey [Funke] [excised] and all other friends.

Yours ever in the Lord,
Vivekananda.

1895.115 — YOUR HIGHNESS

To the Maharaja of Limdi:

Cathiawad, Bombay, Chicago,
14th Dec., '95.

YOUR HIGHNESS,

The gentleman whom I have the pleasure of introducing to you was the chairman of the Parliament of Religions held in Chicago.

He is a holy and noble gentleman. We owe him a deep debt of gratitude; and as he is going to make a tour through India, I hope your Highness will extend him the same hospitality as he has to us.

Yours with blessings,
Vivekananda.

1895.116 — SIR

To the Dewan of Mysore, Madras (His Excellency Seshahari Iyer, K. C. S. I.):

Chicago,
14th Dec., '95.

DEAR SIR,

The gentleman I have the pleasure of introducing to you was the chairman of the Chicago Parliament of religions.

All India owes him a deep debt of gratitude. He is now on a tour through our country, and I am sure you will help him in seeing your part of the country and oblige.

Yours with blessings,
Vivekananda.

1895.117 — BLESSED AND BELOVED

To Mr. E. T. Sturdy:

228 West 39th Street, New York,
16th December, 1895.

BLESSED AND BELOVED,

All your letters reached by one mail today. Miss Müller also writes me one. She has read in the Indian Mirror that Swami Krishnananda is coming over to England. If that is so, he is the strongest man that I can get.

The classes I had here were six in the week, besides a question class. The general attendance varies between 70 to 120. Besides every Sunday I have a public lecture. The last month my lectures were in a small hall holding about 600. But 900 will come as a rule, 300 standing, and about 300 going off, not finding room. This week therefore I have a bigger hall, with a capacity of holding 1200 people.

There is no admission charged in these lectures, but a collection covers the rent. The newspapers have taken me up this week, and altogether I have stirred up New York considerably this year. If I could have remained here this summer and organised a summer place, the work would be going on sure foundations here. But as I intended to come over in May to England, I shall have to leave it unfinished. If, however, Krishnananda comes to England, and you find him strong and able, and if you find the work in London will not be hurt by my absence this summer, I would rather be here this summer.

Again, I am afraid my health is breaking down under constant work. I want some rest. We are so unused to these Western methods, especially the keeping to time. I will leave you to decide all these. The Brahmavâdin is going on here very satisfactorily. I have begun to write articles on Bhakti; also send them a monthly account of the work. Miss Müller wants to come to America. I do not know whether she will or not. Some friends here are publishing my Sunday lectures. I have sent you a few copies of the first one. I shall send you next mail a few of the next two lectures, and if you like them I shall ask them to send you a number. Can you manage to get a few hundred copies sold in England? That will encourage them in publishing the subsequent ones.

Next month I go to Detroit, then to Boston, and Harvard University. Then I shall have a rest, and then I come to England, unless you think that things go on without me and with Krishnananda.

Ever yours with love and blessings,
Vivekananda.

1895.118 — ALASINGA

228 W. 39th St., New York,
20th December, 1895.

DEAR ALASINGA,

...Have patience and be faithful unto death. Do not fight among yourselves. Be perfectly pure in money dealings...We will do great things yet...So long as you have faith and honesty and devotion, everything will prosper.

...In translating the Suktas, pay particular attention to the Bhâshyakâras (commentators), and pay no attention whatever to the orientalists. They do not understand a single thing about our Shâstras (scriptures). It is not given to dry philologists to understand philosophy or religion...For instance the word Ânid-avâtam in the Rig-Veda was translated — "He lived without breathing". Now, here the reference is really to the chief Prâna, and Avâtam has the root-meaning for unmoved, that is, without vibration. It describes the state in which the universal cosmic energy, or Prana, remains before the Kalpa (cycle of creation) begins: vide — the Bhashyakaras. Explain according to our sages and not according to the so-called European scholars. What do they know?

...Be bold and fearless, and the road will be clear...Mind, you have nothing whatsoever to do with the Theosophists. If you all stand by me and do not lose patience, I assure you, we shall do great work yet. The great work will be in England, my boy, by and by. I feel you sometimes get disheartened, and I am afraid you get temptations to play in the hands of the Theosophists. Mind you, the Guru-Bhakta will conquer the world — this is the one evidence of history... It is faith that makes a lion of a man. You must always remember how much work I have to do. Sometimes I have to deliver two or three lectures a day — and thus I make my way against all odds — hard work; any weaker man would die.

... Hold on with faith and strength; be true, be honest, be pure, and don't quarrel among yourselves. Jealousy is the bane of our race.

With love to you and all our friends there,

Yours,
Vivekananda.

1895.119 — SHARAT

To Swami Saradananda:

228 West 39th Street, New York,
23rd December, 1895.

DEAR SHARAT,

Your letter only made me sad. I see you have lost all enthusiasm. I know all of you, your powers and your limitations. I would not have called you to any task which you are incompetent to do. The only task I would have given you was to teach elementary Sanskrit, and with the help of dictionaries and other things assist S. in his translations and teachings. I would have moulded you to it. Anyone could have done as well — only a little smattering of Sanskrit was absolutely necessary. Well, everything is for the best. If it is the Lord's work the right man for the right place will be forthcoming in the right time. None of you need feel disturbed. As for Sanyal, I don't care who takes money or not, but I have a strong hatred for child-marriage. I have suffered terribly from it, and it is the great sin for which our nation has to suffer. As such, I would hate myself if I help such a diabolical custom directly or indirectly. I wrote to you pretty plain about it, and Sanyal had no right to play a hoax upon me about his "law-suit" and his attempts to become free. I am sorry for his playing tricks on me who have never done him any harm. This is the world. What good you do goes for nothing, but if you stop doing it, then, Lord help you, you are counted as a rogue. Isn't it? Emotional natures like mine are always preyed upon by relatives and friends. This world is merciless. This world is our friend when we are its slaves and no more. This world is broad enough for me. There will always be a corner found for me somewhere. If the people of India do not like me, there will be others who do. I must set my foot to the best of my ability upon this devilish custom of child-marriage. No blame will entail on you. You keep at a safe distance if you are afraid. I am sorry, very sorry, I cannot have any partnership with such doings as getting husbands for babies. Lord help me, I never had and never will have. Think of the case of M __ Babu! Did you ever meet a more cowardly or brutal one than that? I can kill the man who gets a husband for a baby. The upshot of the whole thing is—I want bold, daring, adventurous spirits to help me. Else I will work alone. I have a mission to fulfil. I will work it out alone. I do not care who comes or who goes. Sanyal is already done for by Samsâra. Beware, boy! That was all the advice I thought it my duty to give you. Of course, you are great folks now—my words will have no value with you. But I hope the time will come when you will see clearer, know better, and think other thoughts than you are now doing.

Good-bye! I would not bother you any more, and all blessings go with you all. I am very glad I have been of some service to you sometimes if you think so. At least I am pleased with myself for having tried my best to discharge the duties laid on me by my Guru, and well done or ill, I am glad that I tried. So good-bye. Tell Sanyal that I am not at all angry with him, but I am sorry, very sorry. It is not the money—that counts nothing—but the violation of a principle that pained me, and the trick he played on me. Good-bye to him also, and to you all. One chapter of my life is closed. Let others come in their due order. They will find me ready. You need not disturb yourselves at all about me. I want no help from any human being in any country. So good-bye! May the Lord bless you all for ever and ever!

Vivekananda.

1895.120 — CHRISTINA

To Sister Christine:

228 W. 39th Street, New York,
December 24, 1895.

DEAR CHRISTINA,

Merry Christmas and happy New Year to you. I am going today to the country. I return in 10 days.

About the tour through Detroit—I will fix it later on. I am afraid if I go just now, everything here will fall to pieces.

I will come anyway, but I am afraid it will be later than I expected.

My love to Mrs. Phelps, Mrs. Phunkey [Funke] and all our friends and Christmas greetings.

Ever yours in the Lord,
Vivekananda.

PS—Kripananda sends his greetings too.

1895.121 — MRS. OLE BULL

To Mrs. Ole Bull:

228 W. 39, New York,
24 December, 1895.

Merry Christmas and happy New Year to you, dear Mrs. Bull. And may peace and health rest on you and yours for ever. I am going out of town today and will be back in ten days.

My love to all.

Yours affectionately,
Vivekananda.

1895.122 — SISTER

New York,
29th Dec., 1895.

DEAR SISTER, (Miss S. Farmer)

In this universe where nothing is lost, where we live in the midst of death in life, every thought that is thought, in public or in private, in crowded thoroughfares or in the deep recesses of primeval forests, lives. They are continuously trying to become self-embodied, and until they have embodied themselves, they will struggle for expression, and any amount of repression cannot kill them. Nothing can be destroyed — those thoughts that caused evil in the past are also seeking embodiment, to be filtered through repeated expression and, at last, transfigured into perfect good.

As such, there is a mass of thought which is at the present time struggling to get expression. This new thought is telling us to give up our dreams of dualism, of good and evil in essence, and the still wilder dream of suppression. It teaches us that higher direction and not destruction is the law. It teaches us that it is not a world of bad and good, but good and better — and still better. It stops short of nothing but acceptance. It teaches that no situation is hopeless, and as such accepts every form of mental, moral, or spiritual thought where it already stands, and without a word of condemnation tells it that so far it has done good, now is the time to do better. What in old times was thought of as the elimination of bad, it teaches as the transfiguration of evil and the doing of better. It, above all, teaches that the kingdom of heaven is already in existence if we will have it, that perfection is already in man if he will see it.

The Greenacre meetings last summer were so wonderful, simply because you opened yourself fully to that thought which has found in you so competent a medium of expression, and because you took your stand on the highest teaching of this thought that the kingdom of heaven already exists.

You have been consecrated and chosen by the Lord as a channel for converting this thought into life, and every one that helps you in this wonderful work is serving the Lord.

Our scripture teaches that he who serves the servants of the Lord is His highest worshipper. You are a servant of the Lord, and as a disciple of Krishna I will always consider it a privilege and worship to render you any service in the carrying out of your inspired mission wherever I be.

Ever your affectionate brother,
Vivekananda.

1895.123 — FRIEND

To Mr. E. T. Sturdy:

RIDGELY MANOR,
29th December, 1895.

DEAR FRIEND,

By this time the copies of the lectures must have reached you. Hope they may be of some use.

I think, in the first place, there are so many difficulties to overcome; in the second place, they think that they are fit for nothing — that is the national disease; thirdly, they are afraid to face the winter at once; the Tibet man they don't think is a very strong man to work in England. Some one will come sooner or later.

Yours in the Sat,
Vivekananda.

PS — My Christmas greetings to all our friends — to Mrs. and Mr. Johnson, to Lady Margesson, Mrs. Clark, Miss Hawes, Miss Müller, Miss Steel, and all the rest.

Kiss baby for me and bless him. My greetings to Mrs. Sturdy. We will work. "Wah guru ki fateh."

1895.124 — RAKHAL[1]

U.S.A.,
(End of?) 1895.

MY DEAR RAKHAL,

Just now I got your letter and was glad to go through it. No matter whether there is any work done in India or not, the real work lies here. I do not want anybody to come over now. On my return to India I shall train a few men, and after

---

1 Translated from Bengali.

that there will be no danger for them in the West. Yes, it was of Gunanidhi that I wrote. Give my special love and blessings to Hari Singh and others. Never take part in quarrels and disputes. Who on earth possesses the power to put the Raja of Khetri down? — The Divine Mother is at his elbow! I have received Kali's letter too. It will be very good indeed if you can start a centre in Kashmir. Wherever you can, open a centre... Now I have laid the foundations firm here and in England, and nobody has the power to shake them. New York is in a commotion this year. Next year will come the turn of London. Even big giants will give way, who counts your pigmies! Gird up your loins and set yourselves to work! We must throw the world into convulsions with our triumphal shouts. This is but the beginning, my boy. Do you think there are men in our country, it is a Golgotha! There is some chance if you can impart education to the masses. Is there a greater strength than that of Knowledge? Can you give them education? Name me the country where rich men ever helped anybody! In all countries it is the middle classes that do all great works. How long will it take to raise the money? Where are the men? Are there any in our country? Our countrymen are boys, and even must treat them as such... There are some few religious and philosophical books left — the remnants of the mansion that has been burnt down; take them with you, quick and come over to this country...

Never fear! The Divine Mother is helping me! This year such work is going to be turned out that you will be struck dumb to hear of it!

What fear! Whom to fear! Steel your hearts and set yourselves to work!

Yours affectionately,
Vivekananda.

PS — Sarada is talking of bringing out a Bengali magazine. Help it with all your might. It is not a bad idea. You must not throw cold water on anybody's project. Give up criticism altogether. Help all as long as you find they are doing all right, and in cases where they seem to be going wrong, show them their mistakes gently. It is criticising each other that is at the root of all mischief. That is the chief factor in breaking down organizations...

1895.125 — ALASINGA

1895.

DEAR ALASINGA,

We have no organisation, nor want to build any. Each one is quite independent to teach, quite free to preach whatever he or she likes.

If you have the spirit within, you will never fail to attract others. Theosophists' method can never be ours, for the very simple reason that they are an organised sect, we are not.

Individuality is my motto. I have no ambition beyond training individuals up. I know very little; that little I teach without reserve; where I am ignorant, I confess it as such, and never am I so glad as when I find people being helped by Theosophists, Christians, Mohammedans, or anybody in the world. I am a Sannyasin; as such I consider myself as a servant, not as a master in the world... If people love me, they are welcome, if they hate, they are also welcome.

Each one will have to save himself, each one to do his own work. I seek no help, I reject none. Nor have I any right in the world to be helped. Whosoever has helped me or will help, it will be their mercy to me, not my right, and as such I am eternally grateful.

When I became a Sannyasin, I consciously took the step, knowing that this body would have to die of starvation. What of that, I am a beggar. My friends are poor, I love the poor, I welcome poverty. I am glad that I sometimes have to starve. I ask help of none. What is the use? Truth will preach itself, it will not die for the want of the helping hands of me! "Making happiness and misery the same, making success and failure the same, fight thou on" (Gita). It is that eternal love, unruffled equanimity under all circumstances, and perfect freedom from jealousy or animosity that will tell. That will tell, nothing else.

Yours,
Vivekananda.

1896

1896.1 — MRS. BULL

To Mrs. Ole Bull:

228 W. 39th Street, New York,
The 3rd Jan., '96.

DEAR MRS. BULL,

I have had a letter from Mr. Trine asking me to have some classes at the Procopeia in February. I do not see my way to go to Boston in February, however I may like it. I have given up for the present my plan of going to Detroit and Chicago in February. Later on I will try. Miss [Josephine] Locke will see to my having classes in Chicago and I have some friends in Detroit I may go to Baltimore for a few days in the meanwhile. I enjoyed my visit with the Leggetts exceedingly. It has braced me for further work. I am very well both physically and mentally.

Wishing you a happy New Year,

I remain yours affectionately,
Vivekananda.

1896.2 — MRS. FUNKEY

To Mrs. Charles (Mary) Funke:

228 W. 39, New York,
The 6th Jan., 1896.

DEAR MRS. FUNKEY [FUNKE],

Many, many thanks for the sweet flowers. It recalls to me the beautiful times we had at the Thousand Islands and presages many such summer gatherings.

The work here had begun in right earnest, and we will advance it farther this year than in the last.

I am therefore uncertain as to the exact date of my coming to Detroit. I will come, however, very soon.

Yours ever in the Lord,
Vivekananda.

1896.3 — SISTER

To Miss Mary Hale:

New York,
6th January, 1896.

DEAR SISTER,

Many thanks for your kind New Year's greetings. I am glad to learn you enjoyed your six weeks with the Esq. although they be only golf playing. I have been in the midst of the genuine article in England. The English people received me with open arms, and I have very much toned down my ideas about the English race. First of all, I found that those fellows as Lund etc. who came over from England to attack me were nowhere. Their existence is simply ignored by the English people. None but a person belonging to the English Church is thought to be genteel. Again, some of the best men of England belonging to the English Church and some of the highest in position and fame became my truest friends. This was quite another sort of experience from what I met in America, was it not?

The English people laughed and laughed when I told them about my experience with the Presbyterians and other fanatics here and my reception in hotels etc. I also found at once the difference in culture and breeding between the two countries and came to understand why American girls go in shoals to be married to Europeans. Everyone was kind to me there, and I have left many noble friends of both sexes anxiously waiting my return in the spring.

As to my work there, the Vedantic thought has already permeated the higher classes of England. Many people of education and rank, and amongst them not a few clergymen, told me that the conquest of Rome by Greece was being re-enacted in England.

There are two sorts of Englishmen who have lived in India. One consisting of those who hate everything Indian, but they are uneducated. The other, to whom India is the holy land, its very air is holy. And they try to out-Herod Herod in their Hinduism. They are awful vegetarians, and they want to form a caste in England. Of course, the majority of the English people are firm believers in caste. I had eight classes a week apart from public lectures, and they were so crowded that a good many people, even ladies of high rank, sat on the floor and did not think anything of it. In England I find strong-minded men and women to take up the work and carry it forward with the peculiar English grip and energy. This year my work in New York is going on splendidly. Mr. Leggett is a very rich man of New York and very much interested in me. The New Yorker has more steadiness than any other people in this country, so I have determined to make my centre here. In this country my teachings are thought to be queer by the "Methodist" and "Presbyterian" aristocracy. In England it is the highest philosophy to the English Church aristocracy.

Moreover those talks and gossips, so characteristic of the American woman, are almost unknown in England. The English woman is slow; but when she works up to an idea, she will have a hold on it sure; and they are regularly carrying on my work there and sending every week a report — think of that! Here is I go away for a week, everything falls to pieces. My love to all — to Sam and to yourself. May the Lord bless you ever and ever!

Your affectionate brother,
Vivekananda.

1896.4 — MRS. BULL

To Mrs. Ole Bull:

228 W. 39th Street, New York,
10 January, 1896.

DEAR MRS. BULL,

I have received your letter and also another from the Secretary of the Harvard Metaphysical Club.

I will be only too glad to come to Boston for the Harvard lecture especially — but these are the difficulties in the way: First, the work here will fall to pieces; secondly, I have begun to write in right earnest. I want to finish some text books to be the basis of work when I am gone. I want to hurry through four little text books before I go.

Of course it is impossible to come this month as the notices of the four Sunday lectures are out. In the first week of February I have again a lecture at Brooklyn at Dr. Janes's. My idea now is to make a tour to Boston, Detroit, and Chicago in March and then come back to New York a week or so and then start for England. In March I will be able to stay a few weeks at each of these places. Of course it is true that [as] yet I have no competent persons here to carry on the work like Sturdy in England, nor any sincere friend to stand by me except you.

I will do anything you want me to, and if you think it is good for me to come to Boston in February, I am ready.

Ever yours with gratitude, love, and blessings,
Vivekananda.

PS — I have not much faith in that Procopeia business, (The Procopeia Club) except as a nucleus to work from.

My love to Miss Hamlin and all the other friends there.

1896.5 — BLESSED AND BELOVED

To Mr. E. T. Sturdy:

228 West 39th Street, New York,
16th January, 1896.

BLESSED AND BELOVED,

Many many thanks for the books. The Sankhya Karika is a very good book, and the Kurma Purana, though I do not find in it all expected, has a few verses on Yoga. The words dropped in my last letter were Yoga-Sutra, which I am translating with notes from various authorities. I want to incorporate the chapter in Kurma Purana in my notes. I have very enthusiastic accounts of your classes from Miss MacLeod.

Mr. Galsworthy seems to be very much interested now.

I have begun my Sunday lectures here and also the classes. Both are very enthusiastically received. I make them all free and take up a collection to pay the hall etc. Last Sunday's lecture was very much appreciated and is in the press. I shall send you a few copies next week. It was the outline of our work.

As my friends have engaged a stenographer (Goodwin), all these class lessons and public lectures are taken down. I intend to send you a copy of each. They may suggest you some ideas.

My great want here is a strong man like you, possessing intellect, and ability, and love. In this nation of universal education, all seem to melt down into a mediocrity, and the few able are weighed down by the eternal money-making.

I have a chance of getting a piece of land in the country, and some buildings on it, plenty of trees and a river, to serve as a summer meditation resort. That, of course, requires a committee to look after it in my absence, as also the handling of money and printing and other matters.

I have separated myself entirely from money questions, yet without it the movement cannot go on. So necessarily I have to make over everything executive to a committee, which will look after these things in my absence. Steady work is not in the line of the Americans. The only way they work, is in a herd. So let them have it. As to the teaching part, my friends will go over this country from place to place, each one independent, and let them form independent circles. That is the easiest way to spread. Then, when there will be sufficient strength, we shall have yearly gatherings to concentrate our energies.

The committee is entirely executive and it is confined to New York alone…

Ever yours with love and blessings,
Vivekananda.

1896.6 — ALASINGA

23rd January, 1896.

DEAR ALASINGA,

By this time you must have got enough of matter on Bhakti from me. The last copy, dated 21st December, of Brahmavadin is in. I have been smelling something since the last few issues of the Brahmavadin. Are you going to join the Theosophists? This time you simply gave yourselves up. Why, you get in a notice of the Theosophists' lectures in the body of your notes! Any suspicion of my connection with the Theosophists will spoil my work both in America and England, and well it may. They are thought by all people of sound mind to be wrong, and true it is that they are held so, and you know it full well. I am afraid you want to overreach me. You think you can get more subscribers in England by advertising Annie Besant? Fool that you are.

I do not want to quarrel with the Theosophists, but my position is entirely ignoring them. Had they paid for the advertisement? Why should you go forward to advertise them? I shall get more than enough subscribers in England when I go next.

Now, I would have no traitors, I tell you plainly, I would not be played upon by any rogue. No hypocrisy with me. Hoist your flag and give public notice in your paper that you have given up all connections with me, and join the ... camp of the Theosophists or cease to have anything whatsoever to do with them. I give you very plain words indeed. I shall have one man only to follow me, but he must be true and faithful unto death. I do not care for success or no success. I am tired of this nonsense of preaching all over the world. Did any of Annie Besant's people come to my help when I was in England? Fudge! I must keep my movement pure or I will have none.

Yours,
Vivekananda.

PS — Reply sharp your decision. I am very decided on this point. You ought to have told me so before, had your intentions been such from the very beginning. The Brahmavadin is for preaching Vedanta and not Theosophy. I almost lose my patience when I see these underhand dealings. This is the world — those whom you love best and help most try to cheat you.

1896.7 — CHRISTINA

To Sister Christine:

24th Jan. ~~'95.~~ ['96.]

DEAR CHRISTINA,

I have not heard from you [for] long. Hope everything is going on well with you and Mrs. Phunkey [Funke].

Did you receive my poem? I had a letter from Mrs. Phelps today. I am coming to Detroit next March early, as I will have to finish my February course in New York. The public lectures will be printed as they are delivered right along. The class lectures will very soon be collected and edited in little volumes.

May the Lord bless you ever and ever.

Yours ever with love and blessings,
Vivekananda.

1896.8 — SARADA[1]

Jan., 1896.

DEAR SARADA,

...Your idea of the paper is very good indeed. Apply yourself to it heart and soul... Never mind the funds... There are many to preach Christianity and Mohammedanism — you just go through the preaching of your own country's religion. But then if you can get hold of a Mohammedan who is versed in Arabic and have old Arabic books translated, it will be a good plan. There is much of Indian history in the Persian language. If you can have the books translated bit by bit, it will be a good regular item. We want quite a number of writers, then there is the difficult task of getting subscribers. The way out is this: You lead a wandering life; wherever you find Bengali language spoken, thrust the paper on whomsoever you can lay your hands on. Enlist them by vehemence! — they would always turn tail the moment they have to spend something. Never mind anything! Push it on! Begin to contribute articles, all of you who can. It won't do merely to sit idle. You have done a heroic deed! Bravo! Those who falter and vacillate will lag behind, and you will jump straight on top of all! Those that are working for their own salvation will neither have their own nor that of others. Let the commotion that you make be such as to resound to the world's end. There are people who are ready to pick holes in everything, but when it comes to the question of work, not a scent of them can be had! To work! — as far as in you lies! Then I shall go to India and move the whole country. What fear! "Even a snake loses its venom if it is insisted that it has none." These people will go on the negative track, till they are actually reduced to nothing!...

Gangadhar has done right heroic work! Well done! Kali has joined him in work — thrice well done!! Let one go to Madras, and another to Bombay, let the world shake on its hinges! Oh, the grief! If I could get two or three like me, I could have left the world convulsed. As it is, I have to proceed gently. Move the world to its foundations! Send one to China, another to Japan! What will the poor householders do, with their little bits of life? It is for the Sannyasins, Shiva's demons, to rend the skies with their shouts of "Hara! Hara! Shambho!"

Yours affectionately,
Vivekananda.

---

1 Translated from Bengali.

1896.9 — YOGEN[2]

228 W. 39, New York,
24th Jan., 1896.

DEAR YOGEN,

... I am very sorry to heat that your health is not yet all right. Can you go to a very cold climate where there is plenty of snowfall in the winter, Darjeeling, for instance? The severity of the cold will set your stomach right, as it has done in my case. And can you give up altogether the habit of using ghee and spices? Butter digests more quickly than ghee...

Three months more and I go to England, to try once more to make some stir; the following winter to India — and after that, it depends on the Lord.

Put forth all nerve for the magazine that Sarada is wanting to publish. Ask Shashi to look to it. One thing, neither Kali nor anybody else has any need of coming to England at present. I shall train them first when I go to India, and then they may go wherever they please.

We would do nothing ourselves and would scoff at others who try to do something — this is the bane that has brought about our downfall as a nation. Want of sympathy and lack of energy are at the root of all misery, and you must therefore give these two up. Who but the Lord knows what potentialities there are in particular individuals — let all have opportunities, and leave the rest to the Lord. It is indeed very difficult to have an equal love for all, but without it there is no Mukti.

Yours affectionately,
Vivekananda.

1896.10 — MRS. BULL

New York,
25th Jan., 1896.

DEAR MRS. BULL,

Your letter to Sturdy has been sent over to me. It was very kind of you to write that note. This year, I am afraid, I am getting overworked, as I feel the strain. I want a rest badly. So it is very good, as you say, that the Boston work be taken up in the end of March. By the end of April I will start for England.

Land can be had in large plots in the Catskills for very little money. There is a plot of 101 acres for $200. The money I have ready, only I cannot buy the land in my name. You are the only friend in this country in whom I have perfect trust. If you consent, I will buy the land in your name. The students will go there in sum-

2 Translated from Bengali.

mer and build cottages or camps as they like and practice meditation. Later on, if they can collect funds, they may build something up. I am sorry, you cannot come just now. Tomorrow will be the last Sunday lecture of this month. The first Sunday of next month there will be a lecture in Brooklyn; the rest, three in New York, with which I will close this year's New York lectures.

I have worked my best. If there is any seed of truth in it, it will come to life. So I have no anxiety about anything. I am also getting tired of lecturing and having classes. After a few months' work in England I will go to India and hide myself absolutely for some years or for ever. I am satisfied in my conscience that I did not remain an idle Swami. I have a note-book which has travelled with me all over the world. I find these words written seven years ago — "Now to seek a corner and lay myself there to die!" Yet all this Karma remained. I hope I have worked it out. I hope the Lord will give me freedom from this preaching and adding good bondages.

"If you have known the Âtman as the one existence and that nothing else exists, for whom, for what desire, do you trouble yourself?" Through Maya all this doing good etc. came into my brain — now they are leaving me. I get more and more convinced that there is no other object in work except the purification of the soul — to make it fit for knowledge. This world with its good and evil will go on in various forms. Only the evil and good will take new names and new seats. My soul is hankering after peace and rest eternal undisturbed.

"Live alone, live alone. He who is alone never comes into conflict with others — never disturbs others, is never disturbed by others." I long, oh! I long for my rags, my shaven head, my sleep under the trees, and my food from begging! India is the only place where, with all its faults, the soul finds its freedom, its God. All this Western pomp is only vanity, only bondage of the soul. Never more in my life I realised more forcibly the vanity of the world. May the Lord break the bondage of all — may all come out of Maya — is the constant prayer of

Vivekananda.

1896.11 — BLESSED AND BELOVED

To Mr. E. T. Sturdy:

228 West 39th Street, New York,
29th February, 1896.

BLESSED AND BELOVED,

I am coming before May if possible. You need not worry about that. The pamphlet was beautiful. The newspaper cuttings from here will be forwarded if we can get them.

The books and pamphlets here have been got up this way. A committee was formed in New York. They paid all the expenses of stenographing and printing on condition the books will belong to them. So these pamphlets and books are theirs. One book, the Karma-Yoga has been already published; the Raja-Yoga, a much bigger one, is in the course of publication; the Jnana-Yoga may be published later on. These will be popular books, the language being that of talk, as you have seen already. I have purged everything that is objectionable, and they help me in getting up the books.

The books are the property of this Committee, of which Mrs. Ole Bull is the principal backer, also Mrs. Leggett.

It is only just that they should have the books as they paid all the expenses. There is no fear of the publishers meddling with them, as they are the publishers themselves.

If any books come from India please keep them.

The stenographer, who is an Englishman named Goodwin, has become so interested in the work that I have now made him a Brahmachârin, and he is going round with me, and we shall come over together to England. He will be very helpful as he has been always.

Yours with all blessings,
Vivekananda.

1896.12 — MRS. BULL

To Mrs. Ole Bull:

228 W. 39, New York,
The 6th of Feb., '96.

DEAR MRS. BULL,

I received your last duly, but owing to many things I have given up the idea of taking rest next month. I go to Detroit the first week of March and then, towards the middle or last week, come to Boston. I have not much faith in working such things as the Procopeia [Club] etc. — because these mixed-up conglomerations of all isms and ities — mostly fads — disturb the steadiness of the mind, and life becomes a mass of frivolities. I am very glad, however, to get an opportunity to talk to the graduates of Harvard. This does not mean that I am not coming to Procopeia. I will come but it will be only for your sake. There is one if, however — and that is if I am physically able. My health has nearly broken down. I have not slept even one night soundly in New York since I came; and this year there is incessant work, both with the pen and the mouth. The accumulated work and worry of years is on me now, I am afraid. Then a big struggle awaits me in England. I wish to go to the bottom of the sea and have a good, long sleep.

To Detroit I must go, dead or alive, as I have disappointed them several times last year. There were big money offers from near Chicago. I have rejected them as I do not any longer believe in paid lectures and their utility in any country. If after Detroit I feel the body able to drag itself on to Boston, I will come, else I will remain in Detroit or some other quiet place and rest to recuperate for the coming work in England. So far I have tried to work conscientiously — let the fruits belong to the Lord. If they were good they will sprout up sooner or later; if bad, the sooner they die the better. I am quite satisfied with my task in life. I have been much more active than a Sannyasin ought to be. Now I will disappear from society altogether. The touch of the world is degenerating me, I am sure, so it is time to be off. Work has no more value beyond purifying the heart. My heart is pure enough; why shall I bother my head about doing good to others? "If you have known the Atman as the one, only existence and nothing else exists, desiring what? — for whose desire you trouble yourself?" This universe is a dream, pure and simple. Why bother myself about a dream? The very atmosphere of the world is poison to the Yogi, but I am waking up. My old iron heart is coming back — all attachments of relatives, friends, disciples are vanishing fast. "Neither through wealth nor through progeny, but by giving up everything as chaff is that immortality attained" — the Vedas. I am so tired of talking too; I want to close my lips and sit in silence for years. All talk is nonsense.

Yours faithfully,
Vivekananda.

1896.13 — SISTER

228 W. 39th Street, New York,
10th February, 1896.

DEAR SISTER[1],

I was astonished at learning that you have not received my letter yet. I wrote immediately after the receipt of yours and also sent you some booklets of three lectures I delivered in New York. These Sunday public lectures are now taken down in shorthand and printed. Three of them made two little pamphlets, several copies of which I have forwarded to you. I shall be in New York two weeks more, and then I go to Detroit to come back to Boston felt a week or two.

My health is very much broken down this year by constant work. I am very nervous. I have not slept a single night soundly this winter. I am sure I am working too much, yet a big work awaits me in England.

I will have to go through it, and then I hope to reach India and have a rest all the rest of my life. I hale tried at least to do my best for the world, leaving the result to the Lord. Now I am longing for rest. Hope I will get some, and the Indian people will give me up. How I would like to become dumb for some years and not talk at all! I was not made for these struggles and fights of the world. I am naturally dreamy and restful. I am a born idealist, can only live in a world of dreams; the

1. Miss Mary Hale.

very touch of fact disturbs my visions arid makes me unhappy. They, will be done!

I am ever ever grateful to you four sisters; to you I owe everything I have in this country. May you be ever blessed and happy. Wherever I be, you will always be remembered with the deepest gratitude and sincerest love. The whole life is a succession of dreams. My ambition is to be a conscious dreamer, that is all. My love to all — to Sister Josephine.

Ever your affectionate brother,
Vivekananda.

1896.14 — BLESSED AND BELOVED

228 W. 39th Street, New York,
13th February, 1896.

BLESSED AND BELOVED[2],

About the Sannyâsin coming over from India, I am sure he will help you in the translation work, also in other work. Later on, when I come, I may send him over to America. Today another Sannyasin has been added to the list. This time it is a man who is a genuine American and a religious teacher of some standing in the country. He was Dr. Street. He is now Yogananda, as his leaning is all towards Yoga.

I have been sending regular reports to the Brahmavâdin from here. They will be published soon. It takes such a long time for things to reach India! Things are growing nobly in India. As there was no hocus-pocus from the beginning, the Vedanta is drawing the attention of the highest classes in American society. Sarah Bernhardt, the French actress, has been playing "Iziel" here. It is a sort of Frenchified life of Buddha, where a courtesan "Iziel" wants to seduce the Buddha, under the banyan — and the Buddha preaches to her the vanity of the world, whilst she is sitting all the time in Buddha's lap. However, all is well that ends well — the courtesan fails. Madame Bernhardt acts the courtesan. I went to see the Buddha business — and Madame spying me in the audience wanted to have an interview with me. A swell family of my acquaintance arranged the affair. There were besides Madame M. Morrel, the celebrated singer, also the great electrician Tesla. Madame is a very scholarly lady and has studied up the metaphysics a good deal. M. Morrel was being interested, but Mr. Tesla was charmed to hear about the Vedantic Prâna and Âkâsha and the Kalpas, which according to him are the only theories modern science can entertain. Now both Akasha and Prana again are produced from the cosmic Mahat, the Universal Mind, the Brahmâ or Ishvara. Mr. Tesla thinks he can demonstrate mathematically that force and matter are reducible to potential energy. I am to go and see him next week, to get this new mathematical demonstration.

In that case, the Vedantic cosmology will be placed on the surest of foundations. I am working a good deal now upon the cosmology and eschatology[3] of the Vedan-

2. E. T. Sturdy.

3. That is, doctrine of the last things — death, judgement, etc.

ta. I clearly see their perfect unison with modern science, and the elucidation of the one will be followed by that of the other. I intend to write a book later on in the form of questions and answers[1]. The first chapter will be on cosmology, showing the harmony between Vedantic theories and modern science.

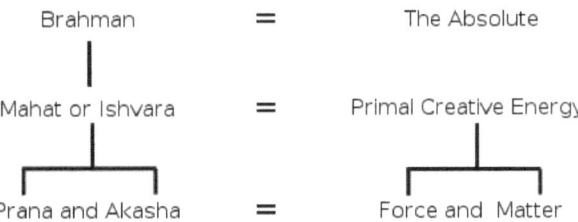

The eschatology will be explained from the Advaitic standpoint only. That is to say, the dualist claims that the soul after death passes on to the Solar sphere, thence to the Lunar sphere, thence to the Electric sphere. Thence he is accompanied by a Purusha to Brahmaloka. (Thence, says the Advaitist, he goes to Nirvâna.)

Now on the Advaitic side, it is held that the soul neither comes nor goes, and that all these spheres or layers of the universe are only so many varying products of Akasha and Prana. That is to say, the lowest or most condensed is the Solar sphere, consisting of the visible universe, in which Prana appears as physical force, and Akasha as sensible matter. The next is called the Lunar sphere, which surrounds the Solar sphere. This is not the moon at all, but the habitation of the gods, that is to say, Prana appears in it as psychic forces, and Akasha as Tanmâtras or fine particles. Beyond this is the Electric sphere, that is to say, a condition in which the Prana is almost inseparable from Akasha, and you can hardly tell whether Electricity is force or matter. Next is the Brahmaloka, where there is neither Prana nor Akasha, but both are merged in the mind stuff, the primal energy. And here—there big neither Prana nor Akasha—the Jiva contemplates the whole universe as Samashti or the sum total of Mahat or mind. This appears as a Purusha, an abstract universal soul, yet not the Absolute, for still there is multiplicity. From this the Jiva finds at last that Unity which is the end. Advaitism says that these are the visions which rise in succession before the Jiva, who himself neither goes nor comes, and that in the same way this present vision has been projected. The projection (Srishti) and dissolution must take place in the same order, only one means going backward, and the other coming out.

Now as each individual can only see his own universe, that universe is created with his bondage and goes away with his liberation, although it remains for others who are in bondage. Now name and form constitute the universe. A wave in the ocean is a wave, only in so far as it is bound by name and form. If the wave subsides, it is the ocean, but those name and form have immediately vanished for ever. So though the name and form of wave could never be without water that was fashioned into the wave by them, yet the name and form themselves were not the

---

1. This was never done. But from his lectures in London in 1896, it is easy to see that his mind was still working on these ideas. (See also Vol. VIII Sayings and Utterances).

wave. They die as soon as ever it returns to water. But other names and forms live in relation to other waves. This name-and-form is called Mâyâ, and the water is Brahman. The wave was nothing but water all the time, yet as a wave it had the name and form. Again this name and form cannot remain for one moment separated from the wave, although the wave as water can remain eternally separate from name and form. But because the name and form can never he separated, they can never be said to exist. Yet they are not zero. This is called Maya.

I want to work; all this out carefully, but you will see at a glance that I am on the right track. It will take more study in physiology, on the relations between the higher and lower centres, to fill out the psychology of mind Chitta (mind-stuff), and Buddhi (intellect), and so on. But I have clear light now, free of all hocus-pocus. I want to give them dry, hard reason, softened in tile sweetest syrup of love and made spicy with intense work, and cooked in the kitchen of Yoga, so that even a baby can easily digest it.

Yours etc.,
Vivekananda.

1896.15 — ALASINGA

U. S. A.,
17th February, 1896.

DEAR ALASINGA,

… I have used some very harsh words in my letters, which you ought to excuse, as you know, I get nervous at times. The work is terribly hard; and the more it is growing, the harder it is becoming. I need a long rest very badly. Yet a great work is before me in England.

Have patience, my son — it will grow beyond all your expectations… Every work has got to pass through hundreds of difficulties before succeeding. Those that persevere will see the light, sooner or later.

I have succeeded now in rousing the very heart of the American civilisation, New York, but it has been a terrific struggle… I have spent nearly, all I had on this New York work and in England. Now things are in such a shape that they will go on. Just as I am writing to you, every one of my bones is paining after last afternoon's long Sunday public lecture. Then you see, to put the Hindu ideas into English and then make out of dry philosophy and intricate mythology and queer startling psychology, a religion which shall be easy, simple, popular, and at the same time meet the requirements of the highest minds — is a task only those can understand who have attempted it. The dry, abstract Advaita must become living — poetic — in everyday life; out of hopelessly intricate mythology must come concrete moral forms; and out of bewildering Yogi-ism must come the most scientific and practical psychology — and all this must be put in a form so that a child may grasp it. That is my life's work. The Lord only knows how far I shall succeed. "To work we have the right, not to the fruits thereof." It is hard work, my boy, hard work! To keep one's self steady in the midst of this whirl of Kâma-Kânchana (lust and gold) and hold on to one's own ideals, until disciples are moulded to conceive of the ideas of realisation and perfect renunciation, is indeed difficult work, my boy. Thank God, already there is great success. I cannot blame the missionaries and others for not understanding me — they hardly ever saw a man who did not care in the least about women and money. At first they could not believe it to be possible; how could they? You must not think that the Western nations have the same ideas of chastity and purity as the Indians. Their equivalents are virtue and courage… People are now flocking to me. Hundreds have now become convinced that there are men who can really control their bodily desires; and reverence and respect for these principles are growing. All things come to him who waits. May you be blessed for ever and ever!

Yours with love,
Vivekananda.

1896.16 — MISS THURSBY

To Miss Emma Thursby:

228 W. 39th Street, New York,
February 26th, 1896.

DEAR MISS THURSBY,

Will you oblige me by giving Mr. Goodwin any particulars you can with reference to the business arrangements made for my 6 lectures with Miss Corbin. He will see her, with the idea of obtaining payment.

Thanking you in anticipation, and with best regards,

Very truly yours,
Vivekananda.

1896.16 — FRIEND

To Shri Giridharidas Mangaldas Viharidas Desai:

228 W. 39th Street, New York

DEAR FRIEND,

Excuse my delay in replying to your beautiful note.

Your uncle was a great soul, and his whole life was given to doing good to his country. Hope you will all follow in his footsteps.

I am coming to India this winter, and cannot express my sorrow that I will not see Haribhai once more.

He was a strong, noble friend, and India has lost a good deal in losing him.

I am going to England very soon where I intend to pass the summer, and in winter next I come to India.

Recommend me to your uncles and friends.

Ever always the well-wisher of your family,
Vivekananda.

PS — My England address is: C/o E. T. Sturdy, Esq., High View, Caversham, Reading, England.

1896.17 — SARADA[1]

Boston,
2nd March, 1896.

DEAR SARADA,

Your letter informed me of everything; but I note that you do not so much as refer to the cable I sent about the celebration. The dictionary that Shashi sent a few months ago has not arrived so far... I am going to England soon. Sharat need not come now at all; for I am myself going to England. I do not want people who take such a long time to make up their minds. I did not invite him for a European tour, and I do not have the money either. So ask him not to come, and none else need.

On perusal of your letter on Tibet, I came to lose all regard for your common sense. In the first place, it is nonsense to say that Notovitch's book is genuine. Did you see any original copy, or bring it to India? Secondly, you say you saw in the Kailas Math the portrait of Jesus and the Samaritan Woman. How do you know that it was Jesus' portrait, and not that of a man in the street? Even taking it for granted, how do you know that it was not put up in the said Math by someone who was a Christian? And your opinions on the Tibetans too are unsound; you did not certainly see the heart of Tibet, but only a fringe of the trade route. In places like those only the dregs of a nation are to be met. If on seeing the Chinabazar and Barabazar quarters of Calcutta, anybody called every Bengali a liar, would that be correct?

Consult Shashi properly when writing any article... What you need is only obedience...

Yours affectionately,
Vivekananda.

---

1 Translated from Bengali.

1896.18 — BLESSED AND BELOVED

To Mr. E. T. Sturdy:

New York,
17th March, 1896.

BLESSED AND BELOVED,

I received your last just now and it frightened me immensely.

The lectures were delivered under the auspices of certain friends who paid for the stenography and all other expenses on condition they alone will have the right to publish them. As such, they have already published the Sunday lectures as well as three books on "Karma-Yoga", "Raja-Yoga", and "Jnana-Yoga". The Raja-Yoga especially has been much altered and re-arranged along with the translation of "Yoga-Sutras of Patanjali". The Raja-Yoga is in the hands of Longmans. The friends here are furious at the idea of these books being published in England; and as they have been made over to them by me legally, I am at a loss what to do. The publication of the pamphlets was not so serious, but the books have been so much re-arranged and changed that the American edition will not recognise the English one. Now pray don't publish these books, as they will place me in a very false position and create endless quarrel and destroy my American work.

By last mail from India I learn that a Sannyasin has started from India. I had a beautiful letter from Miss Müller, also one from Miss MacLeod; the Leggett family has become very attached to me.

I do not know anything about Mr. Chatterji. I hear from other sources that his trouble is money, which the Theosophists cannot supply him with. Moreover the help he will be able to give me is very rudimentary and useless in the face of the fact of a much stronger man coming from India. So far with him. We need not be in a hurry.

I pray you again to think about this publishing business and write some letters to Mrs. Ole Bull and through her ask the opinion of the American friends of the Vedanta, remembering "ours is the Gospel of oneness of all beings", and all national feelings are but wicked superstitions. Moreover I am sure that the person who is always ready to give way to other's opinions finds at last that his opinion has triumphed. Yielding always conquers at last. With love to all our friends,

Yours with love and blessings,
Vivekananda.

PS — I am coming sure in March as early as possible.

1896.19 — SISTER

To Miss Mary Hale:

DEAR SISTER,

I am afraid you are offended and did not answer any of my letters. Now I beg a hundred thousand pardons. By very good luck, I have found the orange cloth and am going to have a coat made as soon as I can. I am glad to hear you met Mrs. Bull. She is such a noble lady and kind friend. Now, sister, there are two very thin Sanskrit pamphlets in the house. Kindly send them over if it does not bother you. The books from India have arrived safe, and I had not to pay any duty on them. I am surprised that the rugs do not arrive yet. I have not been to see Mother Temple any more. I could not find time. Every little bit of time I get I spend in the library.

With everlasting love and gratitude to you all,

Ever your loving brother,
Vivekananda.

PS — Mr. Howe has been a very constant student except the last few days. Kindly give my love to Miss Howe.

1896.20 — CHRISTINA

To Sister Christine:

C/O The Procopeia,
45 St., Botolph Street,
Boston, Mass.,
22nd March, '96.

DEAR CHRISTINA,

Herewith [words excised] to countersign it and put it [words excised]. I am afraid I have made a mistake in writing Miss to your name. In that case you will have to sign also as Miss etc.

I am enjoying Boston very much, especially the old friends here.

They are all kind. Reply promptly. Write fully later on.

With everlasting love and blessings,

Yours etc.,
Vivekananda.

1896.21 — MRS. FUNKEY

To Mrs. Charles (Mary) Funke:

C/O The Procopeia,
45 St., Botolph Street,
Boston, Mass.,
22nd March, '96.

DEAR MRS. FUNKEY [FUNKE],

I had no time to write a line even, I was so busy. I am enjoying Boston immensely, only hard work. The meeting with old friends is very pleasing, no doubt. The so-called class swelled up to 500 people last night and, am afraid, will go on increasing. Everything going on splendidly. Mr. Goodwin as nice as ever. We are all friends here. I go next week to Chicago.

Hope everything is going on well with you there. Kindly give my love to Mrs. Phelps, Mr. Phelps and all the rest of my friends.

With all love and blessings,

Yours,
Vivekananda.

1896.22 — ALASINGA

Boston,
23rd March, 1896.

DEAR ALASINGA,

…One of my new Sannyâsins is indeed a woman… The others are men. I am going to make some more in England and take them over to India with me. These "white" faces will have more influence in India than the Hindus; moreover, they are vigorous, the Hindus are dead. The only hope of India is from the masses. The upper classes are physically and morally dead…

My success is due to my popular style—the greatness of a teacher consists in the simplicity of his language.

…I am going to England next month. I am afraid I have worked too much; my nerves are almost shattered by this long-continued work. I don't want you to sympathise, but only I write this so that you may not expect much from me now. Work on, the best way you can. I have very little hope of being able to do great things now. I am glad, however, that a good deal of literature has been created by taking down stenographic notes of my lectures. Four books are ready… Well, I am satisfied that I have tried my best to do good, and shall have a clear conscience when I retire from work and sit down in a cave.

With love and blessings to all,
Vivekananda.

1896.23 — ALASINGA

U. S. A.,
March, 1896.

DEAR ALASINGA,

... Push on with the work. I will do all I can ... If it pleases the Lord, yellow-garbed Sannyâsins will be common here and in England. Work on, my children.

Mind, so long as you have faith in your Guru, nothing will be able to obstruct your way. That translation of the three Bhâshyas (commentaries) will be a great thing in the eyes of the Westerners.

... Wait, my child, wait and work on. Patience, patience ... I will burst on the public again in good time ...

Yours with love,
Vivekananda.

1896.24 — ALASINGA

U.S.A.
March, 1896.

DEAR ALASINGA,

Last week I wrote you about the Brahmavâdin. I forgot to write about the Bhakti lectures. They ought to be published in a book all together. A few hundreds may be sent to America to Goodyear in New York. Within twenty days I sail for England. I have other big books on Karma, Jnana, and Raja Yogas — the Karma is out already, the Raja will be a very big book and is already in the Press. The Jnana will have to be published, I think, in England.

A letter you published from Kripananda in the Brahmavadin was rather unfortunate. Kripananda is smarting under the blows the Christians have given him and that sort of letter is vulgar, pitching into everybody. It is not in accord with the tone of the Brahmavadin. So in future when Kripananda writes, tone down everything that is an attack upon any sect, however cranky or crude. Nothing which is against any sect, good or bad, should get into the Brahmavadin. Of course, we must not show active sympathy with frauds. Again let me remind you that the paper is too technical to find any subscriber here. The average Western neither knows nor cares to know all about jaw-breaking Sanskrit terms and technicalities. The paper is well fitted for India — that I see. Every word of special pleading should be eliminated from the Editorials, and you must always remember that you are addressing the whole world, not India alone, and that the same world is entirely ignorant of what you have got to tell them. Use the translation of every Sanskrit term carefully and make things as easy as possible.

Before this reaches you I will be in England. So address me c/o E. T. Sturdy, Esq., High View, Caversham, Eng.

Yours etc.,
Vivekananda.

1896.25 — CHRISTINA

To Sister Christine:

1628 Indiana Ave., Chicago, ILL.,
[April 6, 1896.]

DEAR CHRISTINA,

[Line excised.] reply as soon as possible.

I am going forward to New York on Thursday [April 9] and [will] start for England on the 15th of April.

Goodby and love to you all — to Mrs. Funkey [Funke], to Mrs. Phelps and all the rest of our friends.

In this life we meet and part again and again; but the mind is omnipresent and can be, hear, and feel anywhere.

Yours with love and blessings,
Vivekananda.

PS — Give Kripananda and Miss [Martha] Hamilton my love and blessings when you meet them next.

[Written in the margin:] I will go to New York next Friday [April 10].

1896.26 — MRS. BULL

Indiana Ave., Chicago, ILL.,
6th April, 1896.

DEAR MRS. BULL,

Your kind note was duly received. I had beautiful visits with my friends and have already held several classes. I shall have a few more and then start on Thursday.

Everything has been well arranged here, thanks to the kindness of Miss Adams. She is so, so good and kind.

I am suffering from slight fever the last two days; so I can't write a long letter.

My love to all in Boston.

Yours with kind regards,
Vivekananda.

1896.27 — MRS. BULL

124 E. 44th Street, New York,
14th April, 1896.

DEAR MRS. BULL,

... Here is a curious person who comes to me with a letter from Bombay. He is a practical mechanic and his one idea is to see cutlery and other iron manufactories in this country... I do not know anything about him, but even if he be a rogue, I like very much to foster this sort of adventurous spirit among my countrymen. He has money enough to pay his way.

Now, if with all caution testing of his genuineness of spirit, you feel satisfied, all he wants is to get some opportunities of seeing these manufactories. I hope he is true and that you can manage to help him in this.

Yours with kind regards,
Vivekananda.

1896.28 — SARADA[1]

New York,
14th April, 1896.

DEAR SARADA,

Glad to hear everything in your letter. I have got news that Sharat arrived safe. I am in receipt of your letter and the copy of the Indian Mirror. Your contribution is good, go on writing regularly... It is very easy to search for faults, but the characteristic of a saint lies in looking for merits — never forget this... You need a little business faculty... Now what you want is organisation — that requires strict obedience and division of labour. I shall write out everything in every particular from England, for which I start tomorrow. I am determined to make you decent workers thoroughly organised...

The term "Friend" can be used with all. In the English language you have not that sort of cringing politeness common in Bengali, and such Bengali terms translated into English become ridiculous. That Ramakrishna Paramahamsa was God — and all that sort of thing — has no go in countries like this. M — has a tendency to put that stuff down everybody's throat, but that will make our movement a little sect. You keep aloof from such attempts; at the same time, if people worship him as God, no harm. Neither encourage nor discourage. The masses will always have the person, the higher ones the principle; we want both. But principles are universal, not persons. Therefore stick to the principles he taught, let people think whatever

---

1 Translated from Bengali.

they like of his person ... Truce to all quarrels and jealousies and bigotry! These will spoil everything. "But many that are first shall be last; and the last first" "devotees."

Yours affectionately,
Vivekananda.

1896.29 — DR. NANJUNDA RAO

New York,
14th April, 1896.

DEAR DR. NANJUNDA RAO,

I received your note this morning. As I am sailing for England tomorrow, I can only write a few hearty lines. I have every sympathy with your proposed magazine for boys, and will do my best to help it on. You ought to make it independent, following the same lines as the Brahmavâdin, only making the style and matter much more popular. As for example, there is a great chance, much more than you ever dream of, for those wonderful stories scattered all over the Sanskrit literature, to be re-written and made popular. That should be the one great feature of your journal. I will write stories, as many as I can, when time permits. Avoid all attempts to make the journal scholarly — the Brahmavadin stands for that — and it will slowly make its way all over the world, I am sure. Use the simplest language possible, and you will succeed. The main feature should be the teaching of principles through stories. Don't make it metaphysical at all. As to the business part, keep it wholly in your hands. "Too many cooks spoil the broth." In India the one thing we lack is the power of combination, organisation, the first secret of which is obedience.

I have also promised to help starting a magazine in Bengali in Calcutta. Only the first year I used to charge for my lectures The last two years, my work was entirely free of all charges. As such, I have almost no money to send you or the Calcutta people. But I will get people to help you with funds very soon. Go on bravely. Do not expect success in a day or a year. Always hold on to the highest. Be steady. Avoid jealousy and selfishness. Be obedient and eternally faithful to the cause of truth, humanity, and your country, and you will move the world. Remember it is the person, the life, which is the secret of power — nothing else. Keep this letter and read the last lines whenever you feel worried or jealous. Jealousy is the bane of all slaves. It is the bane of our nation. Avoid that always. All blessings attend you and all success.

Yours affectionately,
Vivekananda.

1896.30 — SISTERS

To the Hale Sisters:

6 West 43rd Street, New York,
14th April, 1896.

DEAR SISTERS,

I arrived safe on Sunday and on account of illness could not write earlier. I sail on board the White Star Line Germanic tomorrow at 12 noon. With everlasting memory of love, gratitude and blessings,

I am, your ever loving brother,
Vivekananda.

England

1896.31 — SISTERS

To the Hale Sisters:

High View, Reading,
20th April, 1896.

DEAR SISTERS,

Greetings to you from the other shore. The voyage has been pleasant and no sickness this time. I gave myself treatment to avoid it. I made quite a little run through Ireland and some of the Old English towns and now am once more in Reading amidst Brahma and Maya and Jiva, the individual and the universal soul, etc. The other monk is here; he is one of the nicest of men I see, and is quite a learned monk too. We are busy editing books now. Nothing of importance happened on the way. It was dull, monotonous, and prosaic as my life. I love America more when I am out of it. And, after all, those years there have been some of the best I have yet seen.

Are you trying to get some subscribers for the Brahmavadin? Give my best love and kindest remembrance to Mrs. Adams and Mrs. Conger. Write me as soon as is convenient all about yourselves, and what you are doing, what breaks the monotony of eating, drinking, and cycling. I am in a hurry just now, shall write a bigger letter later; so good-bye and may you be always happy.

Your ever affectionate brother,
Vivekananda.

PS — I will write to Mother Church as soon as I get time. Give my love to Sam and sister Locke.

1896.32 — CHRISTINA

To Sister Christine:

High View, Caversham, Reading, London,
26th April, '96.

DEAR CHRISTINA,

How are things going on with you? I am all safe and sound here in England. Going to begin work from May fourth. How is Mrs. Funkey [Funke]?

Give them all my Love. Write me all about yourself and Mrs. Funkey when you have time. Address me at 63 St., George's Road, S.W. London.

Where is Krip. [Swami Kripananda]? What is he doing now? Has he been able to get up any classes yet? Has his temper gone down?

Give them all my love — and [to] Miss Hamilton and to all my friends and to the Rabbi [Grossman of Detroit].

Yours ever with love and blessings,
Vivekananda.

1896.33 — DEAR[1]

High View, Caversham, Reading,
27th April, 1896.

DEAR, (Members of the Alambazar Math)

... Let me write something for you all. It is not for gaining personal authority that I do this, but for your good and for fulfilling the purpose for which the Lord came. He gave me the charge of you all, and you shall contribute to the great well-being of the world — though most of you are not yet aware of it — this is the special reason of my writing to you. It will be a great pity if any feeling of jealousy or egotism gain ground amongst you. Is it possible for those to establish cordial relations on earth who cannot cordially live with one another for any length of time? No doubt it is an evil to be bound by laws, but it is necessary at the immature stage to be guided by rules; in other words, as the Master used to say that the sapling must be hedged round, and so on. Secondly, it is quite natural for idle minds to indulge in gossip, and faction-mongering, and so forth. Hence I jot down the following hints. If you follow them, you will undoubtedly prosper, but if you don't do so, then there is a danger of all our labours coming to naught.

First let me write about the management of the Math:

1. For the purposes of the Math please hire a commodious house or garden, where everyone may have a small room to himself. There must be a spacious hall where the books may be kept, and a smaller room for meeting the visitors. If possible, there should be another big hall in the house where study of the scriptures and religious discourses will be held every day for the public.

2. Anyone wishing to visit anybody in the Math should see him only and depart, without troubling others.

3. By turns someone should be present in the hall for a few hours every day for the public, so that they may get satisfactory replies to what they come to ask.

4. Everyone must keep to his room and except on special business must not go to others' rooms. Anyone who wishes may go to the Library and read, but it should be strictly forbidden to smoke there or talk with others. The reading should be silent.

1 Translated from Bengali.

5. It shall be wholly forbidden to huddle together in a room and chat the whole day away, with any number of outsiders coming and joining in the hubbub.

6. Only those that are seekers after religion may come and peacefully wait in the Visitors' Hall and when they have seen the particular persons they want, they should depart. Or, if they have any general question to ask, they should refer to the person in charge of that function for the day and leave.

7. Tale-bearing, caballing, or reporting scandals about others should be altogether eschewed.

8. A small room should serve as the office. The Secretary should live in that room, which should contain paper, ink, and other materials for letter-writing. He should keep an account of the income and expenditure. All correspondence should come to him, and he should deliver all letters unopened to their addressees. Books and pamphlets should be sent to the Library.

9. There will be a small room for smoking, which should not be indulged in outside this room.

10. He who wants to indulge in invectives or show temper must do so outside the boundaries of the Math. This should not be deviated from even by an inch.

THE GOVERNING BODY

1. Every year a President should be elected by a majority of votes. The next year, another, and so on.

2. For this year make Brahmananda the President and likewise make another the Secretary, and elect a third man for superintending the worship etc., as well as the arrangement of food.

3. The Secretary shall have another function, viz to keep watch over the general health. Regarding this I have three instructions to give: (i) In every room for each man there shall be a Nair charpoy, mattress, etc. Everyone must keep his room clean. (ii) All arrangements must be made to provide clear and pure water for drinking and cooking purposes, for it is a deadly sin to cook sacramental food in impure or unclean water.

(iii) Give everyone two ochre cloaks of the type that you have made for Saradananda, and see that clothing is kept clean.

4. Anyone wishing to be a Sannyâsin should be admitted as a Brahmacharin first. He should live one year at the Math and one year outside, after which he may be initiated into Sannyâsa.

5. Make over charge of the worship to one of these Brahmacharins, and change them now and then.

DEPARTMENTS

There shall be the following departments in the Math:

I. Study. II. Propaganda. III. Religious Practice.

I. Study — The object of this department is to provide books and teachers for those who want to study. Every morning and evening the teachers should be ready for them.

II. Propaganda — Within the Math, and abroad. The preachers in the Math should teach the inquirers by reading out scriptures to them and by means of question-classes. The preachers abroad will preach from village to village and try to start Maths like the above in different places.

III. Religious Practice — This department will try to provide those who want to practise with the requisites for this. But it should not be allowed that because one has taken to religious practice he will prevent others from study or preaching. Any one infringing this rule shall be immediately asked to clear out, and this is imperative.

The preachers at home should give lessons on devotion, knowledge, Yoga, and work by turns; for this, the days and hours should be fixed, and the routine hung up at the door of the class-room. That is to say, a seeker after devotion may not present himself on the day fixed for knowledge and feel wounded thereby; and so on.

None of you are fit for the Vâmâchâra form of practice. Therefore this should on no account be practised at the Math. Anyone demurring to this must step out of this Order. This form of practice must never even be mentioned in the Math. Ruin shall seize the wicked man, both here and hereafter, who would introduce vile Vamachara into His fold!

SOME GENERAL REMARKS

1. If any woman comes to have a talk with a Sannyasin, she should do it in the Visitors' Hall. No woman shall be allowed to enter any other room — except the Worship-room.

2. No Sannyasin shall be allowed to reside in the Women's Math. Anyone refusing to obey this rule shall be expelled from the Math. "Better an empty fold than a wicked herd."

3. Men of evil character shall be rigorously kept out. On no pretence shall their shadow even cross the threshold of my room. If anyone amongst you become wicked, turn him out at once, whoever he be. We want no black sheep. The Lord will bring lots of good people.

4. Any woman can come to the class-room (or preaching hall) during class time or preaching hour, but must leave the place directly when that period is over.

5. Never show temper, or harbour jealousy, or backbite another in secret. It would be the height of cruelty and hard-heartedness to take note of others' shortcoming instead of rectifying one's own.

6. There should be fixed hours of meals. Everyone must have a seat and a low dining table. He will sit on the former and put his plate on the latter, as is the custom in Rajputana.

THE OFFICE-BEARERS

All the office-bearers you should elect by ballot, as was the mandate of Lord Buddha. That is to say, one should propose that such and such should be the President this year; and all should write on bits of paper 'yes' or 'no' and put them in a pitcher. If the 'yes' have a majority, he should be elected President, and so on. Though you should elect office-bearers in this way, yet I suggest that this year Brahmananda should be President, Nirmalananda, Secretary and Treasurer, Sadananda Librarian, and Ramakrishnananda, Abhedananda, Turiyananda, and Trigunatitananda should take charge of the teaching and preaching work by turns, and so on.

It is no doubt a good idea that Trigunatita has of starting a magazine. But I shall consent to it if only you can work jointly.

About doctrines and so forth I have to say only this, that if anyone accepts Paramahamsa Deva as Avatâra etc., it is all right; if he doesn't do so, it is just the same. The truth about it is that in point of character, Paramahamsa Deva beats all previous records; and as regards teaching, he was more liberal, more original, and more progressive than all his predecessors. In other words, the older Teachers were rather one-sided, while the teaching of this new Incarnation or Teacher is that the best point of Yoga, devotion, knowledge, and work must be combined now so as to form a new society... The older ones were no doubt good, but this is the new religion of this age — the synthesis of Yoga, knowledge, devotion, and work — the propagation of knowledge and devotion to all, down to the very lowest, without distinction of age or sex. The previous Incarnations were all right, but they have been synthesised in the person of Ramakrishna. For the ordinary man and the beginner, steady devotion (Nishthâ) to an ideal is of paramount importance. That is to say, teach them that all great Personalities should be duly honoured, but homage should be paid now to Ramakrishna. There can be no vigour without steady devotion. Without it one cannot preach with the intensity of a Mahâvira (Hanumân). Besides, the previous ones have become rather old. Now we have a new India, with its new God, new religion, and new Vedas. When, O Lord, shall our land be free from this eternal dwelling upon the past? Well, a little bigotry also is a necessity. But we must harbour no antagonistic feelings towards others.

If you consider it wise to be guided by my ideas and if you follow these rules, then I shall supply on all necessary funds... Moreover, please show this letter to Gour-Mâ, Yogin-Mâ, and others, and through them establish a Women's Math. Let Gour-Ma be the President there for one year, and so on. But none of you shall be allowed to visit the place. They will manage their own affairs. They will not have to work at your dictation. I shall supply all necessary expenses for that work also.

May the Lord guide you in the right direction! Two persons went to see the Lord Jagannatha. One of them beheld the Deity — while the other saw some trash that was haunting his mind! My friends, many have no doubt served the Master, but whenever anyone would be disposed to consider himself an extraordinary personage, he should think that although he was associated with Shri Ramakrishna, he has seen only the trash that was uppermost in his mind! Were it not so, he would manifest the results. The Master himself used to quote, "They would sing and dance in the name of the Lord but come to grief in the end." The root of that degeneration is egotism — to think that one is just as great as any other, indeed! "He used to love me too!" — one would plead. Alas, Nick Bottom, would you then be thus translated? Would such a man envy or quarrel with another and degrade himself? Bear in mind that through His grace lots of men will be turned out with the nobility of gods — ay, wherever His mercy would drop!... Obedience is the first duty. Well, just do with alacrity what I ask you to. Let me see how you carry out these few small things. Then gradually great things will come to pass.

Yours,
Vivekananda.

PS — Please read the contents of this letter to all, and let me know whether you consider the suggestions worth carrying out. Please tell Brahmananda that he who is the servant of all is their true master. He never becomes a leader in whose love there is a consideration of high or low. He whose love knows no end, and never stops to consider high or low, has the whole world lying at his feet.

1896.34 — STURDY

Waveney Mansions,
Fairhazel Gardens, London N.W.
April, 1896, Thursday Afternoon.

DEAR STURDY,

I forgot to tell you in the morning that Prof. Max Müller also offered in his letter to me to do everything he could if I went to lecture at Oxford.

Yours affectionately,
Vivekananda.

PS — Have you written for the Artharva-Veda Samhita edited by Shankara Pandurang?

1896.35 — SHASHI[1]

C/O E. T. Sturdy, Esq.
High View, Caversham, Reading,
May (?) 1896.

DEAR SHASHI, (Ramakrishnanada)

   ... This City of London is a sea of human heads — ten or fifteen Calcuttas put together. One is apt to be lost in the mazes unless he arranges for somebody to

---
1 Translated from Bengali.

meet him on arrival... However, let Kali start at once. If he be late in starting like Sharat, better let no one come. It won't do to loiter and procrastinate like that. It is a task that requires the height of Rajas (activity)... Our whole country is steeped in Tamas, and nothing but that. We want Rajas first, and Sattva will come afterwards — a thing far, far removed.

Yours affectionately,
Vivekananda.

1896.36 — MRS. BULL

To Mrs. Ole Bull:

63 St. George's Road, London. S.W.,
May 8, 1896.

DEAR MRS. BULL,

Your last letter to Sturdy at hand. They, I am sorry to say, leave us nowhere. I could not make anything out of them.

What are we to do? Is the book going to be published or not? Prof. [William] James's introduction (Preface to Swami Vivekananda's Râja-Yoga.) is of no use in England. So why wait so long for that; and what use are those long explanations about him?

Our hands are tied down. Why do you not write something plain and decisive? Life is short and time is flying. I am so sorry you are losing sight of that. Your letters are full of explanations [and] directions, but not one word about what is to be done!!! So much red tape about printing a little book!! Empires are managed with less manipulation than that, I am sure!! So kindly write at your earliest something precise about the book and whether it is going to be printed or not, and pray make the writing a little legible.

Poor Sturdy is out of his wits as to what to do; he has gone through the Mss. long ago.

Joking apart, I am very sorry you are not coming over this year. We are in Lady Isabel's house. (The house was rented from Lady Isabel Margesson.) Miss [Henrietta] Müller has taken some rooms in it too. Goodwin is here with us. We have not yet made any big stir here. The classes have begun; they are not yet what we expected. We [have] had only two yet.

We will work on steadily the next 4 or 5 months. Sturdy is as patient and persevering and hopeful as ever.

It is cool enough here yet to have a fire in the grate.

Give my love to Mrs. Adams, Miss Thursby and all other friends. My love to Mr. Fox and blessings.

Yours with love and blessings,
Vivekananda.

1896.37 — ADHYAPAKJI

63 St. George's Road, London, S.W.
16th May, 1896.

DEAR ADHYAPAKJI, (Prof. John Henry Wright. The letter was written on the death of his daughter, aged 16.)

Last mail brought the very very sad news of the blow that has fallen on you.

This is the world my brother — this illusion of Mâyâ — the Lord alone is true. The forms are evanescent; but the spirit, being in the Lord and of the Lord, is immortal and omnipresent. All that we ever had are round us this minute, for the spirit can neither come nor go, it only changes its plane of manifestation.

You are strong and pure and so is Mrs. Wright, and I am sure that the Divine in you has arisen and thrown away the lie and delusion that there can be death for anyone.

"He who sees in this world of manifoldness that one support of everything, in the midst of a world of unconsciousness that one eternal consciousness, in this evanescent world that one eternal and unchangeable, unto him belongs eternal peace."

May the peace of the Lord descend upon you and yours in abundance is the prayer of

Your ever loving friend,
Vivekananda.

1896.38 — SISTER

63 St. George's Road, London,
May, 1896.

DEAR SISTER,

In London once more. The climate now in England is nice and cool. We have fire in the grate. We have a whole house to ourselves, you know, this time. It is small but convenient, and in London they do not cost so much as in America. Don't you know what I was thinking — about your mother! I just wrote her a letter and duly posted it to her, care of Monroe & Co., 7 Rue Scribe, Paris. Some old friends are here, and Miss MacLeod came over from the Continent. She is good as gold, and as kind as ever. We have a nice little family, in the house, with another monk from India. Poor man! — a typical Hindu with nothing of that pluck and go which I have, he is always dreamy and gentle and sweet! That won't do. I will try to put a little activity into him. I have had two classes already — they will go on for four or five months and after that to India I go. But it is to Amerique — there where the heart is. I love the Yankee land. I like to see new things. I do not care a fig to loaf about old ruins and mope a life out about old histories and keep sighing about the ancients. I have too much vigour in my blood for that. In America is the place, the people, the opportunity for everything. I have become horribly radical. I am just going to India to see what I can do in that awful mass of conservative jelly-fish, and start a new thing, entirely new — simple, strong, new and fresh as the first born baby. The eternal, the infinite, the omnipresent, the omniscient is a principle, not a person. You, I, and everyone are but embodiments of that principle, and the more of this infinite principle is embodied in a person, the greater is he, and all in the end will be the perfect embodiment of that and thus all will be one as they are now essentially. This is all there is of religion, and the practice is through this feeling of oneness that is love. All old fogy forms are mere old superstitions. Now, why struggle to keep them alive? Why give thirsty people ditch-water to drink whilst the river of life and truth flows by? This is only human selfishness, nothing else. Life is short — time is flying — that place and people where one's ideas work best should be the country and the people for everyone. Ay, for a dozen bold hearts, large, noble, and sincere!

I am very well indeed and enjoying life immensely.

Yours ever with love,
Vivekananda.

1896.39 — MARY

To Miss Mary Hale:

63 St. George's Road, London, S.W.,
30th May, 1896.

DEAR MARY,

Your letter reached just now. Of course, you were not jealous but all of a sudden were inspired with sympathy for poor India. Well, you need not be frightened. Wrote a letter to Mother Church weeks ago, but have not been able to get a line from her yet. I am afraid the whole party have taken orders and entered a Catholic convent — four old maids are enough to drive any mother to a convent. I had a beautiful visit with Prof. Max Müller. He is a saint — a Vedantist through and through. What think you? He has been a devoted admirer of my old Master for years. He has written an article on my Master in The Nineteenth Century, which will soon come out. We had long talk on Indian things. I wish I had half his love for India. We are going to start another little magazine here. What about The Brahmavadin? Are you pushing it? If four pushful old maids cannot push a journal, I am blowed. You will hear from me now and then. I am not a pin to be lost under a bushel. I am having classes here just now. I begin Sunday lectures from next week. The classes are very big and are in the house. We have rented it for the season. Last night I made a dish. It was such a delicious mixture of saffron, lavender, mace, nutmeg, cubebs, cinnamon, cloves, cardamom, cream, limejuice, onions, raisins, almonds, pepper, and rice, that I myself could not eat it. There was no asafoetida, though that would have made it smoother to swallow.

Yesterday I went to a marriage à la mode. Miss Müller, a rich lady, a friend who has adopted a Hindu boy and to help my work has taken rooms in this house, took us to see it. One of her nieces was married to somebody's nephew I suppose. What tiring nonsense! I am glad you do not marry. Good-bye, love to all. No more time as I am going to lunch with Miss MacLeod.

Yours ever affectionately,
Vivekananda.

1896.40 — MRS. BULL

63 St. George's Road, London,
30th May, 1896.

DEAR MRS. BULL,

… Day before yesterday I had a fine visit with Prof. Max Müller. He is a saintly man and looks like a young man in spite of his seventy years, and his face is without a wrinkle. I wish I had half his love for India and Vedanta. At the same time he is a friend of Yoga too and believes in it. Only he has no patience with humbugs.

Above all, his reverence for Ramakrishna Paramahamsa is extreme, and he has written an article on him for the Nineteenth Century. He asked me, "What are you doing to make him known to the world?" Ramakrishna has charmed him for years. Is it not good news? …

Things are going on here slowly but steadily. I am to begin from next Sunday my public lectures.

Yours ever in grateful affection,
Vivekananda.

1896.41 — MRS. BULL

63 St. George's Road, London S.W.,
5th June, 1896.

DEAR MRS. BULL,

The Raja-Yoga book is going on splendidly. Saradananda goes to the States soon.

I do not like any one whom I love to become a lawyer, although my father was one. My Master was against it, and I believe that that family is sure to come to grief where there are several lawyers. Our country is full of them; the universities turn them out by the hundreds. What my nation wants is pluck and scientific genius. So I want Mohin to be an electrician. Even if he fails in life, still I will have the satisfaction that he strove to become great and really useful to his country… In America alone there is that something in the air which brings out whatever is best in every one... I want him to be daring, bold, and to struggle to cut a new path for himself and his nation. An electrical engineer can make a living in India.

Yours with love,
Vivekananda.

PS — Goodwin is writing to you this mail with reference to a magazine in America. I think something of the sort is necessary to keep the work together, and shall of course do all that I can to help it on in the line he suggests... I think it very probable that he will come over with Saradananda.

1896.42 — MISS NOBLE

63 St. George's Road, London,
7th June, 1896.

DEAR MISS NOBLE,

My ideal indeed can be put into a few words and that is: to preach unto mankind their divinity, and how to make it manifest in every movement of life.

This world is in chain of superstition. I pity the oppressed, whether man or woman, and I pity more the oppressors.

One idea that I see clear as daylight is that misery is caused by ignorance and nothing else. Who will give the world light? Sacrifice in the past has been the Law, it will be, alas, for ages to come. The earth's bravest and best will have to sacrifice themselves for the good of many, for the welfare of all. Buddhas by the hundred are necessary with eternal love and pity.

Religions of the world have become lifeless mockeries. What the world wants is character. The world is in need of those whose life is one burning love, selfless. That love will make every word tell like thunderbolt.

It is no superstition with you, I am sure, you have the making in you of a world-mover, and others will also come. Bold words and bolder deeds are what we want. Awake, awake, great ones! The world is burning with misery. Can you sleep? Let us call and call till the sleeping gods awake, till the god within answers to the call. What more is in life? What greater work? The details come to me as I go. I never make plans. Plans grow and work themselves. I only say, awake, awake!

May all blessings attend you for ever!

Yours affectionately,
Vivekananda.

1896.43 — SHASHI[1]

63 St. George's Road, London S.W.,
24th June, 1896.

DEAR SHASHI,

Max Müller wants all the sayings of Shri Ramakrishna classified, that is, all on Karma in one place, on Vairagya in another place, so on Bhakti, Jnana, etc., etc. You must undertake to do this forthwith… We must take care to present only the universal aspect of his teachings…

Sharat starts for America tomorrow. The work here is coming to a head. We have already got funds to start a London Centre. Next month I go to Switzerland to pass a month or two there, then I shall return to London. What will be the good of my going home? — This London is the hub of the world. The heart of India is here. How can I leave without laying a sure foundation here? Nonsense! For the present, I shall have Kali here, tell him to be ready…

We want great spirit, tremendous energy, and boundless enthusiasm, no womanishness will do. Try to go on exactly as I wrote to you in my last. We want organisation. Organisation is power, and the secret of this is obedience.

Yours affectionately,
Vivekananda.

1896.44 — SHASHI[2]

High View, Caversham, Reading,
3rd July, 1896.

DEAR SHASHI,

Send Kali to England as soon as you get this letter… He will have to bring some books for me. I have only got Rig-Veda Samhitâ. Ask him to bring the Yajur-Veda, Sâma-Veda, Atharva-Samhita, as many of the Brâhmanas as he can get, beginning with the Shatapatha, some of the Sutras, and Yâska's Nirukta…

Let there be no delay as in Sharat's case, but let Kali come at once. Sharat has gone to America, as he had no work to do here. That is to say, he was late by six months, and then when he came, I was here…

Yours affectionately,
Vivekananda.

---

1 Translated from Bengali.
2 Translated from Bengali.

1896.45 — FRIEND AND BROTHER

63 St. George's Road, London, S.W.
6th July, 1896.

DEAR FRIEND AND BROTHER, (To Dr. Lewis I. Janes)

Yours of the 25th June has duly reached and gave me great pleasure. I am so glad to see the noble work progressing. I had learnt with the greatest delight from Mrs. Bull of the work that is going to be done in Cambridge this winter and no better person could have been selected to direct it as yourself. May all power attend you. I will be only too glad to write for the magazine from time to time and my first instalment was to be in a few weeks, when I hope to get some leisure. Certainly it goes without saying that no one of the types we call religious ought to die — they like races require fresh infusion of blood in the form of ideas. It is wonderful to be able to sympathise with others from their standpoints of view.

By this time Goodwin and the other Swami must have reached America. They I trust will be of help to you in your noble work. Godspeed to all good work and infinite blessings on all workers for good.

Yours ever in the truth,
Vivekananda.

1896.46 — FRANKINCENSE

63 St. George's Road, London S.W.,
6th July, 1896.

DEAR FRANKINCENSE, (Mr. Francis H. Leggett whom Swamiji addressed thus)

...Things are going on with me very well on this side of the Atlantic.

The Sunday lectures were quite successful; so were the classes. The season has ended and I too am thoroughly exhausted. I am going to make a tour in Switzerland with Miss Müller. The Galsworthys have been very very kind. Joe (Miss Josephine MacLeod, also referred to as Joe Joe.) brought them round splendidly. I simply admire Joe in her tact and quiet way. She is a feminine statesman or woman. She can wield a kingdom. I have seldom seen such strong yet good common sense in a human being. I will return next autumn and take up the work in America.

The night before last I was at a party at Mrs. Martin's, about whom you must already know a good deal from Joe.

Well, the work is growing silently yet surely in England. Almost every other man or woman came to me and talked about the work. This British Empire with all its drawbacks is the greatest machine that ever existed for the dissemination of ideas.

I mean to put my ideas in the centre of this machine, and they will spread all over the world. Of course, all great work is slow, and the difficulties are too many, especially as we Hindus are the conquered race. Yet, that is the very reason why it is bound to work, for spiritual ideals have always come from the downtrodden. Jews overwhelmed the Roman Empire with their spiritual ideals. You will be pleased to know that I am also learning my lessons every day in patience and, above all, in sympathy. I think I am beginning to see the Divine, even inside the high and mighty Anglo-Indians. I think I am slowly approaching to that state when I should be able to love the very "Devil" himself, if there were any.

At twenty years of age I was the most unsympathetic, uncompromising fanatic; I would not walk on the footpath on the theatre side of the streets in Calcutta. At thirty-three, I can live in the same house with prostitutes and never would think of saying a word of reproach to them. Is it degenerate? Or is it that I am broadening out into the Universal Love which is the Lord Himself? Again I have heard that if one does not sea the evil round him he cannot do good work — he lapses into a sort of fatalism. I do not see that. On the other hand, my power of work is immensely increasing and becoming immensely effective. Some days I get into a sort of ecstasy. I feel that I must bless every one, everything, love and embrace everything, and I do see that evil is a delusion. I am in one of these moods now, dear Francis, and am actually shedding tears of joy at the thought of you and Mrs. Leggett's love and kindness to me. I bless the day I was born. I have had so much of kindness and love here, and that Love Infinite that brought me into being has guarded every one of my actions, good or bad, (don't be frightened), for what am I, what was I ever, but a tool in His hands, for whose service I have given up everything, my beloved ones, my joys, my life? He is my playful darling, I am His playfellow. There is neither rhyme nor reason in the universe! What reason binds Him? He the playful one is playing these tears and laughters over all parts of the play! Great fun, great fun, as Joe says.

It is a funny world, and the funniest chap you ever saw is He — the Beloved Infinite! Fun, is it not? Brotherhood or playmatehood — a school of romping children let out to play in this playground of the world! Isn't it? Whom to praise, whom to blame, it is all His play. They want explanations, but how can you explain Him? He is brainless, nor has He any reason. He is fooling us with little brains and reason, but this time He won't find me napping.

I have learnt a thing or two: Beyond, beyond reason and learning and talking is the feeling, the "Love", the "Beloved". Ay, saké, fill up the cup and we will be mad.

Yours ever in madness,
Vivekananda.

1896.47 — SIR

To Mr. Francis Leggett:

(Swami Vivekananda enclosed the following document in a July 6, 1896 letter written to Francis Leggett.)

63 St. George's Road, London, S.W.,
6th July, 1896.

To Francis Leggett, Esq.:

DEAR SIR,

Herewith I constitute you as my attorney and representative in regards to all publication pamphlets etc., written or dictated by me, their copyright, sale, etc., in the U.S. of America.

Yours affectionately,
Vivekananda.

1896.48 — MRS. BULL

To Mrs. Ole Bull:

63 St. George's Road, London, S.W.,
6th July, 1896.

DEAR MRS. BULL,

I have sent to Mr. Leggett by last mail the power of attorney, and, as you desired, this is to notify you of the fact and absolve you from the responsibilities of the power of attorney which I gave you in America last year.

Yours affectionately,
Vivekananda.

Saradananda and Goodwin have arrived, I am sure, by this time. I have a nice letter from Dr. Jain [Dr. Lewis G. Janes]. I am going to Switzerland for a vacation in a few days. I mean to stay there a month or more. I will return to London in the next fall. I do not know when I go back to India.

Things are growing nicely here.

With love to all.

1896.49 — MOTHER

To Mrs. G. W. Hale:

July 7, 1896.

DEAR MOTHER,

[On the] 18th of this month I start for Switzerland for a holiday. I will come back to London again to work in the Autumn. The work in England bids fair to be much better and deeper than in the U.S. And here in London is the heart of India also. Where are you now? I am passing through Geneva on my way to the Hills. I will be there a day or two.

If you be somewhere near, I will make it a point to come to see you. Did you hear Annie Besant? How did you like her? What about your plans of going to India next winter? What about the innocents (Mary and Harriet Hale and Isabelle and Harriet McKindley.) at home? I haven't had any news of them. My love to Father Pope, Mother Temple (Mrs. James Matthews, Mr. Hale's sister.) and yourself. Kindly answer as I will be only a few days here.

Ever yours with love and gratitude,
Vivekananda.

1896.50 — BABIES

To the Hale Sisters:

London,
7th July, 1896.

DEAR BABIES,

The work here progressed wonderfully. I had one monk here from India. I have sent him to the U.S.A. and sent for another from India. The season is closed; the classes, therefore, and the Sunday lectures are to be closed on the 16th next. And on the 19th I go for a month or so for quiet and rest in the Swiss Mountains to return next autumn to London and begin again. The work here has been very satisfactory. By rousing interest here I really do more for India than in India. Mother wrote to me that if you could rent your flat, she would be glad to take you with her to see Egypt. I am going with three English friends to the Swiss Hills. Later on, towards the end of winter, I expect to go to India with some English friends who are going to live in my monastery there, which, by the by, is in the air yet. It is struggling to materialise somewhere in the Himalayas.

Where are You? Now the summer is in full swing, even London is getting very hot. Kindly give my best love to Mrs. Adams, Mrs. Conger, and all the rest of my friends in Chicago.

Your affectionate brother,
Vivekananda.

1896.51 — MRS. BULL

63 St. George's Road, London S.W.,
8th July, 1896.

DEAR MRS. BULL,

The English people are very generous. In three minutes' time the other evening, my class raised £150 for the new quarters for next autumn's work. They would have given £500 on the spot if wanted, but we want to go slow, and not rush into expense. There will be many hands here to carry on the work, and they understand a bit of renunciation, here — the deep English character.

Yours with best wishes,
Vivekananda.

1896.52 — SIR

[A letter to the editor, which appeared in the July 11, 1896 issue of the Light.]

63, St. George's Road, S.W.

SIR,

Allow me to put a few words in your estimable journal as comments on an article in your paper dated July 4th. I must thank you without reserve for the kind and friendly spirit manifested throughout the article towards me and the philosophy I preach; but, as there is a fear of misconstruction in one part of it — especially by my Spiritualistic friends — I want to clear my position. The truth of correspondence between the living and the dead is, I believe, in every religion, and nowhere more than in the Vedantic sects of India, where the fact of mutual help between the departed and the living has been made the basis of the law of inheritance. I would be very sorry if I be mistaken as antagonistic to any sect or form of religion, so far as they are sincere. Nor do I hold that any system can ever be judged by the frauds and failures that would naturally gather round every method under the present circumstances. But, all the same, I cannot but believe that every thoughtful person would agree with me when I affirm that people should be warned of their dangers, with love and sympathy. The lecture alluded to could but accidentally touch the subject of Spiritualism; but I take this opportunity of conveying my deep admiration for the Spiritualist community for the positive good they have done already, and are doing still: (1) the preaching of a universal sympathy; (2) the still greater work of helping the human race out of doctrines which inculcate fear and not love. Ever ready to co-operate with, and at the service of, all who are striving to bring the light of the spirit,

I remain yours sincerely,
Vive Kananda.

1896.53 — DR. NANJUNDA RAO

England,
14th July, 1896.

DEAR DR. NANJUNDA RAO,

The numbers of *Prabuddha Bharata* have been received and distributed too to the class. It is very satisfactory. It will have a great sale, no doubt, in India. In America I may get also a number of subscribers. I have already arranged for advertising it in America and Goodyear has done it already. But here in England the progress will be slower indeed. The great drawback here is — they all want to start papers of their own; and it is right that it should be so, seeing that, after all, no foreigner will ever write the English language as well as the native Englishman, end the ideas, when put in good English, will spread farther than in Hindu English. Then again it is much more difficult to write a story in a foreign language than an essay. I am trying my best to get you subscribers here. But you must not depend on any foreign help. Nations, like individuals, must help themselves. This is real patriotism. If a nation cannot do that, its time has not yet come. It must wait. It is from Madras that the new light must spread all over India. With this end you must stork. One point I will remark however. The cover is simply barbarous. It is awful and hideous. If it is possible, change it. Make it symbolical and simple, without human figures at all. The banyan tree does not mean awakening, nor does the hill, nor the saint, nor the European couple. The lotus is a symbol of regeneration.

We are awfully behindhand in art especially in that of painting. For instance, make a small scene of spring re-awakening in a forest, showing how the leaves and buds are coming again. Slowly go on, there are hundreds of ideas to be put forward. You see the symbol I made for the Raja-Yoga, printed by Longman Green and Co. You can get it at Bombay. It consists of my lectures on Raja-Yoga in New York.

I am going to Switzerland next Sunday, and shall return to London in the autumn, and take up the work again...I want rest very badly, you know.

Yours with all blessings etc.,
Vivekananda.

1896.54 — MRS. BULL

To Mrs. Ole Bull:

63 St. George's Road,
18th July, '96.

DEAR MRS. BULL,

I received your last note duly — and you already know my gratitude and love for you and that I perfectly agree with most of your ideas and work.

I did not understand, however, one point. You speak of Sturdy and myself being members. Members of what? I, as you well know, can not become a member of any society.

I am very glad to learn that you have been favourably impressed by Saradananda. There is one big mistake you are labouring under. What do you mean of [my] writing to my workers more confidentially and not to you? I seldom write to anyone—I have no time to write. I have no workers. Everyone is independent to work as one likes. I do not bother my head about these little things at all. I can give ideas—that is all; let people work them out any way they like, and Godspeed to all.

"He who works unattached to persons and giving up the fruits of work is a genuine worker"—Gitâ.

Yours Ever with love and gratitude,
Vivekananda.

Switzerland

1896.55 — BLESSED AND BELOVED

To Mr. E. T. Sturdy:

Grand Hotel, Valais, Switzerland.

BLESSED AND BELOVED,

… I am reading a little, starving a good deal, and practising a good deal more. The strolls in the woods are simply delicious. We are now situated under three huge glaciers, and the scenery is very beautiful.

By the by, whatever scruples I may have had as to the Swiss-lake origin of the Aryans have been taken clean off my mind. The Swiss is a Tartar minus a pigtail…

Yours ever affectionately,
Vivekananda.

1896.56 — MRS. BULL

Saas-Grund, Switzerland,
25th July, 1896.

DEAR MRS. BULL,

I want to forget the world entirely at least for the next two months and practice hard. That is my rest… The mountains and snow have a beautifully quieting influence on me, and I am getting better sleep here than for a long time.

My love to all friends.

Yours etc.,
Vivekananda.

1896.57 — SAHJI

C/O. E. T. STURDY, ESQ.,
High View, Caversham, Reading,
5th August, 1896.

DEAR SAHJI, (Lala Badri Sah. The letter was actually written from Switzerland)

Many thanks for your kind greetings. I have an inquiry to make; if you kindly forward me the information I seek, I would be much obliged.

I want to start a Math at Almora or near Almora rather. I have heard that there was a certain Mr. Ramsay who lived in a bungalow near Almora and that he had a garden round his bungalow. Can't it be bought? What is the price? If not to be bought, can it be rented?

Do you know of any suitable place near Almora where I can build my monastery with a garden etc.? I would rather like to have a hill all to myself.

Hoping to get an early reply, I remain, with blessings and love to you and all the rest of my friends in Almora.

Vivekananda.

1896.58 — BLESSED AND BELOVED

To Sister Christine:

[Postmarked: SAAS-FEE],
Switzerland.
5th August, 1896.

BLESSED AND BELOVED,

Surrounded on all sides by eternal snow peaks, sitting on the grass in a beautiful wood, my thoughts go to those I love — so I write.

I am in Switzerland — constantly on the move — getting a much needed rest. It is a miniature Himalayas, and has the same effect of raising the mind up to the Self and driving away all earthly feelings and ties. I am intensely enjoying it. I feel so, so uplifted. I cannot write, but I wish you will have the same for ever — when your feet do not want, as it were, to touch the material earth — when the soul finds itself floating, as it were, in an ocean of spirituality.

Prof. Max Müller has written in the Nineteenth Century an article on my Master. Read it if you can — August number.

I hope you are enjoying this beautiful summer and are perfectly rested after hard work.

My love to all. Blessings to all.

Yours ever with love and blessings,
Vivekananda.

PS — A few Alpine flowers growing almost in the midst of eternal snow I send you, praying that you may attain spiritual hardihood amidst all snows and ice of this life.

1896.59 — BLESSED AND BELOVED

To Mr. E. T. Sturdy:

Switzerland,
5th August, 1896.

BLESSED AND BELOVED,

A letter came this morning from Prof. Max Müller telling me that the article of Shri Ramakrishna Paramahamsa has been published in The XIX Century August number. Have you read it? He asked my opinion about it. Not having seen it yet, I can't write anything to him. If you have it, kindly send it to me. Also The Brahmavadin, if any have arrived. Max Müller wants to know about our plans... and again about the magazine. He promises a good deal of help and is ready to write a book on Shri Ramakrishna Paramahamsa.

I think it is better that you should directly correspond with him about the magazine etc. You will see from his letter which I shall send you as soon as I have replied (after reading The XIX Century) that he is very much pleased with our movement and is ready to help it as much as he can...

Yours with blessings and love,
Vivekananda.

PS — I hope you will consider well the plan for the big magazine. Some money can be raised in America, and we can keep the magazine all to ourselves at the same time. I intend to write to America on hearing about the plan you and Prof. Max Muller decide upon. "A great tree is to be taken refuge in, when it has both fruits and shade. If, however, we do not get the fruit, who prevents our enjoyment of the shade?" So ought great attempts to be made, is the moral.

1896.60 — DEAR __

To Kripananda:

Switzerland,
August, 1896.

DEAR __,

Be you holy and, above all, sincere; and do not for a moment give up your trust in the Lord, and you will see the light. Whatever is truth will remain for ever; whatever is not, none can preserve. We are helped in being born in a time when everything is quickly searched out. Whatever others think or do, lower not your standard of purity, morality, and love of God; above all, beware of all secret organisations. No one who loves God need fear any jugglery. Holiness is the highest and divinest power in earth and in heaven. "Truth alone triumphs, not untruth. Through truth alone is opened the way to God" (Mundaka, III. i. 6). Do not care for a moment who joins hands with you or not, be sure that you touch the hand of the Lord. That is enough...

I went to the glacier of Monte Rosa yesterday and gathered a few hardy flowers growing almost in the midst of eternal snow. I send you one in this letter hoping that you will attain to a similar spiritual hardihood amidst all the snow and ice of this earthly life...

Your dream was very, very beautiful. In dream our souls read a layer of our mind which we do not read in our waking hours, and however unsubstantial imagination may be, it is behind the imagination that all unknown psychic truths lie. Take heart. We will try to do what we can for the good of humanity — the rest depends upon the Lord...

Well, do not be anxious, do not be in a hurry. Slow, persistent and silent work does everything. The Lord is great. We will succeed, my boy. We must. Blessed be His name!...

Here in America are no Ashramas. Would there was one! How would I like it and what an amount of good it would do to this country!

1896.61 — ALASINGA

Switzerland,
6th August, 1896.

DEAR ALASINGA,

I learnt from your letter the bad financial state the Brahmavâdin is in. I will try to help you when I go back to London. You must not lower the tone. Keep up the paper. Very soon I will be able to help you in such a manner as to make you free of this nonsense teacher business. Do not be afraid. Great things are going to be done, my child. Take heart. The Brahmavadin is a jewel — it must not perish. Of course, such a paper has to be kept up by private help always, and we will do it. Hold on a few months more.

Max Müller's article on Shri Ramakrishna has been published in the Nineteenth Century. I will send you a copy as soon as I get it. He writes me very nice letters and wants material for a big work on Ramakrishna's life. Write to Calcutta to send all the material they can to Max Müller.

I have received the communication to the American paper before. You must not publish it in India. Enough of this newspaper blazoning, I am tired of it anyhow. Let us go our own way, and let fools talk. Nothing can resist truth.

I am, as you see, now in Switzerland and am always on the move. I cannot and must not do anything in the way of writing, nor much reading either. There is a big London work waiting for me from next month. In winter I am going back to India and will try to set things on their feet there.

My love to all. Work on, brave hearts, fail not — no saying nay; work on — the Lord is behind the work. Mahâshakti is with you.

Yours with love and blessings,
Vivekananda.

1896.62 — GOODWIN

To Mr. J. J. Goodwin:

Switzerland,
8th August, 1896.

DEAR GOODWIN,

I am now taking rest. I read from different letters a lot about Kripananda. I am sorry for him. There must be something wrong in his head. Let him alone. None of you need bother about him.

As for hurting me, that is not in the power of gods or devils. So be at rest. It is unswerving love and perfect unselfishness that conquer everything. We Vedantists in every difficulty ought to ask the subjective question, "Why do I see that?" "Why can I not conquer this with love?"

I am very glad at the reception the Swami has met with, also at the good work he is doing. Great work requires great and persistent effort for a long time. Neither need we trouble ourselves if a few fail. It is in the nature of things that many should fall, that troubles should come, that tremendous difficulties should arise, that selfishness and all the other devils in the human heart should struggle hard when they are about to be driven out by the fire of spirituality. The road to the Good is the roughest and steepest in the universe. It is a wonder that so many succeed, no wonder that so many fall. Character has to be established through a thousand stumbles.

I am much refreshed now. I look out of the window and see the huge glaciers just before me and feel that I am in the Himalayas. I am quite calm. My nerves have regained their accustomed strength; and little vexations, like those you write of, do not touch me at all. How shall I be disturbed by this child's play? The whole world is a mere child's play — preaching, teaching, and all included. "Know him to be the Sannyasin who neither hates not desires" (Gita, V.3). And what is there to be desired in this little mud-puddle of a world, with its ever-recurring misery, disease, and death? "He who has given up all desires, he alone is happy."

This rest, eternal, peaceful rest, I am catching a glimpse of now in this beautiful spot. "Having once known that the Atman alone, and nothing else, exists, desiring what, or for whose desire, shall you suffer misery about the body?" (Brihadâranyaka, IV. iv. 12.)

I feel as if I had my share of experience in what they call "work". I am finished, I am longing now to get out. "Out of thousands, but one strives to attain the Goal. And even of those who struggle hard, but few attain" (Gita, VII. 3); for the senses are powerful, they drag men down.

"A good world", "a happy world", and "social progress", are all terms equally intelligible with "hot ice" or "dark light". If it were good, it would not be the world. The soul foolishly thinks of manifesting the Infinite in finite matter, Intelligence through gross particles; but at last it finds out its error and tries to escape. This going-back is the beginning of religion, and its method, destruction of self, that is, love. Not love for wife or child or anybody else, but love for everything else except this little self. Never be deluded by the tall talk, of which you will hear so much in America, about "human progress" and such stuff. There is no progress without corresponding digression. In one society there is one set of evils; in another, another. So with periods of history. In the Middle Ages, there were more robbers, now more cheats. At one period there is less idea of married life; at another, more prostitution. In one, more physical agony; in another, a thousandfold more mental. So with knowledge. Did not gravitation already exist in nature before it was observed and named? Then what difference does it make to know that it exists? Are you happier than the Red Indians?

The only knowledge that is of any value is to know that all this is humbug. But few, very few, will ever know this. "Know the Atman alone, and give up all other vain words." This is the only knowledge we gain from all this knocking about the universe. This is the only work, to call upon mankind to "Awake, arise, and stop not till the goal is reached". It is renunciation, Tyâga, that is meant by religion, and nothing else.

Ishwara is the sum total of individuals; yet He Himself also is an individual in the same way as the human body is a unit, of which each cell is an individual. Samashti or the Collective is God. Vyashti or the component is the soul of Jiva. The existence of Ishwara, therefore, depends on that of Jiva, as the body on the cell, and vice versa. Jiva, and Ishwara are co-existent beings. As long as the one exists, the other also must. Again, since in all the higher spheres, except on our earth, the amount of good is vastly in excess of the amount of bad, the sum total or Ishwara may be said to be All-good, Almighty, and Omniscient. These are obvious qualities, and need no argument to prove, from the very fact of totality.

Brahman is beyond both of these, and is not a state. It is the only unit not composed of many units. It is the principle which runs through all, from a cell to God, and without which nothing can exist. Whatever is real is that principle or Brahman. When I think "I am Brahman", then I alone exist. It is so also when you so think, and so on. Each one is the whole of that principle…

A few days ago, I felt a sudden irresistible desire to write to Kripananda. Perhaps he was unhappy and thinking of me. So I wrote him a warm letter. Today from the American news, I see why it was so. I sent him flowers gathered near the glaciers. Ask Miss Waldo to send him some money and plenty of love. Love never dies. The love of the father never dies, whatever the children may do or be. He is my child. He has the same or more share in my love and help, now that he is in misery.

Yours with blessings,
Vivekananda.

1896.63 — BLESSESD AND BELOVED

To Mr. E. T. Sturdy:

Grand Hotel, SAAS FEE,
Valais, Switzerland,
8th August, 1896.

BLESSED AND BELOVED,

A large packet of letters came along with yours. Herewith I send you the letter written to me by Max Müller. It is very kind and good of him.

Miss Müller thinks that she will go away very soon to England. In that case I will not be able to go to Berne for that Purity Congress I have promised. Only if the Seviers consent to take me along, I will go to Kiel and write to you before. The Seviers are good and kind, but I have no right to take advantage of their generosity. Nor can I take the same of Miss Müller, as the expenses there are frightful. As such, I think it best to give up the Berne Congress, as it will come in the middle of September, a long way off.

I am thinking, therefore, of going towards Germany, ending in Kiel, and thence back to England.

Bala Gangadhara Tilak (Mr. Tilak) is the name and Orion that of the book.

Yours,
Vivekananda.

PS — There is also one by Jacobi — perhaps translated on the same lines and with the same conclusions.

PS — I hope you will ask Miss Müller's opinion about the lodgings and the Hall, as I am afraid she will be very displeased if she and others are not consulted.

Miss Müller telegraphed to Prof. Deussen last night; the reply came this morning, 9th August, welcoming me; I am to be in Kiel at Deussen's on the 10th September. So where will you meet me? At Kiel? Miss Müller goes to England from Switzerland. I am going with the Seviers to Kiel. I will be there on the 10th September.

PS — I have not fixed yet anything about the lecture. I have no time to read. The Salem Society most probably is a Hindu community and no faddists.

1896.64 — ALASINGA

Switzerland,
8th August, 1896.

DEAR ALASINGA,

Since writing to you a few days ago I have found my way to let you know that I am in a position to do this for the Brahmavadin. I will give you Rs. 100 a month for a year or two, i.e. £60 or £70 a year, i.e. as much as would cover Rs. 100 a month. That will set you free to work for the Brahmavadin and make it a better success. Mr. Mani Iyer and a few friends can help in raising fund that would cover the printing etc. What is the income from subscription? Can these be employed to pay the contributors and get a fine series of articles? It is not necessary that everybody should understand all that is written in the Brahmavadin, but that they must subscribe from patriotism and good Karma — the Hindus I mean.

Several things are necessary. First there should be strict integrity. Not that I even hint that any of you would digress from it, but the Hindus have a peculiar slovenliness in business matters, not being sufficiently methodical and strict in keeping accounts etc.

Secondly, entire devotion to the cause, knowing that your salvation depends upon making the Brahmavadin a success. Let this paper be your Ishtadevata, and then you will see how success comes. I have already sent for Abhedânanda from India. I hope there will be no delay with him as it was with the other Swami. On receipt of this letter you send me a clear account of all the income and the expenses of the Brahmavadin so that I may judge from it what best can be done. Remember that perfect purity, disinterestedness, and obedience to the Guru are the secret of all success...

A big foreign circulation of a religious paper is impossible. It must be supported by the Hindus if they have any sense of virtue or gratitude left to them.

By the by, Mrs. Annie Besant invited me to speak at her Lodge, on Bhakti. I lectured there one night. Col. Olcott also was there. I did it to show my sympathy for all sects... Our countrymen must remember that in things of the Spirit we are the teachers, and not foreigners — but in things of the world we ought to learn from them.

I have read Max Müller's article, which is a good one, considering that when he wrote it, six months ago, he had no material except Mazoomdar's leaflet. Now he writes me a long and nice letter offering to write a book on Shri Ramakrishna. I have already supplied him with much material, but a good deal more is needed from India.

Work on! Hold on! Be brave! Dare anything and everything!

...It is all misery, this Samsâra, don't you see!

Yours with blessings and love,
Vivekananda.

1896.65 — BLESSED AND BELOVED

To Mr. E. T. Sturdy:

Switzerland,
12th August, 1896.

BLESSED AND BELOVED,

Today I received a letter from America, which I send to you. I have written them that my idea of course is concentration, at least for the present beginning. I have also suggested them that instead of having too many papers, they may start by putting in a few sheets in The Brahmavadin — written in America — and raise the subscription a little which will cover the American expenses. Do not know what they will do.

We will start from here towards Germany next week. Miss Müller goes to England as soon as we have crossed over to Germany.

Capt. and Mrs. Sevier and myself will expect you at Kiel.

I haven't yet written anything nor read anything. I am indeed taking a good rest. Do not be anxious, you will have the article ready. I had a letter from the Math stating that the other Swami is ready to start. He will, I am sure, be just the man you want. He is one of the best Sanskrit scholars we have … and as I hear, he has improved his English much. I had a number of newspaper cuttings from America about Saradananda — I hear from them that he has done very well there. America is a good training ground to bring out all that is in a man. There is such a sympathy in the air. I had letters from Goodwin and Saradananda. S. sends his love to you and Mrs. Sturdy and the baby.

With everlasting love and blessings,
Vivekananda.

1896.66 — SHASHI[1]

Lake Lucerne, Switzerland,
23rd August, 1896.

MY DEAR SHASHI,

Today I received a letter from Ramdayal Babu, in which he writes that many public women attend the Ramakrishna anniversary festival at Dakshineswar, which makes many less inclined to go there. Moreover, in his opinion one day should be appointed for men and another for women. My decision on the point is this:

1. If public women are not allowed to go to such a great place of pilgrimage as Dakshineswar, where else shall they go to? It is for the sinful that the Lord mani-

1 Translated from Bengali.

fests Himself specially, not so much for the virtuous.

2. Let distinctions of sex, caste, wealth, learning, and the whole host of them, which are so many gateways to hell, be confined to the world alone. If such distinctions persist in holy places of pilgrimage, where then lies the difference between them and hell itself?

3. Ours is a gigantic City of Jagannâtha, where those who have sinned and those who have not, the saintly and the vicious, men and women and children irrespective of age, all have equal right. That for one day at least in the year thousand of men and women get rid of the sense of sin and ideas of distinction and sing and hear the name of the Lord, is in itself a supreme good.

4. If even in a place of pilgrimage people's tendency to evil be not curbed for one day, the fault lies with you, not them. Create such a huge tidal wave of spirituality that whatever people come near will be swept away.

5. Those who, even in a chapel, would think this is a public woman, that man is of a low caste, a third is poor, and yet another belongs to the masses — the less be the number of such people (that is, whom you call gentlemen) the better. Will they who look to the caste, sex, or profession of Bhaktas appreciate our Lord? I pray to the Lord that hundreds of public women may come and bow their heads at His feet; it does not matter if not one gentleman comes. Come public women, come drunkards, come thieves and all — His Gate is open to all. "It is easier for a camel to pass through the eye of a needle than for a rich man to enter the Kingdom of God." Never let such cruel, demoniacal ideas have a place in your mind.

6. But then some social vigilance is needed. How are we to do that? A few men (old men, preferably) should take charge as the warders for the day. They will make circuits round the scene of the festival, and in case they find any man or woman showing impropriety of speech or conduct, they will at once expel them from the garden. But so long as they behave like good men and women, they are Bhaktas and are to be respected — be they men or women, honest citizens or unchaste.

I am at present travelling in Switzerland, and shall soon go to Germany, to see Professor Deussen. I shall return to England from there about the 23rd or 24th September, and the next winter will find me back in my country.

My love to you and all.

Yours etc.,
Vivekananda.

1896.67 — MRS. BULL

Lucerne, Switzerland,
23rd August, 1896.

DEAR MRS. BULL,

    I received your last letter today. By this time you must have received my receipt for £5 you sent. I do not know what membership you mean. I have no objection to have my name to be put on the list of membership of any society. As for Sturdy, I do not know what his opinions are. I am now travelling in Switzerland; from hence I go to Germany, then to England, and next winter to India. I am very glad to hear that Saradananda and Goodwin are doing good work in the U.S. As for me, I do not lay any claim to that £500 for any work. I think I have worked enough. I am now going to retire. I have sent for another man from India who will join me next month. I have begun the work, let others work it out. So you see, to set the work going I had to touch money and property, for a time. Now I am sure my part of the work is done, and I have no more interest in Vedanta or any philosophy in the world or the work itself. I am getting ready to depart to return no more to this hell, this world. Even its religious utility is beginning to pall me. May Mother gather me soon to Herself never to come back any more! These works, and doing good, etc., are just a little exercise to cleanse the mind. I had enough of it. This world will be world ever and always. What we are, so we see it. Who works? Whose work? There is no world. It is God Himself. In delusion we call it world. Neither I nor thou nor you — it is all He the Lord, all One. So I do not want anything to do about money matters from this time. It is your money. You spend what comes to you just as you like, and blessings follow you.

Yours in the Lord,
Vivekananda.

PS — I have entire sympathy with the work of Dr. Janes and have written him so. If Goodwin and Saradananda can speed the work in U.S., Godspeed to them. They are in no way bound to me or to Sturdy or to anybody else. It was an awful mistake in the Greenacre programme that it was printed that Saradananda was there by the kind permission (leave of absence from England) of Sturdy. Who is Sturdy or anybody else to permit a Sannyasin? Sturdy himself laughed at it and was sorry too. It was a piece of folly. Nothing short of that. It was an insult to Sturdy and would have proved serious for my work if it had reached India. Fortunately I tore all those notices to pieces and threw them into the gutter, and wondered whether it was the celebrated "Yankee" manners the English people delight in talking about. Even so, I am no master to any Sannyasin in this world. They do whatever it suits them, and if I can help them — that is all my connection with them. I have given up the bondage of iron, the family tie — I am not to take up the golden chain of religious brotherhood. I am free, must always be free. I wish everyone to be free — free as the air. If New York needs Vedanta, or Boston, or any other place in the U.S., it must receive them and keep them and provide for them. As for me, I am as good as retired. I have played my part in the world..

1896.68 — BLESSED AND BELOVED

Lucerne,
23rd August, 1896.

BLESSED AND BELOVED[1],

Today I received a letter from India written by Abhedânanda that in all probability he had started on the 11th August by the B.I.S.N., "S.S.Mombassa". He could not get an earlier steamer; else he would have started earlier. In all probability he would be able to secure a passage on the Mombassa. The Mombassa will reach London about the 15th of September. As you already know, Miss Müller changed the date of my visiting Deussen to the 19th September. I shall not be in London to receive Abhedananda. He is also coming without any warm clothing; but I am afraid by that time it will begin to cool in England, and he will require at least some underwear and an overcoat. You know all about these things much better than I. So kindly keep a look out for this Mombassa. I expect also another letter from him.

I am suffering from a very bad cold indeed. I hope by this time Mohin's money from the Raja has arrived to your care. If so, I do not want the money I gave him back. You may give him the whole of it.

I had some letters from Goodwin and Sâradânanda. They are doing well. Also one from Mrs. Bull regretting that you and I could not be corresponding members of some Society, she is founding at Cambridge. I do remember to have written to her about your and my non-acquiescence in this membership. I have not yet been able to write even a line. I had not a moment's time even to read, climbing up hill and going down dale all the time. We will have to begin the march again in a few days. Kindly give my love to Mohin and Fox when you see them next.

With love to all our friends, Yours ever,
Vivekananda.

---

1. E. T. Sturdy.

1896.69 — NANJUNDA RAO

Switzerland,
26th August, 1896.

DEAR NANJUNDA RAO,

I have just now got your letter. I am on the move. I have been doing a great deal of mountain-climbing and glacier-crossing in the Alps. Now I am going to Germany. I have an invitation from Prof. Deussen to visit him at Kiel. From thence I go back to England. Possibly I will return to India this winter.

What I objected to in the design for the *Prabuddha* Bhârata was not only its tawdriness, but the crowding in of a number of figures without any purpose. A design should be simple, symbolical, and condensed. I will try to make a design for Prabuddha Bharata in London and send it over to you…

The work is going on beautifully, I am very glad to say… I will give you one advice however. All combined efforts in India sink under the weight of one iniquity — we have not yet developed strict business principles. Business is business, in the highest sense, and no friendship — or as the Hindu proverb says "eye-shame" — should be there. One should keep the clearest account of everything in one's charge — and never, never apply the funds intended for one thing to any other use whatsoever — even if one starves the next moment. This is business integrity. Next, energy unfailing. Whatever you do let that be your worship for the time. Let this paper be your God for the time, and you will succeed.

When you have succeeded in this paper, start vernacular ones on the same lines in Tamil, Telugu, Canarese, etc. We must reach the masses. The Madrasis are good, energetic, and all that, but the land of Shankarâchârya has lost the spirit of renunciation, it seems.

My children must plunge into the breach, must renounce the world — then the firm foundation will be laid.

Go on bravely — never mind about designs and other details at present — "With the horse will come the reins". Work unto death — I am with you, and when I am gone, my spirit will work with you. This life comes and goes — wealth, fame, enjoyments are only of a few days. It is better, far better to die on the field of duty, preaching the truth, than to die like a worldly worm. Advance!

Yours with all love and blessings,
Vivekananda.

Germany

1896.70 — FRIEND

To Mr. E. T. Sturdy:

Kiel, Germany,
10th September, 1896.

DEAR FRIEND,

I have at last seen Prof. Deussen... The whole of yesterday was spent very nicely with the Professor, sight-seeing and discussing about the Vedanta.

He is what I should call "a warring Advaitist". No compromise with anything else. "Ishwara" is his bug-bear. He would have none of it if he could. He is very much delighted with the idea of your magazine and wants to confer with you on these subjects in London, where he is shortly going...

Yours in the Lord,
Vivekananda.

England

1896.71 — SISTER

Airlie Lodge, Ridgeway Gardens,
Wimbledon, England,
17th Sept, 1896.

DEAR SISTER, (Miss Harriet Hale)

Your very welcome news reached me just now, on my return here from Switzerland. I am very, very happy to learn that at last you have thought it better to change your mind about the felicity of "Old Maids Home". You are perfectly right now — marriage is the truest goal for ninety-nine per cent of the human race, and they will live the happiest life as soon as they have learnt and are ready to abide by the eternal lesson — that we are bound to bear and forbear and that life to every one must be a compromise.

Believe me, dear Harriet, perfect life is a contradiction in terms. Therefore we must always expect to find things not up to our highest ideal. Knowing this, we are bound to make the best of everything. From what I know of you, you have the calm power which bears and forbears to a great degree, and therefore I am safe to prophesy that your married life will be very happy.

All blessings attend you and your fiancé and may the Lord make him always remember what good fortune was his in getting such a wife as you — good, intelligent, loving, and beautiful. I am afraid it is impossible for me to cross the Atlantic so soon. I wish I could, to see your marriage.

The best I can do in the circumstances is to quote from one of our books: "May you always enjoy the undivided love of your husband, helping him in attaining all that is desirable in this life, and when you have seen your children's children, and the drama of life is nearing its end, may you help each other in reaching that infinite ocean of Existence, Knowledge, and Bliss, at the touch of whose waters all distinctions melt away and we are all one!" (A reminiscence of Kalidasa's Shakuntalam, where Kanva gives his benedictions to Shakuntalâ on the eve of her departure to her husband's place.)

"May you be like Umâ, chaste and pure throughout life — may your husband be like Shiva, whose life was in Uma!"

Your loving brother,
Vivekananda.

1896.72 — SISTER

To Miss Mary Hale:

Airlie Lodge, Ridgeway Gardens,
Wimbledon, England,
17th September, 1896.

DEAR SISTER,

Today I reached London, after my two months of climbing and walking and glacier seeing in Switzerland. One good it has done me — a few pounds of unnecessary adipose tissue have returned back to the gaseous state. Well, there is no safety even in that, for the solid body of this birth has taken a fancy to outstrip the mind towards infinite expansion. If it goes on this way, I would have soon to lose all personal identity even in the flesh — at least to all the rest of the world.

It is impossible to express my joy in words at the good news contained in Harriet's letter. I have written to her today. I am sorry I cannot come over to see her married, but I will be present in "fine body" with all good wishes and blessings. Well, I am expecting such news from you and other sisters to make my joy complete. Now, my dear Mary, I will tell you a great lesson I have learnt in this life. It is this: "The higher is your ideal, the more miserable you are"; for such a thing as an ideal cannot be attained in the world, or in this life even. He who wants perfection in the world is a madman, for it cannot be.

How can you find the Infinite in the finite? Therefore I tell you, Harriet will have a most blessed and happy life, because she is not so imaginative and sentimental as to make a fool of herself. She has enough of sentiment as to make life sweet, and enough of common sense and gentleness as to soften the hard points in life which must come to everyone. So has Harriet McKindley in a still higher degree. She is just the girl to make the best of wives, only this world is so full of idiots that very few can penetrate beyond the flesh! As for you and Isabelle, I will tell you the truth, and my "language is plain".

You, Mary, are like a mettlesome Arab — grand, splendid. You will make a splendid queen — physically, mentally. You will shine alongside of a dashing, bold, adventurous, heroic husband; but, my dear sister, you will make one of the worst of wives. You will take the life out of our easy-going, practical, plodding husbands of the everyday world. Mind, my sister, although it is true that there is more romance in actual life than in any novel, yet it is few and far between. Therefore my advice to you is that until you bring down your ideals to a more practical level, you ought not to marry. If you do, the result will be misery for both of you. In a few months you will lose all regard for a commonplace, good, nice, young man, and then life will become insipid. As to sister Isabelle, she has the same temperament as you; only this kindergarten has taught her a good lesson of patience and forbearance. Perhaps she will make a good wife.

There are two sorts of persons in the world. The one — strong-nerved, quiet, yielding to nature, not given to much imagination, yet good, kind, sweet, etc. For such is this world; they alone are born to be happy. There are others again with high-strung nerves, tremendously imaginative, with intense feeling, always going high one moment and coming down the next. For them there is no happiness. The first class will have almost an even tenor of happiness; the last will have to run between ecstasy and misery. But of these alone what we call geniuses are made. There is some truth in the recent theory that "genius is a sort madness".

Now, persons of this class if they want to be great, they must fight to finish — clear out the deck for battle. No encumbrance — no marriage, no children, no undue attachment to anything except the one idea, and live and die for that. I am a person of this sort. I have taken up the one idea of "Vedanta" and I have "cleared the deck for action". You and Isabelle are made of this metal; but let me tell you, though it is hard, you are spoiling your lives in vain. Either take up one idea, clear the deck, and to it dedicate the life; or be contented and practical; lower the ideal, marry, and have a happy life. Either "Bhoga" or "Yoga" — either enjoy this life, or give up and be a Yogi; none can have both in one. Now or never, select quick. "He who is very particular gets nothing", says the proverb. Now sincerely and really and for ever determine to "clear the deck for fight", take up anything, philosophy or science or religion or literature, and let that be your God for the rest of your life. Achieve happiness or achieve greatness. I have no sympathy with you and Isabelle; you are neither for this nor for that. I wish to see you happy, as Harriet has well chosen, or great. Eating, drinking, dressing, and society nonsense are not things to throw a life upon — especially you, Mary. You are rusting away a splendid brain and abilities, for which there is not the least excuse. You must have ambition to be great. I know you will take these rather harsh remarks from me in the right spirit knowing I like you really as much or more than what I call you, my sisters. I had long had a mind to tell you this, and as experience is gathering I feel like telling you. The joyful news from Harriet urged me to tell you this. I will be overjoyed to hear that you are married also and happy, so far as happiness can be had here, or would like to hear of you as doing great deeds.

I had a pleasant visit with Prof. Deussen in Germany. I am sure you have heard of him as the greatest living German philosopher. He and I travelled together to England and today came together to see my friend here with whom I am to stop for the rest of my stay in England. He (Deussen) is very fond of talking Sanskrit and is the only Sanskrit scholar in the West who can talk in it. As he wants to get a practice, he never talks to me in any other language but Sanskrit.

I have come over here amongst my friends, shall work for a few weeks, and then go back to India in the winter.

Ever your loving brother,
Vivekananda.

1896.73 — ALASINGA

C/O Miss H. Müller,
Airlie Lodge, Ridgeway Gardens,
Wimbledon, England,
22nd September, 1896.

DEAR ALASINGA,

I am sure you have got the article on Ramakrishna, I sent you, by Max Müller. Do not be sorry, he does not mention me there at all, as it was written six months before he knew me. And then who cares whom he mentions, if he is right in the main point. I had a beautiful time with Prof. Deussen in Germany. Later, he and I came together to London, and we have already become great friends.

I am soon sending you an article on him. Only pray do not put that old-fashioned "Dear Sir" before my articles. Have you seen the Râja-Yoga book yet? I will try to send you a design for the coming year. I send you a Daily News article on a book of travel written by the Czar of Russia. The paragraph in which he speaks of India as the land of spirituality and wisdom, you ought to quote in your paper and send the article to the Indian Mirror.

You are very welcome to publish the Jnâna-Yoga lectures, as well as Dr. (Nanjunda Rao) in his Awakened India — only the simpler ones. They have to be very carefully gone through and all repetitions and contradictions taken out. I am sure I will now have more time to write. Work on with energy.

With love to all.

Yours,
Vivekananda.

PS — I have marked the passage to be quoted, the rest of course is useless for a paper.

I do not think it would be good just now to make the paper a monthly one yet, unless you are sure of giving a good bulk. As it is now, the bulk and the matter are all very poor. There is yet a vast untrodden field, namely — the writing of the lives and works of Tulasidâsa, Kabir, Nânak, and of the saints of Southern India. They should be written in a thorough-going, scholarly style, and not in a slipshod, slovenly way. In fact, the ideal of the paper, apart from the preaching of Vedanta, should be to make it a magazine of Indian research and scholarship, of course, bearing on religion. You must approach the best writers and get carefully-written articles from their pen. Work on with all energy.

1896.74 — ALASINGA

14 Grey Coat Gardens,
Westminster, London.
1896.

DEAR ALASINGA,

I have returned about three weeks from Switzerland but could not write you further before. I have sent you by last mail a paper on Paul Deussen of Kiel. Sturdy's plan about the magazine is still hanging fire. As you see, I halve left the St. George's Road place. We have a lecture hall at 39 Victoria Street. C/o E. T. Sturdy will always reach me for a year to come. The rooms at Grey Coat Gardens are only lodgings for self and the other Swami taken for three mouths only. The work in London is growing apace, the classes are becoming bigger as they go on. I have no doubt this will go on increasing at this rate and the English people are steady and loyal. Of course, as soon as I leave, most of this fabric will tumble down. Something will happen. Some strong man will arise to take it up. The Lord knows what is good. In America there is room for twenty preachers on the Vedanta and Yoga. Where to get these preachers and where also the money to bring them? Half the United States can be conquered in ten years, given a number of strong and genuine men. Where are they? We are all boobies over there! Selfish cowards, with our nonsense of lip-patriotism, orthodoxy, and boasted religious feeling! The Madrasis have more of go and steadiness, but every fool is married. Marriage! Marriage! Marriage!... Then the way our boys are married nowadays!... It is very good to aspire to be a nonattached householder; but what we want in Madras is not that just now — but non-marriage...

My child, what I want is muscles of iron and nerves of steel, inside which dwells a mind of the same material as that of which the thunderbolt is made. Strength, manhood, Kshatra-Virya + Brahma-Teja. Our beautiful hopeful boys — they have everything, only if they are not slaughtered by the millions at the altar of this brutality they call marriage. O Lord, hear my wails! Madras will then awake when at least one hundred of its very heart's blood, in the form of its educated young men, will stand aside from the world, gird their loins, and be ready to fight the battle of truth, marching on from country to country. One blow struck outside of India is equal to a hundred thousand struck within. Well, all will come if the Lord wills it.

Miss Müller was the person who offered that money I promised. I have told her about your new proposal. She is thinking about it. In the meanwhile I think it is better to give her some work. She has consented to be the agent for the Brahmavadin and Awakened India. Will you write to her about it? Her address is Airlie Lodge, Ridgeway Gardens, Wimbledon, England. I was living with her over there for the last few weeks. But the London work cannot go on without my living in London. As such I have changed quarters. I am sorry it has chagrined Miss Müller a bit. Cannot help. Her full name is Miss Henrietta Müller. Max Müller is getting very friendly. I am soon going to deliver two lectures at Oxford.

I am busy writing something big on the Vedanta philosophy. I am busy collecting passages from the various Vedas bearing on the Vedanta in its threefold aspect. You can help me by getting someone to collect passages bearing on, first the Advaitic idea, then the Vishishtâdvaitic, and the Dvaitic from the Samhitâs, the Brâhmanas, the Upanishads, and the Purânas. They should be classified and very legibly written with the name and chapter of the book, in each case. It would be a pity to leave the West without leaving something of the philosophy in book form.

There was a book published in Mysore in Tamil characters, comprising all the one hundred and eight Upanishads; I saw it in Professor Deussen's library. Is there a reprint of the same in Devanâgari? If so, send me a copy. If not, send me the Tamil edition, and also write on a sheet the Tamil letters and compounds, and all juxtaposed with its Nagari equivalents, so that I may learn the Tamil letters.

Mr. Satyanathan, whom I met in London the other day, said that there has been a friendly review of my Râja-Yoga book in the *Madras Mail*, the chief Anglo-Indian paper in Madras. The leading physiologist in America, I hear, has been charmed with my speculations. At the same time, there have been some in England, who ridiculed my ideas. Good! My speculations of course are awfully bold; a good deal of them will ever remain meaningless; but there are hints in it which the physiologists had better taken up earlier. Nevertheless, I am quite satisfied with the result. "Let them talk badly of me if they please, but let them talk", is my motto.

In England, of course, they are gentlemen and never talk the rot I had in America. Then again the English missionaries you see over there are nearly all of them from the dissenters. They are not from the gentleman class in England. The gentlemen here, who are religious; all belong to the English Church. The dissenters have very little voice in England and no education. I never hear of those people here against whom you time to time warn me. They are unknown here and dare not talk nonsense. I hope Ram K. Naidu is already in Madras, and you are enjoying good health.

Persevere on, my brave lads. We have only just begun. Never despond! Never say enough!... As soon as a man comes over to the West and sees different nations, his eyes open. This way I get strong workers—not by talking, but by practically showing what we have in India and what we have not. I wish at least that a million Hindus had travelled all over the world!

Yours ever with love,
Vivekananda.

1896.75 — ALASINGA

C/O E. T. Sturdy, Esq., 39 Victoria Street, London,
28th October, 1896.

DEAR ALASINGA,

... I am not yet sure what month I shall reach India. I will write later about it. The new Swami[1] delivered his maiden speech yesterday at a friendly society's meeting. It was good and I liked it; he has the making of a good speaker in him, I am sure.

... You have not yet brought out the — . . Again, books must be cheap for India to have a large sale; the types must be bigger to satisfy the public ... You can very well get out a cheap edition of — if you like. I have not reserved any copyright on it purposely. You have missed a good opportunity by not getting out the — book earlier, but we Hindus are so slow that when we have done a work, the opportunity has already passed away, and thus we are the losers. Your — book came out after a year's talk! Did you think the Western people would wait for it till Doomsday? You have lost three-fourths of the sale by this delay ... That Haramohan is a fool, slower than you, and his printing is diabolical. There is no use in publishing books that way; it is cheating the public, and should not be done. I shall most probably return to India accompanied by Mr. and Mrs. Sevier, Miss Müller, and Mr. Goodwin. Mr. and Mrs. Sevier are probably going to settle in Almora at least for some time, and Goodwin is going to become a Sannyâsin. He of course will travel with me. It is he to whom we owe all our books. He took shorthand notes of my lectures, which enabled the books to be published ... All these lectures were delivered on the spur of the moment, without the least preparation, and as such, they should be carefully revised and edited ... Goodwin will have to live with me ... He is a strict vegetarian.

Yours with love,
Vivekananda.

PS — I have sent a little note to the Indian Mirror today about Dr. Barrows and how he should be welcomed. You also write some good words of welcome for him in the Brahmavadin. All here send love.

1896.76 — INDIAN MIRROR

London,
28th October, 1896.

[On the eve of the lecture-tour of Dr. Barrows in India at the end of 1896, Swami Vivekananda in a letter to the Indian Mirror, *Calcutta, introduced the distinguished visitor to his countrymen and advised them to give him a fitting reception. He wrote among other things as follows:]*

---

1 Swami Abhedananda.

Dr. Barrows was the ablest lieutenant Mr. C. Boney could have selected to carry out successfully his great plan of the Congresses at the World's Fair, and it is now a matter of history how one of these Congresses scored a unique distinction under the leadership of Dr. Barrows.

It was the great courage, untiring industry, unruffled patience, and never-failing courtesy of Dr. Barrows that made the Parliament a grand success.

India, its people, and their thoughts have been brought more prominently before the world than ever before by that wonderful gathering at Chicago, and that national benefit we certainly owe to Dr. Barrows more than to any other man at that meeting.

Moreover, he comes to us in the sacred name of religion, in the name of one of the great teachers of mankind, and I am sure, his exposition of the system of the Prophet of Nazareth would be extremely liberal and elevating. The Christ-power this man intends to bring to India is not that of the intolerant, dominant superior, with heart full of contempt for everything else but its own self, but that of a brother who craves for a brother's place as a co-worker of the various powers already working in India. Above all, we must remember that gratitude and hospitality are the peculiar characteristics of Indian humanity; and as such, I would beg my countrymen to behave in such a manner that this stranger from the other side of the globe may find that in the midst of all our misery, our poverty, and degradation, the heart beats as warm as of yore, when the "wealth of Ind" was the proverb of nations and India was the land of the "Aryas".

1896.77 — CHRISTINA

To Sister Christine:

> Airlie Lodge, Ridgeway Gardens, Wimbledon, England,
> October 6, 1896.

DEAR CHRISTINA,

I am sure you got my letter from Switzerland.

I am now in London, back after having travelled through Germany and Holland.

How are things going with you? Had you a nice summer? How are you physically and spiritually? How is Mrs. Fhunkey [Funke] and all the other friends? Have you any news of Baby? Where is Kr [Kripananda] and what is he doing now?

I have another Sannyasin over here with me now, who will work here whilst I am away to India, where I go this winter.

I will write to you in extenso later; tonight it is so late and I am so weary.

With all love and blessings,

Yours,
Vivekananda.

1896.78 — JOE JOE

C/O Miss Muller,
Airlie Lodge, Ridgeway Gardens,
Wimbledon, England,
7th October, 1896.

DEAR SISTER, (Miss Harriet Hale)

Once more in London, dear Joe Joe, and the classes have begun already. Instinctively I looked about for one familiar face which never had a line of discouragement, never changed, but was always helpful, cheerful, and strengthening — and my mind conjured up that face before me, in spite of a few thousand miles of space. For what is space in the realm of spirit? Well, you are gone to your home of rest and peace. For me, ever-increasing mad work; yet I have your blessings with me always, have I not? My natural tendency is to go into a cave and be quiet, but a fate behind pushes me forward and I go. Whoever could resist fate?

Why did not Christ say in the Sermon on the Mount, "Blessed are they that are always cheerful and always hopeful for they have already the kingdom of heaven"? I am sure, He must have said it, He with the sorrows of a whole world in His heart, He who likened the saintly soul with the child — but it was not noted down; of a thousand things they noted down only one, I mean, remembered.

Most of our friends came — one of the Galsworthys too — i.e. the married daughter. Mrs. Galsworthy could not come today; it was very short notice. We have a hall now, a pretty big one holding about 200 or more. There is a big corner which will be fitted up as the Library. I have another man from India now to help me.

I enjoyed Switzerland immensely, also Germany. Prof. Deussen was very kind — we came together to London and had great fun here. Prof. Max Müller is very, very friendly too. In all, the English work is becoming solid — and respectable too, seeing that great scholars are sympathising. Probably I go to India this winter with some English friends. So far about my own sweet self.

Now what about the holy family? Everything is going on first-rate, I am sure. You must have heard of Fox by this time. I am afraid I rather made him dejected the day before he sailed by telling him that he could not marry Mabel, until he began to earn a good deal of money! Is Mabel with you now? Give her my love. Also give me your present address.

How is Mother? Frankincense, same solid sterling gold as ever, I am sure. Alberta, working at her music and languages, laughing a good deal and eating a good many apples as usual? By the by, I now live mostly on fruits and nuts. They seem to agree with me well. If ever the old doctor, with "land" up somewhere, comes to see you, you may confide to him this secret. I have lost a good deal of my fat. But on days I lecture, I have to go on solid food. How is Hollis? I never saw a sweeter boy — may all blessings ever attend him through life.

I hear your friend Cola is lecturing on Zoroastrian philosophy—surely the stars are not smiling on him. What about your Miss Andreas and our Yoganandla? What news about the brotherhood of the ZZZ's and our Mrs. (forgotten!)? I hear that half a shipload of Hindus and Buddhists and Mohammedans and Brotherhoods and what not have entered the U.S., and another cargo of Mahatma-seekers, evangelists etc. have entered India! Good. India and the U.S. seem to be two countries for religious enterprise. Have a care, Joe; the heathen corruption is dreadful. I met Madam Sterling in the street today. She does not come any more for my lectures, good for her. Too much of philosophy is not good. Do you remember that lady who used to come to every meeting too late to hear a word but button-holed me immediately after and kept me talking, till a battle of Waterloo would be raging in my internal economy through hunger? She came. They are all coming and more. That is cheering.

It is getting late in the night. So goodnight, Joe. (Is strict etiquette to be followed in New York too?) And Lord bless you ever and ever.

"Man's all-wise maker, wishing to create a faultless form whose matchless symmetry should far transcend creation's choicest works, did call together by his mighty will, and garner up in his eternal mind, a bright assemblage of all lovely things, and then, as in a picture, fashioned them into one perfect and ideal form. Such the divine, the wondrous prototype whence her fair shape was moulded into being." (Shakuntalam by Kalidasa, translated by Monier Williams).

That is you, Joe Joe; only I would add, the same the creator did with all purity and nobility and other qualities and then Joe was made.

Ever yours, with love and blessings,
Vivekananda.

PS—Mrs. & Mr. Sevier in whose house (flat) I am writing now, send their kindest regards.

1896.79—MISS S. E. WALDO

Airlie Lodge, Ridgeway Gardens,
Wimbledon,
8th October, 1896.

DEAR, (MISS S. E. WALDO)

...I had a fine rest in Switzerland and made a great friend of Prof. Paul Deussen. My European work in fact is becoming more satisfactory to me than any other work, and it tells immensely on India. The London classes were resumed, and today is the opening lecture. I now have a hall to myself holding two hundred or more...

You know of course the steadiness of the English; they are the least jealous of each other of all nations, and that is why they dominate the world. They have solved the secret of obedience without slavish cringing — great freedom with great law-abidingness.

I know very little of the young man R—. He is a Bengali and can teach a little Sanskrit. You know my settled doctrine. I do not trust any one who has not conquered "lust and gold". You may try him in theoretical subjects, but keep him off from teaching Raja-Yoga — that is a dangerous game except for the regularly trained to play at. Of Saradananda, the blessing of the greatest Yogi of modern India is on him — and there is no danger. Why do you not begin to teach? ... You have a thousand times more philosophy than this boy R—. Send notices to the class and hold regular talks and lectures.

I will be thousand times more pleased to see one of you start than any number of Hindus securing success in America — even one of my brethren. "Man wants Victory from everywhere, but defeat from his own children" ... Make a blaze! Make a blaze!

With all love and blessings,
Vivekananda.

1896.80 — MRS. BULL

Wimbledon,
8th October, 1896.

DEAR MRS. BULL,

... I met in Germany Prof. Deussen. I was his guest at Kiel and we travelled together to London and had some very pleasant meetings here ... Although I am in full sympathy with the various branches of religious and social work, I find that specification of work is absolutely necessary. Our special branch is to preach Vedanta. Helping in other work should be subservient to that one ideal. I hope you will inculcate this in the mind of Saradananda very strongly.

Did you read Max Müller's article on Ramakrishna? ... Things are working very favourably here in England. The work is not only popular but appreciated.

Yours affly.,
Vivekananda.

1896.81 — NOBLE

To Sister Nivedita:

> 14, Greycoat Gardens, Westminster,
> October 29, 1896.

DEAR MISS [MARGARET] NOBLE,

I will be at yours on Friday next, at 4 p.m.

I did not know of any arrangements made to meet anybody Friday last, hence my absence.

> Yours,
> Vivekananda.

1896.82 — MARY

> 14 Greycoat Gardens, Westminster,
> London, England,
> 1st November, 1896.

MY DEAR MARY, (Miss Mary Hale)

"Silver and gold", my dear Mary, "have I none; but such as I have give I thee'" freely, and that is the knowledge that the goldness of gold, the silverness of silver, the manhood of man, the womanhood of woman, the reality of everything is the Lord — and that this Lord we are trying to realise from time without beginning in the objective, and in the attempt throwing up such "queer" creatures of our fancy as man, woman, child, body, mind, the earth, sun, moon, stars, the world, love, hate, property, wealth, etc.; also ghosts, devils, angels and gods, God etc.

The fact being that the Lord is in us, we are He, the eternal subject, the real ego, never to be objectified, and that all this objectifying process is mere waste of time and talent. When the soul becomes aware of this, it gives up objectifying and falls back more and more upon the subjective. This is the evolution, less and less in the body and more and more in the mind — man the highest form, meaning in Sanskrit manas, thought — the animal that thinks and not the animal that "senses" only. This is what in theology is called "renunciation". The formation of society, the institution of marriage, the love for children, our good works, morality, and ethics are all different forms of renunciation. All our lives in every society are the subjection of the will, the thirst, the desire. This surrender of the will or the fictitious self — or the desire to jump out of ourselves, as it were — the struggle still to objectify the subject — is the one phenomenon in this world of which all societies and social forms are various modes and stages. Love is the easiest and smoothest way towards the self-surrender or subjection of the will and hatred, the opposite.

People have been cajoled through various stories or superstitions of heavens and hells and Rulers above the sky, towards this one end of self-surrender. The philosopher does the same knowingly without superstition, by giving up desires.

An objective heaven or millennium therefore has existence only in the fancy — but a subjective one is already in existence. The musk-deer, after vain search for the cause of the scent of the musk, at last will have to find it in himself.

Objective society will always be a mixture of good and evil — objective life will always be followed by its shadow death, and the longer the life, the longer will also be the shadow. It is only when the sun is on our own head that there is no shadow. When God and good and everything else is in us, there is no evil. In objective life, however, every bullet has its billet — evil goes with every good as its shadow. Every improvement is coupled with an equal degradation. The reason being that good and evil are not two things but one, the difference being only in manifestation — one of degree, not kind.

Our very lives depend upon the death of others — plants or animals or bacilli! The other great mistake we often make is that good is taken as an ever-increasing item, whilst evil is a fixed quantity. From this it is argued that evil being diminished every day, there will come a time when good alone will remain. The fallacy lies in the assumption of a false premise. If good is increasing, so is evil. My desires have been much more than the desires of the masses among my race. My joys have been much greater than theirs — but my miseries a million times more intense The same constitution that makes you feel the least touch of good makes you feel the least of evil too. The same nerves that carry sensations of pleasure carry the sensations of pain too — and the same mind feels both. The progress of the world means more enjoyment and more misery too. This mixture of life and death, good and evil, knowledge and ignorance is what is called Maya — or the universal phenomenon. You may go on for eternity inside this net, seeking for happiness — you find much, and much evil too. To have good and no evil is childish nonsense. Two ways are left open — one by giving up all hope to take up the world as it is and bear the pangs and pains in the hope of a crumb of happiness now and then. The other, to give up the search for pleasure, knowing it to be pain in another form, and seek for truth — and those that dare try for truth succeed in finding that truth as ever present — present in themselves. Then we also discover how the same truth is manifesting itself both in our relative error and knowledge — we find also that the same truth is bliss which again is manifesting itself as good and evil, and with it also we find real existence which is manifesting itself as both death and life.

Thus we realise that all these phenomena are but the reflections, bifurcated or manifolded, of the one existence, truth-bliss-unity — my real Self and the reality of everything else. Then and then only is it possible to do good without evil, for such a soul has known and got the control of the material of which both good and evil are manufactured, and he alone can manifest one or the other as he likes, and we know he manifests only good. This is the Jivan-mukta — the living free — the goal of Vedanta as of all other philosophies.

Human society is in turn governed by the four castes — the priests, the soldiers, the traders, and the labourers. Each state has its glories as well as its defects. When the priest (Brahmin) rules, there is a tremendous exclusiveness on hereditary grounds; the persons of the priests and their descendants are hemmed in with all sorts of safeguards — none but they have any knowledge — none but they have the right to impart that knowledge. Its glory is that at this period is laid the foundation of sciences. The priests cultivate the mind, for through the mind they govern.

The military (Kshatriya) rule is tyrannical and cruel, but they are not exclusive; and during that period arts and social culture attain their height.

The commercial (Vaishya) rule comes next. It is awful in its silent crushing and blood-sucking power. Its advantage is, as the trader himself goes everywhere, he is a good disseminator of ideas collected during the two previous states. They are still less exclusive than the military, but culture begins to decay.

Last will come the labourer (Shudra) rule. Its advantages will be the distribution of physical comforts — its disadvantages, (perhaps) the lowering of culture. There will be a great distribution of ordinary education, but extraordinary geniuses will be less and less.

If it is possible to form a state in which the knowledge of the priest period, the culture of the military, the distributive spirit of the commercial, and the ideal of equality of the last can all be kept intact, minus their evils, it will be an deal state. But is it possible?

Yet the first three have had their day. Now is the time for the last — they must have it — none can resist it. I do not know all the difficulties about the gold or silver standards (nobody seems to know much as to that), but this much I see that the gold standard has been making the poor poorer, and the rich richer. Bryan was right when he said, "We refuse to be crucified on a cross of gold." The silver standard will give the poor a better chance in this unequal fight. I am a socialist not because I think it is a perfect system, but half a loaf is better than no bread.

The other systems have been tried and found wanting. Let this one be tried — if for nothing else, for the novelty of the thing. A redistribution of pain and pleasure is better than always the same persons having pains and pleasures. The sum total of good and evil in the world remains ever the same. The yoke will be lifted from shoulder to shoulder by new systems, that is all.

Let every dog have his day in this miserable world, so that after this experience of so-called happiness they may all come to the Lord and give up this vanity of a world and governments and all other botherations.

With love to you all,

Ever your faithful brother,
Vivekananda.

1896.83 — ALASINGA

14 Grey Coat Gardens, Westminster, S. W.,
11th November, 1896.

DEAR ALASINGA,

I shall most probably start on the 16th of December, or may be a day or two later. I go from here to Italy, and after seeing a few places there, join the steamer at Naples. Miss Müller, Mr. and Mrs. Sevier, and a young man called Goodwin are accompanying me. The Seviers are going to settle at Almora. So is Miss Müller. Sevier was an officer in the Indian army for 5 years. So he knows India a good deal. Miss Müller was a Theosophist who adopted Akshay. Goodwin is an Englishman, through whose shorthand notes it has been possible for the pamphlets to be published.

I arrive at Madras first from Colombo. The other people go their way to Almora. I go from thence direct to Calcutta. I will write you the exact information when I start.

Yours affly.,
Vivekananda.

PS — The first edition of Râja-Yoga is sold out, and a second is in the press. India and America are the biggest buyers.

1896.84 — MRS. BULL

Greycoat Gardens,
Westminster, London, S.W.,
13th November, 1896.

DEAR MRS. BULL,

... I am very soon starting for India, most probably on the 16th of December. As I am very desirous to see India once before I come again to America, and as I have arranged to take several friends from England with me to India, it is impossible for me to go to America on my way, however I might have liked it.

Dr. Janes is doing splendid work indeed. I can hardly express my gratitude for the many kindnesses and the help he has given me and my work... The work is progressing beautifully here.

You will be interested to know that the first edition of Raja-Yoga is sold out, and there is a standing order for several hundreds more.

Yours etc.,
Vivekananda.

1896.85 — ALASINGA

39 Victoria Street, London, S. W.,
20th November, 1896.

DEAR ALASINGA,

I am leaving England on the 16th of December for Italy, and shall catch the North German Lloyd S. S. Prinz Regent Luitpold at Naples. The steamer is due at Colombo on the 14th of January next.

I intend to see a little of Ceylon, and shall then go to Madras. I am being accompanied by three English friends — Capt. and Mrs. Sevier and Mr. Goodwin. Mr. Sever and his wife are going to start a place near Almora in the Himalayas which I intend to make my Himalayan Centre, as well as a place for Western disciples to live as Brahmachârins and Sannyâsins. Goodwin is an unmarried young man who is going to travel and live with me, he is like a Sannyasin.

I am very desirous to reach Calcutta before the birthday festival of Shri Ramakrishna... My present plan of work is to start two centres, one in Calcutta and the other in Madras, in which to train up young preachers. I have funds enough to start the one in Calcutta, which being the scene of Shri Ramakrishna's life-work, demands my first attention. As for the Madras one, I expect to get funds in India.

We will begin work with these three centres; and later on, we will get to Bombay and Allahabad. And from these points, if the Lord is pleased, we will invade not only India, but send over bands of preachers to every country in the world. That should be our first duty. Work on with a heart. 39 Victoria will be the London headquarters for some time to come, as the work will be carried on there. Sturdy had a big box of Brahmavâdin I did not know before. He is now canvassing subscribers for it.

Now we have got one Indian magazine in English fixed. We can start some in the vernaculars also. Miss M. Noble of Wimbledon is a great worker. She will also canvass for both the Madras papers. She will write you. These things will grow slowly but surely. Papers of this kind are supported by a small circle of followers. Now they cannot be expected to do too many things at a time — they have to buy the books, find the money for the work in England, subscribers for the paper here, and then subscribe to Indian papers. It is too much. It is more like trading than teaching. Therefore you must wait, and yet I am sure there will be a few subscribers here. Again, there must be work for the people here to do when I am gone, else the whole thing will go to pieces. Therefore there must be a paper here, so also in America by and by. The Indian papers are to be supported by the Indians. To make a paper equally acceptable to all nationalities means a staff of writers from all nations; and that means at least a hundred thousand rupees a year.

You must not forget that my interests are international and not Indian alone. I am in good health; so is Abhedananda.

With all love and blessings,
Vivekananda.

1896.86 — LALAJI

39 Victoria Street, London S.W.,
21st November, 1896.

DEAR LALAJI, (Lala Badri Sah)

I reach Madras about the 7th of January; after a few days in the plains I intend to come up to Almora.

I have three English friends with me. Two of them, Mr. and Mrs. Sevier, are going to settle in Almora. They are my disciples, you know, and they are going to build the Goliath for me in the Himalayas. It was for that reason I asked you to look for some suitable site. We want a whole hill, with a view of the snow-range, all to ourselves. It would of course take time to fix on the site and complete the building. In the meanwhile will you kindly engage a small bungalow for my friends? The bungalow ought to accommodate three persons. I do not require a large one. A small one would do for the present. My friends will live in this bungalow in Almora and then go about looking for a site and building.

You need not reply to this letter, as before your reply will reach me, I shall be on my way to India. I will write to you from Madras as soon as I reach there.

With love and blessings to you all,

Yours,
Vivekananda.

1896.87 — DEAR __

C/O E. T Sturdy, Esq.,
High View, Caversham, Reading,
1896.

DEAR __,

… Can anything be done unless everybody exerts himself to his utmost? "Goddess of Wealth resorts to." No need of looking behind. FORWARD! We want infinite energy, infinite zeal, infinite courage, and infinite patience, then only will great things be achieved …

With love and blessings to you all,

Yours affectionately,
Vivekananda.

1896.88 — SISTERS

39 Victoria St., London S.w.,
28th Nov., 1896.

DEAR SISTERS, (Misses Mary and Harriet Hale)

...I feel impelled to write a few lines to you before my departure for India. The work in London has been a roaring success. The English are not so bright as the Americans, but once you touch their heart, it is yours for ever. Slowly have I gained, and it is strange that in six months' work altogether I would have a steady class of 120 persons apart from public lectures. Here every one means work — the practical Englishman. Capt. and Mrs. Sevier and Mr. Goodwin are going to India with me to work and spend their own money on it! There are scores here ready to do the same: men and women of position, ready to give up everything for the idea, once they feel convinced! And last though not the least, the help in the shape of money to start my "work" in India has come and more will follow. My ideas about the English have been revolutionized. I now understand why the Lord has blessed them above all other races. They are steady, sincere to the backbone, with great depths of feeling — only with a crust of stoicism on the surface; if that is broken, you have your man.

Now I am going to start a centre in Calcutta and another in the Himalayas. The Himalayan one will be an entire hill about 7,000 ft. high — cool in summer, cold in winter. Capt. and Mrs. Sevier will live there, and it will be the centre for European workers, as I do not want to kill them by forcing on them the Indian mode of living and the fiery plains. My plan is to send out numbers of Hindu boys to every civilised country to preach — get men and women from foreign countries to work in India. This would be a good exchange. After having established the centres, I go about up and down like the gentleman in the book of Job.

Here I must end to catch the mail. Things are opening for me. I am glad, and I know so you are. Now all blessings be yours and all happiness.

With eternal love,
Vivekananda.

PS — What about Dharmapala? What is he doing? Give him my love if you meet him.,

1896.89 — JOE

To Miss Josephine MacLeod:

Grey Coat Gardens,
Westminster, S.W., London,
3rd December, 1896.

DEAR JOE,

Many, many thanks, dear Joe Joe, for your kind invitation; but the Dear God has disposed it this way, viz I am to start for India on the 16th with Captain and Mrs. Sevier and Mr. Goodwin. The Seviers and myself take steamer at Naples. And as there will be four days at Rome, I will look in to say good-bye to Alberta.

Things are in a "hum" here just now; the big hall for the class, 39 Victoria, is full and yet more are coming.

Well, the good old country now calls me; I must go. So good-bye to all projects of visiting Russia this April.

I just set things a-going a little in India and am off again for the ever beautiful U.S. and England etc.

So very kind of you to send Mabel's letter — good news indeed. Only I am a little sorry for poor Fox. However, Mabel escaped him; that is better.

You did not write anything about how things are going on in New York. I hope it is all well there. Poor Cola! is he able now to make a living?

The coming of Goodwin was very opportune, as it captured the lectures here which are being published in a periodical form. Already there have been subscribers enough to cover the expenses.

Three lectures next week, and my London work is finished for this season. Of course, everybody here thinks it foolish to give it up just now the "boom" is on, but the Dear Lord says, "Start for Old India". I obey.

To Frankincense, to Mother, to Holister and everyone else my eternal love and blessings, and with the same for you,

Yours ever sincerely,
Vivekananda.

1896.90 — ALBERTA

14 Greycoat Gardens,
Westminster, London S.W.,
3rd Dec., 1896.

DEAR ALBERTA,

Herewith I enclose a letter of Mabel to Joe Joe to you. I have enjoyed the news in it very much and so I am sure you will.

I am to start from here for India on the 16th and to take the steamer at Naples. I will, therefore, be in Italy for some days and in Rome for three or four days. I will be very happy to look in to say good-bye to you.

Capt. and Mrs. Sevier from England are going to India with me, and they will be with me in Italy of course. You saw them last summer.

I intend to return to the U.S. and to Europe thence in about a year.

With all love and blessings,
Vivekananda.

1896.91 — MISS NOBLE

To Sister Nivedita:

14, Greycoat Gardens, Westminster, S.W.,
5 December, 1896.

DEAR MISS NOBLE,

Many thanks for sending the kind present from Mr. Beatty. I have written to him acknowledging his beautiful gift.

As for you, my dear, noble, kind friend, I only would say this — we Indians lack in many things, but there is none on earth to beat us in gratefulness. I remain,

Ever yours gratefully,
Vivekananda.

1896.92 — MRS. BULL

39 Victoria Street, London,
9th Dec., 1896.

DEAR MRS. BULL,

It is needless to express my gratitude at your most generous offer. I don't want to encumber myself with a large amount of money at the first start, but as things progress on I will be very glad to find employment for that sum. My idea is to start on a very small scale. I do not know anything yet. I will know my bearings when on the spot in India. From India I will write to you more details about my plans and the practical way to realise them. I start on the 16th and after a few days in Italy take the steamer at Naples.

Kindly convey my love to Mrs. Vaughan and Saradananda and to the rest of my friends there. As for you, I have always regarded you as the best friend I have, and it will be the same all my life.

With all love and blessings,

Yours,
Vivekananda.

1896.93 — FRANKINCENSE

13th Dec., 1896.

DEAR FRANKINCENSE,

So Gopâla has taken the female form! It is fit that it should be so — the time and the place considering. May all blessings follow her through life. She was keenly desired, prayed for, and she comes as a blessing to you and to your wife for life. I have not the least doubt.

I wish I could have come to America now if only to fulfil the form "the sages of the East bringing presents to the Western baby". But the heart is there with all prayers and blessings, and the mind is more powerful than the body.

I am starting on the 16th of this month and take the steamer at Naples. Will see Alberta in Rome surely. With all love to the holy family,

Yours ever in the Lord,
Vivekananda.

1896.94 — MADAM

London,
13th December, 1896.

DEAR MADAM,[1]

We have only to grasp the idea of gradation of morality and everything becomes clear.

Renunciation — non-resistance — non-destructiveness — are the ideals to be attained through less and less worldliness, less and less resistance, less and less destructiveness. Keep the ideal in view and work towards it. None can live in the world without resistance, without destruction, without desire. The world has not come to that state yet when the ideal can be realised in society.

The progress of the world through all its evils making it fit for the ideals, slowly but surely. The majority will have to go on with this slow growth — the exceptional ones will have to get out to realise the idea in the present state of things.

Doing the duty of the time is the best way, and if it is done only as a duty, it does not make us attached.

Music is the highest art and, to those who understand is the highest worship.

We must try our best to destroy ignorance and evil. Only we have to learn that evil is destroyed by the growth of good.

Yours faithfully,
Vivekananda.

---

1. An American Lady.

Italy

1896.95 — ALBERTA

Hotel Minerva, Florence,
20th Dec., 1896.

DEAR ALBERTA,

Tomorrow we reach Rome. I will most possibly come to see you day after tomorrow as it will be late in the night when we reach Rome. We stop at the Hotel Continental.

With all love and blessings,
Vivekananda.

1896.96 — RAKHAL

To Swami Brahmananda:

Hotel Minerva, Florence,
20th December, 1896.

DEAR RAKHAL,

As you see, by this time I am on my way. Before leaving London, I got your letter and the pamphlet. Take no heed of Mazoomdar's madness. He surely has gone crazy with jealousy. Such foul language as he has used would only make people laugh at him in a civilised country. He has defeated his purpose by the use of such vulgar words.

All the same, we ought not to allow Hara Mohan or any one else to go and fight Brahmos and others in our name. The public must know that we have no quarrel with any sect, and if anybody provokes a quarrel, he is doing it on his own responsibility. Quarrelling and abusing each other are our national traits. Lazy, useless, vulgar, jealous, cowardly, and quarrelsome, that is what we are, Bengalis. Anyone who wants to be my friend must give up these. Neither do you allow Hara Mohan to print any book, because such printing as he does is only cheating the public.

If there are oranges in Calcutta, send a hundred to Madras care of Alasinga, so that I may have them when I reach Madras.

Mazoomdar writes that the Sayings of Shri Ramakrishna published in The Brahmavadin are not genuine and are lies! In that case ask Suresh Dutt and Ram Babu to give him the lie in The Indian Mirror. As I did not do anything about the collection of the Uktis (Sayings), I cannot say anything.

Yours affectionately,
Vivekananda.

PS — Don't mind these fools; "No fool like an old fool" is the proverb. Let them bark a little. Their occupation is gone. Poor souls! Let them have a little satisfaction in barking.

1896.97 — SIR

To the Editor of *Light of the East*:

1896.

DEAR SIR,

Many thanks for your kindly sending me several copies of the *Light of the East*. I wish the paper all success.

As you have asked for my suggestion [that] I can make towards improving the paper — I must frankly state that in my life-long experience in the work, I have always found "Occultism" injurious and weakening to humanity. What we want is strength. We Indians, more than any other race, want strong and vigorous thought. We have enough of the superfine in all concerns. For centuries we have been stuffed with the mysterious; the result is that our intellectual and spiritual digestion is almost hopelessly impaired, and the race has been dragged down to the depths of hopeless imbecility — never before or since experienced by any other civilised community. There must be freshness and vigour of thought behind to make a virile race. More than enough to strengthen the whole world exists in the Upanishads. The Advaita is the eternal mine of strength. But it requires to be applied. It must first be cleared of the incrustation of scholasticism, and then in all its simplicity, beauty and sublimity be taught over the length and breadth of the land, as applied even to the minutest detail of daily life. "This is a very large order"; but we must work towards it, nevertheless, as if it would be accomplished to-morrow. Of one thing I am sure — that whoever wants to help his fellow beings through genuine love and unselfishness will work wonders.

Yours truly,
Vivekananda.

1897

India

1897.1 — MARY

To Miss Mary Hale:

Dampfer, "Prinz-Regent Leopold"
3rd January, 1897.

DEAR MARY,

I received your letter forwarded from London in Rome. It was very very kind of you to write such a beautiful letter, and I enjoyed every bit of it. I do not know anything about the evolution of the orchestra in Europe. We are nearing Port Said after four days of frightfully bad sailing from Naples. The ship is rolling as hard as she can, and you must pardon my scrawls under such circumstances.

From Suez begins Asia. Once more Asia. What am I? Asiatic, European, or American? I feel a curious medley of personalities in me. You didn't write anything about Dharmapala, his goings and doings. I am much more interested in him than in Gandhi.

I land in a few days at Colombo and mean to "do" Ceylon a bit. There was a time when Ceylon had more than 20 million inhabitants and a huge capital of which the ruins cover nearly a hundred square miles!

The Ceylonese are not Dravidians but pure Aryans. It was colonised from Bengal about 800 B.C., and they have kept a very clear history of their country from that time. It was the greatest trade centre of the ancient world, and Anuradhapuram was the London of the ancients.

I enjoyed Rome more than anything in the West, and after seeing Pompeii I have lost all regard for the so-called "Modern Civilisation". With the exception of steam and electricity they had everything else and infinitely more art conceptions and executions than the Moderns.

Please tell Miss Locke that I was mistaken when I told her that sculpturing of the human figure was not developed in India as among the Greeks. I am reading in Fergusson and other authorities that in Orissa or Jagannath, which I did not visit, there are among the ruins human figures which for beauty and anatomical skill would compare with any production of the Greeks. There is a colossal figure of Death, a huge female skeleton covered with a shrivelled skin — the awful fidelity to anatomical details are frightening and disgusting. Says my author, one of the female figures in the niche is exactly like the Venus de Medici and so on. But you must remember that everything almost has been destroyed by the iconoclastic Mohammedan, yet the remnants are more than all European debris put together! I have travelled eight years and not seen many of the masterpieces.

Tell sister Locke also that there is a ruined temple in a forest in India which and the Parthenon of Greece Fergusson considers as the climax of architectural art—each of its type—the one of conception, the other of conception and detail. The later Mogul buildings etc., the Indo-Saracenic architecture, does not compare a bit with the best types of the ancients...

With all my love,
Vivekananda.

PS—Just by chance saw Mother Church and Father Pope at Florence. You know of it already.

1897.2—CHRISTINA

To Sister Christine:

On Board Prinz Regent Luitpold,
3rd January, 1897.

DEAR CHRISTINA,

By two p.m. today I reach Port Said. Asia once more. I have not heard from you [for] long. Hope everything is going on well with you. How are Mrs. Funke, Mrs. Phelps, and all other friends?

My love to all.

Write when you feel like it,
Vivekananda.

1897.3—MADRAS COMITTEE

To the Madras Committee:

[After Swami Vivekananda Colombo on Friday, January 15, 1897, the Madras Committee, which was planning a reception for the Swami, sent the following message: "Motherland rejoices to welcome you back". In reply, Swami Vivekananda sent a wire.]

[Postmarked: January 15, 1897.]

MY LOVE AND GRATITUDE TO MY COUNTRYMEN.

1897.4 — MARY

Ramnad,
30th Jan., 1897.

MY DEAR MARY,

Things are turning out most curiously for me. From Colombo in Ceylon, where I landed, to Ramnad, the nearly southernmost point of the Indian continent where I am just now as the guest of the Raja of Ramnad, my journey has been a huge procession — crowds of people, illuminations, addresses, etc., etc. A monument forty feet high is being built on the spot where I landed. The Raja of Ramnad has presented his address to "His most Holiness" in a huge casket of solid gold beautifully worked. Madras and Calcutta are on the tiptoe of expectation as if the whole nation is rising to honour me. So you see, Mary, I am on the very height of my destiny, yet the mind turns to quietness and peace, to the days we had in Chicago, of rest, of peace, and love; and that is why I write just now, and may this find you all in health and peace! I wrote a letter to my people from London to receive Dr. Barrows kindly. They accorded him a big reception, but it was not my fault that he could not make any impression there. The Calcutta people are a hard-headed lot! Now Barrows thinks a world of me, I hear! Such is the world.

With all love to mother, father, and you all,

I remain, yours affly.,
Vivekananda.

1897.5 — RAKHAL

To Swami Brahmananda:

Madras,
12th February, 1897.

DEAR RAKHAL,

I am to start by S.S. Mombasa next Sunday. I had to give up invitations from Poona and other places on account of bad health. I am very much pulled down by hard work and heat.

The Theosophists and others wanted to intimidate me. Therefore I had to give them a bit of my mind. You know they persecuted me all the time in America, because I did not join them. They wanted to begin it here. So I had to clear my position. If that displeases any of my Calcutta friends, "God help them". You need not be afraid, I do not work alone, but He is always with me. What could I do otherwise?

Yours,
Vivekananda.

PS — Take the house if furnished.

1897.6 — GENTLEMEN

To the Hindu Students of Trichinapally:

[February 16, 1897.]

GENTLEMEN,

I have received your address with great pleasure and sincerely thank you for the kind expressions contained therein.

I much regret, however, that time effectually prevents my paying even a short visit to Trichinopoly at present. In the autumn, however, I propose making a lecture tour throughout India, and you may rely upon it that I shall then not fail to include Trichinopoly in the programme.

Again thanking you, and with my blessings to all.

Sincerely yours,
Vivekananda.

1897.7 — MRS. BULL

Alambazar Math, Calcutta,
25th Feb., 1897.

DEAR MRS. BULL,

Saradananda sends £20 to be placed in the famine relief in India. But as there is famine in his own home, I thought it best to relieve that first, as the old proverb says. So it has been employed accordingly.

I have not a moment to die as they stay, what with processions and tomtomings and various other methods of reception all over the country; I am almost dead. As soon as the Birthday is over I will fly off to the hills. I received an address from the Cambridge Conference as well as one from the Brooklyn Ethical Association. One from the Vedanta Association of New York, as mentioned in Dr. Janes's letter, has not yet arrived.

Also there is a letter from Dr. Janes suggesting work along the line of your conference, here in India. It is almost impossible for me to pay any attention to these things. I am so, so tired. I do not know whether I would live even six months more or not, unless I have some rest.

Now I have to start two centres, one in Madras, the other in Calcutta. The Madras people are deeper and more sincere, and, I am sure, will be able to collect funds from Madras itself. The Calcutta people are mostly enthusiastic (I mean the aristocracy) through patriotism, and their sympathy would never materialise. On the other hand, the country is full of persons, jealous and pitiless, who would leave no stones unturned to pull my work to pieces.

But as you know well, the more the opposition, the more the demon in me is roused. My duty would not be complete if I die without starting the two places, one for the Sannyasins, the other for the women.

I have already £500 from England about, £500 from Mr. Sturdy, and if your money be added to it, I am sure I will be able to start the two. I think, therefore, you ought to send the money as soon as possible. The safest way is to put the money in a bank in America in your and my name jointly, so that either of us may draw it. In case I die before the money is employed, you will be able to draw it all and put it to the use I wanted. So that, in case of my death, none of my people would be able to meddle with it. The English money has been put in the bank in the same position in the joint names of Mr. Sturdy and myself.

With love to Saradananda and eternal love and gratitude to yourself,

Yours etc.,
Vivekananda.

1897.8 — CHRISTINA

To Sister Christine:

Darjeeling,,
[Return Address: Alambazar Math, Calcutta],
16th March, 1897.

DEAR CHRISTINA,

Many, many thanks for the photograph and the poem. I never saw anything half as beautiful. The work I had to do to reach Calcutta from Ceylon was so immense that I could not earlier acknowledge your precious gift. The work has broken me down completely, and I have got "diabetes", an incurable disease, which must carry me off — at least in a few years.

I am now writing to you from Darjeeling, the nearest hill station to Calcutta, with a climate as cool as London. It has revived me a bit. If I live, I will come to America next year or so.

How are things going on with you all? How are Mrs. Funkey [Funke] and Mrs. Phelps?

Are you laying by a few dollars whenever you can? That is very important.

I am in a hurry for the mail. You will be glad to know that the Indian people have, as it were, risen in a mass to honour me. I am the idol of the day. Mr. Goodwin is going to publish in book form all the addresses given to me and the speeches in reply. The demonstrations all over have been simply unique.

Yours with all love,
Vivekananda.

1897.9 — SHARAT CHANDRA CHAKRAVARTI[1]

To Sj. Sharat Chandra Chakravarti, B.A.:

Darjeeling,
19th March, 1897.

SALUTATION TO BHAGAVAN RAMAKRISHNA!

May you prosper! May this letter conveying blessings and cordial embrace make you happy! Nowadays this fleshy tabernacle of mine is comparatively well. Meseems, the snow-capped peaks of the Himalayas, the Chief among mountains, bring even the moribund back to life. And the fatigue of the journeys also seems to have somewhat abated. I have already felt that yearning for Freedom — potent enough to put the heart into turmoil — which your letter suggests you are experiencing. It is this yearning that gradually brings on a concentration of the mind on the eternal Brahman. "There is no other way to go by." May this desire blaze up more and more in you, until all your past Karma and future tendencies are absolutely annihilated. Close upon the heels of that will follow, all on a sudden, the manifestation of Brahman, and with it the destruction of all craving for the sense-world. That this freedom-in-life is approaching for your welfare is easily to be inferred from the strength of your fervour. Now I pray to that world-teacher, Shri Ramakrishna, the Preacher of the gospel of universal synthesis, to manifest himself in the region of your heart, so that, having attained the consummation of your desires, you may with an undaunted heart try your best to deliver others from this dreadful ocean of infatuation. May you be ever possessed of valour! It is the hero alone, not the coward, who has liberation within his easy reach. Gird up your loins, ye heroes, for before you are your enemies — the dire army of infatuation. It is undoubtedly true that "all great achievements are fraught with numerous impediments"; still you should exert your utmost for your end. Behold, how men are already in the jaws of the shark of infatuation! Oh, listen to their piteous heart-rending wails. Advance, forward, O ye brave souls, to set free those that are in fetters, to lessen the burden of woe of the miserable, and to illumine the abysmal darkness of ignorant hearts! Look, how the Vedanta proclaims by beat of drums, "Be fearless!" May that solemn sound remove the heart's knot of all denizens of the earth.

Ever your well-wisher,
Vivekananda.

---

1 Translated from Bengali.

1897.10 — MRS. BULL

To Mrs. Ole Bull:

Alambazar Math, Calcutta,
[Darjeeling],
26th March, 1897.

DEAR MRS. BULL,

The demonstrations and national jubilations over me are over — at least I had to cut them short, as my health broke completely down. The result of this steady work in the West and the tremendous work of a month in India upon the Bengalee constitution is "diabetes". It is a hereditary foe and is destined to carry me off, at best, in a few years' time. Eating only meat and drinking no water seems to be the only way to prolong life — and, above all, perfect rest for the brain. I am giving my brain the needed rest in Darjeeling, from where I am writing you now.

I am so glad to hear about Saradananda's success. Give him my best love and do not allow him [to] do too much work. The Bengalee body is not the same as the American.

Mr. Chatterjy (Mohini) came to see me in Calcutta, and he was very friendly. I gave him your message. He is quite willing to work with me. Nothing more to write, only I am bent upon seeing my monastery started; and as soon as that is done, I come to America once more.

By the by, I will send to you a young lady from England — one Gertrude Orchard. She has been a governess, but she has talent in art etc., and I wished her to try her chance in America. I will give her a letter to you and Mrs. [Florence] Adams.

With my love to Mrs. Adams, Miss Thursby, Miss Farmer (the noble sister) and all the rest of our friends.

With eternal love and gratitude,

Yours affectionately,
Vivekananda.

1897.11 — RAM RAM[2]

To Pandit Ram Ram Samjami:

Darjeeling,
[April] 1897.

DEAR RAM RAM,

I received your first letter in Calcutta. I was busy there, and so it seems that I forgot to reply. You have deplored this in your letter, but that is not right. I do not

2 Translated from Bengali.

forget anyone — especially those who have received grace from "Him".

While I was in England, I received your Avadhuta-Gitâ. It is beautifully printed. You mentioned Karma-Yoga — I do not have that book with me. It was printed in Madras. If there are any copies at the Math, I shall ask them to send one to you.

I have been very sick, so right now I am staying at Darjeeling. As soon as I feel better, I shall return to Calcutta...

Please accept my special love. I pray for your welfare always.

Yours etc.,
Vivekananda.

1897.12 — MISS NOBLE

To Sister Nivedita:

Darjeeling,
3rd April, 1897.

DEAR MISS NOBLE,

I have just found a bit of important work for you to do on behalf of the downtrodden masses of India.

The gentleman I take the liberty of introducing to you is in England on behalf of the Tiyas, a plebeian caste in the native State of Malabar.

You will realize from this gentleman what an amount of tyranny there is over these poor people, simply because of their caste.

The Indian Government has refused to interfere on grounds of non-interference in the internal administration of a native State. The only hope of these people is the English Parliament. Do kindly everything in your power to help this matter [in] being brought before the British Public.

Ever yours in the truth,
Vivekananda.

1897.13 — HONOURED MADAM

ॐ तत् सत्

Rose Bank,
The Maharaja of Burdwan's House,
Darjeeling,
6th April, 1897.

HONOURED MADAM[1],

I feel much obliged for the Bhârati sent by you, and consider myself fortunate

---
1. Shrimati Sarala Ghoshal — Editor, *Bharati*

that the cause, to which my humble life has been dedicated, has been able to win the approbation off highly talented ladies like you.

In this battle of life, men are rare who encourage the initiator off new thought, not to speak of women who would offer him encouragement, particularly in our unfortunate land. It is therefore that the approbation of an educated Bengali lady is more valuable than the loud applause of all the men of India.

May the Lord grant that many women like you be born in this country, and devote their lives to the betterment of their motherland!

I have something to say in regard to the article you have written about me in the *Bharati*. It is this. It has been for the good of India that religious preaching in the West has been and will be done. It has ever been my conviction that we shall not be able to rise unless the Western people come to our help. In this country no appreciation of merit can yet be found, no financial strength, and what is most lamentable of all, there is not a bit of practicality.

There are many things to be done, but means are wanting in this country. We have brains, but no hands. We have the doctrine of Vedanta, but we have not the power to reduce it into practice. In our books there is the doctrine of universal equality, but in work we make great distinctions. It was in India that unselfish and disinterested work of the most exalted type was preached but in practice we are awfully cruel, awfully heartless — unable to think of anything besides our own mass-of-flesh bodies.

Yet it is only through the present state of things that it is possible to proceed to work. There is no other way. Every one has the power to judge of good end evil, but he is the hero who undaunted by the waves of Samsâra — which is full of errors, delusions, and miseries — with one hand wipes the tears, and with the other, unshaken, shows the path of deliverance. On the one hand there is the conservative society, like a mass of inert matter; on the other the restless, impatient, fire-darting reformer; the way to good lies between the two. I heard in Japan that it was the belief of the girls of that country that their dolls would be animated if they were loved with all their heart. The Japanese girl never breaks her doll. O you of great fortune! I too believe that India will awake again if anyone could love with all his heart the people of the country — bereft of the grace of affluence, of blasted fortune, their discretion totally lost, downtrodden, ever-starved, quarrelsome, and envious. Then only will India awake, when hundreds of large-hearted men and women, giving up all desires of enjoying the luxuries of life, will long and exert themselves to their utmost for the well-being of the millions of their countrymen who are gradually sinking lower and lower in the vortex of destitution and ignorance. I have experienced even in my insignificant life that good motives, sincerity, and infinite love can conquer the world. One single soul possessed of these virtues can destroy the dark designs of millions of hypocrites and brutes.

My going to the West again is yet uncertain; if I go, know that too will be for India. Where is the strength of men in this country? Where is the strength of money? Many men and women of the West are ready to do good to India by serving even the lowest Chandâlas, in the Indian way, and through the Indian religion. How many such are there in this country? And financial strength! To meet the expenses or my reception, the people of Calcutta made me deliver a lecture and sold tickets!... I do not blame nor censure anybody for this, I only want to show that our well-being is impossible without men and money coming from the West.

Ever grateful and ever praying to the Lord for your welfare,
Vivekananda.

1897.14 — LALAJEE

To Lala Badri Sah of Almora:

Darjeeling,
7th April, '97.

DEAR LALAJEE,

Just received your kind invitation through telegram. Perhaps you have already heard that I have been attacked by "Diabetes", a fell disease.

That unsettled all our plans, and I had to run up to Darjeeling, it being very cool and very good for the disease.

I have felt much better since, and the doctors therefore do not want me to move about, as that brings about a relapse. If my present state of health continues for a month or two, I think I will be in a condition to come down to the plains and come to Almora to see you all. I am very sorry that I have caused you a good deal of trouble, but you see it could not be helped — the body was not under my control.

With all love to yourself and other friends in Almora.

Yours affectionately,
Vivekananda.

1897.15 — SHASHI[1]

To Swami Ramakrishnananda:

Darjeeling,
20th April, 1897.

DEAR SHASHI,

All of you have doubtless reached Madras by this time. I should think Biligiri is certainly taking great care of you, and that Sadananda serves you as your attendant. In Madras the worship should be done in a completely Sattvic manner, without a trace of Rajas in it. I hope Alasinga has by now returned to Madras. Don't enter into wrangles with anybody — always maintain a calm attitude. For the present let the worship of Shri Ramakrishna be established and continued in the house of Bili-

1 Translated from Bengali.

giri. But see that the worship does not become very elaborate and long. Time thus saved should be utilised in holding classes and doing some preaching. It is good to initiate as many as you can. Supervise the work of the two papers, and help in whatever way you can. Biligiri has two widowed daughters. Kindly educate them and make special efforts that through them more such widowed women get a thorough grounding in their own religion and learn a little English and Sanskrit. But all this work should be done from a distance. One has to be exceedingly careful before young women. Once you fall, there is no way out, and the sin is unpardonable.

I am very sorry to hear that Gupta was bitten by a dog; but I hear that the dog was not a mad one, so there is no cause for alarm. In any case, see that he takes the medicine sent by Gangadhar.

Early morning, finish daily your worship and other duties briefly, and calling together Biligiri with his family, read before them the Gita and other sacred books. There is not the least necessity for teaching the divine Love of Râdhâ and Krishna. Teach them pure devotion to Sitâ-Râm and Hara-Pârvati. See that no mistake is made in this respect. Remember that the episodes of the divine relationship between Radha and Krishna are quite unsuitable for young minds. Specially Biligiri and other followers of Râmânujâchârya are worshippers of Rama; so see to it that their innate attitude of pure devotion is never disturbed.

In the evenings give some spiritual teaching like that to the general public. Thus gradually "even the mountain is crossed". See that an atmosphere of perfect purity is always maintained, and that there enters not the slightest trace of Vâmâchâra. For the rest, the Lord Himself will guide you, there is no fear. Give to Biligiri my respectful salutations and loving greetings, and convey my salutations to similar devotees.

My illness is now much less — it may even be cured completely, if the Lord wills. My love, blessings, and greetings to you.

Yours affectionately,
Vivekananda.

PS — Please tender my specially affectionate greetings and blessings to Dr. Nanjunda Rao and help him as much as you can. Try your best to particularly encourage the study of Sanskrit among the non-Brahmins.

1897.16 — MARY

Darjeeling,
April 28, 1897.

DEAR MARY,

A few days ago I received your beautiful letter. Yesterday came the card announcing Harriet's marriage. Lord bless the happy pair!

The whole country here rose like one man to receive me. Hundreds of thousands of persons, shouting and cheering at every place, Rajas drawing my carriage, arches all over the streets of the capitals with blazing mottoes etc.,!!! The whole thing will soon come out in the form of a book, and you will have a copy soon. But unfortunately I was already exhausted by hard work in England; and this tremendous exertion in the heat of Southern India prostrated me completely. I had of course to give up the idea of visiting other parts of India and fly up to the nearest hill station, Darjeeling. Now I feel much better, and a month more in Almora would complete the cure. By the bye, I have just lost a chance of coming over to Europe. Raja Ajit Singh and several other Rajas start next Saturday for England. Of course, they wanted hard to get me to go over with them. But unfortunately the doctors would not hear of my undertaking any physical or mental labour just now. So with the greatest chagrin I had to give it up, reserving it for a near future.

Dr. Barrows has reached America by this time, I hope. Poor man! He came here to preach the most bigoted Christianity, with the usual result that nobody listened to him. Of course they received him very kindly; but it was my letter that did it. I could not put brains into him! Moreover, he seems to be a queer sort of man. I hear that he was mad at the national rejoicings over my coming home. You ought to have sent a brainier man anyway, for the Parliament of Religions has been made a farce of in the Hindu mind by Dr. Barrows. On metaphysical lines no nation on earth can hold a candle to the Hindus; and curiously all the fellows that come over here from Christian land have that one antiquated foolishness of an argument that because the Christians are powerful and rich and the Hindus are not, so Christianity must be better than Hinduism. To which the Hindus very aptly retort that, that is the very reason why Hinduism is a religion and Christianity is not; because, in this beastly world it is blackguardism and that alone which prospers, virtue always suffers. It seems, however advanced the Western nations are in scientific culture, they are mere babies in metaphysical and spiritual education. Material science can only give worldly prosperity, whilst spiritual science is for eternal life. If there be no eternal life, still the enjoyment of spiritual thoughts as ideals is keener and makes a man happier, whilst the foolery of materialism leads to competition and undue ambition and ultimate death, individual and national.

This Darjeeling is a beautiful spot with a view of the glorious Kanchenjanga (28,146 ft.) now and then when the clouds permit it, and from a near hilltop one can catch a glimpse of Gauri Shankar (29,000 ft?) now and then. Then, the people here too are so picturesque, the Tibetans and Nepalese and, above all, the beautiful Lepcha women. Do you know one Colston Turnbull of Chicago? He was here a few weeks before I reached India. He seems to have had a great liking for me, with the result that Hindu people all liked him very much. What about Joe, Mrs. Adams, Sister Josephine, and all the rest of our friends? Where are our beloved Mills? Grinding slow but sure? I wanted to send some nuptial presents to Harriet, but with your "terrible" duties I must reserve it for some near future. Maybe I shall meet them in Europe very soon. I would have been very glad, of course, if you could announce your engagement, and I would fulfil my promise by filling up half a dozen papers in one letter...

My hair is turning grey in bundles, and my face is getting wrinkled up all over; that losing of flesh has given me twenty years of age more. And now I am losing flesh rapidly, because I am made to live upon meat and meat alone — no bread, no rice, no potatoes, not even a lump of sugar in my coffee!! I am living with a Brahmin family who all dress in knickerbockers, women excepted of course! I am also in knickers. I would have given you a surprise if you had seen me bounding from rock to rock like a chamois, or galloping might and main up and down mountain roads.

I am very well here, for life in the plains has become a torture. I cannot put the tip of my nose out into the streets, but there is a curious crowd!! Fame is not all milk and honey!! I am going to train a big beard; now it is turning grey. It gives a venerable appearance and saves one from American scandal-mongers! O thou white hair, how much thou canst conceal, all glory unto thee, Hallelujah!

The mail time is nearly up, so I finish. Good dreams, good health, all blessings attend you.

With love to father and mother and you all,

Yours,
Vivekananda.

1897.17 — MRS. BULL

Alambazar Math, Calcutta,
May 5th, 1897.

DEAR MRS. BULL,

I have been to Darjeeling for a month to recuperate my shattered health. I am very much better now. The disease disappeared altogether in Darjeeling. I am going tomorrow to Almora, another hill station, to perfect this improvement.

Things are looking not very hopeful here as I have already written you — though the whole nation has risen as one man to honour me and people went almost mad over me! The practical part cannot be had in India. Again, the price of the land has gone up very much near Calcutta. My idea at present is to start three centres at three capitals. These would be my normal schools, from thence I want to invade India.

India is already Ramakrishna's whether I live a few years more or not.

I have a very kind letter from Prof. Janes in which he points out my remarks about degraded Buddhism. You also write that Dharmapala is very wroth about it. Mr. Dharmapala is a good man, and I love him; but it would be entirely wrong for him to go into fits over things Indian.

I am perfectly convinced that what they call modern Hinduism with all its ugliness is only stranded Buddhism. Let the Hindus understand this clearly, and then it would be easier for them to reject it without murmur. As for the ancient form which the Buddha preached, I have the greatest respect for it, as well as for His person. And you well know that we Hindus worship Him as an Incarnation. Neither is the Buddhism of Ceylon any good. My visit to Ceylon has entirely disillusioned me, and the only living people there are the Hindus. The Buddhists are all much Europeanised — even Mr. Dharmapala and his father had European names, which they have since changed. The only respect the Buddhists pay to their great tenet of non-killing is by opening "butcher-stalls" in every place! And the priests encourage this. The real Buddhism, I once thought, would yet do much good. But I have given up the idea entirely, and I clearly see the reason why Buddhism was driven out of India, and we will only be too glad if the Ceylonese carry off the remnant of this religion with its hideous idols and licentious rites.

About the Theosophists, you must remember first that in India Theosophists and Buddhists are nonentities. They publish a few papers and make a lot of splash and try to catch Occidental ears...

I was one man in America and another here. Here the whole nation is looking upon me as their authority — there I was a much reviled preacher. Here Princes draw my carriage, there I would not be admitted to a decent hotel. My utterances here, therefore, must be for the good of the race, my people — however unpleasant they might appear to a few. Acceptance, love, toleration for everything sincere and honest — but never for hypocrisy. The Theosophists tried to fawn upon and flatter me as I am the authority now in India, and therefore it was necessary for me to stop my work giving any sanction to their humbugs, by a few bold, decisive words; and the thing is done. I am very glad. If my health had permitted, I would have cleared India by this time of these upstart humbugs, at least tried my best... Let me tell you that India is already Ramakrishna's and for a purified Hinduism I have organised my work here a bit.

Yours,
Vivekananda.

1897.18 — MISS NOBLE

To Sister Nivedita:

Alambazar Math, Calcutta,
5th May, 1897.

MY DEAR MISS NOBLE,

Your very very kind, loving, and encouraging letter gave me more strength than you think of.

There are moments when one feels entirely despondent, no doubt — especially when one has worked towards an ideal during a whole life's time and just when there is a bit of hope of seeing it partially accomplished, there comes a tremendous thwarting blow. I do not care for the disease, but what depresses me is that my ideals have not had yet the least opportunity of being worked out. And you know, the difficulty is money.

The Hindus are making processions and all that, but they cannot give money. The only help I got in the world was in England, from Miss Müller, and Mr. Sevier. I thought there that a thousand pounds was sufficient to start at least the principal centre in Calcutta, but my calculation was from the experience of Calcutta ten or twelve years ago. Since then the prices have gone up three or four times.

The work has been started anyhow. A rickety old little house has been rented for six or seven shillings, where about twenty-four young men are being trained. I had to go to Darjeeling for a month to recover my health, and I am glad to tell you I am very much better, and would you believe it, without taking any medicine, only by the exercise of mental healing! I am going again to another hill station tomorrow, as it is very hot in the plains. Your society is still living, I am sure. I will send you a report, as least every month, of the work done here. The London work is not doing well at all, I hear, and that was the main reason why I would not come to England just now — although some of our Rajas going for the Jubilee tried their best to get me with them — as I would have to work hard again to revive the interest in Vedanta. And that would mean a good deal more trouble physically.

I may come over for a month or so very soon however. Only if I could see my work started here, how gladly and freely would I travel about!

So far about work. Now about you personally. Such love and faith and devotion and appreciation like yours, dear Miss Noble, repays a hundred times over any amount of labour one undergoes in this life. May all blessings be yours. My whole life is at your service, as we may say in our mother tongue.

It never was and never will be anything but very very welcome, any letters from you and other friends in England. Mr. and Mrs. Hammond wrote two very kind and nice letters and Mr. Hammond a beautiful poem in The Brahmavadin, although I did not deserve it a bit. I will write to you again from the Himalayas, where thought will be clear in sight of the snows and the nerves more settled than in this burning plains. Miss Müller is already in Almora. Mr. and Mrs. Sevier go to Simla. They have been in Darjeeling so long. So things come and go, dear friend. Only the Lord is unchangeable and He is Love. May He make our heart His eternal habitation is the constant prayer of,

Vivekananda.

1897.19 — RAKHAL

To Swami Brahmananda:

Almora,
20th May, 1897.

MY DEAR RAKHAL,

From your letter I got all the important news. I got a letter from Sudhir also and also one from Master Mahashay. I have also got two letters from Nityananda

(Yogen Chatterjee) from the famine areas.

Even now money is floating on the waters, as it were,... but it will surely come. When it comes, buildings, land, and a permanent fund—everything will come all right. But one can never rest assured until the chickens are hatched; and I am not now going down to the hot plains within two or three months. After that I shall make a tour and shall certainly secure some money. This being so, if you think that the [land with a] frontage of eight Kâthâs cannot be acquired..., there is no harm in paying the earnest money to the middle-man vendor as though you were losing it for nothing. In all these matters use your own discretion; I cannot give any further advice. There is particularly a chance of making mistake through hurry... Tell Master Mahashay that I quite approve of what he had said.

Write to Gangadhar that if he finds it difficult to get alms etc. there, he should feed himself by spending from his own pocket, and that he should publish a weekly letter in Upen's paper (The Basumati). In that case others also may help.

I understand from a letter of Shashi... he wants Nirbhayananda. If you think this course to be the best, then send Nirbhayananda and bring back Gupta... Send Sashi a copy of the Bengali Rules and Regulations of the Math or an English version of it, and write to him to see that the work there is done in accordance with the Rules and Regulations.

I am glad to learn that the Association in Calcutta is going on nicely. It does not matter if one or two keep out. Gradually everyone will come. Be friendly and sympathetic with everybody. Sweet words are heard afar; it is particularly necessary to try and make new people come. We want more and more new members.

Yogen is doing well. On account of the great heat in Almora, I am now in an excellent garden twenty miles from there. This place is comparatively cool, but still warm. The heat does not seem to be particularly less than that of Calcutta...

The feverishness is all gone. I am trying to go to a still cooler place. Heat or the fatigue of walking, I find, at once produces trouble of the liver. The air here is so dry that there is a burning sensation in the nose all the time, and the tongue becomes, as it were, a chip of wood. You have stopped criticising; otherwise I would have gone to a colder place by this time just for the fun of it. "He constantly neglects diet restrictions"—what rot do you talk? Do you really listen to the words of these fools? It is just like your not allowing me to take Kalâi-dâl (black pulses), because it contains starch! And what is more—there will be no starch if rice and Roti (bread) are eaten after frying them! What wonderful knowledge, my dear. The fact of the matter is my old nature is coming back—this I am seeing clearly. In this part of the country now, an illness takes on the colour and fashion of this locality; and in that part of the country, it takes on the colour and fashion of the illnesses in that locality. I am thinking of making my meals at night very light; I shall eat to the full in the morning and at noon; at night milk, fruits, etc. That is why I am staying in this orchard, "in expectation of fruits"! Don't you see?

Now don't be alarmed. Does a companion of Shiva die so quickly? Just now the evening lamp has been lighted, and singing has to be done throughout the whole night. Nowadays my temper also is not very irritable, and feverishness is all due to the liver — I see this clearly. Well, I shall make that also come under control — what fear? ... Bravely brace yourself up and do work; let us create a mighty commotion.

Tender my love to all at the Math. At the next meeting of the Association give my greetings to everybody and tell them that though I am not physically present there, yet my spirit is where the name of our Lord is sung — " goes the round on the earth" — because, you see, the Atman is omnipresent.

Yours affectionately,
Vivekananda.

1897.20 — SUDHIR

Almora,
20th May, 1897.

DEAR SUDHIR,

Your letter gave me much pleasure. One thing, perhaps, I forget to tell you — to keep a copy of the letter you sent me. Also all important communications to the Math from different persons and to different persons should be copied and preserved.

I am very glad to learn that things are going on well, that the work there is steadily progressing as well as that of Calcutta.

I am all right now except for the fatigue of the travel which I am sure will go off in a few days.

My love and blessings to you all.

Yours,
Vivekananda.

1897.21 — DOCTOR SHASHI

Almora,
29th May, 1897.

MY DEAR DOCTOR SHASHI, (Bhushan Ghosh)

Your letter and the two bottles containing the medicines were duly received. I have begun from last evening a trial of your medicines. Hope the combination will have a better effect than the one alone.

I began to take a lot of exercise on horseback, both morning and evening. Since that I am very much better indeed. I was so much better the first week of my gymnastics that I have scarcely felt so well since I was a boy and used to have kusti (wrestling) exercises. I really began to feel that it was a pleasure to have a body.

Every movement made me conscious of strength—every movement of the muscles was pleasurable. That exhilarating feeling has subsided somewhat, yet I feel very strong. In a trial of strength I could make both G. G. and Niranjan go down before me in a minute. In Darjeeling I always felt that I was not the same man. Here I feel that I have no disease whatsoever, but there is one marked change. I never in my life could sleep as soon as I got into bed. I must toss for at least two hours. Only from Madras to Darjeeling (during the first month) I would sleep as soon as my head touched the pillow. That ready disposition to sleep is gone now entirely, and my old tossing habit and feeling hot after the evening meal have come back. I do not feel any heat after the day meal. There being an orchard here, I began to take more fruit than usual as soon as I came. But the only fruit to be got here now is the apricot. I am trying to get more varieties from Naini Tâl. There has not been any thirst even though the days are fearfully hot... On the whole my own feeling is one of revival of great strength and cheerfulness, and a feeling of exuberant health, only I am afraid I am getting fat on a too much milk diet. Don't you listen to what Yogen writes. He is a hypochondriac himself and wants to make everybody so. I ate one-sixteenth of a barphi (sweetmeat) in Lucknow, and that according to Yogen was what put me out of sorts in Almora! Yogen is expected here in a few days. I am going to take him in hand. By the by, I am very susceptible to malarious influences. The first week's indisposition at Almora might have been caused to a certain extent by my passage through the Terai. Anyhow I feel very, very strong now. You ought to see me, Doctor, when I sit meditating in front of the beautiful snow-peaks and repeat from the Upanishads:

"न तस्य रोगो न जरा न मृत्युः प्राप्तस्य योगाग्निमयं शरीरम्—He has neither disease, nor decay, nor death; for, verily, he has obtained a body full of the fire of Yoga."

I am very glad to learn of the success of the meetings of the Ramakrishna Mission at Calcutta. All blessings attend those that help in the great work...

With all love, Yours in the Lord,
Vivekananda.

1897.22—SIR[1]

Almora,
30th May, 1897.

DEAR SIR,

I hear some unavoidable domestic grief has come upon you. To you, a man of wisdom, what can this misery do? Yet the amenities of friendly intercourse, incidental to relative existence in this world, require my making mention of it. Those moments of grief, however, very often bring out a better spiritual realisation. As if for a while the clouds withdraw and the sun of truth shines out. In the case

---

1 Translated from Bengali.

of some, half of the bondage is loosened. Of all bandages the greatest is that of position — the fear of reputation is stronger than the fear of death; but even this bondage appears to relax a little. As if the mind sees for a moment that it is much better to listen to the indwelling Lord than to the opinions of men. But again the clouds close up, and this indeed is Mâyâ.

Though for a long time I had no direct correspondence with you, yet I have often been receiving from others almost all the news about you. Some time ago you kindly sent me to England a copy of a translation of the Gita. The cover only bore a line of your handwriting. The few words in acknowledgment of this gift, I am told, raised doubts in your mind about my old affection towards you.

Please know these doubts to be groundless. The reason of that laconic acknowledgment is that I was given to see, during four or five years, only that one line of your handwriting on the cover of an English Gita, from which fact I thought, if you had no leisure to write more, would you have leisure enough to read much? Secondly, I learnt, you were particularly the friend of white-skinned missionaries of the Hindu religion and the roguish black natives were repelling! There was apprehension on this score. Thirdly, I am a Mlechchha, Shudra, and so forth; I eat anything and everything, and with anybody and everybody — and that in public both abroad and here. In my views, besides, much perversion has supervened — one attributeless absolute Brahman, I see, I fairly understand, and I see in some particular individuals the special manifestations of that Brahman; if those individuals are called by the name of God, I can well follow — otherwise the mind does not feel inclined towards intellectual theorisings such as the postulated Creator and the like.

Such a God I have seen in my life, and his commands I live to follow. The Smritis and the Puranas are productions of men of limited intelligence and are full of fallacies, errors, the feelings of class and malice. Only parts of them breathing broadness of spirit and love are acceptable, the rest are to be rejected. The Upanishads and the Gita are the true scriptures; Rama, Krishna, Buddha, Chaitanya, Nanak, Kabir, and so on are the true Avatâras, for they had their hearts broad as the sky — and above all, Ramakrishna. Ramanuja, Shankara etc., seem to have been mere Pundits with much narrowness of heart. Where is that love, that weeping heart at the sorrow of others? — Dry pedantry of the Pundit — and the feeling of only oneself getting to salvation hurry-scurry! But is that going to be possible, sir? Was it ever likely or will it ever be so? Can anything be attained with any shred of "I" left anyhow?

Another great discrepancy: the conviction is daily gaining on my mind that the idea of caste is the greatest dividing factor and the root of Maya; all caste either on the principle of birth or of merit is bondage: Some friends advise, "True, lay all that at heart, but outside, in the world of relative experience, distinctions like caste must needs be maintained." ... The idea of oneness at heart (with a craven impotence of effort, that is to say), and outside, the hell-dance of demons — oppression and persecution — ay, the dealer of death to the poor, but if the Pariah be wealthy enough, "Oh, he is the protector of religion!"

Over and above, I come to see from my studies that the disciplines of religion are not for the Shudra; if he exercises any discrimination about food or about going out to foreign lands, it is all useless in his case, only so much labour lost. I am a Shudra, a Mlechchha, so I have nothing to do with all that botheration. To me what would Mlechchha's food matter or Pariah's? It is in the books written by priests that madnesses like that of caste are to be found, and not in books revealed from God. Let the priests enjoy the fruits of their ancestors' achievement, while I follow the word of God, for my good lies there.

Another truth I have realised is that altruistic service only is religion, the rest, such as ceremonial observances, are madness—even it is wrong to hanker after one's own salvation. Liberation is only for him who gives up everything for others, whereas others who tax their brains day and night harping on "my salvation", "my salvation", wander about with their true well-being ruined, both present and prospective; and this I have seen many a time with my own eyes. Reflecting on all these sundry matters, I had no heart for writing a letter to you. If notwithstanding all these discrepancies, you find your attachment for me intact, I shall feel it to be a very happy issue indeed.

Yours etc.,
Vivekananda.

1897.23 — BADRI SAH

To Lala Badri Sah:

Devaldhar Bagicha,
Thursday, [June, 1897.]

DEAR BADRI SAH,

I have been very sorry to learn that you are not well. It would please me very much if you would come down here for a few days, at any rate, with us; and I am sure it would do you good.

Yours with blessings,
Vivekananda.

1897.24 — MR.__

Almora,
1st June, 1897.

DEAR MR.__,

The objections you show about the Vedas would be valid if the word Vedas meant Samhitâs. The word Vedas includes the three parts, the Samhitas, the Brâhmanas, and the Upanishads, according to the universally received opinion in India. Of these, the first two portions, as being the ceremonial parts, have been nearly put out of sight; the Upanishads have alone been taken up by all our philosophers and founders of sects.

The idea that the Samhitas are the only Vedas is very recent and has been started by the late Swâmi Dayânanda. This opinion has not got any hold on the orthodox population.

The reason of this opinion was that Swami Dayananda thought he could find a consistent theory of the whole, based on a new interpretation of the Samhitas, but the difficulties remained the same, only they fell back on the Brahmanas. And in spite of the theories of interpretation and interpolation a good deal still remains.

Now if it is possible to build a consistent religion on the Samhitas, it is a thousand times more sure that a very consistent and harmonious faith can be based upon the Upanishads, and moreover, here one has not to go against the already received national opinion. Here all the Âchâryas (Teachers) of the past would side with you, and you have a vast scope for new progress.

The Gita no doubt has already become the Bible of Hinduism, and it fully deserves to be so; but the personality of Krishna has become so covered with haze that it is impossible today to draw any life-giving inspiration from that life. Moreover, the present age requires new modes of thought and new life.

Hoping this will help you in thinking along these lines.

I am yours with blessings,
Vivekananda.

1897.25 — SHUDDHANANDA[1]

Almora,
1st June, 1897.

DEAR SHUDDHANANDA,

Glad to know from your letter that all are doing well there, and to go through the news in detail. I too am in better health; the rest you will know from Dr. Shashi Bhushan. Let the teaching go on for the present in the method revised by Brahmananda, and if any changes ar needed in future, have them done. But it should never be lost sight of that this must be done with the consent of all.

I am now living in a garden belonging to a merchant situated a little to the north of Almora. Before me are the snow-peaks of the Himalayas looking, in the reflection of the sun, like a mass of silver, a delight to the heart. By taking free air, regular diet, and plenty of exercise, I have grown strong and healthy in body. But I hear the Yogananda is very ill. I am inviting him to come here But then, he fears the mountain air and water. I wrote to him today, saying, "Stay in this garden for some

---

1 Translated from Bengali.

day' and if you find your illness shows no improvement, you may go to Calcutta." He will do as he pleases.

At Almora, every evening Achyutananda gathers the people together and reads to them the Gita and other Shâstras. Many residents of the town, as also soldiers from the cantonment, come there daily. I learn also that he is appreciated by all.

The Bengali interpretation that you have given of the Shloka interpretation in question is this: "When (the land) is flooded with water, what is the use of drinking water?" If the law of nature be such that when a land is flooded with water, drinking it is useless, that through certain air passages or through any other recondite way people's thirst may be allayed, then only can this novel interpretation be relevant, otherwise not. It is Shankara whom you should follow. Or you may explain it in this way: As, even when whole tracts are flooded with water, small pools are also of great use to the thirsty (that is to say, just a little water suffices him, and he says, as it were, "Let the vast sheet of water be, even a little of water will satisfy my object."), of identical use are the whole Vedas to a learned Brahmin. As even when the land is overflooded, one's concern lies in drinking the water and no more, so in all the Vedas illumination alone is the concern.

Here is another interpretation which hits better the meaning the author wishes to convey: Even when the land is overflooded, it is only that water which is drinkable and salutary, that people seek for, and no other kind. There are various kinds of water, which differ in quality and properties — even though the land be flooded over — according to the differences in property of their substratum, the soil. Likewise a skilful Brahmin, too, will, for the quenching of the worldly thirst, choose from that sea of words known as the Vedas, which is flooded over with diverse courses of knowledge, that which alone will be of potence to lead to liberation. And it is the knowledge of the Brahman which will do this.

With blessing and good wishes.

Yours,
Vivekananda.

1897.26 — MARIE

To Marie Halboister:

Almora,
2nd June, 1897.

DEAR MARIE,

I begin here my promised big chatty letter with the best intention as to its growth, and if it fails, it will be owing to your own Karma. I am sure you are enjoying splendid health. I have been very, very bad indeed; now recovering a bit — hope to recover very soon.

What about the work in London? I am afraid it is going to pieces. Do you now and then visit London? Hasn't Sturdy got a new baby?

The plains of India are blazing now. I cannot bear it. So I am here in this hill station—a bit cooler than the plains.

I am living in a beautiful garden belonging to a merchant of Almora—a garden abutting several miles of mountains and forests. Night before last a leopard came here and took away a goat from the flock kept in this garden. It was a frightful din the servants made and the barking of the big Tibet watchdogs. These dogs are kept chained at a distance all night since I am here, so that they may not disturb my sleep with their deep barks. The leopard thus found his opportunity and got a decent meal, perhaps, after weeks. May it do much good to him!

Do you remember Miss Müller? She has come here for a few days and was rather frightened when she heard of the leopard incident. The demand for tanned skins in London seems very great, and that is playing havoc with our leopards and tigers more than anything else.

As I am writing to you, before me, reflecting the afternoon's flow, stand long, long lines of huge snow peaks. They are about twenty miles as the crow flies from here, and forty through the circuitous mountain roads.

I hope your translations have been well received in the Countess's paper. I had a great mind and very good opportunity of coming over to England this Jubilee season with some of our Princes, but my physicians would not allow me to venture into work so soon. For going to Europe means work, isn't it? No work, no bread.

Here the yellow cloth is sufficient, and I would have food enough. Anyhow I am taking a much desired rest, hope it will do me good.

How are you going on with your work? With joy or sorrow? Don't you like to have a good rest, say for some years, and no work? Sleep, eat, and exercise; exercise, eat, and sleep—that is what I am going to do some months yet. Mr. Goodwin is with me. You ought to have seen him in his Indian clothes. I am very soon going to shave his head and make a full-blown monk of him.

Are you still practising some of the Yogas? Do you find any benefit from them? I learn that Mr. Martin is dead. How is Mrs. Martin—do you see her now and then?

Do you know Miss Noble? Do you ever see her? Here my letter comes to an end, as a huge dust storm is blowing over me, and it is impossible to write. It is all your Karma, dear Marie, for I intended to write so many wonderful things and tell you such fine stories; but I will have to keep them for the future, and you will have to wait.

Ever yours in the Lord,
Vivekananda.

1897.27 — MISS NOBLE

Almora,
3rd June, 1897.

DEAR MISS NOBLE,

...As for myself I am quite content. I have roused a good many of our people, and that was all I wanted. Let things have their course and Karma its sway. I have no bonds here below. I have seen life, and it is all self—life is for self, love for self, honour for self, everything for self. I look back and scarcely find any action I have done for self—even my wicked deeds were not for self. So I am content; not that I feel I have done anything specially good or great, but the world is so little, life so mean a thing, existence so, so servile—that I wonder and smile that human beings, rational souls, should be running after this self—so mean and detestable a prize.

This is the truth. We are caught in a trap, and the sooner one gets out, the better for one. I have seen the truth—let the body float up or down, who cares?

It is a beautiful mountain park I am living in now. On the north, extending almost all along the horizon, are peak after peak of the snow-clad Himalayas—forests abounding. It is not cold here, neither very warm; the evenings and mornings are simply delicious. I should like to be here this summer, and when the rains set in, I go down to the plains to work.

I was born for the life of a scholar—retired, quiet, poring over my books. But the Mother dispenses otherwise—yet the tendency is there.

Yours etc.,
Vivekananda.

1897.28 — RAKHAL[1]

Almora,
14th June, 1897.

DEAR RAKHAL,

I am wholly in sympathy with the subject-matter of the letter of Charu that you have sent me.

In the proposed Address to the Queen-Empress the following points should be noted:

1. That it must be free from exaggeration, in other words, statements to the effect that she is God's regent and so forth, which are so common to us natives.

2. That all religions having been protected during her reign, we have been able fearlessly to preach our Vedantic doctrines both in India and England.

---

1 Translated from Bengali.

3. Her kindness towards the Indian poor — as, for instance, her inspiring the English to unique acts of charity by contributing herself to the cause of famine-relief.

4. Prayer for her long life and for the continual growth of happiness and prosperity among the people of her dominions.

Have this written in correct English and send it to me at Almora, and I shall sign it and send it to Simla. Let me know to whom it should be addressed at Simla.

Yours etc.,
Vivekananda.

PS — Let Shuddhananda preserve a copy of the weekly letters that he writes to me from the Math.

1897.29 — AKHANDANANDA[2]

Almora,
15th June, 1897.

MY DEAR AKHANDANANDA,

I am getting detailed reports of you and getting more and more delighted. It is that sort of work which can conquer the world. What do differences of sect and opinion matter? Bravo! Accept a hundred thousand embraces and blessings from me. Work, work, work — I care for nothing else. Work, work, work, even unto death! Those that are weak must make themselves great workers, great heroes — never mind money, it will drop from the heavens. Let them whose gifts you will accept, give in their own name if they like, no harm. Whose name, and what is it worth? Who cares for name? Off with it! If in the attempt to carry morsels of food to starving mouths, name and possession and all be doomed even — अहो भग्यमहो भाग्यम् — thrice blessed art thou! It is the heart, the heart that conquers, not the brain. Books and learning, Yoga and meditation and illumination — all are but dust compared with love. It is love that gives you the supernatural powers, love that gives you Bhakti, love that gives illumination, and love, again, that reads to emancipation. This indeed is worship, worship of the Lord in the human tabernacle, "नेदं यदिदमुपासते — not this that people worship". (That is things other than God.) This is but the beginning, and unless we spread over the whole of India, nay, the whole earth, in that way, where lies the greatness of our Lord!

Let people see whether or not the touch of our Lord's feet confers divinity on man! It is this that is called liberation-in-life — when the last trace of egoism and selfishness is gone. Well done! Glory to the Lord! Gradually try to spread. If you can, go to Calcutta, and raise a fund with the help of another band of boys; set one or two of them to work at some place, and begin somewhere else. Spread in that way, and go on inspecting them. You will see that the work will gradually become permanent, and spread of religion and education will follow as a matter of course.

2 Translated from Bengali.

I have given particular instructions to them in Calcutta. Do that kind of work, and I shall carry you on my shoulders—bravo! You will see that by degrees every district will become a centre—and that a permanent one. I am soon going down to the plains. I am a fighter, and shall die in the battlefield. Does it behave me to sit up here like a zenana lady?

Yours with all love,
Vivekananda.

1897.30 — RAKHAL[1]

Almora,
20th June, 1897.

DEAR RAKHAL,

Glad to learn that you are better in health than before. Well, it is seldom that Brother Yogen reports the bare truths, so do not at all be anxious to hear them. I am all right now, with plenty of muscular strength, and no thirst... The liver, too, acts well. I am not certain as to what effects Shashi (Babu)'s medicine had. So I have stopped using it. I am having plenty of mangoes. I am getting exceptionally adept in riding, and do not feel the least pain or exhaustion even after a run of twenty or thirty miles at a stretch. Milk I have altogether stopped for fear of corpulence.

Yesterday I came to Almora, and shall not go any more to the garden. Henceforth I am to have three meals a day in the English fashion, as Miss Müller's guest...

Shuddhananda writes to say that they are going on with Ruddock's Practice of Medicine or something of that sort. What nonsense do you mean by having such things taught in the class? A set of common apparatus for physics and another for chemistry, an ordinary telescope and a microscope—all these can be had for Rupees 150 to 200. Shashi Babu may give a lecture on practical chemistry once a week, and Hariprasanna on physics etc. And buy all the good scientific books that you can have in Bengali, and have them read

Yours affectionately,
Vivekananda.

1897.31 — MISS NOBLE

To Sister Nivedita:

Almora,
20th June, 1897.

MY DEAR MISS NOBLE,

... Let me tell you plainly. Every word you write I value, and every letter is wel-

1 Translated from Bengali.

come a hundred times. Write whenever you have a mind and opportunity, and whatever you like, knowing that nothing will be misinterpreted, nothing unappreciated. I have not had any news of the work for so long. Can you tell me anything? I do not expect any help from India, in spite of all the jubilating over me. They are so poor!

But I have started work in the fashion in which I myself was trained—that is to say, under the trees, and keeping body and soul together anyhow. The plan has also changed a little. I have sent some of my boys to work in the famine districts. It has acted like a miracle. I find, as I always thought, that it is through the heart, and that alone, that the world can be reached. The present plan is, therefore, to train up numbers of young men (from the highest classes, not the lowest. For the latter I shall have to wait a little), and the first attack will be made by sending a number of them over a district. When these sappers and miners of religion have cleared the way, there will then be time enough to put in theory and philosophy.

A number of boys are already in training, but the recent earthquake has destroyed the poor shelter we had to work in, which was only rented, anyway. Never mind. The work must be done without shelter and under difficulties... As yet it is shaven heads, rags, and casual meals. This must change, however, and will, for are we not working for it, head and heart?...

It is true in one way that the people here have so little to give up—yet renunciation is in our blood. One of my boys in training has been an executive engineer, in charge of a district. That means a very big position here. He gave it up like straw!...

With all love,

Yours in the Truth,
Vivekananda.

1897.32—MOTHER

To Mrs. Francis Leggett:

Almora,
20 June, '97.

DEAR MOTHER,

Herewith I take the liberty to introduce to you Miss Tremayne of London, a particular friend of mine going over to the States.

Any help given to her would greatly oblige.

Yours in the Lord,
Vivekananda.

1897.33 — MRS. BULL

To Mrs. Ole Bull:

Almora,
20 June, '97.

DEAR MRS. BULL,

Herewith I take the liberty of introducing Miss Tremayne of London.

I like nothing so much as being serviceable to young and energetic persons — and any help given to her in America will greatly oblige.

Yours in the Lord,
Vivekananda.

1897.34 — FRIEND

To Mr. Sokanathan, Colombo:

ALMORA,
30th June, 1897.

MY DEAR FRIEND,

The bearer of this note, Swami Shivananda, is [being] sent to Ceylon, as promised by me during my sojourn. He is quite fit for the work entrusted to his care, of course, with your kind help.

I hope you will introduce him to other Ceylon friends.

Yours ever in the Lord,
Vivekananda.

1897.35 — SARAT CHANDRA[1]

Almora,
3rd July, 1897.

Constant salutation be to Shri Ramakrishna, the Free, the Ishvara, the Shiva-form, by whose power we and the whole world are blessed.

Mayest thou live long, O Sharat Chandra[2]!

Those writers of Shâstra who do not tend towards work say that all-powerful destiny prevails; but others who are workers consider the will of man as superior. Knowing that the quarrel between those who believe in the human will as the remover of misery and others who rely on destiny is due to indiscrimination — try to

---

1 Translated from Bengali.

2. Sharat Chandra Chakravarty, a disciple of Swamiji.

ascend the highest peak of knowledge.

It has been said that adversity is the touchstone of true knowledge, and this may be said a hundred times with regard to the truth: "Thou art That." This truly diagnoses the Vairâgya (dispassion) disease. Blessed is the life of one who has developed this symptom. In spite of your dislike I repeat the old saying: "Wait for a short time." You are tired with rowing; rest on your oars. The momentum will take the boat to the other side. This has been said in the Gita (IV. 38), "In good time, having reached perfection in Yoga, one realises That in one's own heart;" and in the Upanishad, "Neither by rituals, nor by progeny, nor by riches, but by renunciation alone a few (rare) people attained immortality" (Kaivalya, 2). Here, by the word renunciation Vairagya is referred to. It may be of two kinds, with or without purpose. If the latter, none but worm-eaten brains will try for it. But if the other is referred to, then renunciation would mean the withdrawal of the mind from other things and concentrating it on God or Atman. The Lord of all cannot be any particular individual. He must be the sum total. One possessing Vairagya does not understand by Atman the individual ego but the All-pervading Lord, residing as the Self and Internal Ruler in all. He is perceivable by all as the sum total. This being so, as Jiva and Ishvara are in essence the same, serving the Jivas and loving God must mean one and the same thing. Here is a peculiarity: when you serve a Jiva with the idea that he is a Jiva, it is Dayâ (compassion) and not Prema (love); but when you serve him with the idea that he is the Self, that is Prema. That the Atman is the one objective of love is known from Shruti, Smriti, and direct perception. Bhagavân Chaitanya was right, therefore, when he said, "Love to God and compassion to the Jivas". This conclusion of the Bhagavan, intimating differentiation between Jiva and Ishvara, was right, as He was a dualist. But for us, Advaitists, this notion of Jiva as distinct from God is the cause of bondage. Our principle, therefore, should be love, and not compassion. The application of the word compassion even to Jiva seems to me to be rash and vain. For us, it is not to pity but to serve. Ours is not the feeling of compassion but of love, and the feeling of Self in all.

For thy good, O Sharman, may thine be Vairagya, the feeling of which is love, which unifies all inequalities, cures the disease of Samsâra, removes the threefold misery, inevitable in this phenomenal world, reveals the true nature of all things, destroys the darkness of Mâyâ, and which brings out the Selfhood of everything from Brahma to the blade of grass!

This is the constant prayer of Vivekananda.

Ever bound to thee in love,
Vivekananda.

1897.36 — MISS NOBLE

To Sister Nivedita:

Almora,
4th July, 1897.

MY DEAR MISS NOBLE,

I am being played upon curiously by both good and evil influences from London these times here... On the other hand, your letters are full of life and sunshine, and bring strength and hope to my spirits, and they sadly want these now. God knows.

Although I am still in the Himalayas, and shall be here for at least a month more, I started the work in Calcutta before I came, and they write progress every week.

Just now I am very busy with the famine, and except for training a number of young men for future work, have not been able to put more energy into the teaching work. The "feeding work" is absorbing all my energy and means. Although we can work only on a very small scale as yet, the effect is marvellous. For the first time since the days of Buddha, Brahmin boys are found nursing by the bed-side of cholera-stricken pariahs.

In India, lectures and teaching cannot do any good. What we want is Dynamic Religion. And that, "God willing", as the Mohammedans say, I am determined to show... I entirely agree with the prospectus of your Society, and you may take for granted my agreement with everything you will do in the future. I have entire faith in your ability and sympathy. I already owe you an immense debt, and you are laying me every day under infinite obligations. My only consolation is that it is for the good of others. Else I do not deserve in the least the wonderful kindness shown to me by the Wimbledon friends. You good, steady, genuine English people, may the Lord always bless you. I appreciate you every day more and more from a distance. Kindly convey my love everlasting to __ and all the rest of our friends there.

With all love, yours ever in the Truth,
Vivekananda.

1897.37 — SHIVANANDA[1]

To Swami Shivananda:

Almora,
The 9th July, 1897.

DEAR SHIVANANDA, (This address was written in English)

I haven't received any word of your arrival yet. I heard that Alasinga has gone there with his relations by way of Jaipur. We stayed at the Binsar Dak Bungalow [rest-house] for two or three days, and then I left for Shyamdhura. At this, Miss

---

1 Translated from Bengali.

[Henrietta] Müller got infuriated and left for Almora. Terribly upset, Miss Müller accused Shivananda of telling her first that I shall live with a friend as his guest and of renting later such a big house for the season at 80 rupees without consulting her. Very cross with everybody, she has been reproving one and all but has cooled down a little when I said I would pay half of the rent...

Shashi himself [Swami Ramakrishnananda] should handle the entire amount of 100 rupees which the Raja of Ramnad is donating (every month); he should send a detailed account of the monthly income and expenditure to the Math — otherwise there won't be any check. Advise him to spend as little as necessary on Thakur's worship, for the money is [primarily] "for propagation of Truth".

The phrase "for propagation of Truth" was written in English.)

In case Gupta [Swami Sadananda] has lost his mental balance, ask him to come to Almora—but only when the boy selected for Shashi reaches there. I received a letter from R. A. [Rajam Aiyer?]. The money he sent has reached the Math. I have received two volumes of Ramanuja's commentary. Advise him to send me the third. Ask G. G. [Narasimhachari] to send me similar commentaries by Madhva and others, if he can.

A public meeting will have to be organized at Madras to present an address of welcome to the Raja [Ajit Singh] of Khetri and to Pratap Singh of Jodhpur for their boldness in visiting England as well as for representing their principalities in India in the Jubilee celebration. This has to be done on their return to India, but for that you have to endeavour from now on. Please go to Colombo and arrange a similar public meeting there.

Give my love to Kidi [Singaravelu Mudaliar] and Doctor [Nanjunda Rao]; ask Kidi why he hasn't written to me. What is wrong with him? Has he lost his devotion? Bear this in mind that you should not assume a teacher's place in the beginning. Do all your work with humility; otherwise everything will crumble to pieces. Please see that there is no opposition, criticism or obstacles to Shashi's work in Madras, for everybody should obey him—whoever may be in charge of a particular centre. If Shashi goes to Ceylon, he will have to obey your authority, etc. Make sure that every centre sends a weekly report to the Math. I have not seen a single one from Shashi yet. "O Rama! How hard it is to turn a donkey into a horse, even by beating!"

Above all "obedience" and "esprit de corps".[2] The work cannot succeed unless there is perfect obedience to the authority of the Order and sacrifice of individual views for the sake of the Order. Trinair gunatvam âpannair badhyante mattadantinah — "Blades of grass woven into a rope can restrain even mad elephants".

With love to Sashi and Gupta,
Vivekananda.

---

2. Swami Vivekananda wrote this sentence in English. The French Phrase *esprit de corps* means "the spirit of loyalty".

1897.38 — SISTER

Almora,
9th July, 1897.

DEAR SISTER[1],

I am very sorry to read between the lines the desponding tone of your letter, and I understand the cause; thank you for your warning, I understand your motive perfectly. I had arranged to go with Ajit Singh to England; but the doctors not allowing, it fell thorough. I shall be so happy to learn that Harriet has met him. He will be only too glad to meet any of you.

I had also a lot of cuttings from different American papers fearfully criticising my utterances about American women and furnishing me with the strange news that I had been outcasted! As if I had any caste to lose, being a Sannyâsin!

Not only no caste has been lost, but it has considerably shattered the opposition to sea-voyage — my going to the West. If I should have to be outcasted, it would be with half the ruling princes of India and almost all of educated India. On the other hand, a leading Raja of the caste to which I belonged before my entering the order got up a banquet in my honour, at which were most of the big bugs of that caste. The Sannyasins, on the other hand, may not dine with any one in India, as it would be beneath the dignity of gods to dine with mere mortals. They are regarded as Nârâyanas, while the others are mere men. And dear Mary, these feet have been washed and wiped and worshipped by the descendants of kings, and there has been a progress through the country which none ever commanded in India.

It will suffice to say that the police were necessary to keep order if I ventured out into the street! That is outcasting indeed! Of course, that took the starch out of the missionaries, and who are they here? — Nobodies. We are in blissful ignorance of their existence all the time. I had in a lecture said something about the missionaries and the origin of that species except the English Church gentlemen, and in that connection had to refer to the very churchy women of America and their power of inventing scandals. This the missionaries are parading as an attack on American women en masse to undo my work there, as they well know that anything said against themselves will rather please the U.S. people. My dear Mary, supposing I had said all sorts of fearful things against the "Yanks" — would that be paying off a millionth part of what they say of our mothers and sisters? "Neptune's waters" would be perfectly useless to wash off the hatred the Christian "Yanks" of both sexes bear to us "heathens of India" — and what harm have we done them? Let the "Yanks" learn to be patient under criticism and then criticise others. It is a well-known psychological fact that those who are ever ready to abuse others cannot bear the slightest touch of criticism from others. Then again, what do I owe them? Except your family, Mrs. Bull, the Leggetts, and a few other kind persons, who else has been kind to me? Who came forward to help me work out my ideas? I had

---

1. Miss Mary Hale.

to work till I am at death's door and had to spend nearly the whole of that energy in America, so that the Americans may learn to be broader and more spiritual. In England I worked only six months. There was not a breath of scandal save one, and that was the working of an American woman, which greatly relieved my English friends — not only no attacks but many of the best English Church clergymen became my firm friends, and without asking I got much help for my work, and I am sure to get much more. There is a society watching my work and getting help for it, and four respectable persons followed me to India to help my work, and dozens were ready, and the next time I go, hundreds will be.

Dear, dear Mary, do not be afraid for me… The world is big, very big, and there must be some place for me even if the "Yankees" rage. Anyhow, I am quite satisfied with my work. I never planned anything. I have taken things as they came. Only one idea was burning in my brain — to start the machine for elevating the Indian masses — and that I have succeeded in doing to a certain extent. It would have made your heart glad to see how my boys are working in the midst of famine and disease and misery — nursing by the mat-bed of the cholera stricken Pariah and feeding the starving Chandâla — and the Lord sends help to me and to them all. "What are men?" He is with me, the Beloved, He was when I was in America, in England, when I was roaming about unknown from place to place in India. What do I care about what they talk — the babies, they do not know any better. What! I, who have realised the Spirit and the vanity of all earthly nonsense, to be swerved from my path by babies' prattle! Do I look like that?

I had to talk a lot about myself because I owned that to you. I feel my task is done — at most three or four years more of life are left. I have lost all wish for my salvation. I never wanted earthly enjoyments. I must see my machine in strong working order, and then knowing sure that I have put in a lever for the good of humanity, in India at least, which no power can drive back, I will sleep, without caring what will be next; and may I be born again and again, and suffer thousands of miseries so that I may worship the only God that exists, the only God I believe in, the sum total of all souls — and above all, my God the wicked, my God the miserable, my God the poor of all races, of all species, is the special object of my worship.

"He who is in you and is outside of you, who works through every hand, who walks through every foot, whose body you are, Him worship, and break all other idols.

"He who is the high and the low, the saint and the sinner, the god and the worm, Him worship, the visible, the knowable, the real, the omnipresent, break all other idols.

"In whom there is neither past life nor future birth, nor death nor going or coming, in whom we always have been and always will be one, Him worship, break all other idols.

"Ay, fools, neglecting the living Gods and His infinite reflection with which the world is full, and running after, imaginary shadows! Him worship, the only visible, and break all other idols."

My time is short. I have got to unbreast whatever I have to say, without caring if it smarts some or irritates others. Therefore, my dear Mary, do not be frightened at whatever drops from my lips, for the power behind me is not Vivekananda but He the Lord, and He knows best. If I have to please the world, that will be injuring the world; the voice of the majority is wrong, seeing that they govern and make the sad state of the world. Every new thought must create opposition — in the civilised a polite sneer, in the vulgar savage howls and filthy scandals.

Even these earthworms must stand erect, even children must see light. The Americans are drunk with new wine. A hundred waves of prosperity have come and gone over my country. We have learned the lesson which no child can yet understand. It is vanity. This hideous world is Maya. Renounce and be happy. Give up the idea of sex and possessions. There is no other bond. Marriage and sex and money the only living devils. All earthly love proceeds from the body. No sex, no possessions; as these fall off, the eyes open to spiritual vision. The soul regains its own infinite power. How I wish I were in England to see Harriet. I have one wish left — to see you four sisters before I die, and that must happen.

Yours ever affly.,
Vivekananda.

1897.39 — JOE JOE

To Miss Josephine MacLeod:

Almora,
10th July, 1897.

MY DEAR JOE JOE,

I am glad to learn that you have at last found out that I have time to read your letters.

I have taken to the Himalayas, tired of lecturing and orating. I am so sorry the doctors would not allow my going over with the Raja of Khetri to England, and that has made Sturdy mad.

The Seviers are at Simla and Miss Müller here in Almora.

The plague has subsided, but the famine is still here, and as it looks (on account of no rain as yet), it may wear yet a terrible aspect.

I am very busy from here directing work by my boys in some of the famine districts.

Do come by all means; only you must remember this. The Europeans and the Hindus (called "Natives" by the Europeans) live as oil and water. Mixing with Natives is damning to the Europeans.

There are no good hotels to speak of even at the capitals. You will have to travel with a number of servants about you (cost cheaper than hotels). You will have to bear with people who wear only a loin cloth; you will see me with only a loin cloth about me. Dirt and filth everywhere, and brown people. But you will have plenty of men to talk to you philosophy. If you mix with the English much here, you will have more comforts but see nothing of the Hindus as they are. Possibly I will not be able to eat with you, but I promise that I will travel to good many places with you and do everything in my power to make your journey pleasant. These are what you expect; if anything good comes, so much the better. Perhaps Mary Hale may come over with you. There is a young lady, Miss Campbell, Orchard Lake, Orchard Island, Michigan, who is a great worshipper of Krishna and lives alone in that Island, fasting and praying. She will give anything to be able to see India once, but she is awfully poor. If you bring her with you, I will anyhow manage to pay her expenses. If Mrs. Bull brings old Landsberg with her, that will be saving that fool's life as it were.

Most probably I may accompany you back to America. Kiss Holister for me and the baby. My love to Alberta, to the Leggetts, and to Mabel. What is Fox doing? Give him my love when you see him. To Mrs. Bull and S. Saradananda my love. I am as strong as ever, but it all depends upon leading a quiet life ever afterwards. No hurly-burly any more.

I had a great mind to go to Tibet this year; but they would not allow me, as the road is dreadfully fatiguing. However, I content myself with galloping hard over precipices on mountain ponies. (This is more exciting than your bicycle even, although I had an experience of that at Wimbledon.) Miles and miles of uphill and miles and miles of downhill, the road a few feet broad hanging over sheer precipices several thousand feet deep below.

Ever yours in the Lord,
Vivekananda.

PS — The best time to come is to arrive in India by October or beginning of November. December, January, and February you see things all over and then start by the end of February. From March it begins to get hot. Southern India is always hot.

Goodwin has gone to work in Madras on a paper to be started there soon.

1897.40 — RAKHAL[1]

Salutation to Bhagavan Ramakrishna!

Almora,
10th July, 1897.

DEAR RAKHAL,

Today I send back the proofs of the objects of our Association that you sent me,

---

[1] Translated from Bengali.

corrected. The rules and regulations portion (which the members of our Association had read) is full of mistakes. Correct it very carefully and reprint it, or people will laugh.

... The kind of work that is going on at Berhampore is exceedingly nice. It is those works that will triumph — can doctrines and dogmas touch the heart? Work, work — live the life; what do doctrines and opinions count? Philosophy and Yoga and penance — the worship-room — your sunned rice or vegetable offerings — all these constitute the religion of one man or one country; doing good to others is the one great, universal religion. Men and women, young and old, down to the Pariah, nay, the very animal — all can grasp this religion. Can a merely negative religion be of any avail? The stone is never unchaste, the cow never tells a lie, nor do trees commit theft or robbery, but what does it matter? Granted that you do not steal, nor tell a lie, nor lead an unchaste life, but meditate four hours a day and religiously ring the bell for twice as many hours — yet, what matters it after all? That work, little as it is, that you have done, has brought Berhampore to your feet for ever — now people will do whatever you wish them to. Now you will no longer have to argue to the people that "Ramakrishna is God." Without it what will mere lectures do? — Do fine words butter any parsnips? If you could do like that in ten districts, all the ten would become yours to have and hold. Therefore, like the intelligent boy that you are, lay your greatest stress, for the present, on that work department, and try heart and soul to augment the utility of that alone. Organise a number of boys to go from door to door, let them fetch, in the manner of the Alakhiâ Sâdhus, whatever they can get — money, or worn out clothes, or rice and eatables, or anything. Then distribute them. That is work, work indeed. After that people will have faith, and will then do what they are told.

Whatever is left over after defraying the expenses of the Calcutta meeting, remit for famine relief, or help with it the countless poor that live in the slums of Calcutta; let Memorial Halls and things of that kind go to the dogs. The Lord will do what He thinks best. I am at present in excellent health ...

Why are you not collecting materials? — I shall go down and start the paper myself. Kindness and love can buy you the whole world; lectures and books and philosophy all stand lower than these.

Please write to Shashi to open a work department like this for the service of the poor.

... Curtail the expenses of worship to a rupee or two per mensem. The children of the Lord are dying of starvation ... Worship with water and Tulasi leaves alone, and let the allowance for His Bhoga (food offerings) be spent in offering food to the Living God who dwells in the persons of the poor — then will His grace descend on everything. Yogen felt unwell here; so today he started for Calcutta. I shall again go to Dewaldhar tomorrow. Please accept my love and tender it to all.

Yours affectionately,
Vivekananda.

1897.41 — SHUDDHANANDA

Almora,
11th July, 1897.

MY DEAR SHUDDHANANDA,

I was very glad to receive your last report. I have very little criticism to make except that you ought to write a bit more legibly.

I am quite satisfied with the work done so far, but it must be pushed forward. I have not learnt as yet of the suggestion I made before as to getting a set of chemical and physical apparatus and starting classes in elementary and experimental Chemistry and Physics, especially in Physiology.

What about the other suggestion of buying sets of all the scientific books that have been translated into Bengali?

It now seems to me that there must at least be three Mahantas (heads) elected at a time — one to direct the business part, one the experimental, the other the intellectual part.

The difficulty is to get the director of education. Brahmananda and Turiyananda may well fill the other two. Of visitors I am sorry to learn that you are only getting Babus from Calcutta. They are no good. What we want are brave young men who will work, not tomfools.

Ask Brahmananda to write to both Abhedananda and Saradananda to send weekly reports to the Math without fail, also to send Bengali articles and notes for the would-be paper. Is G. C. Ghosh getting up things for the paper? Work on with a will and be ready.

Akhandananda is working wonderfully at Mahula, but the system is not good. It seems they are frittering away their energies in one little village and that only doling out rice. I do not hear that any preaching has been done along with this helping. All the wealth of the world cannot help one little Indian village if the people are not taught to help themselves. Our work should be mainly educational, both moral and intellectual. I have not learnt anything abut it — only so many beggars are helped! Ask Brahmananda to open centres in different districts so as to cover the largest space with our small means.

And then, so far it seems to have been ineffectual, for they have not succeeded in rousing the people of the place to start societies to educate the people, so that they may learn to be self-reliant, frugal, and not given to marrying, and thus save themselves from future famine. Charity opens the heart, but work on through that wedge.

The easiest way is to take a hut — make it a temple of Guru Maharaj! Let the poor come here to be helped, also to worship. Let there be Kathâ (Puranic recitals) morning and evening there — through that you may teach all you want to teach the people. By degrees the people will be interested. They will keep up the temple themselves; maybe the hut temple will evolve into a great institution in a few years. Let those that go to relief-work first select a central spot in each district and start such a hut-temple, from which all our little work is to proceed.

Even the greatest fool can accomplish a task if it be after his heart. But the intelligent man is he who can convert every work into one that suits his taste. No work is petty. Everything in this world is like a banyan-seed, which, though appearing tiny as a mustard-seed, has yet the gigantic banyan tree latent within it. He indeed is intelligent who notices this and succeeds in making all work truly great. *This paragraph only is translated from Bengali.*

Moreover, they have to see that cheats do not get the food of the deserving. India is full of lazy rogues, and curious, they never die of hunger, they always get something. Ask Brahmananda to write this to everyone in relief-work — they must not be allowed to spend money to no good. We want the greatest possible good work permanent from the least outlay.

Now you see you must try to think out original ideas — else, as soon as I die, the whole thing will tumble to pieces. For example, you hold a meeting to consider, "How we can reap the best permanent results out of the small means at our disposal." Let all have notice a few days before and let each suggest something and discuss all the suggestions, criticising them; and then send me a report.

Lastly, you must remember I expect more from my children than from my brethren. I want each one of my children to be a hundred times greater than I could ever be. Everyone of you must be a giant — must, that is my word. Obedience, readiness, and love for the cause — if you have these three, nothing can hold you back.

With love and blessings,
Vivekananda.

1897.42 — RAKHAL[1]

To Swami Brahmananda:

Deuldhar, Almora,
13th July, 1897.

MY DEAR RAKHAL,

Going to Almora from here I made special efforts for Yogen. But he left for the plains as soon as he had recovered a little. From Subhala valley he will write to me of his safe arrival there. As it is impossible to procure a Dandi (a carrying chair) or any other conveyance, Latu could not go. Achyut and myself have again come back to this place. Today my health is a little bad owing to this riding on horseback at breakneck speed in the sun. I took Shashi Babu's medicine for two weeks — I find no special benefit... The pain in the liver is gone, and owing to plenty of exercise my hands and legs have become muscular, but the abdomen is distending very

1 Translated from Bengali.

much. I feel suffocated while getting up or sitting down. Perhaps this is due to the taking of milk. Ask Shashi if I can give up milk. Previously I suffered from two attacks of sunstroke. From that time, my eyes become red if I expose myself to the sun, and the health continues to be bad for two or three days at a stretch.

I was very pleased to get all the news from the Math, and I also heard that the famine relief work is going on well. Please let me know if any money has been received from the office of the Brahmavadin for famine relief. Some money will be sent soon from here also. There is famine in many other places as well, so it is not necessary to stay so long in one place. Tell them to move to other localities and write to each man to go to a separate place. All such work is real work. If the field is made ready in this way, the seeds of spiritual knowledge can be sown. Remember this always—that the only answer to those conservative fanatics who abuse us is such work. I have no objection to getting the thing printed as Shashi and Sarada have suggested.

You yourselves come to a decision as to what the name of the Math should be... The money will come within seven weeks; but I have no further news about the land. In this matter it seems to me that it will be good if we can get the garden of Kristo Gopal in Cossipore. (Where Shri Ramakrishna passed his last days.) What do you say? In future great works will be accomplished. If you agree with me, don't let this matter out to anybody either within the Math or outside, but quietly make inquiries. The work is spoiled if plans are not kept secret. If it can be bought with fifteen or sixteen thousand, then buy at once—of course, only if you think it good. If something more is demanded, make some advance payment and wait for those seven weeks. My view is that for the present it is better to buy it. Everything else will come by and by. All our associations centre round that garden. In reality that is our first Math. Let the thing be done very privately.

A work can be judged by its results only, just as one can infer the nature of previous mental tendencies by their resultant in present behaviour...

Undoubtedly the price of the land of the garden at Cossipore has increased; but our purse has, on the other hand, dwindled. Do something or other, but do it quickly. All work is spoilt by dilatoriness. This garden also has to be acquired—if not today, tomorrow—however big the Math on the banks of the Ganga may be. It will be still better if you can broach the subject through a proxy. If they hear that we are willing to buy, they will bid high. Do the work very confidentially. Be fearless; Shri Ramakrishna is our helper, what fear? Give my love to all.

Yours affectionately,
Vivekananda.

PS—(on the cover):... Make special efforts for Cossipore... Give up the land at Belur. Should the poor (The famine-stricken people for whom the Mahabodhi Society agreed to pay, on condition that the work would be done in its name.) die of starvation while you people at the top are indulging in controversy regarding to whom the credit should go? If "Mahabodhi" takes all the credit, let it. Let the poor be benefited. That the work is going on well is good news. Work on with greater energy. I am beginning to send articles. The saccharine and lime have reached.

1897.43 — MISS NOBLE

Almora,
23rd July, 1897.

MY DEAR MISS NOBLE,

Excuse these few lines. I shall write more fully as soon as I reach some place. I am on my way from the hills to the plains.

I do not understand what you mean by frankness without familiarity — I for one will give anything to get rid of the last lingering bit of Oriental formality in me and speak out like a child of nature. Oh, to live even for a day in the full light of freedom, to breathe the free air of simplicity! Is not that the highest purity?

In this world we work through fear of others, we talk through fear, we think through fear, alas! we are born in a land of enemies. Who is there who has been able to get rid of this feeling of fear, as if everyone is a spy set specially to watch him? And woe unto the man who pushes himself forward! Will it ever be a land of friends? Who knows? We can only try.

The work has already begun and at present famine-relief is the thing next to hand. Several centres have been opened and the work goes on; famine-relief, preaching, and a little teaching. As yet of course it is very very insignificant, the boys in training are being taken out as opportunity is offering itself. The sphere of action at present is Madras and Calcutta. Mr. Goodwin working in Madras. Also one has gone to Colombo. From the next week a monthly report of the whole work will be forwarded to you if it has not already reached you. I am away from the centre of work, so things go a little slow, you see; but the work is satisfactory on the whole.

You can do more work for us from England than by coming here. Lord bless you for your great self-sacrifice for the poor Indians.

I entirely agree with you that the work in England will look up when I am there. But all the same it is not proper to leave India before the machine is moving at some rate and I am sure that there are many to guide it in my absence. That will be done in a few months. "God willing", as the Mussulmans say. One of my best workers is now in England, the Raja of Khetri. I expect him soon in India, and he will be of great service to me no doubt.

With everlasting love and blessings,

Yours,
Vivekananda.

1897.44 — AKHANDANANDA[1]

Salutation to Bhagavan Ramakrishna!

Almora,
24th July, 1897.

MY DEAR AKHANDANANDA,

I am very glad to receive your letter and go through the contents. Your wishes about the orphanage are very good and Shri Maharaj (Shri Ramakrishna.) will not fail to fulfil them at an early date. Try your best to found a permanent centre... Never worry about money. Tomorrow I shall leave Almora for the plains; and wherever there will be made some stir, I shall open a subscription list for famine — set your mind easy on that score. When in every district there will be a Math on the model of our Math in Calcutta, then will my heart's desire be fulfilled. Let not the work of preaching, too, be at a standstill, and greater even than preaching, is the work of imparting education. By means of lectures and the like, the village people must be taught religion, history, and such other subjects — specially history. To help our educational work there is a Society in England, which, as I find from reports, is doing excellent work. In time we shall get help of this kind from everywhere, don't be frightened. They only do work who think that help will come, directly they are on the field of work.

All strength is in you, have faith in it. It will not go unmanifested. Accept my heartiest love and blessings, and convey them to the Brahmachârin. Write now and then fiery letters to the Math, so that all may take heart and work. Victory to the Guru!

Yours affectionately,
Vivekananda.

1897.45 — MARIE

To Marie Halboister:

Almora,
25th July, 1897.

MY DEAR MARIE,

I have time, will, and opportunity now to clear my promise. So my letter begins. I have been very weak for some time, and with that and other things my visit to England this Jubilee season had to be postponed.

I was very sorry at first not to be able to meet my nice and very dear friends once more, but Karma cannot be avoided, and I had to rest contented with my Himalayas. It is a sorry exchange, after all; for the beauty of the living spirit shining through the human face is far more pleasurable than any amount of material beauty.

Is not the soul the Light of the world?

---

1 Translated from Bengali.

The work in London had to go slow—for various reasons, and last though not the least was l'argent, mon amie! When I am there l'argent comes in somehow, to keep the mare going. Now everybody shrugs his shoulder. I must come again and try my best to revive the work.

I am having a good deal of riding and exercise, but I had to drink a lot of skimmed milk per prescription of the doctors, with the result that I am more to the front than back! I am always a forward man though—but do not want to be too prominent just now, and I have given up drinking milk.

I am glad to learn that you are eating your meals with good appetite.

Do you know Miss Margaret Noble of Wimbledon? She is working hard for me. Do correspond with her if you can, and you help me a good deal there. Her address is, Brantwood, Worple Road, Wimbledon.

So you saw my little friend Miss Orchard and you liked her too—good. I have great hopes for her. And how I should like to be retired from life's activities entirely when I am very old, and hear the world ringing with the names of my dear, dear young friends like yourself and Miss Orchard etc.!

By and by, I am glad to find that I am aging fast, my hair is turning grey. "Silver threads among the gold"—I mean black—are coming in fast.

It is bad for a preacher to be young, don't you think so? I do, as I did all my life. People have more confidence in an old man, and it looks more venerable. Yet the old rogues are the worst rogues in the world, isn't it?

The world has its code of judgment which, alas, is very different from that of truth's.

So your "Universal Religion" has been rejected by the Revue de deux Mondes. Never mind, try again some other paper. Once the ice is broken, you get in at a quick rate, I am sure. And I am so glad that you love the work: it will make its way, I have no doubt of it. Our ideas have a future, ma chere Marie—and it will be realised soon.

I think this letter will meet you in Paris—your beautiful Paris—and I hope you will write me lots about French journalism and the coming "World's Fair" there.

I am so glad that you have been helped by Vedanta and Yoga. I am unfortunately sometimes like the circus clown who makes others laugh, himself miserable!

You are naturally of a buoyant temperament. Nothing seems to touch you. And you are moreover a very prudent girl, inasmuch as you have scrupulously kept yourself away from "love" and all its nonsense. So you see you have made your good Karma and planted the seed of your lifelong well-being. Our difficulty in life is that we are guided by the present and not by the future. What gives us a little pleasure now drags us on to follow it, with the result that we always buy a mass of pain in the future for a little pleasure in the present.

I wish I had nobody to love, and I were an orphan in my childhood. The greatest misery in my life has been my own people—my brothers and sisters and mother etc. Relatives are like deadly clogs to one's progress, and is it not a wonder that people will still go on to find new ones by marriage!!!

He who is alone is happy. Do good to all, like everyone, but do not love anyone. It is a bondage, and bondage brings only misery. Live alone in your mind — that is happiness. To have nobody to care for and never minding who cares for one is the way to be free.

I envy so much your frame of mind — quiet, gentle, light, yet deep and free. You are already free, Marie, free already — you are Jivanmukta. I am more of a woman than a man, you are more of a man than woman. I am always dragging other's pain into me — for nothing, without being able to do any good to anybody — just as women, if they have no children, bestow all their love upon a cat!!!

Do you think this has any spirituality in it? Nonsense, it is all material nervous bondage — that is what it is. O! to get rid of the thraldom of the flesh!

Your friend Mrs. Martin very kindly sends me copies of her magazine every month — but Sturdy's thermometer is now below zero, it seems. He seems to be greatly disappointed with my non-arrival in England this summer. What could I do?

We have started two Maths (monasteries) here, one in Calcutta, the other in Madras. The Calcutta Math (a wretched rented house) was awfully shaken in the late earthquake.

We have got in a number of boys, and they are in training; also we have opened famine relief in several places and the work is going on apace. We will try to start similar centres in different places in India.

In a few days I am going down to the plains and from thence go to the Western parts of the mountains. When it is cooler in the plains, I will make a lecture tour all over and see what work can be done.

Here I cannot find any more time to write — so many people are waiting — so here I stop, dear Marie, wishing you all joy and happiness.

May you never be lured by flesh is the constant prayer of —

Ever yours in the Lord,
Vivekananda.

1897.46 — MOTHER

Almora,
28th July, 1897.

MY DEAR MOTHER[1],

Many many thanks for your beautiful and kind letter. I wish I were in London to be able to accept the invitation with the Raja of Khetri. I had a great many dinners to attend in London last season. But it was fated not to be, and my health did not permit my going over with the Raja.

1. Mrs. Leggett.

So Alberta is once more at home in America. I owe her a debt of gratitude for all she did for me in Rome. How is Holli? To both of them my love, and kiss the new baby for me, my youngest sister.

I have been taking some rest in the Himalayas for nine months. Now I am going down to the plains to be harnessed once more for work.

To Frankincense and Joe Joe and Mabel my love, and so to you eternally.

Yours ever in the Lord,
Vivekananda.

1897.47 — SHASHI[1]

To Swami Ramakrishnananda:

Almora,
29th July, 1897.

DEAR SHASHI,

I got information that your work there is going on very well. Get a thorough mastery of the three Bhâshyas (commentaries), and also study well European philosophy and allied subjects — see to it without fail. To fight with others one requires sword and shield — this fact should never be forgotten. I hope Sukul has now reached there and is attending on you all right. If Sadananda does not like to stay there, send him to Calcutta. Don't forget to send to the Math every week a report of the work including income and expenditure and other information.

Alasinga's sister's husband borrowed four hundred rupees from Badridas here, promising to send it back as soon as he reached Madras; inquire from Alasinga and tell him to send it quickly. For I am leaving this place the day after tomorrow — whether for Mussoorie Hills or somewhere else I shall decide later.

Yesterday I delivered a lecture in the circle of the local English people, and all were highly pleased with it. But I was very much pleased with the lecture in Hindi that I delivered the previous day — I did not know before that I could be oratorical in Hindi.

Are there any new boys joining the Math? If so, then carry on the work in the same manner as it is being done in Calcutta. At present don't use up your wisdom too much, lest it should become completely exhausted — you can do that later on.

Pay particular attention to your health, but too much coddling of the body will, on the contrary, also spoil the health. If there is not the strength of knowledge, nobody would care twopence for your ringing of the bell — this is certain; and knowing this for certain equip yourself accordingly. My heart's love and blessings to you and to Goodwin and others.

Yours affectionately,
Vivekananda.

1 Translated from Bengali.

1897.48 — MISS NOBLE

Almora,
29th July, 1897.

MY DEAR MISS NOBLE,

A letter from Sturdy reached me yesterday, informing me that you are determined to come to India and see things with your own eyes. I replied to that yesterday, but what I learnt from Miss Muller about your plans makes this further note necessary, and it is better that it should be direct.

Let me tell you frankly that I am now convinced that you have a great future in the work for India. What was wanted was not a man, but a woman — a real lioness — to work for the Indians, women specially.

India cannot yet produce great women, she must borrow them from other nations. Your education, sincerity, purity, immense love, determination, and above all, the Celtic blood make you just the woman wanted.

Yet the difficulties are many. You cannot form any idea of misery, the superstition, and the slavery that are here. You will be in the midst of a mass of half-naked men and women with quaint ideas of caste and isolation, shunning the white skin through fear or hatred and hated by them intensely. On the other hand, you will be looked upon by the white as a crank, and every one of your movements will be watched with suspicion.

Then the climate is fearfully hot; our winter in most places being like your summer, and in the south it is always blazing.

Not one European comfort is to be had in places out of the cities. If in spite of all this, you dare venture into the work, you are welcome, a hundred times welcome. As for me, I am nobody here as elsewhere, but what little influence I have shall be devoted to your service.

You must think well before you plunge in; and after work, if you fail in this or get disgusted, on my part I promise you, I will stand by you unto death whether you work for India or not, whether you give up Vedanta or remain in it. "The tusks of the elephant come out, but never go back"; so are the words of a man never retracted. I promise you that. Again, I must give you a bit of warning. You must stand on your own feet and not be under the wings of Miss Muller or anybody else. Miss Muller is a good lady in her own way, but unfortunately it got into her head, when she was a girl, that she was a born leader and that no other qualifications were necessary to move world but money! This idea is coming on the surface again and again in spite of herself, and you will find it impossible to pull on with her in a few days. She now intends to take a house in Calcutta for herself and yourself and other European or American friends who may come.

It is very kind and good of her, but her Lady Abbess plan will never be carried out for two reasons — her violent temper and overbearing conduct, and her awfully vacillating mind. Friendship with many is best at a distance, and everything goes well with the person who stands on his own feet.

Mrs. Sevier is a jewel of a lady—so good, so kind! The Seviers are the only English people who do not hate the natives, Sturdy not excepted. Mr. and Mrs. Sevier are the only persons who did not come to patronise us, but they have no fixed plans yet. When you come, you may get them to work with you, and that will be really helpful to them and to you. But after all it is absolutely necessary to stand on one's own feet.

I learn from America that two friends of mine, Mrs. Ole Bull of Boston and Miss MacLeod, are coming on a visit to India this autumn. Miss MacLeod you already know in London, that Paris-dressed young American lady; Mrs. Ole Bull is about fifty and has been a kind friend to me in America. I may suggest that your joining the party may while away the tedium of the journey, as they also are coming by way of Europe.

I am glad to receive a note at least from Sturdy after long. But it was so stiff and cold. It seems he is disappointed at the collapse of the London work.

With everlasting love,

Yours ever in the Lord,
Vivekananda.

1897.49 — AKHANDANANDA[1]

Almora,
30th July, 1897.

MY DEAR AKHANDANANDA,

According to your instructions, I write a letter to Mr. Levinge, the Dist. Magistrate. Besides, you will write a big letter to the Indian Mirror, describing in detail his method of work (having got the same revised by Dr. Shashi), and send a copy of it to the gentleman named above. Our fools only search for people's shortcomings. Let them see some virtues too.

I am leaving this place next Monday...

What do you talk of the difficulty in getting orphans? Better ask for four or five men from the Math, if you like; you can find some orphans in two days, if you seek from village to village.

Of course we must have a permanent centre. And can anything be done in this country unless the—help? Do not mix in politics etc., nor have any connection with them. At the same time you need not have any quarrel with anybody. You must put your body, mind, and all you have to some one work. Here I gave a lecture to a European audience in English, and another to the Indian residents in Hindi. This was my maiden speech in Hindi, but everyone liked it for all that. Of

1 Translated from Bengali.

course the Westerners, as is their wont, were in raptures over it, as coming from a "nigger"! "Oh, how wonderful!" and that sort of thing. Next Saturday there will be another lecture for the Europeans. A big Association has been set on foot here — let us wait and see how far it works in future. The object of the Association is to impart education and religion.

Monday next, trip to Bareilly then to Saharanpur, next to Ambala, thence, most probably, to Mussoorie with Captain Sevier, and as soon as it is a little cool, return to the plains and journey to Rajputana etc. Go on working at top speed. Never fear! I, too, have determined to work. The body must go, no mistake about that. Why then let it go in idleness? It is better to wear out than rust out. Don't be anxious even when I die, my very bones will work miracles. We must spread over the whole of India in ten years, short of this it is no good. To work like an athlete! Victory to the Guru! Money and all will come of themselves, we want men, not money. It is man that makes everything, what can money do? — Men we want, the more you get, the better... Here, for instance, was M — who brought together a lot of money, but there was no man, and what good did he achieve?

Yours affectionately,
Vivekananda.

1897.50 — JOE

The Math, Belur,
11th August, 1897.

DEAR JOE[2],

...Well, the work of the Mother will not suffer; because it has been built and up to date maintained upon truth, sincerity, and purity. Absolute sincerity has been its watchword.

Yours with all love,
Vivekananda.

1897.51 — SHASHI[3]

To Swami Ramakrishnananda:

Ambala,
19th August, 1897.

DEAR SHASHI,

I am very much pained to hear that the work in Madras is not prospering for want of funds. I am glad to learn that the amount borrowed by Alasinga's broth-

2. Miss MacLeod.
3 Translated from Bengali.

er-in-law (sister's husband) has been received back in Almora. Goodwin has written to me to inform the Reception Committee to take some money for expenses from the amount that is left as a result of the lecture. It is a very mean thing to spend the money received on the occasion of that lecture for the purpose of the Reception—and I do not like to tell anybody anything about this matter. I have understood quite well what the people of our country are when it comes to money-matters... On my behalf, you personally talk with the friends there and politely make them understand that it is all right if they can find ways and means to bear the expenses; but if they cannot do so, all of you come back to the Math at Calcutta or go to Ramnad and establish the Math there.

I am now going to the hills at Dharamsala. Niranjan, Dinu, Krishnalal, Latu, and Achyut will stay at Amritsar. Why did you not, all these days, send Sadananda to the Math? If he is still there, then send him to the Punjab on receipt of a letter from Niranjan from Amritsar. I intend to start work in the Punjab after a few days' more rest in the Punjab hills. The Punjab and Rajputana are indeed fields for work. I shall write to you again soon after starting work...

My health was very bad recently. Now I am very slowly recovering. It will be all right, if I stay in the hills for some more days. My love to you and to Alasinga, G. G., R. A., Goodwin, Gupta, Sukul, and all others.

Yours affectionately,
Vivekananda.

1897.52 — MRS. BULL

The Math (The letter was actually written from Ambala.),
19th August, 1897.

DEAR MRS. BULL,

... My health is indifferent, and although I have some rest, I do not think I shall be able to regain my usual vigour till winter next. I had a letter from Joe saying that you are both coming to India. I, of course, will be very glad to see you in India, only you ought to know from the first that India is the dirtiest and unhealthiest hole in the world, with scarcely any European comforts except in the big capitals.

I learn from England that Mr. Sturdy is sending Abhedananda to New York. It seems that the English work is impossible without me. Only a magazine will be started and worked by Mr. Sturdy. I had arranged to come to England this season, but I was foolishly prevented by the doctors. In India the work is going on.

I do not think any European or American will be of any service here just now, and it will be hard for any Westerner to bear the climate. Annie Besant with her exceptional powers works only among the Theosophists, and thus she submits to all the indignities of isolation which a Mlechchha is made to undergo here. Even Goodwin smarts now and then and has to be called to order. Goodwin is doing good work, as he is a man and can mix with the people. Women have no place in men's society here, and she can do good only among her own sex in India. The English friends that came over to India have not been of any help as yet, and do not know whether they will be of any in the future. With all these, if anybody wants to try, she is welcome.

If Saradananda wants to come, he may, and I am sure he will be of very good service to me just now in organising the work, now that my health is broken. There is a young English woman, Miss Margaret Noble, very eager to come to India to learn the state of things, so that she may do some work when she is back home. I have written her to accompany you in case you come via London. The great difficulty is that you can never understand the situation here from a distance. The two types are so entirely different in all things that it is not possible to form any idea from America or England.

You ought to think that you are starting for the interior of Africa, and if you meet anything better, that will be unexpected.

Ever yours etc.,
Vivekananda.

1897.53 — MOTHER[1]

1897.

DEAR MOTHER, (Shrimati Indumati Mitra)

Please be not anxious because I could not write to you and could not go to Belgaon. I was suffering very much from illness and it was impossible for me to go then. Now thanks to my travels in the Himalayas, I have greatly regained my health. I shall soon resume work. In two weeks I am going to the Punjab, and just after delivering a lecture or two at Lahore and Amritsar, I shall start via Karachi for Gujarat, Cutch, etc. I shall surely see you at Karachi.

This Kashmir is a veritable heaven on earth. Nowhere else in the world is such a country as this. Mountains and rivers, trees and plants, men and women, beasts and birds — all vie with one another for excellence. I feel a pang at heart not to have visited it so long. Please write to me in detail how you are doing, mentally and physically, and accept my special blessings. I am constantly hating your welfare at heart, know this for certain.

Yours sincerely,
Vivekananda.

1 Translated from Bengali.

1897.54 — RAKHAL[1]

To Swami Brahmananda:

Amritsar,
2nd September, 1897.

MY DEAR RAKHAL,

Yogen tells me in a letter to buy the house at Baghbazar for Rs. 20,000. Even if we buy that house, there are still a lot of difficulties; for example, we shall have to break it down in part and make the drawing room into a big hall, and similar alterations and repairs. Moreover the house is very old and ramshackle. However, consult Girish Babu and Atul and do what you decide to be best. Today I am leaving by the two o'clock train with all my party for Kashmir. The recent stay at Dharamsala Hills has improved my health much, and the tonsillitis, fever, etc. have completely disappeared. From a letter of yours I got all the news. Niranjan, Latu, Krishnalal, Dinanath, Gupta, and Achyut are all going to Kashmir with me.

The gentleman from Madras who donated Rs. 1,500 for famine relief wants an account of how exactly the money was expended. Send him such an account. We are doing more or less well.

Yours affectionately,
Vivekananda.

PS — Give my love to all at the Math.

1897.55 — RAKHAL[2]

To Swami Brahmananda:

C/O Rishibar Mukhopadhyaya,
Chief Justice, Srinagar, Kashmir,
13th September, 1897.

MY DEAR RAKHAL,

Now Kashmir. The excellent accounts you heard of this place are all true. There is no place so beautiful as this; and the people also are fair and good-looking, though their eyes are not beautiful. But I have also never seen elsewhere villages and towns so horribly dirty. In Srinagar I am now putting up at the house of Rishibar Babu. He is very hospitable and kind. Send all my letters to his address. In a few days I shall go out somewhere else on excursions; but while returning, I shall come by way of Srinagar, and so shall get the letters also. I have read the letter that you sent regarding Gangadhar. Write to him that there are many orphans in Central India and in Gorakhpur. From there the Punjabis are getting many children. You must

---
1 Translated from Bengali.
2 Translated from Bengali.

persuade Mahendra Babu and get up an agitation about this matter, so that the people of Calcutta are induced to take up the charge of these orphans—such a movement is very desirable. Especially a memorial should be sent to the Government requesting it to see that orphans taken over by the missionaries are returned to the Hindus. Tell Gangadhar to come over; and on behalf of the Ramakrishna Society a tearing campaign should be made. Gird up your loins, and go to every house to carry on the campaign. Hold mass meetings etc. Whether you succeed or not, start a furious agitation. Get all the facts from the important Bengali friends at Gorakhpur by writing to them, and let there be a countrywide agitation over this. Let the Ramakrishna Society be fully established. The secret of the whole thing is to agitate and agitate without respite. I am much pleased to see the orderliness of Sarada's work. Gangadhar and Sarada should not rest satisfied until they have succeeded in creating a centre in every place they visit.

Just now I received a letter from Gangadhar. It is good news that he is determined to start a centre in that district. Write to him saying that his friend, the Magistrate, has sent an excellent reply to my letter. As soon as we come down to the plains from Kashmir, I shall send back Latu, Niranjan, Dinu, and Khoka. For there is no suitable work for them here any more; also within three to four weeks send Shuddhananda, Sushil, and one other to me. Send them to the house of Mr. Shyamacharan Mukhopadhyaya, Medical Hall, Cantonment, Ambala. From there I shall go to Lahore. They should have each two thick gerua-coloured jerseys, and two blankets for bedding. I shall buy them woollen chaddars, and other woollen necessities in Lahore. If the translation of Râja-Yoga has been completed, get it published bearing all the cost... Where the language is obscure, make it very simple and clear, and let Tulsi make a Hindi translation of it if he can. If these books are published, they will help the Math very greatly.

I hope your health is now quite all right. Since reaching Dharamsala I have been all right. I like the cold places; there the body keeps well. I have a desire either to visit a few places in Kashmir and then choose an excellent site and live a quiet life there, or to go on floating on the water. I shall do what the doctor advises. The Raja is not here now. His brother, the one just next to him in age, is the Commander-in-Chief. Efforts are being made to arrange a lecture under his chairmanship. I shall write all about this afterwards. If the meeting for the lecture is held in a day or two, I shall stay back, otherwise I go out again on my travels. Sevier is still at Murree. His health is very bad—going about in the jolting tongas and jutkas. The Bengali gentlemen of Murree are very good and courteous. Give my respects to G. C. Ghosh, Atul, Master Mahashay, and others, and keep up the spirits of everybody. What is the news about the house which Yogen suggested we should buy? In October I shall go down from here and shall deliver a few lectures in the Punjab. After that I may go via Sind to Cutch, Bhuj, and Kathiawar—even down to Poona if circumstances are favourable; otherwise I go to Rajputana via Baroda. From Rajputana I go to the North-Western Province, (In those days this was made up of Uttar Pradesh and part of the Punjab.) then Nepal, and finally Calcutta—this is my present programme. Everything, however, is in God's hands. My love and greetings to all.

Yours affectionately,
Vivekananda.

1897.56 — SHUDDHANANDA

To Swami Shuddhananda:

C/O Rishibar Mukhopadhyaya,
Chief Justice, Srinagar, Kashmir,
15th September, 1897.

MY DEAR SHUDDHANANDA,

We are in Kashmir at last. I need not tell you of all the beauties of the place. It is the one land fit for Yogis, to my mind. But the land is now inhabited by a race who though possessing great physical beauty are extremely dirty. I am going to travel by water for a month seeing the sights and getting strong. But the city is very malarious just now, and Sadananda and Kristolal have got fever. Sadananda is all right today, but Kristolal has fever yet. The doctor came today and gave him a purgative. He will be all right by tomorrow, we hope; and we start also tomorrow. The State has lent me one of its barges, and it is fine and quite comfortable. They have also sent orders to the Tahsildars of different districts. The people here are crowding in banks to see us and are doing everything they can to make us comfortable.

A clipping from The Indian Mirror, quoting passages from an article written by Dr. Barrows in an American paper, has been sent over to me by somebody without a name and asking me what reply to give. I send back the cutting to Brahmananda with my answer to the passages which are damned lies!

I am glad to learn you are doing well there and going on with your usual work. I also had a letter from Shivananda giving the details of work there.

After a month I go back to the Punjab, and I will expect three of you at Ambala. In case a centre is founded, one of you will be left in charge. Niranjan, Latu, and Kristolal will be sent back.

I intend to make a rapid march through the Punjab and Sind via Kathiawar and Baroda, back to Rajputana, and thence to Nepal and last Calcutta.

Write to me C/o Rishibar Babu at Srinagar. I will get the letter on my way back.

With love to all and blessings,

Yours,
Vivekananda.

1897.57 — HARIPADA[1]

To Sri Haripada Mitra:

Srinagar, Kashmir,
1897.

DEAR HARIPADA,

My health has been very bad for the last nine months, and the heat made it still worse. So I have been wandering over the hills from place to place. Now I am in Kashmir. I have travelled far and wide, but I have never seen such a country. I shall soon leave for the Punjab and again go to work. From Sadananda I have heard all the news about you and continue to get it. I am sure to go to Karachi after visiting the Punjab. So we shall meet in person there.

With blessings,
Vivekananda.

1897.58 — MISS MACLEOD

To Miss Josephine MacLeod:

Srinagar, Kashmir,
30th September, 1897.

MY DEAR MISS MACLEOD,

Come soon if you intend to come really. From November to the middle of February India is cool; after that it is hot. You will be able to see all you want within that time, but to see all takes years.

I am in a hurry; therefore excuse this hasty card. Kindly tender my love to Mrs. Bull and my good wishes and earnest thoughts for Goodwin's speedy recovery. My love to Mother, to Alberta, to the baby, to Holister, and last, not the least, to Franky.

Yours in the Lord,
Vivekananda.

1897.59 — RAKHAL

To Swami Brahmananda:

Srinagar, Kashmir,
30th September, 1897.

DEAR RAKHAL,

I received your affectionate letter and also the letter from the Math. I am leaving for the Punjab in two or three days. I have received the foreign mail. The following

---

1 Translated from Bengali.

are my answers to Miss Noble's questions in her letter:

1. Nearly all the branches have been started, but the movement is only just beginning.

2. Most of the monks are educated. Those that are not are also having secular education. But above all, to do good, perfect unselfishness is absolutely necessary. To ensure that, more attention is given to spiritual exercises than to anything else.

3. Secular educators: We get mostly those who have already educated themselves. What is needed is training them into our method and building up of character. The training is to make them obedient and fearless; and the method is to help the poor physically first and then work up to higher regions of mentality.

Arts and Industries: This part of the programme alone cannot be begun for want of funds. The simplest method to be worked upon at present is to induce Indians to use their own produce and get markets for Indian artware etc. in other countries. This should be done by persons who are not only not middlemen themselves, but will devote the entire proceeds of this branch to the benefit of the workmen.

4. Wandering from place to place will be necessary till "people come to education". The religious character of the wandering monks will carry with it a much greater weight than otherwise.

5. All castes are open to our influence. So long the highest only have been worked upon. But since the work department is in full operation in different famine-centres, we are influencing the lower classes more and more.

6. Nearly all the Hindus approve our work, only they are not used to practical co-operation in such works.

7. Yes, from the very start we are making no distinction in our charities or other good works between the different religions of India.

Reply to Miss N. according to these hints.

See that there is no remissness whatever in the medical treatment of Yogen — if necessary spend money by drawing on the capital. Did you go and meet Bhavanath's wife?

If Brahmachari Hariprasanna can come, it will be very helpful. Mr. Sevier has become very impatient about acquiring a house somewhere; it will be good if something is done quickly about it! Hariprasanna is an engineer; so he will be able to do something quickly about it. Also he understands better about the suitability of places. They (the Seviers) like to have a place somewhere near about Dehra Dun or Mussoorie; that is to say, the place must not be too cold and must be habitable throughout the year. So send Hariprasanna at once straight to Sj. Shyamapada Mukherjee, Medical Hall, Ambala Cantonment. As soon as I go down to the Punjab, I shall send Mr. Sevier along with him. I am returning (to the Math) in a trice after a tour of the Punjab, Karachi, and then via Rajputana, not via Kathiawar and Gujarat — to Nepal. Tulsi has gone to Madhya Bharat — is it for the famine-relief work?…

My blessings and love to all. I have got the news that Kali has reached New York; but he has not written any letter. Sturdy writes that his work had increased so much that people were amazed—and a few persons have also written me praising him highly. However, there is not so much difficulty in America; the work will go on somehow or other. Send Shuddhananda and his brother along with Hariprasanna. Of the party only Gupta and Achyut will accompany me.

Yours affectionately,
Vivekananda.

1897.60 — SHASHI[1]

To Swami Ramakrishnananda:

Srinagar, Kashmir,
30th September, 1897.

MY DEAR SHASHI,

Now I am returning from a visit to places in Kashmir. In a day or two I shall leave for the Punjab. As my health is now much better, I have decided to tour again in the same way as before. Not too much lecturing—one or two lectures, perhaps, in the Punjab, otherwise none. The people of our country have not yet offered me even as much as a pice for my travelling expenses—and to cap it all, to take with you a whole party, well, you can easily understand how troublesome it all is. It is also a matter of shame to have to draw upon only the English disciples. So, as before, I start out "with only a blanket". In this place there is no need for any person like Goodwin, as you can see.

A monk from Ceylon, P. C. Jinawar Vamar by name, has written to me among other things that he wants to visit India. Perhaps he is the same monk who comes of the Siamese royal family. His address is Wellawatta, Ceylon. If convenient, invite him to Madras. He believes in the Vedanta. It will not be so difficult to send him to other places from Madras. It is also good to have such a person in the Order. My love and blessings to you and all others.

Yours affectionately,
Vivekananda.

PS—The Maharaja of Khetri is reaching Bombay on the 10th October. Don't forget to present him an address of welcome.

---

1 Translated from Bengali.

1897.61 — RAKHAL

To Swami Brahmananda:

Srinagar, Kashmir,
30th September, 1897.

DEAR RAKHAL,

I understand from a letter of Gopal Dada that you have seen that piece of land at Konnagar. It seems that that site is rent-free and measures 16 bighas (about 5 acres), and that the price is below eight or ten thousand rupees. Do what you think best after considering the healthiness and other factors. In a day or two I shall leave for the Punjab. So don't write any more letters to me at this address. I shall telegraph to you my next address. Don't forget to send Hariprasanna. Tell Gopal Dada thus: "Your health will soon be all right—winter is coming, what fear? Eat well and be merry." Write a letter to Mrs. C. Sevier at Spring Dale, Murree, as to Yogen's present state of health, marking on the cover "to await arrival". Give my love and blessings to all.

Yours affectionately,
Vivekananda.

PS—The Maharaja of Khetri reaches Bombay on the 10th October. Don't forget to give him an address of welcome.

1897.62 — MARGO

To Sister Nivedita:

Srinagar, Kashmir,
1st October, 1897.

DEAR MARGO,

Some people do the best work when led. Not every one is born to lead. The best leader, however, is one who "leads like the baby". The baby, though apparently depending on everyone, is the king of the household. At least, to my thinking, that is the secret... Many feel, but only a few can express. It is the power of expressing one's love and appreciation and sympathy for others, that enables one person to succeed better in spreading the idea than others...

I shall not try to describe Kashmir to you. Suffice it to say, I never felt sorry to leave any country except this Paradise on earth; and I am trying my best, if I can, to influence the Raja in starting a centre. So much to do here, and the material so hopeful!...

The great difficulty is this: I see persons giving me almost the whole of their love. But I must not give anyone the whole of mine in return, for that day the work would be ruined. Yet there are some who will look for such a return, not having the breadth of the impersonal view. It is absolutely necessary to the work that I should have the enthusiastic love of as many as possible, while I myself remain entirely impersonal. Otherwise jealousy and quarrels would break up everything. A leader must be impersonal. I am sure you understand this. I do not mean that one should be a brute, making use of the devotion of others for his own ends, and laughing in his sleeve meanwhile. What I mean is what I am, intensely personal in my love, but having the power to pluck out my own heart with my own hand, if it becomes necessary, "for the good of many, for the welfare of many", as Buddha said. Madness of love, and yet in it no bondage. Matter changed into spirit by the force of love. Nay, that is the gist of our Vedanta. There is but One, seen by the ignorant as matter, by the wise as God. And the history of civilisation is the progressive reading of spirit into matter. The ignorant see the person in the non-person. The sage sees the non-person in the person. Through pain and pleasure, joy and sorrow, this is the one lesson we are learning…

Yours ever with love and truth,
Vivekananda.

1897.63 — SARADA[1]

Murree,
10th October, 1897.

DEAR SARADA,

I am sorry to learn from your letter that you are not doing well. If you can make an unpopular man popular, then I call you a clever fellow. There is no prospect of work there in the future; it would have been better had you gone rather to Dacca, or some other place. However, it is a good thing that the work will close in November. If you get very badly off in health, you should better come away. There is much field for work in the Central Provinces; and even without famine, there is no lack of poverty-stricken people in our country. Wherever it is, if you can choose a site with an eye to prospect, you are sure to turn out good work. However, be not sorry. What one does has no destruction — no, never. Who knows, at that very place the future may reap golden results.

I shall very soon begin my work in the plains. I have now no need of travelling over the mountains.

Keep watch over your health.

Yours affectionately,
Vivekananda.

---

[1] Translated from Bengali.

1897.64 — AKHANDANANDA[1]

Murree,
10th October, 1897.

MY DEAR AKHANDANANDA,

I am very glad to receive your letter. You need not make a big plan for the present, but do only what is possible under existing circumstances. Gradually the way will open to you. We must certainly have the orphanage, no hesitating in that. We must not leave the girls in the lurch either. But then we must have a lady superintendent for an orphanage of girls. I believe Mother will be a very good hand for that. Or engage for this task some aged widow of the village who has no issue. And there must be separate places for the boys and girls. Captain Sevier is ready to send you money to help in this. Nedou's Hotel, Lahore — that is his address. If you write to him, write the words, "To wait arrival", on the letter. I am soon going to Rawalpindi, tomorrow or the day after; then I visit Lahore and other places via Jammu, and return to Rajputana via Karachi etc.

I am doing well.

Yours affectionately,
Vivekananda.

PS — You must admit Mohammedan boys, too, but never tamper with their religion. The only thing you will have to do is to make separate arrangements for their food etc., and teach them so that they may be moral, manly, and devoted to doing good to others. This indeed is religion.

Shelve your intricate philosophical speculations for the present. In our country we at present need manhood and kindness. " — The Lord is the Essence of unutterable love." But instead of saying" say, " — He is ever manifest as Love in all beings." What other God — the creation of your mind — are you then going to worship! Let the Vedas, the Koran, the Puranas, and all scriptural lumber rest now for some time — let there be worship of the visible God of Love and Compassion in the country. All idea of separation is bondage, that of non-differentiation is Mukti. Let not the words of people dead-drunk with worldliness terrify you. " — Be fearless" "Ignore the ordinary critics as worms!" Admit boys of all religions — Hindu, Mohammedan, Christian, or anything; but begin rather gently — I mean, see that they get their food and drink a little separately, and teach them only the universal side of religion.

Be mad over this, and strike others with this madness! This life has no other end. Preach His name, let His teachings penetrate the world to the very bone. Never forget. Repeat this Mantra in your heart of hearts unceasingly, as you go the round of your daily duties.

---

1 Translated from Bengali.

1897.65 — RAKHAL[2]

Murree,
10th October, 1897.

DEAR RAKHAL,

Reached Murree from Kashmir in the evening of the day before yesterday. Everybody had an enjoyable time of it, only Krishnalal (Dhirananda) and Gupta (Sadananda) suffered now and then from fever, which, however, was but slight. This Address is to be sent to the Raja of Khetri. Have it printed in gilt etc. The Raja is expected at Bombay about the 21st or 22nd of October. None of us is staying at Bombay at present — if there be any, send him a copy so that he may present the same to the Raja even on Board the ship, or somewhere in the city of Bombay. Send the superior copy to Khetri. Have this passed in a meeting and if any change is needed, no harm. Then sign it, all of you, only leaving a blank for my name, and I shall sign it on going to Khetri. Let no pains be spared in this.

...Captain Sevier says he is very anxious for a site. He wishes to have a spot near Mussoorie or in some other central place, as soon as possible...The thing is that we do not want a place which is too cold, at the same time it must not be too hot. Dehra Dun is unbearable in summer, but pleasant in winter; Mussoorie itself is, I dare say, not the right place for many in winter. Above or below it, that is, in British or Garhwal territory, some land is sure to be found. At the same time there must be a supply of water at the place throughout the year, for drinking purposes and for everyday use. My plan is this: With only Achyutananda and Gupta I go from Murree to Rawalpindi, thence to Jammu, thence to Lahore, and from Lahore straight to Karachi...Give my hearty love and blessings to Shashi Babu. I see that Master Mahashaya has buckled to work after such a long time. Alive him my special love and greetings. To see him, with his feminine retiringness, stirred to work, my courage has gone up by leaps and bounds. I am writing to him tomorrow even. Victory to the Lord! — To work! To work!

Yours affectionately,
Vivekananda.

1897.66 — JAGMOHANLAL

Murree,
11th October, 1897.

MY DEAR JAGAMOHANLAL,

...Leave words when you start for Bombay to somebody to take care of three Sannyasins I am sending to Jaipur. Give them food and good lodging. They will be there till I come. They are fellows — innocent, not learned. They belong to me,

2 Translated from Bengali.

and one is my Gurubhâi (brother-disciple). If they like, take them to Khetri where I will come soon. I am travelling now quietly. I will not even lecture much this year. I have no more faith in all this noise and humbug which brings no practical good. I must make a silent attempt to start my institution in Calcutta; for that I am going to visit different centres quietly to collect funds.

Yours with blessings,
Vivekananda.

1897.67 — RAKHAL[1]

To Swami Brahmananda:

Murree,
11th October, 1897.

MY DEAR RAKHAL,

I feel I have been working as if under an irresistible impulse for the last ten days, beginning from Kashmir. It may be either a physical or a mental disease. Now I have come to the conclusion that I am unfit for further work... I now understand that I have been very harsh to all of you. But I knew, however, that you would bear with all my shortcomings; in the Math there is no one else who will do so. I have been increasingly harsh to you. Whatever has happened is now past — it is all the result of past Karma. What is the good of my repentance? I do not believe in it. It is all Karma. Whatever of Mother's work was to be accomplished through me, She made me do, and has now flung me aside breaking down my body and mind. Her will be done!

Now I retire from all this work. In a day or two I shall give up everything and wander out alone; I shall spend the rest of my life quietly in some place or other. Forgive me if you all will, or do what you like.

Mrs. Bull has given much of the money. She has implicit confidence in Sharat. Do the work of the Math with Sharat's advice; or do as you will.

But I have all along been like a hero — I want my work to be quick like lightning, and firm as adamant. Likewise shall I die also. Therefore kindly do my work for me — no question of success or defeat enters here at all. I have never retreated in a fight — shall I now...? There is success and failure in every work. But I am inclined to believe that one who is a coward will be born after death as an insect or a worm, that there is no salvation for a coward even after millions of years of penance. Well, shall I after all be born as a worm?... In my eyes this world is mere play — and it will always remain as such. Should one spend six long months brooding over the questions of honour and disgrace, gain and loss pertaining to this?... I am a man of action. Simply advice upon advice is being given — this one says this, that one says that; again that man threatens, and this one frightens! This life is not, in my view,

---

1 Translated from Bengali.

such a sweet thing that I would long to live through so much care and caution and fear. Money, life, friends, and relatives, and the love of men and myself—if one wants to enter into work fully assured beforehand of all these—if one has to be so much ridden with fear, then one will get just what Gurudeva used to say, "The crow thinks itself very clever but..." (The crow thinks itself very clever, but it cannot help eating filth.)—well, he will get that. After all, what is the purpose behind all these—money and wealth, Maths and institutions, preaching and lecturing? There is only one purpose in the whole of life—education. Otherwise what is the use of men and women, land and wealth?

So loss of money, or loss of anything else—I cannot bother about, and I will not. When I fight, I fight with girded loins—that much I fully understand; and I also understand that man, that hero, that god, who says, "Don't care, be fearless. O brave one, here I am by your side!" To such a man-god I offer a million salutations. Their presence purifies the world, they are the saviours of the world. And the others who always wail, "Oh, don't go forward, there is this danger, there is that danger"—those dyspeptics—they always tremble with fear. But through the grace of the Divine Mother my mind is so strong that even the most terrible dyspepsia shall not make me a coward. To cowards what advice shall I offer?—nothing whatsoever have I to say. But this I desire, that I should find shelter at the feet of those brave souls who dared to do great deeds even though they failed to succeed, of those heroes who never quailed nor shirked, of those fighters who never disobeyed orders through fear or pride. I am the child of the Divine Mother, the source of all power and strength. To me, cringing, fawning, whining, degrading inertia and hell are one and the same thing. O Mother of the Universe, O my Gurudeva, who would constantly say, "This is a hero!"—I pray that I may not have to die a coward. This is my prayer, O brother. "—certainly there is, or there will be born one equal to me"; some one or other will certainly arise from these thousands of devotees of Shri Ramakrishna who will be like me, and who will be able to understand me.

O hero, awake, and dream no more. Death has caught you by the forelock...still fear not. What I have never done—fleeing from the battle—well, will that happen today? For fear of defeat shall I retreat from the fight? Defeat is the ornament the hero adorns himself with. What, to acknowledge defeat without fighting! O Mother, Mother!...Not one capable of even playing second fiddle and yet the mind filled with petty self-importance, "We understand everything"...Now I retire;...everything I leave in your control. If Mother sends me men again in whose heart there is courage, in whose hands strength, in whose eyes there is fire, real children of the Mother—if She gives me even one such, then I shall work again, then I shall return. Otherwise, I shall take it that, by Mother's will, this is the end. I am in a tremendous hurry, I want to work at hurricane speed, and I want fearless hearts.

I have rebuked poor Sarada severely. What to do?...I do scold; but I also have much to complain...Almost suffocated by short breathing, standing and standing, I have written an article for him...It is all good, otherwise how will renunciation come?...Will Mother in the end kill me with attachment? I have offended all of you—do what you want.

I bless you all with a full heart. May Mother enshrine Herself in your hearts as strength: — the support that is fearlessness — may She make you all fearless. This I have seen in life — he who is over-cautious about himself falls into dangers at every step; he who is afraid of losing honour and respect, gets only disgrace; he who is always afraid of loss always loses... May all good attend you all.

Yours affectionately,
Vivekananda.

1897.68 — RAKHAL[1]

To Swami Brahmananda:

Murree,
12th October, 1897.

MY DEAR RAKHAL,

I wrote at length in yesterday's letter. I think it desirable to give you special directions about certain matters... (1) To all those who collect money and send it to the Math... the acknowledgment of the amounts will be issued from the Math. (2) The acknowledgment must be in duplicate, one for the sender, and one for filing in the Math. (3) There must be a big register in which all the names and addresses of the donors will be entered. (4) Accounts, accurate to the last pie, must be kept of the amounts that are donated to the Math Fund, and fully accurate accounts should be obtained from Sarada and others to whom money is given. For lack of accurate account-keeping... see that I am not accused as a cheat. These accounts should afterwards be published. (5) Immediately go and register a will under lawyer's advice to the effect that in case you and I die then Hari and Sharat will succeed to all that there is in our Math.

I have not yet got any news from Ambala, whether Hariprasanna and others have reached there or not. Give the other half-sheet of this letter to Master Mahashay.

Yours affectionately,
Vivekananda.

---

1 Translated from Bengali.

1897.69 — M __

C/O. Lala Hansraj, Rawalpindi,
Oct., 1897.

DEAR M __,

C'est bon, mon ami — now you are doing just the thing, Come out, man! No sleeping an life; time is flying. Bravo! That is the way.

Many thanks for your publication. Only, I am afraid it will not pay its way in a pamphlet form... Never mind, pay or no pay — let it see the blaze of daylight. You will have many blessings on you and many more curses — but that is always the way of the world!

This is the time.

Yours in the Lord,
Vivekananda.

1897.70 — MISS NOBLE

To Sister Nivedita:

Jammu,
3rd November, 1897.

MY DEAR MISS NOBLE, (This was the last letter received in England by Sister Nivedita.)

...Too much sentiment hurts work. "Hard as steel and soft as a flower" is the motto.

I shall soon write to Sturdy. He is right to tell you that in case of trouble I will stand by you. You will have the whole of it if I find a piece of bread in India — you may rest assured of that. I am going to write to Sturdy from Lahore, for which I start tomorrow. I have been here for 15 days to get some land in Kashmir from the Maharaja. I intend to go to Kashmir again next summer, if I am here, and start some work there.

With everlasting love,

Yours,
Vivekananda.

1897.71 — RAKHAL[1]

To Swami Brahmananda:

Lahore,
11th November, 1897.

MY DEAR RAKHAL,

The lecture at Lahore is over somehow. I shall start for Dehra Dun in a day or two. I have now postponed my tour to Sind, as none of you are agreeable to it, and also because of various other obstacles. Somebody has opened my two letters from England on the way. So don't send me letters any further for the present. Send them after I have written for them from Khetri. If you go to Orissa, then make arrangements that some one will do all the work as your representative — say Hari, especially now, when I am daily expecting letters from America.

Perhaps the will that I asked you to make in favour of Hari and Sharat has now been made.

Probably I shall leave Sadananda and Sudhir here after establishing a Society. Now no more lecturing — I go in a hurry straight to Rajputana.

The establishment of the Math must have precedence over everything.

Without regular exercise the body does not keep fit; talking, talking all the time brings illness — know this for certain. My love to all.

Yours affectionately,
Vivekananda.

1897.72 — MOTHER[2]

Lahore,
15th November, 1897.

DEAR MOTHER, (Shrimati Indumati Mitra)

It is a matter of deep regret that in spite of my earnest wishes, I do not find it feasible to go to Karachi this time and see you. First, because Captain and Mrs. Sevier, who have come from England and are travelling with me for the last nine months nearly, are very anxious to buy some land at Dehra Dun and start an orphanage there. It is their special request that I should go and open the work. This makes it unavoidable to go to Dehra Dun.

Secondly, owing to my kidney troubles I cannot count upon a long life. Even now it is one of my desires to start a Math in Calcutta, towards which as yet I could do nothing. Moreover, the people of my country have withheld the little help that they used to give to our Math of late. They have got a notion that I have brought

1 Translated from Bengali.
2 Translated from Bengali.

plenty of money from England! Over and above that, it is impossible to celebrate Shri Ramakrishna's festival this year, for the proprietors of Rasmani's garden would not let me go there, as I am returned from the West! Hence my first duty lies in seeing the few friends we have in Rajputana and trying my best to have a centre in Calcutta. For these reasons I have been very sorry to postpone my tour to Sindh tat present. I shall try my best to go there via Rajputana and Kathiawar. Please do not be sorry. Never for a day do I forget you all. But duty must be done first. It will ease me of my anxiety when a Math is established in Calcutta. Then I can hope that the work for which I struggled all my life through all sorts of privation and suffering will not die out after I cease to live in this body. I start for Dehra Dun this very day. After a week's stay there, to Rajputana, thence to Kathiawar, and so on.

Yours sincerely,
Vivekananda.

1897.73 — RAKHAL[3]

To Swami Brahmananda:

Lahore,
15th November, 1897.

MY DEAR RAKHAL,

I hope you and Hari are now in good health. The work in Lahore went off with great éclat. Now I go to Dehra Dun. The Sind tour is postponed. I have yet no news whether Dinu, Latu, and Krishnalal have reached Jaipur. Babu Nagendranath Gupta will collect subscriptions and donations from here and send them to the Math to meet expenses. Send him regular receipts. Let me know if you have received anything from Murree, Rawalpindi, and Sialkot.

Reply to me C/o Post Master, Dehra Dun. Other letters you may send me after hearing from me from Dehra Dun. My health is good; only I have to get up at night once or twice. I am having sound sleep; sleep is not spoiled even after exhausting lectures; and I am doing exercise every day… There is no trouble at all. Now, come on, work with redoubled energy. Keep an eye on that big piece of land — in all secrecy. We are making regular efforts so that big Utsava (Celebration — of Shri Ramakrishna's birthday.)can be held there. My love to all.

Yours affectionately,
Vivekananda.

PS — It will be a very good thing if Master Mahashay will write now and then about us in The Tribune, so that Lahore will not become cold again — now it is quite warmed up. Spend money a little economically; pilgrimage expenses should be borne by you personally; preaching and propaganda expenses should be charged to the Math.

3 Translated from Bengali.

1897.74 — MOTHER[1]

Dehra Dun,
24th November, 1897.

DEAR MOTHER, (Shrimati Indumati Mitra)

I have duly received your letter and that of dear Haripada. Of course you have ample reason to feel sorry for, but you see, I couldn't help it. And what took me here also became a fiasco; neither could I go to Sindh. It is the Lord's will. Now, I have an idea of proceeding to Calcutta through Rajputana, Kathiawar, and Sindh. But some difficulty may crop up on the way. If all goes well, I am certainly coming to Sindh. You must have undergone a lot of difficulty in coming to Hyderabad by arranging for leave etc. Any least trouble undergone, is bound to produce its excellent results. Friday next I shall leave this place, and have a mind to go via Saharanpur to Rajputana direct. I am doing well now, and trust you too are in health and peace of mind...

With best love and blessings to yourself and Haripada,

Yours sincerely,
Vivekananda.

1897.75 — BABURAM[2]

To Swami Premananda:

Dehra Dun,
24th November, 1897.

MY DEAR BABURAM,

I got all news about you from Hariprasanna. I am especially pleased to hear that Rakhal and Hari are now quite well.

Now Babu Raghunath Bhattacharya of Tehri is suffering very much from some pain in the neck; I also have been suffering for a long time from some pain at the back of my neck. If you can get hold of some very old ghee, then send some of it to him at Dehra Dun and some of it to me also at my Khetri address. You are sure to get it from Habu or Sharat (lawyer). Address it to Babu Raghunath Bhattacharya, Dehra Dun, N.W.P... and it will reach him.

The day after tomorrow I am leaving for Saharanpur; from there to Rajputana.

Yours affectionately,
Vivekananda.

PS — My love to all.

---

1 Translated from Bengali.
2 Translated from Bengali.

1897.76 — M. __

Dehra Dun,
24th November, 1897.

MY DEAR M. __[3],

Many many thanks for your second leaflet (leaves from the *Gospel*). It is indeed wonderful. The move is quite original, and never was the life of a great Teacher brought before the public untarnished by the writer's mind, as you are presenting this one. The language also is beyond all praise, so fresh, so pointed, and withal so plain and easy.

I cannot express in adequate terms how I have enjoyed the leaflets. I am really in a transport when I read them. Strange, isn't it? Our Teacher and Lord was so original, and each one of us will have to be original or nothing. I now understand why none of us attempted his life before. It has been reserved for you, this great work. He is with you evidently.

With all love and Namaskâra,
Vivekananda.

PS — The Socratic dialogues are Plato all over; you are entirely hidden. Moreover, the dramatic part is infinitely beautiful. Everybody likes it here and in the West.

1897.77 — RAKHAL[4]

To Swami Brahmananda:

Delhi,
30th November, 1897.

MY DEAR RAKHAL,

Part of the money that Miss Müller promised has reached Calcutta. The balance will come afterwards in a short while. We have also some amount. Miss Müller will deposit the money in your name as well as mine with Messrs. Grindlay & Co. As you have got the power of attorney, you alone can draw all the money. As soon as the money is deposited, you yourself with Hari go to Patna and meet that gentleman and by some means or other influence him; and if the price of the land is reasonable, buy it. If it cannot be had, try for some other plot of ground. I am trying to get some money in these parts too. We must hold the big festival on our own plot of ground — remember this must be your first and foremost work, come what may.

You have shown great pluck; the work you have done these last eight or nine months does you great credit. Now you must see to it that a Math and a centre in

3. Mahendra Nath Gupta, author of *The Gospel of Sri Ramakrishna*.
4 Translated from Bengali.

Calcutta are steadily established before everything else. Work hard to this end but quietly and in secret. Get information about the Cossipore house also. Tomorrow I am going to Khetri via Alwar. My health is good, even though I have caught a cold. Send all letters to Khetri. My love to all.

Yours affectionately,
Vivekananda.

PS—What about the will I asked you to make in favour of Sharat and Hari? Or will you buy the land and other things in my name, and I shall make a will?

1897.78 — RAKHAL[1]

To Swami Brahmananda:

Delhi,
8th December, 1897.

MY DEAR RAKHAL,

We shall start for Khetri tomorrow. Gradually the luggage has greatly increased. After Khetri I intend to send everybody to the Math. I could get done through them none of the work which I had hoped. That is to say, it is quite certain that none of them can do anything if he always remains with me. Unless each goes about independently, he will not be able to do anything. The fact is, who will care for them if they are in my company? Only waste of time. So I am sending them to the Math.

Keep as a fund for some permanent work the balance of the money left after the famine relief. Do not spend that money for any other purpose, and after giving the full accounts of the famine work, note down thus, "So much balance is left for some other good work"...

Work I want—I don't want any humbug. To those who have no desire to work I say, "My dear fellow, now go and follow your own way." As soon as I reach Khetri, I will send you the power of attorney with my signature if the document has reached there meanwhile. Open only those letters from America which bear the Boston postmark, not the others. Send all my letters to Khetri. I shall get money in Rajputana itself; no cause for anxiety on that score. Try energetically for the piece of land; we must have the celebration on our own ground this time.

Is the money in the Bengal Bank, or have you kept it elsewhere? Be very careful about money matters; keep detailed accounts, and regarding money know for certain that one cannot rely even on one's own father.

Give my love to all. Write to me how Hari is doing. Recently I met at Dehra Dun the Udâsi Sâdhu, Kalyân Dev, and a few others. I hear the people at Hrishikesh are very eager to see me and are asking again and again about me.

Yours affectionately,
Vivekananda.

1 Translated from Bengali.

1897.79 — RAKHAL[2]

To Swami Brahmananda:

Khetri,
14th December, 1897.

MY DEAR RAKHAL,

I have today sent your power of attorney with my signature… Draw the money as early as you can, and wire to me as soon as you have done so. A Raja of a place in Bundelkhand named Chatrapur has invited me. I shall visit the place on my way to the Math. The Raja of Limbdi, too, is writing earnestly. I cannot avoid going there also. I shall make a lightning tour of Kathiawar — that is what it will come to. I shall feel great relief as soon as I reach Calcutta… There is no news from Boston as yet; perhaps Sharat is coming; anyway, whenever any news comes from anywhere, write to me immediately.

Yours affectionately,
Vivekananda.

PS — How is Kanai? I hear that his health is not good. Pay special attention to him and see that nobody is unduly bossed over. Write to me about your health as well as Hari's.

1897.80 — CHRISTINA

To Sister Christine:

Khetri,
13th December, 1897.

MY DEAR CHRISTINA,

How funny all these dreams and evil prognostications of yours! You don't want to send me evil influences by thinking that way of me! I will be only too glad to lose 50 lbs. of my weight. A little rest puffs me up, and I am the same bloated monk as ever.

I am all right except [for] a bad cold the last few days, owing to exposure and travel in the desert. I thank you for the letter though. I am pleased with it enormously, as it shows the mind.

Give Mrs. Funkey [Funke], Baby [Stella Campbell], and all the rest my love, and, as you know, yourself —

Yours ever in the Lord,
Vivekananda.

PS — I will write a better note when this cold has left.

---

2 Translated from Bengali.

1897.81 — SHIVANANDA[1]

To Swami Shivananda:

Jaipur,
27th December, 1897.

MY DEAR SHIVANANDA,

Mr. Setlur of Girgaon, Bombay, whom you know very well from Madras writes to me to send somebody to Africa to look after the religious needs of the Indian emigrants in Africa. He will of course send the man and bear all expenses.

The work will not be congenial at present, I am afraid, but it is really the work for a perfect man. You know the emigrants are not liked at all by the white people there. To look after the Indians, and at the same time maintain cool—headedness so as not to create more strife—is the work there. No immediate result can be expected, but in the long run it will prove a more beneficial work for India than any yet attempted. I wish you to try your luck in this. If you agree, please write to Setlur, about your willingness and ask for more information, mentioning this letter. And godspeed to you! I am not very well, but am going to Calcutta in a few days and will be all right.

Yours in the Lord,
Vivekananda.

---

1 Translated from Bengali.

1898

1898.1 — SISTER CHRISTINE

To Sister Christine:

Jodhpur, Rajputana,
4th January, 1898.

Love and greetings etc. to thee, dear Christina, and a happy New Year. May it find you younger in heart, stronger in body, and purer in spirit.

I am still travelling in and out of season. Lecturing some, working a good deal.

Have you seen Mr. [Edward T.] Sturdy of England, who, I learn, has been to Detroit? Did you like him?

I am quite well and strong. Hope to meet you this blessed year again in America.

I am going to Calcutta in a few days, where I intend to be the rest of this cold weather. Next summer, I start for England or America most probably.

Yours ever in the Lord,
Vivekananda.

1898.2 — MISS NOBLE

To Sister Nivedita:

Calcutta,
30th January, 1898.

MY DEAR MISS NOBLE,

This is to introduce Prof. M. Gupta, who has been already introduced to you on board the boat that brought you over to shore.

He has very kindly consented to devote an hour or more every day to teach you Bengali. I need not state that he is a genuine, good and great soul.

Yours ever in the Lord,
Vivekananda.

PS — I am afraid you felt badly today.

1898.3 — RAJAJI

To Raja Pyari Mohan Mukherjee:

The Math, Belur,
25th February, 1898.

MY DEAR RAJAJI,

My gratitude for your very kind invitation to speak. I had a talk with Mr. Bhattacharya on the subject a few days back, and I am trying my best as a result to find time for your Society. I also promised to let them know the result on Sunday.

A friend to whom I owe much is here, presumably, to take me to his place in Darjeeling.

There are some American friends come, and every spare moment is occupied in working for the new Math and several organisations therein, and I expect to leave India next month for America.

Believe me, I am trying my best to be able to take advantage of this invitation of yours and shall communicate the result to you on Sunday through Mr. Bhattacharya.

Yours with love and blessings,
Vivekananda.

1898.4 — SHASHI

To Swami Ramakrishnananda:

Math, Belur, Howrah P.o.,
25th February, 1898.

MY DEAR SHASHI,

Our congratulations for the successful carrying out of the Mahotsava (Big celebration of Shri Ramakrishna's birthday.) in Madras. Hope you had a good gathering and plenty of spiritual food. We are all so glad that you have girded yourself to teach more of spirituality to the Madras people than those finger twistings and kling phat (Cryptic Mantras or sound formulae.) you are so fond of. Really your lecture on Shriji (Shri Ramakrishna.) was splendid. I could only catch a report in the Madras Mail in Khandwa, and the Math people have not had any. Why don't you send us over a copy?

I learn that you complain about my silence, is it? I have written you more letters, however, than you ever wrote me, from Europe and America even. You ought to give me all the news you can from Madras every week. Simplest way is to put down a few lines and a few items of news every day on a sheet.

My health has not been all right of late; at present it is much better. Calcutta is unusually cool just now, and the American friends who are here are enjoying it ever so much. Today we take possession of the land we have bought, and though it is not practicable to have the Mahotsava on it just now, I must have something on it on Sunday. Anyhow, Shriji's relics must be taken to our place for the day and worshipped. Gangadhar is here and asks me to write to you that though he has succeeded in getting some subscriptions for the Brahmavadin, the delivery being very irregular, he is afraid of losing them also soon. I received your letter of recommendation for the young man with the old story of "having nothing to eat, Your Honour"; only added in the Madras edition: "got a number of children too", for generating whom no recommendation was needed! I would be very glad to help him, but the fact is, I have no money; every cent I had I have made over to Raja, (Rakhal or Swami Brahmananda.) as they all say I am a spendthrift and are afraid of keeping money with me. I have, however, sent the letter to Rakhal if he can find the way to help your friend, the young man, in having some more children. He writes that the Christians will help him out if he becomes a convert, but he won't. Perhaps he is afraid that his conversion will make Hindu India lose one of her brightest jewels and Hindu society the benefit of his propagating power to eternal misery!

The boys here are rather seedy owing to the unusual amount of pure and cool air they are made to breathe in and live on the bank of the Ganga in the new Math. Sarada has his malaria brought over from Dinajpur. I made him eat a dose of opium the other day without much benefit to him except his brain which progressed for some hours towards its natural direction, namely, idiocy. Hari also has a touch; I hope it will take off a good bit of their avoirdupois. By the by, we have once more started the dancing business here, and it would make your heart glad to see Hari and Sarada and my own good self in a waltz. How we keep balance at all is a wonder to me.

Sharat has come and is hard at work as usual. We have got some good furniture now, and a big jump from the old Châtâi (mat) in the old Math to nice tables and chairs and three Khâts (cots), mind you. We have curtailed the Pujâ (worship) work a good deal, and the amount of pruning your klings and phats and svâhâs have undergone would make you faint. The puja occupied only the day, and they slept soundly all night. How are Tulsi and Khoka? Are they more tractable with you than under Rakhal? You may run in to Calcutta for a few days giving charge to Tulsi, but it is so expensive, and then you must go back, as Madras has to be thoroughly worked up. I am going to America again with Mrs. Bull in a few months.

Give my love to Goodwin and tell him that we are going to see him at any rate on our way to Japan. Shivananda is here, and I have toned down a bit his great desire to go to the Himalayas for food! Is Tulsi contemplating the same? The bandicoot-hole will be a sufficient cave for him, I suppose.

So the Math here is a fait accompli, and I am going over to get more help… Work on with energy. India is a rotten corpse inside and outside. We shall revive it by the blessings of Shri Maharaj. With all love,

Ever yours in the Lord,
Vivekananda.

1898.5 — MARY

To Miss Mary Hale:

Math, Belur,
Howrah District, Bengal, India,
2nd March, 1898.

MY DEAR MARY,

You have news of me already, I hope, through the letter I wrote to Mother Church. You are all so kind, the whole family, to me, I must have belonged to you in the past, as we Hindus say. My only regret is that the millionaires do not materialise: and I want them so badly just now that I am growing decrepit and old and hot in the midst of building and organising. Though Harriet has got one of a million virtues, a few millions of cash virtue would have made it more shining, I am sure; so you do not commit the same mistake.

A certain young couple had everything favourable to make them man and wife except that the bride's father was determined not to give his daughter to anyone who had not a million. The young people were in despair when a clever matchmaker came to the rescue. He asked the bridegroom whether he was willing to part with his nose on payment of a million — which he refused. The matchmaker then swore before the bride's father that the bridegroom had in store goods worth several millions, and the match was completed. Don't you take like millions.

Well, well, you could not get the millionaire, so I could not get the money; so I had to worry a good deal and work hard to no purpose; so I got the disease. It requires brains like mine to find out the true cause — I am charmed with myself!

Well, it was in Southern India, when I came from London and when the people were feting and feasting and pumping all the work out of me, that an old hereditary disease made its appearance. The tendency was always there, and excess of mental work made it "express" itself. Total collapse and extreme prostration followed, and I had to leave Madras immediately for the cooler North; a day's delay meant waiting for a week in that awful heat for another steamer. By the by, I learnt afterwards that Mr. Barrows arrived in Madras next day and was very much chagrined at not finding me as he expected, though I helped getting up an address for him and arranged for his reception. Poor man, he little knew I was at death's door then.

I have been travelling in the Himalayas all through last summer; and a cold climate, I found immediately, brought me round; but as soon as I come into the heat of the plains I am down again. From today the heat in Calcutta is becoming intense, and I will soon have to fly. This time to cool America as Mrs. Bull and Miss MacLeod are here. I have bought a piece of land for the institution on the river Ganga near Calcutta, on which is a little house where they are living now; within a stone's throw is the house where the Math is situated at present in which we live.

So I see them every day and they are enjoying it immensely à L'Inde. They intend making a trip to Kashmir in a month, and I am going with them as a guide and friend and philosopher perhaps, if they are willing. After that we all sail for the land of freedom and scandal.

You need not be alarmed with me as the disease will take two or three years at worst to carry me off. At best it may remain a harmless companion. I am content. Only I am working hard to set things all right and always so that the machine moves forward when I am off the stage. Death I have conquered long ago when I gave up life. My only anxiety is the work, and even that to the Lord I dedicate, and He knows best.

Ever yours in the Lord,
Vivekananda.

1898.6 — CHRISTINA

To Sister Christine:

The Math, Beloor,
Howrah Dist., Bengal, India,
11th March, 1898.

MY DEAR CHRISTINA,

I simply wonder what has become of you. It is an age [that] I did not hear from you, and I expected so much after Sturdy's visit to Detroit. How did you like the man? What about Baby and the Devendorfs? How is Mrs. Funkey [Funke]? What are you going to do this summer? Take rest, dear Christina; I am sure you require it badly.

Mrs. Bull of Boston and Miss MacLeod of New York are now in India. We have changed our Math from the old, nasty house to a house on the banks of the Ganges. This is much more healthy and beautiful. We have also got a good piece of land very near on the same side where Mrs. Bull and Miss MacLeod are putting up now. It is wonderful how they accommodate themselves to our Indian life of privation and hardship! My, these Yanks can do anything! After the luxuries of Boston and New York, to be quite content and happy in this wretched little house!! We intend to travel a bit together in Kashmir, and then I come to America with them and am sure to get a hearty welcome from my friends. What do you think? Is it welcome news to you? Of course, I cannot undergo the same amount of work as before; that, dear Christina, I am sorry, I will no more be able to do. I will do a little work and [take] a good deal of rest. No more getting crowds and making noise, but quiet, silent, personal work will be all I intend to do.

This time I will quietly come and quietly go away, seeing only my old friends, and no noise.

Write soon, as I am so anxious.

Yours ever in the Lord,
Vivekananda.

"There are two sorts of persons—one sort has the heart of water, the other of stone. The one easily takes an impression, and as easily throws it off; the other seldom takes an impression, but once it takes, it is there for ever. Nay, the more they struggle to cast it off, the more it cuts deep into the stone soul."—R. K. [Ramakrishna] Paramahamsa

1898.7—MARGARET

To Sister Nivedita:

Math, Belur, Howrah, Bengal,
16th March, 1898.

MY DEAR MARGARET,

It is needless to let you know, you have fulfilled all my expectations in your last lecture.

It appears to me that the platform is the great field where you will be of great help to me, apart from your educational plans. I am glad to learn that Miss [Henrietta] Müller is going to have a place on the river. Are you also going to Darjeeling? So you will all the better work after a trip up there! Next season I am planning a series of lectures for you all over India.

Ever yours with all love and blessings,
[Stamp with Swamiji's portrait]
The Calcutta boy

1898.8—SHASHI

To Swami Ramakrishnananda:

Math, Belur, (Howrah),
March, 1898.

MY DEAR SHASHI,

I forgot to write you about two things. 1. That Tulsi ought to learn shorthand from Goodwin, at least the beginning. 2. I had to write a letter almost every mail to Madras while I was out of India. I have in vain written for a copy of those letters. Send me all those letters. I want to write out my travels. Do not fail, and I shall send them back as soon as they have been used up. The Dawn can manage with 200 subscribers to come out regularly on Rs. 40 an issue expenditure. This is a great fact to know. The P.B. (Prabuddha Bhârata) seems to be very disorganised; try best to organise it. Poor Alasinga, I am sorry for him. Only thing I can do is to make him entirely free for a year so that he may devote all his energy to the Brahmavadin work. Tell him not to worry; I have him always in mind, poor child; his devotion I can never repay.

I am thinking of going to Kashmir again with Mrs. Bull and Miss MacLeod. (I) return to Calcutta and start for America from here.

Miss Noble is really an acquisition. She will soon surpass Mrs. Besant as a speaker, I am sure.

Do look after Alasinga. I have an idea that he is breaking himself with work. Tell him, the best work is only done by alternate repose and work. Give him all my love. We had two public lectures in Calcutta, one from Miss Noble and the other from our Sharat. Both of them did very well indeed; there was great enthusiasm, which shows that the Calcutta public has not forgotten us. Some of the members of the Math had a touch of influenza. They are all right now. The thing is working nicely. Shri (Holy) Mother is here, and the European and American ladies went the other day to see her, and what do you think, Mother ate with them even there! Is not that grand? The Lord is watching over us; there is no fear; do not lose your nerves, keep your health and take things easy. It is always good to give a few strong strokes and rest on your oars. Rakhal is living with the new land and buildings. I was not satisfied with the Mahotsava this year. What it should be is a grand mixture of all the different phases here. We shall try it next year — I shall send instructions. With love to all of you there and blessings.

Vivekananda.

1898.9 — DHIRA MATA

To Mrs. Ole Bull:

Darjeeling,
The 4th April, '98.

MY DEAR DHIRA MATA,

I am afraid you are getting roasted down there in the heat of Calcutta. Here it is nice and cool and rather chill when it rains, which it does almost every day. Yesterday the view of the snows was simply superb, and it is the most picturesque city in the world; there is such a mass of colour everywhere, especially in the dress of the Lepchas and Bhutias and the Paharees. Had it not been for the awful, corrugated iron roofs everywhere, it would have been twenty times more picturesque.

My health was not bad in Calcutta; here it is the same — only, the sugar has entirely disappeared, the specific gravity being only 13. I slept very well last night too; but the morning ride up, or climb, of a few miles is proving too much for my adipose tissues. The flannel clothes only made me worse, so I have given them up and have gone to my summer dress and am all right.

I have sent you Sturdy's letter already — poor fellow — I do not know what to do for him. He is really "living in a desert of his own making" — you see, one thing is not good for every one. Marriage has indeed proved a hell for Sturdy. And he can not come, although "he is skirting the coast of India". Lord help the poor boy. May

He cut all his bonds and make him free soon. Aye, it is good that he is feeling the bondage—and not "hugging and kissing its spokes of agony".

I gave a little lecture to the Hindus here yesterday, and I told them all their defects purposely and with their permission. I hope it will make them howl.

Miss Müller has taken a bungalow here and she is coming on Wednesday. I do not know whether Miss Noble is coming with her. She [Miss Noble] had better be your guest in Kashmir as according to our plan.

Have you got that place yet or changed [places]? I am going to Kashmir anyway, as I have promised.

I will be here only a few days and then I come to Calcutta, to be there only a week—and [then] I start for the N.W. Of course this is not the time to see anything in the N.W.P.; (North-West Provinces, now Uttar Pradesh.) everything is burning there. Yet that heat is much healthier than that of Bengal.

Yours ever in the Lord,
Vivekananda.

1898.10 — JAGMOHAN

To Munshi Jagmohanlal:

Ballen Ville, Darjeeling,
15 April, 1898.

MY DEAR JAGMOHAN,

If you can find out all the letters that I addressed to H.H. on my way to—and stay in—Japan, Europe and America, please do send them carefully packed, under registered cover, to my address in the Math, as early as possible.

With blessing to you, I remain,

Yours truly,
Vivekananda.

1898.11 — JOE JOE

To Miss Josephine MacLeod:

Darjeeling,
18th April, 1898.

MY DEAR JOE JOE,

I was down with fever brought upon, perhaps, by excessive mountain climbing and the bad health in the station.

I am better today and intend leaving this in a day or two. In spite of the great heat there, I used to sleep well in Calcutta and had some appetite. Here both have vanished — this is all the gain.

I could not see Miss Müller yet on the subject of Marguerite; but I intend to write her today. She is making all arrangements to receive her here. Mr. Gupta is also invited to teach them Bengali. She may now do something about her. I shall, however, write.

It will be easy for Marguerite to see Kashmir any time during her stay; but if Miss M. is not willing, there will be a big row again to injure both her and Marguerite.

I am not sure whether I go to Almora again. Much riding it seems is sure to bring on a relapse. I will wait for you at Simla — whilst you pay your visit to the Seviers. We will think on it when I am in. I am so glad to learn that Miss Noble delivered an address at the R.K. Mission. With all love to the Trinity,

Ever yours in the Lord,
Vivekananda.

1898.12 — MISS MACLEOD

To Miss Josephine MacLeod:

Darjeeling,
19th April, '98.

MY DEAR MISS MACLEOD,

Miss Müller is very glad to learn that you intend inviting Miss Noble to join our party to Kashmir.

It has her hearty approval. On her way back, Miss Müller will start something for her in Calcutta. She need not come to Darjeeling at all.

Hope you are enjoying the baking quite a bit. I start this week most probably.

Yours ever in the Lord,
Vivekananda.

1898.13 — SIR

To the Officer in Charge of Telegrams, Srinagar:

April 19, 1898.

SIR,

Please allow Miss M'cLeod [MacLeod] or her agent to receive any telegrams that you have received for me and receipt the same.

Yours truly,
Vivekananda.

1898.14 — RAKHAL[1]

To Swami Brahmananda:

Darjeeling,
23rd April, 1898.

MY DEAR RAKHAL,

My health was excellent on my return from Sandukphu (11,924 ft.) and other places; but after returning to Darjeeling, I had first an attack of fever, and after recovering from that, I am now suffering from cough and cold. I try to escape from this place every day; but they have been constantly putting it off for a long time. However, tomorrow, Sunday, I am leaving; after halting at Kharsana for a day I start again for Calcutta on Monday. I shall send you a wire after starting. We should hold an annual meeting of the Ramakrishna Mission, and also one for the Math. In both the meetings the accounts of famine relief must be submitted, and the report of the famine relief must be published. Keep all this ready.

Nityagopal says, managing an English magazine will not cost much. So let us first get this one out, and we shall see to the Bengali magazine afterwards. All these points will have to be discussed. Is Yogen willing to shoulder the responsibility of running the paper? Shashi writes that if Sharat goes some time to Madras, they may make a lecture tour jointly. Oh, how hot it is now! Ask Sharat if G. G., Sarada, Shashi Babu, and others have got their articles ready. Give my love and blessing to Mrs. Bull, Miss MacLeod, and Nivedita.

Yours affectionately,
Vivekananda.

1898.15 — JOE JOE

To Miss Josephine MacLeod:

Darjeeling,
29th April, 1898.

MY DEAR JOE JOE,

I have had several attacks of fever, the last being influenza.

It has left me now, only I am very weak yet. As soon as I gather strength enough to undertake the journey, I come down to Calcutta.

On Sunday I leave Darjeeling, probably stopping for a day or two at Kurseong, then direct to Calcutta. Calcutta must be very hot just now. Never mind, it is all the better for influenza. In case the plague breaks out in Calcutta, I must not go anywhere; and you start for Kashmir with Sadananda. How did you like the old gentleman, Devendra Nath Tagore? Not as stylish as "Hans Baba" with Moon God

---

1 Translated from Bengali.

and Sun God of course. What enlightens your insides on a dark night when the Fire God, Sun God, Moon God, and Star Goddesses have gone to sleep? It is hunger that keeps my consciousness up, I have discovered. Oh, the great doctrine of correspondence of light! Think how dark the world has been all these ages without it! And all this knowledge and love and work and all the Buddhas and Krishnas and Christs—vain, vain have been their lives and work, for they did not discover that "which keeps the inner light when the Sun and Moon were gone to the limbo" for the night! Delicious, isn't it?

If the plague comes to my native city, I am determined to make myself a sacrifice; and that I am sure is a "Darn sight, better way to Nirvâna" than pouring oblations to all that ever twinkled.

I have had a good deal of correspondence with Madras with the result that I need not send them any help just now. On the other hand I am going to start a paper in Calcutta. I will be ever so much obliged if you help me starting that. As always with undying love,

Ever yours in the Lord,
Vivekananda.

1898.16 — MARGOT

Almora,
20th May, 1898.

DEAR MARGOT (Margaret E. Noble or Sister Nivedita)

... Duty has no end, and the world is extremely selfish.

Be of good cheer. "Never a worker of good came to grief." ...

Ever yours etc.,
Vivekananda.

1898.17 — RAKHAL[2]

To Swami Brahmananda:

Almora,
20th May, 1898.

MY DEAR RAKHAL,

I have got all the news from your letter and have replied to your wire already. Niranjan and Govindalal Shah will wait at Kathgodam for Yogen-Ma. After I reached Naini Tal, Baburam went from here to Naini Tal on horseback against everybody's advice, and while returning, he also accompanied us on horseback. I was far behind as I was in a Dandi. When I reached the dak bungalow at night,

---

2 Translated from Bengali.

I heard that Baburam had again fallen from the horse and had hurt one of his arms—though he had no fractures. Lest I should rebuke him, he stayed in a private lodging house. Because of his fall, Miss MacLeod gave him her Dandi and herself came on the horse. He did not meet me that night. Next day I was making arrangements for a Dandi for him, when I heard that he had already left on foot. Since then I have not heard of him. I have wired to one or two places, but no news. Perhaps he is putting up at some village. Very well! They are experts in increasing one's worries.

There will be a Dandi for Yogen-Ma; but all the rest will have to go on foot.

My health is much better, but the dyspepsia has not gone, and again insomnia has set in. It will be very helpful if you can soon send some good Ayurvedic medicine for dyspepsia.

Since only one or two sporadic cases of plague have occurred there, there is plenty of accommodation in the Government plague hospital, and there is a talk of having hospitals in every Ward. Taking all this into consideration, do what the situation demands. But remember that something said by somebody in Baghbazar does not constitute public opinion ... Take care that funds do not run short in times of need and that there is no waste of money. For the present buy a plot of ground for Ramlal in the name of Raghuvir (The family deity of Shri Ramakrishna's birthpalce, Kamarpukur, Ramlal being his nephew.) after careful consideration ... Holy Mother will be the Sebâit (worshipper-in-charge); after her will come Ramlal, and Shibu will succeed them as Sebait; or make any other arrangement that seems best. You can, if you think it right, begin the construction of the building even now. For it is not good to live in a new house for the first one or two months, as it will be damp ... The anti-erosion wall can be completed afterwards. I am trying to raise money for the magazine. See that the sum of Rs. 1,200 which I gave for the magazine is kept only for that account.

All the others are well here. Sadananda sprained his foot yesterday. He says he will be all right by the evening. The climate at Almora is excellent at this time. Moreover the bungalow rented by Sevier is the best in Almora. On the opposite side Annie Besant is staying in a small bungalow with Chakravarty. Chakravarty is now the son-in-law of Gagan (of Ghazipur). One day I went to see him. Annie Besant told me entreatingly that there should be friendship between her organisation and mine all over the world, etc., etc. Today Besant will come here for tea. Our ladies are in a small bungalow near by and are quite happy. Only Miss MacLeod is a little unwell today. Harry Sevier is becoming more and more a Sadhu as the days pass by ... Brother Hari sends you his greetings and Sadananda, Ajoy, and Suren send you their respectful salutations. My love to you and all the others.

Yours affectionately,
Vivekananda.

PS—Give my love to Sushil and Kanai and all the others.

1898.18 — MR. J. J. GOODWIN'S MOTHER

To Mr. J. J. Goodwin's mother:

[On receiving news of the untimely death of Josiah J. Goodwin, Swami Vivekananda sent the following paragraph along with the poem "Requiescat in Pace" (This poem has been previously published in Complete Works, IV.) to the newspapers as well as to Goodwin's mother.]

Almora,
June, 1898.

With infinite sorrow I learn the sad news of Mr. Goodwin's departure from this life, the more so as it was terribly sudden and therefore prevented all possibilities of my being at his side at the time of death. The debt of gratitude I owe him can never be repaid, and those who think they have been helped by any thought of mine ought to know that almost every word of it was published through the untiring and most unselfish exertions of Mr. Goodwin. In him I have lost a friend true as steel, a disciple of never — failing devotion, a worker who knew not what tiring was, and the world is less rich by one of those few who are born, as it were, to live only for others.

[UNSIGNED]

1898.19 — YOUR HIGHNESS

Almora,
9th June, 1898.

Your Highness, (Maharaja of Khetri.)

Very sorry to learn that you are not in perfect health. Sure you will be in a few days.

I am starting for Kashmir on Saturday next. I have your letter of introduction to the Resident, but better still if you kindly drop a line to the Resident telling him that you have already given an introduction to me.

Will you kindly ask Jagamohan to write to the Dewan of Kishangarh reminding him of his promise to supply me with copies of Nimbârka Bhâshya on the *Vyâsa-Sutras* and other Bhashyas (commentaries) through his Pandits.

With all love and blessings,

Yours,
Vivekananda.

PS — Poor Goodwin is dead. Jagamohan knows him well. I want a couple of tiger skins, if I can, to be sent to the Math as present to two European friends. These seem to be most gratifying presents to Westerners.

1898.20 — FRIEND

Almora,
10th June, 1898.

MY DEAR FRIEND[1],

I appreciate your letter very much and am extremely happy to learn that the Lord is silently preparing wonderful things for our motherland.

Whether we call it Vedantism or any ism, the truth is that Advaitism is the last word of religion and thought and the only position from which one can look upon all religions and sects with love. I believe it is the religion of the future enlightened humanity. The Hindus may get the credit of arriving at it earlier than other races, they being an older race than either the Hebrew or the Arab; yet practical Advaitism, which looks upon and behaves to all mankind as one's own soul, was never developed among the Hindus universally.

On the other hand, my experience is that if ever any religion approached to this equality in an appreciable manner, it is Islam and Islam alone.

Therefore I am firmly persuaded that without the help of practical Islam, theories of Vedantism, however fine and wonderful they may be, are entirely valueless to the vast mass of mankind. We want to lead mankind to the place where there is neither the Vedas, nor the Bible, nor the Koran; yet this has to be done by harmonising the Vedas, the Bible and the Koran. Mankind ought to be taught that religions are but the varied expressions of THE RELIGION, which is Oneness, so that each may choose that path that suits him best.

For our own motherland a junction of the two great systems, Hinduism and Islam — Vedanta brain and Islam body — is the only hope.

I see in my mind's eye the future perfect India rising out of this chaos and strife, glorious and invincible, with Vedanta brain and Islam body.

Ever praying that the Lord may make of you a great instrument for the help of mankind, and especially of our poor, poor motherland.

Yours with love,
Vivekananda.

1898.21 — STURDY

To Mr. E. T. Sturdy:

Kashmir,
3rd July, 1898.

DEAR STURDY,

Both the editions had my assent, as it was arranged between us that we would

1. Written to Mohammed Sarfaraz Husain of Naini Tal.

not object to anybody's publishing my books. Mrs. Bull knows about it all and is writing to you.

I had a beautiful letter from Miss Souter the other day. She is as friendly as ever. With love to the children, Mrs. Sturdy, and yourself

Ever yours in the Lord,
Vivekananda.

1898.22 — MISS MACLEOD / MRS. BULL

To Miss Josephine MacLeod or Mrs. Ole Bull:

Seshnag, Chandanbari, Kashmir,
[En route from Srinagar to Amarnath],
[Mid of July, 1898.]

I send back the old Dandi (A simple palanquin.) as it is difficult to carry it through. I have got another like Margaret's. Please send it back to the Tahsildar of Vernag, Khand Chand, Esq., whom you already know. We are all right. Margot has discovered some new flowers and is happy. There is not much ice so the road is good.

Yours affectionately,
Vivekananda.

PS — Keep this Dandi till I come and pay the coolies (2) 4 Rs., 2 annas each.

1898.23 — RAKHAL[2]

To Swami Brahmananda:

Srinagar,
17th July, 1898.

MY DEAR RAKHAL,

I got all the news from your letter... My opinion regarding what you have written about Sarada is only that it is difficult to make a magazine in Bengali paying; but if all of you together canvass subscribers from door to door, it may be possible. In this matter do as you all decide. Poor Sarada has already been disappointed once. What harm is there if we lose a thousand rupees by supporting such an unselfish and very hardworking person? What about the printing of Raja-Yoga? As a last resort, you may give it to Upen on certain terms of sharing the profit in the sales... About money matters, the advice given previously is final. Henceforward do what you consider best regarding expenditure and other things. I see very well

---

2 Translated from Bengali.

that my policy is wrong, and yours is correct, regarding helping others; that is to say, if you help with money too much at a time, people instead of feeling grateful remark on the contrary that hey have got a simpleton to bank upon. I always lost sight of the demoralising influence of charity on the receiver. Secondly, we have no right to deviate even slightly from the purposes for which we collect the donations. Mrs. Bull will get her rosary all right if you send it care of Chief Justice Rishibar Mukhopadhyaya, Kashmir. Mr. Mitra and the Chief Justice are taking every care of them. We could not get a plot of ground in Kashmir yet, but there is a chance that we shall do so soon. If you can spend a winter here, you are sure to recoup your health. If the house is a good one and if you have enough fuel and warm clothing, then life in a land of snow is nothing but enjoyable. Also for stomach troubles a cold climate is an unfailing remedy. Bring Yogen with you; for the earth here is not stony, it is clay like that of Bengal.

If the paper is brought out in Almora, the work will progress much; for poor Sevier will have something to do, and the local people also will get some work. Skilful management lies in giving every man work after his own heart. By all the means in our power the Nivedita Girls' School in Calcutta should be put on a firm footing. To bring Master Mahashay to Kashmir is still a far cry, for it will be long before a college is established here. But he has written that it is possible to start a college in Calcutta, with him as the principal, at an initial expense of a thousand rupees. I hear that you all also favour this proposal. In this matter do what you all consider best. My health is all right. I have to get up seldom at night, even though I take twice a day rice and potatoes, sugar, or whatever I get. Medicine is useless — it has no action on the system of a Knower of Brahman! Everything will be digested — don't be afraid.

The ladies are doing well, and they send you their greetings. Two letters from Shivananda have come. I have also received a letter from his Australian disciple. I hear that the outbreak of plague in Calcutta has completely subsided.

Yours affectionately,
Vivekananda.

1898.24 — YOUR HIGHNESS

C/O Risibar Mookerjee,
Chief Judge, Kashmir,
17th September, 1898.

Your Highness, (Maharaja of Khetri.)

I have been very ill here for two weeks. Now getting better. I am in want of funds. Though the American; friends are doing everything they can to help me, I feel shame to beg from them all the time, especially as illness makes one incur contingent expenses. I have no shame; to beg of one person in the world and that is yourself. Whether you give or refuse, it is the same to me. If possible send some money kindly. How are you? I am going down by the middle of October.

Very glad to learn from Jagamohan the complete recovery of the Kumâr (Prince) Saheb. Things are going on well with me; hoping it is the same with you.

Ever yours in the Lord,
Vivekananda.

1898.25 — RAKHAL[1]

To Swami Brahmananda:

Srinagar,
1st August, 1898.

MY DEAR RAKHAL,

You are always under a delusion, and it does not leave you because of the strong influence, good or bad, of other brains. It is this: whenever I write to you about accounts, you feel that I have no confidence in you... My great anxiety is this: the work has somehow been started, but it should go on and progress even when we are not here; such thoughts worry me day and night. Any amount of theoretical knowledge one may have; but unless one does the thing actually, nothing is learnt. I refer repeatedly to election, accounts, and discussion so that everybody may be prepared to shoulder the work. If one man dies, another — why another only, ten if necessary — should be ready to take it up. Secondly, if a man's interest in a thing is not roused, he will not work whole-heartedly; all should be made to understand that everyone has a share in the work and property, and a voice in the management. This should be done while there is yet time. Give a responsible position to everyone alternately, but keep a watchful eye so that you can control when necessary; thus only can men be trained for the work. Set up such a machine as will go on automatically, no matter who dies or lives. We Indians suffer from a great defect, viz we cannot make a permanent organisation — and the reason is that we never like to share power with others and never think of what will come after we are gone.

I have already written everything regarding the plague. Mrs. Bull and Miss Müller and others are of opinion that it is not desirable to spend money uselessly when hospitals have been started in every Ward. We lend our services as nurses and the like. Those that pay the piper must command the tune.

The Maharaja of Kashmir has agreed to give us a plot of land. I have also visited the site. Now the matter will be finalised in a few days, if the Lord wills. Right now, before leaving, I hope to build a small house here. I shall leave it in the charge of Justice Mukherjee when departing. Why not come here with somebody else and spend the winter? Your health will improve, and a need, too, will be fulfilled. The money I have set apart for the press will be sufficient for the purpose, but all will be as you decide. This time I shall surely get some money from N.W.P., Rajputana,

---

1 Translated from Bengali.

and other places. Well, give as directed… money to a few persons. I am borrowing this amount from the Math and will pay it back to you with interest.

My health is all right in a way. It is good news that the building work has begun. My love to all.

Yours affectionately,
Vivekananda.

1898.26 — YOUR HIGHNESS

To Maharaja Ajit Singh, the Raja of Khetri:

Srinagar,
10 August, 1898.

YOUR HIGHNESS,

I have long not heard any news of you. How are things going on with you both bodily and mentally?

I have been to see Shri Amarnathji. It was a very enjoyable trip and the Darshana was glorious.

I will be here about a month more, then I return to the plains. Kindly ask Jagmohan to write to the Dewan Saheb of Kishangarh to get for me the copies of Nimbârka Bhâshya which he promised.

With all love,

Yours,
Vivekananda.

1898.27 — MARGOT

Kashmir,
25th Aug., 1898.

DEAR MARGOT (Margaret E. Noble or Sister Nivedita)

It is a lazy life I am leading for the last two months, floating leisurely in a boat, which is also my home, up and down the beautiful Jhelum, through the most gorgeous scenery God's world can afford, in nature's own park, where the earth, air, land, grass, plants, trees, mountains, snows, and the human form, all express, on the outside at least, the beauty of the Lord — with almost no possessions, scarcely a pen or an inkstand even, snatching up a meal whenever or wherever convenient, the very ideal of a Rip Van Winkle!…

Do not work yourself out. It is no use; always remember — "Duty is the midday sun whose fierce rays are burning the very vitals of humanity." It is necessary for a time as a discipline; beyond that, it is a morbid dream. Things go on all right whether we lend them our helping hands or not. We in delusion only break ourselves. There is a false sentiment which goes the extreme of unselfishness, only to injure others by its submission to every evil. We have no right to make others selfish by our unselfishness; have we?...

Yours etc.,
Vivekananda.

1898.28 — MARY

To Miss Mary Hale:

Srinagar, Kashmir,
28th August, 1898.

MY DEAR MARY,

I could not make an earlier opportunity of writing you, and knowing that you were in no hurry for a letter, I will not make apologies. You are learning all about Kashmir and ourselves from Miss MacLeod's letter to Mrs. Leggett, I hear — therefore needless going into long rigmaroles about it.

The search for Heinsholdt's Mahatmas in Kashmir will be entirely fruitless; and as the whole thing has first to be established as coming from a creditable source, the attempt will also be a little too early. How are Mother Church and Father Pope and where? How are you ladies, young and old? Going on with the old game with more zest now that one has fallen off the ranks? How is the lady that looks like a certain statue in Florence? (I have forgotten the name) I always bless her arms when I think of the comparison.

I have been away a few days. Now I am going to join the ladies. The party then goes to a nice quiet spot behind a hill, in a forest, through which a murmuring stream flows, to have meditation deep and long under the deodars (trees of God) cross-legged à la Buddha.

This will be for a month or so, when by that time our good work will have spent its powers and we shall fall from this Paradise to earth again; then work out our Karma a few months and then will have to go to hell for bad Karma in China, and our evil deeds will make us sink in bad odours with the world in Canton and other cities. Thence Purgatory in Japan? And regain Paradise once more in the U.S. of America. This is what Pumpkin Swami, brother of the Coomra Swami, foretells (in Bengali Coomra means squash). He is very clever with his hands. In fact his cleverness with his hands has several times brought him into great dangers.

I wished to send you so many nice things, but alas! the thought of the tariff makes my desires vanish "like youth in women and beggars' dreams".

By the by, I am glad now that I am growing grey every day. My head will be a full-blown white lotus by the time you see me next.

Ah! Mary, if you could see Kashmir—only Kashmir; the marvellous lakes full of lotuses and swans (there are no swans but geese—poetic licence) and the big black bee trying to settle on the wind-shaken lotus (I mean the lotus nods him off refusing a kiss—poetry), then you could have a good conscience on your death-bed. As this is earthly paradise and as logic says one bird in the hand is equal to two in the bush, a glimpse of this is wiser, but economically the other better; no trouble, no labour, no expense, a little namby-pamby dolly life and later, that is all.

My letter is becoming a bore... so I stop. (It is sheer idleness). Good night.

Ever yours in the Lord,
Vivekananda.

My address always is:
Math, Belur,
Howrah Dist., Bengal, India.

1898.29 — HARIPADA[1]

To Shri Haripada Mitra:

Srinagar, Kashmir,
17th September, 1898.

DEAR HARIPADA,

I got all news from your letter and wire. That you may easily pass your examination in Sindhi is my prayer to the Lord.

Recently my health was very bad, and so I have been delayed, otherwise I had intended to leave for the Punjab this week. The doctor had advised me not to go to the plains at the present time, as it is very hot there. Perhaps I may reach Karachi by about the last week of October. Now I am doing somewhat well. There is nobody else with me now excepting two American friends—ladies. Probably I shall part from them at Lahore. They will wait for me in Calcutta or in Rajputana. I shall probably visit Cutch, Bhuj, Junagad, Bhavnagar, Limbdi, and Baroda and then proceed to Calcutta. My present plan is to go to America via China and Japan in November or December, but it is all in the hands of the Lord. The above-mentioned American friends bear all my expenses, and I shall take from them all my expenses including railway fare up to Karachi. But if it is convenient to you, send me Rs. 50 by wire C/o Rishibar Mukhopadhyaya, Chief Justice, Kashmir State, Srinagar. It will be a great help to me, for I have incurred much extra expense of late owing to illness, and I feel a little ashamed to have to depend always on my foreign devotees. With best wishes,

Yours affectionately,
Vivekananda.

---

1 Translated from Bengali.

1898.30 — YOUR HIGHNESS

Lahore,
16th October, 1898.

Your Highness, (Maharaja of Khetri.)

The letter that followed my wire gave the desired information; therefore I did not wire back about my health in reply to yours.

This year I suffered much in Kashmir and am now recovered and going to Calcutta direct today. For the last ten years or so I have not seen the Puja of Shri Durgâ in Bengal which is the great affair there. I hope this year to be present.

The Western friends will come to see Jaipur in a week or two. If Jagamohan be there, kindly instruct him to pay some attention to them and show them over the city and the old arts.

I leave instructions with my brother Saradananda to write to Munshiji before they start for Jaipur.

How are you and the Prince? Ever as usual praying for your welfare,

I remain yours affectionately,
Vivekananda.

PS — My future address is Math, Belur, Howrah Dist. Bengal.

1898.31 — HARIPADA[2]

To Shri Haripada Mitra:

Lahore,
16th October, 1898.

MY DEAR HARIPADA,

In Kashmir my health has completely broken down, and I have not witnessed the Durga-Puja for the last nine years; so I am starting for Calcutta. I have for the present given up the plan of going to America. I think I shall have plenty of time to go to Karachi during the winter.

My brother-disciple Saradananda will send Rs. 50 from Lahore to Karachi. Don't yield to sorrow — everything is in God's hands. Certainly I won't go anywhere this year without meeting all of you. My blessings to all.

Yours affectionately,
Vivekananda.

---

2 Translated from Bengali.

1898.32 — CHRISTINA

To Sister Christine:

> The Math, Beloor, Howrah Dist.,
> 25th October, 1898.

MY DEAR CHRISTINA,

How are you? I am very anxious about your health. I have long not had any letter from you.

My health again failed badly. I had, therefore, to leave Kashmir in haste and come to Calcutta. The doctors say I ought not go tramping again this winter. That is such a disappointment, you know. However, I am coming to the U. S. this summer. Mrs. Bull and Miss MacLeod enjoyed this year's trip to Kashmir immensely, and now they are having a glimpse of the old monuments and buildings of Delhi, Agra, Jeypore [Jaipur], etc.

Do write a nice, long letter if you have time, and do not work yourself to death. Duty is duty, no doubt; but we have our duties, not only to our mother etc., but to others also. Sometimes one duty asks for physical sacrifice, whilst the other insists on great care for our health. Of course, we follow the stronger motive, and [I] do not know which will prove stronger in your case. Anyhow, take great care of your body, now that your sisters have come to your help.

How do you manage the family? — the expenses etc? Write me all you like to write. Give me a long chat, will you? Do!

I am getting better every day — and then the long months before I can start for the U.S. Never mind, "Mother" knows what is best for us. She will show the way. I am now in Bhakti. As I am growing old, Bhakti is taking the place of Jnâna. Did you get the new Awakened India? How do you like it?

> Ever yours in the Lord,
> Vivekananda.

1898.33 — YOUR HIGHNESS

> Math, Belur, Howrah Dist., Bengal,
> 26th October, 1898.

Your Highness, (Maharaja of Khetri.)

I am very very anxious about your health. I had a great desire to look in on my way down, but my health failed completely, and I had to run down in all haste. There is some disturbance with my heart, I am afraid.

However I am very anxious to know about your health. If you like I will come over to Khetri to see you. I am praying day and night for your welfare. Do not lose heart if anything befalls, the "Mother" is your protection. Write me all about yourself... How is the Kumar Saheb?

With all love and everlasting blessings,

Ever yours in the Lord,
Vivekananda.

1898.34 — YOUR HIGHNESS

The Math, Belur, Howrah Dist.,
November (?), 1898.

Your Highness, (Maharaja of Khetri.)

Very glad to learn that you and the Kumar are enjoying good health As for me, my heart has become very weak. Change, I do not think, will do me any good, as for the last 14 years I do not remember to have stopped at one place for 3 months at a stretch. On the other hand if by some chance I can live for months in one place, I hope it will do me good. I do not mind this. However, I feel that my work in this life is done. Through good and evil, pain and pleasure, my life-boat has been dragged on. The one great lesson I was taught is that life is misery, nothing but misery. Mother knows what is best. Each one of us is in the hands of Karma; it works itself out — and no nay. There is only one element in life which is worth having at any cost, and it is love. Love immense and infinite, broad as the sky and deep as the ocean — this is the one great gain in life. Blessed is he who gets it.

Ever yours in the Lord,
Vivekananda.

1898.35 — JOE

To Miss Josephine MacLeod:

57 Ram Kanta Bose Street, Calcutta,
12th November, 1898.

MY DEAR JOE,

I have invited a few friends to dinner tomorrow, Sunday...

We expect you at tea. Everything will be ready then.

Shri Mother is going this morning to see the new Math. I am also going there. Today at 6 p.m. Nivedita is going to preside. If you feel like it, and Mrs. Bull strong, do come.

Ever yours in the Lord,
Vivekananda.

1898.36 — YOUR HIGHNESS

Maharaja Ajit Singh, the Raja of Khetri:

Math Belur,
22 November, 1898.

YOUR HIGHNESS,

Many thanks for your kind note and the Nimbarka Bhashya—reached through Jaga Mohan Lalji.

I approach your Highness today on a most important business of mine, knowing well that I have not the least shame in opening my mind to you, and that I consider you as my only friend in this life. If the following appeals to you, good; if not, pardon my foolishness as a friend should.

As you know already, I have been ailing since my return. In Calcutta your Highness assured me of your friendship and help for me personally and [advised me] not to be worried about this incurable malady. This disease has been caused by nervous excitement; and no amount of change can do me good, unless the worry and anxiety and excitement are taken off me.

After trying these two years a different climate, I am getting worse every day and now almost at death's door. I appeal to your Highness's work, generosity and friendship. I have one great sin rankling always in my breast, and that is [in order] to do a service to the world, I have sadly neglected my mother. Again, since my second brother has gone away, she has become awfully worn-out with grief. Now my last desire is to make Sevâ [give service] and serve my mother, for some years at least. I want to live with my mother and get my younger brother married to prevent extinction of the family. This will certainly smoothen my last days as well as those of my mother. She lives now in a hovel. I want to build a little, decent home for her and make some provision for the youngest, as there is very little hope of his being a good earning man. Is it too much for a royal descendent of Ramchandra to do for one he loves and calls his friend? I do not know whom else to appeal to. The money I got from Europe was for the "work", and every penny almost has been given over to that work. Nor can I beg of others for help for my own self. About my own family affairs—I have exposed myself to your Highness, and none else shall know of it. I am tired, heartsick and dying. Do, I pray, this last great work of kindness to me, befitting your great and generous nature and [as] a crest to the numerous kindnesses you have shown me. And as your Highness will make my last days smooth and easy, may He whom I have tried to serve all my life ever shower His choicest blessings on you and yours.

Ever yours in the Lord,
Vivekananda.

PS—This is strictly private. Will you please drop a wire to me whether you will do it or not?

1898.37 — YOUR HIGHNESS

To Maharaja Ajit Singh, the Raja of Khetri:

Math Beloor, Howrah District,
1 December, 1898.

YOUR HIGHNESS,

Your telegram has pleased me beyond description, and it is worthy of your noble self. I herewith give you the details of what I want.

The lowest possible estimate of building a little home in Calcutta is at least ten thousand rupees. With that it is barely possible to buy or build a house in some out-of-the-way quarter of the town — a little house fit for four or five persons to live in.

As for the expenses of living, the 100 Rs. a month your generosity is supplying my mother is enough for her. If another 100 Rs. a month be added to it for my lifetime for my expenses — which unfortunately this illness has increased, and which, I hope, will not be for long a source of trouble to you, as I expect only to live a few years at best — I will be perfectly happy. One thing more will I beg of you — if possible, the 100 Rs. a month for my mother be made permanent, so that even after my death it may regularly reach her. Or even if your Highness ever gets reasons to stop your love and kindness for me, my poor old mother may be provided [for], remembering the love you once had for a poor Sâdhu.

This is all. Do this little work amongst the many other noble deeds you have done, knowing well whatever else can be proved or not, the power of Karma is self-evident to all. The blessings of this good Karma shall always follow you and yours. As for me, what shall I say — whatever I am in the world has been almost all through your help. You made it possible for me to get rid of a terrible anxiety and face the world and do some work. It may be that you are destined by the Lord to be the instrument again of helping yet grander work, by taking this load off my mind once more.

But whether you do this or not, "once loved is always loved". Let all my love and blessings and prayers follow you and yours, day and night, for what I owe you already; and may the Mother, whose play is this universe and in whose hands we are mere instruments, always protect you from all evil.

Ever yours in the Lord,
Vivekananda.

1898.38 — DEAR __

The Math, Belur,
15th Dec., 1898.

DEAR __,

... The Mother is our guide and whatever happens or will happen is under Her ordination ...

Yours etc.,
Vivekananda.

1898.39 — DHIRA MATA

Baidyanath, Deoghar,
29th Dec., 1898.

MY DEAR DHIRA MATA, (Mrs. Ole Bull)

You know already my inability to accompany you. I cannot gather strength enough to accompany you. The cold in the lungs continues, and that is just what makes me unfit for travel. On the whole I hope to improve here.

I find my cousin has been all these years cultivating her mind with a will, and she knows all that the Bengali literature can give her, and that is a good deal, especially of metaphysics. She has already learnt to sign her name in English and the Roman alphabet. It is now real brain work to teach her, and therefore I have desisted. I am trying simply to idle away my time and force myself to take rest.

Ere this I had only love for you, but recent development proves that you are appointed by the Mother to watch over my life; hence, faith has been added to love! As regards me and my work, I hold henceforth that you are inspired, and I will gladly shake off all responsibilities from my shoulder and abide by what the Mother ordains through you.

Hoping soon to join you in Europe or America, I remain,

Ever your loving son,
Vivekananda.

1899

1899.1 — MOTHER[1]

Deoghar, Vaidyanath.
3rd January, 1899.

DEAR MOTHER[2],

Some very important questions have been raised in your letter. It is not possible to answer them fully in a short note, still I reply to them as briefly as possible.

(1) Rishi, Muni, or God — none has power to force an institution on society. When the needs of the times press hard on it, society adopts certain customs for self-preservation. Rishis have only recorded those customs As a man often resorts even to such means as are good for immediate self-protection but which are very injurious in the future, similarly society also not unfrequently saves itself for the time being, but these immediate means which contributed to its preservation turn out to be terrible in the long run.

For example, take the prohibition of widow-marriage in our country. Don't think that Rishis or wicked men introduced the law pertaining to it. Notwithstanding the desire of men to keep women completely under their control, they never could succeed in introducing those laws without betaking themselves to the aid of a social necessity of the time. Of this custom two points should be specially observed: (a) Widow-marriage takes place among the lower classes. (b) Among the higher classes the number of women is greater than that of men.

Now, if it be the rule to marry every girl, it is difficult enough to get one husband apiece; then how to get, in succession, two or three for each? Therefore has society put one party under disadvantage, i.e. it does not let her have a second husband, who has had one; if it did, one maid would have to go without a husband. On the other hand, widow-marriage obtains in communities having a greater number of men than women, as in their case the objection stated above does not exist. It is becoming more and more difficult in the West, too, for unmarried girls to get husbands.

Similar is the case with the caste system and other social customs.

So, if it be necessary to change any social custom the necessity underlying it should be found out first of all, and by altering it, the custom will die of itself. Otherwise no good will be done by condemnation or praise.

(2) Now the question is: Is it for the good of the public at large that social rules are framed or society is formed? Many reply to this in the affirmative; some, again, may hold that it is not so. Some men, being comparatively powerful, slowly bring all others under their control and by stratagem, force, or adroitness gain their own objects. If this be true, what can be the meaning of the statement that there is danger in giving liberty to the ignorant? What, again, is the meaning of liberty?

Liberty does not certainly mean the absence of obstacles in the path of misap-

---

1 Translated from Bengali.
2. Shrimati Mrinalini Bose.

propriation of wealth etc. by you and me, but it is our natural right to be allowed to use our own body, intelligence, or wealth according to our will, without doing any harm to others; and all the members of a society ought to have the same opportunity for obtaining wealth, education, or knowledge. The second question is: Those who say that if the ignorant and the poor be given liberty, i.e. full right to their body, wealth, etc., and if their children have the same opportunity to better their condition and acquire knowledge as those of the rich and the highly situated, they would become perverse—do they say this for the good of society or blinded by their selfishness? In England too I have heard, "Who will serve us if the lower classes get education?"

For the luxury of a handful of the rich, let millions of men and women remain submerged in the hell of want and abysmal depth of ignorance, for if they get wealth and education, society will be upset!

Who constitute society? The millions—or you, I, and a few others of the upper classes?

Again, even if the latter be true, what ground is there for our vanity that we lead others? Are we omniscient?

"उध्दरेदात्मनात्मानं—One should raise the self by the self." Let each one work out one's own salvation. Freedom in all matters, i.e. advance towards Mukti is the worthiest gain of man. To advance oneself towards freedom—physical, mental, and spiritual—and help others to do so, is the supreme prize of man. Those social rules which stand in the way of the unfoldment of this freedom are injurious, and steps should be taken to destroy them speedily. Those institutions should be encouraged by which men advance in the path of freedom.

That in this life we feel a deep love at first sight towards a particular person who may not be endowed with extraordinary qualities, is explained by the thinkers of our country as due to the associations of a past incarnation.

Your question regarding the will is very interesting: it is the subject to know. The essence of all religions is the annihilation of desire, along with which comes, of a certainty, the annihilation of the will as well, for desire is only the name of a particular mode of the will. Why, again, is this world? Or why are these manifestations of the will? Some religions hold that the evil will should be destroyed and not the good. The denial of desire here would be compensated by enjoyments hereafter. This reply does not of course satisfy the wise. The Buddhists, on the other hand, say that desire is the cause of misery, its annihilation is quite desirable. But like killing a man in the effort to kill the mosquito on his cheek, they have gone to the length of annihilating their own selves in their efforts to destroy misery according to the Buddhistic doctrine.

The fact is, what we call will is an inferior modification of something higher. Desirelessness means the disappearance of the inferior modification in the form of will and the appearance of that superior state. That state is beyond the range of mind and intellect. But though the look of the gold mohur is quite different from that of the rupee and the pice, yet as we know for certain that the gold mohur is greater than either, so, that highest state — Mukti, or Nirvâna, call it what you like — though out of the reach of the mind and intellect, is greater than the will and all other powers. It is no power, but power is its modification, therefore it is higher. Now you will see that the result of the proper exercise of the will, first with motive for an object and then without motive, is that the will-power will attain a much higher state.

In the preliminary state, the form of the Guru is to be meditated upon by the disciple. Gradually it is to be merged in the Ishta. By Ishta is meant the object of love and devotion... It is very difficult to superimpose divinity on man, but one is sure to succeed by repeated efforts. God is in every man, whether man knows it or not; your loving devotion is bound to call up the divinity in him.

Ever your well-wisher,
Vivekananda.

1899.2 — MARGOT

To Sister Nivedita:

3 p.m. Sunday,
[Early 1899.]

MY DEAR MARGOT,

I am sorry I cannot come to see Dr. Mahoney — I am ill. I have not yet broken my fast.

Have you stopped teaching my little cousin?

Yours with love,
Vivekananda.

1899.3 — NIVEDITA

To Sister Nivedita:

[Early 1899?]

MY DEAR NIVEDITA,

The address of my cousin is 127 Manicktala Street. The husband's name is Durga Prasanna Bose. The wife's name is most probably not known to the people you will meet in the male department. Therefore it is the custom to ask for the wife of so-and-so.

Manicktala Street is that which runs east and west, south of the tank garden.

Yours with love,
Vivekananda.

1899.4 — CHRISTINA

To Sister Christine:

The Math, Belur, Dist. Howrah, Bengal, India,
26th January, 1899.

MY DEAR CHRISTINA,

Excuse this long delay in replying to your very beautiful note. The fact is, I was once more in the vale of death. The old diabetes has now disappeared. In its place has come what some doctors call asthma, others dyspepsia, owing to nervous prostration. However, it is a most worrying disease, giving one the sensation of suffocation — sometimes for days. I am best only in Calcutta; so I am here for rest and quiet and low diet. If I get well by March, I am going to start for Europe. Mrs. Bull and others are gone; sorry I could not accompany them owing to this disease.

I have carefully weighed your plans for coming over. I will be ever so glad to see you, you know it well; but, my dear, the Indian summer will not suit you, and if you start now it will be midsummer when you reach India. Then, you must not hope of making any living here. It is impossible for me to make a living most times in my own country. Then all the surroundings are so, so wretched and different from what you see around you, e.g. you will find me going about in loin-cloth — will that shock you? Three-fourths of the population only wearing a strip of white cloth about their loins — can you bear that?

I must stop here; I am so weak. If I do not get well by March, I will write you to come, for I wish it ever so much to see you once before I pass away.

Do not be the least anxious, dear. Things must be as "Mother" wishes. Ours is only to obey and work

Ever yours in the Lord,
Vivekananda.

PS — Mrs. Bull will reach Cambridge, Mass., soon. You may write to her there on the particulars.

PPS. I have again lost your address. Please give the correct one in your next.

1899.5 — JOE

The Math, Belur, Howrah, Bengal,
2nd February, 1899.

My Dear Joe[1],

You must have reached N.Y. by this time and are in the midst of your own after a long absence. Fortune has favoured you at every step of this journey — even the sea was smooth and calm, and the ship nearly empty of undesirable company. Well,

---
1. Miss Josephine MacLeod.

with me it is doing otherwise. I am almost desperate I could not accompany you. Neither did the change at Vaidyanath do me any good. I nearly died there, was suffocating for eight days and nights!! I was brought back to Calcutta more dead than alive, and here I am struggling to get back to life again.

Dr. Sarkar is treating me now.

I am not so despondent now as I was. I am reconciled to my fate. This year seems to be very hard for us. Yogananda, who used to live in Mother's house, is suffering for the last month and every day is at death's door. Mother knows best. I am roused to work again, though not personally but am sending the boys all over India to make a stir once more. Above all, as you know, the chief difficulty is of funds. Now that you are in America, Joe, try to raise some funds for our work over here.

I hope to rally again by March, and by April I start for Europe. Again Mother knows best.

I have suffered mentally and physically all my life, but Mother's kindness has been immense. The joy and blessings I had infinitely more than I deserve. And I am struggling not to fail Mother, but that she will always find me fighting, end my last breath will be on the battlefield.

My best love and blessings for you ever and ever.

Ever yours in the Truth,
Vivekananda.

1899.6 — RAJA

To Swami Brahmananda:

The Math, Belur,
Friday, [March(?), 1899.]

MY DEAR RAJA,

Please pay 100 Rs. to Sister Nivedita immediately for plague work and credit it to a separate plague account.

Ever yours in the Lord,
Vivekananda.

1899.7 — S__

To Swami Swarupananda, editor of Prabuddha Bharata, Mayavati:

[March, 1899.]

MY DEAR S[WARUPANANDA],

I have no objection whether Mrs. Sevier's name goes on top or mine or anybody else's; the prospectus ought to go in the name of the Seviers, mustering my name also if necessary. I send you a few lines for your consideration in the prospectus. The rest are all right.

I will soon send the draft deed.

Vivekananda.

1899.8 — MARGOT

To Sister Nivedita:

The Math, Belur,
March 2nd, 1899.

MY DEAR MARGOT,

Will you look into your trunks for a Sanskrit book of mine, which was, you know, in your keeping in Kashmir. I do not find it in our library here.

I have been thinking of your friend Miss [Sarala] Ghosal's coming to see the Math on Sunday. The difficulty is here. The ebb tide will be on till 5 p.m. In that case our big boat can go down easily to bring the party up; and going back, if the party starts long before 5 p.m., say 4 p.m., will be all right. To come up will take at least two hours from Baghbazar. If the party starts from Baghbazar—say at 12 a.m.—and reaches the Math at 2 p.m. for lunch and then starts back by 4 p.m., it will be nice.

If you cannot start as early as that, I will advise you to send the carriage to wait at Baranagore on the other side so that our boat can ferry the party over any time they like. The boat journey in that case will only be on coming.

With all love and blessings,
Vivekananda.

1899.9 — MARGOT

To Sister Nivedita:

The Math, Belur,
March 2nd, 1899.

MY DEAR MARGOT,

I could not come today. I am so, so sorry. The body would not allow—neither can I come to the Boses'. I have written to them.

I have an engagement tomorrow.

Possibly I may see you in the evening.

With all love and blessings,
Vivekananda.

1899.10 — SIR

To Ishwar Chandra Ghosh:

Math, Belur, Howrah Dist.,
6th March, '99.

MY DEAR SIR,

Many thanks for your kind invitation. I am so sorry that so many days' delay should occur in reply to your note.

I was very ill at the time, and the gentleman on whom the duty fell of replying could not do it, it seems. I got notice of it just now.

I am not yet sufficiently recovered to take advantage of your kindness. This winter I had made it a point of visiting your part of the country. But my Karma will have otherwise. I will have to wait to give myself the pleasure of visiting the seat of civilisation of ancient Bengal.

With my thanks again for all your kindness, I remain,

Yours in the Lord,
Vivekananda.

1899.11 — MARY

To Miss Mary Hale:

Math, Belur, Howrah District,
16th March, 1899.

MY DEAR MARY,

Thanks to Mrs. Adams; she roused you naughty girls to a letter at last. "Out of sight out of mind" — as true in India as in America. And the other young lady, who just left her love as she flitted by, deserves a ducking I suppose.

Well, I have been in a sort of merry-go-round with my body which has been trying to convince me for months that it too much exists.

However, no fear, with four mental-healing sisters as I have, no sinking just now. Give me a strong pull and a long pull, will you, all together, and then I am up!

Why do you talk so much about me in your one-letter-a-year and so little about the four witches mumbling Mantras over the boiling pot in a corner of Chicago?

Did you come across Max Müller's new book, Ramakrishna: His Life and Sayings?

If you have not, do, and let Mother see it. How is Mother? Growing grey? And Father Pope? Who have been our last visitors from America do you suppose? "Brother, love is a drawing card" and "Misses Meel"; they have been doing splendid in Australia and elsewhere; the same old "fellies", little changed if any. I wish you could come to visit India—that will be some day in the future. By the by, Mary, I heard a few months ago, when I was rather worrying over your long silence, that you were just hooking a "Willy", and so busy with your dances and parties; that explained of course your inability to write. But "Willy" or no "Willy", I must have my money, don't forget. Harriet is discreetly silent since she got her boy; but where is my money, please? Remind her and her husband of it. If she is Woolley, I am greasy Bengali, as the English call us here—Lord, where is my money?

I have got a monastery on the Ganga now, after all, thanks to American and English friends. Tell Mother to look sharp. I am going to deluge your Yankee land with idolatrous missionaries.

Tell Mr. Woolley he got the sister but has not paid the brother yet. Moreover, it was the fat black queerly dressed apparition smoking in the parlour that frightened many a temptation away, and that was one of the causes which secured Harriet to Mr. Woolley; therefore, I want to be paid for my great share in the work etc., etc. Plead strong, will you?

I do so wish I could come over to America with Joe for this summer; but man proposes and who disposes? Not God surely always. Well, let things slide as they will. Here is Abhayananda, Marie Louse you know, and she has been very well received in Bombay and Madras. She will be in Calcutta tomorrow, and we are going to give her a good reception too.

My love to Miss Howe, Mrs. Adams, to Mother Church, and Father Pope and all the rest of my friends across the seven oceans. We believe in seven oceans—one of milk, one of honey, one of curd, one wine, one sugar-cane juice, one salt, one I forget what. To you four sisters I waft my love across the ocean of honey...

Ever sincerely, your brother,
Vivekananda.

PS—Write when you find time between dances.

1899.12—DEAR __

The Math,
11th April, 1899.

DEAR __,

...Two years of physical suffering have taken away twenty years of my life. Well, but the soul changeth not, does it? It is there, the same madcap Atman, mad upon one idea, intent and intense.

Yours etc.,
Vivekananda.

1899.13 — MADAM[1]

Belur Math,
16th April, 1899.

DEAR MADAM, (Shrimati Sarala Ghosal, B. A.)

Very glad to receive your kind note. If by the sacrifice of some specially cherished object of either myself or my brother-disciples many pure and genuinely patriotic souls come forward to help our cause, rest assured, we will not hesitate in the least to make that sacrifice nor shed a tear-drop — you will see this verified in action. But up till now I have seen nobody coming forward to assist in this way. Only some have wished to put their own hobby in place of ours — that is all. If it really help our country or humanity — not to speak of giving up Guru-worship — believe me, we are prepared to commit any dire iniquity and suffer the eternal damnation of the Christians. But my hairs have turned grey since I began the study of man. This world is a most trying place, and it is long since I have taken to wandering with the lantern of the Grecian Philosopher in hand. A popular song my Master often used to sing comes to my mind:

"He who's a man after one's heart
Betrays himself by his very looks.
Rare indeed is such a one!
He's a man of aesthetic perceptions
Who treads a path contrary to others."

This much from my side. Please know that not one word of it is exaggerated — which you will find to be actually the case. But then I have some doubts about those patriotic souls who can join with us if only we give up the worship of the Guru. Well, if, as they pose, they are indeed panting and struggling so much — almost to the point of dissolution from their body — to serve the country, how can the single accident of Guru-worship stop everything!

This impetuous river with rolling waves which bade fair to sweep away whole hills and mountains — was a bit of Guru-worship sufficient to turn it back to the Himalayas! I put it to you, do you think anything great will come of such patriotism, or any substantial good proceed from such assistance? It is for you to say; I can make nothing out of it. For a thirsty man to weigh so much the merits of water, or for a man about to die of hunger to cogitate so much and turn up his nose at the food presented! Well, people have strange ways of thinking. I, for one, am inclined to think that those people were best in a glass-case; the more they keep away from actual work, the better.

"Love stops not for questions of birth.
Nor the hungry man for stale food."

This is what I know. But I may be wholly mistaken. Well, if this trifle of Guru-worship sticks in one's throat to choke one to death, we had better extricate him

[1] Translated from Bengali.

from this predicament.

However, I have a great longing to talk over these points with you in detail. For talking these things over, affliction and death have given me leave till now, and I hope they will do so yet.

May all your wishes be fulfilled in this New Year!

Yours sincerely,
Vivekananda.

1899.14 — CHRISTINA

To Sister Christine:

The Math, Belur, Dist. Howrah, Bengal, India,
10th May, 1899.

MY DEAR CHRISTINA,

I am getting better again. In my mind the whole of my complaint is bad assimilation of food and nervous exhaustion. The first, I am taking care of; the second will completely pass off when I meet you again. The great joy of meeting old, old friends, you know! Cheer up! There is no cause for anxiety. Do not believe a single desponding line I write now, because I am at times not myself. I get so nervous.

I start this summer for Europe anyway, as you say in America. With all love and blessings,

Yours ever in the Lord,
Vivekananda.

1899.15 — FRIEND

The Math, Alambazar (?),
14th June, 1899.

MY DEAR FRIEND[1],

I want your Highness in that fashion as I am here, you need most of friendship and love just now.

I wrote you a letter a few weeks ago but could not get news of yours. Hope you are in splendid health now. I am starting for England again on the 20th this month.

I hope also to benefit somewhat by this sea-voyage.

May you be protected from all dangers and may all blessings ever attend you!

I am yours in the Lord,
Vivekananda.

PS — To Jagamohan my love and good-bye.

1. Raja Of Khetri.

1899.16 — MISS MACLEOD

To Miss Josephine MacLeod:

[When Swami Vivekananda sailed from Calcutta, he dispatched the following cablegram.]

[Calcutta,
June 21, 1899.]

STARTED. WIRE STURDY.

England

1899.17 — CHRISTINA

To Sister Christine:

Suez,
14th July, 1899.

MY DEAR CHRISTINA,

You see this time I am really out, and hope to reach London in two weeks. I am sure to come to America this year and earnestly hope will have the opportunity of seeing you. I am so materialistic yet, you know! Want to see my friends in the gross body.

I had a beautiful letter from Baby [Stella Campbell] before I left. I am soon going to pen a reply to your care, as directed. I could not write her earlier.

I was so, so bad in health in India. My heart went wrong all the way — what with mountain climbing, bathing in glacier water and nervous prostration! I used to get terrible fits [of asthma] — the last lasting about seven days and nights. All the time I was suffocating and had to stand up.

This trip has almost made a new man of me. I feel much better and, if this continues, hope to be quite strong before I reach America. How are you? What are you doing? Write everything about yourself, c/o E. T. Sturdy Esq., 25 Holland Villas Road, London, W.

With everlasting love and blessings,

Yours ever in the Lord,
Vivekananda.

1899.18 — STURDY

To Mr. E. T. Sturdy:

Port Said,
14th July, 1899.

MY DEAR STURDY,

I got your letter all right just now. I have one from M. Nobel of Paris too. Miss Noble has several from America.

M. Nobel writes to me to defer my visit to him at Paris to some other date, from London, as he will have to be away for a long time. As you know sure, I shall not have many friends staying now in London, and Miss MacLeod is so desirous I should come. A stay in England under these circumstances is not advisable. Moreover, I do not have much life left. At least I must go on with that supposition. I mean, if anything has to be done in America, it is high time we bring our scattered influence in America to a head—if not organise regularly. Then I shall be free to return to England in a few months and work with a will till I return to India.

I think you are absolutely wanted to gather up, as it were, the American work. If you can, therefore, you ought to come over with me. Turiyananda is with me. Saradananda's brother is going to Boston... In case you cannot come to America, I ought to go, ought I not?

Yours,
Vivekananda.

1899.19 — CHRISTINA

To Sister Christine:

Marseilles,
23rd July, 1899.

MY DEAR CHRISTINA,

Your very, very welcome wire just came. By next Sunday we arrive in London, Albert Dock. We are a party of four: myself, another Sannyasin, a Calcutta boy going to study in America, and Miss [Margaret] Noble. Miss Noble is a young lady from Wimbledon, near London, who has been working in India on the education of girls.

Our stay in England will not be long, I am afraid, as this is neither the season nor am I in fit condition to work much. Anyhow, we will be in London a few weeks—at least myself—then go to the U.S. We will talk over all this and infinite things besides when we meet. I do not think even English summer days are long enough for all the chatter I will assail you with.

We go to Wimbledon for a day or two, and then I come back to London and find lodgings for myself and make plans.

Come to the Dock if that is possible and discreet. Yes, it is discreet, as there is a lady in the party and others will come to meet her. Only, Christina, don't if you feel the least tired or unwell. I hope you are enjoying London immensely.

The Orientals do not like any effusion of feeling. They are trained to hide all expression.

Is Mrs. Funkey [Mary Caroline Funke] with you? If so, give her my best love.

I am much, much better just now. I am really quite another man this time. I was nearly dead in Calcutta when I started, but this voyage has improved me immensely.

Hoping soon to see you,

Ever yours in the Lord,
Vivekananda.

1899.20 — SISTER CHRISTINE

To Sister Christine:

TELEGRAM
TO:

Christina Grinnstidel [Greenstidel],
23 Crowhurst Rd., Angell Rd., Briaton, LDN.
30 July, 1899.

GOLCONDA DUE DOCKS 6 AM MONDAY. (Vide Swami Vivekananda's letter dated)

1899.21 — JOE

To Miss Josephine MacLeod:

THE LYMES,
WOODSIDES, WIMBLEDON,
3rd August, 1899.

MY DEAR JOE,

We are in at last. Turiyananda and I have beautiful lodgings here. Saradananda's brother is with Miss Noble and starts Monday next.

I have recovered quite a bit by the voyage. It was brought about by the exercise on the dumb-bells and monsoon storms tumbling the steamer about the waves. Queer, isn't it? Hope it will remain. Where is our Mother, the Worshipful Brahmini cow of India? She is with you in New York, I think.

Sturdy is away, Mrs. Johnson and everybody. Margo is rather worried at that. She cannot come to U.S. till next month. Already I have come to love the sea. The fish Avatâra is on me, I am afraid — good deal of him in me, I am sure, a Bengali.

How is Alberta, ... the old folks and the rest of them? I had a beautiful letter from dear Mrs. Brer Rabbit; she could not meet us in London; she started before we arrived.

It is nice and warm here; rather too much they say. I have become for the present a Shunyavâdi, a believer in nothingness, or void. No plans, no afterthought, no attempt, for anything, laissez faire to the fullest. Well, Joe, Margo would always take your side on board the steamer, whenever I criticised you or the Divine cow. Poor child, she knows so little! The upshot of the whole is, Joe, that there cannot be any work in London, because you are not here. You seem to be my fate! Grind on, old lady; it is Karma and none can avoid. Say, I look several years younger by this voyage. Only when the heart gives a lurch, I feel my age. What is this osteopathy, anyway? Will they cut off a rib or two to cure me? Not I, no manufacturing of ... from my ribs, sure. Whatever it be, it will be hard work for him to find my bones. My bones are destined to make corals in the Ganga. Now I am going to study French if you give me a lesson every day; but no grammar business — only I will read and you explain in English. Kindly give my love to Abhedananda, and ask him to get ready for Turiyananda. I will leave with him. Write soon.

With all love etc.,
Vivekananda.

1899.22 — MOTHER

To Mrs. Ole Bull:

The Lymes, Woodside,
Wimbledon, England,
6 August, 1899.

MY DEAR MOTHER,

Your letter directed to Sturdy at hand. I am very thankful for your kind words. As for me, I don't know what I am to do next or anything to do at all. On board the steamer I was all right, but since landing [I am] feeling quite bad again. As to mental worry, there has been enough of late. The aunt whom you saw had a deep-laid plan to cheat me, and she and her people contrived to sell me a house for 6,000 Rs., or £400, and I bought [it] for my mother in good faith. Then they would not give me possession, hoping that I would not go to court for the shame of taking forcible possession as a Sannyasin.

I do not think I have spent even one rupee from what you and others gave me for the work. Cap. Sevier gave me 8,000 Rs. with the express desire of helping my mother. This money, it seems, has [also] gone to the dogs. Beyond this, nothing has been spent on my family or even on my own personal expenses — my food etc. being paid for by the Khetri Raja, and more than half of that went to the Math every month. Only, if Brahmananda spends some in the lawsuit [against the aunt], as I must not be robbed that way — if he does, I will make it good anyway, if I live to do it.

The money which I got in Europe and America by lecturing alone, I spent just as I like; but every cent I got for the work has been accounted for and is in the Math, and the whole thing ought to be clear as daylight if Brahmananda never cheated me. I don't believe he will ever cheat me. I got a letter at Aden from Saradananda that they were preparing an account. I have not received any yet.

I have no plans yet, nor care to make any. Neither do I wish to work. Let the Mother find other workers. I have my burden enough already.

Ever your devoted son,
Vivekananda.

1899.23 — RAKHAL[1]

To Swami Brahmananda:

London,
10th August, 1899.

MY DEAR RAKHAL,

I got a lot of news from your letter. My health was much better on the ship, but, after landing, owing to flatulence it is rather bad now... There is a lot of difficulty here — all friends have gone out of town for the summer. In addition my health is not so good, and there is a lot of inconvenience regarding food etc. So in a few days I leave for America. Send an account to Mrs. Bull as to how much was spent on purchase of land, how much on buildings, how much on maintenance etc.

Sarada writes that the magazine is not going well... Let him publish the account of my travels, and thoroughly advertise it beforehand — he will have subscribers rushing in. Do people like a magazine if three-fourths of it are filled with pious stuff? Anyway pay special attention to the magazine. Mentally take it as though I were not. Act independently on this basis. "We depend on the elder brother for money, learning, everything" — such an attitude is the road to ruin. If all the money even for the magazine is to be collected by me and all the articles too are from my pen — what will you all do? What are our Sahibs then doing? I have finished my part. You do what remains to be done. Nobody is there to collect a single penny, nobody to do any preaching, none has brains enough to take proper care of his own affairs, none has the capacity to write one line, and all are saints for nothing!... If this be your condition, then for six months give everything into the hands of the boys — magazine, money, preaching work, etc. If they are also not able to do anything, then sell off everything, and returning the proceeds to the donors go about as mendicants. I get no news at all from the Math. What is Sharat doing? I want to see work done. Before dying, I want to see that what I have established as a result of my lifelong struggle is put in a more or less running condition. Consult the Committee in every detail regarding money matters. Get the signatures of the Committee for every item of expenditure. Otherwise you also will be in for a bad name. This much is customary that people want some time or other an account of their donations. It is very wrong not to have it ready at every turn... By such lethargy in the beginning, people finally become cheats. Make a committee of all those who are in the Math, and no expenditure will be made which is not countersigned by them — none at all! I want work, I want vigour — no matter who lives or dies. What are death and life to a Sannyasin?

If Sharat cannot rouse up Calcutta,... if you are not able to construct the embankment this year, then you will see the fun! I want work — no humbug about it. My respectful salutations to Holy Mother.

Yours affectionately,
Vivekananda.

---

1 Translated from Bengali.

1899.24 — MARIE

To Miss Marie Halboister:

C/O Miss Noble,
21A High Street, Wimbledon.
August, 1899.

MY DEAR MARIE,

I am in London again. This time not busy, not hustling about but quietly settled down in a corner — waiting to start for the U.S. America on the first opportunity. My friends are nearly all out of London in the country and elsewhere, and my health not sufficiently strong.

So you are happy in the midst of your lakes and gardens and seclusion in Canada. I am glad, so glad to know that you are up again on top of the tide. May you remain there for ever!

You could not finish the Raja-Yoga translation yet — all right, there is no hurry. Time and opportunity must come if it is to be done you know, otherwise we vainly strive.

Canada must be beautiful now, with its short but vigorous summer, and very healthy.

I expect to be in New York in a few weeks, and don't know what next. I hope to come back to England next spring.

I fervently wish no misery ever came near anyone; yet it is that alone that gives us an insight into the depths of our lives, does it not?

In our moments of anguish, gates barred for ever seem to open and let in many a flood of light.

We learn as we grow. Alas! we cannot use our knowledge here. The moment we seem to learn, we are hurried off the stage. And this is Mâyâ!

This toy world would not be here, this play could not go on, if we were knowing players. We must play blindfolded. Some of us have taken the part of the rogue of the play, some heroic — never mind, it is all play. This is the only consolation. There are demons and lions and tigers and what not on the stage, but they are all muzzled. They snap but cannot bite. The world cannot touch our souls. If you want, even if the body be torn and bleeding, you may enjoy the greatest peace in your mind.

And the way to that is to attain hopelessness. Do you know that? Not the imbecile attitude of despair, but the contempt of the conqueror for things he has attained, for things he struggled for and then throws aside as beneath his worth.

This hopelessness, desirelessness, aimlessness, is just the harmony with nature. In nature there is no harmony, no reason, no sequence; it was chaos before, it is so still.

The lowest man is in consonance with nature in his earthy-headness; the highest the same in the fullness of knowledge. All three aimless, drifting, hopeless — all three happy.

You want a chatty letter, don't you? I have not much to chat about. Mr. Sturdy came last two days. He goes home in Wales tomorrow.

I have to book my passage for N.Y. in a day or two.

None of my old friends have I seen yet except Miss Souter and Max Gysic, who are in London. They have been very kind, as they always were.

I have no news to give you, as I know nothing of London yet. I don't know where Gertrude Orchard is, else would have written to her. Miss Kate Steel is also away. She is coming on Thursday or Saturday.

I had an invitation to stay in Paris with a friend, a very well-educated Frenchman, but I could not go this time. I hope another time to live with him some days.

I expect to see some of our old friends and say good day to them.

I hope to see you in America sure. Either I may unexpectedly turn up in Ottawa in my peregrinations or you come to N.Y.

Good-bye, all luck be yours.

Ever yours in the Lord,
Vivekananda.

U.S.A

1899.25 — ISABEL

To Miss Isabelle McKindley:

Ridgely Manor, Stone Ridge, N.Y.,
31st August, '99.

MY DEAR ISABEL,

Many thanks for your kind note. I will be so, so glad to see you. Miss M'cLeod [MacLeod] is going to write you to stop a day and a night here on your way to the West.

My love to the holy family in Chicago, and hope surely to be able to come West and have great fun.

So you are in Greenacre at last. Is this the first year you have been there? How do you like the place? [You have] seen Miss Farmer, of course. Kindly convey her my kindest regards and to all the rest of my friends there.

Ever yours affectionately,
Vivekananda.

1899.26 — MRS. BULL

Ridgely,
4th Sept., 1899.

DEAR MRS. BULL,

...Mother knows best, that is all about me...

Yours etc.,
Vivekananda.

1899.27 — MOTHER

To Mrs. Ole Bull:

Ridgely Manor,
4th September, 1899.

MY DEAR MOTHER,

It is an awful spell of the bad turn of fortune with me last six months. Misfortune follows me ever wherever I go. In England, Sturdy seems to have got disgusted with the work; he does not see any asceticism in us from India. Here no sooner I reach than Olea gets a bad attack.

Shall I run up to you? I know I cannot be of much help, but I will try my best in being useful.

I hope everything will soon come right with you, and Olea will be restored to perfect health even before this reaches you. Mother knows best; that is all about me.

Ever yours affectionately,
Vivekananda.

1899.28 — STURDY

To Mr. E. T. Sturdy:

Ridgely Manor,
14th September, 1899.

MY DEAR STURDY,

I have simply been taking rest at the Leggetts' and doing nothing. Abhedananda is here. He has been working hard.

He goes in a day or two to resume his work in different places for a month. After that he comes to New York to work.

I am trying to do something in the line you suggested, but don't know how far an account of the Hindus will be appreciated by the Western public when it comes from a Hindu...

Mrs. Johnson is of opinion that no spiritual person ought to be ill. It also seems to her now that my smoking is sinful etc., etc. That was Miss Müller's reason for leaving me, my illness. They may be perfectly right, for aught I know — and you too — but I am what I am. In India, the same defects plus eating with Europeans have been taken exception to by many. I was driven out of a private temple by the owners for eating with Europeans. I wish I were malleable enough to be moulded into whatever one desired, but unfortunately I never saw a man who could satisfy everyone. Nor can anyone who has to go to different places possibly satisfy all.

When I first came to America, they ill-treated me if I had not trousers on. Next I was forced to wear cuffs and collars, else they would not touch me etc., etc. They thought me awfully funny if I did not eat what they offered etc., etc...

In India the moment I landed they made me shave my head and wear "Kaupin" (loin cloth), with the result that I got diabetes etc. Saradananda never gave up his underwear — this saved his life, with just a touch of rheumatism and much comment from our people.

Of course, it is my Karma, and I am glad that it is so. For, though it smarts for the time, it is another great experience of life, which will be useful, either in this or in the next...

As for me, I am always in the midst of ebbs and flows. I knew it always and preached always that every bit of pleasure will bring its quota of pain, if not with compound interest. I have a good deal of love given to me by the world; I deserve a good deal of hatred therefore. I am glad it is so — as it proves my theory of "every wave having its corresponding dip" on my own person.

As for me, I stick to my nature and principle — once a friend, always a friend — also the true Indian principle of looking subjectively for the cause of the objective.

I am sure that the fault is mine, and mine only, for every wave of dislike and hatred that I get. It could not be otherwise. Thanking you and Mrs. Johnson for thus calling me once more to the internal,

I remain as ever with love and blessings,
Vivekananda.

1899.29 — CHRISTINA

To Sister Christine:

Ridgely Manor,
20th September, 1899.

DEAR CHRISTINA,

I am much better, thank you. Hitherto, excepting three days, there has not been any wet weather to speak of here. Miss [Margaret] Noble came yesterday, and we are having a jolly good time. I am very, very sorry to say I am growing fat again. That is bad. I will eat less and grow thin once more.

You are again at work — so do I find — only with a little variation of the old occupation. Better rest than mere idling. Do you like my new poem? (Vide letter.) Miss Noble thinks it is nice. But that is her way with everything I do. So you also say. I will now send my writings to missionary papers to get a fierce criticism.

With all love to you and Mrs. Funkey [Funke],

Ever yours affectionately,
Vivekananda.

1899.30 — MARY

To Miss Mary Hale:

Ridgely Manor,
September, 1899.

MY DEAR MARY,

Yes, I have arrived. I had a letter from Isabelle from Greenacre. I hope to see her soon and Harriet. Harriet Woolley has been uniformly silent. Never mind, I will bide my time, and as soon as Mr. Woolley becomes a millionaire, demand my money. You did not write any particulars about Mother Church and Father Pope, only the news of something about me in some newspapers. I have long ceased to take any interest in papers; only they keep me before the public and get a sale of my books "anyway" as you say. Do you know what I am trying to do now? Writing a book on India and her people—a short chatty simple something. Again I am going to learn French. If I fail to do it this year, I cannot "do" the Paris Exposition next year properly. Well, I expect to learn much French here where even the servants talk it.

You never saw Mrs. Leggett, did you? She is simply grand. I am going to Paris next year as their guest, as I did the first time.

I have now got a monastery on the Ganga for the teaching of philosophy and comparative religion and a centre of work.

What have you been doing all this time? Reading? Writing? You did not do anything. You could have written lots by this time. Even if you had taught me French, I would be quite a Froggy now, and you did not, only made me talk nonsense. You never went to Greenacre. I hope it is getting strength every year.

Say, you 24 feet and 600 lbs. of Christian Science, you could not pull me up with your treatments. I am losing much faith in your healing powers. Where is Sam? "Bewaring" all this time as he could; bless his heart, such a noble boy!

I was growing grey fast, but somehow it got checked. I am sorry, only a few grey hairs now; a research will unearth many though. I like it and am going to cultivate a long white goaty. Mother Church and Father Pope were having a fine time on the continent. I saw a bit on my way home. And you have been Cinderella-ing in Chicago—good for you. Persuade the old folks to go to Paris next year and take you along. There must be wonderful sights to see; the French are making a last great struggle, they say, before closing business.

Well, you did not write me long, long. You do not deserve this letter, but—I am so good you know, especially as death is drawing near—I do not want to quarrel with anyone. I am dying to see Isabelle and Harriet. I hope they have got a great supply of healing power at Greenacre Inn and will help me out of my present fall. In my days the Inn was well stored with spiritual food, and less of material stuff. Do you know anything of osteopathy? Here is one in New York working wonders really.

I am going to have my bones searched by him in a week. Where is Miss Howe? She is such a noble soul, such a friend. By the by, Mary, it is curious your family, Mother Church and her clergy, both monastic and secular, have made more impression on me than any family I know of. Lord bless you ever and ever.

I am taking rest now, and the Leggetts are so kind. I feel perfectly at home. I intend to go to New York to see the Dewy procession. I have not seen my friends there.

Write me all about yourselves. I so long to hear. You know Joe Joe of course. I marred their visit to India with my constant break-downs, and they were so good, so forgiving. For years Mrs. Bull and she have been my guardian angels. Mrs. Bull is expected here next week.

She would have been here before this, but her daughter (Olea) had a spell of illness. She suffered much, but is now out of danger. Mrs. Bull has taken one of Leggett's cottages here, and if the cold weather does not set in faster than usual, we are going to have a delightful month here even now. The place is so beautiful — well wooded and perfect lawns.

I tried to play golf the other day; I do not think it difficult at all — only it requires good practice. You never went to Philadelphia to visit your golfing friends? What are your plans? What do you intend to do the rest of your life? Have you thought out any work? Write me a long letter, will you? I saw a lady in the streets of Naples as I was passing, going along with three others, must be Americans, so like you that I was almost going to speak to her; when I came near I saw my mistake. Good-bye for the present. Write sharp...

Ever your affectionate brother,
Vivekananda.

1899.31 — MARY

To Miss Mary Hale:

Ridgely Manor,
3rd October, 1899.

MY DEAR MARY,

Thanks for your very kind words. I am much better now and growing so every day. Mrs. Bull and her daughter are expected today or tomorrow. We hope thus to have another spell of good time — you are having yours all the time, of course. I am glad you are going to Philadelphia, but not so much now as then — when the millionaire was on the horizon. With all love,

Ever your affectionate brother,
Vivekananda.

1899.32 — MOTHER CHURCH

To Mrs. G. W. Hale:

Ridgely Manor,
5 October, 1899.

MY DEAR MOTHER CHURCH,

Many, many thanks for your kind words.

I am so glad you are working on as ever. I am glad because the wave of optimism has not caught you yet. It is all very well to say everything is right, but that is apt to degenerate into a sort of laissez-faire. I believe with you that the world is evil—made more hideous with a few dashes of good.

All our works have only this value, that they awaken some to the reality of this horror—and [those] flee for refuge to some place beyond, which is called God, or Christ, or Brahma, or Buddha, etc. Names do not make much difference.

Again, we must always remember ours is only to work—we never attain results. How can we? Good can never be done without doing evil. We cannot breathe a breath without killing thousands of poor little animals. National prosperity is another name for death and degradation to millions of other races. So is individual prosperity the beggaring of many. The world is evil—and will ever remain so. It is its nature, and cannot be changed—"Which one of you by taking thought ... " etc. (Matthew 6.27.)

Such is truth. The wisdom is therefore in renunciation, that is, to make the Lord our all in all. Be a true Christian, Mother—like Christ, renounce everything and let the heart and soul and body belong to Him and Him alone. All this nonsense which people have built round Christ's name is not His teaching. He taught to renounce. He never says the earth is an enjoyable place. And your time has come to get rid of all vanities—even the love of children and husband—and think of the Lord and Him alone.

Ever your Son,
Vivekananda.

1899.33 — MOTHER

To Mrs. G. W. Hale:

[Ridgely Manor], New York, N.Y.,
23 October, 1899.

MY DEAR MOTHER,

I was taking a few days' complete rest and so am late in replying to your very kind note. Accept my congratulations on the anniversary of your marriage. I pray many, many such returns may come to you.

I am sure my previous letter was coloured by the state of my body, as indeed is the whole of existence to us. Yet, Mother, there is more pain than pleasure in life. If not, why do I remember you and your children almost every day of my life, and not many others? Happiness is liked so much because it is so rare, is it not? Fifty percent of our life is mere lethargy, ennui; of the rest, forty percent is pain, only ten happiness—and this for the exceptionally fortunate. We are oft-times mixing up this state of ennui with pleasure. It is rather a negative state, whilst both pleasure and pain are nearer positive, though not positive.

Pleasure and pain are both feeling, not willing. They are only processes which convey to the mind excitements or motives of action. The real positive action is the willing, or impulse to work, of the mind—begun when the sensation has been taken in (pleasure and pain); thus the real is neither pleasure nor pain. It has no connection with either. Quite different from either. The barking of the dog awakens his master to guard against a thief or receive his dearest friend. It does not follow, therefore, that the dog and his master are of the same nature or have any degree of kinship. The feelings of pleasure or pain similarly awaken the soul to activity, without any kinship at all.

The soul is beyond pain, beyond pleasure, sufficient in its own nature. And no hell can punish it, nor any heaven can bless it. So far philosophy.

I am coming soon to Chicago, and hope to say "Lord bless you" to you and your children. All love as usual to my Christian relatives, scientific or quacks.

Vivekananda.

1899.34 — CHRISTINA

To Sister Christine:

C/O F. H. Leggett, Esq.,
Ridgely Manor, Stone Ridge, Ulster Co., N.Y.,
25th October, 1899.

DEAR CHRISTINA,

What is the matter with you? Write me a line to tell me how you are and what you are doing now.

I am tired of this place, and will come down to New York for a few days soon. I start thence for Chicago and, if you like, will stop at Detroit on my way to How-do-you-do. I am much better, indeed quite a different man, though not completely cured — for that, time is necessary.

Yours,
Vivekananda.

1899.35 — CHRISTINA

To Sister Christine:

Ridgely Manor,
30th October, 1899.

MY DEAR CHRISTINA,

Did you not get my last letter? I am very anxious to know how you are. Write a line to tell me you are in very good health.

I am afraid the previous one was misdirected, so I send this c/o Mrs. Funkey [Funke].

Do write soon. I am thinking of Battle Creek food. Baby insists on that. Do you think it will do me any good? Write soon.

Ever yours in the Lord,
Vivekananda.

PS — Where is this Battle Creek? Is it near Detroit? I am seriously thinking of giving it a trial. I am not bad, but unfit for any exertion, even for a walk. This sort of life is no good to live. I [will] try Battle Creek, and if that fails, get out quick.

Write me about Battle Creek.

1899.36 — OPTIMIST

To Miss Mary Hale:

Ridgely Manor,
30th October, 1899.

MY DEAR OPTIMIST,

I received your letter and am thankful that something has come to force optimistic laissez faire into action. Your questions have tapped the very source of pessimism, however. British rule in modern India has only one redeeming feature, though unconscious; it has brought India out once more on the stage of the world; it has forced upon it the contact of the outside world. If it had been done with an eye to the good of the people concerned, as circumstances favoured Japan with, the results could have been more wonderful for India. No good can be done when the main idea is blood-sucking. On the whole the old regime was better for the people, as it did not take away everything they had, and there was some justice, some liberty.

A few hundred, modernised, half-educated, and denationalised men are all the show of modern English India — nothing else. The Hindus were 600 million in number according to Ferishta, the Mohammedan historian, in the 12th century — now less than 200 million.

In spite of the centuries of anarchy that reigned during the struggles of the English to conquer, the terrible massacre the English perpetrated in 1857 and 1858, and the still more terrible famines that have become the inevitable consequence of British rule (there never is a famine in a native state) and that take off millions, there has been a good increase of population, but not yet what it was when the country was entirely independent — that is, before the Mohammedan rule. Indian labour and produce can support five times as many people as there are now in India with comfort, if the whole thing is not taken off from them.

This is the state of things — even education will no more be permitted to spread; freedom of the press stopped already, (of course we have been disarmed long ago), the bit of self-government granted to them for some years is being quickly taken off. We are watching what next! For writing a few words of innocent criticism, men are being hurried to transportation for life, others imprisoned without any trial; and nobody knows when his head will be off.

There has been a reign of terror in India for some years. English soldiers are killing our men and outraging our women — only to be sent home with passage and pension at our expense. We are in a terrible gloom — where is the Lord? Mary, you can afford to be optimistic, can I? Suppose you simply publish this letter — the law just passed in India will allow the English Government in India to drag me from here to India and kill me without trial. And I know all your Christian governments will only rejoice, because we are heathens. Shall I also go to sleep and become optimistic? Nero was the greatest optimistic person! They don't think it worth while to write these terrible things as news items even! If necessary, the news agent of Reuter gives the exactly opposite news fabricated to order! Heathen-murdering is only a legitimate pastime for the Christians! Your missionaries go to preach God and dare not speak a word of truth for fear of the English, who will kick them out the next day.

All property and lands granted by the previous governments for supporting education have been swallowed up, and the present Government spends even less than Russia in education. And what education?

The least show of originality is throttled. Mary, it is hopeless with us, unless there really is a God who is the father of all, who is not afraid of the strong to protect the weak, and who is not bribed by wealth. Is there such a God? Time will show.

Well, I think I am coming to Chicago in a few weeks and talk of things fully! Don't quote your authority.

With all love, ever your brother,
Vivekananda.

PS — As for religious sects — the Brahmo Samaj, the Arya Samaj, and other sects have been useless mixtures; they were only voices of apology to our English masters to allow us to live! We have started a new India — a growth — waiting to see what comes. We believe in new ideas only when the nation wants them, and what will be true for us. The test of truth for this Brahmo Samaj is "what our masters approve"; with us, what the Indian reasoning and experience approves. The struggle has begun — not between the Brahmo Samaj and us, for they are gone already, but a harder, deeper, and more terrible one.

1899.37 — MARGOT

Ridgely,
1st Nov., 1899.

DEAR MARGOT, (Margaret E. Noble or Sister Nivedita)

...It seems there is a gloom over your mind. Never mind, nothing is to last for ever. Anyhow life is not eternal. I am so, so thankful for it. Suffering is the lot of the world's best and bravest—yet, for aeons yet—till things are righted; if possible, here—at least it is a discipline which breaks the dream. In my sane moments I rejoice for my sufferings. Some one must suffer here;—I am glad it is I, amongst others of nature's sacrifices.

Yours etc.,
Vivekananda.

1899.38 — CHRISTINA

To Sister Christine:

Ridgely Manor,
4th November, 1899.

MY DEAR CHRISTINA,

The letter was all right in reaching. It was only my nervousness. I am sure you will understand and excuse this. I eagerly expect t o see you in Cambridge. I am going to New York next week. Thence I go for a few days to Washington and then to Cambridge. Do come. And mind you, I must learn German. I am determined to be a French and German scholar. French, I think, I can manage with the help of a dictionary. If I can do that much German in a month, I will be so glad.

It naturally takes time for a letter to reach from here. We have one delivery and one posting a day.

With all love,

Ever yours in the Lord,
Vivekananda.

My eternal love and blessings to Mrs. Funkey [Funke].

1899.39 — CHRISTINA

To Sister Christine:

21 West 34th Street, New York,
10th November, 1899.

MY DEAR CHRISTINA,

I received your letter just now. I am now in New York. Dr. [Egbert] Guernsey analysed my urine yesterday, and there was no sugar or albumen in it. So my kidneys are all right, at least at present. The heart is only nervous, requires calming!—some cheerful company and good, loving friends and quiet. The only difficulty is the dyspepsia, and that is the evil. For instance, I am all right in the morning and can walk miles, but in the evening it is impossible to walk after a meal—the gas—that depends entirely up on food, does it not? I ought to try the Battle Creek food. If I come to Detroit, there will be quiet and Battle Creek food for me.

But if you come to Cambridge with all the instructions of the Battle Creek food, I will have it prepared there; or, between you and me, we will cook it. I am a good hand at that. You don't know a thing about cooking. Well, you may help in cleaning the plates etc. I always get money when I need it badly. "Mother" always sees to that. So, no danger on that head. I am not in the least danger of life, the Doctors agree — only if this dyspepsia goes away. And that is "food", "food", "food", and no worry. Oh, what a worry I have had! Say we go somewhere else and make a little party and keep house ourselves. In Cambridge, Mrs. Bull has a quiet separate place — her studio house. You can have rooms there. I wish you to know Mrs. Bull. She is a saint, a real saint, if ever there was one. Wait for my next letter. I will write today again, or tomorrow after seeing Mrs. Bull.

Ever yours in the Lord,
Vivekananda.

1899.40 — MRS. BULL

To Mrs. Ole Bull:

180 W. 59, C/O E. Guernsey, M.D.,
12 November, 1899.

DEAR MRS. BULL,

I am laid up with a bad cold. The clothes are not ready — they will be next week. I don't know what my next step will be. Dr. Guernsey is very kind. Several Doctors have examined me and none could detect any organic disease.

Even the kidney complications for the present have disappeared.

Well, the whole thing is then dyspepsia. I want ever so much to try Battle Creek food. There is a restaurant which cooks only Battle Creek food. Do you think it should be best for me to try it just now? If so, I go to Detroit. In that case, send me my terracotta, thick cashmere coat.

Ever yours in the Lord,
Vivekananda.

Had three treatments already from Helmer. Going to take some next week. None can do anything for this "wind". That is why dieting should be tried at any cost.

1899.41 — CHRISTINA

To Sister Christine:

C/O Dr. E. Guernsey,
180 West 59th Street, New York,
12th November, 1899.

CHRISTINA,

Mrs. Bull has gone to Boston without seeing me. I am with the Guernseys. All today laid up with colds.

Oh, these nasty colds. The doctor here declares my case as entirely one of nervous exhaustion. Even the dyspepsia is entirely nervous.

I will be a few days yet here, and then I don't know where I go. I have a great mind to try health food. As for you, write unreservedly where you [would] like me to be. If you think it best for me to come to Detroit, write or wire on receipt of this. I will come immediately. Only difficulty is now the dyspepsia.

With love to Mrs. Funkey [Funke],

Ever yours with blessings,
Vivekananda.

PS — If Cambridge is best, say that immediately.

1899.42 — MARGOT

New York,
15th Nov., 1899.

DEAR MARGOT, (Margaret E. Noble or Sister Nivedita)

... On the whole I don't think there is any cause for anxiety about my body. This sort of nervous body is just the instrument to play great music at times and at times to moan in darkness.

Yours etc.,
Vivekananda.

1899.43 — STURDY

C/O F. H. Leggett,
21 West Thirty-Fourth Street New York
Nov., 1899.

MY DEAR STURDY,

This is not to defend my conduct. Words cannot wipe off the evils I have done, nor any censor stop from working the good deeds, if any.

For the last few months I have been hearing so much of the luxuries I was given to enjoy by the people of the West — luxuries which the hypocrite myself has been enjoying, although preaching renunciation all the while: luxuries, the enjoyment of which has been the great stumbling-block in my way, in England at least. I nearly hypnotised myself into the belief that there has at least been a little oasis in the dreary desert of my life, a little spot of light in one whole life of misery and gloom; one moment of relaxation in a life of hard work and harder curses — even that oasis, that spot, that moment was only one of sense-enjoyment!!

I was glad, I blessed a hundred times a day those that had helped me to get it, when, lo, your last letter comes like a thunderclap, and the dream is vanished. I begin to disbelieve your criticisms — have little faith left in all this talk of luxuries and enjoyments and other visions memory calls up. These I state. Hope you will send it round to friends, if you think fit, and correct me where I am wrong.

I remember your place at Reading, where I was fed with boiled cabbage and potatoes and boiled rice and boiled lentils, three times a day, with your wife's curses for sauce all the time. I do not remember your giving me any cigar to smoke — shilling or penny ones. Nor do I remember myself as complaining of either the food or your wife's incessant curses, though I lived as a thief, shaking through fear all the time, and working every day for you.

The next memory is of the house on St. George's Road — you and Miss Muller at the head. My poor brother was ill there and Miss Müller drove him away. There too I don't remember to have had any luxuries as to food or drink or bed or even the room given to me.

The next was Miss Müller's place. Though she has been very kind to me, I was living on nuts and fruits. The next memory is that of the black hole of London where I had to work almost day and night and cook the meals oft-times for five or six, and most nights with a bite of bread and butter.

I remember Mrs. Sturdy giving me a dinner and a night's lodging in her place, and then the next day criticising the black savage — so dirty and smoking all over the house.

With the exception of Capt. and Mrs. Sevier, I do not remember even one piece of rag as big as a handkerchief I got from England. On the other hand, the incessant demand on my body and mind in England is the cause of my breakdown in health. This was all you English people gave me, whilst working me to death; and now I am cursed for the luxuries I lived in!! Whosoever of you have given me a coat? Whosoever a cigar? Whosoever a bit of fish or flesh? Whosoever of you dare say I asked food or drink or smoke or dress or money from you? Ask, Sturdy, ask for God's sake, ask your friends, and first ask your own "God within who never sleeps."

You have given me money for my work. Every penny of it is there. Before your eyes I sent my brother away, perhaps to his death; and I would not give him a farthing of the money which was not my private property.

On the other hand, I remember in England Capt. and Mrs. Sevier, who have clad me when I was cold, nursed me better than my own mother would have, borne with me in my weakness, my trials; and they have nothing but blessings for me. And that Mrs. Sevier, because she did not care for honours, has the worship of thousands today; and when she is dead millions will remember her as one of the great benefactresses of the poor Indians. And they never cursed me for my luxuries, though they are ready to give me luxuries, if I need or wish.

I need not tell you of Mrs. Bull, Miss MacLeod, Mr. and Mrs. Leggett. You know their love and kindness for me; and Mrs. Bull and Miss MacLeod have been to our country, moved and lived with us as no foreigner ever did, roughing it all, and they do not ever curse me and my luxuries either; they will be only too glad to have me eat well and smoke dollar cigars if I wish. And there Leggetts and Bulls were the people whose bread whose money bought my smokes and several times paid my rent, whilst I was killing myself for your people, when you were taking my pound of flesh for the dirty hole and starvation and reserving all this accusation of luxury.

"The clouds of autumn make great noise but send no rain; The clouds of the rainy season without a word flood the earth."

See Sturdy, those that have helped or are still helping have no criticism, no curses: it is only those who do nothing, who only come to grind their own axes, that curse, that criticise. That such worthless, heartless, selfish, rubbish criticise, is the greatest blessing that can come to me. I want nothing so much in life as to be miles off from these extremely selfish axe-grinders.

Talking of luxuries! Take these critics up one after the other — It is all flesh, all flesh and no spirit anywhere. Thank God, they come out sooner or later in their true colours. And you advise me to regulate my conduct, my work, according to the desires of such heartless, selfish persons, and are at your wit's end because I do not!

As to my Gurubhais (brother-disciples), they do nothing but what I insist on their doing. If they have shown any selfishness anywhere, that is because of my ordering them, not what they would do themselves.

Would you like your children put into that dark hole you got for me in London, made to work to death, and almost starved all the time? Would Mrs. Sturdy like that? They are Sannyasins, and that means, no Sannyasin should unnecessarily throw away his life or undertake unnecessary hardship.

In undergoing all this hardship in the West we have been only breaking the rules of Sannyasa. They are my brothers, my children. I do not want them to die in holes for my sake. I don't, by all that is good and true I don't, want them starved and worked and cursed for all their pains.

A word more. I shall be very glad if you can point out to me where I have preached torturing the flesh. As for the Shâstras (scriptures), I shall be only too glad if a Shâstri (Pundit) dares oppose us with the rules of life laid down for Sannyasins and Paramahamsas.

Well, Sturdy, my heart aches. I understand it all. I know what you are in — you are in the clutches of people who want to use you. I don't mean your wife. She is too simple to be dangerous. But, my poor boy, you have got the flesh-smell — a little money — and vultures are around. Such is life.

You said a lot about ancient India. That India still lives, Sturdy, is not dead, and that living India dares even today to deliver her message without fear or favour of the rich, without fear of anybody's opinion, either in the land where her feet are in chains or in the very face of those who hold the end of the chain, her rulers. That India still lives, Sturdy, India of undying love, of everlasting faithfulness, the unchangeable, not only in manners and customs, but also in love, in faith, in friendship. And I, the least of that India's children, love you, Sturdy, with Indian love, and would any day give up a thousand bodies to help you out of this delusion.

Ever yours,
Vivekananda.

1899.44 — STURDY

To Mr. E. T. Sturdy:

C/O F. Leggett Esq.,
Ridgely Manor, Ulster County, N.Y.

MY DEAR STURDY,

Your last letter reached me after knocking about a little through insufficient address.

It is quite probable that very much of your criticism is just and correct. It is also possible that some day you may find that all this springs from your dislike of certain persons, and I was the scapegoat.

There need be no bitterness, however, on that account, as I don't think I ever posed for anything but what I am. Nor is it ever possible for me to do so, as an hour's contact is enough to make everybody see through my smoking, bad temper, etc. "Every meeting must have a separation" — this is the nature of things. I carry no feeling of disappointment even. I hope you will have no bitterness. It is Karma that brings us together, and Karma separates.

I know how shy you are, and how loath to wound others' feelings. I perfectly understand months of torture in your mind when you have been struggling to work with people who were so different from your ideal. I could not guess it before at all, else I could have saved you a good deal of unnecessary mental trouble. It is Karma again.

The accounts were not submitted before, as the work is not yet finished; and I thought of submitting to my donor a complete account when the whole thing was finished. The work was begun only last year, as we had to wait for funds a long time, and my method is never to ask but wait for voluntary help.

I follow the same idea in all my work, as I am so conscious of my nature being positively displeasing to many, and wait till somebody wants me. I hold myself ready also to depart at a moment's notice. In the matter of departure thus, I never feel bad about it or think much of it, as, in the constant roving life I lead, I am constantly doing it. Only so sorry, I trouble others without wishing it. Will you kindly send over if there is any mail for me at your address?

May all blessings attend you and yours for ever and ever will be the constant prayer of

Vivekananda.

1899.45 — MRS. BULL

To Mrs. Ole Bull:

C/O E. Guernsey, M.D.,
The Madrid, 180 W. 59,
15th November, 1899.

MY DEAR MRS. BULL,

After all I decide to come to Cambridge just now. I must finish the stories I began. The first one I don't think was given back to me by Margo.

My clothes will be ready the day after tomorrow, and then I shall be ready to start; only my fear is, it will be for the whole winter a place for becoming nervous and not for quieting of nerves, with constant parties and lectures. Well, perhaps you can give me a room somewhere, where I can hide myself from all the goings on in the place. Again I am so nervous of going to a place where indirectly the Indian Math will be. The very name of these Math people is enough to frighten me. And they are determined to kill with these letters etc.

Anyhow, I come as soon as I have my clothes — this week. You need not come to New York for my sake. If you have business of your own, that is another matter. I had a very kind invitation from Mrs. Wheeler of Montclair. Before I start for Boston, I will have a turn-in in Montclair for a few hours at least.

I am much better and am all right; nothing the matter with me except my worry, and now I am sure to throw that all overboard.

Only one thing I want — and I am afraid I cannot get it of you — there should be no communication about me in your letters to India even indirect. I want to hide for a time or for all time. How I curse the day that brought me celebrity!

With all love,
Vivekananda.

1899.46 — RAKHAL[1]

To Swami Brahmananda:

U.S.A.,
20th November, 1899.

MY DEAR RAKHAL,

Got some news from Sharat's letter... Get experience while still there is a chance; I am not concerned whether you win or lose... I have no disease now. Again... I am going to tour from place to place. There is no reason for anxiety, be fearless. Everything will fly away before you; only don't be disobedient, and all success will be yours... Victory to Kâli! Victory to the Mother! Victory to Kali! Wâh Guru,

---

1 Translated from Bengali.

Wah Guru ki Fateh (Victory unto the Guru)!

...Really, there is no greater sin than cowardice; cowards are never saved—that is sure. I can stand everything else but not that. Can I have any dealings with one who will not give that up?...If one gets one blow, on must return ten with redoubled fury...Then only one is a man...The coward is an object to be pitied.

I bless you all; today, on this day sacred to the Divine Mother, on this night, may the Mother dance in your hearts, and bring infinite strength to your arms. Victory to Kali! Victory to Kali! Mother will certainly come down—and with great strength will bring all victory, world victory. Mother is coming, what dear? Whom to fear? Victory to Kali! At the tread of each one of you the earth will tremble...Victory to Kali! Again onward, forward! Wah Guru! Victory to the Mother! Kali! Kali! Kali! Disease, sorrow, danger, weakness—all these have departed from you all. All victory, all good fortune, all prosperity yours. Fear not! Fear not! The threat of calamity is vanishing, fear not! Victory to Kali! Victory to Kali!

Vivekananda.

PS—I am the servant of the Mother, you are all servants of the Mother—what destruction, what fear is there for us? Don't allow egoism to enter your minds, and let love never depart from your hearts. What destruction can touch you? Fear not. Victory to Kali! Victory to Kali!

1899.47 — MARY

To Miss Mary Hale:

1 East 39 St., New York,
20th November, 1899.

MY DEAR MARY,

I start tomorrow most probably for California. On my way I would stop for a day or two in Chicago. I send a wire to you when I start. Send somebody to the station, as I never was so bad as now in finding my way in and out.

Ever your brother,
Vivekananda.

1899.48 — CHRISTINA

To Sister Christine:

21 West 34th Street, New York,
21st November, 1899.

MY DEAR CHRISTINA,

Circumstances have so fallen that I have to start for California tomorrow. It is for my physical benefit too; as the doctor says, I had better be off where the severe winter of the North cannot reach.

Well, thus my plans are made and marred. Anyway—come over to Cambridge when you feel like it. Mrs. Bull will only be too happy to do anything for you she can.

I hope to stop in Detroit on my way back. The Lord's will—as we say.

Ever yours in the Lord,
Vivekananda.

1899.49 — BRAHMANANDA

To Swami Brahmananda:

21 West 34 St., New York,
21st November, 1899.

MY DEAR BRAHMANANDA,

The accounts are all right. I have handed them over to Mrs. Bull who has taken charge of reporting the different parts of the accounts to different donors. Never mind what I have said in previous harsh letters. They would do you good. Firstly, they will make you business-like in the future to keep regular and clear accounts and get the brethren into it. Secondly, if these scolding don't make you brave, I shall have no more hopes of you. I want to see you die even, but you must make a fight. Die in obeying commands like a soldier, and go to Nirvana, but no cowardice.

It is necessary that I must disappear for some time. Let not anyone write me or seek me during that time, it is absolutely necessary for my health. I am only nervous, that is all, nothing more.

All blessings follow you. Never mind my harshness. You know the heart always, whatever the lips say. All blessings on you. For the last year or so I have not been in my senses at all. I do not know why. I had to pass through this hell—and I have. I am much better—well, in fact. Lord help you all. I am going to the Himalayas soon to retire for ever. My work is done.

Ever yours in the Lord,
Vivekananda.

PS—Mrs. Bull sends her love.

1899.50 — MRS. LEGGETT

Chicago,
26th Nov., 1899.

MY DEAR MRS. LEGGETT,

Many, many thanks for all your kindness and especially the kind note. I am going to start from Chicago on Thursday next, and got the ticket and berth ready for that day.

Miss Noble is doing very well here, and working her way out. I saw Alberta the other day. She is enjoying every minute of her stay here and is very happy. Miss Adams (Jane Adams), as ever is an angel.

I shall wire to Joe Joe before I start and read all night.

With all love to Mr. Leggett and yourself,

Ever yours affectionately,
Vivekananda.

1899.51 — DHIRA MATA

To Mrs. Ole Bull:

Chicago,
30 November, 1899.

MY DEAR DHIRA MATA,

I am going to leave this place tonight. They have given me a new trunk — a big one. The Maspero book is with me, only the second volume. The first volume must be in Boston. Kindly send it c/o Joe [Miss Josephine MacLeod].

They have been very kind. Madame [Emma] Calvé, came to see me day before yesterday. She is a great woman.

I have nothing to write here except that Margo [Sister Nivedita] is doing very well, except some people were complaining last night that she frightened them with her assertion that Swami can not make mistakes!!!

Hope things are going on with you very well. This is in haste. I write in length from California.

Ever your son,
Vivekananda.

My love to Mrs. [Olea] Vaughn. (Mrs. Ole Bull's daughter.)

1899.52 — MOTHER

Chicago,
30th Nov., 1899.

MY DEAR MOTHER, (Mrs. Leggett.)

Nothing new — except Madame Calvé's visit. She is a great woman. I wish I saw more of her. It is a grand sight to see a giant pine struggling against a cyclone. Is it not?

I leave here tonight. These lines in haste as A__ is waiting. Mrs. Adams is kind as usual. Margot doing splendidly. Will write more from California.

With all love to Frankincense,

Ever your son,
Vivekananda.

1899.53 — MOTHER

To Mrs. G. W. Hale:

The California Limited,
Santa Fe Route,
1 December, 1899.

MY DEAR MOTHER,

Excuse this scrawl as the train is dancing.

I passed a good night and hope to have a good time all through. With all love for the sisters and Mr. [Clarence] Woolley (Husband of Mrs. Hale's daughter Harriet.) and Bud and Father Pope.

With love,
Vivekananda.

1899.54 — MARGOT

To Sister Nivedita:

The California Limited,
Santa Fe Route,
December 2nd, 1899.

MY DEAR MARGOT,

Two nights are passed — today the third will come. If it proves as pleasant and somnolent as the last two, I [shall] rejoice.

The scenery today I am passing through is much like the neighborhood of Delhi, the beginning of a big desert, bleak hills, scanty, thorny shrubs, very little water. The little streams are frozen, but during the middle of the day it is hot. Must be [illegible] I presume, in summer.

I send this to the care of Mrs. Adams, (Probably Mrs. Milward Adams.) as I don't know your address. The Chicago work will not give you much, I am sure, except in education in the methods here, which I am sure will work out soon.

With all love and blessings,
Vivekananda.

1899.55 — MOTHER

To Mrs. G. W. Hale:

Los Angeles,
6 December, 1899.

MY DEAR MOTHER,

A few lines to say my safe arrival and am going to resume my usual work of lecturing here.

I am much better than I was in Chicago and hope soon to become well again.

I cannot tell you how I enjoyed once more the little visit with my American Mother and Sisters.

Harriet has scored a triumph really. I am charmed with Mr. Woolley — only hope Mary will be equally fortunate. It gives me a new lease of life to see people happy. May they all be happy.

Ever with love, your son,
Vivekananda.

1899.56 — MARGOT

Los Angeles,
6th Dec., 1899.

DEAR MARGOT,

Your sixth has arrived, but with it yet no change in my fortune. Would change be any good, do you think? Some people are made that way, to love being miserable. If I did not break my heart over people I was born amongst, I would do it for somebody else. I am sure of that. This is the way of some, I am coming to see it. We are all after happiness, true, but that some are only happy in being unhappy — queer, is it not? There is no harm in it either, except that happiness and unhappiness are both infectious. Ingersoll said once that if he were God, he would make health catching, instead of disease, little dreaming that health is quite as catching as disease, if not more! That is the only danger. No harm in the world in my being happy, in being miserable, but others must not catch it. This is the great fact. No sooner a prophet feels miserable for the state of man than he sours his face, beats his breast, and calls upon everyone to drink tartaric acid, munch charcoal, sit upon a dungheap covered with ashes, and speak only in groans and tears! — I find they all have been wanting. Yes, they have. If you are really ready to take the world's burden, take it by all means. But do not let us hear your groans and curses. Do not frighten us with your sufferings, so that we came to feel we were better off with our own burdens. The man who really takes the burden blesses the world and goes his own way. He has not a word of condemnation, a word of criticism, not because there was no evil but that he has taken it on his own shoulders willingly, voluntarily. It is the Saviour who should "go his way rejoicing, and not the saved".

This is the only light I have caught this morning. This is enough if it has come to live with me and permeate my life.

Come ye that are heavy laden and lay all your burden on me, and then do whatever you like and be happy and forget that I ever existed.

Ever with love,

Your father,
Vivekananda.

1899.57 — CHRISTINA

To Sister Christine:

921 West 21St Street, Los Angeles,
9th December, 1899.

MY DEAR CHRISTINA,

After all, it is good for me, and good for those I love, that I should come here. Here at last in California! One of our poets says: "Where is Benares, where is Kashmir, where Khorasan, where Gujarat! O Tulsi! thus, man's past Karma drags him on". And I am here. After all it is best, isn't it? Are you going to Boston? I am afraid you are not. I have not unsettled any of your plans, have I? — unnecessary expenses? Well, if any, I will make it up. Only the trouble is yours. I am ashamed of my eccentricities. Well, how are you? What are you doing? How are things going with you? Sleep if you can; it is better to sleep than get awakened. I pray that all good may come to thee — all peace, all strength to do and suffer. I have a great deal of strength to do, but very little to suffer.

I am so selfish again, always thinking of my own sufferings and paying no heed to others. Pray for me; send strong thoughts that I may have strength to suffer. I know you will. Now, I mean to remain a few weeks in this city. After that, "Mother" knows. I am physically much better now than I have been for months. The weakness of the heart is nearly gone. The dyspepsia is also much better, and [there is] very little. I can walk miles now without feeling it in the heart. If this continues, I expect to have a new lease on life. I am so, so sorry of asking you to come to Boston and flying away. If you are there, I hope you will enjoy the place and the meetings. If you have given it up — well, did you take leave and not go to Boston? My! what a bungle! Well, I ask a thousand pardons, if such is the case. Things must look brighter anyway, sooner or later. What of these little, few days of life!

How is Mrs. Funke? Loads of love for her. How long a leave [do] you get at Christmas? When does it begin? If you feel inclined and willing, write me a long note, will you? But don't tell my friends my whereabouts. I want to be off from the world for a time, if I can. Will you kindly send Mr. Freer's address to Mrs. Bull?

She needs it. I had a lecture here last night. The hall was not crowded, as there was very little ad[vertisement], but a fairly good — sized audience though. I hope they were pleased. If I feel better, I am going to have classes in this city soon. I am on the business path this time, you know. Want a few dollars quick, if I can.

Ever yours in the Lord,
Vivekananda.

1899.58 — MRS. BULL

12th Dec., 1899.

MY DEAR MRS. BULL,

You are perfectly right; I am brutal, very indeed. But about the tenderness etc., that is my fault. I wish I had less, much less of that — that is my weakness — and alas! all my sufferings have come from that. Well, the municipality is trying to tax us out — good; that is my fault as I did not make the Math public property by a deed of trust. I am very sorry I use harsh language to my boys, but they also know I love them more than anybody else on earth. I may have had Divine help — true; but oh, the pound of blood every bit of Divine help has been to me!! I would be gladder and a better man without that. The present looks very gloomy indeed; but I am a fighter and must die fighting, not give way — that is why I get crazy at the boys. I don't ask them to fight, but not to hinder my fight.

I don't grudge my fate. But oh! now I want a man, one of my boys, to stand by me and fight against all odds! Don't you vex yourself; if anything is to be done in India, my presence is necessary; and I am much better in health; possibly the sea will make me better. Anyway I did not do anything this time in America except bother my friends. Possibly Joe will help me out with the passage, and I have some money with Mr. Leggett. I have hopes of collecting some money in India yet. I did not see any of my friends in different parts of India. I have hope of collecting the fifteen thousand that will make up the fifty thousand, and a deed of trust will bring down the municipal taxes. If I cannot collect that — it is better to struggle and die for it than vegetate here in America. My mistakes have been great; but everyone of them was from too much love. How I hate love! Would I never had any Bhakti! Indeed, I wish I could be an Advaitist, calm and heartless. Well, this life is done. I will try in the next. I am sorry, especially now, that I have done more injury to my friends than there have been blessings on them. The peace, the quiet I am seeking, I never found.

I went years ago to the Himalayas, never to come back; and my sister committed suicide, the news reached me there, and that weak heart flung me off from that prospect of peace! It is the weak heart that has driven me out of India to seek some help for those I love, and here I am! Peace have I sought, but the heart, that seat of Bhakti, would not allow me to find it. Struggle and torture, torture and struggle. Well, be it then. since it is my fate, and the quicker it is over, the better. They say I am impulsive, but look at the circumstances!!! I am sorry I have been the cause of pain to you, to you above all, who love me so much, who have been so, so kind. But it is done—was a fact. I am now going to cut the knot or die in the attempt.

Ever your son,
Vivekananda.

PS—As Mother wants it, so let it be. I am going to beg of Joe a passage via San Francisco to India. If she gives it, I start immediately via Japan. It would take a month. In India, I think, I can raise some money to keep things straight or on a better footing—at least to leave things where I get them all muddled. The end is getting very dark and very much muddled; well, I expected it so. Don't think I give in in a moment. Lord bless you; if the Lord has made me His hack to work and die on the streets, let Him have it. I am more cheerful just now after your letter than I was for years—Wah Guru ki Fateh! Victory unto the Guru!! Yes, let the world come, the hells come, the gods come, let Mother come, I fight and do not give in. Râvana got his release in three births by fighting the Lord Himself! It is glorious to fight Mother.

All blessings on you and yours. You have done for me more, much more, than I deserved ever.

Love to Christine and Turiyananda.

1899.59—BRAHMANANDA

To Swami Brahmananda:

[Swami Vivekananda sent the following cablegram to his brother-monk.]

[Postmarked: December 13, 1899]

PERFECTLY CURED. BLESS ALL. VIVEKANANDA.

1899.60—DHIRA MATA

To Mrs. Ole Bull:

22nd December, 1899.

MY DEAR DHIRA MATA,

I have a letter from Calcutta today, from which I learn your cheques have arrived; a great many thanks and grateful words also came.

Miss Souter of London sends me a printed New Year's greetings. I think she must have got the accounts you sent her by this time.

Kindly send Saradananda's letters that have come to your care.

As for me, I had a slight relapse of late, for which the healer has rubbed several inches of my skin off.

Just now I am feeling it, the smart. I had a very hopeful note from Margo. I am grinding on in Pasadena; hope some result will come out of my work here. Some people here are very enthusiastic; the Raja-Yoga book did indeed great services on this coast. I am mentally very well; indeed I never really was so calm as of late. The lectures for one thing do not disturb my sleep, that is some gain. I am doing some writing too. The lectures here were taken down by a stenographer, the people here want to print them.

I learn they are well and doing good work at the Math — from Swami Saradananda's letter to Joe. Slowly as usual plans are working; but Mother knows, as I say. May She give me release and find other workers for Her plans. By the by, I have made a discovery as to the mental method of really practising what the Gita teaches, of working without an eye to results. I have seen much light on concentration and attention and control of concentration, which if practised will take us out of all anxiety and worry. It is really the science of bottling up our minds whenever we like. Now what about yourself, poor Dhira Mata! This is the result of motherhood and its penalties; we all think of ourselves, and never of the Mother. How are you? How are things going on with you? What about your daughter? about Mrs. Briggs?

I hope Turiyananda is completely recovered now and working. Poor man, suffering is the lot! Never mind; there is a pleasure in suffering even, when it is for others, is there not? Mrs. Leggett is doing well; so is Joe; I — they say — I too am. May be they are right. I work anyway and want to die in harness; if that be what Mother wants, I am quite content.

Ever your son,
Vivekananda.

1899.61 — MARGOT

921, 21St Street, Los Angeles,
23rd December, 1899.

DEAR MARGOT, (Margaret E. Noble or Sister Nivedita)

Yes, I am really getting well under the manipulations of magnetic healing! At any rate I am all right. There was, never anything serious with my organs — it was nerves and dyspepsia.

Now I walk miles every day, at any time — before or after meals. I am perfectly well — and am going to remain so, I am sure.

The wheel is turning up, Mother is working it up. She cannot let me go before Her work is done — and that is the secret.

See, how England is working up. After this blood-letting, (Swamiji refers to the Boer war.) people will then have time of thinking better and higher things than "war", "war", "war". That is our opportunity. We run in quick, get hold of them by the dozens and then set the Indian work in full swing.

I pray that England will lose Cape Colony, so that she will be able to concentrate her energy on India. These capes and promontories never are of any use to England except in puffing up a false pride and costing her hordes in money and blood.

Things are looking up. So get ready. With all love to the four sisters and to you,

Yours etc.,
Vivekananda.

1899.62 — CHRISTINA

To Sister Christine:

921 West 21St Street, Los Angeles,
27th December, 1899.

DEAR CHRISTINA,

So you are awake and can't go to sleep any more. Good! Keep awake, wide awake. It was good I came here. For, in the first place, I am cured. What do you think of this — able to walk, and every day walk three miles after a heavy dinner! Good! Isn't it?

I am making money fast — twenty-five dollars a day now. Soon I will work more and get fifty dollars a day. In San Francisco I hope to do still better — where I go in two or three weeks. Good again — better, say I — as I am going to keep the money all to myself and not squander it any more. And then I will buy a little place in the Himalayas — a whole hill — about say, six thousand feet high with a grand view of the eternal snows. There must be springs and a tiny lake. Cedars — the Himalayan cedar forests — and flowers, flowers everywhere. I will have a little cottage; in the middle, my vegetable gardens, which I will work myself — and — and — and — my books — and see the face of man only once in a great while. And the world may go to ruin round about my ears, I would not care. I will have done with all my work — secular or spiritual — and retire. My! how restless I have been all my life! Born nomad. I don't know; this is the present vision. The future is to come yet. Curious — all my dreams about my own happiness are, as it were, bound to come to nothing; but about others' well-being — they as a rule prove true.

I am so glad you are happy and peaceful under Mrs. Bull's hospitable roof. She is a great, great woman — one whom to see is a pilgrimage.

No snow here — exactly like northern India in winter. Some days, even warmer — cool in the morning and evening, in the middle of the day, warm, in the sun, hot. The roses are about us, gardens everywhere, and the beautiful palms. But I like the snow: crisp, crackling under the feet, white, white, white — all round white!

I don't think I have anything with the kidneys or the heart. The whole thing was about indigestion and it is now nearly cured. A month more, and I will be strong like a lion and hardy like a mule. The poor English are getting it hot from the Boers. Mourning in every home in England and still the war goes on. Such is human folly. How long will it take for man to become civilized! Will wars ever cease? Mother knows! The New Year is sure to bring about a great change. Pray some good may come to India. I send you all joy, all love, all success for the New Year and many, many more to come.

So you did well, you think, by coming to Mrs. Bull. I am glad. I wanted you to know Mrs. Bull thoroughly. Remain there as long as you can. It will do you good, I am sure. Take heart and be of cheer, for next year is sure to bring many joys and a hundred blessings.

Yours truly,
Vivekananda.

1899.63 — DHIRA MATA

To Mrs. Ole Bull:

921 W. 21St Street, Los Angeles,
27th December, 1899.

BELOVED DHIRA MATA,

An eventful and happy New Year to you and many such returns!

I am much better in health — able enough to work once more. I have started work already and have sent to Saradananda some money — Rs. 1,300 already — as expenses for the law suit. I shall send more, if they need it. I had a very bad dream this morning and had not any news of Saradananda for three weeks. Poor boys! How hard I am on them at times. Well, they know, in spite of all that, I am their best friend.

Mr. Leggett has got a little over £500 I had with Sturdy on account of Raja-Yoga and the Maharaja of Khetri. I have now about a thousand dollars with Mr. Leggett. If I die, kindly send that money to my mother. I wired to the boys three weeks ago that I was perfectly cured. If I don't get any worse, this much health as I have now will do well enough. Do not worry at all on my account; I am up and working with a will.

I am sorry I could not write any more of the stories. I have written some other things and mean to write something almost every day.

I am very much more peaceful and find that the only way to keep my peace is to teach others. Work is my only safety valve.

I only want some clear business head to take care of the details as I push onwards and work on. I am afraid it will be a long time to find such in India, and if there are any, they ought to be educated by somebody from the West.

Again, I can only work when thrown completely on my own feet. I am at my best when I am alone. Mother seems to arrange so. Joe believes great things are brewing—in Mother's cup; hope it is so.

Joe and Margot have developed into actual prophets, it seems. I can only say, every blow I had in this life, every pang, will only become joyful sacrifice if Mother becomes propitious to India once more.

Miss Greenstidel writes a beautiful letter to me, about you most of it. She thinks a lot about Turiyananda too. Give Turiyananda my love. I am sure he will work well. He has the pluck and stamina.

I am going soon to work in California; when I leave I shall send for Turiyananda and make him work on the Pacific coast. I am sure here is a great field. The Raja-Yoga book seems to be very well known here. Miss Greenstidel had found great peace under your roof and is very happy. I am so glad it is so. May things go a little better with her every day. She has a good business head and practical sense.

Joe has unearthed a magnetic healing woman. We are both under her treatment. Joe thinks she is pulling me up splendidly. On her has been worked a miracle, she claims. Whether it is magnetic healing, California ozone, or the end of the present spell of bad Karma, I am improving. It is a great thing to be able to walk three miles, even after a heavy dinner.

All love and blessings to Olea. My love to Dr. Janes and other Boston friends.

Ever your son,
Vivekananda.

1899.64—MARY

To Miss Mary Hale:

C/O Mrs. Blodgett,
921, West 21st St., Los Angeles,
27th December, 1899.

MY DEAR MARY,

Merry Christmas and Happy New Year and many, many glorious returns of such for your birthday. All these wishes, prayers, greetings in one breath. I am cured, you will be glad to know. It was only indigestion and no heart or kidney affection, quoth the healers; nothing more. And I am walking three miles a day—after a heavy dinner.

Say—the person healing me insisted on my smoking! So I am having my pipe nicely and am all the better for it. In plain English the nervousness etc. was all due to dyspepsia and nothing more.

... I am at work too; working, working, not hard; but I don't care, and I want to make money this time. Tell this to Margot, especially the pipe business. You know who is healing me? No physician, no Christian Science healer, but a magnetic healing woman who skins me every time she treats me. Wonders—she performs operations by rubbing — internal operations too, her patients tell me.

It is getting late in the night. I have to give up writing separate letters to Margot, Harriet, Isabelle, and Mother Church. Wish is half the work. They all know how I love them dearly, passionately; so you become the medium for my spirit for the time, and carry them my New Year's messages.

It is exactly like Northern Indian winter here, only some days a little warmer; the roses are here and the beautiful palms. Barley is in the fields, roses and many other flowers round about the cottage where I live. Mrs. Blodgett, my host, is a Chicago lady — fat, old, and extremely witty. She heard me in Chicago and is very motherly.

I am so sorry, the English have caught a Tartar in South Africa. A soldier on duty outside a camp bawled out that he had caught a Tartar. "Bring him in", was the order from inside the tent. "He will not come", replied the sentry. "Then you come yourself", rang the order again. "He will not let me come either". Hence the phrase "to catch a Tartar". Don't you catch any.

I am happy just now and hope to remain so for all the rest of my life. Just now I am Christian Science — no evil, and "love is a drawing card".

I shall be very happy if I can make a lot of money. I am making some. Tell Margot, I am going to make a lot of money and go home by way of Japan, Honolulu, China, and Java. This is a nice place to make money quick in; and San Francisco is better, I hear. Has she made any?

You could not get the millionaire. Why don't you start for half or one-fourth million? Something is better than nothing. We want money; he may go into Lake Michigan, we have not the least objection. We had a bit of an earthquake here the other day. I hope it has gone to Chicago and raised Isabelle's mud-puddle up. It is getting late. I am yawning, so here I quit.

Good-bye; all blessings, all love,
Vivekananda.

1900

1900.1 — DHIRA MATA

To Mrs. Ole Bull:

17th January, 1900.

MY DEAR DHIRA MATA,

I received yours with the enclosures for Saradananda; and there was some good news. I hope to get some more news this week. You did not write anything about your plans. I had a letter from Miss Greenstidel expressing her deep gratitude for your kindness — and who does not? Turiyananda is getting well by this time, I hope.

I have been able to remit Rs. 2,000 to Saradananda, with the help of Miss MacLeod and Mrs. Leggett. Of course they contributed the best part. The rest was got by lectures. I do not expect anything much here or anywhere by lecturing. I can scarcely make expenses. No, not even that; whenever it comes to paying, the people are nowhere. The field of lecturing in this country has been overworked; the people have outgrown that.

I am decidedly better in health. The healer thinks I am now at liberty to go anywhere I choose, the process will go on, and I shall completely recover in a few months. She insists on this, that I am cured already; only nature will have to work out the rest.

Well, I came here principally for health. I have got it; in addition I got Rs. 2,000, to defray the law expenses. Good.

Now it occurs to me that my mission from the platform is finished, and I need not break my health again by that sort of work.

It is becoming clearer to me that I lay down all the concerns of the Math and for a time go back to my mother. She has suffered much through me. I must try to smooth her last days. Do you know, this was just exactly what the great Shankarâchârya himself had to do! He had to go back to his mother in the last few days of her life! I accept it, I am resigned. I am calmer than ever. The only difficulty is the financial part. Well, the Indian people owe something. I will try Madras and a few other friends in India. Anyhow, I must try, as I have forebodings that my mother has not very many years to live. Then again, this is coming to me as the greatest of all sacrifices to make, the sacrifice of ambition, of leadership, of fame. I am resigned and must do the penance. The one thousand dollars with Mr. Leggett and if a little more is collected, will be enough to fall back upon in case of need. Will you send me back to India? I am ready any time. Don't go to France without seeing me. I have become practical at least compared to the visionary dreams of Joe and Margot. Let them work their dreams out for me — they are not more than dreams. I want to make out a trust-deed of the Math in the names of Saradananda, Brahmananda, and yourself. I will do it as soon as I get the papers from Saradananda. Then I am quits. I want rest, a meal, a few books, and I want to do some scholarly work. Mother shows this light vividly now. Of course you were the one to whom She showed it first. I would not believe it then. But then, it is now shown that — leaving my mother was a great renunciation in 1884 — it is a greater renunciation to go back to my mother now. Probably Mother wants me to undergo the same that She made the great Âchârya undergo in old days. Is it? I am surer of your guidance than of my own. Joe and Margot are great souls, but to you Mother is now sending the light for my guidance. Do you see light? What do you advise? At least do not go out of this country without sending me home.

I am but a child; what work have I to do? My powers I passed over to you. I see it. I cannot any more tell from the platform. Don't tell it to anyone — not even to Joe. I am glad. I want rest; not that I am tired, but the next phase will be the miraculous touch and not the tongue — like Ramakrishna's. The word has gone to you and the voice to Margo. No more it is in me. I am glad. I am resigned. Only get me out to India, won't you? Mother will make you do it. I am sure.

Ever your son,
Vivekananda.

1900.2 — MARGOT

Los Angeles, California,
24th Jan., 1900.

DEAR MARGOT, (Margaret E. Noble or Sister Nivedita)

I am afraid that the rest and peace I seek for will never come. But Mother does good to others through me, at least some to my native land, and it is easier to be reconciled to one's fate as a sacrifice. We are all sacrifices — each in his own way. The great work is going on — no one can see its meaning except that it is a great sacrifice. Those that are willing escape a lot of pain. Those who resist are broken into submission and suffer more. I am now determined to be a willing one.

Yours etc.,
Vivekananda.

1900.3 — MARGO

To Sister Nivedita:

Los Angeles,
[Early February, 1900.]

DEAR MARGO [MARGOT],

You have the Gopâla. Add the Sâvitri story to that. I send you four more herewith. They ought to make a nice volume. Work on them a bit, will you. If you get a publisher in Chicago, all right; if not, Mr. Leggett promised to publish them sometime ago.

Yours,
Vivekananda.

PS — The preliminary parts should be struck off.

1900.4 — DHIRA MATA

To Mrs. Ole Bull:

Los Angeles,
15th February, 1900.

DEAR DHIRA MATA,

Before this reaches you, I am off to San Francisco. You already know all about the work. I have not done much work, but my heart is growing stronger every day, physically and mentally. Some days I feel I can bear everything and suffer everything. There was nothing of note inside the bundle of papers sent by Miss Müller. I did not write her, not knowing her address. Then again, I am afraid.

I can always work better alone, and am physically and mentally best when entirely alone! I scarcely had a day's illness during my eight years of lone life away from my brethren. Now I am again getting up, being alone. Strange, but that is what Mother wants me to be. "Wandering alone like the rhinoceros", as Joe likes it. I think the conferences are ended. Poor Turiyananda suffered so much and never let me know; he is so strong and good. Poor Niranjan, I learn from Mrs. Sevier, is so seriously ill in Calcutta that I don't know whether he has passed away or not. Well, good and evil both love company; queer, they come in strings. I had a letter from my cousin telling me her daughter (the adopted little child) was dead. Suffering seems to be the lot of India! Good. I am getting rather callous, rather stilted, of late. Good. Mother knows. I am so ashamed of myself — of this display of weakness for the last two years! Glad it is ended.

Ever your loving son,
Vivekananda.

1900.5 — NIVEDITA

C/O Miss Mead,
447 Douglas Building,
Los Angeles, California,
15th Feb., 1900.

MY DEAR NIVEDITA,

Yours of the — reached me today at Pasadena. I see Joe has missed you at Chicago — although I have not heard anything from them yet from New York.

There was a bundle of English newspapers from England with a line on the envelope expressing good wishes for me and signed, F.H.M. Nothing important was in those, however. I would have written a letter to Miss Müller, but I do not know the address; then I was afraid to frighten her.

In the meanwhile, Mrs. Leggett started a plan of a $100 subscription each a year for ten years to help me, and headed the list with her $100 for 1900, and got 2 others here to do the same. Then she went on writing letters to all my friends asking each to join in it. When she went on writing to Mrs. Miller I was rather shy — but she did it before I knew. A very polite but cold letter came to her in reply from Mrs. Hale, written by Mary, expressing their inability and assuring her of their love for me. I am afraid Mrs. Hale and Mary are displeased. But it was not my fault at all!!

I get news from Mrs. Sevier that Niranjan is seriously ill in Calcutta. I do not know if he has passed away. Well — but I am strong now, Margo, stronger than ever I was mentally. I was mentally getting a sort of ironing over my heart. I am getting nearer a Sannyasin's life now. I have not had any news from Saradananda for two weeks. I am glad you got the stories; rewrite them if you think so — get them published if you find anybody to do it and take the proceeds, if any, for your work. I do not want any I have got a few hundred dollars here. Going to San Francisco next week, and hope to do better there. Tell Mary when you see her next that I had nothing whatsoever to do with the proposal of $100 a year subscription to Mrs. Hale. I am so grateful to them.

Well, money will come for your school, never fear — it has got to come; if it does not come, who cares? One road is quite as good as the other. Mother knows best. I don't know whether I am very soon going to the East or not. If I have an opportunity, of course I will go to Indiana.

The international scheme is a good one and by all mean join it, and be the medium of getting some Indian women's clubs to join it through you, which is better...

Things shall look up for us, never mind. As soon as the war is finished we go to England and try to do a big work there. What do you think? Shall I write to Mother Superior? If so, send her whereabouts. Has she written to you? Sturdies and "Shakies" will all come round — hold on.

You are learning your lessons — that is all I want. So am I; the moment we are fit, money and men must flow towards us. Between my nerves and your emotion we may make a mess of everything just now. So Mother is curing my nerves and drilling you into level-headedness — and then we go. This time good is coming in chunks, I am sure. We will make the foundations of the old land shake this time.

...I am getting cool as a cucumber — let anything come, I am ready. The next move — any blow shall tell — not one miss — such is the next chapter.

With all love,
Vivekananda.

1900.6 — MARY

To Miss Mary Hale:

> Pasadena,
> 20th February, 1900.

MY DEAR MARY,

Your letter bearing the sad news of Mr. Hale's passing away reached me yesterday. I am sorry, because in spite of monastic training, the heart lives on; and then Mr. Hale was one of the best souls I met in life. Of course you are sorry, miserable, and so are Mother Church and Harriet and the rest, especially as this is the first grief of its kind you have met, is it not? I have lost many, suffered much, and the most curious cause of suffering when somebody goes off is the feeling that I was not good enough to that person. When my father died, it was a pang for months, and I had been so disobedient. You have been very dutiful; if you feel anything like that, it is only a form of sorrow.

Just now I am afraid life begins for you, Mary, in earnest. We may read books, hear lectures, and talk miles, but experience is the one teacher, the one eye-opener. It is best as it is. We learn, through smiles and tears we learn. We don't know why, but we see it is so; and that is enough. Of course Mother Church has the solace of her religion. I wish we could all dream undisturbed good dreams.

You have had shelter all your life. I was in the glare, burning and panting all the time. Now for a moment you have caught a glimpse of the other side. My life is made up of continuous blows like that, and hundred times worse, because of poverty, treachery, and my own foolishness! Pessimism! You will understand it, how it comes. Well, well, what shall I say to you, Mary? You know all the talks; only I say this and it is true — if it were possible to exchange grief, and had I a cheerful mind, I would exchange mine for your grief ever and always. Mother knows best.

> Your ever faithful brother,
> Vivekananda.

1900.7 — AKHANDANANDA[1]

> California,
> 21st February, 1900.

MY DEAR AKHANDANANDA,

I am very glad to receive your letter and go through the details of news. Learning and wisdom are superfluities, the surface glitter merely, but it is the heart that is the seat of all power. It is not in the brain but in the heart that the Atman, possessed of knowledge, power, and activity, has Its seat. "शतं चैका च हृदयस्य

---

1 Translated from Bengali.

नाड्य: — The nerves of the heart are a hundred and one" etc. The chief nerve-centre near the heart, called the sympathetic ganglia, is where the Atman has Its citadel. The more heart you will be able to manifest, the greater will be the victory you achieve. It is only a few that understand the language of the brain, but everyone from the Creator down to a clump of grass, understands the language that comes from the heart. But then, in our country, it is a case of rousing men that are, as it were, dead. It will take time, but if you have infinite patience and perseverance, success is bound to come. No mistake in that.

How are the English officials to blame? Is the family, of whose unnatural cruelty you have written, an isolated one in India? Or, are there plenty of such? It is the same story all over the country. But then, it is not as a result of pure wickedness that the selfishness commonly met with in our country has come. This bestial selfishness is the outcome of centuries of failure and repression. It is not real selfishness, but deep-rooted despair. It will be cored at the first inkling of success. It is only this that the English officials are noticing all round, so how can they have faith at the very outset? But tell me, do they not sympathise with any real work that they meet with?...

In these days of dire famine, flood, disease, and pestilence, tell me where your Congressmen are. Will it do merely to say, "Hand the government of the country over to us"? And who is there to listen to them? If a man does work, has he to open his mouth to ask for anything? If there be two thousand people like you working in several districts, won't it be the turn of the English themselves to consult you in matters of political moment?" A — was not allowed to open a centre, but what of that! Has not Kishengarh allowed it? — Let him work on without ever opening his lips; there is no use of either telling anything to anybody, or quarrelling with any. Whoever will assist in this work of the Divine Mother of the universe, will have Her grace, and whoever will oppose it will not only be laying the axe to his own prospects. — all in good time. Many a little makes a mickle. When a great work is being done, when the foundations are laid or a road constructed, when superhuman energy is needed — it is one or two extraordinary men who silently and noiselessly work through a world of obstacles and difficulties. When thousands of people are benefited, there is a great tomtoming, and the whole country is loud in notes of praise. But then the machine has already been set agoing, and even a boy can work it, or a fool add to it some impetus. Grasp this that, that benefit done to a village or two, that orphanage with its twenty orphans, those ten or twenty workers — all these are enough; they form the nucleus, never to be destroyed. From these, hundreds of thousands of people will be benefited in time. Now we want half a dozen lions, then excellent work will be turned out by even hundreds of jackals...

If orphan girls happen to come to your hands for shelter, you must take them in above all else. Otherwise, Christian missionaries will take them, poor things, away! What matters it that you have no particular arrangements for them? Through the Divine Mother's will, they will be provided for. When you get a horse, never you worry about the whip... Get together whomsoever you can lay your hands on, no picking and choosing now — everything will be set right in course of time. In every attempt there are many obstacles to cope with, but gradually the path becomes smooth.

Convey to the European officer many thanks from me. Work on fearlessly — there is a hero! Bravo! Thrice well done! The starting of a centre at Bhagalpur that you have written about is no doubt a good idea — enlightening the schoolboys and things of that sort. But our mission is for the destitute, the poor, and the illiterate peasantry and labouring classes, and if, after everything has been done for them first, there is spare time, then only for the gentry. Those peasants and labouring people will be won over by love. Afterwards it will be they who will collect small sums and start missions at their own villages, and gradually, from among those very men, teachers will spring.

Teach some boys and girls of the peasant classes the rudiments of learning and infuse a number of ideas into their brains. Afterwards the peasants of each village will collect funds and have one of these in their village. " — this holds good in all spheres. We help them to help themselves. That they are supplying you with your daily bread is a real bit of work done. The moment they will come to understand their own condition and feel the necessity of help and improvement, know that your work is taking effect and is in the right direction, while the little good that the moneyed classes, out of pity, do to the poor, does not last, and ultimately it does nothing but harm to both parties. The peasants and labouring classes are in a moribund condition, so what is needed is that the moneyed people will only help them to regain their vitality, and nothing more. Then leave the peasants and labourers to look to their own problem, to grapple with and solve it. But then you must take care not to set up class-strife between the poor peasants, the labouring people, and wealthy classes. Make it a point not to abuse the moneyed classes. " — The wise man should achieve his own object."

Victory to the Guru! Victory to the Mother of the Universe! What fear! Opportunity, remedy, and its application will present themselves. I do not care about the result, well or ill. I shall be happy if only you do this much of work. Wordy warfares, texts and scriptures, doctrines and dogmas — all these I am coming to loathe as poison in this my advanced age. Know this for certain that he who will work will be the crown on my head. Useless bandying of words and making noise is taking away our time, is consuming our life-energy, without pushing the cause of humanitarianism a step further. — Away with fear! Bravo! There is a hero indeed! May the blessed Guru be enthroned in your heart, and the Divine Mother guide your hands.

Yours affectionately,
Vivekananda.

1900.8 — JOE

To Miss Josephine MacLeod:

1231 Pine Street, San Francisco,
March 2nd, 1900.

DEAR JOE,

Your note enclosing two from France and three from India just received. I have had general good news and am happy.

Financially, I have got $300 in Los Angeles. About Mrs. Bowler, she has about a hundred odd dollars in cash. Mrs. Hendrick and she have not paid up as yet. That money — $300 in all — is with her. She will send it to me whenever I write.

Rev. Benjamin Fay Mills, a very popular Unitarian preacher in Oakland, invited me from here and paid the fare to San Francisco. I have spoken twice in Oakland to 1500 people each time. Last time I got from collection $30. I am going to have classes at 50 cents admission each.

San Francisco had one lecture the other night [February 23] at 50¢ each. It paid its expenses. This Monday [Sunday?] I am going to speak free — after that a class.

I went to see Mrs. Hurst [Hearst]. She was not at home. I left a card — so with Prof. Le Conte

Mary [Hale] writes that you wrote her of my coming any day to the East. I don't know. Here I have a large following — ready — made by my books. Will get some money, not much. St. Francis [Francis Leggett] may put the money in the bank for me — but can that be done without my signature? And I am here? It is good if it can be done. Did you see any possibility of my books being sold for good to any publisher?

The French invitation is all right. But it seems impossible to write any decent paper on the subject we chose. Because if I have to lecture and make money, very little time will be left for anything else. Again, I can not find any books (Sanskrit) here. So let me try to make a little money if I can and go to France all the same, but send them no paper. No scholarly work can be done in this haphazard and hurried fashion. It means time and study.

Shall I write to Mr. [Gerald] Nobel an acknowledgement and thanks? Write to me fully on these subjects if you can before you leave [for Europe]. My health is going on the same way. The gas is there more or less and this city is all climbing up[hill] — that tires me much.

With all love,

Yours affectionately,
Vivekananda.

PS — Did anybody else respond to Mrs. Leggett's call?

1900.9 — MARY

To Miss Mary Hale:

1251 Pine Street, San Francisco,
2nd March, 1900.

DEAR MARY,

Very kind of you to write to invite me to Chicago. I wish I could be there this minute. But I am busy making money; only I do not make much. Well, I have to make enough to pay my passage home at any rate. Here is a new field, where I find ready listeners by hundreds, prepared beforehand by my books.

Of course money making is slow and tedious. If I could make a few hundreds, I would be only too glad. By this time you must have received my previous note. I am coming eastward in a month or six weeks, I hope.

How are you all? Give Mother my heartfelt love. I wish I had her strength, she is a true Christian. My health is much better, but the old strength is not there yet. I hope it will come some day, but then, one had to work so hard to do the least little thing. I wish I had rest and peace for a few days at least, which I am sure I can get with the sisters at Chicago. Well, Mother knows best, as I say always. She knows best. The last two years have been specially bad. I have been living in mental hell. It is partially lifted now, and I hope for better days, better states. All blessings on you and the sisters and Mother. Mary, you have been always the sweetest notes in my jarring and clashing life. Then you had the great good Karma to start without oppressive surroundings. I never know a moment's peaceful life. It has always been high pressure, mentally. Lord bless you.

Ever your loving brother,
Vivekananda.

1900.10 — DHIRA MATA

To Mrs. Ole Bull:

1502 Jones Street, San Francisco,
4th March, 1900.

DEAR DHIRA MATA,

I have not had a word from you for a month. I am in Frisco. The people here have been prepared by my writing beforehand, and they come in big crowds. But it remains to be seen how much of that enthusiasm endures when it comes to paying at the door. Rev. Benjamin Fay Mills invited me to Oakland and gave me big crowds to preach to. He and his wife have been reading my works and keeping track of my movements all the time. I sent the letter of introduction from Miss Thursby to Mrs. Hearst. She has invited me to one of her musicals Sunday next.

My health is about the same; don't find much difference; it is improving, perhaps, but very imperceptibly. I can use my voice, however, to make 3,000 people hear me, as I did twice in Oakland, and get good sleep too after two hours of speaking.

I learn Margot is with you. When are you sailing for France? I will leave here in April and go to the East. I am very desirous of getting to England in May if I can. Must not go home before trying England once more.

I have nice letters from Brahmananda and Saradananda; they are all doing well. They are trying to bring the municipality to its senses; I am glad. In this world of Maya one need not injure, but "spread the hood, without striking". That is enough.

Things must get round; if they don't, it is all right. I have a very nice letter from Mrs. Sevier too. They are doing fine in the mountains. How is Mrs. Vaughan? When is your conference to close? How is Turiyananda?

With everlasting love and gratitude.

Your son,
Vivekananda.

1900.11 — NIVEDITA

San Francisco,
4th March, 1900.

DEAR NIVEDITA,

I don't want to work. I want to be quiet and rest. I know the time and the place; but the fate or Karma, I think, drives me on — work, work. We are like cattle driven to the slaughter-house — hastily nibbling a bite of grass on the roadside as they are driven along under the whip. And all this is our work, our fear — fear, the beginning of misery, of disease, etc. By being nervous and fearful we injure others, by being so fearful to hurt we hurt more. By trying so much to avoid evil we fall into its jaws.

What a mass of namby-pamby nonsense we create round ourselves!! It does us no good, it leads us on to the very thing we try to avoid — misery...

Oh, to become fearless, to be daring, to be careless of everything!...

Yours etc.,
Vivekananda.

1900.12 — DHIRA MATA

To Mrs. Ole Bull:

1502 Jones Street, San Francisco,
7th March, 1900.

DEAR DHIRA MATA,

Your letter, enclosing one from Saradananda only and the accounts, came. I am very much reassured by all the news I since received from India. As for the accounts and the disposal of the Rs. 30,000, do just what you please. I have given over the management to you, the Master will show you what is best to do. The money is Rs. 35,000; the Rs. 5,000, for building the cottage on the Ganga, I wrote to Saradananda not to use just now. I have already taken Rs. 5,000 of that money. I am not going to take more. I had paid back Rs. 2,000 or more of that Rs. 5,000 in India. But it seems, Brahmananda, wanting to show as much of the Rs. 35,000 intact as he could, drew upon my Rs. 2,000; so I owe them Rs. 5,000 still on that score.

Anyway, I thought I could make money here in California and pay them up quietly. Now I have entirely failed in California financially. It is worse here than in Los Angeles. They come in crowds when there is a free lecture and very few when there is something to pay.

I have some hopes yet in England. It is necessary for me to reach England in May. There is not the least use in breaking my health in San Francisco for nothing. Moreover, with all Joe's enthusiasm, I have not yet found any real benefit from the magnetic healer, except a few red patches on my chest from scratching! Platform work is nigh gone for me, and forcing it is only hastening the end. I leave here very soon, as soon as I can make money for a passage. I have 300 dollars in hand, made in Los Angeles. I will lecture here next week and then I stop. As for the Math and the money, the sooner I am released of that burden the better.

I am ready to do whatever you advise me to do. You have been a real mother to me. You have taken up one of my great burdens on yourself — I mean my poor cousin. I feel quite satisfied. As for my mother, I am going back to her — for my last days and hers. The thousand dollars I have in New York will bring Rs. 9 a month; then I bought for her a bit of land which will bring about Rs. 6; and her old house — that will bring, say, Rs. 6. I leave the house under litigation out of consideration, as I have not got it. Myself, my mother, my grandmother, and my brother will live on Rs. 20 a month easy. I would start just now, if I could make money for a passage to India, without touching the 1,000 dollars in New York.

Anyhow I will scrape three or four hundred dollars — 400 dollars will be enough for a second class passage and for a few weeks' stay in London. I do not ask you to do anything more for me; I do not want it. What you have done is more, ever so much more than I deserve. I have given my place solemnly to you in Shri Ramakrishna's work. I am out of it. All my life I have been a torture to my poor mother. Her whole life has been one of continuous misery. If it be possible, my last attempt should be to make her a little happy. I have planned it all out. I have served the Mother all my life. It is done; I refuse now to grind Her axe. Let Her find other workers — I strike.

You have been one friend with whom Shri Ramakrishna has become the goal of life — that is the secret of my trust in you. Others love me personally. But they little dream that what they love me for is Ramakrishna; leaving Him, I am only a mass of foolish selfish emotions. Anyway this stress is terrible, thinking of what may come next, wishing what ought to come next. I am unequal to the responsibility; I am found wanting. I must give up this work. If the work has not life in it, let it die; if it has, it need not wait for poor workers like myself.

Now the money, Rs. 30,000, is in my name, in Government Securities. If they are sold now, we shall lose fearfully, on account of the war; then, how can they be sent over here without being sold there? To sell them there I must sign them. I do not know how all this is going to be straightened out. Do what you think best about it all. In the meanwhile, it is absolutely necessary that I execute a will in your favour for everything, in case I suddenly die. Send me a draft will as soon as possible and I shall register it in San Francisco or Chicago; then my conscience will be safe. I don't know any lawyer here, else I would have got it drawn up; neither have I the money. The will must be done immediately; the trust and things have time enough for them.

Ever your son,
Vivekananda.

1900.13 — JOE

To Miss Josephine MacLeod:

1502 Jones Street, San Francisco,
7th March, 1900.

DEAR JOE,

I learn from Mrs. Bull's letter that you are in Cambridge.

I also learn from Miss Helen that you did not get the stories sent on to you. I am sorry. Margot has copies she may give you. I am so so in health. No money. Hard work. No result. Worse than Los Angeles.

They come in crowds when the lecture is free—when there is payment, they don't. That's all. I have a relapse—for some days—and am feeling very bad. I think lecturing every night is the cause. I hope to do something in Oakland at least to work out my passage to New York, where I mean to work for my passage to India. I may go to London if I make money here to pay a few months' lodging there.

Will you send me our General's address? Even the name slips from memory now!

Good-bye. May see you in Paris, may not. Lord bless you, you have done for me more than I ever deserve.

With infinite love and gratitude,

Yours,
Vivekananda.

1900.14 — CHRISTINA

To Sister Christine:

1719 Turk Street, San Francisco, California,
12th March, 1900.

DEAR CHRISTINA,

Just now received a letter from you through New York. I, the other day, wrote you one c/o Mrs. Funke, as I was not sure which of your addresses in my notebook was the correct one! Mental telepathy or foolishness — what is it?

By this time you must have got mine. There is nothing particular about me, except things are going on at the same rate — very little money — making, a good deal of work, and moving about. I leave here in April and come to Chicago for a few days, then to Detroit and then, through New York, go to England. I hope you are all right. I am very calm and peaceful mentally, and hope to remain so for the rest of my life.

How are Mrs. Funkey [Funke] and the rest of our friends?

With all love,
Vivekananda.

1900.15 — RAKHAL[1]

To Swami Brahmananda:

San Francisco,
12th March, 1900.

MY DEAR RAKHAL,

I got a letter from you some time ago. A letter from Sharat reached me yesterday. I saw a copy of the invitation letters for the birthday anniversary of Gurudeva (Divine Master). I am frightened hearing that Sharat is troubled by rheumatism. Alas, sickness, sorrow, and pain have been my companions for the last two years. Tell Sharat that I am not going to work so hard any more. But he who does not work enough to earn his food will have to starve to death!...I hope Durgaprasanna has done by this time whatever was necessary for the compound wall... The raising of a compound wall is not, after all, a difficult thing. If I can, I shall build a small house there and serve my old grandmother and mother. Evil actions leave none scot-free; Mother never spares anybody. I admit my actions have been wrong. Now, brother, all of you are Sâdhus and great saints, kindly pray to the Mother that I do not have to shoulder all this trouble and burden any longer. Now I desire a little peace — it seems there is no more strength left to bear the burden of work and responsibility — rest and peace for the few days that I shall yet live! Victory to

---

1 Translated from Bengali.

the Guru! Victory to the Guru!... No more lectures or anything of that sort. Peace!

As soon as Sharat sends the trust-deed of the Math, I shall put my signature to it. You all manage — truly I require rest. This disease is called neurasthenia, a disease of the nerves. Once it comes, it continues for some years. But after a complete rest for three or four years it is cured. This country is the home of the disease, and here it has caught me. However, it is not only no fatal disease, but it makes a man live long. Don't be anxious on my account. I shall go on rolling. But there is only this sorrow that the work of Gurudeva is not progressing; there is this regret that I have not been able to accomplish anything of his work. How much I abuse you all and speak harshly! I am the worst of men! Today, on the anniversary of his birthday, put the dust of your feet on my head — and my mind will become steady again. Victory to the Guru! Victory to the Guru! You are my only refuge — you are my only refuge! Now that my mind is steady, let me tell you that this resignation is the permanent attitude of my mind. All other moods that come are, you should know, only disease. Please don't allow me to work at all any longer. Now I shall quietly do Japa and meditation for some time — nothing more. Mother knows all else. Victory to the Mother of the Universe!

Yours affectionately,
Vivekananda.

1900.16 — MARY

To Miss Mary Hale:

1719 Turk Street, San Francisco,
12th March, 1900.

DEAR MARY,

How are you? How is Mother, and the sisters? How are things going on in Chicago? I am in Frisco, and shall remain here for a month or so. I start for Chicago early in April. I shall write to you before that of course. How I wish I could be with you for a few days; one gets tired of work so much. My health is so so, but my mind is very peaceful and has been so for some time. I am trying to give up all anxiety unto the Lord. I am only a worker. My mission is to obey and work. He knows the rest.

"Giving up all vexations and paths, do thou take refuge unto Me. I will save you from all dangers" (Gita, XVIII.66).

I am trying hard to realise that. May I be able to do it soon.

Ever your affectionate brother,
Vivekananda.

1900.17 — DHIRA MATA

To Mrs. Ole Bull:

1719 Turk Street, San Francisco,
12th March, 1900.

MY DEAR DHIRA MATA,

Your letter from Cambridge came yesterday. Now I have got a fixed address, 1719 Turk Street, San Francisco. Hope you will have time to pen a few lines in reply to this. I had a manuscript account sent me by you. I sent it back as you desired; besides that, I had no other accounts. It is all right.

I had a nice letter from Miss Souter from London. She expects to have Mr... to dine with her.

So glad to hear of Margot's success. I have given her over to you, and am sure you will take care of her. I will be here a few weeks more and then go East. I am only waiting for the warm season.

I have not been at all successful financially here, but am not in want. Anyway, things will go on as usual with me, I am sure; and if they don't, what then?

I am perfectly resigned. I had a letter from the Math; they had the Utsava yesterday. I do not intend to go by the Pacific. Don't care where I go, and when. Now perfectly resigned; Mother knows; a great change, peacefulness is coming on me. Mother, I know, will see to it. I die a Sannyasin. You have been more than mother to me and mine. All love, all blessings be yours for ever, is the constant prayer of

Vivekananda.

PS — Kindly tell Mrs. Leggett that my address for some weeks now will be, 1719 Turk Street, San Francisco.

1900.18 — MOTHER

1719 Turk Street, San Francisco,
17th March, 1900.

MY DEAR MOTHER (Mrs. Leggett.),

So glad to get your nice letter. Well, you may be sure I am keeping in touch with my friends. Yet a delay may sometimes cause nervousness.

Dr. and Mrs. Hiller returned to the city, much benefited, as they declare, by Mrs. Melton's rubbings. As for me, I have got several huge red patches on my chest. What materialises later on as to complete recovery, I will let you know. Of course, my case is such that it will take time to come round by itself.

So thankful to you and to Mrs. Adams for the kindness. I will surely go and call on them in Chicago.

How are things going on with you? I have been following the "Put up or shut up" plan here, and so far it has not proved bad. Mrs. Hansborough, the second of the three sisters, is here, and she is working, working, working—to help me. Lord bless their hearts. The three sisters are three angels, are they not? Seeing such souls here and there repays for all the nonsense of this life.

Well, all blessings to you for ever is my prayer. You are one of the angels also, say I.

With love to Miss Kate,

Ever your son,
Vivekananda.

PS—How is the "Mother's child"?

How is Miss Spencer? All love to her. You know already I am a very bad correspondent, but the heart never fails. Tell this to Miss Spencer.

1900.19 — MOTHER

1719 Turk Street, San Francisco,
17th March, 1900.

DEAR MOTHER, (Mrs. Leggett)

I had a letter from Joe asking me to send my signature on four slips of paper, so that Mr. Leggett may put my money in the bank for me. As I cannot possibly reach her in time, I send the slips to you.

I am getting better in health and doing financially something. I am quite satisfied. I am not at all sorry that more people did not respond to your call. I knew they would not. But I am eternally thankful to you for all your kindness. May all blessings follow you and yours for ever.

It is better that my mail be sent to 1231 Pine Street, C/o the Home of Truth. For though I be moving about, that place is a permanent establishment, and the people there are very kind to me.

I am so glad to learn that you are very well now. Mrs. Melton has left Los Angeles—I am informed by Mrs. Blodgett. Has she gone to New York? Dr. and Mrs. Hiller came back to San Francisco day before yesterday. They declare themselves very much helped by Mrs. Melton. Mrs. Hiller expects to get completely cured in a short time.

I had a number of lectures here already and in Oakland. The Oakland lectures paid well. The first week in San Francisco was not paying, this week is. Hope the next week will pay also. I am so glad to hear the nice arrangement made by Mr. Leggett for the Vedanta Society. He is so good.

With all love,

Yours,
Vivekananda.

PS — Do you know anything about Turiyananda? Has he got completely cured?

1900.20 — MARY

To Miss Mary Hale:

1719 Turk Street, San Francisco,
22nd March, 1900.

MY DEAR MARY,

Many thanks for your kind note. You are correct that I have many other thoughts to think besides Indian people, but they have all to go to the background before the all-absorbing mission — my Master's work.

I would that this sacrifice were pleasant. It is not, and naturally makes one bitter at times; for know, Mary, I am yet a man and cannot wholly forget myself; hope I shall some time. Pray for me.

Of course I am not to be held responsible for Miss MacLeod's or Miss Noble's or anybody else's views regarding myself or anything else, am I? You never found me smart under criticism.

I am glad you are going over to Europe for a long period. Make a long tour, you have been long a house-dove.

As for me, I am tired on the other hand of eternal tramping; that is why I want to go back home and be quiet. I do not want to work any more. My nature is the retirement of a scholar. I never get it! I pray I will get it, now that I am all broken and worked out. Whenever I get a letter from Mrs. Sevier from her Himalayan home, I feel like flying off the Himalayas. I am really sick of this platform work and eternal trudging and seeing new faces and lecturing.

You need not bother about getting up classes in Chicago. I am getting money in Frisco and will soon make enough for my passage home.

How are you and the sisters? I expect to come to Chicago some time towards the first part of April.

Yours,
Vivekananda.

1900.21 — NIVEDITA

San Francisco,
25th March, 1900.

DEAR NIVEDITA,

I am much better and am growing very strong. I feel sometimes that freedom is near at hand, and the tortures of the last two years have been great lessons in many ways. Disease and misfortune come to do us good in the long run, although at the time we feel that we are submerged for ever.

I am the infinite blue sky; the clouds may gather over me, but I am the same infinite blue.

I am trying to get a taste of that peace which I know is my nature and everyone's nature. These tin pots of bodies and foolish dreams of happiness and misery — what are they?

My dreams are breaking. Om Tat Sat!

Yours,
Vivekananda.

1900.22 — MARGOT

1719 Turk Street, San Francisco,
28th March, 1900.

MY DEAR MARGOT, (Margaret E. Noble or Sister Nivedita)

I am so glad at your good fortune. Things have got to come round if we are steady. I am sure you will get all the money you require here or in England.

I am working hard; and the harder I work, the better I feel. This ill health has done me a great good, sure. I am really understanding what non-attachment means. And I hope very soon to be perfectly non-attached.

We put all our energies to concentrate and get attached to one thing; but the other part, though equally difficult, we seldom pay any attention to — the faculty of detaching ourselves at a moment's notice from anything.

Both attachment and detachment perfectly developed make a man great and happy.

I am so glad at Mrs. Leggett's gift of $1,000. She is working up, wait. She has a great part to play in Ramakrishna's work, whether she knows it or not.

I enjoyed your accounts of Prof. Geddes, and Joe has a funny account of a clairvoyant. Things are just now beginning to turn...

This letter, I think, Will reach you at Chicago...

I had a nice letter from Max Gysic, the young Swiss who is a great friend of Miss Souter. Miss Souter also sends her love, and they ask to know the time when I come over to England. Many people are inquiring, they say.

Things have got to come round — the seed must die underground to come up as the tree. The last two years were the underground rotting. I never had a struggle in the jaws of death, but it meant a tremendous upheaval of the whole life. One such brought me to Ramakrishna, another sent me to the U.S., this has been the greatest of all. It is gone — I am so calm that it astonishes me sometimes!! I work every day morning and evening, eat anything any hour — and go to bed at 12 p.m. in the night — but such fine sleep!! I never had such power of sleeping before!

Yours with all love and blessings,
Vivekananda.

1900.23 — MARY

To Miss Mary Hale:

1719 Turk Street, San Francisco,
28th March, 1900.

WELL BLESSED MARY,

This is to let you know "I am very happy". Not that I am getting into a shadowy optimism, but my power of suffering is increasing. I am being lifted up above the pestilential miasma of this world's joys and sorrows; hey are losing their meaning. It is a land of dreams; it does not matter whether one enjoys or weeps; they are but dreams, and as such, must break sooner or later. How are things going on with you folks there? Harriet is going to have a good time at Paris. I am sure to meet her over there and parler fransaise! I am getting by heart a French dictionnaire! I am making some money too; hard work morning and evening; yet better for all that. Good sleep, good digestion, perfect irregularity.

You are going to the East. I hope to come to Chicago before the end of April. If I can't, I will surely meet you in the East before you go.

What are the McKindley girls doing? Eating grapefruit concoctions and getting plump? Go on, life is but a dream. Are you not glad it is so? My! They want an eternal heaven! Thank God, nothing is eternal except Himself. He alone can bear it, I am sure. Eternity of nonsense!

Things are beginning to hum for me; they will presently roar. I shall remain quiet though, all the same. Things are not humming for you just now. I am so sorry, that is, I am trying to be, for I cannot be sorry for anything and more. I am attaining peace that passeth understanding, which is neither joy nor sorrow, but something above them both. Tell Mother that. My passing through the valley of death, physical, mental, last two years, has helped me in this. Now I am nearing that Peace, the eternal silence. Now I mean to see things as they are, everything in that peace, perfect in its way. "He whose joy is only in himself, whose desires are only in himself, he has learned his lessons." This is the great lesson that we are here to learn through myriads of births and heavens and hells — that there is nothing to be asked for, desired for, beyond one's Self. "The greatest thing I can obtain is my Self." "I am free", therefore I require none else for my happiness. "Alone through eternity, because I was free, am free, and will remain free for ever." This is Vedantism. I preached the theory so long, but oh, joy! Mary, my dear sister, I am realising it now every day. Yes, I am — "I am free." "Alone, alone, I am the one without a second."

PS—Now I am going to be truly Vivekananda. Did you ever enjoy evil! Ha! ha! you silly girl, all is good! Nonsense. Some good, some evil. I enjoy the good and I enjoy the evil. I was Jesus and I was Judas Iscariot; both my play, my fun. "So long as there are two, fear shall not leave thee." Ostrich method? Hide your heads in the sand and think there is nobody seeing you! All is good! Be brave and face everything—come good, come evil, both welcome, both of you my play. I have no good to attain, no ideal to clench up to, no ambition to fulfil; I, the diamond mine, am playing with pebbles, good and evil; good for you—evil, come; good for you-good, you come too. If the universe tumbles round my ears, what is that to me? I am Peace that passeth understanding; understanding only gives us good or evil. I am beyond, I am peace.

Ever yours in the Sat-Chit-Ânanda,
Vivekananda.

1900.24—HARIBHAI[1]

To Swami Turiyananda:

San Francisco,
March, 1900.

DEAR HARIBHAI,

I have just received a bill of lading from Mrs. Banerji. She has sent some Dâl (pulses) and rice. I am sending the bill of lading to you. Give it to Miss Waldo; she will bring all these things when they come.

Next week I am leaving this place for Chicago; thence I go over to New York. I am getting on somehow... Where are you putting up now? What are you doing?

Yours affectionately,
Vivekananda.

1900.25—JOE

To Miss Josephine MacLeod:

1719 Turk Street, San Francisco,
30th March, 1900.

MY DEAR JOE,

Many thanks for the prompt sending of the books. They will sell quick, I believe. You have become worse than me in changing your plans, I see. I wonder why I have not got any Awakened India yet. My mail is getting so knocked about, I am afraid.

I am working hard—making some money—and am getting better in health. Work morning and evening, go to bed at 12 p.m. after a heavy supper!—and

---

1 Translated from Bengali.

trudge all over the town! And get better too!

So Mrs. Milton is there, give her my love, will you? Has not Turiyananda's leg got all right?

I have sent Margot's letter to Mrs. Bull as she wanted. I am so happy to learn of Mrs. Leggett's gift to her. Things have got to come round; anyway, they are bound to, because nothing is eternal.

I will be a week or two more here if I find it paying, then go to a place near by called Stockton and then — I don't know. Things are going anyhow.

I am very peaceful and quiet, and things are going anyway-just they go.

With all love,
Vivekananda.

PS — Miss Waldo is just the person to undertake editing Karma-Yoga with additions etc.

1900.26 — HARIBHAI[2]

To Swami Turiyananda:

DEAR HARIBHAI,

I am glad to hear that your leg is all right and that you are doing splendid work. My body is going on all right. The thing is, I fall ill when I take too much precaution. I am cooking, eating whatever comes, working day and night, and I am all right and sleeping soundly!

I am going over to New York within a month. Has Sarada's magazine gone out of circulation? I am not getting it any longer. Awakened also has gone to sleep, I think. They are not sending it to me any more. Let that go. There is an outbreak of plague in our country; who knows who is alive and who is dead! Well, a letter from Achu has come today. He had hidden himself in the town of Ramgarh in Sikar State. Someone told him that Vivekananda was dead; so he has written to me! I am sending him a reply.

All well here. Hope this finds you and all others well.

Yours affectionately,
Vivekananda.

---

2 Translated from Bengali.

1900.27 — JOE

To Miss Josephine MacLeod:

1719 Turk Street, San Francisco, Calif.
April, 1900.

MY DEAR JOE,

Just a line before you start for France. Are you going via England? I had a beautiful letter from Mrs. Sevier in which I find that Miss Müller sent simply a paper without any other words to Kali who was with her in Darjeeling.

Congreave is the name of her nephew, and he is in the Transvaal war; that is the reason she underlined that, to show her nephew fighting the Boers in Transvaal. That was all. I cannot understand it any more now than then, of course.

I am physically worse than at Los Angeles, mentally much better, stronger, and peaceful. Hope it will continue to be so.

I have not got a reply to my letter to you; I expect it soon.

One Indian letter of mine was directed by mistake to Mrs. Wheeler; it came all right to me in the end. I had nice notes from Saradananda; they are doing beautifully over there. The boys are working up; well, scolding has both sides, you see; it makes them up and doing. We Indians have been so dependent for so long that it requires, I am sorry, a good lot of tongue to make them active. One of the laziest fellows had taken charge of the anniversary this year and pulled it through. They have planned and are successfully working famine works by themselves without my help... All this comes from the terrific scolding I have been giving, sure!

They are standing on their own feet. I am so glad. See Joe, the Mother is working.

I sent Miss Thursby's letter to Mrs. Hearst. She sent me an invitation to her musical. I could not go. I had a bad cold. So that was all. Another lady for whom I had a letter from Miss Thursby, an Oakland lady, did not reply. I don't know whether I shall make enough in Frisco to pay my fare to Chicago! Oakland work has been successful. I hope to get about $100 from Oakland, that is all. After all, I am content. It is better that I tried... Even the magnetic healer had not anything for me. Well, things will go on anyhow for me; I do not care how... I am very peaceful. I learn from Los Angeles, Mrs. Leggett has been bad again. I wired to New York to learn what truth was in it. I will get a reply soon, I expect.

Say, how will you arrange about my mail when the Leggetts are over on the other side? Will you so arrange that they reach me right?

I have nothing more to say; all love and gratitude is yours; already you know that. You have already done more than I ever deserved. I don't know whether I go to Paris or not, but I must go to England sure in May. I must not go home without trying England a few weeks more. With all love,

Ever yours in the Lord,
Vivekananda.

PS — Mrs. Hansborough and Mrs. Appenul have taken a flat for a month at 1719 Turk Street. I am with them, and shall be a few weeks.

1900.28 — DHIRA MATA

To Mrs. Ole Bull:

1719 Turk Street, San Francisco,
1st April, 1900.

DEAR DHIRA MATA,

Your kind note came this morning. I am so happy to learn that all the New York friends are being cured by Mrs. Milton. She has been very unsuccessful, it seems, in Los Angeles, as all the people we introduced tell me. Some are in a worse state than before the skin paring. Kindly give Mrs. Milton my love; her rubbings used to do me good at the time at least. Poor Dr. Hiller! We send him over post-haste to Los Angeles to get his wife cured. You ought to have seen him the other morning and heard him too! Mrs. Hiller, it appears, is many times worse for all the rubbings given; and she is only a few bones; and, above all, the doctor had to spend 500 dollars in Los Angeles. That makes him feel very bad. I, of course, would not write this to Joe; she is happy in her dreams of having done so much good to poor sufferers. But oh, if she could hear the Los Angeles folks and this old Dr. Hiller, she would change her mind at once and learn wisdom from an old adage not to recommend medicine to any one. I am so glad I did not write of old Dr. Hiller's alacrity in getting over to Los Angeles when he heard of this cure from Joe. She ought to have seen the old man dance about my room, with greater alacrity! 500 dollars was too much for the old man; he is a German; he dances about, slaps his pockets and says, "You can'th have goth the five hundred, buth for this silly cure!"

Then there are poor people who paid her three dollars a rubbing sometimes and now complimenting Joe and myself. Don't tell this to Joe. You and she can afford to lose money on anyone. So also the old German doctor, but the poor boy finds it a bit hard. The old doctor is now persuaded that some devils are misarranging his affairs of late. He had counted on so much to have me as his guest, and his wife righted, but he had to run to Los Angeles and that upset the whole plan; and now, though he tries his best to get me in as his guest, I fight shy, not of him, but of his wife and sister-in-law. He is sure, "Devils must be in it"; he has been a Theosophical student. I told him to write to Miss MacLeod to hunt up a devil-driver somewhere so that he might run with his wife and spend another five hundred! Doing good is not always smooth!

As for me, I get the fun out of it — as long as Joe pays — bone-cracker, or skin-parer, or any system whatever. But this was not fair of Joe — after having got in all these people to get rubbed down, to run off and let me bear all the compliments! I am glad she is not introducing any outsiders to be skinned. Otherwise Joe would be gone to Paris, leaving poor Mr. Leggett to collect the compliments. I sent in a Christian Science healer to Dr. Hiller as a make-up of Joe's misdemeanour, but his wife slammed the door in her face and would have nothing to do with queer healing.

Anyhow, I sincerely hope and pray Mrs. Leggett will be well this time. Did they analyse the sting?

I hope the will will arrive soon; I am a bit anxious about it. I expected to get a draft trust-deed also by this mail from India; no letters came, not even Awakened India, though I find Awakened India has reached San Francisco.

I read in the papers the other day of 500 deaths in one week of plague in Calcutta! Mother knows what is good.

So Mr. Leggett has got the V. Society up. Good.

How is Olea? Where is Margot? I wrote her a letter the other day to 21 W. 34, N.Y. I am so happy that she is making headway. With all love,

Ever your son,
Vivekananda.

PS — I am getting all the work I can do and more. I will make my passage, anyhow. Though they cannot pay me much, yet they pay some, and by constant work I will make enough to pay my way and have a few hundred in the pocket anyhow. So you needn't be the least anxious about me.

1900.29 — MARGOT

To Sister Nivedita:

U.S.A.,
6th April, 1900.

DEAR MARGOT,

Glad you have returned. Gladder you are going to Paris. I shall go to Paris of course, only don't know when. Mrs. Leggett thinks I ought to immediately, and take up studying French. Well, take what comes. So you do too.

Finish your books, and in Paris we are going to conquer the Froggies. How is Mary? Give her my love. My work here is done. I will come in fifteen days to Chicago if Mary is there. She is going away to the East soon.

With blessings,
Vivekananda.

PS — The mind is omnipresent and can be heard and felt anywhere.

1900.30 — AMERICAN FRIEND

To an American friend:

San Francisco,
7th April, 1900.

... I am more calm and quiet now than I ever was. I am on my own feet, working hard and with pleasure. To work I have the right. Mother knows the rest.

You see, I shall have to stay here, longer than I intended, and work. But don't be disturbed. I shall work out all my problems. I am on my own feet now, and I begin to see the light. Success would have led me astray, and I would have lost sight of the truth that I am a Sannyasin. That is why Mother is giving me this experience.

My boat is nearing the calm harbour from which it is never more to be driven out. Glory, glory unto Mother! I have no wish, no ambition now. Blessed be Mother! I am the servant of Ramakrishna. I am merely a machine. I know nothing else. Nor do I want to know. Glory, glory unto Shri Guru!

1900.31 — MOTHER

1719 Turk Street, San Francisco,
7th April, 1900.

DEAR MOTHER, (Mrs. Leggett)

Accept my congratulations for the news of the cause of the wound being completely removed. I have no doubt of your being perfectly cured this time.

Your very kind note cheered me a good deal. I do not mind at all whether people come round to help me or not; I am becoming calm and less worried.

Kindly convey my best love to Mrs. Melton. I am sure to recover in the long run. My health has been improving in the main, though there are occasional relapses. Each relapse becoming less, both in tone and in time.

It is just like you to have Turiyananda and Siri treated. The Lord has blessed you for your great heart. May all blessings ever follow you and yours.

It is perfectly true that I should go to France and work on French. I hope to reach France in July or earlier. Mother knows. May all good ever follow you, is the constant prayer of

Your son,
Vivekananda.

1900.32 — DHIRA MATA

To Mrs. Ole Bull:

>1719 Turk Street, San Francisco,
>8th April, 1900.

DEAR DHIRA MATA,

Here is a long letter from A__. He seems to be entirely upset. I am sure a little kindness will completely win him over. He thinks that you want to drive him out of New York, etc. He awaits my orders. I have told him to trust you in everything and remain in New York till I come.

I think, as things stand in New York, they require my presence. Do you? In that case I shall come over soon.

I have been making enough money to pay my passage. I will stop on my way at Chicago and Detroit.

Of course by that time you will be off. A__ has done good work so far; and, of course, you know I do not meddle with my workers at all.

The man who can work has an individuality of his own and resists any pressure there. That is my reason in leaving workers entirely free. Of course you are on the spot and know best. Advise me what to do.

The remittance to Calcutta has duly reached. I got news of it by this mail. My cousin sends her respects and thanks, but she is sorry she cannot write English.

I am getting better every day, and even walking uphill. There are falls now and then, but the duration is decreasing constantly. My thanks to Mrs. Milton.

I had a little note from Siri Gryanander. Poor girl, she is so thankful to be trusted. That is just like Mrs. Leggett — good, good, good. Money is not evil after all — in good hands. I hope fervently Siri will completely recover, poor child.

I will leave here in about two weeks. I go to a place called Star Klon and then start for the East. It may be I may go to Denver also. With all love to Joe,

>Ever your son,
>Vivekananda.

PS — I do not any more doubt my ultimate cure; you ought to see me working like a steam engine cooking, eating anything and everything, and, all the same, sleeping well and keeping well!

I have not done any writing — no time. I am so glad Mrs. Leggett is much better and walking about naturally. I expect her complete recovery soon and pray for it.

PS — I had a nice letter from Mrs. Sevier; they are going on splendidly with the work. Plague has broken out severely at Calcutta, but no hullabaloo over it this time.

PS — Did you reveal to A__ that I have given over to you the charge of the entire work? Well, you know best how to do things; but he seems to be hurt at that.

1900.33 — SISTER CHRISTINE

To Sister Christine:

1719 Turk Street, San Francisco,
[April 9, 1900]

Hello! What's the matter with you — gone to sleep? Have not had any news of you for a long time.

I am getting better every day, and one of these days — say in a few weeks — I am coming straight to say how-d'you-do. Well, I will be here two weeks more, then to a place called Stockton — thence to the East. I may stop a few days in Chicago. I may not.

Beginning of May, I come [for] sure to Detroit. I will, of course, write to you. How is life going on with you — grinding, as usual? Any improvements? Write a chatty letter if you feel like. I am dying to get news.

Ever yours in the Truth,
Vivekananda.

1900.34 — JOE

To Miss Josephine MacLeod:

1719 Turk Street, San Francisco,
10th April, 1900.

DEAR JOE,

There is a squabble in New York, I see. I got a letter from A__ stating that he was going to leave New York. He thought Mrs. Bull and you have written lots against him to me. I wrote him back to be patient and wait, and that Mrs. Bull and Miss MacLeod wrote only good things about him.

Well, Joe Joe, you know my method in all these rows; to leave all rows alone! "Mother" sees to all such things. I have finished my work. I am retired, Joe. "Mother" will work now Herself. That is all.

Now, as you say, I am going to send all the money I have made here. I could do it today, but I am waiting to make it a thousand. I expect to make a thousand in Frisco by the end of this week. I will buy a draft on New York and send it or ask the bank the best way to do it.

I have plenty of letters from the Math and the Himalayan centre. This morning came one from Swarupananda. Yesterday one from Mrs. Sevier.

I told Mrs. Hansborough about the photos.

You tell Mr. Leggett from me to do what is best about the Vedanta Society matter. The only thing I see is that in every country we have to follow its own method. As such, if I were you, I would convene a meeting of all the members and sympathisers and ask them what they want to do. Whether they want to organise or not, what sort of organisation they want if any, etc. But Lordy, do it on your own hook. I am quits. Only if you think my presence would be of any help I can come in fifteen days.

I have finished my work here; only, out of San Francisco, Stockton is a little city I want to work a few days in; then I go East. I think I should rest now, although I can have $100 a week average in this city, all along. This time I want to let upon New York the charge of the Light Brigade.

With all love,

Ever yours affectionately,
Vivekananda.

PS — If the workers are all averse to organising, do you think there is any benefit in it? You know best. Do what you think best. I have a letter from Margot from Chicago. She asks some questions; I am going to reply.

1900.35 — AMERICAN FRIEND

To an American friend:

Alameda, California,
12th April, 1900.

Mother is becoming propitious once more. Things are looking up. They must.

Work always brings evil with it. I have paid for the accumulated evil with bad health. I am glad. My mind is all the better for it. There is a mellowness and a calmness in life now, which was never there before. I am learning now how to be detached as well as attached, and mentally becoming my own master...

Mother is doing Her own work; I do not worry much now. Moths like me die by the thousand every instant. Her work goes on all the same. Glory unto Mother!... Alone and drifting about in the will-current of the Mother has been my whole life. The moment I have tried to break this, that moment I have been hurt. Her will be done!...

I am happy, at peace with myself, and more of the Sannyasin than I ever was before. The love for my own kith and kin is growing less every day, and that for Mother increasing. Memories of long nights of vigil with Shri Ramakrishna under the Dakshineswar Banyan are waking up once more. And work? What is work? Whose work? Whom shall I work for?

I am free. I am Mother's child. She works, She plays. Why should I plan? What should I plan? Things came and went, just as She liked, without my planning. We are Her automata. She is the wirepuller.

1900.36 — MR. LEGGETT

17th April, 1900.

MY DEAR MR. LEGGETT,

Herewith I send the executed Will to you. It has been executed as desired by her, and of course, as usual, I am requesting you for the trouble of taking charge of it.

You and yours have been so uniformly kind to me. But you know, dear friend, it is human nature to ask for more favours (now that they have come) where it gets from.

I am only a man, your child.

I am so sorry A__ has made disturbances. He does that now and then, at least used to. I do not venture to meddle, for fear of creating more trouble. You know how to manage him best. By the time you receive this letter, I will be off from San Francisco. Will you kindly send my Indian mail C/o Mrs. Hale, 10 Aster Street, Chicago, and to Margot in the same place? Margot writes very thankfully of your gift of a thousand dollars for her school.

May all blessings ever follow you and yours for your uniform kindness to me and mine, is the constant prayer of

Yours affectionately,
Vivekananda.

PS — I am so glad to learn that Mrs. Leggett has already recovered.

1900.37 — JOE

Alameda, California,
18th April, 1900.

MY DEAR JOE,

Just now I received yours and Mrs. Bull's welcome letter. I direct this to London. I am so glad Mrs. Leggett is on the sure way to recovery.

I am so sorry Mr. Leggett resigned the presidentship.

Well, I keep quiet for fear of making further trouble.

You know my methods are extremely harsh and once roused I may rattle A — too much for his peace of mind.

I wrote to him only to tell him that his notions about Mrs. Bull are entirely wrong.

Work is always difficult; pray for me Joe that my works stop for ever, and my whole soul be absorbed in Mother. Her works, She knows.

You must be glad to be in London once more — the old friends, give them all my love and gratitude.

I am well, very well mentally. I feel the rest of the soul more shall that of the body. The battles are lost and won, I have bundled my things and am waiting for the great deliverer.

"Shiva, O Shiva, carry my boat to the other shore."

After all, Joe, I am only the boy who used to listen with rapt wonderment to the wonderful words of Ramakrishna under the Banyan at Dakshineswar. That is my true nature; works and activities, doing good and so forth are all superimpositions. Now I again hear his voice; the same old voice thrilling my soul. Bonds are breaking — love dying, work becoming tasteless — the glamour is off life. Only the voice of the Master calling. — "I come Lord, I come." "Let the dead bury the dead, follow thou Me." — "I come, my beloved Lord, I come."

Yes, I come. Nirvana is before me. I feel it at times — the same infinite ocean of peace, without a ripple, a breath.

I am glad I was born, glad I suffered so, glad I did make big blunders, glad to enter peace. I leave none bound, I take no bonds. Whether this body will fall and release me or I enter into freedom in the body, the old man is gone, gone for ever, never to come back again! The guide, the Guru, the leader, the teacher has passed away; the boy, the student, the servant is left behind.

You understand why I do not want to meddle with A—. Who am I to meddle with anyone, Joe? I have long given up my place as a leader — I have no right to raise my voice. Since the beginning of this year I have not dictated anything in India. You know that. Many thanks for what you and Mrs. Bull have been to me in the past. All blessings follow you ever! The sweetest moments of my life have been when I was drifting: I am drifting again — with the bright warm sun ahead and masses of vegetation around — and in the heat everything is so still, so calm — and I am drifting languidly — in the warm heart of the river! I dare not make a splash with my hands or feet — for fear of breaking the marvellous stillness, stillness that makes you feel sure it is an illusion!

Behind my work was ambition, behind my love was personality, behind my purity was fear, behind my guidance the thirst of power! Now they are vanishing, and I drift. I come! Mother, I come! In Thy warm bosom, floating wheresoever Thou takest me, in the voiceless, in the strange, in the wonderland, I come — a spectator, no more an actor.

Oh, it is so calm! My thoughts seem to come from a great, great distance in the interior of my own heart. They seem like rains, distant whispers, and peace is upon every thing, sweet, sweet peace — like that one feels for a few moments just before falling into sleep, when things are seen and felt like shadows — without fear, without love, without emotion. Peace that one feels alone, surrounded with statues and pictures — I come! Lord, I come!

The world is, but not beautiful nor ugly, but as sensations without exciting any emotion. Oh, Joe, the blessedness of it! Everything is good and beautiful; for things are all losing their relative proportions to me — my body among the first. Om That Existence!

I hope great things to come to you all in London and Paris. Fresh joy—fresh benefits to mind and body.

With love as ever to you and Mrs. Bull,

Yours faithfully,
Vivekananda.

1900.38 — JOE

To Miss Josephine MacLeod:

Alameda, California,
20th April, 1900.

MY DEAR JOE,

Received your note today. I wrote you one yesterday but directed it to England thinking you will be there.

I have given your message to Mrs. Betts. I am so sorry this little quarrel came with A__. I got also his letter you sent. He is correct so far as he says, "Swami wrote me 'Mr. Leggett is not interested in Vedanta and will not help any more. You stand on your own feet.'" It was as you and Mrs. Leggett desired me to write him from Los Angeles about New York — in reply to his asking me what to do for funds.

Well, things will take their own shape, but it seems in Mrs. Bull's and your mind there is some idea that I ought to do something. But in the first place I do not know anything about the difficulties. None of you write me anything about what that is for, and I am no thought-reader. You simply wrote me a general idea that A__ wanted to keep things in his hands. What can I understand from it? What are the difficulties? Regarding what the differences are about, I am as much in the dark as about the exact date of the Day of Destruction! And yet Mrs. Bull's and your letters show quite an amount of vexation! These things get complicated sometimes, in spite of ourselves. Let them take their shape.

I have executed and sent the will to Mr. Leggett as desired by Mrs. Bull.

I am going on, sometimes well and at other times ill. I cannot say, on my conscience, that I have been the least benefited by Mrs. Milton. She has been good to me, I am very thankful. My love to her. Hope she will benefit others.

For writing to Mrs. Bull this fact, I got a four page sermon, as to how I ought to be grateful and thankful, etc., etc. All that is, sure, the outcome of this A__ business! Sturdy and Mrs. Johnson got disturbed by Margot, and they fell upon me. Now A__ disturbs Mrs. Bull and, of course, I have to bear the brunt of it. Such is life!

You and Mrs. Leggett wanted me to write him to be free and independent and that Mr. Leggett was not going to help them. I wrote it — now what can I do? If John or Jack does not obey you, am I to be hanged for it? What do I know about this Vedanta Society? Did I start it? Had I any hand in it? Then again, nobody condescends to write me anything about what the affair is! Well, this world is a great fun.

I am glad Mrs. Leggett is recovering fast. I pray every moment for her complete recovery. I start for Chicago on Monday. A kind lady has given me a pass up to New York to be used within three months. The Mother will take care of me. She is not going to strand me now after guarding me all my life.

Ever yours gratefully,
Vivekananda.

1900.39 — MARY

To Miss Mary Hale:

23rd April, 1900.

MY DEAR MARY,

I ought to have started today but circumstances so happened that I cannot forgo the temptation to be in a camp under the huge red-wood trees of California before I leave. Therefore I postpone it for three or four days. Again after the incessant work I require a breath of God's free air before I start on this bone-breaking journey of four days.

Margot insists in her letter that I must keep my promise to come to see Aunt Mary in fifteen days. It will be kept — only in twenty days instead of fifteen. By that I avoid the nasty snowstorm Chicago had lately and get a little strength too.

Margot is a great partisan of Aunt Mary it seems, and other people besides me have nieces and cousins and aunts.

I start tomorrow to the woods. Woof! get my lungs full of ozone before getting into Chicago. In the meanwhile keep my mail for me when it comes to Chicago and don't send it off here like a good girl as you are.

I have finished work. Only a few days' rest, my friends insist — three or four — before facing the railway.

I have got a free pass for three months from here to New York; no expense except the sleeping car; so, you see, free, free!

Ever yours gratefully,
Vivekananda.

1900.40 — MARY

To Miss Mary Hale:

30th April, 1900.

MY DEAR MARY,

Sudden indisposition and fever prevent my starting for Chicago yet. I will start as soon as I am strong for the journey. I had a letter from Margot the other day. Give her kindly my love, and know yourself my eternal love. Where is Harriet? Still in Chicago? And the McKindley sisters?

To all my love,
Vivekananda.

1900.41 — AUNT ROXY

2nd May, 1900.

DEAR AUNT ROXY, (Mrs. Blodgett of Los Angeles)

Your very, very kind letter came. I am down again with nerves and fever, after six months of hard work. However, I found out that my kidneys and heart are as good as ever. I am going to take a few days' rest in the country and then start for Chicago.

I have just written to Mrs. Milward Adams and also have given an introduction to my daughter, Miss Noble, to go and call upon Mrs. Adams and give her all information she wants about the work.

Well, dear good mother, may all blessings attend you and peace. I just want a bit of peace badly — pray for me. With love to Kate,

Ever your son,
Vivekananda.

PS — Love to Miss Spencer — the Basaquisitz(?), Mrs. S__, and the other friends.

A heap of loving pats on the head to Tricks.

1900.42 — NIVEDITA

To Sister Nivedita:

2nd May, 1900.

MY DEAR NIVEDITA,

I have been very ill — one more relapse brought about by months of hard work. Well, it has shown me that I have no kidney or heart disease whatsoever, only overworked nerves. I am, therefore, going today in the country for some days till I completely recover, which I am sure will be in a few days.

In the meanwhile I do not want to read any India letters with the plague news etc. My mail is coming to Mary; either she or you keep them (you, if she goes away) till I return.

I am going to throw off all worry, and glory unto Mother.

Mrs. C. P. Huntington, a very, very wealthy lady, who has helped me, came; wants to see and help you. She will be in New York by the first of June. Do not go away without seeing her. If I cannot come early enough, I will send you an introduction to her.

Give my love to Mary. I am leaving here in a few days.

Ever yours with blessings,
Vivekananda.

PS — The accompanying letter is to introduce you to Mrs. M. C. Adams, wife of Judge Adams. Go to see her immediately. Much good may come out of it. She is well known; find out her address.

1900.43 — MARGOT

To Sister Nivedita:

C/O Dr. Logan,
770 Oak Street, San Francisco, California,
17th May [1900].

DEAR MARGOT,

I am sorry, I cannot come to Chicago yet for a few days. The doctor (Dr. Logan) says I must not undertake a journey till completely strong. He is bent on making me strong. My stomach is very, very good and nerves fine. I am getting on. A few days more and I will be all right. I received your letter with the enclosed.

If you leave for New York soon, take my mail with you. I am coming to New York direct. If you leave New York before I leave, put my mail in a cover and deposit with Turiyananda, and tell him to keep it for me and not to open it on any account, nor any one of my Indian letters. Turiyananda will take charge. Also see that my clothes and books are at the Vedanta Society's rooms in New York.

I will write you more soon — an introduction to Mrs. Huntington. This affair should be private.

With love and blessings,
Vivekananda.

PS — As I have got to stop at Chicago for my ticket, will you ask anybody to take me in for a day or two, if Mrs. Hale is gone East by that time?

1900.44 — MARGOT

To Sister Nivedita:

> 770 Oak Street, San Francisco, California,
> 18th May, 1900.

DEAR MARGOT,

Enclosed find the letter of introduction to Mrs. Huntington. She can, if she likes, make your school a fact with one stroke of her pen. May Mother make her do it!

I am afraid I will have to go direct to New York, as by that time the Hales will be off. I cannot start for two weeks at least yet. Give the Hales my love.

With love and blessings,

> Yours,
> Vivekananda.

PS — I received your letter, including Yum's [Miss Josephine MacLeod's].

1900.45 — MOTHER

To Mrs. Ole Bull (in London):

> San Francisco,
> 18 May, 1900.

MY DEAR MOTHER,

Many thanks for Joe's [Miss Josephine MacLeod's] and your letters. I have again a bad relapse — and [am] struggling out of it. This time I am perfectly certain that with me all diseases are nervous. I want rest for two, three years — and not the least bit of work between. I will take rest with the Seviers in the Himalayas.

Mrs. [James Henry] Sevier gave me 6,000 Rs. for family — this was distributed between my cousin, aunt, etc. The 5,000 Rs. for buying the house was borrowed from the Math funds. Do not stop the remittance you send to my cousin, whatever Saradananda may say to the contrary. Of course I do not know what he says.

I have long given up the idea of a little house on the Ganges, as I have not the money.

But I have got some in Calcutta and some with the Leggetts, and if you give a thousand more, that will be a fund for my own personal expenses (as you know I never took Math money) as well as for my mother. Kindly write to Saradananda to give up the little house plan. I am not going to write any more for weeks yet — till I completely recover. I hope to get over [it] in a few weeks from now — it was a terrible relapse. I am with a Doctor friend [Dr. Milburn H. Logan], and he is taking every care of me.

Tell Joe that going amongst different people with a message also does not belong to the Sannyasin; for a Sannyasin, [there] is quiet and retirement, scarcely seeing the face of man.

I am now ripe for that, physically at least. If I don't go into retirement, nature will force me to it. Many thanks that temporal things have been so well arranged by you.

With all love to Joe and yourself—

Your Son,
Vivekananda.

1900.46 — CHRISTINA

To Sister Christine:

C/O Dr. Logan,
770 Oak Street, San Francisco, California,
19th May, 1900.

DEAR CHRISTINA,

How are you? When is your vacation to commence? I am still in California. Hope to start for the East in two or three weeks more.

Write me all about yourself and how things are going on. How is Mrs. Funkey [Funke]? And the other friends?

Yours as ever,
Vivekananda.

1900.47 — ABHEDANANDA

To Swami Abhedananda:

C/O Dr. Logan, M.d.,
770 Oak Street, San Francisco, Cal.,
[May 19, 1900?]

MY DEAR ABHEDANANDA,

I am very, very glad to hear about the new home of the Vedanta Society. As things stand, I will have to come to New York direct from here—without stoppage—but it will be two or three weeks yet, I am afraid. Things are coming up so fast that I can not but change my plans and stop a few more days.

I am trying my best to get one of you for a flying visit to this Coast—it is a great country for Vedanta.

Get all my books and clothes etc., in your home. I am coming soon. My love to Mrs. Crane. Is she still living on beef-steak and hot water? Miss [Sarah Ellen]

Waldo and Mrs. Coulston write about the publication of a new edition of Karma-Yoga. I have written to Miss Waldo all about it. The money in hand from the sale of books ought to be spent, of course.

Do you see my books and clothes all safe there? They were with Mrs. Bull in Boston.

With all love,
Vivekananda.

1900.48 — NIVEDITA

To Sister Nivedita:

San Francisco,
26th May, 1900.

DEAR NIVEDITA,

All blessings on you. Don't despond in the least. Shri wah Guru! Shri wah Guru! You come of the blood of a Kshatriya. Our yellow garb is the robe of death on the field of battle. Death for the cause is our goal, not success. Shri wah Guru!...

Black and thick are the folds of sinister fate. But I am the master. I raise my hand, and lo, they vanish! All this is nonsense. And fear? I am the Fear of fear, the Terror of terror, I am the fearless secondless One, I am the Rule of destiny, the Wiper-out of fact. Shri wah Guru! Steady, child, don't be bought by gold or anything else, and we win!

Vivekananda.

1900.49 — CHRISTINA

To Sister Christine:

Vedanta Society,
102 East 58th Street, New York,
9th June, 1900.

DEAR CHRISTINA,

I could not write more, as the last few weeks of my stay in California was one more relapse and great suffering. However, I got one great benefit out of it inasmuch as I came to know I have really no disease, except worry and fear. My kidneys are as sound as any other healthy man's. All the symptoms of Bright's disease etc., are only brought on by nerves.

I wrote you one, however, from 770 Oak Street, San Francisco, to which I did not get any reply. Of course, I was bedridden then and my address book was not in the place I was in. There was a mistake in number. I cannot believe you did not reply willingly.

As you see, now I am in New York, and will be here a few days. I have an invitation from Mrs. Walton of Cleveland, Ohio. I have accepted it. She writes me you are also invited and have accepted her invitation. Well, we will meet in Cleveland then. I am sure to see you before I go to Europe — either there or anywhere you wish. If you don't think it would be possible for you to come to Ohio, I will come to any other place you want me to come to say goodbye.

When is your school going to close? Write me all about your plans — do!

Miss Noble wants me very much to go to Cleveland. I would be very, very glad to get a few weeks' seclusion and rest before I start with friends who do not disturb me at all. I know I will find rest and peace that way, and you can help me any amount in that. In Cleveland, of course, there will be a few friends always and much talkee-talkee as a matter of course. So if you think I will have real peace and rest elsewhere, just write all about it.

My reply to the Cleveland lady depends on your letter.

How I wish I were in Detroit or elsewhere just now, among friends who I know are good and true always. This is weakness; but when the physical vitality is lowered and the nerves all unstrung, I feel so, so much to depend upon somebody. You will be glad to learn I made a little money in the West. So I will be quite able to pay my expenses.

Write soon.

Yours affectionately,
Vivekananda.

1900.50 — CHRISTINA

To Sister Christine:

Vedanta Society,
102 East 58th Street, New York,
13th June, 1900.

DEAR CHRISTINA,

There is no cause for any anxiety. As I wrote, I am healthier than ever; moreover, all the past fear of kidney troubles has passed away. "Worry" is the only disease I have, and I am conquering it fast.

I will be here a week or two, and then I come to Detroit. If things so happen that I cannot come, I will sure send for you. Anyway, I am not going to leave this country before seeing you. Sure, sure — I must see you first, and then go to Europe.

Things are looking cheerful once more, and good luck, like ill, also comes in bunches. So I am sure it will be smooth sailing every way now, for some time at least.

With love to Mrs. Funkey [Funke],

Ever yours in the Truth,
Vivekananda.

1900.51 — CHRISTINA

To Sister Christine:

Vedanta Society,
102 East 58th Street, New York,
15th June, 1900.

MY DEAR CHRISTINA,

I am getting better every day, only this New York is a bad place for sleep. Again, I am working some, though not hard, to get the old friends together and put the thing in shape.

Now, you know, I will in a week or so finish this work and then be ready for a real quiet of a week or two or more.

Detroit, alas! will be no better than New York. With so many old friends! How can you avoid friends whom you really love?

I will have perfect freedom at yours — sure — but how can I avoid seeing friends and the eternal visiting and paying visits and much talkee-talkee? Do you know any other place within eight or ten hours (I want to avoid night rides) of riding from New York where I can be quiet and free from the people? (Lord bless them.) I am dead tired seeing people just now. Just think of that and everything else; if, after all, you think Detroit is the best place for me, I am ready to come.

Yours truly,
Vivekananda.

PS — I am also thinking of a quiet place.

1900.52 — MARY

To Miss Mary Hale:

1921 W. 21 Street, Los Angeles,
17th June, 1900.

MY DEAR MARY,

It is true I am much better, but not yet completely recovered; anyway, the complexion of the mind is one belonging to everyone that suffers. It is neither gas nor anything else.

Kâli worship is not a necessary step in any religion. The Upanishads teach us all there is of religion. Kali worship is my special fad; you never heard me preach it, or read of my preaching it in India. I only preach what is good for universal humanity. If there is any curious method which applies entirely to me, I keep it a secret and there it ends. I must not explain to you what Kali worship is, as I never taught it to anybody.

You are entirely mistaken if you think the Boses are rejected by the Hindu people. The English rulers want to push him into a corner. They don't of course like that sort of development in the Indian race. They make it hot for him, that is why he seeks to go elsewhere.

By the "anglicised" are meant people who by their manners and conduct show that they are ashamed of us poor, old type Hindus. I am not ashamed of my race or my birth or nationality. That such people are not liked by the Hindus, I cannot wonder.

Ceremonials and symbols etc. have no place in our religion which is the doctrine of the Upanishads, pure and simple. Many people think the ceremonial etc. help them in realising religion. I have no objection.

Religion is that which does not depend upon books or teachers or prophets or saviours, and that which does not make us dependent in this or in any other lives upon others. In this sense Advaitism of the Upanishads is the only religion. But saviours, books, prophets, ceremonials, etc. have their places. They may help many as Kali worship helps me in my secular work. They are welcome.

The Guru, however, is a different idea. It is the relation between the transmitter and the receiver of force — psychic power and knowledge. Each nation is a type, physically and mentally. Each is constantly receiving ideas from others only to work them out into its type, that is, along the national line. The time has not come for the destruction of types. All education from any source is compatible with the ideals in every country; only they must be nationalised, i.e. fall in line with the rest of the type manifestation.

Renunciation is always the ideal of every race; only other races do not know what they are made to do by nature unconsciously. Through the ages one purpose runs sure. And that will be finished with the destruction of this earth and the sun! And worlds are always in progress indeed! And nobody as yet developed enough in any one of the infinite worlds to communicate with us! Bosh! They are born, show the same phenomena, and die the same death! Increasing purpose! Babies! Live in the land of dreams, you babies!

Well, now about me. You must persuade Harriet to give me a few dollars every month, and I will have some other friends do the same. If I succeed, I fly off to India. I am dead tired of the platform work for a living. It does not please me any more. I retire and do some writing if I can do some scholarly work.

I am coming soon to Chicago, hope to be there in a few days. Say, would not Mrs. Adams be able to get up a class for me to pay my passage back?

Of course I shall try different places. So much of optimism has come to me, Mary, that I should fly off to the Himalayas if I had wings.

I have worked for this world, Mary, all my life, and it does not give me a piece of bread without taking a pound of flesh.

If I can get a piece of bread a day, I retire entirely; but this is impossible — this is the increasing purpose that is unfolding all the devilish inwardness, as I am getting older!

PS—If ever a man found the vanity of things, I have it now. This is the world, hideous, beastly corpse. Who thinks of helping it is a fool! But we have to work out our slavery by doing good or evil; I have worked it out, I hope. May the Lord take me to the other shore! Amen! I have given up all thoughts about India or any land. I am now selfish, want to save myself!

"He who revealed unto Brahmâ (the first of the gods) the Vedas, who is manifest in every heart, unto Him I take refuge, hoping deliverance from bondage."

Ever yours in the Lord,
Vivekananda.

1900.53 — NIVEDITA

New York,
20th June, 1900.

DEAR NIVEDITA,

…Well, Mother seems to be kind again and the wheel is slowly rising up…

Yours etc.,
Vivekananda.

1900.54 — MARY

To Miss Mary Hale:

Vedanta Society,
146 E. 55th Street, New York,
23rd June, 1900.

MY DEAR MARY,

Many, many thanks for your beautiful letter. I am very well and happy and same as ever. Waves must come before a rise. So with me. I am very glad you are going to pray. Why don't you get up a Methodist camp-meeting? That will have quicker effect, I am sure.

I am determined to get rid of all sentimentalism, and emotionalism, and hang me if you ever find me emotional. I am the Advaitist; our goal is knowledge — no feelings, no love, as all that belongs to matter and superstition and bondage. I am only existence and knowledge.

Greenacre will give you good rest. I am sure. I wish you all joy there. Don't for a moment worry on my account. "Mother" looks after me. She is bringing me fast out of the hell of emotionalism, and bringing me into the light of pure reason. With everlasting wishes for your happiness,

PS — Margot starts on the 26th. I may follow in a week or two. Nobody has any power over me, for I am the spirit. I have no ambition; it is all Mother's work; I have no part.

I could not digest your letter as the dyspepsia was rather bad last few days.

Non-attachment has always been there. It has come in a minute. Very soon I stand where no sentiment, no feeling, can touch me.

Ever your brother,
Vivekananda.

1900.55 — CHRISTINA

To Sister Christine:

Vedanta Society,
102 East 58th Street, New York,
27th June, 1900.

DEAR CHRISTINA,

This is my plan just now. I will have to remain in New York a few days yet to see my books through. I am going to publish another edition of Karma-Yoga and the London lectures in a book form. Miss Waldo is editing them, and Mr. Leggett will publish.

Then, I think, if I am to remain in this country a few weeks more, it is better that you get a rest and change. Newport is a celebrated seaside place — four hours from New York. I am invited there. I will go there this week and, as promised, I [will] find quiet and retirement and freedom. I will try to find a place for you and wire you as soon as found.

I am sure in Detroit you cannot have rest. A little change of place and quiet from time to time is a great factor in renewing one's vigour.

Well, if you think that you would have better rest and quiet in Detroit, drop a line and I come. It is only seventeen hours from New York to Detroit, and I am quite strong to undertake it. I am free to go already; only I really want you to take a good, long rest for some weeks at least.

Don't be afraid of expenses. Mother has amply provided that and will provide, so long I am unselfish.

Think [over] all the pros and cons, and write at your earliest convenience.

I am going to Newport anyway, just to see what it looks like. I will write you all about [it] as soon as I am there.

Ever yours in the Lord,
Vivekananda.

1900.56 — MRS. HANSBROUGH

To Mrs. Alice (Shanti) Hansbrough:

The Vedanta Society,
102 East 58th Street, New York, N.Y.,
[End of June, 1900]

DEAR MRS. HANSBROUGH,

I have not written you a line since you left San Francisco. I am well and things are going on well with me.

I am in New York once more, where they have got now a home for the Society and their headquarters. I and the other Swamis also live there.

A San Francisco lady [Miss Minnie C. Boock] now here owns a plot of land near Mt. Hamilton, 12 miles east of Lick observatory — 160 acres in area. She is going to make us a present of it. It would be nice for a summer gathering for us in California. If friends like to go there now, I will send them the written authority. Will you write to Mrs. Aspinall and Miss Bell etc., about it? I am rather desirous it should be occupied this summer as soon as possible. There is only a log cabin on the land; for the rest they must have tents.

I am sorry I can not spare a Swami yet.

With all love to you and Mrs. [Carrie Mead] Wyckoff and the baby of the family.

Ever yours in the Truth,
Vivekananda.

PS — Tell Helen [the youngest Mead sister] — I thank her for her kind invitation, but [am] so sorry [I] can not accept it now. After all, you three sisters have become a part of my mind forever. What about the club?

1900.57 — NIVEDITA

New York,
2nd July, 1900.

DEAR NIVEDITA,

... Mother knows, as I always say. Pray to Mother. It is hard work to be a leader — one must crush all one's own self under the feet of the community ...

Yours etc.,
Vivekananda.

1900.58 — SISTER CHRISTINE

To Sister Christine:

[On July 3, 1900, before departing for Detroit with Swami Turiyananda and Miss Minnie Boock, Swami Vivekananda dispatched a telegram.]

[POSTMARKED: NEW YORK,
July 3, 1900.]

STARTED REACH TOMORROW WEDNESDAY 2 P.M. COME STATION WABASH.

Swami Vivekananda.

1900.59 — MRS. HANSBROUGH

To Mrs. Alice (Shanti) Hansbrough:

102 E. 58th Street, New York,
3rd July, 1900.

MY DEAR MRS. HANSBROUGH,

This is to introduce Swami Turiyananda. The lady who gave the piece of land for Vedanta work belongs to Los Angeles. She has taken Turiyananda with her. He is a great spiritual teacher — but has no experience in platform work.

The best thing would be to help him to start a centre for quiet and rest and meditation in the land near San Jose.

With all love to the holy Trinity.

Ever yours in the Lord,
Vivekananda.

1900.60 — SISTER

To Miss Mary Hale:

102 E. 58th Street, New York,
11th July, 1900.

MY DEAR DEVOTED SISTER,

I was glad to get your note as also to learn that you were going to Greenacre. Hope you will have much profit. I have been much censured by everyone for cutting off my long hair. I am sorry. You forced me to do it.

I had been to Detroit and came back yesterday. Trying as soon as possible to go to France, thence to India. Very little news here; the work is closed. I am taking regularly my meals and sleeping—that is all.

Ever faithful and loving brother,
Vivekananda.

PS—Write to the girls to send my mails, if any, at Chicago.

1900.61—TURIYANANDA

To Swami Turiyananda:

102 E. 58th Street, New York,
18th July, 1900.

MY DEAR TURIYANANDA,

Your letter reached me redirected. I stayed in Detroit for three days only. It is frightfully hot here in New York. There was no Indian mail for you last week. I have not heard from Sister Nivedita yet.

Things are going on the same way with us. Nothing particular. Miss Müller cannot come in August. I will not wait for her. I take the next train. Wait till it comes. With love to Miss Boocke,

Yours in the Lord,
Vivekananda.

PS—Kali went away about a week ago to the mountains. He cannot come back till September. I am all alone, and washing; I like it. Have you seen my friends? Give them my love.

1900.62—JOE

To Miss Josephine MacLeod:

102 E. 58th Street, New York,
20th July, 1900.

DEAR JOE,

Possibly before this reaches you I shall be in Europe, London or Paris as the chance of steamer comes.

I have straightened out my business here. The works are at Mr. Whitmarsh's suggestion in the hands of Miss Waldo.

I have to get the passage and sail. Mother knows the rest.

My intimate friend did not materialise yet and writes she will come some time in August, and she is dying to see a Hindu, and her soul is burning for Mother India.

I wrote her I may see her in London. Mother knows again. Mrs. Huntington sends love to Margot and expects to hear from her if she is not too busy with her scientific exhibits.

With all love to "sacred cow" of India, to yourself, to the Leggetts, to Miss (what's her name?), the American rubber plant.

Ever yours in the Lord,
Vivekananda.

1900.63 — JOE

To Miss Josephine MacLeod:

102 E. 58th Street, New York,
24th July, 1900.

DEAR JOE,

The sun = Knowledge. The stormy water = Work. The lotus = Love. The serpent = Yoga. The swan = the Self. The Motto = May the Swan (the Supreme Self) send us that. It is the mind-lake. (This explains the design on the Ramakrishna Math and Mission seal, printed on the title page of this volume — Ed.) How do you like it? May the Swan fill you with all these anyway.

I am to start on Thursday next, by the French steamer La Champagne. The books are in the hands of Waldo and Whitmarsh. They are nearly ready.

I am well, getting better — and all right till I see you next week.

Ever yours in the Lord,
Vivekananda.

1900.64 — ABHEDANANDA

To Swami Abhedananda:

102 E. 58th Street, New York,
24 July, 1900.

DEAR ABHEDANANDA,

I would have gladly remained here, but sastây kisti mât. Got a fine berth — one room all to myself — on a fine vessel. As soon as August comes it will be a terrible Bhida [crowd] as the companies are reducing prices.

Things are going quite all right. Mr. Johnson has returned to their house, and all the rooms are full except two. You write to Mrs. Crane whether you want to get them or not.

You need not feel the least anxiety about the N.Y. work; it will go as a marriage bull next season. Give my love to Mrs. [Mary B.] Coulston and explain to her the circumstances.

With all love,
Vivekananda.

1900.65 — TURIYANANDA

To Swami Turiyananda:

102 E. 58th Street, New York,
25th July, 1900.

DEAR TURIYANANDA,

I received a letter from Mrs. Hansborough telling me of your visit to her. They like you immensely, and I am sure you have found in them genuine, pure, and absolutely unselfish friends.

I am starting for Paris tomorrow. Things all turn that way. Kali is not here. He is rather worried at my going away, but it has got to be.

Address your next letter to me care of Mr. Leggett, 6 Place des États-Unis, Paris, France.

Give my love to Mrs. Wyckoff, Hansborough, and to Helen. Revive the clubs a bit and ask Mrs. Hansborough to collect the dues as they fall and send them to India. Sarada writes they are having rather hot times. My kind regards for Miss Boocke.

With all love,

Ever yours in the Lord,
Vivekananda.

1900.66 — DEAR __ [1]

To a Brahmacharin (Brahmachari Harendra Nath) of the Advaita Ashrama, Mayavati:

New York,
August, 1900.

DEAR __,

I had a letter from you several days ago, but I could not reply earlier. Mr. Sevier speaks well of you in his letter. I am very pleased at this.

Write to me in minute detail who all are there, and what each one is doing. Why don't you write letters to your mother? What is this? Devotion to the mother is the

---

1 Translated from Bengali.

root of all welfare. How is your brother getting on with his studies at Calcutta? The Sannyasin-names of those there escape my memory—how to address each? Give my love to all conjointly. I got the news that Khagen has now fully recovered. This is happy news. Write to me whether the Seviers are attending to your comforts and other details. I am glad to know that Dinu's health is all right. The boy Kali has a tendency to become fat; but this will all surely go away by constantly climbing up and down the hills there. Tell Swarup that I am very much pleased with his conducting of the paper. He is doing splendid work. Give to all others also my love and blessings. Tell everybody that my health is now all right. From here I shall go to England and from there to India very shortly.

With all blessings,
Vivekananda.

France

1900.67 — CHRISTINA

To Sister Christine:

> À bord du Paquebot La Champagne,
> Friday morning, 9 a.m.,
> 3rd August, 1900.

DEAR CHRISTINA,

It is foggy this morning. We are in the channel—expect to reach [Le Havre] at 12 a.m. [noon]. It has been a very bad voyage—rolling and raining and dark nearly all the time. Terrible rolling all through. Only last night I had good sleep. On other occasions the rolling makes me sleep well, but this time I don't know what was the matter; the mind was so whirling. Anyway, I am well and soon to reach land.

Hope to reach Paris this evening.

I send this to Detroit, expecting you there.

> With all love and blessings,
> Vivekananda.

1900.68 — MRS. LEGGETT

To Mrs. Francis Leggett:

[Swami Vivekananda sent the following telegram on Friday, August 3, 1900, when the S.S. Champagne (which he had boarded in New York on July 26) docked at Le Havre, France.]

> [Postmarked: Friday, August 3, 1900]

ARRIVE A HUIT HEURES STLAZARE — VIVEKANANDA

[Translation: "I arrive at eight o'clock (p.m.) St. Lazare — Vivekananda".]

1900.69 — HARI[1]

To Swami Turiyananda:

6, Place des États-Unis, Paris,
13th August, 1900.

DEAR BROTHER HARI,

I got your letter from California. So three persons are getting spiritual trances; well, it is not bad. Even out of that much good will come. Shri Ramakrishna knows! Let things happen as they will. His work He knows, you and I are but servants and nothing else.

I am sending this letter to San Francisco — care of Mrs. C. Panel. Just now I got some news from New York. They are well. Kali is on tour. Write in detail about your health and work in San Francisco. And don't be indifferent to the question of sending money to the Math. See that money goes certainly every month, from Los Angeles and San Francisco.

I am on the whole doing well. I am shortly starting for England. I get news of Sharat. Recently he had an attack of dysentery. The rest are all well. This time few got malaria; nor is it so prevalent on the banks of the Ganga. This year, owing to the scarcity of rain, there is fear of famine in Bengal also.

By the grace of Mother, go on doing work, brother. Mother knows, and you know — but I am off! Now I am going to take a rest.

Yours affectionately,
Vivekananda.

1900.70 — CHRISTINE

To Sister Christine:

6, Place des États-Unis,
14th August, 1900.

DEAR CHRISTINE,

Your letter from New York reached just now. You must have got mine from France, directed to 528 Congress.

Well — it was a dreary, funeral-like time. Just think what it is to a morbid man like me!

I am going to the Exposition, etc., trying to pass time. Had a lecture here. Père Haycinth [Hyacinthe], the celebrated clergy — man here, seems to like me much. Well, well what? Nothing. Only, you are so good, and I am a morbid fool — that is all about it. But "Mother" — She knows best. I have served Her through weal

---

1 Translated from Bengali.

or woe. Thy will be done. Well, I have news of my lost brother [Mahendranath Datta]. He is a great traveller, that is good. So you see, the cloud is lifting slowly. My love to your mother and sister and to Mrs. Funkey [Funke].

With love,
Vivekananda.

1900.71 — JOHN FOX

To Mr. John Fox:

Boulevarrd Hans Swan, Paris,
14th August, 1900.

JOHN FOX, ESQ.,
6 Dr. Wolf Street,
Dorchester, Mass, U.S., America.

Kindly write Mohin (Mahendranath Datta, younger brother of Swamiji.) that he has my blessings in whatever he does. And what he is doing now is surely much better than lawyering, etc. I like boldness and adventure and my race stands in need of that spirit very much. Only as my health is failing and I do not expect to live long, Mohin must see his way to take care of mother and family. I may pass away any moment. I am quite proud of him now.

Yours affectionately,
Vivekananda.

1900.72 — NIVEDITA

To Sister Nivedita:

6, Place des États-Unis, Paris,
23rd August, 1900.

DEAR NIVEDITA,

The manuscript accounts of the Math just reached. It is delightful reading. I am so pleased with it.

I am going to print a thousand or more to be distributed in England, America and India. I will only add a begging paragraph in the end.

What do you think the cost will be?

With love to you and Mrs. Bull,
Vivekananda.

1900.73 — CHRISTINE

To Sister Christine:

6, Place des États-Unis, Paris,
23rd August, 1900.

DEAR CHRISTINE,

What is the matter with you? Are you ill? Unhappy? What makes you silent? I had only one little note from you in all this time.

I am getting a bit nervous about you — not much. Otherwise I am enjoying this city. Did Mrs. A. P. Huntington write you?

I am well — keeping well as far as it is possible with me.

With love,
Vivekananda.

1900.74 — NIVEDITA

6, Place des États-Unis, Paris,
25th Aug., 1900.

DEAR NIVEDITA,

Your letter reached me just now. Many thanks for the kind expressions.

I gave a chance to Mrs. Bull to draw her money out of the Math; and as she did not say anything about it, and the trust deeds were waiting here to be executed, I got them executed duly at the British Consulate; and they are on their way to India now.

Now I am free, as I have kept no power or authority or position for me in the work. I also have resigned the presidentship of the Ramakrishna Mission.

The Math etc., belong now to the immediate disciples of Ramakrishna except myself. The presidentship is now Brahmananda's — next it will fall on Premananda etc., etc., in turn.

I am so glad a whole load is off me, now I am happy. I have served Ramakrishna through mistakes and success for 20 years now. I retire for good and devote the rest of my life to myself.

I no longer represent anybody, nor am I responsible to anybody. As to my friends, I had a morbid sense of obligation. I have thought well and find I owe nothing to anybody; if anything, I have given my best energies, unto death almost, and received only hectoring and mischief-making and botheration. I am done with everyone here and in India.

Your letter indicates that I am jealous of your new friends. You must know once for all, I am born without jealousy, without avarice, without the desire to rule—whatever other vices I am born with.

I never directed you before; now, after I am nobody in the work, I have no direction whatever. I only know this much: So long as you serve "Mother" with a whole heart, She will be your guide.

I never had any jealousy about what friends you made. I never criticised my brethren for mixing up in anything. Only I do believe the Western people have the peculiarity of trying to force upon others whatever seems good to them, forgetting that what is good for you may not be good for others. As such, I am afraid you might try to force upon others whatever turn your mind might take in contact with new friends. That was the only reason I sometimes tried to stop any particular influence, and nothing else.

You are free, have your own choice, your own work…

Friends or foes, they are all instruments in Her hands to help us work out our own Karma, through pleasure or pain. As such "Mother" bless them all.

With all love and blessings,

Yours affectionately,
Vivekananda.

1900.75 — NIVEDITA

Paris,
28th August, 1900.

DEAR NIVEDITA,

Such is life—grind, grind; and yet what else are we to do? Grind, grind! Something will come—some way will be opened. If it does not, as it probably never will—then, then—what then? All our efforts are only to stave off, for a season, the great climax—death! Oh, what would the world do without you, Death! Thou great healer!

The world, as it is, is not real, is not eternal, thank the Lord!! How can the future be any better? That must be an effect of this one—at least like this, if not worse!

Dreams, oh dreams! Dream on! Dream, the magic of dream, is the cause of this life, it is also the remedy. Dream' dream; only dream! Kill dream by dream!

I am trying to learn French, talking to—here. Some are very appreciative already. Talk to all the world—of the eternal riddle, the eternal spool of fate, whose thread-end no one finds and everyone seems to find, at least to his own satisfaction, at least for a time—to fool himself a moment, isn't it?

Well, now great things are to be done! Who cares for great things? Why not do small things as well? One is as good as the other. The greatness of little things, that is what the Gita teaches—bless the old book!!…

I have not had much time to think of the body. So it must be well. Nothing is ever well here. We forget them at times, and that is being well and doing well...

We play our parts here—good or bad. When the dream is finished and we have left the stage, we will have a hearty laugh at all this—of this only I am sure.

Yours etc.,
Vivekananda.

1900.76 — BROTHER HARI[1]

To Swami Turiyananda:

6, Place des États-Unis, Paris,
August, 1900.

DEAR BROTHER HARI,

Now I am staying on the sea-coast of France. The session of the Congress of History of Religions is over. It was not a big affair; some twenty scholars chattered a lot on the origin of the Shâlagrâma and the origin of Jehovah, and similar topics. I also said something on the occasion.

My body and mind are broken down; I need rest badly. In addition, there is not a single person on whom I can depend; on the other hand so long as I live, all will become very selfish depending upon me for everything... Dealing with people entails constant mental uneasiness... I have cut myself off by a will. Now I am writing to say that nobody will have sole power. All will be done in accordance with the view of the majority... If a trust-deed on similar lines can be executed, then I am free... What you are doing is also Guru Maharaj's work. Continue to do it. Now I have done my part. Don't write to me any more about those things; do not even mention the subject. I have no opinions whatever to give on that subject...

Yours affectionately,
Vivekananda.

PS—Convey my love to all.

1900.77 — HARI[2]

To Swami Turiyananda:

6, Place des États-Unis,
Da Forest P.O., Santa Clara Co., Paris, France,
1st September, 1900.

MY DEAR HARI,

I learnt everything from your letter. Earlier I had an inkling of some trouble

---

1 Translated from Bengali.
2 Translated from Bengali.

between the full-fledged Vedantist and the Home of Truth — someone wrote that. Such things do occur; wisdom consists in carrying on the work by cleverly keeping all in good humour.

For some time now I have been living incognito. I shall stay with the French to pick up their language. I am somewhat freed from worries; that is to say, I have signed the trust-deed and other things and sent them to Calcutta. I have not reserved any right or ownership for myself. You now possess everything and will manage all work by the Master's grace.

I have no longer any desire to kill myself by touring. For the present I feel like settling down somewhere and spending my time among books. I have somewhat mastered the French language; but if I stay among the French for a month or two, I shall be able to carry on conversation well. If one can master this language and German sufficiently, one can virtually become well acquainted with European learning. The people of France are mere intellectualists, they run after worldly things and firmly believe God and souls to be superstitious; they are extremely loath to talk on such subjects. This is a truly materialistic country! Let me see what that Lord does. But this country is at the head of Western culture, and Paris is the capital of that culture.

Brother, free me from all work connected with preaching. I am now aloof from all that, you manage it yourselves. It is my firm conviction that Mother will get work done through all of you a hundredfold more than through me.

Many days ago I received a letter from Kali. He must have reached New York by now. Miss Waldo sends news now and then.

I keep sometimes well and sometimes bad. Of late I am again having that massage treatment by Mrs. Milton, who says, "You have already recovered!" This much I see — whatever the flatulence, I feel no difficulty in moving, walking, or even climbing. In the morning I take vigorous exercise, and then have a dip in cold water.

Yesterday I went to see the house of the gentleman with whom I shall stay. He is a poor scholar, has his room filled with books and lives in a flat on the fifth floor. And as there are no lifts in this country as in America, one has to climb up and down. But it is no longer trying to me.

There is a beautiful public park round the house. The gentleman cannot speak English; that is a further reason for my going. I shall have to speak French perforce. It is all Mother's will. She knows best what She wants to have done. She never speaks out, "only keeps mum". But this much I notice that for a month or so I have been having intense meditation and repetition of the Lord's name.

Please convey my love to Miss Boocke, Miss Bell, Mrs. Aspinel, Miss Beckham, Mr. George, Dr. Logan, and other friends and accept it yourself. My love to all in Los Angeles also.

Yours,
Vivekananda.

1900.78 — MOTHER

6, Place des États-Unis, Paris,
3rd Sept., 1900.

DEAR MOTHER, (Mrs. Francis Leggett)

We had a congress of cranks here in this house.

The representatives came from various countries, from India in the south, to Scotland in the north, with England and America buttressing the sides.

We were having great difficulty in electing the president, for though Dr. James (Professor William James) was there, he was more mindful of the blisters raised on him by Mrs. Melton (probably a magnetic healer) than solution of world problems.

I proposed Joe (Josephine MacLeod), but she refused on the ground of non-arrival of her new gown — and went to a corner to watch the scene, from a coign of vantage.

Mrs. (Ole) Bull was ready, but Margot (Sister Nivedita) objected to this meeting being reduced to a comparative philosophy class.

When we were thus in a fix — up sprung a short, square, almost round figure from the corner, and without any ceremony declared that all difficulties will be solved, not only of electing a president but of life itself, if we all took to worshipping the Sun God and Moon God. He delivered his speech in five minutes; but it took his disciple, who was present, fully three quarters of an hour to translate. In the meanwhile, the master began to draw the rugs in your parlour up in a heap, with the intention, as he said, of giving us an ocular demonstration of the power of "Fire God", then and there.

At this juncture Joe interposed and insisted that she did not want a fire sacrifice in her parlour; whereupon the Indian saint looked daggers at Joe, entirely disgusted at the behaviour of one he confidently believed to be a perfect convert to fire worship.

Then Dr. James snatched a minute from nursing his blisters and declared that he would have something very interesting to speak upon Fire God and his brethren, if he were not entirely occupied with the evolution of Meltonian blisters. Moreover his great Master, Herbert Spencer, not having investigated the subject before him, he would stick to golden silence.

"Chutney is the thing", said a voice near the door. We all looked back and saw Margot. "It is Chutney," she said, "Chutney and Kali, that will remove all difficulties of Life, and make it easy for us to swallow all evils, and relish what is good." But she stopped all of a sudden and vehemently asserted that she was not going to speak any further, as she has been obstructed by a certain male animal in the audience in her speech. She was sure one man in the audience had his head turned towards the window and was not paying the attention proper to a lady, and though as to herself she believed in the equality of the sexes, yet she wanted to know the reason of that disgusting man's want of due respect for women. Then one and all declared that they had been giving her the most undivided attention, and all above the equal right, her due, but to no purpose. Margot would have nothing to do with that horrible crowd and sat down.

Then Mrs. Bull of Boston took the floor and began to explain how all the difficulties of the world were from not understanding the true relation between the sexes. She said, "The only panacea was a right understanding of the proper persons, and then to find liberty in love and freedom in liberty and motherhood, brotherhood, fatherhood, Godhood, love in freedom and freedom in love, in the right holding up of the true ideal in sex."

To this the Scotch delegate vehemently objected and said that as the hunter chased the goatherd, the goatherd the shepherd, the shepherd the peasant, and the peasant drove the fisher into the sea, now we wanted to fish out of the deep the fisher and let him fall upon the peasant, the peasant upon the shepherd, and so on; and the web of life will be completed and we will be all happy. He was not allowed to continue his driving businesss long. In a second everyone was on his feet, and we could only hear a confusion of voices — "Sun God and Moon God", "Chutney and Kali," "Freedom holdings up right understanding, sex, motherhood", "Never, the fisherman must go back to the shore", etc. Whereupon Joe declared that she was yearning to be the hunter for the time and chase them all out of the house if they did not stop their nonsense.

Then was peace and calm restored, and I hasten to write you about it.

Yours affectionately,
Vivekananda.

1900.79 — ALBERTA

6, Place des États-Unis, Paris,
10th September, 1900.

DEAR ALBERTA,

I am surely coming this evening and of course will be very glad to meet the princess (probably Princess Demidoff) and her brother. But if it be too late to find my way out here, you will have to find me a place to sleep in the house.

Yours with love and blessings,
Vivekananda.

1900.80 — CHRISTINA

To Sister Christine:

6, Place des États-Unis, Paris,
15th September, 1900.

DEAR CHRISTINA,

Your letter was very reassuring. I am so glad this summer did you good. So you did not get enamoured of New York City.

Well, I am getting enamoured of Paris. I now am living with a M. Jules Bois, a French savant, who has been a student and admirer of my works.

He talks very little English; in consequence, I have to trot out my jargon French and am succeeding well, he says. I can now understand if he will talk slowly.

Day after tomorrow I go to Bretagne [Brittany] where our American friends are enjoying the sea breeze — and the massage.

I go with M. Bois for a short visit; après cet [after that] I don't know where I go. I am getting quite Frenchy, connaissezvous [do you know]? I am also studying grammaire and hard at work. [Sentence torn off] In a few months I hope to be Frenchy, but by that time I will forget it by staying in England.

I am strong, well and content — no morbidity.

Au revoir,
Vivekananda.

1900.81 — TURIYANANDA[1]

To Swami Turiyananda:

6, Place des États-Unis, Paris,
September, 1900.

MY DEAR TURIYANANDA,

Just now I received your letter. Through Mother's will all work will go on; don't be afraid. I shall soon leave for some other place. Perhaps I shall be on a tour of Constantinople and other places for some time. Mother knows what will come next. I have received a letter from Mrs. Wilmot. From this, too, it appears that she is very enthusiastic. Sit firm and free from worries. Everything will be all right. If hearing the Nada etc. does anyone harm, he can get rid of it if he gives up meditation for a time and takes to fish and meat. If the body does not become progressively weak, there is no cause for alarm. Practice should be slow.

I shall leave this place before your reply comes. So do not send the reply to this letter here. I have received all the issues of Sarada's paper, and wrote to him lots a

---

1 Translated from Bengali.

few weeks ago. I have a mind to send more later on. There is no knowing where my next stop will be. This much I can say that I am trying to be free from care.

I received a letter from Kali, too, today. I shall send him a reply tomorrow. The body is somehow rolling on. Work makes it ill, and rest keeps it well — that is all. Mother knows. Nivedita has gone to England. She and Mrs. Bull are collecting funds. She has a mind to run a school at Kishengarh with the girls she had there. Let her do what she can. I do not intervene any more in any matter — that is all.

My love to you. But I have nothing more to advise as regards work.

Yours in service,
Vivekananda.

1900.82 — ALBERTA

Perros Guirec Bertagne,
22nd September, 1900.

To Miss Alberta Sturges on her 23rd birthday:

> The mother's heart, the hero's will,
> The softest flower's sweetest feel;
> The charm and force that ever sway
> The altar fire's flaming play;
> The strength that leads, in love obeys;
> Far-reaching dreams, and patient ways,
> Eternal faith in Self, in all
> The sight Divine in great in small;
> All these, and more than I could see
> Today may "Mother" grant to thee.

Ever yours with love and blessings,
Vivekananda.

DEAR ALBERTA,

This little poem is for your birthday. It is not good, but it has all my love. I am sure, therefore, you will like it.

Will you kindly send a copy each of the pamphlets there to madame Besnard, Clairoix, Bres Compiegne, Oise, and oblige?

Your well-wisher,
Vivekananda.

1900.83 — MADEMOISELLE[1]

6, Place des États-Unis, Paris,
October, 1900.

My Dear Mademoiselle,

I have been very happy and content here. I am having the best of times after many years. I find life here with Mr. Bois very satisfactory—the books, the calm, and the absence of everything that usually troubles me.

But I don't know what kind of destiny is waiting for me now.

My letter is funny, isn't it? But it is my first attempt.

Yours faithfully,
Vivekananda.

1900.84 — SISTER CHRISTINE[2]

To Sister Christine:

6, Place des États-Unis, Paris,
14th October, 1900.

God bless you at each step, my dear Christine, such is my constant prayer!

Your letter, so beautiful and so calm, has given me that fresh energy which I am often losing.

I am happy, yes, I am happy, but the cloud has not left me entirely. It sometimes comes back, unfortunately, but it no longer has the morbidity it used to have.

I am staying with a famous French writer, M. Jules Bois. I am his guest. As he is a man making his living with his pen, he is not rich; but we have many great ideas in common and feel happy together.

He discovered me a few years ago and has already translated some of my pamphlets into French. We shall in the end find what we are looking for, isn't it?

Thus, I shall travel with Madame Calve, Miss MacLeod, and M. Jules Bois. I shall be the guest of Madame Calve, the famous singer. We shall go to Constantinople, the Near East, Greece, and Egypt. On our way back, we shall visit Venice.

It may be that I shall give a few lectures in Paris after my return, but they will be in English with an interpreter. I have no time any more, nor the power to study a new language at my age. I am an old man, isn't it?

Mrs. Funke is ill. I think she works too hard. She already had some nervous trouble. I hope she will soon be well.

I am sending all the money I earned in America to India. Now I am free, the

---

1 Translated from the original in French.
2 Translated from the original in French.

begging-monk as before. I have also resigned from the Presidentship of the Monastery. Thank God, I am free! It is no more for me to carry such a responsibility. I am so nervous and so weak.

"As the birds which have slept in the branches of a tree wake up, singing when the dawn comes, and soar up into the deep blue sky, so is the end of my life."

I have had many difficulties, and also some very great successes. But all my difficulties and suffering count for nothing, as I have succeeded. I have attained my aim. I have found the pearl for which I dived into the ocean of life. I have been rewarded. I am pleased.

Thus it seems to me that a new chapter of my life is opening. It seems to me that Mother will now lead me slowly and softly. No more effort on roads full of obstacles, now it is the bed prepared with birds' down. Do you understand that? Believe me, I feel quite sure.

The experience of all my life, up to now, has taught me, thank God, that I always find what I am looking for with eagerness. Sometimes it is after much suffering, but it does not matter! All is forgotten in the softness of the reward. You are also going through troubles, my friend, but you shall have your reward. Alas! What you now find is not a reward but an additional affliction.

As to myself, I see the cloud lifting, vanishing, the cloud of my bad Karma. And the sun of my good Karma rises — shining, beautiful, and powerful. This will also be the case for you, my friend. My knowledge of this language has not the power to express my emotion. But which language can really do so?

So I drop it, leaving it to your heart to clothe my thought with a soft, loving, and shining language. Good night, gute Nacht!

Your devoted friend,
Vivekananda.

PS — We shall leave Paris for Vienna on October 29th. Mr. Leggett is leaving for the United States by next week. We shall notify the Post Office to forward our letters to our further destinations.

1900.85 — MOTHER

To Mrs. Ole Bull,
66, rue Ampère,
22nd October, 1900.

DEAR MOTHER,

I am sorry to learn you are not well. Hope you will soon be better. Things seem to turn out better for me.

Mr. Maxim of the gun fame is very much interested in me, and he wants to put in his book on China and the Chinese something about my work in America. I have not any documents with me; if you have, kindly give them to him. He will come to see you and talk it over with you. Canon Hawes [Reverend Hugh Reginald Haweis] also keeps track of my work in England. So much about that. It may be that Mother will now work up my original plan of international work. In that case, you will find your work of the Conference has not been in vain.

It seems that after this fall in my health, physical and mental, it is going to open out that way—larger and more international work. Mother knows best.

My whole life has been divided into successive depressions and rises—and so, I believe, is the life of everyone. I am glad, rather than not, these falls come. I understand it all; still, I suffer and grumble and rage!! Perhaps that is a part of the cause of the next upheaval.

I think you will be in America by the time we return; if not, I will see you in London again. Anyhow, adieu for the present. We start day after tomorrow for Egypt etc. And all blessings ever be on you and yours is, as always, my prayer.

Your son,
Vivekananda.

PS—To Margot [Sister Nivedita] my love, and I am sure she will succeed.

India

1900.86 — ALBERTA

To Miss Alberta Sturges:

[Swami Vivekananda sent the following postcard.]

[Constantinople,
November 1, 1900.]

DEAR ALBERTA,

How are you? I am having a grand Turkish time.

Vivekananda.

1900.87 — MARGO

To Sister Nivedita:

[On a picture postcard showing dervishes and local fish merchants, Swami Vivekananda wrote the following note.]

[Postmarked: Constantinople,
November 1, 1900.]

DEAR MARGO [Margot], the blessings of the howling dervishes go with you — Yours in the Lord,

Vivekananda.

PS — All love to Mrs. Bull.

1900.88 — CHRISTINA

To Sister Christine:

[On a postcard, picturing the old decayed fortress walls of Istanbul, Swami Vivekananda wrote the following note.]

[Postmarked: November 1, 1900.]

DEAR CHRISTINA,

I am having a good time here. So I hope you also are having in Detroit —

Vivekananda.

1900.89 — SISTER CHRISTINE

To Sister Christine:

[On a postcard, showing the temple of Hepaistos, popularly called Thesion, Swami Vivekananda wrote.]

[Postmarked: Athens,
November 11, 1900.]

Great fun. I write without the possibility of being written to, as I am changing place all the time. How do you do?

Vivekananda.

1900.90 — JOE

To Miss Josephine MacLeod:

Port Tewfick
26th November, 1900.

DEAR JOE,

The steamer was late; so I am waiting. Thank goodness, it entered the Canal this morning at Port Said. That means it will arrive some time in the evening if everything goes right.

Of course it is like solitary imprisonment these two days, and I am holding my soul in patience.

But they say the change is thrice dear. Mr. Gaze's agent gave me all wrong directions. In the first place, there was nobody here to tell me a thing, not to speak of receiving me. Secondly, I was not told that I had to change my Gaze's ticket for a steamer one at the agent's office, and that was at Suez, not here. It was good one way, therefore, that the steamer was late; so I went to see the agent of the steamer and he told me to exchange Gaze's pass for a regular ticket.

I hope to board the steamer some time tonight. I am well and happy and am enjoying the fun immensely. How is Mademoiselle? Where is Bois? Give my everlasting gratitude and good wishes to Mme. Calve. She is a good lady.

Hoping you will enjoy your trip.

Ever affectionately yours,
Vivekananda.

1900.91 — JOE

The Math, Belur,
11th Dec., 1900.

DEAR JOE,

I arrived night before last. Alas! my hurrying was of no use.

Poor Captain Sevier passed away, a few days ago — thus two great Englishmen gave up their lives for us — us the Hindus. Thus is martyrdom if anything is. Mrs. Sevier I have written to just now, to know her decision.

I am well, things are well here — every way. Excuse this haste. I will write longer ere long.

Ever yours in truth,
Vivekananda.

1900.92 — MOTHER

To Mrs. Ole Bull:

The Math, Belur,
Howrah Dist., Bengal,
15 December, 1900.

MY DEAR MOTHER,

Three days ago I reached here. It was quite unexpected — my visit, and everybody was so surprised.

Things here have gone better than I expected during my absence, only Mr. Sevier has passed away. It was a tremendous blow, sure, and I don't know the future of the work in the Himalayas. I am expecting daily a letter from Mrs. Sevier who is there still.

How are you? Where are you? My affairs here will be straightened out shortly, I hope, and I am trying my best to straighten them out.

The remittance you send my cousin should henceforth be sent to me direct, the bills being drawn in my name. I will cash them and send her the money. It is better the money goes to her through me.

Saradananda and Brahmananda are much better and this year there is very little malaria here. This narrow strip on the banks of the river is always free from malaria. Only when we get a large supply of pure water the conditions will be perfected here.

Vivekananda.

1900.93 — NIVEDITA

The Math, Belur, Howrah,
19th Dec., 1900.

DEAR NIVEDITA,

Just a voice across the continents to say, how do you do? Are you not surprised? Verily I am a bird of passage. Gay and busy Paris, grim old Constantinople, sparkling little Athens, and pyramidal Cairo are left behind, and here I am writing in my room on the Ganga, in the Math. It is so quiet and still! The broad river is dancing in the bright sunshine, only now and then an occasional cargo boat breaking the silence with the splashing of the oars. It is the cold season here, but the middle of the day is warm and bright every day. But it is the winter of Southern California. Everything is green and gold, and the grass is like velvet; yet the air is cold and crisp and delightful.

Yours etc.,
Vivekananda.

1900.94 — JOE

The Math, Belur, Howrah,
26th Dec., 1900.

DEAR JOE,

This mail brought your letter including that of Mother and Alberta. What the learned friend of Alberta says about Russia is about the same I think myself. Only there is one difficulty of thought: Is it possible for the Hindu race to be Russianised?

Dear Mr. Sevier passed away before I could arrive. He was cremated on the banks of the river that flows by his Ashrama, à la Hindu, covered with garlands, the Brahmins carrying the body and boys chanting the Vedas.

The cause has already two martyrs. It makes me love dear old England and its heroic breed. The Mother is watering the plant of future India with the best blood of England. Glory unto Her!

Dear Mrs. Sevier is calm. A letter she wrote me to Paris comes back this mail. I am going up tomorrow to pay her a visit. Lord bless her, dear brave soul!

I am calm and strong. Occasion never found me low yet Mother will not make me now depressed.

It is very pleasant here, now the winter is on. The Himalayas will be still more beautiful with the uncovered snows.

The young man who started from New York, Mr. Johnston, has taken the vow of a Brahmachârin and is at Mayavati.

Send the money to Saradananda in the Math, as I will be away in the hills.

They have worked all right as far as they could; I am glad, and feel myself quite a fool on account of my nervous chagrin.

They are as good and as faithful as ever, and they are in good health. Write all this to Mrs. Bull and tell her she was always right and I was wrong, and I beg a hundred thousand pardons of her.

Oceans of love for her and for M__

I look behind and after

And find that all is right. In my deepest sorrows

There is a soul of light.

All love to M__, Mrs. C__, to Dear J.B.__, and to you, Dear Joe, Pranâms.

Vivekananda.

1900.95 — SHASHI[1]

Math, Belur,
26th December, 1900.

DEAR SHASHI[2],

I got all the news from your letter. If your health is bad, then certainly you should not come here; and also I am going to Mayavati tomorrow. It is absolutely necessary that I should go there once.

If Alasinga comes here, he will have to await my return. I do not know what those here are deciding about Kanai. I shall return shortly from Almora, and then I may be able to visit Madras. From Vaniyambadi I have received a letter. Write to the people there conveying my love and blessings, and tell them that on my way to Madras I shall surely visit them. Give my love to all. Don't work too hard. All is well here.

Yours affectionately,
Vivekananda.

---

1 Translated from Bengali.

2. Swami Ramakrishnananda.

1900.96 — YOUR HIGHNESS

To Maharaja Ajit Singh, the Raja of Khetri:

> The Math, Beloor,
> Howrah Dist.,
> [December, 1900.]

YOUR HIGHNESS,

Very glad to learn that you and the Coomar [the Royal Prince] are enjoying good health. As for me, my heart has become very weak. Change, I do not think, will do me any good, as for the last 14 years I do not remember to have stopped at one place for three months at a stretch. On the other hand, if by some chance I can live for months in one place, I hope it will do me good. I do not mind this, however; I feel that my work in this life is done. Through good and evil, pain and pleasure, my life — boat has been dragged on. The one great lesson I was taught is that life is misery, nothing but misery. Mother knows what is best. Each one of us is in the hands of Karma — it works out itself, and no nay. There is only one element in life which is worth having at any cost — and it is love. Love immense and infinite, broad as the sky and deep as the ocean. This is the one great gain in life. Blessed is he who gets it.

> Ever yours in the Lord,
> Vivekananda.

1901

1901.1 — MOTHER

Prabuddha Bharata Office,
Advaita Ashrama,
Mayavati (Via Almora),
Kumaon, Himalayas,
6th January, 1901.

MY DEAR MOTHER[1],

I send you forthwith a translation of the Nâsadiya Hymn sent by Dr. Bose through you. I have tried to make it as literal as possible.

I hope Dr. Bose has recovered his health perfectly by this time.

Mrs. Sevier is a strong woman, and has borne her loss quietly and bravely. She is coming over to England in April, and I am going over with her.

I ought to come to England as early as I can this summer; and as she must go to attend to her husband's affairs, I accompany her.

This place is very, very beautiful, and they have made it simply exquisite. It is a huge place several acres in area, and is very well kept. I hope Mrs. Sevier will be in a position to keep it up in the future. She wishes it ever so much, of course.

My last letter from Joe informed me that she was going up the... with Mme Calvé.

I am very glad to learn that Margot is leaving her lore for future use. Her book has been very much appreciated here, but the publishers do not seem to make any effort at sale.

The first day's touch of Calcutta brought the asthma back; and every night I used to get a fit during the two weeks I was there. I am, however, very well in the Himalayas.

It is snowing heavily here, and I was caught in a blizzard on the way; but it is not very cold, and all this exposure to the snows for two days on my way here seems to have done me a world of good.

Today I walked over the snow uphill about a mile, seeing Mrs. Sevier's lands; she has made beautiful roads all over. Plenty of gardens, fields, orchards, and large forests, all in her land. The living houses are so simple, so clean, and so pretty, and above all so suited for the purpose.

Are you going to America soon? If not, I hope to see you in London in three months.

Kindly give my best wishes to Miss Olcock and kindly convey my undying love to Miss Müller the next time you see her; so to Sturdy. I have seen my mother, my cousin, and all my people in Calcutta.

Kindly send the remittance you send my cousin to me — in my name so that I

1. Mrs. Ole Bull.

shall cash the cheque and give her the money. Saradananda and Brahmananda and the rest were well in the Math when I last left them.

All here send love.

Ever your loving son,
Vivekananda.

PS — Kali has taken two sacrifices; the cause has already two European martyrs. Now, it is going to rise up splendidly.

My love to Alberta and Mrs. Vaughan. The snow is lying all round six inches deep, the sun is bright and glorious, and now in the middle of the day we are sitting outside, reading. And the snow all about us! The winter here is very mild in spite of the snow. The air is dry and balmy, and the water beyond all praise.

1901.2 — STURDY

Mayavati, Himalayas,
15th January, 1901.

MY DEAR STURDY,

I learn from Saradananda that you have sent over Rs. 1,529-5-5 to the Math, being the money that was in hand for work in England. I am sure it will be rightly used.

Capt. Sevier passed away about three months ago. They have made a fine place here in the mountains and Mrs. Sevier means to keep it up. I am on a visit to her, and I may possibly come over to England with her.

I wrote you a letter from Paris. I am afraid you did not get it.

So sorry to learn the passing away of Mrs. Sturdy. She has been a very good wife and good mother, and it is not ordinarily one meets with such in this life.

This life is full of shocks, but the effects pass away anyhow, that is the hope.

It is not because of your free expression of opinion in your last letter to me that I stopped writing. I only let the wave pass, as is my wont. Letters would only have made a wave of a little bubble.

Kindly tender my regards and love to Mrs. Johnson and other friends if you meet them.

And I am ever yours in the Truth,
Vivekananda.

1901.3 — MOTHER

The Math, Belur, Howrah Dist., Bengal,
26th January, 1901.

MY DEAR MOTHER[1],

Many thanks for your very encouraging words. I needed them very much just now. The gloom has not lifted with the advent of the new century, it is visibly thickening. I went to see Mrs. Sevier at Mayavati. On my way I learnt of the sudden death of the Raja of Khetri. It appears he was restoring some old architectural monument at Agra, at his own expense, and was up some tower on inspection. Part of the tower came down, and he was instantly killed.

The three cheques have arrived. They will reach my cousin when next I see her.

Joe is here, but I have not seen her yet.

The moment I touch Bengal, especially the Math, the asthmatic fits return! The moment I leave, I recover!

I am going to take my mother on pilgrimage next week. It may take months to make the complete round of pilgrimages. This is the one great wish of a Hindu widow. I have brought only misery to my people all my life. I am trying at least to fulfil this one wish of hers.

I am so glad to learn all that about Margot; everybody here is eager to welcome her back.

I hope Dr. Bose has completely recovered by this time.

I had a beautiful letter also from Mrs. Hammond. She is a great soul.

However, I am very calm and self-possessed this time and find everything better than I ever expected.

With all love,

Ever your son,
Vivekananda.

1901.4 — SHASHI

Math, Belur.

MY DEAR SHASHI, (Swami Ramakrishnananda)

I am going with my mother to Rameswaram, that is all. I don't know whether I shall go to Madras at all. If I go, it will be strictly private. My body and mind are completely worked out; I cannot stand a single person. I do not want anybody. I have neither the strength nor the money, nor the will to take up anybody with me. Bhaktas (devotees) of Guru Maharaj or not, it does not matter. It was very foolish of you even to ask such a question. Let me tell you again, I am more dead than

1. Mrs. Ole Bull

alive, and strictly refuse to see anybody. If you cannot manage this, I don't go to Madras. I have to become a bit selfish to save my body.

Let Yogin-Ma and others go their own way. I shall not take up any company in my present state of health.

Yours in love,
Vivekananda.

1901.5 — MOTHER

The Math, Belur, Howrah Dist., Bengal,
2nd February, 1901.

My Dear Mother[1],

Several days ago I received your letter and a cheque for Rs. 150 included. I will tear up this one, as the three previous cheques I have handed over to my cousin.

Joe is here, and I have seen her twice; she is busy visiting. Mrs. Sevier is expected here soon en route to England. I expected to go to England with her, but as it now turns out, I must go on a long pilgrimage with my mother.

My health suffers the moment I touch Bengal; anyhow, I don't much mind it now; I am going on well and so do things about me.

Glad to learn about Margot's success, but, says Joe, it is not financially paying; there is the rub. Mere continuance is of little value, and it is a far cry from London to Calcutta. Well, Mother knows. Everybody is praising Margot's Kali the Mother; but alas! they can't get a book to buy; the booksellers are too indifferent to promote the sale of the book.

That this new century may find you and yours in splendid health and equipment for a yet greater future is and always has been the prayer of your son.

Vivekananda.

1901.6 — JOE

Belur Math, Dist. Howrah,
14th February, 1901.

My Dear Joe, (Miss Josephine MacLeod)

I am ever so glad to hear that Bois is coming to Calcutta. Send him immediately to the Math. I will be here. If possible I will keep him here for a few days and then let him go again to Nepal.

Yours etc.,
Vivekananda.

---

1. Mrs. Ole Bull.

1901.7 — JOE

The Math, Belur,
Howrah, Bengal,
17th February, 1901.

DEAR JOE, (Miss Josephine MacLeod)

Just now received your nice long letter. I am so glad that you met and approve Miss Cornelia Sorabji. I knew her father at Poona, also a younger sister who was in America. Perhaps her mother will remember me as the Sannyasin who used to live with the Thakore Sahib of Limbdi at Poona.

I hope you will go to Baroda and see the Maharani.

I am much better and hope to continue so for some time. I have just now a beautiful letter from Mrs. Sevier in which she writes a whole lot of beautiful things about you.

I am so glad you saw Mr. Tata and find him so strong and good.

I will of course accept an invitation if I am strong enough to go to Bombay.

Do wire the name of the steamer you leave by for Colombo. With all love,

Yours affectionately,
Vivekananda.

1901.8 — MOTHER

To Mrs. Ole Bull (in London):

Dacca,
20 March, 1901.

MY DEAR MOTHER,

At last I am in Eastern Bengal. This is the first time I am here, and never before knew Bengal was so beautiful. You ought to have seen the rivers here — regular rolling oceans of fresh water, and everything so green — continual production. The villages are the cleanest and prettiest in all India.

Joe [Miss Josephine MacLeod] is perhaps by this time in Japan. I received a long and beautiful letter from Margot. Tell Margot that there has been of late a regular fall of fortune on the Kashmir Raja; things are all changing to his benefit. Mr. Mookherjey is now Governor of Kashmir. Saradananda had a bad fever. He is well now, but weak. He possibly goes to Darjeeling for a change. Mrs. [M. N.] Banerjey, who is at Calcutta, is very anxious to take him to the hills. Mohin [Mahendranath Datta], my brother, is in India, in Karachi near Bombay, and he corresponds with Saradananda. He writes to say he is going to Burma, China, etc. The traders who lure him have shops in all those places. I am not at all anxious about him. He is a very selfish man.

I have no news from Detroit. I received one letter from Christina nine months ago, but I did not reply. Perhaps that may have vexed her.

I am peaceful and calm — and am finding every day the old begging and trudging life is the best for me after all.

Mrs. Sevier I left at Belur. She is the guest of Mrs. Banerjey, who has rented Nilambar Mookherjey's house on the river (the old Math). She goes very soon to Europe.

Things are going on, as is in the nature of things. To me has come resignation.

With all love,

Ever your Son,
Vivekananda.

PS — All blessings on Margot's work. Mother is leading, I am sure.

1901.9 — MOTHER

Dacca,
29th March, 1901.

MY DEAR MOTHER[1],

By this time you must have received my other note from Dacca. Saradananda has been suffering badly from fever in Calcutta, which has become simply a hell of demons this year. He has recovered and is now in the Math which, thank God, is one of the healthiest places in our Bengal.

I do not know what conversation took place between you and my mother; I was not present. I suppose it was only an eager desire on her part to see Margot, nothing else.

My advice to Margot would be to mature her plans in England and work them out a good length before she comes back. Good solid work must wait.

Saradananda expects to go to Darjeeling to Mrs. Banerji, who has been in Calcutta for a few days, as soon as he is strong enough.

I have no news yet of Joe from Japan. Mrs. Sevier expects to sail soon. My mother, aunt, and cousin came over five days ago to Dacca, as there was a great sacred bath in the Brahmaputra river. Whenever a particular conjunction of planets takes place, which is very rare, a huge concourse of people gather on the river on a particular spot. This year there has been more than a hundred thousand people; for miles the river was covered with boats.

The river, though nearly a mile broad at the place, was one mass of mud! But it was firm enough, so we had our bath and Pujâ (worship), and all that.

I am rather enjoying Dacca. I am going to take my mother and the other ladies

---

1 Mrs. Ole Bull..

to Chandranath, a holy place at the easternmost corner of Bengal.

I am rather well and hope you and your daughter and Margot are also enjoying splendid health.

With everlasting love,

Ever your son,
Vivekananda.

PS — My cousin and mother send you and Margot their love. PS. I do not know the date.

1901.10 — SIR

To Ramesh Chandra Dutta:

The Math, P.o. Belur, Dist. Howrah, Bengal,
4 April, 1901.

DEAR SIR,

I am so very glad to learn from a person of your authority of the good work Sister Nivedita is doing in England. I join in earnest prayer with the hopes you entertain of her future services to India by her pen.

I have not the least desire that she should leave her present field of utility and come over to India.

I am under a deep debt of gratitude to you, Sir, for your befriending my child, and hope you will never cease to advise her as to the length of her stay in England and the line of work she ought to undertake.

Her book on Kâli has been very popular in India. The debt our Motherland already owes you is immense, and we are anxiously awaiting the new book of yours.

May all blessings ever attend you and yours is the constant prayer of—

Yours humbly,
Vivekananda.

1901.11 — MARGOT

To Sister Nivedita:

The Math, Belur, Howrah District, Bengal,
4 April, 1901.

DEAR MARGOT,

A letter came just now from Mr. R. Dutt [Ramesh Dutta] praising you and your work in England very much and asking me to wish you to stop longer in England.

It requires no imagination to learn that I am overjoyed at all the news about you Mr. Dutt so kindly sends.

Of course, you stay as long as you think you are working well. Yum [Miss Josephine MacLeod] had some talk about you with Mother [Holy Mother, Sarada Devi], and she desired you to come over. Of course, it was only her love and anxiety to see you — that was all; but poor Yum has been much too serious for once, and hence all these letters. However, I am glad it should happen, as I learnt so much about your work from Mr. Dutt, who can't be accused of a relative's blind love.

I have written to Mrs. Bull already about this matter. I am now at last in Dacca and had some lectures here. I depart for Chandranath tomorrow, near Chittagong, the farthest eastern extremity of Bengal. My Mother, aunt, cousin, another cousin's widow, and nine boys are with me. They all send you love.

I had just now a few lines from Mrs. Bull, also a letter from Mr. Sturdy. As it would be almost impossible for me to write for some days now, I ask you to thank Mrs. Bull for me for her letter, and tell her kindly that I have just now a long letter from Miss [Christina] Greenstidel of Detroit. She mentions a beautiful letter from Mrs. Bull. Sturdy writes about the publication of any further edition of Raja-Yoga by Longmans. I leave that consideration with Mrs. Bull. She may talk over the matter with Sturdy and do what she thinks proper.

Please give Sturdy my best love, and tell him I am on the march and will take time to reply to his letter; in the meanwhile the business will be looked after by Mrs. Bull.

With everlasting love and blessings,
Vivekananda.

1901.12 — CHRISTINE

To Sister Christine:

The Math, Belur, Howrah Dist., Bengal,
[April 4, 1901]

DEAR CHRISTINE,

The subsequent proceedings have been so much interesting; and the interest has been growing so rapidly of late, that one could scarcely utter a word.

I am glad to learn of Mrs. [Ole] Bull's sweet letter to you; she is an angel. You are peaceful and happy — good. I am growing towards it too.

I am en route to Chandranath on pilgrimage.

I have been anxiously awaiting a letter from you, and it seemed it would never come.

I am sure to be happy — can't help thinking so. After so much struggle, the result must come. Things take their own course; it is I who am to brighten up, I find.

And I am trying my best. And you can help me by writing nice letters now and then; will you?

Margot [Sister Nivedita] is doing splendid work in England with Mrs. Bull's backing. Things are going on nicely.

I am sleeping better and the general health is not bad.

With everlasting love and blessings,
Vivekananda.

PS — Please enquire of Miss [Sarah Ellen] Waldo about the publication of Karma and Jnâna Yogas and write.

1901.13 — INTRODUCTION

Letter of Introduction:

Gauhati,
April 17, 1901.

I have great pleasure in certifying the great amiability and helpfulness of the brothers Shivakanta and Lakshmikanta, Pandas of Shri Kamakhya Peetham.

They are men who help most and are satisfied with the least.

I can unhesitatingly recommend them to the Hindu public visiting this most holy shrine.

Swami Vivekananda.

1901.14 — CHRISTINE

To Sister Christine:

The Math, Belur, Howrah Dist., Bengal,
13th May, 1901.

DEAR CHRISTINE,

I arrived in the Math yesterday. This morning came your short note. You must have got my letters by this time, and [I] hope this will give you a taste of how sometimes silence is gold.

I have beautiful letters from everywhere this morning and am quite happy. I paid a long visit of two months to Assam and different parts of eastern Bengal. For combined mountain and water scenery, this part of the country is unrivalled.

Either I am to go to Europe this summer, and thence to the U.S., or you come over to India — things are all getting ready to that end. Mother knows Her ways. For one thing, I am calm, very calm, and hope to keep a hold on this state for a long time; and you are my best help to keep this poise, are you not? I will write more in my next; just now these few lines — and a hundred pardons I beg for their scantiness. Yet silence tells more sometimes than all the speech in the world.

With all love and blessings,

Ever yours in the Lord,
Vivekananda.

1901.15 — MOTHER

To Mrs. Ole Bull:

The Math, Belur,
13 May, 1901.

DEAR MOTHER,

I reached Calcutta yesterday. This morning arrived your letter containing three cheques for my cousin. They shall reach her regularly.

I have not had any letter from Joe [Miss Josephine MacLeod] from Japan, but several I find awaiting me from on board steamer. She also sends me a newspaper cutting to be sent to Professor Geddes. I enclose it in this letter and expect you to direct it to Prof. Geddes.

Saradananda has been three weeks in Darjeeling, where he has improved greatly. I wish he will remain some time longer there. Mr. Bannerjy is the kindest of hosts.

Mrs. Sevier is in London at 2, Maisemore Mansions, Canfield Gardens, London, N.W.

You are right: my experiences are bringing about calmness — great calmness.

Mrs. Patterson and children are off to Europe. General [C. B. Patterson] is alone and very desirous that I would call. I will the next time I go to town.

My cousin and mother and the rest send love, and my eternal love you know always.

Ever your son,
Vivekananda.

PS — All love and blessings for Margot [Sister Nivedita].

1901.16 — SWARUP

The Math,
15th May, 1901.

MY DEAR SWARUP, (Ânanda)

Your letter from Naini Tal is quite exciting. I have just returned from my tour through East Bengal and Assam. As usual I am quite tired and broken down.

If some real good comes out of a visit to H. H. of Baroda I am ready to come over, otherwise I don't want to undergo the expense and exertion of the long journey Think it well over and make inquiries, and write me if you still think it would be best for the Cause for me to come to see H. H...

Yours with love and blessings,
Vivekananda.

1901.17 — MARY

The Math, Belur, Howrah Dist.,
Bengal, India, 18th May, 1901.

MY DEAR MARY[1],

Sometimes it is hard work to be tied to the shoestrings of a great name. And that was just what happened to my letter. You wrote on the 22nd January, 1901. You tied me to the latchet of a great name, Miss MacLeod. Consequently the letter has been following her up and down the world. Now it reached me yesterday from Japan, where Miss MacLeod is at present. Well, this, therefore, is the solution of the sphinx's riddle. "Thou shalt not join a great name with a small one."

So, Mary, you have been enjoying Florence and Italy, and I do not know where you be by this time. So, fat old "laidy", I throw this letter to the mercy of Monroe & Co., 7 rue Scribe.

Now, old "laidy"—so you have been dreaming away in Florence and the Italian lakes. Good; your poet objects to its being empty though.

Well, devoted sister, how about myself? I came to India last fall, suffered all through winter, and went this summer touring through Eastern Bengal and Assam—through a land of giant rivers and hills and malaria—and after hard work of two months had a collapse, and am now back to Calcutta slowly recovering from the effects of it.

The Raja of Khetri died from a fall a few months ago. So you see things are all gloomy with me just now, and my own health is wretched. Yet I am sure to bob up soon and am waiting for the next turn.

I wish I were in Europe, just to have a long chat with you, and then return as quick to India; for, after all, I feel a sort of quiet nowadays, and have done with three-fourths of my restlessness.

My love to Harriet Woolley, to Isabel, to Harriet McKindley; and to mother my eternal love and gratitude. Tell mother, the subtle Hindu's gratitude runs through generations.

Ever yours in the Lord,
Vivekananda.

PS—Write a line when you feel like it.

1. Miss Mary Hale.

1901.18 — SHASHI[1]

Math, Belur, Dist., Howrah,
3rd June, 1901.

MY DEAR SHASHI[2],

Reading your letter I felt like laughing, and also rather sorry. The cause of the laughter is that you had a dream through indigestion and made yourself miserable, taking it to be real. The cause of my sorrow is that it is clear from this that your health is not good, and that your nerves require rest very badly.

Never have I laid a curse on you, and why should I do so now? All your life you have known my love for you, and today are you doubting it? True, my temper was ever bad, and nowadays owing to illness it occasionally becomes terrible — but know this for certain that my love can never cease.

My health nowadays is becoming a little better. Have the rains started in Madras? When the rains begin a little in the South, I may go to Madras via Bombay and Poona. With the onset of the rains the terrible heat of the South will perhaps subside.

My great love to you and all others. Yesterday Sharat returned to the Math from Darjeeling — his health is much better than it was before. I have come here after a tour of East Bengal and Assam. All work has its ups and downs, its periods of intensity and slackness. Again it will rise up. What fear?...

Whatever that may be, I say that you stop your work for some time and come straight back to the Math. After you have taken a month's rest here, you and I together will make a grand tour via Gujarat, Bombay, Poona, Hyderabad, Mysore to Madras. Would not that be grand? If you cannot do this, stop your lectures in Madras for a month. Take a little good food and sleep well. Within two or three months I shall go there. In any case, reply immediately as to what you decide to do.

Yours with blessings,
Vivekananda.

1901.19 — MRS. HANSBROUGH

To Mrs. Alice (Shanti) Hansbrough:

The Math, Howrah Dist., Bengal,
3rd June, 1901.

DEAR MRS. HANSBROUGH,

The contribution of six pounds and three shillings to the Math by the Los Angeles club has duly reached. Swami Brahmananda will write to you a separate ac-

1 Translated from Bengali.
2. Swami Ramakrishnananda

knowledgement. But as I happen to be here just now and have not had long any direct communication with you, I feel like having a chat with you as of yore, even though it be through the post. Now how are you and the Baby and the holy Trinity and the oldest who brings up the rear?

How are all our Los Angeles friends? Poor Mrs. [Emeline F.] Bowler, I hear, has passed away. She was an angel. Where is Miss Strickney? Please tender her my sincerest love, gratitude and prayers when you meet her next.

How are all the San Francisco friends? How is our Madam (Mrs. Benjamin Aspinall.)—the noble, the unselfish? What is she doing now? Quietly gone back to her Home of Truth work?

Are you pleased with Turiyananda and his work? Is the [Shanti] Ashrama progressing?

With everlasting love and blessings,

Ever yours in the Lord,
Vivekananda.

1901.20—JOE

The Math, Belur, Howrah Dist.,
14th June, 1901.

DEAR JOE[3],

I am so glad you are enjoying Japan—especially Japanese art. You are perfectly correct in saying that we will have to learn many things from Japan. The help that Japan will give us will be with great sympathy and respect, whereas that from the West unsympathetic and destructive. Certainly it is very desirable to establish a connection between India and Japan.

As for me, I was thrown *hors de combat* in Assam. The climate of the Math is just reviving me a bit. At Shillong—the hill sanatorium of Assam—I had fever, asthma, increase of albumen, and my body swelled to almost twice ills normal size. These symptoms subsided, however, as soon as I reached the Math. It is dreadfully hot this year; but a bit of rain has commenced, and I hope we will soon have the monsoon in full force. I have no plans just now, except that the Bombay Presidency wants me so badly that I think of going there soon. We are thinking of starting touring through Bombay in a week or so.

The 300 dollars you speak of sent by Lady Betty have not reached me yet, nor have I any intimation of its arrival from General Patterson.

He, poor man, was rather miserable, after his wife and children sailed for Europe and asked me to come and see him, but unfortunately I was so ill, and am so afraid of going into the City that I must wait till the rains have set in.

Now, Joe dear, if I am to go to Japan, this time it is necessary that I take Sara-

3. Miss Josephine MacLeod.

dananda with me to carry on the work. Also I must have the promised letter to Li Huang Chang from Mr. Maxim; but Mother knows the rest. I am still undecided.

So you went to Alanquinan to see the foreteller? Did he convince you of his powers? What did he say? Write particular *s'il vous plait*.

Jules Bois went as far as Lahore, being prevented from entering Nepal. I learn from the papers that he could not bear the heat and fell ill; then he took ship et *bon voyage*. He did not write me a single line since we met in the Math. You also are determined to drag Mrs. Bull down to Japan from Norway all the way — *bien, Mademoiselle, vous êtes use puissante magicienne, sans doute*.[1] Well, Joe, keep health and spirits up; the Alanquinan man's words come out true most of them; and *gloire et honneur* await you — and Mukti. The natural ambition of woman is through marriage to climb up, leaning upon a man; but those days are gone. You shall be great without the help of any man, just as you are, plain, dear Joe — our Joe, everlasting Joe...

We have seen enough of this life to care for any of its bubbles have we not Joe? For months I have been practicing to drive away all sentiments; therefore I stop here, and good-bye just now. It is ordained by Mother we work together; it has been already for the good of many; it shall be for the good of many more; so let it be. It is useless planning, useless high flights; Mother will find Her own way;... rest assured.

Ever yours with love and heart's blessings,
Vivekananda.

PS — Just now came a cheque for Rs. 300 from Mr. Okakura, and the invitation. It is very tempting, but Mother knows all the same.

1901.21 — FRIEND

To Mr. Okakura Kakuzo:

The Math, Belur, Howrah Dis., Bengal,
18th June, 1901.

DEAR FRIEND,

Allow me to call you a friend. We must have been such in some past birth. Your cheque for 300 rupees duly reached and many thanks for the same.

I am just thinking of going to Japan, but with one thing or another and my precarious health, I cannot expedite matters as I wish.

Japan to me is a dream — so beautiful that it haunts one all his life.

With all love and blessings,
Vivekananda.

Kakudzo [Kakuzo] Okakura Esq., Tokyo, Japan.

1. Well, Miss, you are undoubtedly a powerful magician.

1901.22 — JOE

The Math, Belur,
18th June, 1901.

DEAR JOE, (Miss Josephine MacLeod)

I enclose with yours an acknowledgement of Mr. Okakura's money—of course I am up to all your tricks.

However, I am really trying to come, but you know—one month to go—one to come—and a few days' stay! Never mind, I am trying my best. Only my terribly poor health, some legal affairs, etc., etc., may make a little delay.

With everlasting love,
Vivekananda.

1901.23 — JOE

The Math, Belur, Howrah, Bengal,
1901.

DEAR JOE, (Miss Josephine MacLeod)

I can't even in imagination pay the immense debt of gratitude I owe you. Wherever you are you never forget my welfare; and, there, you are the only one that bears all my burdens, all my brutal outbursts.

Your Japanese friend has been very kind, but my health is so poor that I am rather afraid I have not much time to spare for Japan. I will drag myself through the Bombay Presidency even if only to say, "How do you do?" to all kind friends.

Then two months will be consumed in coming and going, and only one month to stay; that is not much of a chance for work, is it?

So kindly pay the money your Japanese friend has sent for my passage. I shall give it back to you when you come to India in November.

I have had a terrible collapse in Assam from which I am slowly recovering. The Bombay people have waited and waited till they are sick—must see them this time.

If in spite of all this you wish me to come, I shall start the minute you write.

I had a letter from Mrs. Leggett from London asking whether the £300 have reached me safe. They have, and I had written a week or so before to her the acknowledgment, C/o Monroe & Co., Paris, as per her previous instructions.

Her last letter came to me with the envelope ripped up in a most barefaced manner! The post offices in India don't even try to do the opening of my mail decently.

Ever yours with love,
Vivekananda.

1901.24 — CHRISTINA

To Sister Christine:

The Math, Belur, Dist. Howrah, Bengal,
[End of June 1901]

DEAR CHRISTINA,

Your very welcome letter just reached. A few days ago a precious little bit of poem also reached. I wish it ever so much you were the writer thereof. Anyhow, most of us feel, though unable to express; and then, "There are thoughts that lie too deep for tears". Regularity in anything is not in my line of life, but that need not make you irregular. I pray you to drop a few lines every now and then. Of course, when I am not in this body, I am sure the news will reach you, and then you will have to stop writing.

Miss MacLeod wishes me to join her in Japan, but I am not sure. Most probably I am not going, especially as I expect both her and Mrs. Ole Bull in India, in November. Two whole months consumed in coming and going; only one month's stay in Japan — that does not pay, I am afraid.

Say, I am getting enormously fat about the middle — alas!

Mrs. [Charlotte] Sevier, who is now in England, returns in a few months to India. She has invited Mrs. Bull etc. to be her guests in the Himalayas. I wish they could be there during summer.

I have manfully borne the terrific heat of my country in the plains, and now I am facing the deluging rains of my country. Do you know how I am taking rest? I have got a few goats and sheep and cows and dogs and cranes! And I am taking care of them the whole day! It is not trying to be happy; what for? Why should one not be unhappy as well — both being nonsense? — but just to kill time.

Do you correspond with Mrs. Bull or Nivedita?

Don't worry, don't be anxious; for me the "Mother" is my protection and refuge; and everything must come round soon, better than my fondest dreams can paint.

With all love,
Vivekananda.

1901.25 — MARY

The Math,
5th July, 1901.

My Dear Mary[1],

I am very thankful for your very long and nice letter, especially as I needed just such a one to cheer me up a bit. My health has been and is very bad. I recover for

1. Miss Mary Hale.

a few days only; then comes the inevitable collapse. Well, this is the nature of the disease anyway.

I have been touring of late in Eastern Bengal and Assam. Assam is, next to Kashmir, the most beautiful country in India, but very unhealthy. The huge Brahmaputra winding in and out of mountains and hills, studded with islands, is of course worth one's while to see.

My country is, as you know, the land of waters. But never did I realise before what that meant. The rivers of East Bengal are oceans of rolling fresh water, not rivers, and so long that steamers work on them for weeks. Miss MacLeod is in Japan. She is of course charmed with the country and asked me to come over, but my health not permitting such a long voyage, I desisted. I have seen Japan before.

So you are enjoying Venice. The old man must be delicious; only Venice was the home of old Shylock, was it not?

Sam is with you this year—I am so glad! He must be enjoying the good things of Europe after his dreary experience in the North. I have not made any interesting friends of late, and the old ones that you knew of, have nearly all passed away, even the Raja of Khetri. He died of a fall from a high tower at Secundra, the tomb of Emperor Akbar. He was repairing this old grand piece of architecture at his own expense at Agra, and one day while on inspection, he missed his footing, and it was a sheer fall of several hundred feet. Thus we sometimes come to grief on account of our zeal for antiquity. Take care, Mary, don't be too zealous for your piece of Indian antiquity.

In the Mission Seal, the snake represents mysticism; the sun knowledge; the worked up waters activity; the lotus love; the swan the soul in the midst of all.

With love to Sam and to mother,

Ever with love,
Vivekananda.

PS—My letter had to be short; I am out of sorts all the time; it is the body!

1901.26 — CHRISTINE

The Math, Belur,
6th July, 1901.

DEAR CHRISTINE,

Things come to me by fits—today I am in a fit of writing. The first thing to do is, therefore, to pen a few lines to you. I am known to be nervous, I worry much; but it seems, dear Christine, you are not far behind in that trick. One of our poets says, "Even the mountains will fly, the fire will be cold, yet the heart of the great will never change." I am small, very, but I know you are great, and my faith is always in your true heart. I worry about everything except you. I have dedicated you to the Mother. She is your shield, your guide. No harm can reach you — nothing hold you down a minute. I know it.

Ever yours in the Lord,
Vivekananda.

1901.27 — CHRISTINE

To Sister Christine:

The Math, Belur, Dist. Howrah, Bengal,
6th August, 1901.

Letters are sometimes, dear Christina, like mercy — good to the one that sends and the other that receives.

I am so happy that you are calm and resigned as ever. You are ever that. "Mother knows", indeed; only I know that "Mother" not only knows, but does — and is going to do something very fine for me in the near future. What do you think will be very good for me on earth? Silver? Gold? Pooh! I have got something infinitely better; but a little gold will not be amiss to keep my jewel in proper surroundings, and it is coming, don't you think so?

I am a man who frets much, but waits all the same; and the apple comes to my mouth by itself. So, it is coming, coming, coming.

Now, how are you? Growing ever thinner, thinner, thinner, eh? Do have a very good appetite and good sleep in anticipation of the coming good time — to be in trim for welcoming its advent.

How did the heat feel this year? We read all sorts of horrible stories about American heat waves. You have beaten the world's records, even in heat — that's Yankee push, surely.

Well, you are right as about taste: I renounce the yellow of gold and the white of silver, but stick to amber always — that is to my taste.

Amber and corals I always hated; but of late I am awakening to their beauty. One learns as he lives, is it not?

I am going to Darjeeling tomorrow for a few days and will write to you from there. Now gute Nacht [good night] and au revoir [good-bye] for the present.

Ever yours truly,
Vivekananda.

1901.28 — CHRISTINE

To Sister Christine:

The Math, Belur, Dist. Howrah, Bengal,
27th August, 1901.

DEAR CHRISTINE,

I am expecting a long, long letter from you; and, like all expectations of mine, [it] will not be realized, I fear.

Well, I need not bother you with the usual string of questions: How are you? What are you doing all this summer? etc. I am sure the Mother will [do] so much as to keep you in good health at least.

Now, Christina, for many reasons this letter happens to be short, very. It is written with the special purpose that as soon as you get this, send me your latest photograph.

Did you write to Miss [Sarah Ellen] Waldo about the publication of the books? I get no news and, what is more important, no money (that is between you and me) from the sale.

Did you have any news of Margot [Sister Nivedita], of Mrs. [Ole] Bull etc.? And are you happy? I sometimes feel I am, other times it is clouded. Well, it is all the body, after all — material. Goodbye.

Yours with love and blessings,
Vivekananda.

PS — Do send the photo as soon as possible.

1901.29 — MARY

The Math, Belur, Howrah Dist., Bengal,
27th August, 1901.

MY DEAR MARY[1],

I would that my health were what you expected — at least to write you a long letter. It is getting worse, in fact, every day, and so many complications and botherations without that. I have ceased to notice it at all.

I wish you all joy in your lovely Swiss chalet — splendid health, good appetite, and a light study of Swiss or other antiquities just to liven things up a bit. I am so glad you are breathing the free air of the mountains, but sorry that Sam is not in the best of health. Well, there is no anxiety about it, he has naturally such a fine physique...

"Women's moods and man's luck — the gods themselves do not know, what to

1. Miss Mary Hale.

speak of man?" My instincts may be very feminine, but what I am exercised with just this moment is, that you get a little bit of manliness about you. Oh! Mary, your brain, health, beauty, everything is going to waste just for lack of that one essential—assertion of individuality. Your haughtiness, spirit, etc. are all nonsense, only mockery; you are at best a boarding-school girl, no backbone! no backbone!

Alas! this lifelong leading-string business! This is very harsh, very brutal; but I can't help it. I love you, Mary, sincerely, genuinely; I can't cheat you with namby-pamby sugar candies. Nor do they ever come to me.

Then again, I am a dying man; I have no time to fool in. Wake up, girl. I expect now from you letters of the right slashing order; give it right straight; I need a good deal of rousing.

I did not hear anything of the MacVeaghs when they were here. I have not had any direct message from Mrs. Bull or Niveditâ, but I hear regularly from Mrs. Sevier, and they are all in Norway as guests of Mrs. Bull.

I don't know when Nivedita comes to India or if she ever comes back.

I am in a sense a retired man; I don't keep much note of what is going on about the Movement; then the Movement is getting bigger, and it is impossible for one man to know all about it minutely.

I now do nothing, except trying to eat and sleep and nurse my body the rest of the time. Good-bye, dear Mary; hope we shall meet again somewhere in this life, but, meeting or no meeting, I remain,

Ever your loving brother,
Vivekananda.

1901.30—BLESSED AND BELOVED

The Math, Belur, Howrah,
29th August, 1901.

BLESSED AND BELOVED[1],

I am getting better, though still very weak... The present disturbance is simply nervous. Anyhow I am getting better every day.

I am so much beholden to mother[2] for her kind proposal, only I am told by everybody in the Math that Nilambar Babu's place and the whole of the village of Belur at that becomes very malarious this month and the next. Then the rent is so extravagant. I would therefore advise mother to take a little house in Calcutta if she decides to come. I may in all probability go and live there, as it is not good for me to catch malaria over and above the present prostration. I have not asked the opinion of Saradananda or Brahmananda yet. Both are in Calcutta. Calcutta is healthier these two months and very much less expensive.

1. Shri M. N. Banerji.
2. Holy Mother—Shri Sarada Devi.

After all, let her do as she is guided by the Lord. We can only suggest and may be entirely wrong.

If she selects Nilambar's house for residence, do first arrange the rent etc. beforehand. "Mother" knows best. That is all I know too.

With all love and blessings,

Ever yours in the Lord,
Vivekananda.

1901.31 — CHRISTINE

To Sister Christine:

The Math, Belur, Dist. Howrah, Bengal,
2nd September, 1901.

MY DEAR CHRISTINE,

I have been looking at one of your old photos — the only one you sent four or five years ago; and then I remember how changed and reduced you looked last summer; and it came to me that you must be awfully thin now, as it seems very hard for you to get rid of anxieties. This is simply foolish. Things will, of course, take their shape. We only make ourselves miserable by moping. It is very hard to manipulate one's philosophy to contribute to one's daily need. So it is with you, as with me. But it is easiest to take the teacher's chair and read a lecture. And that has been my life's business!! Indeed, that is the reason why there are more disciples up to the mark than teachers. The upshot of all this is that you must create a huge appetite, then gorge, then sleep and grow fat, fat, fat. Plump is the English word, is it not?

As for me, I am very happy. Of course, Bengal brings the asthma now and then, but it is getting tame, and the terrible things — Bright's disease and diabetes — have disappeared altogether. Life in any dry climate will stop the asthma completely, I am sure. I get reduced, of course, during a fit, but then it takes me no time to lay on a few layers of fat. I have a lot of cows, goats, a few sheep, dogs, geese, ducks, one tame gazelle, and very soon I am going to have some milk buffaloes. These are not your American bison, but huge things — hairless, half-aquatic in habits, and [that] give an enormous quantity of very rich milk.

Within the last few months, I got two fits [of asthma] by going to two of the dampest hill stations in Bengal — Shillong and Darjeeling. I am not going to try the Bengalee mountains any more.

Mrs. Bull and Nivedita are in Norway. I don't know when they [will] come over to India. Miss MacLeod is in Japan. I have not heard from her [for] a long while. They all are expected here in November, and will have a "hot time in this old town" etc. I pray you can come, and the Mother will open the door for it. I cannot but say my prayers mostly have been heard, up to date.

Well now, Christina, send me one of your latest photos next mail, will you? I want to see how much of fat you have accumulated in one year.

Anyhow, I will have to go to America with Mrs. Bull, I am sure. [Excision] By the by, excusez-moi, our Calcutta is never so hot as your Detroit or New York, with its added advantage — we are not required by our society to wear many things. The old Greeks used to think that wearing too many clothes and [feeling] shame to show any part of the body a peculiarity of barbarians! So the Hindus think, down to the present day. We are the most scantily clothed people in the whole world. Bless the Lord! How one would live otherwise in our climate!

3rd September —

I left the letter unfinished last night. The foreign English mail starts day after tomorrow. So begin again. The moon is not up yet, but there is a sunless glow upon the river. Our mighty Ganges (She is indeed mighty now, during the rains) is splashing against the walls of the house. Numerous tiny boats are flitting up and down in the dark; they have come to fish for our shads, which come up the river this season.

How I wish you were here to taste our shads — one of the most delicate fish in the world. It is raining outside — pouring. But the moment this downpour ceases, I rain through every pore — it is so hot yet. My whole body is covered by big patches of prickly heat. Thank goodness there are no ladies about! If I had to cover myself in this state of things, I surely would go crazy.

I have also my theme, but I am not despondent. I am sure very soon to pan it out into a beautiful ecstasy [excision]. I am half crazy by nature; then my overtaxed nerves make me outrageous now and then. As a result I don't find anybody who would patiently bear with me! I am trying my best to make myself gentle as a lamb. I hope I shall succeed in some birth. You are so gentle. Sometimes I did frighten you very much, did I not, Christina? I wish I were as gentle as you are. Mother knows which is best.

I would not take any supper tonight, as I ate rather heartily of the aforesaid shad! Then I have to think, think, think on my theme; and some subjects I think best in bed because the whole is made clear to me in dream. Therefore, I am going to bed, and gute Nacht, bonsoir, etc., etc. No, no, it is now about 10 a.m. in Detroit. Therefore, a very happy day to you. May all good realities reach you today while I am expecting dreams.

Ever yours with love and blessings,
Vivekananda.

1901.32 — NIVEDITA

The Math, Belur,
7th Sept., 1901.

DEAR NIVEDITA,

We all work by bits, that is to say, in this cause. I try to keep down the spring, but something or other happens, and the spring goes whirr, and there you are — thinking, remembering, scribbling, scrawling, and all that!

Well, about the rains — they have come down now in right earnest, and it is a deluge, pouring, pouring, pouring night and day. The river is rising, flooding the banks; the ponds and tanks have overflowed. I have just now returned from lending a hand in cutting a deep drain to take off the water from the Math grounds. The rain-water stands at places some feet high. My huge stork is full of glee, and so are the ducks and geese. My tame antelope fled from the Math and gave us some days of anxiety in finding him out. One of my ducks unfortunately died yesterday. She had been gasping for breath more than a week. One of my waggish old monks says, "Sir, it is no use living in this Kali-Yuga when ducks catch cold from damp and rain, and frogs sneeze!"

One of the geese had her plumes falling off. Knowing no other method, I left her some minutes in a tub of water mixed with mild carbolic, so that it might either kill or heal; and she is all right now.

Yours etc.,
Vivekananda.

1901.33 — BLESSED AND BELOVED

The Math, Belur, Howrah Dist.,
7th September, 1901.

BLESSED AND BELOVED[1],

I had to consult Brahmananda and others, and they were everyone in Calcutta, hence the delay in replying to your last.

The idea of taking a house for a whole year must be worked out with deliberation. As on the one hand there is some risk of catching malaria in Belur this month, in Calcutta on the other hand there is the danger of plague. Then again one is sure to avoid fever if one takes good care not to go into the interior of this village, the immediate bank of the river being entirely free from fever. Plague has not come to the river yet, and all the available places in this village are filled with Marwaris during the plague season.

Then again you ought to mention the maximum rent you can pay, and we seek

---

1. Shri M. N. Banerji.

the house accordingly. The quarter in the city is another suggestion. For myself, I have almost become a foreigner to Calcutta. But others will soon find a house after your mind. The sooner you decide these two points: (1) Whether mother stays at Belur or Calcutta, (2) If Calcutta, what rent and quarter, the better, as it can be done in a trice after receiving your reply.

Yours with love and blessings,
Vivekananda.

PS—We are all right here. Moti has returned after his week's stay in Calcutta. It is raining here day and night last three days. Two of our cows have calved.

1901.34—CHRISTINE

To Sister Christine:

The Math, Belur, Dist. Howrah, Bengal,
25th September, 1901.

DEAR CHRISTINE,

I could not write you last mail, excusez [excuse]. But I have been expecting one from you for a long time. Hope one will come this mail.

I am just thinking of going over to Japan, as Miss [Josephine] MacLeod is so insistent. Perhaps something will be done; who knows?

From Japan, of course, a peep into America seems inevitable.

Not much news of Mrs. [Ole] Bull or Margot [Sister Nivedita]. Margot is rested, well, and strong. She will come to India some day, perhaps. I am soon expecting Mrs. [Charlotte] Sevier though. Her work is needing her. Her beautiful home in the Himalayan forests is a temptation, especially now when a huge tiger is roaming in her compound and killed a horse, a buffalo, and her pair of mastiffs in broad daylight; a number of bears [are] playing havoc with her vegetable garden; and lots of porcupines [are] doing mischief everywhere!!! She went out of the way to buy land in a forest—she and her husband liked it so much.

There is not much to write this week. Words only tire one, except one which is inexhaustible, infinite.

So, goodbye till next week.

Ever with love and blessings,
Vivekananda.

PS—Just now comes a telegram from Miss MacLeod and a letter also. She is so insistent that I am thinking of going over to Japan. In that case, we cross over to America this winter, and thence to England.

1901.35 — CHRISTINA

To Sister Christine:

The Math, Belur, Dist. Howrah, Bengal,
8th October, 1901.

DEAR CHRISTINA,

Yours of September 9 came to hand yesterday. I congratulate you on your successful visit to the Huron Lake; a few more of them (according to your letter) will force you to sympathize with our condition — oh, the gasping and the melting and the puffing and all the rest of them!

However, nothing in the world like a plump, ripe fruit.

I had to give up my trip to Japan: firstly, because I am not in a working trim yet; secondly, [I] don't much care to make such a long voyage (one month) alone; thirdly, what am I to talk to them, I wonder.

Our heat too has been fierce and is continuing unusually long this year. I am blacker than a Negro by this time.

The California work is progressing famously. They want one or two men more. I would send, if I could, but I have not any more spare men. Poor Turiyananda is suffering from malaria yet, and is awfully overworked.

Do you know whether they published my Jnana-Yoga or not? I got a copy of a second edition of Karma-Yoga only.

I am bobbing up and down in the current of life. Today it is rather down, so I finish the letter here.

Yours with all love and blessings,
Vivekananda.

1901.36 — CHRISTINA

To Sister Christine:

The Math, Belur, Dist. Howrah, Bengal,
14th October, 1901.

MY DEAR CHRISTINA,

Just now came a letter from Mrs. Bull, but none from you, as I expected one this mail.

Mrs. Bull writes, "I wrote Christina recently to ask her if she were to be free in case the opportunity opened for her to go to the East. I send you her reply".

I went through several times your letter to Mrs. Bull. It surely was horrible; and you have been all this time hiding the real state of affairs from me and posing great cheerfulness!!

You will be a precious fool to lose the opportunity if such comes and is offered by Mrs. Bull. You will only have to take a year's leave. The rest will all be arranged by Mrs. Bull, including, I am sure, all your anxiety for those you will have to leave behind in Detroit.

You have been good, too good to be human, and you are so, still. But it is no use making oneself unnecessarily miserable. "Mother's will", surely, if the chance comes; and it has got to come, I know.

I would not write you about my health; for after all this hide and seek, even though it was for my good, I think you have not much of a right to know the truth about my health.

But to some things you have eternal rights, and amongst others, to my eternal love and blessings,

Vivekananda.

1901.37 — JOE

The Math, Belur, Howrah,
8th November, 1901.

My Dear Joe[1],

By this this time you must have received the letter explaining the word abatement. I did not write the letter nor send the wire. I was too ill at the time to do either. I have been ever since my trip to East Bengal almost bedridden. Now I am worse than ever with the additional disadvantage of impaired eyesight. I would not write these things, but some people require details, it seems.

Well, I am so glad that you are coming over with your Japanese friends — they will have every attention in my power. I will most possibly be in Madras. I have been thinking of leaving Calcutta next week and working my way gradually to the South.

I do not know whether it will be possible to see the Orissan temples in company with your Japanese friends. I do not know whether I shall be allowed inside myself — owing to my eating "Mlechchha" food. Lord Curzon was not allowed inside.

However, your friends are welcome to what I can do always. Miss Müller is in Calcutta. Of course she has not visited us.

Yours with all love,
Vivekananda.

---

1. Miss Josephine MacLeod.

1901.38 — MARGO

To Sister Nivedita:

The Math, P.O. Belur, Howrah,
12th November, 1901.

MY DEAR MARGO [Margot],

Since the Durgâ Pujâ I have been very ill, and so could not reply to your letter earlier.

We had a grand Puja here of Durga, lasting nearly four days; but, alas, I was down with fever all the time.

We had a grand image, and a huge Puja it was. Then we had the Lakshmi Puja following close, and then night before yesterday, we had the Kali Puja. It is always after midnight — this Puja. I am better now, and we will find a house for you as soon as you come.

I am so glad you are accompanying Mrs. [Ole] Bull. She requires all care; and she always thinks of herself the last. Joe [Miss Josephine MacLeod] is coming to India shortly — at Christmas time with some Japanese friends. I am expected to meet her in Madras.

I am going off to the N.W.P. [North-Western Provinces] etc. soon, as Bengal is malarious — now that the rains are over.

Mrs. Bull has been a mother to us all, and any time and service spent for her is as nothing to what she has been doing for us all. Remain with her as long as she wants you — the work can wait well; "Mother" sees to her work. We needn't be anxious.

By the by, Miss [Henrietta] Müller is here in Calcutta. She wrote a letter to Akhandananda, with whom she has been in regular correspondence — care of the Math. So I sent some flowers and fruits and a letter of welcome to her hotel. I have not had a reply yet.

Mrs. [Charlotte] Sevier, I expect, has already started. Swarupananda had his heart weakened by the constant uphill and downhill. He is here and improving.

Things are going on well with us, slowly but surely. The boys of late have been very active, and it is work only that tells and nothing else.

Yours with all love and blessings,
Vivekananda.

1901.39 — CHRISTINA

To Sister Christine:

The Math, P.O. Belur, Howrah,
12th November, 1901.

DEAR CHRISTINA,

The morning's mail brought me a photograph from Detroit. I thank the sender very much for promptness. Well, I liked it much. But the old one is the profile view; this, the front. Then again, the phenomenal fat seems to be only imaginary on somebody's part. In a way, I am more used to the old one, and, as such, I cannot slight an old friend. So let me say both are good. The one is an evolution of the other — for the better. I expected a line but it has not arrived yet; [it] may tomorrow. We have a proverb here: "One river is equal to forty miles". There is only a river between Calcutta and our Math, and yet such a round — about way for the mail. Sometimes it comes dribbling for days.

Mrs. [Ole] Bull and Nivedita must have started for the U.S. by this time. Nivedita is sure to see you in Detroit. Mrs. Bull is anxious to induce you to join her Indian party via Japan. If you can take leave for some months, do come. Mother will arrange anyhow; I need not trouble myself.

Mrs. Sevier has started already, it seems — alone.

We had grand Pujas (worships) here in our Math this year. The biggest of our Pujas is the Mother worship, lasting nearly four days and nights. We brought a clay image of Mother with ten hands, standing with one foot on a lion, the other on a demon. Her two daughters — the Goddess of Wealth and the Goddess of Learning and Music — on either side on lotuses; beneath, her two sons — the God of War and that of Wisdom.

Thousands of people were entertained, but I could not see the Puja, alas! I was down with high fever all the time. Day before yesterday, however, came the Puja of Kali. We had an image, too, and sacrificed a goat and burned a lot of fireworks. This night every Hindu home is illuminated, and the boys go crazy over fireworks. There are, of course, several cases of severe burns in the hospitals. We had less fireworks but more Puja, recitation of Mantras, offering of flowers, food and songs. It lasted only one night.

I am expected to leave Calcutta and Bengal in a few days, as this country becomes very malarious this month, after the rains. It is pleasant and cool now, and the north Himalayan wind is blowing.

We have fenced in a lot of our grounds to protect our vegetables from our cows and goats and sheep. The other day one of my [a portion excised] ... but the mother was either so wicked or [a portion excised] ... that she would not look at her young. I tried to keep them alive on cow's milk, but the poor things died in the night! Two of my ducks are sitting on their eggs. As this is their first time, and the male does not help them a bit, I am trying my best to keep up their strength by good feeding. We cannot keep chickens here — they are forbidden to us.

With all love,
Vivekananda.

1901.40 — CHRISTINE

To Sister Christine:

The Math, P.O. Belur, Howrah,
25th November, 1901.

DEAR CHRISTINE,

It seems your bottle of nerve tonic did not do you much good, your assurances to the contrary. It must have been a curious error. I must have been down with fever or asthma or something else at that time. Still a thousand, thousand pardons. This was my first, and it will be my last, offence. Your letter that went to Miss [Josephine] MacLeod has not come back yet. Perhaps Miss MacLeod is bringing the letter with her, as she is coming over to India from Japan herself, accompanied by her Japanese converts (male, of course, as she is a lady missionary).

Well, well, I so wish things would so arrange themselves that I could see you once more. Mother knows. By the by, my right eye is failing me badly. I see very little with that one. It will be hard for me for some time either to read or write; and as it is getting worse every day, my people are urging me to go to Calcutta and consult a doctor. I will go soon, as soon as I recover from a bad cold I have on.

I am so glad you were so taken by Abhedananda; only I thought one Hindu was good for a lifetime.

Poor Miss Joe [Miss Josephine MacLeod] — so she remains ignorant as to the real cause of my not going over to Japan! You need not be the least anxious — there is no harm done; and if there were, Joe and especially Mrs. [Ole] Bull make it their life's duty to befriend those I love.

I will try your tonic when it arrives; and the gift, I pray, will even be followed by the giver, for surely a [words excised] ... is more stimulating and healing than dead drugs.

With all love,
Vivekananda.

1901.41 — CHRISTINE

To Sister Christine:

The Math, P.O. Belur, Howrah,
27th November, 1901.

DEAR CHRISTINE,

It is almost sure, I did not write any letter to you that week in which [I] made that infamous blunder. As I wrote you two letters a few days previously, it is not at all probable that I wrote you another. Then Miss [Josephine] MacLeod [would have] sent the letter back. I must have written only one letter that week to Miss MacLeod, giving her my reasons for not going to Japan; and somehow it so happened that the hand wrote the most familiar name on the envelope. So you need not expect any letter of yours back from Japan, as there was none; and if there were, you shall have it.

I am just under another spell of catarrh and asthma. Yesterday a cyclone blew over the place, and several trees and a bit of the roof are damaged. It is gloomy yet and cold. You know it is almost impossible to write with the asthma on. So au revoir [good-bye].

Vivekananda.

1901.42 — CHRISTINE

To Sister Christine:

The Math, P.O. Belur, Howrah,
12th December, 1901.

DEAR CHRISTINE,

Well, then, you wanted to know all about my state of health, and you insist. You shall have it.

You know, the last three years I have been getting albuminuria now and then. It is not constant, nor is it yet of any organic character. The kidneys are structurally all right. Only they throw out albumen now and then.

This is worse than throwing out sugar in diabetes. Albumen poisons the blood, attacks the heart and does all sorts of mischief. Catching cold always increases it. This time it has caused a small blood vessel in the right eye to burst, so that I scarcely see with that eye.

Then the circulation has become very rapid. The doctors have put me to bed; and I am forbidden to eat meat, to walk or even stand up, to read and write.

Already there is some benefit in this lying-down process, as I sleep a lot and have a good appetite and am digesting my meals. Curious, is it not, that inactivity should bring on sleep and appetite? There is no cause to be anxious at all.

Mrs. [Charlotte] Sevier arrived in Calcutta three days ago; and by the last advice from Nivedita, Mrs. Bull and she will start on the 13th December, if they can secure berths, or on the 30th December at least. I pray Mrs. Bull has already invited you and that you have got your year's leave and are coming over, and that you will get this letter in India redirected. If Mother does not fulfil this prayer, sure She will take me across the water soon, and [line excised] ... The doctor says if I keep to my bed for three months, I will get completely cured.

Now, don't worry. If good days are not coming, we will make them, that is all. Hang it! I must have good days now and, that too, very soon. You know, I always keep my word. Mother must do it, or I throw Her overboard. I am not so submissive as you are.

Our old-school physicians pour in tons of iron and other metals — including gold, silver, pearls, etc. — down our throats. I should be a man of iron by this time; perhaps yours will be the last touch to make my body one of steel.

This is our best season for eating turtles, but they are all black. The green [ones] can only be found in America. Alas! I am prevented from the taste of meat.

Now, noble heart, take courage. Don't mope: you have buffeted [too] many a storm in life, old war horse, to be like a silly boarding-school girl. Things must go all right. I am not going to die or to be ill just now; I am determined to be healthy. You know my grit.

Miss [Josephine] MacLeod sent you your letter. What was it about? Was there anything queer? I am glad she had it. She writes beautifully about you. She has already started, and we will have a jolly good company this winter here in Calcutta.

Mrs. [Ole] Bull, Miss MacLeod, Mrs. Sevier and Nivedita and I will be overjoyed if somebody else will be thrown into the bargain. I can't get any more value, eh? I must stop. Am going to look after my geese and ducks just for five minutes, breaking the doctor's command to lie down all the time. One of the geese is a silly, fearful bird, always despondent and anxious. She likes to be all alone by herself and is miserable — very much like another goose I know in another place.

> Here my story ends
> And spinach top bends.
> Why is spinach withering?
> Because the goat is browsing.
> Why is the goat browsing?
> Because no grass is growing.
> Why no grass is growing?
> The gardener is not watering.
> Why there is no watering?
> The Master is not commanding.

Why is he not commanding?

An ant has bitten the Master!

This is a nursery rhyme told after a story, and it is true of us all. It is only an ant bite, after all — the trouble here; is it not?

Ever yours,
Vivekananda.

1901.43 — CHRISTINE

To Sister Christine:

The Math, Belur, Dist. Howrah, Bengal,,
18th December, 1901.

DEAR CHRISTINE,

I am much better, and the rest is doing me good. I have found out that lying in bed all the time gives me as much sleep as wanted and good digestion too. Albumen and sugar vanish immediately [when] I begin taking rest.

Mrs. Bull and Nivedita start for India from Marseilles today, and unless they change their plan, [they] must be in India before this reaches you — two weeks before.

Herewith I send you four hundred and eighty dollars by cheque drawn on Thomas Cook & Son, Broadway, New York. They have no branch office in Detroit. On receipt of this, you write to Thomas Cook & Son, Broadway, New York, that you have got a cheque from India — mentioning the amount and number — drawn by Thomas Cook & Son on the firm of Thomas Cook & Son, and want to be advised as to how to cash it. Don't send the cheque ahead. (Excuse all these details. I feel you are a baby in business, though I am worse.) This is to pay your "passage to India" if you think fit to accept Mrs. Sevier's invitation. If you get leave and come, I am sure you will find somebody who is coming to England, at least. Then from there, again, somebody who is coming to Egypt. You come with them as far as Italy, thence direct on a boat to India.

Second-class passage across the Atlantic is all right, but the second class from Italy to Bombay is rather bad. There are always a few rough men and fast women. There is money enough for travelling first class all through, if you so like.

The Mother will see to it, even as [She did when] this money came. Drop me a line as soon as you engage your passage — better a week ahead; otherwise I don't see how the letter can reach me. The vessel to India you get from London; and possibly a letter may reach me with the name of the vessel, etc. In any case, however, you wire me as soon as you land and get into a good hotel. You will find many persons to receive you — and me too, most probably.

In case, however, things take another turn and you cannot come, no matter. Do with the money just as it pleases you.

It is very probable that after Miss [Josephine] MacLeod and Mrs. [Ole] Bull have been through India, they are going home via Japan; and, of course, I am going with them. In that case I will be in California next fall.

It will be a nice trip, and would it not be a fine tour round the world if you get leave and come?

Do just as the Mother opens the way for you, and do not worry.

Yours with all love and blessings,
Vivekananda.

1901.44 — SISTER CHRISTINE

To Sister Christine:

The Math, Belur, Dist. Howrah, Bengal,
25th December, 1901.

A Merry Christmas and Happy New Year is the usual congratulation. Alas! The stars brought you a tremendous blow. (Sister Christine's mother had passed away.) Blessed be the name of the Lord. After all, it is only "Thy will be done" — our only refuge. I will not insult you by offering you consolation — you know it all already. Only this line to remind you of one who is in entire sympathy with you and who knows that all your plans must be good in joy or sorrow, as you are dedicated to the eternal Mother. Well, the Mother phenomenal has merged in the Mother absolute, eternal. Thy will be done.

By this time you must have made a decision, or, rather, the "Mother" has shown you the way, surely. I rest content.

The soldier of the Queen has gone abroad to fight for Her cause, leaving all he loves to Her care. The soldier is to look to his duty. The Queen of the Universe knows the rest.

With all love as usual,
Vivekananda.

1902

1902.1 — SWARUP

Gopal Lal Villa,
Benares (Varanasi) Cantonment,
9th February, 1902.

MY DEAR SWARUP, (ânanda)

... In answer to Châru's letter, tell him to study the *Brahma-Sutras* himself. What does he mean by the *Brahma-Sutras* containing references to Buddhism? He means the Bhâshyas, of course, or rather ought to mean, and Shankara was only the last Bhâshyakâra (commentator). There are references, though in Buddhistic literature, to Vedanta, and the Mahâyâna school of Buddhism is even Advaitistic. Why does Amara Singha, a Buddhist, give as one of the names of Buddha — Advayavâdi? Charu writes, the word Brahman does not occur in the Upanishads! *Quelle bêtise!*

I hold the Mahayana to be the older of the two schools of Buddhism.

The theory of Mâyâ is as old as the Rik-Samhitâ. The Shvetâshvatara Upanishad contains the word "Maya" which is developed out of Prakriti. I hold that Upanishad to be at least older than Buddhism.

I have had much light of late about Buddhism, and I am ready to prove:

(1) That Shiva-worship, in various forms, antedated the Buddhists, that the Buddhists tried to get hold of the sacred places of the Shaivas but, failing in that, made new places in the precincts just as you find now at Bodh-Gayâ and Sârnâth (Varanasi).

(2) The story in the Agni Purâna about Gayâsura does not refer to Buddha at all — as Dr. Rajendralal will have it — but simply to a pre-existing story.

(3) That Buddha went to live on Gayâshirsha mountain proves the pre-existence of the place.

(4) Gaya was a place of ancestor-worship already, and the footprint-worship the Buddhists copied from the Hindus.

(5) About Varanasi, even the oldest records go to prove it as the great place of Shiva-worship; etc., etc.

Many are the new facts I have gathered in Bodh-Gaya and from Buddhist literature. Tell Charu to read for himself, and not be swayed by foolish opinions.

I am rather well here, in Varanasi, and if I go on improving in this way, it will be a great gain.

A total revolution has occurred in my mind about the relation of Buddhism and Neo-Hinduism. I may not live to work out the glimpses, but I shall leave the lines of work indicated, and you and your brethren will have to work it out.

Yours with all blessings and love,
Vivekananda.

1902.2 — MRS. OLE BULL

Gopal Lal Villa,
Benares (Varanasi) Cantonment,
10th February, 1902.

Welcome to India once more, dear mother[1] and daughter. A copy of a Madras journal that I received through the kindness of Joe delighted me exceedingly, as the reception Nivedità had in Madras was for the good of both Nivedita and Madras. Her speech was indeed beautiful.

I hope you are resting well after your long journey, and so is Nivedita. I wish it so much that you should go for a few hours to a few villages west of Calcutta to see the old Bengali structures made of wood, bamboo, cane, mica, and grass.

These are the bungalows, most artistic. Alas! the name is travestied nowadays by every pigsty appropriating the name.

In old days a man who built a palace still built a bungalow for the reception of guests. The art is dying out. I wish I could build the whole of Nivedita's School in that style. Yet it is good to see the few that yet remained, at least one.

Brahmananda will arrange for it, and you have only to take a journey of a few hours.

Mr. Okakura has started on his short tour. He intends to visit Agra, Gwalior, Ajanta, Ellora, Chittore, Udaipur, Jaipur, and Delhi.

A very well-educated rich young man of Varanasi, with whose father we had a long-standing friendship, came back to this city yesterday. He is especially interested in art, and spending purposely a lot of money in his attempts to revive dying Indian arts. He came to see me only a few hours after Mr. Okakura left. He is just the man to show him artistic India (i.e. what little is left), and I am sure he will be much benefited by Okakura's suggestions. Okakura just found a common terracotta water-vessel here used by the servants. The shape and the embossed work on it simply charmed him, but as it is common earthenware and would not bear the journey, he left a request with me to have it reproduced in brass. I was at my wit's end as to what to do. My young friend comes a few hours after, and not only undertakes to have it done but offers to show a few hundreds of embossed designs in terracotta infinitely superior to the one Okakura fancied.

He also offers to show us old paintings in that wonderful old style. Only one family is left in Varanasi who can paint after the old style yet. One of them has painted a whole hunting scene on a pea, perfect in detail and action!

I hope Okakura will come to this city on his return and be this gentleman's guest and see a bit of what is left.

Niranjan has gone with Mr. Okakura, and as he is a Japanese, they don't object to his going into any temple. It seems that the Tibetans and the other Northern

---

1. Mrs. Ole Bull.

Buddhists have been coming here to worship Shiva all along.

They allowed him to touch the sign of Shiva and worship. Mrs. Annie Besant tried once, but, poor woman, although she bared her feet, put on a Sari, and humiliated herself to the dust before the priests, she was not admitted even into the compound of the temple. The Buddhists are not considered non-Hindus in any of our great temples. My plans are not settled; I may shift from this place very soon.

Shivananda and the boys send you all their welcome, regards, and love.

I am, as ever, your most affectionate son

Vivekananda.

1902.3 — SISTER NIVEDITA

Benares (Varanasi),
12th February, 1902.

May all powers come unto you[2]! May Mother Herself be your hands and mind! It is immense power — irresistible — that I pray for you, and, if possible, along with it infinite peace...

If there was any truth in Shri Ramakrishna, may He take you into His leading, even as He did me, nay, a thousand times more!

Vivekananda.

1902.4 — RAKHAL[3]

Gopal Lal Villa,
Benares (Varanasi) Cantonment,
12th February, 1902.

MY DEAR RAKHAL[4],

I was glad to get all the detailed news from your letter. Regarding Nivedita's School, I have written to her what I have to say. My opinion is that she should do what she considers to be best.

Don't ask my opinion on any other matter either. That makes me lose my temper. Just do that work for me — that is all. Send money, for at present only a few rupees are left.

Kanai (Nirbhayananda) lives on Mâdhukari[5], does his Japa at the bathing ghat, and comes and sleeps here at night; Nyedâ does a poor man's work and comes and

---

2. Sister Nivedita.
3 Translated from Bengali.
4. Swami Brahmananda.
5. Cooked food obtained by begging from several houses.

sleeps here at night. "Uncle[1]" and Niranjan have gone to Agra. I may get their letter today.

Continue doing your work as the Lord guides. Why bother about the opinion of this man and that? My love to all.

Yours affectionately.
Vivekananda.

1902.5 — RAKHAL[2]

Gopal Lal Villa,
Benares (Varanasi) Cantonment,
18th February, 1902.

MY DEAR RAKHAL, (Swami Brahmananda)

You must have received by this time my letter of yesterday containing an acknowledgment of the money. The main object of this letter is to write about—. You should go and meet him as soon as you get this letter... Get a competent doctor and have the disease diagnosed properly. Now where is Vishnu Mohini, the eldest daughter of Ram Babu[3]? She has recently been widowed...

Anxiety is worse than the disease. Give a little money—whatever is needed. If in this hell of a world one can bring a little joy and peace even for a day into the heart of a single person, that much alone is true; this I have learnt after suffering all my life; all else is mere moonshine...

Reply very soon. "Uncle[4]" and Niranjan have written a letter from Gwalior... Here it is now becoming hot gradually. This place was cooler than Bodh-Gaya... I was very pleased to hear that the Saraswati-Puja was celebrated by Nivedita with great success. If she wants to open the school soon, let her do so. Readings from the sacred books, worship, study—see that all these are being maintained. My love to all.

Yours affectionately,
Vivekananda.

---

1. Mr. Okakura was endearingly so called. "Kura" approximating to "Khurhâ" in Bengali which means uncle; Swamiji out of fun calls him uncle.

2 Translated from Bengali.

3. Ram Chandra Datta, a disciple of Shri Ramakrishna.

4. See note (4) previous page.

1902.6 — RAKHAL[5]

Gopal Lal Villa,
Benares (Varanasi) Cantonment,
21st February, 1902.

MY DEAR RAKHAL,

I received a letter from you just now. If mother and grandmother desire to come, send them over. It is better to get away from Calcutta now when the season of plague is on. There is wide-spread plague in Allahabad; I do not know if it will spread to Varanasi this time... Tell Mrs. Bull from me that a tour to Ellora and other places involves a difficult journey, and it is now very hot. Her body is so tired that it is not proper to go on a tour at present. It is several days since I received a letter from "Uncle[6]" The last news was that he had gone to Ajanta. Mahant also has not replied, perhaps he will do so with the reply to Raja Pyari Mohan's letter...

Write me in detail about the matter of the Nepal Minister. Give my special love and blessings to Mrs. Bull, Miss MacLeod, and all others. My love and greetings to you, Baburam[7] and all others. Has Gopal Dada[8] got the letter? Kindly look after the goat a bit.

Yours affectionately,
Vivekananda.

PS — All the boys here send you their respectful salutations.

1902.7 — BRAHMANANDA[9]

Gopal Lal Villa,
Benares (Varanasi) Cantonment,
24th February, 1902.

This morning I got a small American parcel sent by you[10]. I have received no letter, neither the registered one you refer to nor any other. Whether the Nepalese gentleman came and what happened — I have not been able to know anything at all about it. To write a simple letter so much trouble and so much delay!... Now I shall be relieved if I get the accounts. That also I get who knows after how many months!...

Yours affectionately,
Vivekananda.

5 Translated from Bengali.
6. See note (4) previous page.
7. Swami Premananda.
8. Swami Advaitananda.
9 Translated from Bengali.
10. Swami Brahmananda.

1902.8 — JOE

The Math,
21st April, 1902.

DEAR JOE, (Miss Josephine MacLeod)

It seems the plan of going to Japan seems to have come to nought. Mrs. Bull is gone, you are going. I am not sufficiently acquainted with the Japanese.

Sadananda has accompanied the Japanese to Nepal along with Kanai. Christine could not start earlier, as Margot could not go till the end of this month.

I am getting on splendidly, they say, but yet very weak and no water to drink. Anyhow the chemical analysis shows a great improvement. The swelling about the feet and the complaints have all disappeared.

Give my infinite love to Lady Betty and Mr. Leggett, to Alberta and Holly—the baby has my blessings from before birth and will have for ever.

How did you like Mayavati?

Write me a line about it.

With everlasting love,
Vivekananda.

1902.9 — JOE

The Math,
Belur, Howrah,
15th May, 1902.

DEAR JOE[1],

I send you the letter to Madame Calvé… I am somewhat better, but of course far from what I expected. A great idea of quiet has come upon me. I am going to retire for good—no more work for me. If possible, I will revert to my old days of begging.

All blessings attend you, Joe; you have been a good angel to me.

With everlasting love,
Vivekananda.

---

1. Miss Josephine MacLeod.

1902.10 — DHIRA MATA

The Math,
14th June, 1902.

DEAR DHIRÂ MÂTÂ[2],

...In my opinion, a race must first cultivate a great respect for motherhood, through the sanctification and inviolability of marriage, before it can attain to the ideal of perfect chastity. The Roman Catholics and the Hindus, holding marriage sacred and inviolate, have produced great chaste men and women of immense power. To the Arab, marriage is a contract or a forceful possession, to be dissolved at will, and we do not find there the development of the idea of the virgin or the Brahmachârin. Modern Buddhism — having fallen among races who had not yet come up to the evolution of marriage — has made a travesty of monasticism. So until there is developed in Japan a great and sacred ideal about marriage (apart from mutual attraction and love), I do not see how there can be great monks and nuns. As you have come to see that the glory of life is chastity, so my eyes also have been opened to the necessity of this great sanctification for the vast majority, in order that a few lifelong chaste powers may be produced...

I wanted to write many things, but the flesh is weak... "Whosoever worships me, for whatsoever desire, I meet him with that."...

Vivekananda

1902.11 — CHRISTINE

To Sister Christine:

The Math, Belur, Dist. Howrah,
27th May, 1902.

MY DEAR CHRISTINE,

I am sorry I could not visit the mountains this time. My health, though not improved as much as I [had] wished, is not bad. The liver has been benefited — [that] is a great gain. The rains will commence very soon in the hills. So it is useless for me to take all the trouble of that terrible route.

I am so happy to learn the mountains are doing you good. Eat a lot, sleep as much as you can, and get plump. Stuff yourself till you get plump or you burst.

So the place did not suit Mr. Okakura [Kakuzo] — why? There must have been something to annoy him very much that he left the place so abruptly. Did he not like the scenery? Was it not sublime enough for him? Or the Japanese do not like sublimity at all? They only like beauty.

One of the boys writes that the little boy is getting disobedient etc. Mrs. Sevier

2. Mrs. Ole Bull.

wants me to take him down. So I do. I have asked Sadananda and another monk (whom I want for work here) to go to Almora and wait for the monsoon, and when it breaks, to come down.

If you feel you are becoming the least burdensome to Mrs. Sevier, write me immediately. It would be a sin to put further pressure on her — she does so much for me. However, she likes you very much and writes that you look be-au-ti-ful in saris.

I have just now two kids and three lambs added to the family. There was one more kid, but he got himself drowned in the yellow fish tank. How is Margot? Is she still there, or gone away with Mr. Okakura? How is she pulling on with the boys?

What do you do the whole day? How do you pass the day? Write me all details, and frequently; but do not expect long letters from me often.

Give my love to Mrs. Sevier, to Margot and the rest, and you may take a few spoonfuls, if you like,

With only this,
Vivekananda.

PS — Have an eye on the little chap. The boys are already jealous of him. They did spoil another boy that way before.

1902.12 — CHRISTINE

To Sister Christine:

The Math, Belur, Dist. Howrah,
14th June, 1902.

MY DEAR CHRISTINE,

Your letters had to wait a few days, as I was out of town in a village. Well, many thanks for all the information I got. Mr. Okakura [Kakuzo] has been to the Math, but I was away. He will be in Calcutta a few weeks more and then goes to Bombay. He intends taking a house near the city to learn intimately the customs of Bengalees. I am so glad to learn Margo's [Sister Nivedita's] intention to stop at Mayavati longer. She really requires good rest, and she had none in Europe, I am sure of that. If she were amenable to my advice as of old, I would take away every book and every scrap of paper from her, make her walk some, eat a lot and sleep a lot more. As to talking, I would have the merriest conversation all the while.

I have a beautiful letter from Mrs. Sevier, and [am] so happy to learn that she loves you more and more. But plumpness is the criterion, mon amie [my friend], for a' [all] that.

So there was a great flutter in our dovecote owing to my letters, but things must have assumed their old form by this time. The boy, my nephew, is going to be sometime yet in the Ashrama; make him talk English with a good accent — do. No foreign language can be learnt properly unless you talk in it from childhood.

Mr. Bose is still there, I hope; and you must have liked him immensely. He is a man, a brick. Tender him my best regards, will you?

Have you any water in the lakes now? Do you get the snows clearer? It has been raining all through this summer here. We had very few burning days, only a number of stuffy ones. Our rains also have nearly set in. In a week the deluge will commence in earnest.

As for me, I am much stronger than before; and when seven miles of jolting in a bullock-cart and railway travel of thirty-four miles did not bring back the dropsy to the feet, I am sure it is not going to return.

But anyway, it is the Math that suits me best just now.

With all love,
Vivekananda.

1902.13 — CHRISTINE

To Sister Christine:

The Math, Belur, Dist. Howrah,
15th June, 1902.

DEAR CHRISTINE,

Just now received your note. I am quite easy in my mind so long [as] you live with Mrs. [Charlotte] Sevier at Mayavati. You know, anxiety is one thing I must avoid to recover. I will be very anxious if you are in Calcutta, at Baghbazar. I am slowly recovering. Stay with Mrs. Sevier as long as you can. Don't come down with Margot [Sister Nivedita].

With love,
Vivekananda.

1902.14 — CHRISTINE

To Sister Christine:

The Math, Belur, Dist. Howrah,
21st June, 1902.

MY DEAR CHRISTINE,

You have not the least cause to be anxious. I am getting on anyhow and am quite strong. As to diet, I find I have to restrict myself and not follow the prescription of my doctor to eat anything I like. The pills continue, however. Will you ask the boys if they can get "Amalaki" [Emblic myrobalan] fruits in the place now? We cannot get them in the plains now. They are rather sour and puckery eaten raw; but make marmalade of whole [ones] — delicious. Then they are the best things for fermentation I ever get.

No anxiety on the score of Marie Louise's arrival in Calcutta. She has not yet made any noise.

Things go on the same. I am trying to go to Monghyr — a place near Calcutta and said to be very salubrious.

We will think of your coming to Baghbazar after Nivedita has fairly started; till then keep quiet and lay on food.

With all love to yourself, the boys and Mother [Mrs. Charlotte Sevier],

Vivekananda.

PS — I am laying on adipose tissues fast — especially about the abdominal regions: "It is fearful to see!"

NAME INDEX

Index of Proper Names

A

Abhedananda (Swami) 46, 201, 299, 603, 613

Akhandananda 35, 43, 44, 125, 294, 310, 438, 454, 459, 471, 572

Alambazar Monastery disciple(s) 153, 356

Alasinga Perumal 73, 77, 88, 121, 131, 139, 145, 165, 177, 185, 186, 192, 198, 209, 211, 226, 239, 242, 246, 255, 258, 259, 270, 284, 292, 307, 311, 321, 326, 335, 344, 349, 350, 377, 381, 391, 392, 394, 402, 403

Alberta Sturges (Miss) 274, 313, 406, 409, 624, 626, 630

An American Friend 592, 595

An American Lady 408

Atul Chandra Ghosh 43

B

Bagley, John J. 128

Balaram Bose 22, 26, 28, 30, 32, 33, 39, 42

Banerji, M. N. (Shri) 659

Bhushan Ghosh (Doctor) 430

Blodgett (Mrs., Aunt Roxy) 600

Brahmananda (Swami, Rakhal) 220, 284, 288, 297, 302, 304, 325, 409, 416, 439, 448, 451, 463, 466, 469, 472, 473, 475, 477, 478, 480, 481, 482, 497, 498, 502, 504, 533, 551, 553, 559, 580, 678, 679, 680

Bull, Ole (Mrs., Dhira Mata) 176, 184, 189, 194, 224, 229, 240, 244, 249, 257, 259, 260, 261, 268, 283, 287, 295, 298, 312, 316, 319, 324, 332, 334, 338, 340, 351, 352, 361, 364, 369, 371, 372, 374, 384, 398, 402, 407, 417, 420, 426, 441, 461, 494, 502, 513, 532, 536, 546, 551, 554, 558, 559, 562, 568, 570, 576, 577, 582, 590, 593, 602, 629, 632, 640, 642, 643, 644, 645, 649, 677, 682

C

Carus, Paul 260, 268

D

Dewan of Mysore 320

Dharmapala 210

F

Farmer, S. 324

Fox, John 618

Frankincense 408

Funke, Charles (Mary) 332, 349

G

Goodwin, J. J. 378

Goodwin J. J.'s Mother 500

Govinda Sahay 56, 217

Greenstidel, Christina 282, 283, 316, 318, 319, 323, 336, 348, 351, 355, 375, 395, 415, 418, 482, 488, 492, 509, 521, 527, 529, 530, 531, 538, 542, 545, 546, 552, 557, 561, 580, 594, 603, 604, 605, 606, 609, 611, 616, 617, 619, 625, 627, 630, 631, 647, 648, 655, 656, 657, 658, 660, 663, 664, 667, 668, 669, 671, 672, 682, 683, 684, 685

H

Halboister, Marie 435, 454, 534

Hale, George W. (Mrs.) 92, 93, 107, 108, 109, 112, 118, 120, 122, 127, 128, 129, 134, 143, 144, 147, 148, 152, 157, 160, 161, 163, 167, 168, 173, 176, 178, 185, 188, 193, 194, 195, 198, 206, 208, 241, 243, 250, 251, 252, 258, 271, 272, 275, 277, 278, 279, 370, 540, 541, 555, 556

Hale, Harriet 388, 396

Hale, Mary 113, 119, 138, 165, 175, 194, 207, 210, 236, 262, 263, 265, 332, 341, 348, 363, 389, 399, 414, 416, 424, 445, 491, 506, 524, 538, 540, 543, 552, 563, 572, 576, 581, 584, 586, 599, 600, 606, 608, 611, 650, 655, 658

Hale Sisters 110, 111, 146, 149, 150, 158, 254, 354, 355, 370, 405

Hansbrough, Alice (Shanti) 610, 611

Harendra Nath (Brahmachari) 614

Haridas Viharidas Desai 60, 61, 63, 69, 70, 71, 105, 135, 187, 196, 204, 345

Haripada Mitra (Sri) 93, 95, 466, 507, 508

I

Indian Mirror (The) 394

Indumati Mitra (Shrimati) 71, 462, 477, 479

Ishwar Chandra Ghosh 524

J

Jagmohanlal 472

Janes, Lewis I. 249, 251, 367

K

Kakuzo, Okakura 653

Kidi 178, 200, 264

Kripananda 376

L

Lala Badri Sah 404, 423, 433

Landsberg, Leon 174

Leggett, Francis H. (Mrs.) 246, 254, 262, 273, 285, 301, 367, 369, 440, 456, 553, 554, 582, 583, 592, 596, 616, 623

Light of the East (Editors of) 371, 410

M

MacLeod, Josephine (Joe Joe) 267, 296, 299, 306, 308, 317, 406, 447, 460, 466, 495, 496, 497, 502, 510, 521, 528, 531, 575, 579, 587, 589, 594, 596, 598, 612, 613, 631, 632, 633, 643, 644, 652, 654, 665, 681

Mademoiselle 627

Madhusudan Chattopadhyaya 68

Madras Comittee 415

Madras Disciple(s) 103, 141, 179, 214, 285

Maharaja Ajit Singh (Raja of Khetri) 213, 274, 500, 503, 505, 508, 509, 510, 511, 512, 527, 635

Maharaja of Limdi 319

Maharaj (Pandit) 62

Mahendra Nath Gupta 480

Manmatha Nath Bhattacharya 168

McKindley, Harriet 113

McKindley, Isabelle 103, 124, 126, 159, 184, 191, 242, 245, 306, 536

Mohammed Sarfaraz Husain of Naini Tal 501

Mrinalini Bose (Shrimati) 518

Munshi Jagmohanlal 495

N

Narasimhachariar G. G. 224

Noble, Margaret Elizabeth (Sister Nivedita) 365, 399, 407, 421, 427, 437, 439, 443, 453, 458, 469, 476, 488, 493, 498, 505, 520, 523, 544, 547, 555, 556, 560, 569, 570, 577, 584, 585, 591, 600, 601, 602, 604, 608, 610, 618, 619, 620, 630, 633, 646, 662, 666, 678

O

Officer in Charge of Telegrams, Srinagar 496

P

Pramadadas Mitra 4, 5, 6, 10, 11, 12, 14, 15, 18, 19, 20, 21, 22, 29, 31, 32, 33, 35, 50

Premananda (Swami) 479

R

Raja Pyari Mohan Mukherjee 488

Ramakrishna (Swami, Shashi) 10, 100, 114, 190, 230, 269, 303, 322, 360, 366, 382, 423, 428, 457, 460, 468, 489, 493, 522, 634, 642, 651

Ramesh Chandra Dutta 646

Ram Ram Samjami (Pandit) 420

Rao Bahadur Narasimhachariar 138

Rao Nanjunda 68, 200, 353, 372, 386

S

Sadananda (Swami) 34

Sanyal 239

Sarada 228, 337, 346, 352, 470

Sarada Devi (Shri) 659

Saradananda 130

Sarala Ghoshal (Shrimati) 421, 526

Satish Chandra Mukherji 27

Sharat Chandra Chakravarti 50, 52, 419, 441

Shivananda (Swami) 218, 443, 483

Shuddhananda (Swami) 434, 450, 465

Sokanathan 441

Sturdy, E. T. (Mr.) 247, 248, 253, 279, 280, 292, 308, 309, 310, 313, 314, 317, 320, 325, 334, 339, 342, 347, 360, 374, 376, 380, 382, 387, 501, 529, 537, 547, 550, 641

Sturges, William 276

Sudhir 430

Swarup 649, 676

Swarupananda (Swami) 522

T

Thursby, Emma 191, 227, 345

Trichinapally (Hindu Students of) 417

Tulsiram Ghosh 47

Turiyananda (Swami, Hari) 587, 588, 612, 614, 617, 621, 625

V

Vehemia Chand Limbdi 190

W

Waldo, S. E. 397

Woods (Mrs.) 87, 92

Wright, John Henry 82, 85, 88, 124, 127, 130, 133, 134, 238, 362

Y

Yajneshwar Bhattacharya 26

Yogen 338

Discovery Publisher is a multimedia publisher whose mission is to inspire and support personal transformation, spiritual growth and awakening. We strive with every title to preserve the essential wisdom of the author, spiritual teacher, thinker, healer, and visionary artist.

www.ingramcontent.com/pod-product-compliance
Lightning Source LLC
Chambersburg PA
CBHW031956220426
43664CB00005B/44